THE DAWN OF CIVILIZATION

THE DAWN OF

THE FIRST WORLD SURVEY OF

TEXTS BY

EDITED BY STUART PIGGOTT

THAMES AND HUDSON · LONDON

CIVILIZATION

HUMAN CULTURES IN EARLY TIMES

GRAHAME CLARK

JAMES MELLAART

M.E.L. MALLOWAN

CYRIL ALDRED

WILLIAM CULICAN

SETON LLOYD

M.S.F. HOOD

SIR MORTIMER WHEELER

WILLIAM WATSON

ANTHONY CHRISTIE

E.D. PHILLIPS

T.G.E. POWELL

G.H.S. BUSHNELL

940 illustrations

172 in colour

110 original reconstructions

645 photographs and drawings

48 maps and chronological charts

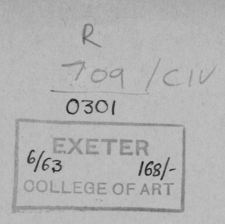
Designed and produced by **Thames and Hudson**

Editorial S. T. England BA, J. V. S. Megaw MA (Assistant Editor),
E. C. Peters, I. R. Sutton BA and Rose Thompson BA

Index M. Beryl Bailey ALA, MSIND

Design Ian Mackenzie Kerr ARCA

Colour Reconstructions Gaynor Chapman ARCA

Maps Charles Hasler MSIA and Shalom Schotten

Architectural Drawings P. P. Pratt and Martin E. Weaver,
Architectural Association, London

Line Illustrations Diana Holmes NDD, Marjory Maitland Howard FZS,
Margaret Scott BSC, Hubert J. Pepper ATD, FRAI, FZS, and Philip R. Ward,
Department of Oriental Antiquities, British Museum

Photography Josephine Powell, Eileen Tweedy, John R. Freeman and Edwin Smith

Blocks Gilchrist Bros. Ltd., Leeds; City Engraving Company Ltd., Hull;
Chemigraphische Kunstanstalt Erwin Vogt K. G., Düsseldorf;
Klischee-Werkstätten Der Industriedienst GmbH & Co., Wiesbaden;
Klischeefabrik Ludwig Fein, Cologne; Peukert & Co., Klischeefabrik, Cologne;
Cliches Schwitter A. G., Basle

Printed in Germany by DuMont Presse, Cologne

Paper Samum Polyton Woodfree Art and Apex Smooth Buff,
supplied by Frank Grunfeld Ltd., London

Bound by Van Rijmenam N. V., The Hague, Holland

© THAMES AND HUDSON LIMITED LONDON 1961

FOREWORD

ALMOST exactly three years ago the initial scheme for *The Dawn of Civilization* saw its first light—not unsuitably—amongst the stones of Stonehenge. Now as the project reaches its final stages, these lines are being written in the shadow of London's British Museum. This chance link between the library shelves and showcases of Bloomsbury and the grey sarsens of Salisbury Plain is in a way emblematic of the aims of this book—to bring together not only the visible remains of man's past achievements but the less impressive though no less important minutiae of the scholar, the pot-sherds, plans, and sections which are the archaeologist's basic tools no less than his trowel.

The Dawn of Civilization has been from the start a co-operative venture; nor could it have been otherwise. In the first place, the editing of such a complex volume has been made possible only by the unremitting work of Mr J. V. S. Megaw, who has acted throughout as my Assistant Editor. He has undertaken innumerable tasks of research, liaison and co-ordination, and above all has made himself mainly responsible, in co-operation with the authors, for the illustrations which we feel form so essential and notable a part of the work. Here, with infinite patience and the eyes of an expert, Mrs Eva Neurath has made us steer a strict course between the archaeologically necessary and the artistically valuable.

In a subject where the expert all too often seems to be one who learns more and more about less and less it has been our good fortune to work with authors, all scholars in their own right, but whose interests also embrace fields outside their own. As a result each separate chapter though designed as an entity contributes to the general underlying theme of man's development as a social animal. The co-operation of the authors has gone far beyond the arduous preparation of texts; their advice—and criticism—has been invaluable in the collection and preparation of illustrations and material for the running captions for the half-tone sections which have been the responsibility of the publishers. These last have been prepared as a parallel commentary to the main texts, to describe in words the points made by the pictorial matter; if the captions succeed in this aim the Editor at least will be gratified. With regard to the texts in general, Mr Max Parrish has been a tower of strength, as helpful as he has been self-effacing. One note of warning; in three years much work has been done on old material and much new found and thus it must be remembered that time and not always carelessness is responsible for some

omissions and inaccuracies which may present themselves to the discerning reader. As we go to press Hacılar has revealed new splendours and Knossos added more problems to those of past seasons, while in Africa the dawn of man himself is receding ever further.

The illustrations have presented a major task solved not only by the travels of photographers (whose commissions in one case led by Land-Rover from Athens to Karachi) and architects preparing reconstructions sometimes on the very sites concerned, but also through the kindness of those many government departments, institutions, and individuals mentioned by name in the *List and Sources of Illustrations*. Over and above these it would only be courtesy to single out for their ready assistance in affording special photographic facilities the Directors of the Government Archaeological Services of Cyprus, Greece, Iran, Iraq, the Lebanon, Pakistan, and Turkey. The Chinese People's Association for Cultural Relations with Foreign Countries, the Griffith Institute, Ashmolean Museum, Oxford, the Society for Cultural Relations with the U. S. S. R., and the Trade Delegation of the U. S. S. R. in the U. K. have been agents in obtaining some unique source material. Mr Megaw feels that on countless occasions he may have tried, but not it is hoped exhausted, the patience of many friends and colleagues. In this connection he is particularly grateful to the following members of the staff of the British Museum: Dr R. D. Barnett, Mr J. W. Brailsford, Mr Adrian Digby, Mr R. A. Higgins, Mr T. G. H. James, and Dr D. J. Wiseman. Learned libraries have also rendered sterling service, chief amongst them being those of the Institute of Archaeology, University of London (Miss Joan du Plat Taylor and Miss G. C. Talbot), the Department of Egyptology, University College, London (Miss K. E. Cynthia Cox), and the Society of Antiquaries of London (Mr John Hopkins). If any source has gone unacknowledged through ignorance or neglect the fault is entirely that of the Editor and Assistant Editor. They must be held responsible for such omissions.

Finally I have written elsewhere in this volume that it has been our purpose throughout not only to interest but to excite. If this should indeed be the impact of *The Dawn of Civilization* on both scholar and layman then we shall feel that three years have not been spent in vain.

STUART PIGGOTT

London–Edinburgh–Harvard March 1961

CONTENTS

A visual time-table of the periods covered by the chapters of this book

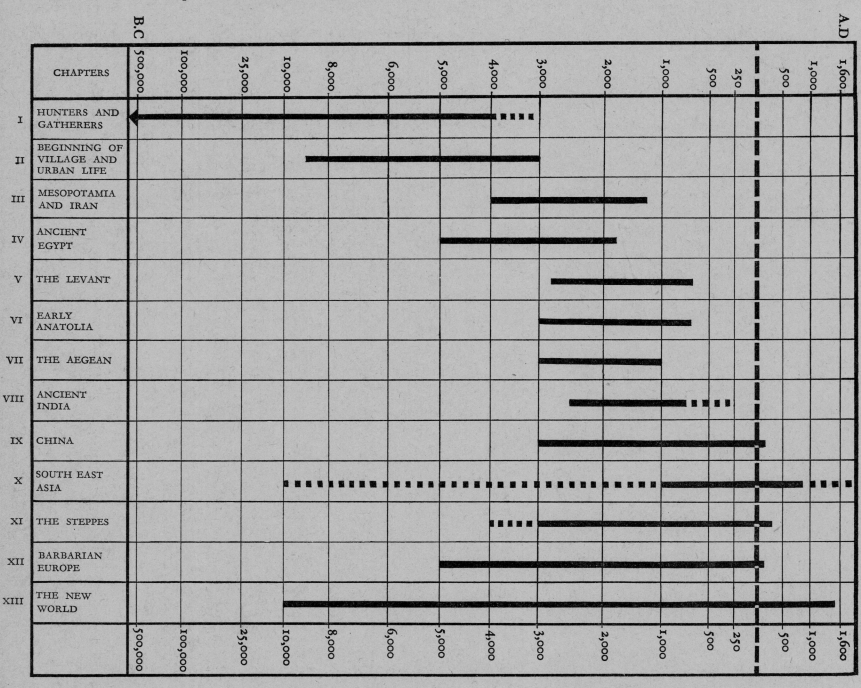

Introduction: the man-made world

STUART PIGGOTT

What is Civilization?

THE GREAT CIVILIZATIONS of the past—Egyptian, Assyrian, Persian, Greek, Roman—did not spring into being out of the void. Their tremendous cultural and material achievements were due, not to the emergence of superior human beings, but rather to the methodical application and development of skills and technologies inherited from those who preceded them. This book, the product of several years' work by some of the foremost scholars in archaeology and early history, tells the story of those peoples who laid the foundations upon which were built all the civilizations of antiquity. This is the theme of *The Dawn of Civilization*.

However, before turning to examine this dawn we must briefly consider civilization itself. The definition of 'civilization' has been the frequent concern of philosophers, historians and others ever since man was sufficiently self-conscious and analytical to wonder about the nature of his own achievement. As with the perception of the historical past itself, the definition will of course vary in accordance with the philosophy of history adopted by the enquirer. In this book, 'civilization' is used to mean a society which has worked out a solution to the problem of living in a relatively large permanent community, at a level of technological and social development above that of the hunting band, the family farmstead, the rustic, self-sufficient village or the pastoral tribe. Civilization is something artificial and man-made, the result of making tools of increasing complexity in response to the enlarging concepts of community life evolving in men's minds.

It is with such societies that our book largely deals, though not entirely, for it is impossible to rule a hard-and-fast line between civilized and non-civilized in antiquity, or to understand what contributed to the classical civilization of the Mediterranean lands on the one hand, and that of China and Indonesia on the other, without taking the story beyond the threshold of civilization and into its incipient or full achievement. In this borderland of social evolution archaeology still has an important part to play.

Archaeology today is no longer a matter of chance digging inspired by the hope of rich loot, but the deliberate pursuit of ordered knowledge in which excavation takes its place as a field technique for obtaining the raw material, on which a working hypothesis can be based, and from which inferences can be drawn. The recent developments in archaeological techniques in the field and in the laboratory, make it possible for us to reconstruct, in varying degrees of likelihood, the ways of life of those long-vanished men and women of remote antiquity who made the first steps away from savagery and barbarism and toward civilization. In this book we present these reconstructions in words and pictures, side-by-side with illustrations of all possible aspects of the material achievements of the ancient peoples with whom we deal, in so far as these survive.

Cultural Variety

For much of our story we have to rely to a great extent on the evidence of developing technology, the products of manual skill and craftsmanship, because in the absence of written records no other approach is possible. We shall be struck, in observing the early development of human societies, by the way in which within some of them a tradition of technological innovation had become early established and soon accepted as socially desirable, whereas in others once a satisfactory adaptation of the human society to its natural environment had been achieved, technology remained more or less stationary. But this does not mean that we should regard these societies as 'failures'; they solved their problems, and the frequent long persistence with little alteration of particular elements in their material culture is surely a tribute to the skill with which the adaptation of the human to the natural circumstances were in fact made. This is, after all, a characteristic of human societies today as in antiquity. 'Every human society everywhere', as Ruth Benedict has observed, 'has made such a selection of its cultural institutions. Each, from the point of view of another, ignores fundamentals and exploits irrelevancies. One culture hardly recognizes monetary values; another has made them fundamental in every field of behaviour. In one society technology is unbelievably slighted even in those aspects of life which seem necessary to ensure survival; in another, equally simple, technological achievements are complex and fitted with admirable nicety to the situation. One builds an enormous cultural superstructure upon adolescence, one upon death, one upon after-life.' The types of society in remote antiquity which each in their way laid foundations for later civilizations are varied and diverse, as we shall see in the chapters of this book.

To understand our heritage of civilization, we must first appreciate what lay behind the mature achievement of the ancient world. The earliest European literature is that of a people still within the barbarian world of prehistory. In Homer, 'the manliest warriors weep copiously and publicly . . . . the noblest behave like savages in battle . . . . women are an avowed aim and approved prize of war . . . . piracy, raiding at large for human and other booty, is an honourable trade . . . . the prince is honoured like a god by his people, yet lives close to nature . . . . he superintends in the harvest field and herds cattle.' Here, in the literature which was to form the basis of the great classical tradition, we are in a world which can hardly be understood if seen from the narrow view-point of what would usually be considered that of a 'civilized' observer, but which takes its place naturally enough when seen as an expression of Late Bronze Age and Early Iron Age Europe, with overtones derived from the cultural traditions of Minoans and the other peoples in the Eastern Mediterranean area.

A 'Model' of the Past

At this point we must pause and consider for a moment a question fundamental to any thought about history or prehistory. What is our knowledge of the past and how do we obtain it? The past no longer exists for us, even the past of yesterday: we call it the past because of this very quality. This means that we can never have direct knowledge of the past. We have only information or evidence from which we can construct a picture, whether we are concerned with what took place on the field of Waterloo, or in a Stone Age hunter's camp fifty thousand years ago. A scientist constructs a theory or a working hypothesis to explain and give significance to the facts obtained from controlled observations. The historian or prehistorian has the evidence of the past to interpret, and so he, like the scientist, makes a working hypothesis to explain it. This will be as near to an historical 'truth' as can be attained, and like the scientist he will modify or even abandon it if new evidence demands it.

There is more than one way of looking at the past. Here it is useful to think in scientific terms once again. When scientists are concerned with a large general problem such as the nature of the physical universe or the phenomena of outer space, they mentally construct a general framework within which further observations and reasoning can take place, and in which their observations fall into a significant pattern. This they would call a *model*. The model is valid in so far as it makes sense of the observed phenomena, and the inferences made from these. More than one model can exist at a time, each 'true' in its own way.

Now this idea of the 'model' to give significance to a number of facts and inferences can of course be applied to our knowledge of the past. In order to give the raw material of the archaeologist or the archivist significance, it has to be interpreted: stone axe-heads or clay tablets inscribed in cuneiform script are meaningless in themselves, and their study is hardly at a higher level than stamp collecting if they are not used as data from which meaningful inferences may be drawn. And such inferences can only be made within the terms of a model of the past, a method of looking at it, a way of describing what is seen. This is constructing prehistory or history out of archaeological material.

For a model to 'work', it has to be thought out in close relationship to the evidence it uses. It would clearly be nonsense, for instance, to use a model of the past based on variations in language for peoples of whose speech we are totally ignorant because it is nowhere recorded in writing. Our view of the past is directly conditioned by the means of approach we use, and by the type of evidence we employ. If we use purely archaeological evidence (that is to say, the surviving relics of the material culture of extinct communities, exclusive of any literary documents that may or may not exist), we will get only one sort of a view of the past. As we are dealing with the material products of man's craft and skill, our viewpoint will be a material one: we are mainly concerned with technology, and our model will be to a large extent a technological one. Our picture of the past will be in fact a materialistic one. If on the other hand we have written documents of some kind, we can give an added dimension to our view of the past, by using the documentary evidence to obtain information on those human activities which are not directly reflected in the material objects they made and used.

All this has a practical bearing on any reading about, or investigation of the past that any of us may undertake. If we are to understand what the historian or prehistorian is getting at, we must remember that we can perceive the past in varying ways and that the sort of past we see is conditioned by the type of evidence on which it is based. When we look at the prehistoric past, for instance, we are obliged by the nature of archaeological evidence to construct a story which almost entirely deals with techniques, and in which pots and tools, houses and tombs, weapons and ornaments, are the evidence for the developments in crafts and skills from generation to generation, or in one region as compared with another. Much of the content of this book has had to be constructed in these terms as a technological model of the past. Of course it has its limitations, but it does enable the reader to judge how man came to grips with his natural environment in more than one region in a similar manner, or again, how his reactions varied in response to the peculiar challenge the type of environment presented to him. All these assaults by man upon his surroundings, every exploitation of his fellow-animals or of the familiar plants around him, each intrusion of human will into the natural order of things, mark the emergence of man as an animal differentiated from the rest of his kind by the deliberate intention behind his acts, rather than a blind response to instinct. Civilization, however defined, is something essentially artificial and man-made, and to that extent self-conscious. A human community is one deliberately organised, and not the outcome of such a pattern of reflexes as produced the ant-heap or the bee-hive.

This survey of man's craftsmanship in antiquity is illuminated from very early times by works of art which today still have the capacity to stir our emotions and to give us aesthetic delight over the long millennia. We can trace the working of man's varied artistic genius in the surviving examples from societies whose material culture and social structure are of the simplest, and if we can never know what impulses lay behind the creation of the Old Stone Age animal drawings, or the subtle patterns of prehistoric painted pottery, we can nevertheless enjoy the achievement and value the contribution made by these nameless artists to our artistic heritage today. So too, save with peoples with a written record, we can know hardly anything of the religion of early man.

Inference from Material Remains

From archaeological evidence we can infer a certain amount, sometimes a surprisingly large amount, about the probable solutions made by peoples in remote antiquity to the problems posed in the contest with their natural environment, problems of subsistence and survival. Again, we see something of the geographical grouping of various societies and their contacts with other groups by trade and migration. We can see, too, how many of the really basic contributions to civilization were the products of anonymous peoples, often at a very early stage of technological development; peoples without a written record and so beyond the range of perception of the past based solely on literary sources, but nevertheless worthy to take their place among the founders of civilization. In the words of St Jerome, 'we should not despise those small things without which the greater could not stand.'

Much of our story is of anonymous peoples, for the prehistoric, or non-literate, past must always be one without names for person, place or people. It is because of this that archaeologists and prehistorians

have had to invent words and phrases to describe the material with which they deal. Terms such as the Palaeolithic period, the Middle Bronze Age, the Early Iron Age, are useful labels when used with discretion and an understanding of their limitations, but they can be deceptive if they are used in any but a local sense to imply the technological stage arrived at by peoples in the particular region, and not in a sense of strict chronology. If you use another model of the past you may sometimes get another name: the Hittite Empire covers the Middle and Late Bronze Age of Anatolia, but we know this only because of documentary records, used in terms of an historical model.

Chronology

This brings us to the interesting question of dates in prehistory and early history. On the whole, the dates used in this book are of three kinds, different because each is the result of using a particular method of determining the actual position in the time-scale of the events or circumstances involved. The first, and most familiar, type of date is one given in years and calculated from historical evidence (that is to say, from evidence which is ultimately documentary in its nature). These are the familiar dates like AD 1066 for the Norman Conquest of England, or 480 BC for the battle of Salamis, but they are also the less familiar and less precise dates such as 1850 BC for the beginning of the Egyptian New Kingdom, which some authorities would place at 1570 BC; or 1740 BC for the beginning of the Hittite Empire, arrived at by reckoning back from a reasonably fixed date of 1590 BC for the death of the fifth king of the dynasty. Nevertheless, for all essential purposes, these are historical dates, arrived at from historical evidence within a reasonable margin of error.

When one is dealing with communities who are either literally prehistoric (existing at a time when there was no writing anywhere in the world) or non-literate (existing side-by-side with peoples with some form of a written record) dates in years can be obtained only by a more roundabout method. History begins when writing begins: about 3000 BC in Mesopotamia for instance, or the nineteenth century AD for the Australian aborigines. It is usually possible to work out, for any region, the sequence in which the various prehistoric communities occupied the area, by means of such archaeological techniques as the observation of stratigraphy (the superimposition of the remains of one culture upon another), or by typology (comparsion of the various types of objects used by the people concerned). Then, by means of further comparisons, and such evidence as is afforded by the interchange of objects between one community and another, the various sequences can be placed in the right relation to each other. This is what archaeologists call a 'relative chronology', and it can be expressed in terms of sequences, but not in actual dates BC or AD.

Methods of Dating

To convert a relative chronology into one with dates, or in other words to make it an 'absolute chronology', the same processes of comparison and sequences have to be carried on to a point when one or more such sequences can be linked to one which is in fact historical, and so has its absolute chronology. Such cross-contacts can often be best established by a study of the objects traded between one community and another. A particularly good example of such a method of dating relates to the Mycenaeans. Amber, which occurs naturally on the coasts of the Baltic, was much traded in the form of beads and other ornaments not only in northern and central Europe, among prehistoric and non-literate tribes, but as far to the south-east as the Aegean, where it was acquired by such peoples as the Mycenaeans in early Greece. Now, the Mycenaeans have not got an absolute chronology based on their own records (though they were literate in at least the later stages of their civilization), but they and the Minoans were sufficiently closely linked to Egypt, a country with a true historical chronology, for us to construct an absolute chronology for the Aegean which we can use with some confidence. So that when we find the remains of amber necklaces of types made in northern Europe (and indeed in England) buried in Mycenaean tombs, we can infer the approximate time that these were in fashion in the north by using the Mycenaean chronology, and so convert our relative sequences into a scheme with at least a date fixed by these means here and there. It so happens that in this particular instance (the Aegean links with north-west Europe between about 1600 and 1400 BC) we have a cross-check, for the other side of the trade exchange is seen in objects of Aegean origin or derivation appearing in the north at the time the distinctive amber beads were also in fashion. For much of our dating in prehistoric Europe and Asia we have had to use evidence much less precise than the example just given, but even so some fairly satisfactory correlations have been established, and a skeleton chronology worked out, although it will be observed that there are differences even amongst experts.

But what can be done when no contacts, however indirect, can be obtained between non-literate cultures and those with an historical chronology? What if the communities in question flourished at a time which geological considerations show to have been wholly before literacy anywhere, or where the remoteness of the region studied was such that contacts were virtually impossible to establish? This was a particularly difficult problem to surmount when one came to the American continent and its pre-literate or non-literate communities. It was in fact from America that the answer came, and in a wholly unexpected manner. A new method of obtaining an absolute chronology of the past, at least for the last 30,000 years, was discovered as a more or less accidental by-product of atomic research.

There is present in the carbon dioxide of the air a radio-active form (isotope) of carbon, which has an atomic weight of 14 (C 14) instead of 12, that of normal carbon (C 12). The radio-active carbon is absorbed by living vegetation, so this too contains C 14 in the same constant proportions as the atmosphere. As all animals are directly or indirectly eaters of vegetable matter, they too contain the same proportion. When the living organism dies, it ceases to absorb further C_{14}, and, as with all radio-active substances, it then starts disintegrating without renewal. All such radio-active substances have a life-period, at the end of which disintegration of the original substance will be complete; in the case of C_{14} the disintegration is at such a rate that after 5700 years only half the original amount will be left, after about 11,400 years only a quarter, and so on. It follows that if it were possible to estimate with accuracy the point of radio-active decay reached in an ancient sample of, say, wood-charcoal, one could give a date before the present time at which the organic material died and ceased to absorb C 14, in other words the date when the tree was cut down and burnt.

Such an estimation is in fact possible by means of complicated laboratory techniques, and a large series of dates for the prehistoric and ancient world are now available to form the framework for an absolute time-scale. In using these dates we must remember two things. In the first place, individual dates from single samples are naturally less reliable than groups of dates from the same or similar archaeological contexts. Secondly, a C_{14} date has invariably to be given in terms of what is technically known as a standard deviation in plus or minus terms. This is a statistical expression and means that there is a high degree of probability that the true date lies somewhere between the two extremes. In a date given as 2710 plus or minus 130 years before the present, for example, there is a two-to-one chance that the true age lies between 2580 and 2840 years.

These, then, are some of the methods which have been used to construct the essential time-scales for the human past. They are essential, because the study of the past is a study in the time dimension. Without knowing the relative and absolute dates of the human cultures of antiquity which we study, we cannot set them in their true perspective, nor assess their relationship one to another. But once we can add an accurately measured time dimension to our observation of past societies we can see how they fall into place in relation to their predecessors and their successor. We have our perspective, and we can look more clearly into the complex story of our remote ancestors, the contributors to the civilizations which were to come.

It may help the reader if at this stage attention is drawn to a few general points. We have seen something of the necessarily imperfect nature of the archaeological record, where so much depends on the accident of survival, and where at best we are only presented with the material culture of the nameless peoples of the past. With the best will in the world, the chapters in this book present a patchy story, with inevitable overlapping when the same points need emphasis in different parts of the text. The chronological sequence, as we have seen, can be obtained indirectly by tracing the contacts between non-literate communities and those having a written history, or more directly, by the radio-carbon method. Without chronology we are nowhere: we must know the dimension in time for our ancient societies and also their distribution in geographical space before we consider the nature of the contacts between them.

The Technique of Digging

Much of the information contained in this book is based on the results of stratified sites—in other words, places where settlement has been continuous over the centuries, each successive group of people building their village or town on the ruins of its predecessor. This sequence of settlement can be recovered by the techniques of scientific excavation, with the oldest obviously at the bottom, the latest at the top, like the layers of letters in an undisturbed waste-paper basket. These successive phases or periods, defined in the soil by the remains of the structures and broken or lost objects of the abandoned settlements, form the 'levels' of the archaeologist, and are often numbered in a conventional series, such as Troy I or Troy VI, usually from below upwards, and so from the earlier to the later.

Pottery

It may seem odd that so much of the evidence used in this book turns out to be broken bits of pottery. But there is a very good reason for this. 'What is important is what is persistent', said a Victorian scientist in another connection, and the phrase might well have been coined to apply to pottery as the archaeologist sees it. As a substance, the baked clay of which pots are made is relatively fragile, and can be broken into pieces, but these pieces are extremely durable. So that straight away, we have in pottery a substance with a high survival-value. The next thing to remember is that, within a very short time of its first invention, pottery became essential, cheap (because made of such a common substance as clay) and abundant. The very fact that it broke relatively easily meant that a constant supply of new pots had to be available which, in their turn, would go into the rubbish-heap in fragments. Archaeologists have been taunted with being students of ancient dust-bins and their contents, and this is to some extent true: the commonest thing in the rubbish was broken pottery.

So far, so good. But there is more in pottery than that. Each community, every region, each successive phase of occupation is denoted by a different type or style of pottery. In simple communities there is extreme conservatism in all craftsmanship, and each group of people has a limited and recognisable style in pottery (and of course in all other branches of handicraft, such as stone or metal tools and weapons, or the type of cart or house they build). There is nothing mysterious in the ability of the archaeologist to recognise a distinctive type of pottery in fragments, any more than that of the art historian to recognise a fragment of a picture as being of the period and place of Giotto, rather than those of Cézanne. After all, most of us have some sort of capacity for recognising this quality in the works of man, whether it is deciding on the date and make of a vintage motor-car, distinguishing a phrase of Bach from one of Bix Beiderbecke, or (to come back to pottery) recognising a piece of Chelsea china among a heap of pieces from Woolworth's. It is the same with all the products of human craftsmanship which go to make up the subject-matter of archaeology: the realisation that (as an art historian put it) 'not everything is possible in every period' of human activity, but that each community has its distinctive style with its limitations and its achievements.

The chapters that follow do not make a wholly consecutive or unbroken narrative. In the present imperfect state of our knowledge this would be impossible, and the necessity of moving from one significant area to another would alone prevent it. What we have tried to do is to describe the dawn of civilization in the main formative regions of the world. These beginnings of what we have called civilization are varied in type, and they came into being at different periods of antiquity. So often the peoples we are describing existed side-by-side with others who had long passed their 'dawn' stage, and were in the full maturity of their historical life. These latter are outside our scope here, but they have to be mentioned from time to time in order to place the other simpler societies in their right setting.

Landmarks

Certain themes recur, indicating the basic technological discoveries and achievements which we can perceive in the ancient past. There is the critical change in economy from that of hunting and food-gathering to that of pastoralism or settled agriculture: we watch this taking place in the Old and in the New World independently, and in the complex pattern of Old World prehistory we can see the varied ways in which this solution to the problem of large and stable human communities was reached. Hard on the heels of the development of agriculture came the invention of metallurgy, primarily based on copper and tin, and their alloy, bronze. With this went the necessity for extensive trade in raw materials and finished products, breaking down the virtual self-sufficiency of the stone-using village, and at once extending the possibilities of technological development in the metal-using community, and making it potentially less stable, since supplies from outside became the subject of political control, and could be cut off by war or policy. A bronze-using economy was peculiarly subject to these hazards, in the same manner as an oil-using people today, and one of the incidental results of the utilization of iron was to restore something of economic self-sufficiency to many communities, since iron ore is so incomparably more abundant than are those of copper and tin.

Vanity and snobbery are themes as recurrent in prehistory and early history as they are today, finding their expression in the use of precious metals such as gold—rare, incorruptible, beautiful and easily worked—or the magic, electrical, attractive amber. Not much is known of the gold sources in the ancient world, but it must be remembered that once a certain amount of the metal had been won and worked, it was easier to acquire by piracy or looting than by prospecting. Great quantities of gold must have been melted down and refashioned from generation to generation in antiquity: perpetually reborn in new splendour for the delight of mankind, it was dealt with in a manner more civilized than that of storage in bank vaults.

The domestication of farmyard animals such as cattle, sheep, goats and pigs goes back to the beginning of agriculture itself, but the horse, an animal not of the Fertile Crescent but of the steppe lands on its northern fringe, was not domesticated until later times. Its use, after all, was limited. A small agile type of pony has no advantage over the ox as a draught animal, mare's milk is not superior to cow's, and in the settled village economy the horse had little place. Among the pastoralists the horse could be tamed for traction at greater speed than oxen, and eventually used as an animal for riding. But it was warfare that gave the horse its chance. Speed and agility in drawing the warrior's chariot, and later the mounted bowman, could be provided by the horse alone; and ancient warfare, both in the Near East and in Europe, was revolutionised by the use of the horse as a traction animal from about 1600 BC onwards.

The basic elements of artificial forms of locomotion were early appreciated. The boat, the sledge and the ski were known among the North European hunters and fishers before the beginning of agriculture in the Near East, though it was in this latter region that wheeled vehicles seem to have been invented before 3000 BC. We know little of early ships, which in their very nature are not likely to survive, but every settlement on an island presupposes shipping of some kind, and representations of ships on early decorated pottery or textiles in Egypt are among the first pieces of evidence we have of the type of vessel, the use of oars or of a sail.

Writing

Amongst these basic skills and inventions, whose development we have shown visually in the chart on pages 16 and 17, perhaps the greatest invention of all was that of writing, the discovery that a set of conventional symbols could be constructed whereby human speech could be recorded in permanent form. This discovery, so far as the Old World was concerned, was made in Mesopotamia, around 3000 BC, and as with all inventions, it came about in response to a particular need. The early Mesopotamian communities had developed rapidly from villages to towns, and with such development the social structure had become correspondingly complex. Commercial transactions were no longer on the simple level of barter between individuals, but with the beginnings of a bureaucracy centred on the temples, were becoming impersonal, large-scale, and long-term. Some notation to record the receipt of temple dues in kind, to reckon with mercantile affairs, to provide a check on defaulters or those engaged in sharp practice was necessary once the system had arrived at a stage when all these things could no longer be kept in a man's memory.

Writing, then, was primarily the product of societies with a strong sense of private and public property. Only in such a society had it a use. An imaginative literature, the tales of heroes, the genealogies of chieftains, the dictates of the gods can all be conveyed and transmitted by an oral, word-of-mouth, tradition, and were so composed and handed down in antiquity, from the *Iliad* and the *Odyssey* to the northern sagas, and the Irish tales composed in the early centuries AD and still part of the Celtic oral tradition in the British Isles.

Climate

A question which is often asked concerns the climate of a particular region at a particular point in remote antiquity. What is not always realised is that any estimation of ancient climatic conditions is so complex a problem that it may in the present state of evidence be called insoluble. Variations of climate in the past can be traced only by their influence on the natural environment as represented by plants and animals, and for more recent prehistoric antiquity the influence of climate has to be distinguished from the influence of man on the landscape: the deforestation of an area by man (and goats) may well alter the climatic balance of the region. In the critical regions of the Mediterranean and the Near East we know least of climatic change, since archaeologists working in these areas have made the recovery of works of art their primary objective, and innumerable large-scale excavations have been conducted in which the environmental evidence was ignored, and indeed destroyed. In northern Europe we know a great deal more of the main phases of climatic change from Glacial times onwards, but even here the subject bristles with uncertainties.

Migrations

Readers thinking only in terms of the modern world may be surprised to encounter in this book so many references to the movements of peoples: small-scale settlements or wholesale migrations inferred from the evidence of archaeology and sometimes of linguistics as well. We are accustomed to think of human communities as being essentially permanent and stable, and forget that this permanence and stability is, particularly in Europe, a relatively late achievement, dating in fact only from the early Middle Ages so far as we in North-West Europe are concerned. The life of the hunter-fishers was one of complete mobility, their movements being dictated by the seasonal migrations of the animals on which they depended for food. With the advent of animal and plant domestication in the ancient Near East, the prerequisites of settled life were available, and the village and urban civilizations which grew up in Mesopotamia or Egypt were the first communities to achieve this stability. Even an agriculturalist cannot always maintain a fixed settlement, if the land he tills becomes exhausted and he has no knowledge of the techniques of fallow or manuring; the village must move, and crop another area of virgin land until that too is exhausted. In such manner the earliest stone-using agricultural communities of Central Europe moved across the country from the middle Danube to the lower Rhine.

Another element of instability was of course necessarily present in pastoral communities such as those of the steppe lands, whose rhythm of life was dictated, almost in the manner of the hunters of the last Ice Ages, by the animals which now formed their flocks and herds. In both simple agriculture and advanced pastoralism, then, there was a mobile quality which would allow of the movement of tribes or smaller groups of people, and such movement would be taken for granted. In relation to the available land for crops or pasture the human population was tiny, and there was room for all. And within the general framework of this accepted mobility there would fit the more deliberate and warlike movements of warrior bands, out to gain prestige and loot like the Vikings by sea and the Teutonic peoples by land in post-Roman Europe, when the removal of imposed rule by a static form of economy allowed a relapse into the more normal and accustomed mobility of the pre-Roman world.

Languages

It is in terms of this mobility of ancient peoples that we can see something of the likely stages in the transmission of certain groups of related languages in Eurasia from somewhere before 2000 BC. Language 'families' of related dialects must have grown up from the most ancient times, but we can perceive their existence only when we have written records attesting the languages either directly (by being written in the particular language with which we are concerned) or indirectly, as when words and names of places or persons in one language are quoted in another.

By about 2500 BC the main language group in the Ancient Near East was that of the Semitic variants, but beyond and to the north of the relatively high civilizations with these forms of speech was a large group of related dialects, or languages of a quite different type. These were languages which were to have a remarkably wide and effective dispersal, for by 1000 BC, to take a convenient round date, they must have been spoken from India in the east to Central and Western Europe.

It is from the fact of this wide geographical dispersal that the related languages in question have been classed as Indo-European. Philologists, working with archaeologists and ancient historians, are beginning to define, however roughly, the areas within which the related languages could have developed from a common stock, and the sequence and routes of the various movements of peoples which took the languages to their ancient, and often their modern homeland. Somewhere between the Carpathians and the Caucasus seems a possible place of origin for the Indo-European group of languages, with Hittite and Celtic and the Italic language behind Latin as among the earlier of the variants to be transmitted to Anatolia, Central Europe and Italy respectively. Later movements would have taken Sanskrit to India and Greek to the Aegean; later still the Germanic languages were to develop in Central Europe in close contact with Celtic, and the Slav tongues to acquire their distinctive forms.

Conclusions

What, if anything, can be said in general about the achievements and failures of man before history, in the usually accepted sense, takes up the tale? The first thing that must be rembered is the fact, emphasised already in this Introduction, that material evidence will give material results. You cannot, from archaeological evidence, inform yourself on man's ideas, beliefs, fears or aspirations. You cannot understand what his works of art or craftmanship signified to him: indeed this is also true of many historically documented communities in the ancient world. Without a written record, and one in some detail, you can have no knowledge of social or political systems, of ethical or legal codes. Even when the evidence for these, or some of these, is available, it may be extremely difficult to interpret, simply because our knowledge of the intellectual and emotional context in which it was framed is itself so tenuous.

Perhaps all we can really perceive is the history of technology, making and doing as expressed in material objects. We can certainly see how in some communities, notably the earliest agricultural societies of the Ancient East, technical innovation was set at a premium. As heirs to these societies, most of us accept such a view unquestioningly; but many societies in antiquity did not, and some still today regard the innovator with the gravest suspicion and genuine hostility whether he comes from outside or from among themselves. If we start making value judgements about the past, from the viewpoint that technical development is an unquestioned good, we class these societies as the failures. But that is just what we should not do. We should not expect to seek in history either a justification or an explanation of our own thoughts and actions, except in so far as we inherit a complex mass of unapprehended mental attitudes which go back not only to Greece and Rome, not only to Ur and Memphis, but back beyond this to the hunters and fishers of the Ice Ages. What we like to call our thinking may be as much conditioned by the fears and prejudices of the mammoth-hunter or the neolithic peasant as by the religious aspirations of the early Semites or the speculative thoughts of the Greeks.

The final point to be made is that this book has been deliberately planned as a co-operative inquiry into the human past. The answer to those who may wonder why it could not have been the work of one man is that specialisation due to increasing knowledge makes it inevitable that a survey of the foundations of civilizations on a world-wide basis must be the work of several scholars each familiar with his own field. Nor is this a negative virtue, for there is no one absolute 'truth' about historical events, and still less for those concerning the prehistoric past. What we *can* know is limited by the evidence at our disposal, and by the way that evidence is interpreted. So many men, so many differences in approach to the story of the early past of man in the Old and New Worlds, give us, because of its composite nature, a truer view than that of a single scholar with a single line of inquiry. Differences in emphasis and selection, and in assessing this or that contribution to the sum of human development, are both salutary and stimulating; they are but one aspect of this book, which has been written not only to inform, but also to excite.

BASIC SKILLS OF THE HUNTER AND FOOD GATHERER

The making of recognisable tools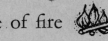

Use of fire

Earliest known wooden spears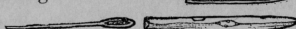

Earliest evidence for bows and arrows

Earliest domestication of dog

Earliest fishing nets and boats with paddles

Sledges on runners

Skis

SKILLS DEVELOPED FROM AGRICULTURE AND PASTORALISM

First cultivation of cereal crops

Domestication of sheep, goats and cattle

Domestication of horse

Earliest cultivated rice

Manufacture of linen

Manufacture of cotton

Manufacture of wool

Basketry

Sailing boats

Use of solid and tripartite wheels

Use of spoked wheels

Metal working in copper, bronze and gold

Metal working in iron

Making of pottery

Making of faience

Making of glass

THE ARTS

Representational art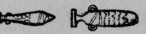

Human portraiture

Writing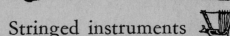

Blown instruments

Stringed instruments

Landmarks of man's cultural achievements 500,000–1,000 BC

IN THIS CHART we have selected some of the most important technological discoveries and developments made by the diverse groups which form the theme of this book.

The *Basic Skills* are the achievements of the earliest and most primitive societies, *Agriculture and Pastoralism* and the skills developed by the more settled and gradually urbanized cultures follow next. Finally though representational art and the first music-making go back to the Stone Age, others of the *Arts* such as writing were once more products of the first urban communities.

The illustrations are for the most part of actual objects, the geographical divisions only approximate. Thus 'Africa' should be understood to include the whole continent excepting the Nilotic region.

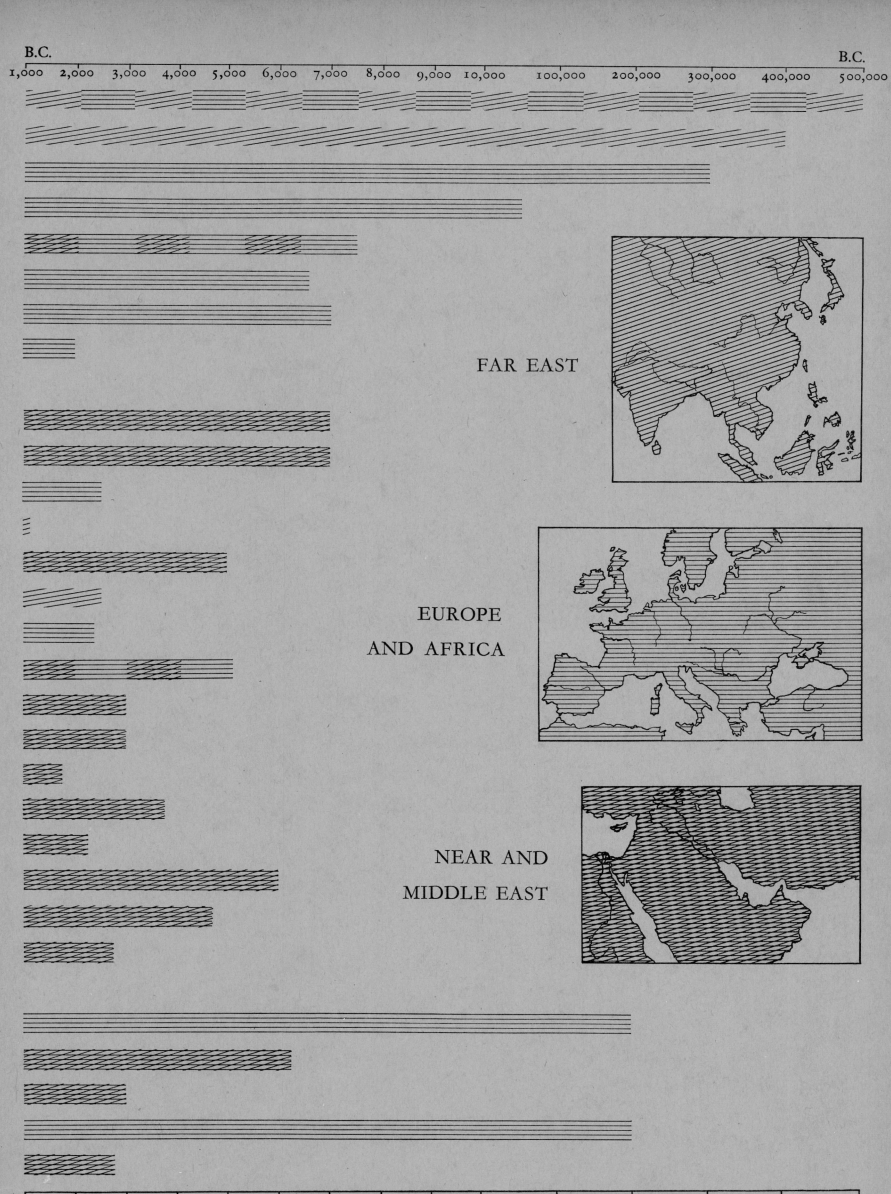

FAR EAST

EUROPE
AND AFRICA

NEAR AND
MIDDLE EAST

I THE FIRST HALF-MILLION YEARS

The hunters and gatherers of the Stone Age

GRAHAME CLARK

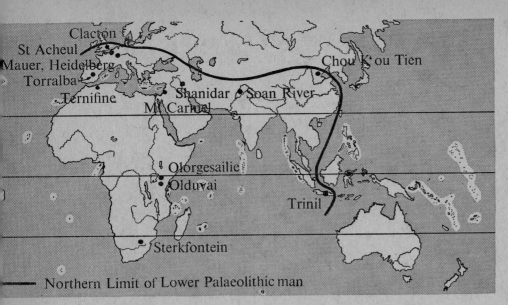

Clacton
St Acheul
Mauer, Heidelberg
Torralba
Ternifine
Shanidar · Soan River
Mt Carmel
Chou K'ou Tien

Olorgesailie
Olduvai

Trinil

Sterkfontein

——— Northern Limit of Lower Palaeolithic man

Oban
Star Carr · Mullerup
Gagarino
Kostienki
La Madeleine · Angles-sur-l'Anglin · Dolni Vĕstonice
Sauveterre-la-Lemance · Szeleta
La Solutré
Altamira · Lascaux · Niaux
Tuc d'Audoubert · La Portel
Mas-d'Azil
Wady-en-Natuf · Jericho

〰〰〰 Known final limit of ice sheets

᭄ ----- Shore line at end of Palæolithic period

On this reference page are (above) a map of the sites where remains of Lower Palaeolithic man have been found, and (right) some sites of importance for periods both before and after the major climatic changes of c. 10,000 BC. Below is a diagram showing the technological development of Man from his probable first appearance on earth: the vast expanse of time from 1,000,000 to 100,000 BC has been visually compressed.

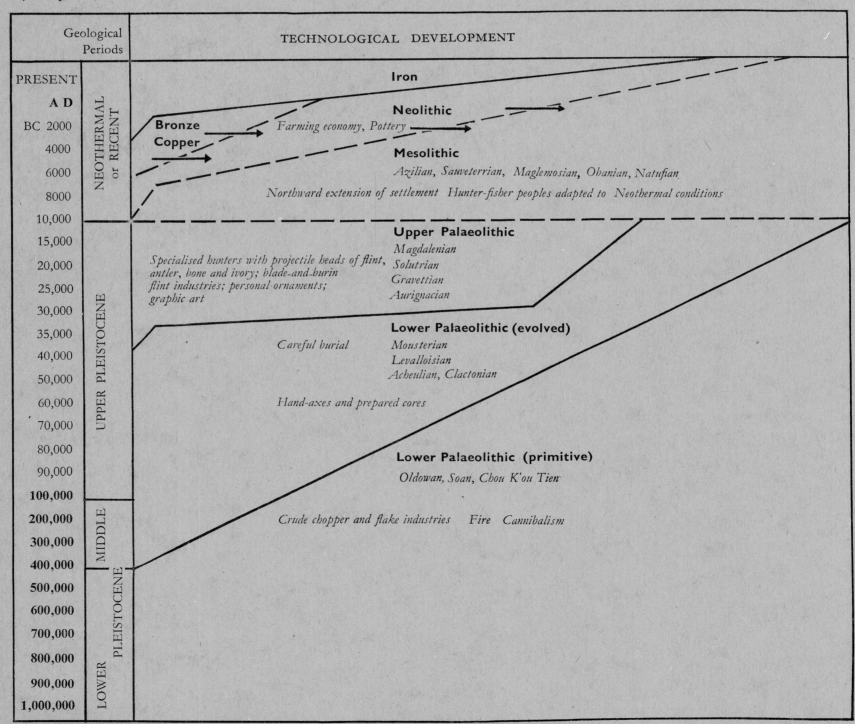

Geological Periods		TECHNOLOGICAL DEVELOPMENT

PRESENT AD — **Iron**

BC 2000 — **Neolithic**

Bronze
Copper — *Farming economy, Pottery* —

4000 — **Mesolithic**

6000 — *Azilian, Sauveterrian, Maglemosian, Obanian, Natufian*

8000 — *Northward extension of settlement Hunter-fisher peoples adapted to Neothermal conditions*

(NEOTHERMAL or RECENT)

10,000

15,000 — **Upper Palaeolithic**
Magdalenian

Specialised hunters with projectile heads of flint,
20,000 — *antler, bone and ivory; blade-and-burin* *Solutrian*
flint industries; personal ornaments;
25,000 — *graphic art* *Gravettian*
Aurignacian

30,000

35,000 — **Lower Palaeolithic (evolved)**

Careful burial *Mousterian*
40,000 — *Levalloisian*
Acheulian, Clactonian
50,000

60,000 — *Hand-axes and prepared cores*

70,000

(UPPER PLEISTOCENE)

80,000

90,000 — **Lower Palaeolithic (primitive)**
Oldowan, Soan, Chou K'ou Tien

100,000

200,000 — *Crude chopper and flake industries   Fire   Cannibalism*

(MIDDLE)

300,000

400,000

500,000

600,000

700,000

800,000

900,000

1,000,000

(LOWER PLEISTOCENE)

The creature that was to become Man

may have been on this earth already over a million years ago. The creature that certainly was modern man, *Homo sapiens*, first appeared between 30 and 40,000 years ago. During the long ages between, while the ice was spreading down from the poles and retreating again, an ape-like being seems to have descended from the trees to live mainly on the ground. He already had both eyes looking towards the front, and to avoid danger on the ground he had to be able to look round quickly in all directions. To do this was easiest when standing upright on two legs; so he learnt to walk upright. With both fore-limbs now free, he could use objects to hand as tools. Later he learnt to *make* tools for future use, and because these tools began to appear in standardized form we infer that he could use sounds not just to express emotions (as the apes do today), but also to convey information to his fellows and to train his growing young. He was not especially fleet of foot, nor were his teeth adapted for fighting: only by cunning could he escape his enemies. So gradually, by the slow processes of evolution, the size of his brain increased.

The first tool-making humans of whom we have a clear picture lived perhaps 400,000 years ago. Their remains were found at Chou K'ou Tien near Peking, including an almost complete human skull, remains of more than forty persons, crude stone implements and the bones of many animals, especially deer. The reconstruction above, by Maurice Wilson, is based on these discoveries.

The humans were about 5 feet tall, of much the same build as modern man. They were hunters who had learnt to make fire, for hearths and charred long bones have been found. The man squatting in the foreground is making a quartz pebble tool, crudely shaped by chipping away flakes with a hammer stone. An upturned skull contains mulberries gathered from the trees beyond the cave entrance.

The Peking human was a thorough-going cannibal. He extracted marrow from the bones of both men and animals, and from the way he enlarged the opening at the base of the human skull it is clear he had a special taste for the brain. It was a practice, however, which sharply distinguished him from the apes. They were, and still are, mainly vegetarian.

This early human type, who has been given the name *Pithecanthropus*, was a hunter who could find many animals for food: bones have been traced of deer, antelope, horse, wild pig, bison, water-buffalo, elephant, rhinoceros and monkey, as well as several species of carnivore. The only weapons he had for the chase were the crudely shaped stones described below and wooden spears with the pointed end hardened in the fire. But he had one advantage which was to be decisive: he could match strength with cunning, for his brain was now nearly twice the size of that of any known predecessor. (1)

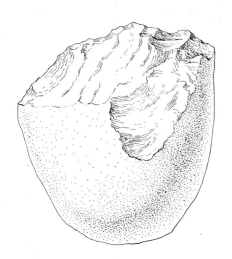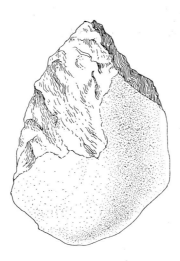

The first tools made by man are sometimes hard to distinguish from natural stones. This drawing, from an actual example found at Olduvai, East Africa, illustrates how they were made first by breaking stones until one was left with a sharp ridge, and then by chipping both sides of the core to form a jagged edge. Such tools have been found in South Africa and from India to Europe. (2)

21

The giant men and beasts of East Africa lived a quarter of a million years ago. Evidence for them has been found in the Olduvai Gorge, and it is on the discoveries in the lower levels of the thick sequence of old lake deposits there that the reconstruction above is based. The wart-hogs shown were almost as big as a rhinoceros; accompanying them were giant varieties of giraffe, horse, pig, sheep and baboon.

The country is dry and barren, with rocky and sandy soil. The hunters have settled in an open-air hunting camp at the water-holes. With only wooden spears and sharpened flints as weapons, they probably drove their huge quarry towards prepared pit-fall traps or the clayey beds of streams, to immobilize the animals before attacking them. Neither men nor women wore clothing, nor is there any evidence of personal adornment. (3)

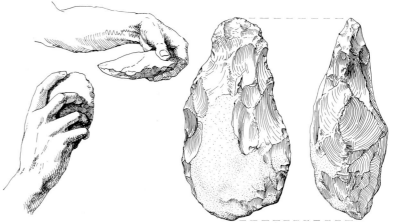

The slowly growing skill of Man is well illustrated by the emergence of the hand-axes. They developed from the crude chopper tools of the first humans to flaked stones, still made by repeated blows from a hammer stone, with jagged working edges on either side of a pointed end (left). Later secondary flaking was done by means of a soft cylinder of bone or wood, which removed shallower flakes and produced a thinner tool with a more even, carefully shaped working edge all round. At about the same time we find that tortoise-shaped cores were first made and smaller tools struck from them, perhaps to be further shaped into scrapers or points (extreme right).

The tools, grasped directly in the hand (the most versatile and accommodating of holders), seem to have been used for digging up roots, cutting meat and shaping wood. (4)

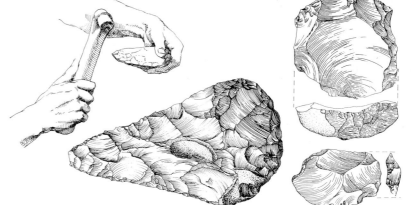

23

appeared much later, about 25,000 BC. By this time *Homo sapiens*, modern man, was making objects to adorn himself, and occasionally his valuables in bone and ivory were decorated with simple geometrical patterns. But more significant perhaps were the small figurines of women that have been found over a wide area from South Russia to Italy and France. They were carved in the round from stone or from mammoth ivory, or they were modelled in clay and hardened in the fire. These are not portraits: the heads are often blank knobs only, the arms puny, the legs tapered. The emphasis on sexual characteristics, full breasts, prominent buttocks and signs of pregnancy, suggest a concern with fertility and the reproduction of the artists' own kind. Their purpose is not known, but for the first time man is expressing his emotions and anxieties in effective works of art.

The baked mud and bone statuette (above left) is typical. It came from a mammoth hunters' settlement in Moravia, where clay animals were also found. (5)

The ivory figurine (centre) was found at Lespugue, southern France. (6)

A mammoth's tusk, also from Moravia, has survived in part (right). A fine tool has been used to cut on it a primitive figure, with triangular head and enlarged pelvic area, in geometrical style. (7)

The elaborate coiffure on the ivory head (left) is in sharp contrast with the token heads of the figurines opposite. It is perhaps one of the earliest attempts at human portraiture. The head was found in the Landes, France and is less than an inch and a half long. (8)

The mammoth hunters of southern Russia are typical of the people of this time. The reconstruction below is based upon discoveries at Pushkari, where the people lived, not in caves but on open sites in tents of skin supported by poles and held down by stones or mammoth bones. They were fully clothed in skins and warmed by fires inside the dwellings. They carved in ivory and bone, making small implements such as awls or bodkins as well as personal ornaments. Remains of these people are spread over Europe as far as Italy, France and Spain. (9)

The most splendid artistic achievements of Early Man were accomplished while the ice still covered large tracts of Northern Europe. They are the remarkable and revealing paintings, engravings and reliefs found in the caves of south-western France, Spain and Italy. They date from between 10,000 and 25,000 years ago.

The enduring backgrounds for this early art were the walls, ceilings and occasionally the floors of caves deep in the rock, often far from the possible reach of daylight (the paintings at Niaux in the Dordogne begin 550 yards from the entrance and continue as far as 1,200 yards or more). They must have been drawn by the flickering light of fire or torch.

The paintings are the work of gifted men, with their frequent realistic detail, rapid and convincing movement, and use of colour and shading. The existence of well-defined styles, in region and in time, suggest that the art was transmitted from master to pupils. But such a society could not maintain full-time artists, and it would be quite wrong to assess the paintings as art created for art's sake. What then was their purpose?

A clue to the meaning of cave art can perhaps be obtained from the famous dancing figure found in Les Trois Frères in the Ariège. The original, and a drawing from it, are shown below (left). It is a painting in black of a bearded figure wearing a mask and antlers of a red deer, the skin of a horse or wolf and a long, bushy tail. The suggestion that the dance was part of a magic ritual is inescapable. (10)

A crouching cave bear, found modelled in clay at Montespan, Haute Garonne, is a further clue to the early artists' purpose. The actual skull was found between the paws. Stabbing marks are clearly visible in the clay animals' flanks, and the scene which they suggest is reconstructed inside the fold opposite. The model is covered with a bear's pelt and head. Men dressed in animal masks and skins perform a dance in which the bear is killed in mime by ritual stabbing. No clothing other than the skins is worn.

To understand the art of Early Man we must look today at a society like that of the Australian aborigines, among whom art is not an amusement or a means of self-expression, but part of the rites and ceremonies seeking reassurance in birth, death, fertility and the propitiation of evil forces — rituals which involve mime, dancing and the recitation of legends. Early man lived by success in the hunt, his most important source of food and clothing. With his primitive equipment it must have been a constant source of problems and anxiety. We might expect him therefore to seek confidence and success from magic. Animals which were direct rivals, or difficult to find and kill, are the more frequently represented; fish, easily caught, and plants, not important for food, are rare. Although we cannot be certain, it seems likely that dances with masked figures were performed in magical rites. Cave art could have been part of these rites, or the setting in which they took place. (11)

In the famous caves at Lascaux, on the wall at the entrance to the main gallery, was found the painting above. A bison faces to the right, at bay, its back pierced by darts, implying sympathetic magic. The drawing is in two colours, the darts incised. Running towards the left is a bistre horse with black mane, its rear engraved over the bison.

The cave artists frequently painted or engraved one subject over another; by studying these much has been discovered of sequence in the paintings. As early as 20,000 years ago, wavy lines were painted on rock or traced on clay by the finger. Outline drawings and paintings appeared, with some flat-wash, the beginnings of work in two colours, and also low-reliefs. The bison and horse above are examples of two-colour work of the middle period. In the second cycle the low-reliefs died out, to be succeeded by fine engravings with thin shading. The climax of achievement was reached in the splendid multi-coloured paintings of Altamira or Font de Gaume.

The paintings were coloured with various kinds of ochre, manganese and charcoal, for which bone containers have been found. (13)

On a low cave roof at Altamira appears a multi-coloured 'picture gallery' containing more than 100 overlapping figures. On the opposite page are some of a group of bison which form part of it. The artist made clever use of the bosses on the roof to obtain the effect of relief, as elsewhere he has placed wounds at natural drip marks. (12)

old
out ▶

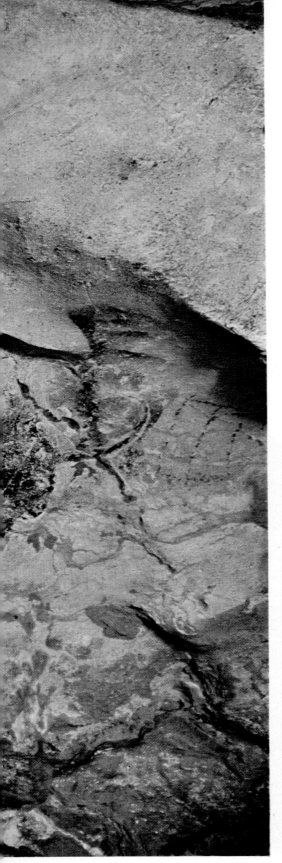

The reliefs, carved by stone from stone, are shown in two examples below. In one, two ibex are interlocked in battle; in the other, a boar is followed by a wild horse. These reliefs are in the combined cave and rock-shelter at Le Roc-de-Sers, Charente. (14)

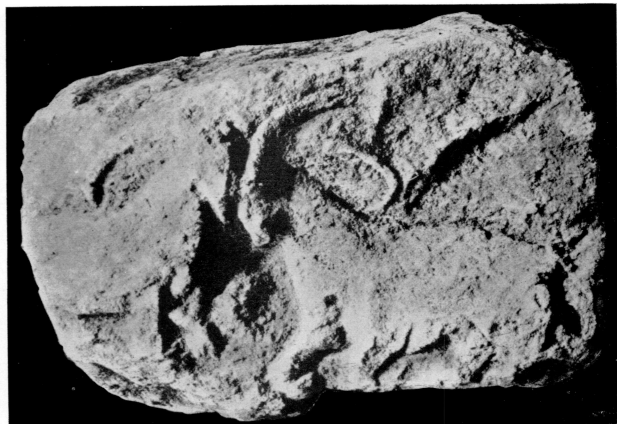

The final retreat of the ice

between 9000 and 8000 BC brought profound changes rapidly to the people of Europe and the Mediterranean lands. The rain belts passed from north Africa and south-west Asia, leaving the lands arid and forcing the people into emigration or a radical readjustment of their mode of living. The temperate and fertile areas crept northwards in the wake of the receding ice, became covered with extensive forests and provided food and shelter for a rich fauna. The old world was breaking up and a new one, ripe for dramatic development, was slowly forming.

The response of the hunters to these changes was most positive in the north of Europe, where the Baltic was still a lake and the North Sea largely dry land. They liked to live near open water, and hunted the game which abounded in the forests: elk, aurochs, red deer, wild pig and roe deer. They fished with spears and by hooks and nets. Their weapons were made from bone, antler or wood; they made great use of the forest trees, cut down by primitive flint axes set in handles. They had no cave art (there are no caves), but decorated their tools, weapons and ornaments readily.

The human figure (right), engraved on a mattock head made from a stag antler, echoes in its triangular head the decoration on a mammoth tusk of about 18,000 years earlier (pl. 7). The mattock head was found in Denmark. (16)

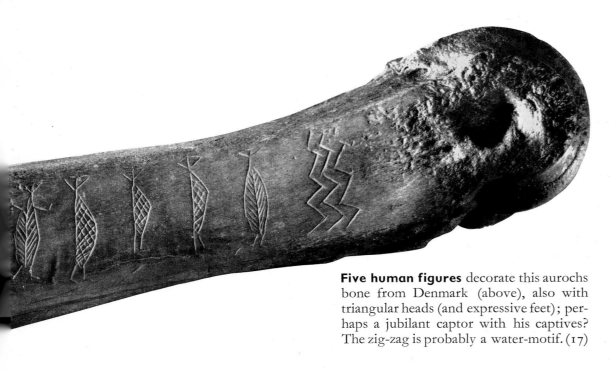

Five human figures decorate this aurochs bone from Denmark (above), also with triangular heads (and expressive feet); perhaps a jubilant captor with his captives? The zig-zag is probably a water-motif. (17)

The barbed harpoon below (left), which follows on those of the cave artists, was made from an antler, and is typical; it was found with three others and an antler axe in a bog in Denmark. The wooden longbow (right) is also from Denmark; arrows were tipped and barbed with flints. (15)

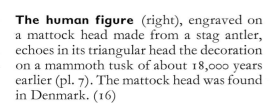

Many weapons and tools have been found. Above is a dug-out canoe from the Netherlands; a Carbon 14 test gave a date of 6300 BC, making it the earliest in the world. Below is the head of a tree-felling axe from Denmark, with its flint blade set into an antler holder. The drawing of the grubbing mattock of antler shows how the wooden handles were attached (left). To the right are birch bark floats and sections of a bast fish-net found in Finland (similar knots are used by fishermen in North Europe today). The drawing below shows a bone fish-hook from Denmark and a paddle from North Germany. (18)

The lake-side dwellers of the North lived the kind of life shown in the reconstruction below. It is based upon discoveries at Star Carr in Yorkshire, in Denmark and in Schleswig-Holstein. The men are tall and well-built, with prominent brows and pale brown hair. They paddle a dug-out canoe and catch pike by spear or by seine nets (in the canoe). Two women skin and cut up an elk. The round huts, made perhaps of branches rammed into the ground and pulled together at the top, were frequently built on a platform of brush-wood. The forest is of pine and birch, with alders in the foreground. A man fells them with a flint-bladed axe. Dogs seem not yet to have been trained to hunt for man; they are companions and scavengers. Beavers are at work on a dam; a red deer and a wild pig are in the forest; duck, a crested grebe and cranes feed on the lake. There are no cultivated crops and there is no pottery. (19)

In south-western Europe at this time, change was slow and development even arrested. The conventional designs (above), on pebbles in red ochre found in the Ariège, date from c. 8000 BC; they may represent human figures and contrast markedly with the great artistic flowering of the earlier age of cave art. (20)

The sea-fishers of the North came later. The reconstruction on the right is based on discoveries at a settlement in Oban, c. 2500 BC. Large numbers of shell refuse-heaps from such settlements are known on the Scandinavian and British coasts. The man in the foreground has caught sea fish with a bone harpoon on a line, from a boat of seal skins stretched over a wooden frame. In the background, a man clubs a seal, whose bones are very frequent. A great auk stands on the sea's edge; white-tailed eagles fly above. While the men in the North lived like this, the first Neolithic settlements were developing in the South. (21)

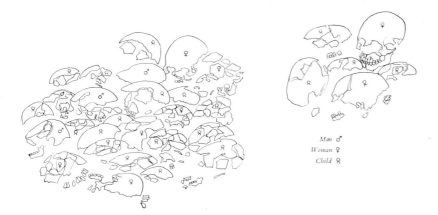

Man ♂
Woman ♀
Child ♀

Thirty-three human skulls of this time were found in two depressions in a cave at Ofnet, in Bavaria. They were covered with red ochre and faced west. Of twenty-seven in the larger pit, four are identified in the key as men, seven as women and fifteen as children. The smaller pit contains three children and two women. The evidence suggests that all met a violent death. Near the skull in the left bottom corner lie the perforated shells of a necklace. These shells are illustrated separately below; they are similar to those found at Mugharet el-Wad, Transjordan. (22)

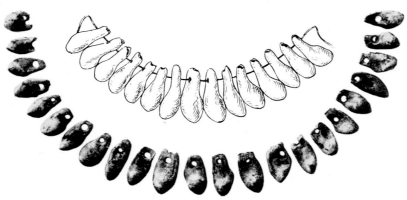

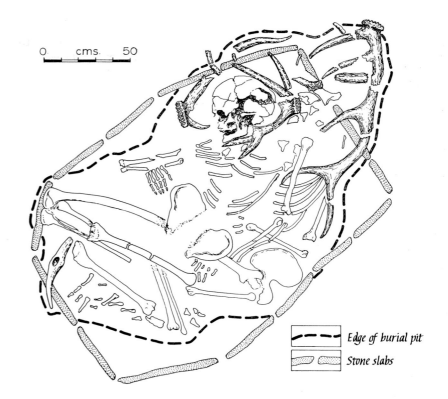

0   cms.   50

The grave of a man of about 4000 BC is shown in the drawing on the right. It is stone-lined and has a crest of antler crowns, and was one of ten graves containing 23 skeletons found among the refuse of the settlement on Téviec, an island off the coast of Morbihan, Brittany. (23)

— — — Edge of burial pit

▨▨▨ Stone slabs

The hunters and gatherers of the Stone Age

GRAHAME CLARK

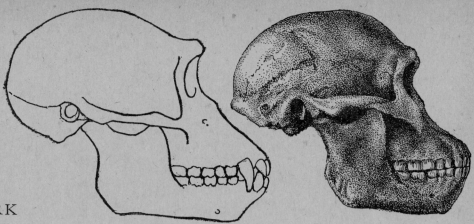

Ape and 'pre-man': skull of chimpanzee (left) and of Australopithe-cus transvaalensis. *The former is enlarged, for comparison. (fig. 1)*

Speech and Tools

WHEN did our remote forebears cross the threshold of humanity? There is a very real sense in which man made himself—by developing his own resources he succeeded in escaping more and more from the trammels both of his external environment and of the animal appetites inherited as a part of his own organism. As he added to his culture early man was confronted with a progressively wider range of choice: indeed one might say that prehistory is exciting precisely because it allows us to watch, alongside the development of material achieve-ments, the growth of man's awareness of his own situation, an aware-ness that implied from the beginning an element of conscious choice.

Culture in the broadest sense may be defined as a learnt mode of behaviour inherited by virtue of belonging to a social group. In this sense it is far older than the emergence of even the earliest primate: one may recall, for example, that bird song includes distinct local cultures within the general pattern of the species as a whole. Man is thus not distinguished from the other animals through the possession of culture, but rather through the *progressive* character of his culture. The possibility of *enlarging* and *transmitting* a growing body of culture depends above all on the ability to invent and employ symbols. Experts are agreed that one of the biggest drawbacks suffered by the great apes in comparison with even the simplest human communities is their limited range of communication. It is true that chimpanzees have a very wide 'register of emotional expression' and that they are able to communicate not only their emotional states but also definite desires; yet, as Köhler has emphasized, 'their gamut of phonetics is entirely "subjective", and can only express emotions, never designate or describe objects'. In their heroic enterprise of rearing the chimpanzee Vicki from the age of three days to three years, Dr and Mrs Hayes found it possible to train her to commands, but failed after eighteen months of intensive tuition to get her to identify her nose, eyes, hands or feet. The possibility of transmitting and so of accumulating any considerable body of culture hardly existed, therefore, until the homi-nids (the family of Man, from the time when it divided from that of the apes) had developed *words* as symbols. This can be said with certainty even though there is no direct means for studying the earliest development of speech. We can infer it from the appearance of tools of standardized form, though even here one should not forget the possibility of learning through direct imitation.

Man's capacity for making *tools* to supplement his limbs is another basic distinction, this time one which finds a place in the archaeologi-cal records. Although the one presumably developed from the other, there is a world of difference between *tool-using* and *tool-making*. If we define tool-using as the use by an animal of objects from its environment to serve its own purposes we must admit that very lowly organisms could be classified as falling within this category. Thus, even the great apes can use tools, and are often ingenious in manipulating sticks and strings or in stacking boxes, though their use even of these reveals grave limitations: it is not merely that they rely more upon blind im-provisation than upon insight, but their activities are directed exclus-ively to securing visible objectives. Tool-making on the other hand implies an element of foresight or at least a willingness to devote labour to making things ready to use at some future, undefined time. Moreover the tools themselves are not simply existing objects used for special purposes: they are artificial creations and, however elemen-tary, they exhibit the styles prevailing in the communities of their makers.

The transition from using whatever lay at hand to fashioning tools is difficult to detect, because it was gradual and ill-defined; natural fragments of flint or stone might for example be adapted for use with only the minimum of artificial modification. There is also a special difficulty here: natural and artificial flints unfortunately often resemble each other and in the past mistakes have been made. Flints that used to be thought examples of early human workmanship are now known to occur in certain types of natural deposit of widely varying geologi-cal age and in some cases it is even possible to observe them at the present day in process of formation. Many factors, therefore, have to be taken into consideration in estimating the value of such discoveries.

It is still an open question at what stage in their evolution the homi-nids began to make tools. They had certainly been *using* them from a very remote period, although even an approximate date is difficult to fix. At some time during Late Tertiary times, groups of ape-like creatures seem to have descended from the trees that had previously been their home and begun to live mainly on the ground. How this crucial step came to be taken cannot be known for certain. Probably it happened in savannah country, when the ape ancestors had to go down to the ground from time to time in order to cross from one clump of trees to the next.

The creature already had the advantage of binocular vision (i.e. both eyes looking to the front). From now on he became more and more an eye-animal, and less and less dependent upon his sense of smell. To avoid danger on the ground he had to be able to look round quickly in all directions. The easiest way to do this was to stand upright on two legs, and this position gradually became habitual, as can be proved from the study of the skeleton throughout the various stages of Man's evolution. This was of great importance for the future, since it left the fore-limbs free for the handling of tools. Intelligence now came to have survival value, and by the slow processes of biological mutation the brain size increased.

The stage of transition is well represented by the genus *Australo-pithecus (fig. 1)*. It was at this period that pre-man was making his tenta-tive beginnings at all the activities that were eventually to lead to civili-zation: tool-making, the formation of social units and a form of speech. The ability consciously to communicate information meant that experience became cumulative, and each successive generation could draw on that of its predecessors for its technical skill.

Of *Australopithecus* about 100 individuals are known. The skeleton shows that he habitually stood on two legs. The cranial capacity had increased and the skull was assuming a more definitely human appear-ance. Intelligence was now the chief means of defence. *Australo-pithecus* could not rely on flight to save himself from predators nor were his teeth adapted for fighting. Only his ability to use tools and to defeat his enemies by cunning enabled him to survive. We must not assume, however, that Man is descended from *Australopithecus*; more probably the ancestor of present-day Man was a distinct but related branch.

At Sterkfontein in the Transvaal, teeth of *Australopithecus (fig. 1)* have been discovered together with primitive pebble-tools. Some scholars infer from this that he made the tools himself, but it is, of course, just as likely that he was the victim of the maker of the tools who himself may have been human. The same uncertainty applies to remains of an Australopithecine recently recovered from a tool-bearing stratum at Olduvai in Tanganyika.

The earliest creatures known for certain to have been toolmakers were of the genus *Pithecanthropus (fig. 2)*, whose average brain size was almost twice that of *Australopithecus*. They represent the stage in Man's evolution attained during Middle Pleistocene times, although once again we must not assume that the line of descent is direct. The anthropians lived during the Middle Pleistocene Age; the best documented examples are from Java and Peking and of these only the latter certainly made tools (pl. 1).

Food and Hunting

The Peking discoveries provide us with our first clear picture of tool-using human-beings, at a date perhaps 400,000 years ago. The material included traces of *Pithecanthropus* himself, crude stone implements, material from hearths and the remains of food. Such food-remains show a significant fact that at once distinguishes him from the apes: these are mainly vegetarian, whereas *Pithecanthropus* was a meat-eater. The hunting of animals seems to have been one of the means by which man realized his potentialities. Among the animals whose bones have been found are deer, antelope, horse, wild pig, bison, water-buffalo, elephant, rhinoceros and monkey, as well as several species of carnivore. The association of these with ash layers indicative of hearths, the way the bones were broken open for marrow and the presence of a variety of scratches and cut-marks all make it clear that in the main at any rate they represent traces of animals killed for food. The deposit also shows that man had learnt to produce fire and to use it for warmth and for protection (pl. 1).

How was *Pithecanthropus* able to gain a mastery over so wide a range of animals, many of them fleeter and stronger than himself? The answer is two-fold: by his brain and by his culture. The only weapons which on present evidence can certainly be attributed to Lower Palaeolithic man are wooden spears with the pointed end hardened in the fire, like those found in interglacial deposits at Clacton, Essex, and Lohringen, Lower Saxony. Since we know that *Pithecanthropus* employed fire, one may safely assume him able to make wooden weapons. There is on the other hand no evidence whatever, either from the Peking or any other Lower Palaeolithic industry, for the manufacture of separate heads for projectiles made from antler, bone or stone. Fire may very well have been used to stampede or head off game and in conjunction with this the concerted operations of even quite a small band of hunters may well have been sufficient to drive animals over steep places and so disable them. Another way of catching game, especially effective in the case of very large animals, was to employ traps that might consist of little more than pits and stakes, such as could hardly be expected to survive in the archaeological record of geologically remote ages, unless by the most fortunate chance.

Cultural Limitations

The technical means by which *Pithecanthropus* managed to gain so remarkable a mastery over the other animals with whom he competed for food and on whose flesh he largely subsisted were meagre indeed. The stone tools found by his hearths are so crude that many could hardly be recognized as such otherwise than by their association with ash and food refuse. This is no doubt partly due to the difficult character of the raw materials available, notably quartz, greenstone and coarse chert. Among the few recognizable forms may be noted rough flakes, some with 'bipolar' scars caused by crushing between two boulders, and crude chopper tools made by striking a few flakes in either direction from the edge of a flake or pebble. There are signs that antler and bone were utilized and even on occasion cut into sections for convenience, but there is no evidence that these materials were used as raw materials for carefully made implements. Another striking lack is the absence of any trace of personal adornment even so simple as a perforated tooth.

A yet more obvious limitation in thought is implied by the absence of any trace of burial. The whole of the surviving skeletal material relating to *Pithecanthropus pekinensis* himself—and upwards of forty individuals are represented—consists of food refuse. Considering the very large volume of soil minutely examined and the complete absence of even a single tooth of any other type of hominid, it is hardly possible to maintain that *Pithecanthropus* was the victim of any but his own fellows. The only inference we can draw is that he was a thorough-going cannibal; he systematically broke open long bones to extract marrow and from the way he enlarged the occipital opening at the base of the skull it is clear that he had a special taste for the brain.

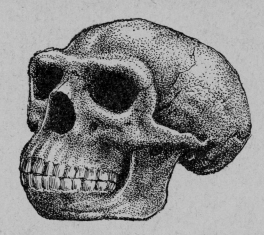

The first known tool-maker : Pithecanthropus pekinensis. *Reconstruction of skull found at Chou K'ou Tien. (fig. 2)*

Progress in Tool-making

Stone industries characterized by crude chopping tools and flakes were widely distributed in the warmer parts of the Old World inhabited by hominids of broadly Pithecanthropian type. The most significant new development of the Middle Pleistocene was the emergence of the hand-axe or *coup-de-poing* (pl. 4). This was made by thinning down a nodule or thick flake on two faces to form an edge that was usually confined to one end but might in highly evolved specimens run all the way round. Since, apart from a few flakes and nondescript forms, this was the only finished implement-type, it can be assumed that it was used for a variety of purposes. The assumption is that hand-axes were probably grasped directly in the hand, the most versatile and accommodating of holders, and used for such purposes as grubbing up roots, cutting up game and shaping wood. They were made from all kinds of raw materials including, in addition to flint and obsidian, the more difficult quartzes, quartzites, lavas and even granites. Yet the degree of standardization of hand-axes of varying stages of development over wide geographical zones is often remarkable. There is no doubt that Africa was the cradle of the hand-axe industries. It is not merely that their geographical distribution is centred on Africa, with extensions into south-west Europe and restricted parts of southern Asia, but it is only there that a continuous history of axe-making can be demonstrated.

One of the most complete sequences of examples is that obtained from Olduvai in Tanganyika, where the erosion of a great gorge through the Serengeti plains exposed a thick sequence of tuffs and old lake sediments laid down in the course of Middle Pleistocene times. The lowermost bed (I), made up of layers of tuffs formed by volcanic ashes that had settled in shallow water, yielded crude chopper tools, made as a rule by striking a few flakes from one or two directions off water-worn pebbles, together with flakes removed by such blows (pl. 2). In the bed above this (II) the pebble tools continued, but at this stage we begin to see the first essays in hand-axes: flaking not unlike that on the choppers has been directed to making jagged working edges on either side of a pointed end, producing hand-axes similar to examples from Abbeville in France. By the top of this bed hand-axes appeared with carefully shaped working edges all the way round; (this style is called 'Acheulian' from St Acheul in France, where specimens were first discovered). Acheulian types of hand-axe are common in the third, higher bed (III), and in the upper layers there is in addition a type of cleaver with a sharp working end formed by the intersection of major flake scars, a type better adapted to granular rocks than to flint and one which is more commonly found in Africa than in Europe. In the final bed (IV) the hand-axes were finely flaked, but, as in the final stages of the Acheulian in Europe, they grew smaller (pl. 4).

The Olduvai sequence, valuable as it is for demonstrating the continuity of the hand-axe tradition in east central Africa, does not tell us much about other aspects of the lives of the tool-makers. For this we must turn to old lake beds close by early camping-places, because these are likely to preserve traces of the rubbish from which we are able to deduce something of their way of life. The most definite impression one receives is that the Lower Palaeolithic hand-axe people

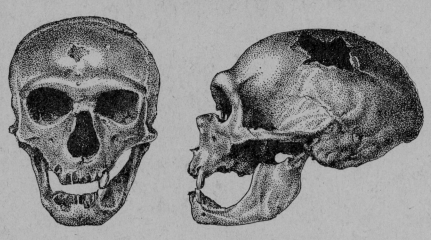

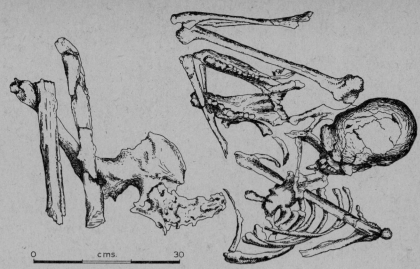

Neanderthal Man: skull of one of the earliest representatives of the genus Homo, *from La Chapelle-aux-Saints. (fig. 3)*

Skeleton from Mount Carmel, where a cemetery provided the earliest evidence of organized burial. (fig. 4)

were as powerful hunters as we have seen *Pithecanthropus* to have been in north China. Thus at Torralba in Spain they accounted for elephant and rhinoceros as well as for smaller quarry like ox, stag and horse; and at Olorgesailie near Nairobi, Kenya, they killed and smashed open the skulls of hippopotamus and of giant varieties of horse, pig, sheep and baboon. These people lived as far back as 250,000 years ago.

Towards the end of the Middle Pleistocene phase in the northern zone of the hand-axe province, the emphasis in working flint and stone began to shift towards flake rather than core tools, i.e. utilizing the fragments broken off a lump of rock instead of the piece that remained. Even in the chopper and hand-axe industries flakes must have been produced in the course of working and it is likely that many of these were used; indeed, in the case of the Clactonian culture of western and central Europe it has been seriously debated whether the heavier pieces were in fact choppers, of which the flakes were by-products, or simply cores incidental to the production of flakes. Contemporaneously and often in closest association with evolved Acheulian hand-axes, we begin to find flakes that have been removed from carefully dressed tortoise-shaped cores, a technique named after the locality of Levallois where they were discovered (pl. 4). Flakes struck from such cores bear traces of the trimming of their parent cores in the form of faceting: they might be used as they were struck or they might be trimmed into shape to form scrapers or points. Further, it would seem that the old Clactonian tradition still persisted and each of these techniques, used in varying degrees by the makers of the Acheulian hand-axes, contributed to the stone industries of early Late Pleistocene times.

These industries, of which variants of that named after the site of Le Moustier in France were notable examples, were made by the earliest representatives of the genus *Homo* or Man properly so-called, namely *Homo neanderthalensis (fig. 3)* and parallel forms. Neanderthal man of the type found in many European centres was something of a special variant adapted perhaps to the extreme climate of the northern parts of the then inhabited world. Related forms from south-western Asia seem to have stood nearer the main line of evolution that led up from the anthropians to modern man *(Homo sapiens)* who first appeared in his modern guise between 30 and 40,000 years ago *(fig. 5)*.

The First Burials

From what we are able to learn from deposits in the caves he occupied, Neanderthal man and his relations in Palestine and other parts of south-west Asia were subject to many of the limitations that applied to *Pithecanthropus* and to his immediate successors. The types of flint implement were still few in number, no standard forms of antler or bone tools were made and apart from the wooden spear, a wound from which was noted in the thigh-bone of one of the Mount Carmel skeletons, no specialized weapons—certainly none with hafted heads—were used. Even more noteworthy, no object of personal adornment has been found, nor any trace of art.

The only new departure of importance was the practice of careful burial of the dead, of which we have evidence in a number of single graves and, on the terrace of the MughVaret es-Skhul, Mount Carmel, a cemetery containing the bodies of ten individuals, ranging from children of three and four to a man of over fifty years of age *(fig. 4)*.

The practice of careful burial in itself allows us to infer some awareness of death as a personal fate, an awareness which may well presage the dawn of religious feeling. In the jaws of a great wild boar apparently clasped in the arms of one of the adult male burials at Mount Carmel, we may see an indication of solicitude for the dead that marks a new stage in the unfolding of human sensibility.

The Aurignacian Culture

It was not until the latter part of the Late Pleistocene, hardly less than thirty to thirty-four thousand years ago, that *Homo sapiens* emerged in his modern guise as the bearer of an advanced hunting culture, based on the use of effective weapons. Precisely when and where the new traditions took shape is still uncertain, but new flint industries had certainly appeared in Palestine and Syria, at any rate in a tentative form, before the development of that known technically as the Levalloiso-Mousterian of the Mount Carmel caves. The new blade-and-burin cultures are marked by a preponderance of regular blades (that is flakes with more or less parallel flake scars, detached probably by punches from well prepared cores), and by burins or graving-tools, with a chisel-like edge formed by striking one or more flakes into the main axis of the blade. The first well defined and widely distributed blade-and-burin culture is named after the French locality of Aurignac, but this is due to nothing more than the priority of French workers in the field of prehistory: in fact the Aurignacian culture almost certainly developed in western Asia, where the thickest deposits are found and which was therefore presumably the centre of the total distribution. Recent exploration has shown that the Aurignacian extended as far east as northern Iraq and Afghanistan and the pattern of finds suggests that it reached western Europe, where it spread as far as the Pyrenees and Cantabria, by way of the Balkans and central Europe.

Although the 'blade-and-burin' people were in due course destined to enlarge dramatically the potentialities of human life, the Aurignacians themselves showed few signs of the glories to come. Like their immediate forebears they were accustomed to live in caves. Some of their most characteristic tools, which were not much more varied than those of the Levalloiso-Mousterians, namely the beaked burin and the rostrate scraper, may have been used for working wood, though no direct evidence for this has survived. The only advance to which they can lay incontrovertible claim lies in the improvement of their weapons, as witnessed by the manufacture of bone points split at the base to engage a shaft; these constitute the first standardized artifacts made from bone.

The Gravettian Culture

Very different in character and showing much more significant signs of increased mental development was the culture that was first recognized in France overlying the Aurignacian and commonly termed Gravettian. Once again the site from which the culture is named turns out to be situated near the western limit of distribution of a culture, which in this case seems to have been centred on an area comprising the south Russian plain and central Europe, spreading to Italy, France and Spain at a time when the head of the present Adriatic was dry land.

The Gravettians lived on open sites in artificial dwellings by the

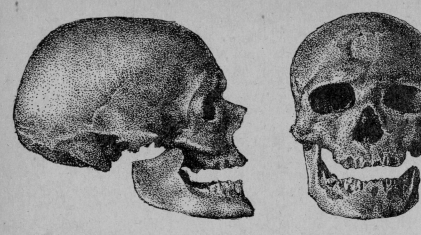

The emergence of the artist: skull of Homo sapiens, *found at Cro-Magnon, Dordogne. (fig. 5)*

great rivers of south Russia and on the loess of central Europe. This was a new development contrasting markedly with the habits of earlier primitive man. It was perhaps the simple consequence of their having gone to occupy lands without caves. As a general rule basic family units were housed separately, either in groups of individual dwellings or in rows of dwellings joined together, but each with separate fire-places. The floors, more or less oval in plan, were usually scooped a few inches into the subsoil. Only occasional post-holes have been observed and there is no evidence that there was any elaborate super-structure built on a frame; it is much more likely that the huts were roofed by earth resting on branches supported by a few uprights wedged against the floor or by skins held up by a few poles and weight-ed down on the edge by heavy bones or stones (pl. 9).

The main quarry in these regions was the mammoth, which we must suppose was first disabled by fall-traps of some kind, but smaller game were also taken.

Gravettian flint-work, though ultimately derived from the same sources as that of the Aurignacians, differed from it markedly in that it included numerous small pieces made from narrow bladelets and shaped by steep, almost vertical retouch: the battered backs of these were designed to protect the finger when used as knives, or alternat-ively, represent the blunt side of flints intended to be inserted in wood-en shafts or handles. Bone and ivory, though now more freely used, were restricted to a comparatively small range of implements, notably awls or bodkins and probably skin-working tools, as well as a variety of objects of personal adornment. These now included various forms of bead, bracelet and pin, and perforated shells. Another signi-ficant feature of the bone and ivory objects was the occasional presence of decorative designs of simple geometrical pattern; frequently these comprised incised strokes arranged as marginal fringes, criss-cross lines and linear chevrons or zig-zags *(fig. 6)*, but mammoth ivories have been decorated by means of large numbers of small pits.

In some respects the most notable products of the culture are the small figurines of women, sometimes referred to rather flatteringly

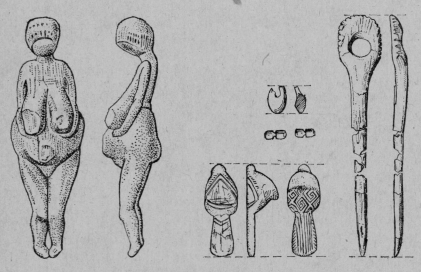

Gravettian artifacts: ivory figurine from Kostienki, Ukraine; stylized figurine from Mezin, Ukraine; bone ornaments (pin and beads) from Kostienki. (fig. 6)

as 'Venuses', that are found over a wide territory from South Russia to Italy and France. These figurines measure only a few inches in height and are carved in the round from a variety of stones and from mam-moth ivory or modelled from clay and hardened in the fire, like pottery (pl. 5, 6). Clearly what interested their makers were the sexual characteristics of the women, full breasts, prominent buttocks and signs of pregnancy: heads were usually shown as mere knobs, though the hair might be represented in conventional fashion and very rarely indeed some features indicated; thighs were shown as plump, but legs were tapered and the feet merely indicated; arms were puny; and clothing, in the rare instances in which the figures were not entirely naked, was confined to a girdle or fringe *(fig. 6)*. We do not know what purpose these figurines served, but they do far more than reveal primitive man's concern with fertility and the reproduction of his own kind; they epitomize his ability to give expression to this concern in three-dimensional works of art that remain effective despite their small scale.

France in Upper Palaeolithic Times

Although the land of France was geographically near one extremity of the territories of the two cultures just discussed, it was the scene of the most splendid achievements of Upper Palaeolithic man. One explanation may well be that in France the two cultures (Aurignacian and Gravettian) came into contact in a country rich in varied game and fish and well provided with caves and rock-shelters. Whatever the cause, it was the limited zone of south-west France and Cantabric Spain that witnessed the rise of the most important regional groups of engraving, painting and relief carving in Upper Palaeolithic Europe. Moreover, it was precisely here that the Upper Palaeolithic culture achieved its greater variety during the final stages of the Pleistocene, up to 10,000–8000 BC.

First there was the Solutrean episode, named after the French locality La Solutré, and marked by the appearance above all of flint points of laurel-leaf form, shaped by shallow flaking on both faces; in these, we have another development from Mousterian sources. But the intrusion of this archaic element failed to break the continuity of culture. Artistic activity persisted and in late Solutrean levels shoul-dered points appear, which, whether with steep retouch or with shallow bifacial flaking, must surely stem ultimately from Gravettian sources.

Second, there was the evolution of a vigorous local culture, named after La Madeleine, at a time when in other parts of the Gravettian territory stagnation if not degeneration was the order of the day. The Magdalenian was centred on France and Cantabria, penetrated south to Valencia and east to Poland in its earlier stages and in its later ones included parts of south-west Germany: its beginnings may go back to 12,000 or even 15,000 BC and it lasted down to 8000 BC. It was characterized by the widespread use of antler and bone as raw materials for hunting gear: various types of lance-head and of harpoon-head *(fig. 7)* were made; and during the middle stages of the culture spear-throwers hooked at one end to engage the shaft were frequently given naturalistic carvings of horses, ibex and other game animals, as well as birds and fish. The lavish and extremely skilful manner in which they ornamented some of their most cherished belongings is indeed one of the most notable features of this culture.

Cave Art

In many respects the paintings on the walls, ceilings and occasionally on the floors of certain Upper Palaeolithic caves give us our finest insight into the lives of the hunting peoples of western Europe during the Ice Age. The region where this art was practised was much smaller geographically than that of the blade-and-burin cultures as a whole. For instance it seems to be quite absent from western Asia and the Crimea, from the Carpathians and from central Europe in general. Even in France it was restricted to districts west of the Rhône and south of the Loire; and elsewhere the main localities were Cantabria, Old Castille and Andalusia in Spain, and in Italy the neighbourhood of Tivoli near Rome, Otranto, Palermo and the small island of Levan-zo off the north coast of Sicily. Perhaps the mysterious depths of caves and the irregularities of their walls and ceilings, exaggerated by distant daylight or the flickering illumination of lamps, may in them-selves have stimulated the imagination of the hunter-artists. Engrav-ings and paintings were executed in some instances far from the daylight—at Niaux in the Dordogne the first paintings found were some 550 yards from the entrance and some were as far as 1200 yards or more; again, it is striking how the artists took advantage of surface irregularities of the rock-surfaces, improving bosses to form shoulders or buttocks, utilizing stalagmitic columns for legs and drip-marks for wounds. It is an interesting fact that the regions where cave art was practised are precisely those in which one finds the decoration of personal possessions carried to its highest pitch.

Cave art comprised engraving and painting, either separately or in conjunction; reliefs made by cutting away the rock to varying depths (pl. 14); doodling on clay films on wall, ceiling or floor; and modelling clay figures in full relief. Colouring matter consisted of various kinds of ochre, manganese and charcoal. This would either be mixed with animal fat to bind it together and applied by means of the finger or some kind of brush or pad, or blown on in the form of powder or drawn on direct by a pencil. Flint burins were used for engraving and stone picks or punches, as well as flint tools, for carving. Outlines on stone plaques from the cave deposits may in some cases have served for practice. The existence of well defined regional groups as well as of a chronological succession of styles suggests that the art was transmitted from masters to pupils. It is reasonable to think that those initiated more fully into the art were men naturally gifted in that direction, but it would be quite wrong to imagine that societies so small and with so primitive a basis of subsistence could have supported full-time artists. On the other hand hunters would be likely to enjoy periods of leisure; and these might be more prolonged than, for example, among primitive peasant communities.

In trying to assess the meaning and significance of palaeolithic art we must at all costs avoid judging it in terms of our own modern culture. Palaeolithic man had no idea of 'art for art's sake'. If we wish to understand his attitude we must go, not to the modern artist, but to a society like that of the Australian aborigines. Among these people art is not an amusement or a means of self-expression: it is an adjustment to the rites and ceremonies connected with birth, death, fertility and the propitiation of evil forces. When the aborigines of central Australia engrave and paint rocks they do so as part of a ritual that may involve mime, dancing and the recitation of legends, the total aim of which is to reassure society at large and enhance the confidence of its individual members.

The Upper Palaeolithic hunting peoples of western Europe had two great preoccupations: the need for nourishment and the need to perpetuate their kind. They were concerned with their own fertility and with that of the animals on which they so largely depended; and they were concerned, as they might well be, considering the primitive nature of their equipment, with success in the hunt, on which they depended for their only important source of food and clothing. The Upper Palaeolithic cave-dwellers experienced anxieties common to the rest of mankind; their special claim on our attention is the manner in which they sought to resolve them through the medium of art.

Preoccupation with sex and above all with woman as the symbol of continuity found expression, as we have already noted, in the figurines associated with the Gravettian culture over a very wide geographical range. To these we may add from France some remarkable relief carvings: from Laussel in the Dordogne we have an obese and naked woman with featureless head holding in her right hand a horn, in itself a symbol of fertility, together with three others on separate slabs, one of whom was apparently depicted in the act of giving birth; and from Angles-sur-l'Anglin, Vienne, the recently discovered frieze carved on the limestone wall includes the lower portion of female froms showing frontal views of hips and thighs. On the male side, one might cite the so-called satyr from Le Portel, Ariège, having an erect organ formed by a stalagmitic column, or the clay phalloi found in a recess of the cave of Tuc d'Audoubert near the clay models of a male bison following a female, a motif repeated in the engraving of a bull following a cow at Teyjat.

The predominant theme is that of animals as potential quarry for the hunter. Only rarely, as in the sexual scenes just dealt with, are the animals specially related to each other in any way: as a rule single animals are drawn regardless even of the existence of previous pictures on the same surface. This art was executed by artists with first-hand experience of the chase and its apparent aim was to engender confidence in the hunter and win magical control over intended victims. Most of the animals depicted were herbivores of the kind taken for food, but there is no exact correspondence between the proportion in which the various species are represented in the art and in the dis-

carded remains incorporated in the archaeological deposits: thus bison are common in both, but mammoth, rarely represented in the animal remains found in the caves, is frequently depicted and in the case of wild boar the exact opposite applies—a reflection perhaps of the relative difficulty of securing the beasts, the more difficult requiring the more magic, and vice versa. It may be that fish, including trout and salmon, were only rarely shown because their capture gave rise to no great anxiety, since there are indications that they were taken in considerable numbers and the same is true of certain birds. On the other hand the rarity of representation of insects, snakes and plants may well be a true indication of their lack of importance in the diet of the late glacial hunters.

The hunting motive is sometimes given explicit expression in representations of feathered arrows or darts, like those on the flanks of ibex at Niaux and on horses and bison at Lascaux (pl. 13); and, again, in the indication of wounds, the arrows on a bison outlined on the clay floor at Niaux pointing directly to drip-marks used for the purpose. In the case of certain representations of carnivores, direct rivals of early man, the 'killing' has evidently been carried out in mime, for instance at Montespan clay models of a lion and a bear, the latter accompanied by a skull and probably covered originally by a skin, bore the marks of repeated stabbing by spears, as though, more than 140 yards from the light of day, these enemies of man had been done to death by magic (pl. 11). Significant, if not very frequent, items in the repertory of the cave art are dancing figures of men masked as animals, such as the one with a skin and mask complete with horns of a bison from Les Trois Frères in the Ariége or the more elaborate one with mask and antlers of red deer, beard and tail, probably of horse or wolf, high up in a gallery of the same cave (pl. 10). No doubt masks were used in hunting and it may be that their success caused them to be endowed with magic potency. Although we cannot be certain, it seems likely that dances by masked figures played a part in the magical rites for which the cave art provided a setting and in conjunction with which it may even have been executed.

It is more difficult to relate the art on the walls and ceilings of the Franco-Cantabrian caves and rock-shelters to successive stages in the development of Upper Palaeolithic cultures than it is the decorated objects from the archaeological deposits. On the other hand a study of the 'palimpsests', caused by one work overlying another, makes it possible to learn a good deal about sequence. It is believed that the art passed through two successive cycles. In the first, associated in the main with the Gravettian culture (perhaps 20,000 years ago), wavy lines painted on the rock or traced on clay by the finger; outline drawings and paintings; flat-wash and the beginnings of bichrome painting; and bas reliefs like those from Laussel, are all characteristic. The second or Solutreo-Magdalenian cycle showed continuity in respect of the bas-reliefs, which however were only found during the earlier stages, to be succeeded by fine engravings filled with thin shading: but in the sphere of painting the artists seem to have reverted to simple black outlines, progressing by way of flat-wash and other stages to the splendid polychromes of Altamira (pl. 12) or Font de Gaume, that mark the climax of Magdalenian achievement.

The artistic ebullience of the Magdalenians spread to the decoration of their personal possessions. It was indeed in this sphere that the artistic impulse seems first to have found expression. Yet the Magdalenians went far beyond the Gravettian achievement in this respect and, in addition to decorating more or less lavishly a variety of artifacts mainly of reindeer antler, even went so far as to emphasize by engraved lines the barbs and stems of their harpoon-heads *(fig. 7)*, the expendable ammunition, as one might say, of the day. The ornamentation of the person was another way in which the Gravettians and their successors displayed their aesthetic awareness. A variety of beads, including spacers for multiple necklaces, pendants, pins, bracelets and anklets were made from materials ranging from bone, ivory, stone, amber, brown coal and fish vertebrae to fired clay and shells. It is worth emphasizing that some of the latter are among the earliest indications of distant trade, a pointer to the power of conspicuous consumption as an economic force even in the Ice Age. Certain hints in the cave art and the presence of numerous finely-eyed needles in Magdalenian deposits suggest that sewn skin clothing was worn out-of-doors, as is still the case over a large part of the arctic zone. To judge from the position of shells and other objects in their ceremonial burials, they were laid to rest fully-clothed, sprinkled with ochre, and adorned with the ornaments on which they clearly set store in life.

(fig. 7)

Climatic changes : 9000-8000 BC

One of the most exciting results of the radio-carbon dating of sediments from the close of the Pleistocene and the beginning of the Neothermal or Recent eras has been to emphasize how rapidly and severely the environment was modified during the 9th millennium BC. The regions most profoundly affected were those on the margins of major natural zones of flora and fauna: notably the territories immediately bordering the last major glaciation, which as a result of the final and rapid contraction of the ice-sheets were made temperate by the onset of a more genial climate; regions which, like parts of north Africa and south-western Asia, passed abruptly from pluvial to arid conditions with the shifting of the rain-belt. The contrast between the two is worth emphasizing. Over the former periglacial zone skirting the ice-sheets, and in due course over territories formerly covered by ice there was a marked improvement in the conditions for human settlement: extensive forests provided food and shelter for a rich fauna and the area of settlement grew steadily larger (p. 20). By contrast the peoples occupying territories which suddenly began to have a greatly reduced rainfall were confronted by sharply worsening conditions that could only be met by migration or a dramatic re-adjustment in their mode of living. In either case it is evident that the natural conditions favourable for the Late Pleistocene hunting cultures were, at any rate in these two major zones, completely altered and it is hardly surprising that the period should have been marked by significant changes in the sphere of culture. It meant, in fact, the break-up of the Upper Palaeolithic world, the emergence of a new pattern of hunter-fisher life known as the Mesolithic, and almost at once in the zone of greatest stress, the beginnings of a Neolithic economy on which the future progress of mankind was to depend.

All Mesolithic industries carried forward into the period of climate approximating to modern conditions traditions inherited from the Late Pleistocene and differed merely in the degree to which these were modified in response to changed natural environment. In some regions, such as much of southern Europe, environmental change was so gradual that the transition to the Neothermal period is difficult to define and the modifications in the sphere of culture are correspondingly unexciting. Sometimes, as in the case of the Azilian of the Franco-Cantabrian region, named after Mas d'Azil in the Ariège, the Mesolithic culture soon after 8000 BC was hardly more than a transformation of the final Upper Palaeolithic of the region. Harpoon-heads of antler remained the characteristic type though made of red deer rather than reindeer; art continued, though now reduced to conventional anthropomorphic designs painted in red on pebbles (pl. 20) which may have served a purpose analogous to that of the sacred *churinga* of the Australian aborigines; and the flint industry with its burins, small thumb-nail scrapers and simple microliths with battered backs showed no important innovation. In some respects the equipment of the cultures known as the epi-Gravettian of Spain and the parallel Sauveterrian of France with its close counterparts in neighbouring parts of the continent and over much of Britain is even more meagre and derivative; indeed the mystery is how these people, traces of whom have been recovered from caves and rock-shelters as well as from open sites, managed to gain a living with a flint industry that consisted of narrow microliths (in many cases geometric forms of minute size that can only have formed part of composite tools or weapons), scrapers, burins and ancillary tools, and with only the most modest use of bone and antler. Hunter-fishers of this type were still occupying Britain when the first neolithic farmers arrived perhaps around 2500-3000 BC.

The Maglemosians

On the other hand, the people who succeeded the reindeer hunters on the European plain and who extended settlement further north, made a much more positive response to the opportunities of the newly forested environment. The Maglemosians, to give them the name they acquired from a locality (*Maglemose* meaning big bog) at Mullerup on the Danish island of Sjælland, occupied a territory that extended unbroken from eastern England and Flanders to Denmark, southern Sweden and North Germany, Poland, Esthonia and North-West Russia, round a Baltic which was then a lake, even as the North Sea was largely dry land. They were fond of living close by lakes (pl. 19)—at Star Carr near Scarborough in Yorkshire an early group seems to have occupied a rough platform of birch brushwood on a reed swamp immediately bordering the open water (c. 7500 BC). This habit has caused an unusually large amount of organic evidence to survive, so that in general we know more about their food-supply and many aspects of their material culture than we do about other Mesolithic groups. The Maglemosians lived mainly by hunting the game that abounded in the forests, such as elk, aurochs, red deer, wild pig and roe deer. They used bows with arrows tipped and barbed by flint microliths (*fig. 8*) and spears and barbed antler or bone heads (pl. 15). They also fished, taking pike by spearing them and also using lines with bone hooks and nets made of bast, weighted by stones and supported by wooden or bark floats (pl. 18). Fowling was also carried on; nuts and fruits were gathered in season. Apart from dogs, which so far as we know did no more than provide companionship and act as scavengers, the Maglemosians kept no domestic animals and of course they neither cultivated crops nor made pottery. Not much is known about their dwellings, but traces have been found in Danish bogs of roughly rectangular huts with bark floors and walls of small branches rammed into the ground and pulled together at the top to form a roof.

A feature of their culture was their attack upon the forest trees, which they cut down and utilized by means of primitive axe and adze blades made by flaking down flint nodules mounted in antler sleeves into which wooden handles were set. From wood they made a variety of handles, bows (pl. 15), paddles and probably dug-out canoes. Great use was made also of antler and bone for making mattock-heads, holders for axes and adzes, skin-working tools, fish-hooks, netting-needles, awls and a variety of barbed spearheads (pl. 18). The impression of a vigorous culture is heightened by the art: there were no caves in this region, and so no cave art, but particularly in the West Baltic area the Maglemosians decorated implements, weapons, perforated batons and amulets either with lightly incised lines or with neatly drilled pits, and occasionally carved lumps of amber into animal shapes. In addition to geometric patterns, they introduced conventionalized animal motifs and those anthropomorphic designs (pl. 16, 17), which resemble some of those painted on the Azilian pebbles.

The closing phases of the European Mesolithic age were marked by the growth of coastal cultures in which the resources of the interior were supplemented to varying degrees by the hunting of sea-mammals, such as whales and seals, the catching of sea-fish and the gathering of shell-fish. This can be well seen in the northern parts of Denmark where large numbers of coastal middens are known; on the coast of western Sweden; round the Norwegian coast as far as the northernmost province of Finnmark; on either side of the North Channel in Ulster and western Scotland (pl. 21); and on what are now islands off the coast of Morbihan (pl. 24). North German settlements of this type date between 5000 and 2000 BC. By this time Neolithic peasants had already begun to spread into much of central Europe and the Mesolithic peoples of marginal territories were fast turning over to the new economy. In many parts of Europe the hunter-fishers continued to maintain their old way of life for some while, but after a period of co-existence they were absorbed into the new societies which in this way acquired some of their distinctive local character.

As we have stated earlier the rather sudden change of climate at the close of the Pleistocene presented a challenge to the hunter-fisher peoples of south-west Asia that could be met in a positive manner only by enlarging the basis of subsistence. Too little is known of what happened in most of the region, but we have a fairly good idea of the kind of adjustment made in the strip of territory from Jordan to Syria by the successors of the local Upper Palaeolithic cave-dwellers. The Natufians, so named after the Wady en-Natuf in southern Palestine, lived in many respects like their predecessors; they hunted gazelle, in place of deer; they were skilled flint-workers, making a special type of blade to be inset in wooden spears or arrows, and proficient in shaping antler and bone into such things are barbed spearheads and hooks; were fond of personal ornaments and made some good naturalistic carvings; and accorded ceremonial burial to their dead. On the other hand they began to pay attention on a large scale to plant food. We have found not only stone pestles and mortars, but very significantly flint blades bearing the lustre that comes from harvesting cereals, together with the slotted bone reaping-knife handles in which they were set (chap. II, *fig. 2*). At precisely what stage agriculture began can only be decided when cereals from successive deposits have been subjected to intensive botanical study. All we know for certain is that even the early Natufians harvested cereals and it is surely highly suggestive that Natufians were the earliest settlers to form real urban communities.

(fig. 8)

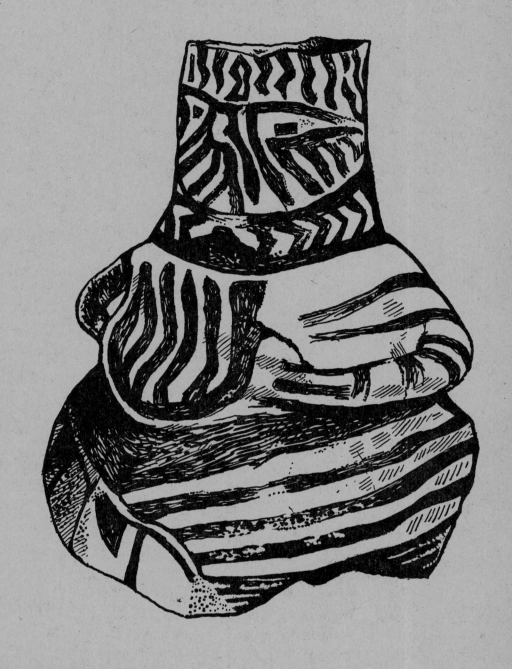

II ROOTS IN THE SOIL

The beginning of village and urban life

JAMES MELLAART

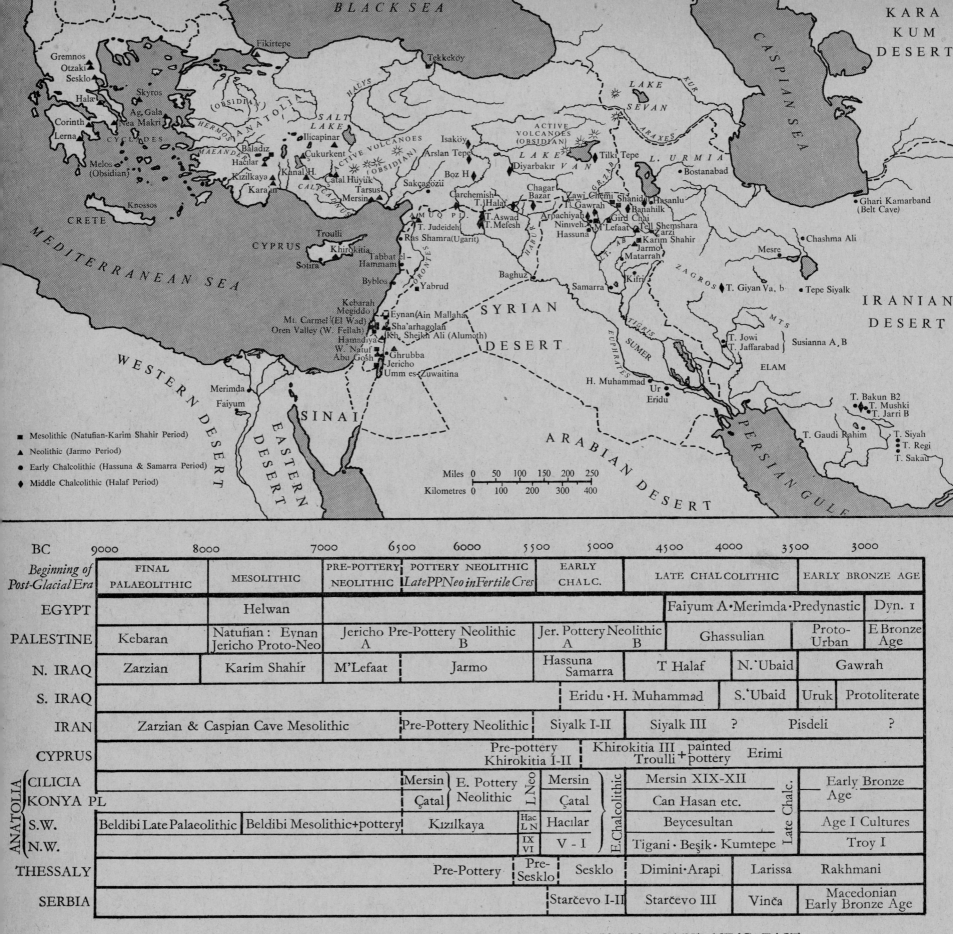

BC	9000	8000	7000	6500	6000	5500	5000	4500	4000	3500	3000
Beginning of Post-Glacial Era	FINAL PALAEOLITHIC	MESOLITHIC	PRE-POTTERY NEOLITHIC	POTTERY NEOLITHIC / *Late PP Neo in Fertile Cres*		EARLY CHALC.		LATE CHALCOLITHIC		EARLY BRONZE AGE	
EGYPT		Helwan						Faiyum A · Merimda · Predynastic			Dyn. 1
PALESTINE	Kebaran	Natufian: Eynan / Jericho Proto-Neo	Jericho Pre-Pottery Neolithic A / B			Jer. Pottery Neolithic A / B		Ghassulian		Proto-Urban	E Bronze Age
N. IRAQ	Zarzian	Karim Shahir	M'Lefaat	Jarmo		Hassuna Samarra		T Halaf	N. Ubaid	Gawrah	
S. IRAQ						Eridu · H. Muhammad		S. Ubaid	Uruk	Protoliterate	
IRAN	Zarzian & Caspian Cave Mesolithic		Pre-Pottery Neolithic		Siyalk I-II		Siyalk III	?	Pisdeli	?	
CYPRUS				Pre-pottery Khirokitia I-II		Khirokitia III / Troulli + painted pottery		Erimi			
CILICIA				Mersin	E. Pottery Neolithic	L. Neo / Mersin		Mersin XIX-XII		Early Bronze Age	
KONYA PL				Çatal		Çatal		Can Hasan etc.			
S.W.	Beldibi Late Palaeolithic	Beldibi Mesolithic + pottery		Kızılkaya		Hac L N / Hacılar		Beycesultan		Age I Cultures	
N.W.						IX VI / V - I		Tigani · Beşik · Kumtepe		Troy I	
THESSALY			Pre-Pottery	Pre-Sesklo	Sesklo		Dimini · Arapi		Larissa	Rakhmani	
SERBIA					Starčevo I-II		Starčevo III		Vinča	Macedonian Early Bronze Age	

TENTATIVE INTERPRETATION OF CULTURAL PROGRESS IN THE NEAR EAST

BC c.9000 Beginning of post-glacial era.

9000–8000 Last occupation of cave-sites by food-gatherers with late Palaeolithic industries.

8000–7000 Gradual move from caves to open-air sites, either semi-permanent camps or first villages (e.g. Eynan and Proto-Neolithic Jericho). First huts and houses, domestication of dog and goat and reaping and storing of grain. Hunting, fishing etc. continue strongly.

7000–6500 Possible beginnings of agriculture—i.e. food-producing—no great progress in domestication. Hunting etc. continues, but now appear the first permanent villages and towns (e.g. Pre-Pottery Neolithic Jericho), fortifications—i.e. urbanization, at least at Jericho, showing some social organisation, if not already local rulers.

6500–5500 Invention of pottery in part of the Near East. Great improvements in architecture. Cities on S. Anatolian plateau. Painted pottery appears in second half of period. Definite growing of grain in part of area, elsewhere economy unchanged.

5500–5000 General use of pottery, mostly painted red-on-cream. Metallurgy in Anatolia and Iran. Fortifications, rulers' castles. Probably first irrigation in S. Mesopotamia. Efficient farming economy.

5000–4000 Gradual spread of metallurgy to Mesopotamia and of village farming to Egypt. Beginnings of religious architecture (Arpachiyah, Eridu).

4000–3000 Development of urbanisation and religious architecture in Mesopotamia during 'Ubaid period. Arrival of new elements in Uruk period, probably Sumerians—initiating Protoliterate period—writing and cylinder seals invented; great advance in representational art. *Fully urban civilization in Sumer only.*

3000 Beginning of historical period in Egypt and Sumer. Dynastic states and national civilizations in those two countries only.

At least eight thousand years
before the birth of Christ, man took the decisive step forward from
a nomadic life of hunting and fishing to a more settled existence
based on agriculture. He began to domesticate animals, and to gather,
if not to cultivate, cereal crops. This entailed, for the first time, living
in communities, in open settlements, then later in villages and even
small fortified towns. The beginnings of this very gradual process
must be looked for, not in Europe, where the hunting and fishing
economy was to continue for several thousand years, but in the
natural habitat of the wild cereals, the sheep, goats, cattle and pigs.
This was the well-watered uplands that fringe the Arabian, Syrian
and Iranian deserts. One of the most important types of these early
village-dwellers are the Natufians, whose remains have been found
at various sites, in particular at Eynan, in the Upper Jordan valley,
and at Jericho. Small-boned, about five feet tall, with delicate features
and long skulls, they are believed to have come into Palestine from
the north. Flint hoes and sickles, often with the characteristic sheen
produced by cutting reeds, grass or grain, prove the harvesting of
crops, but by themselves are no evidence of regular agriculture.
Hunting (with arrows tipped with flint) was still the main way of
procuring food.

They buried their dead under the dwelling-place—whether cave
or settlement—sometimes several bodies together. One of the
most remarkable burials found at Eynan is this last resting-place of a
Natufian chieftain. Under a layer of rocks and paving-stones (left),
surrounded by a plastered and red-painted parapet, lay two complete skeletons extended on their backs, with the legs detached after
death and laid alongside. One of these skeletons, that of an adult
male (right) lay partly covered, partly propped up with stones, facing
towards the snowy peak of Mount Hermon. Funerary rituals of this
sort lasted on at Jericho for another 2,000 years. (1, 2)

The oldest known town in the world is Jericho, at the north end of the
Dead Sea, with a continuous record of occupation nearly ten thous-
and years long. At the lowest occupation level this Natufian shrine
(right) was excavated; it has been dated by the Carbon 14 method
c. 7800 BC. The round hollows in the rough-plastered floor may
have served as grain storage pits. Querns are better evidence for the
preparation, if not the cultivation, of cereals at this early date. (3)

Forty-eight domed huts have been excavated at Khirokitia, Cyprus, and their total number may have approached the thousand mark, implying a population of several thousands—a small town rather than a village. The reconstruction (right) shows part of this town, with the roof of the main hut cut away to show the interior. On a circular limestone foundation and core, mud-brick walls are raised, topped off with a domed roof and covered with mud plaster. From a wooden-framed doorway plastered steps lead down to a beaten mud floor, in the middle of which a fire burns in a baked clay hearth. Two square limestone pillars support a partial upper floor of wooden beams, brushwood and beaten mud. Set into the pillars are wooden-framed niches or cupboards. To the left, a meal is being eaten at a round stone table while pigs rootle near by. In the centre, three women are grinding corn (of which three more are bringing up further supplies) and another is spinning wool, probably from the long-horned sheep that are being driven down the paved, embanked 'main street' of the village. To the right, stone carvers are at work, hollowing out large boulders, using sand and water as an abrasive. Beyond the huts lies a grove of cultivated olive trees. As well as the spinning of wool, the technique of weaving was also known at this time: the striped sleeping mats 'upstairs' are inferred from present-day examples. Over all this scene one must imagine the blinding Mediterranean light, the heat, the dust—and the flies. (4)

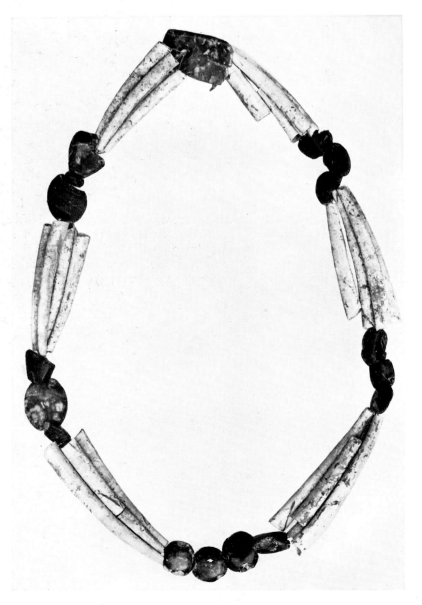

Not as early as Natufian Jericho, Khirokitia is an extremely interesting little township of the same stage in man's development. It has been dated by the Carbon 14 method to about 5500 BC. Again, sheep and goats and possibly pigs were domesticated, and from evidence of sickle blades and querns, agriculture may have been practised. Necklaces have been found, like the one on the left, which is of carnelian beads and the tusk-shaped *dentalium* shells so typical of the period. The earliest inhabitants of Khirokitia made a few clumsy attempts at pottery, but soon abandoned this for the polished stoneware that is their most characteristic product. The examples opposite are made of andesite, a volcanic stone; the design may have been inspired by basketwork. (5-7)

The walls of Jericho

are only partly known, but may have enclosed about eight acres of the first fortified town yet found in the Near East. A huge stone tower, some twenty-seven feet thick and still standing twenty-one feet high, must have been the main lookout post of the town (below, left). Through the centre of the tower descended a stone stairway leading to a passage twelve feet long which presumably ended in a doorway giving access to the tower from ground-level. Up against the tower ran a city wall built of stone, five feet wide at the top and still preserved to a height of twelve feet. In the thousand years that these fortifications lasted, both tower and wall were added to with two more layers of masonry, until the wall reached a height of more than sixteen feet. At two places within the wall, remains of round houses have been found (below, right), the curve of whose walls suggests a domed roof like the beehive huts of Khirokitia (pl. 4).

Eventually, however, the town was taken, the site was abandoned, and it seems possible that there was a gap before newcomers settled there. It is not known who were the conquerors, but the fact that walls and tower had been kept in good repair and even enlarged through more than a thousand years seems to indicate the nearness of an enemy more formidable than some tribe of marauding nomads. It also appears likely that they were the ancestors of the new settlers, whom we know as Tahunians.

Under this second phase Jericho, though still a walled town of about eight acres, took on a very different appearance. Houses were rectangular instead of round, with finely plastered floors and walls. Several buildings seem to have served some cult purposes. Pottery was still unknown, and stone vessels were used.

With features modelled in plaster and eyes inlaid with cowrie shells, this skull from Jericho gives a vivid impression of what the Tahunians of Jericho's second phase looked like. Small-boned, long-headed, they belonged to the same Mediterranean race as the Natufians, from whom they were probably descended. It is not known whether restored skulls of this kind were trophies or a memorial of a revered ancestor. (8, above)

View of the great stone tower, below, with adjacent mud-brick structures to the left. The entrance to the stairway, which may have led to a spring, can be seen in the centre. The successive shells of stone re-building can be seen. (9)

Under this round house, below, of the first Neolithic phase before pottery occurs lie 13 ft. of occupation debris, corresponding in date to the shrine of pl. 3, and like it representing the earliest occupation of Jericho. The house is adjacent to the contemporary tower. (10)

'Mother goddess' or fertility figurines (above) are a typical Neolithic feature over a wide area. The two on the left, in green limestone and brown steatite, come from Çukurkent, the other, a mother-of-pearl pendant, from Hacılar, both in southern Turkey. (11)

The great wall of Jericho with the tower in the background (where the second figure from the top is standing). The two additions of masonry can be clearly seen. In front of the wall is a deep rock-cut ditch, 27 feet wide and nearly seven feet deep (its position is marked by the figure in the foreground). Its cutting must have been a prodigious labour, for there are no signs of picks or hoes. The rock must have been chopped out piecemeal with stone pounders, no doubt aided by the age-old method of splitting with fire and water, as the ancient Egyptians were to do much later. (12, left)

A small rectangular shrine (above) from the second Neolithic phase of Jericho (c. 6000 BC). A polished flattened stone standing in a carefully plastered niche may have been intended as an emblem of a fertility cult. (13)

The exaggerated buttocks of the Neolithic female figurines (above) may be merely the customary stressing of those parts so often found in fertility figurines (cf. pl. 11), but they are also the result of a grain diet, noticeable today in peasant women of Anatolia and Africa. The one on the left is in burnished clay, from Hacılar, Anatolia; the other (three views) white stone from Aegina, Greece. (15)

The invention of pottery

marks the next important step forward in social evolution. At the same period of the Neolithic as the pre-pottery cultures of Jericho and Khirokitia, pottery was being made on the S.W. Anatolian plateau of Southern Turkey, and in Mainland Greece. (Some crude attempts at pottery had been made at an early stage in Khirokitia, probably imitating vessels from Anatolia, but these were soon abandoned in favour of stone vessels.) At first, pottery was not decorated, only burnished or given a brilliant polish. Occasionally a slip was used (a thin paste of clay), but colour variations were mostly the result of firing different clays.

Late in the Neolithic period, however, came the invention of painted pottery throughout what is now Southern Turkey. The use of a red wash on cream-coloured wares led to the development of designs, and a highly imaginative series of patterns made their appearance over a wide area of the Near East and Greece. These designs, together with pottery shapes and techniques, are among the most valuable kinds of evidence to show the routes by which civilization spread. Red-on-cream pottery marks the beginning of the Chalcolithic (copper-and-stone) period, c. 5500 BC, with the spread of metallurgy from the highlands of Anatolia and Iran.

Three successive stages in the development of early pottery in the Anatolian Neolithic period (right). Top: characteristic dark burnished pottery from Çatal Hüyük, on the Konya plain. Centre: typical early cream slipped and burnished wares from the late Neolithic levels at Hacılar. These were the first to offer a suitable surface for painting with the red ochre that had been used for decorative purposes since the time of the cave artists. Bottom: earliest red-on-cream painted pottery, also from Hacılar. This ware is the ancestor of the painted pottery of the copper-stone or Chalcolithic period. (16)

Later painted pottery from the Chalcolithic period in Iran and Iraq, roughly contemporary with Hacılar red-on-cream painted ware. Right: early black-on-buff from Level I of the cemetery at Tepe Siyalk, Iran. Left: later ware which takes its name from Samarra on the Tigris. Iranian influence seems to have been the main source for animals on painted pottery (cf. pl. 34). (17)

Later Siyalk comparable with Level II of the type site black-on-red pottery, contemporary with Samarra ware. (18)

The spread of the technique and the earliest styles of painted pottery from the highlands of Anatolia and Iran can be seen from the map below, which shows the diversity of shapes and styles that developed throughout the region. The dotted areas mark the rough distribution of each major group, the type sites being marked with red dots. The coastal sites of Ugarit, Tabbat el-Hammam, and Byblos mark a contemporary zone of unpainted wares. (19)

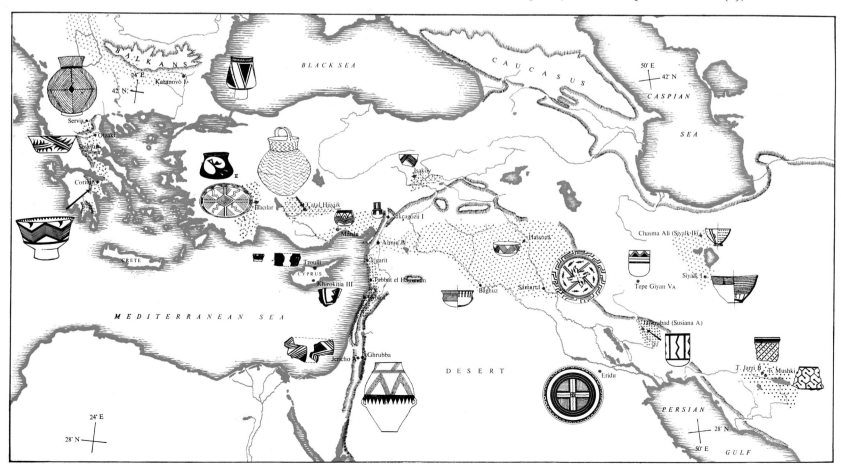

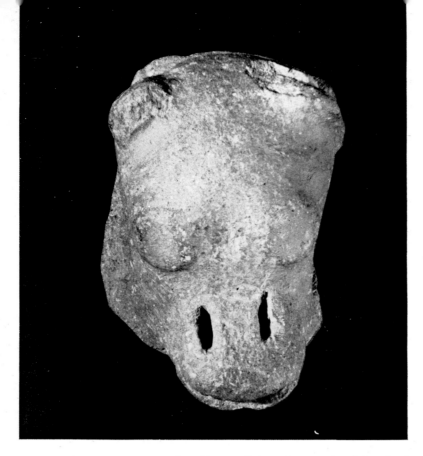

Stoneware was on the wane but still in use, copying pottery shapes. (Left) oval bowl in white marble, with a lug in the form of a ram's head; (right) footed bowl in grained marble. c. 5200 BC. (22)

The standing female figurine below, from the Chalcolithic levels at Hacılar, though only half of it has been preserved, still shows the exaggerated shape of the earlier 'mother goddess' figures. (23)

A tendency to elaborate handles and lugs into animal heads is shown in this red burnished clay pot handle shaped like a pig's head. Bucak, early Chalcolithic (c. 5500 BC). (20)

Unchanged for two thousand years, this polished stone axe in an antler sleeve (above; Hacılar, c. 5000 BC) might have been used by a Mesolithic craftsman about 7500 BC. The burnished yellow clay seal below bears an incised meander pattern, perhaps the owner's mark, or for cloth stamping; Hacılar II. (21)

Crude and unsophisticated by comparison are these comb-ornamented pots from Byblos, on the Lebanon coast. Painted pottery techniques did not reach here until considerably later than 5000 BC. (24)

Surprisingly naturalistic compared with pl. 23 (though not much later in date) are these figurines from the other side of the Aegean. Below, a marble male figurine from Knossos; right, female figurine of red burnished pottery from Lerna, in the Peloponnese. (25, 26)

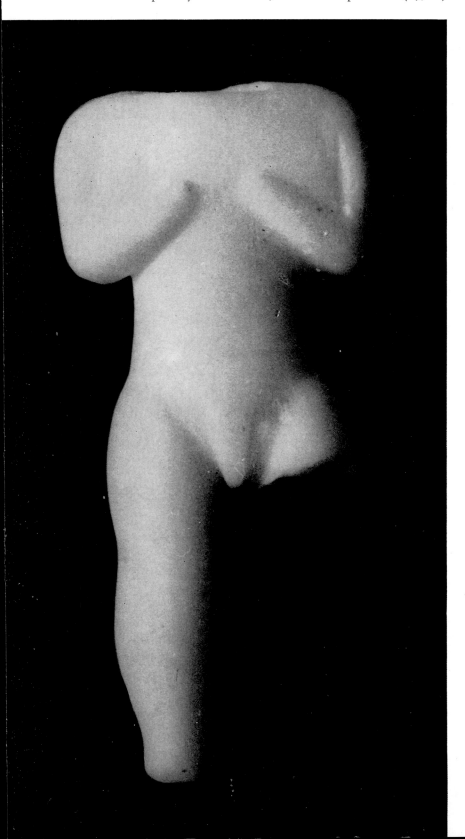

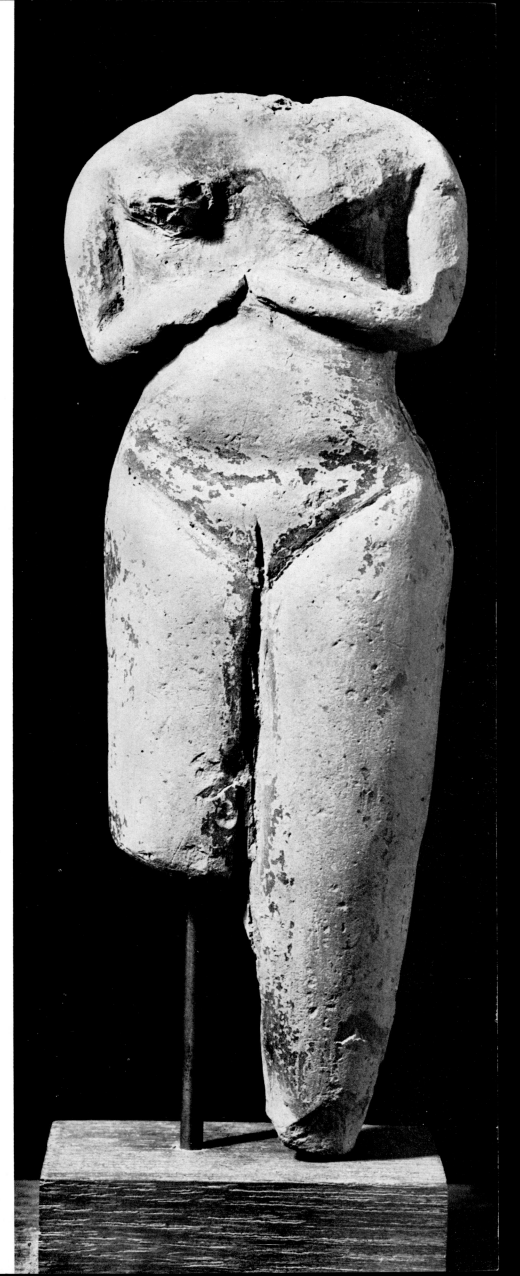

The idea of painting pottery,
which developed towards the end of the Neolithic period, must have spread fast. From the very beginning of the next period, the Chalcolithic, about 5500 BC, we find painted pottery in use in the greater part of the Near East. As we have seen, quite elaborate designs can be found side by side with the plainer burnished red, black or buff wares.

A diversity of shapes and styles can be seen in these five examples of pottery of the later Chalcolithic period from Hacılar. The anthropomorphic pot at the bottom (Level I) probably had some ritual purpose; the eyes are of inlaid obsidian. In the centre group are an ovoid pot with an human-like design, a square-mouthed pot and an oval cup. The design on the dish (top) may have been influenced by basketry. (27-29)

The men were the artists and the women the unskilled labour in the Chalcolithic period potteries, or so we may infer from present-day conditions. This reconstruction of a potter's shop in the second level at Hacılar, c. 5200 BC (with the front wall removed) shows not only how the potters must have worked, but also how the houses were built. The walls were of mud-brick, without foundations, covered with plastered gypsum. The doors were wood-framed, and wooden beams supported a roof of rush matting and clay. In an alcove at the back, formed by one of the stout mud-brick buttresses, a woman can be seen stacking pots, while another is attending to the domed oven outside the door.

Women, it seems, were the hewers of wood and drawers of water,

performing the unskilled jobs such as grinding the ochre, while the more skilled work of shaping the pots, and painting and burnishing them, was performed by the men. Behind a rush matting screen, a woman kneels on a *kilim*, a woven mat whose existence is inferred from designs on pottery of the time; she is grinding ochre on a palette.

The master potter, in the centre holding a pot, wears a necklace of perforated boars' teeth, and two of his assistants, seated on a reed mat, are busily engaged in painting and burnishing. On the floor beside the farther of these two, a clay figurine and a burnishing stick lie ready to hand. Querns and palettes for mixing red and white ochre can also be seen on the floor. (30)

53

The vast area from the Balkans to S.W. Iran showed, about 5000 BC, certain general features in common. Villages, market towns and the citadels of local rulers dotted the more fertile parts of the countryside. Life was based on mixed farming, supplemented by hunting and fishing. Goods and raw materials, such as obsidian, a little copper, marble and other attractive stones, were traded over great distances, probably by nomadic tribes. An early form of metal-working was practised in certain areas, but only the few would be in a position to possess metal. The next step, however—from urban communities to state and national organization—took another 1500 years. Not until the rise of Egypt and Sumer did mankind achieve the stronger political control and the concentration of economic resources that enabled civilization to evolve further.

A high degree of artistry is shown in this polychrome painted plate (above), also from Arpachiyah. It represents the latest stage in the development of painted pottery (c. 4100 BC). (33)

For personal adornment, articles were still produced in stone at the time when men first learned to work in metals in the highlands of Anatolia and Iran. These steatite amulets (above) of the Halaf culture from Arpachiyah, Northern Iraq, take the form of (left) a double-headed axe, and (right) a gable-roofed house, seen from the side. (31)

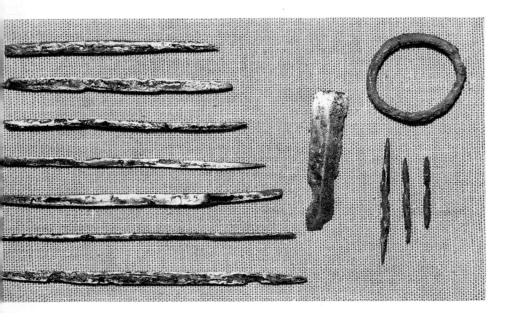

Some of the earliest copper tools known to us (above) were found at Beycesultan, Anatolia (5th millennium BC). Among them was a silver ring; here we may have early evidence of man's desire to accumulate material wealth. The site is discussed further in Chap. VI. (32)

Lively and free, the design on this pot (Siyalk III, Iran, c. 4000 BC) is characteristic of Iranian pottery towards the end of the Chalcolithic period and represents a departure from the more geometric style of ornament found, for instance, at Hacılar. (34, above)

The beginning of village and urban life

JAMES MELLAART

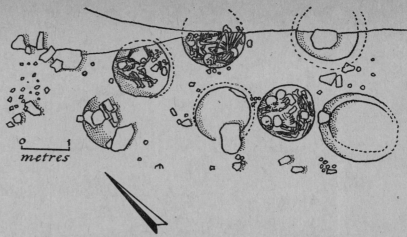

Natufian village of Eynan: circular rock-cut depressions, some of which were re-used for burials. (fig. 1)

The Earliest Agricultural Communities

ALTHOUGH VERY LITTLE is known about the conditions prevailing in the Near East at the end of the Late Glacial phase, dated in Northern Europe to c. 9000–8000 BC, it is quite clear that in this warmer zone the climatic changes were much less severe than in Europe. There the retreat of the glaciers northward brought with them a gradual disappearance of the large herds of herbivorous animals. Palaeolithic man's food supply was replaced by more scattered, less abundant and more agile animals such as deer, wild boar and numbers of smaller animals.

Men adapted themselves to these new conditions in various ways, evolving cultures that are known as 'Mesolithic'. They were still food-gatherers, making their living by hunting, fishing and collecting fruit, berries, nuts and other edible plants. To help in the pursuit of game and fowl the dog was domesticated. The Mesolithic cultures in North-Western Europe can be traced over a period of some seven thousand years, from c. 9000–2000 BC, and in many parts even longer. Eventually they were succeeded, in one region after another, by cultures involving elementary agriculture and the domestication of animals. The two new conceptions of food conservation and production do not appear to have been of European origin, for neither the wild ancestors of sheep and goat, cattle and pigs, nor those of wheat and barley, had their natural habitat there.

The origins of agriculture and stock-breeding must be sought in the area where these grasses and animals were at home, and that is in the Near East. Sheep, goat, cattle and pigs had their natural habitat not in arid regions or deserts, the home of gazelles, jerboas etc., but in the well watered uplands that fringe the Arabian, Syrian and Iranian deserts. The wild ancestors of wheat and barley again are medium altitude grasses, preferring altitudes of 750–1,000 metres above sea level. Of the two main wheat groups in antiquity, the *Einkorn* group ranges in its wild state from the Balkans to West Iran, whereas the *Emmer* group seems to have been at home in North Mesopotamia, Eastern Turkey, Persia, Syria, Palestine and Jordan. The distribution of barley again covers the same area from Anatolia to Afghanistan and from Transcaucasia to Arabia. Denser forests, now reduced by overgrazing and deforestation, imply a slightly higher rainfall, but otherwise the Near East ten thousand years ago appears to have had the same physical aspect it bears today. Against this background, so utterly different from that of Europe at the same time, the momentous developments about to take place—the invention of agriculture and animal domestication, the very foundations of civilization—must be viewed.

The First Villages

The final Palaeolithic cultures of Palestine, Syria and Iraq, dating from between 10,000 and 8700 BC, are mainly found in caves. Most of the mesolithic sites in the same areas, on the other hand, seem to have been open encampments that already had the characteristics of villages (Map, p.42). The two most important types are known as the *Natufian* culture (in Palestine) and the *Karim Shahir* culture (in Iraqi Kurdistan), and they can be dated at around 8000 BC. At the important village site of Eynan (Wadi Mallaha) in the Upper Jordan valley in Israel, three levels of Natufian overlie Palaeolithic remains, suggesting that the later culture developed as an uninterrupted continuation of the earlier. At the Jericho mound, the bottom Mesolithic deposits belong to the Natufian period, and include what may be a burnt Natufian shrine (pl. 3), recently dated by C 14 to 7800 BC.

Of these two cultures the Natufian is the better known. Its origin is uncertain, but some scholars think it came into Palestine from the North. The Natufians were physically of early Mediterranean stock, small boned with delicate features and long (dolicocephalic) skulls. Their average stature was a little over 5 ft. At El Wad on Mt Carmel and in the Oren Valley (Wadi Fellah) the Natufians lived in the open mouths of rock shelters, and on the terraces in front of them. Flimsy structures, traces of walls, pavements, numerous fireplaces and burials between the walls were found at both sites.

The Natufian Culture: Eynan

At Eynan, the beginning of an architectural tradition can be traced. Here there are three successive levels with floors, and circular or oval depressions 1.5 m. in diameter and 0.80 m. in depth, as well as storage pits with white plastered sides widening at the base. One of the circular constructions, probably originally a house, was afterwards used as a tomb and will be described later. Eynan II seems to have been a village of round houses (pl. 4), some measuring 7 m. in diameter, the lower parts of which were sunk below ground level and plastered, while the superstructure probably consisted of reeds, easily available at neighbouring Lake Huleh, where building in reeds has survived till the present day. What was stored in the pits near the houses is not known, nor has any actual grain yet been found on a Natufian site. Nevertheless, hoes made of flint figure among the Natufian tools and so do composite sickle blades made of the same material, often bearing a characteristic sheen or gloss produced by cutting reeds, grass or grain. The individual components of these blades were set end to end in bone hafts of straight sickles, the handles of which were frequently carved in the form of animals, such as the young fawn from El Wad (*fig. 2*) or the two heads in black horn from the Oren Valley site. Storage pits, hoes and sickle blades are by themselves no evidence for agriculture, but the Natufians may well have reaped wild wheat, such as now grows in the Jordan Valley. If the pits were indeed used for storing grain, we can only say that we have no evidence that it was deliberately sown.

The numerous animal bones from Eynan clearly show that hunting was still the main way of procuring food. The animals represented include abundant goat (possibly domesticated), cattle, gazelle, red deer, fallow deer, roe deer, wild horse, boar, hyaena, fox, hare, small carnivores, rodents, birds, fish, tortoises and shellfish, and their remains are evidence that by this date they had all evolved to their modern form. From Mt Carmel we can add bear and leopard, and a domesticated dog of large size, probably descended from a now extinct type of jackal. On the other hand, in the Oren Valley settlement, fishing appears to have been more popular. For hunting, the Natufians used microlithic lunate blades of flint to tip their reed arrows, presumably cut with their sickles. Tanged arrowheads are rare. Microliths formed about 80% of the chipped flint industry.

Among the larger flint tools were burins for engraving, backed blades for cutting, and scrapers (*fig. 2*). Ground stone was used for many articles such as stone vases, the finest piece being a pedestalled basalt vase from Eynan, 0.60 m. high; circular palettes with a small depression on one side containing red ochre, a limestone human figurine (all from Eynan), another stone figurine painted with red ochre from Oren Valley, a human head from El Wad and a crouching animal from Umm es-Zuwaitina in the Judaean Desert. Bone needles were common at Eynan, as well as awls, harpoons, fish-hooks, either single or double, beads and phallus-shaped pendants. Numerous mortars, querns (small hand-mills), pestles and pounders, often coated with red ochre, are found at Natufian sites. It is likely, though not certain, that these were used for grinding food as well as for preparing red paint.

The Natufians buried their dead within the dwelling place, be it cave or settlement, and such burials have been found at Eynan. At Mt Carmel the bodies buried inside the cave lay on their backs, whereas those buried on the terrace were found in a flexed position. Both methods were also practised at Eynan. Sometimes several bodies were buried together; grave goods were on the whole sparse, although some objects usually accompanied the dead, and two of the skulls at Mt Carmel even had elaborate head-dresses of *dentalium* shells. In the bottom level at Eynan a single flint or basalt object was buried with each individual, and headbands or necklaces of the same shells, or of shells and gazelle's knuckle bones, were worn. One of the skulls was surrounded by four gazelle's bones.

The burial customs may strike us as rather gruesome. One grave contained five skulls, and bones representing five legs and seven arms, besides other fragments; another contained five skulls, one of which was painted red, and fragments of other decomposed bodies. Thirty-eight individuals in all have been found. Most tombs contained red ochre. Most remarkable, however, is the burial of a chieftain of the Middle Natufian level at Eynan. The tomb (pl. 1), possibly originally the chieftain's house, is circular, 5 m. in diameter and 0.80 m. deep. Surrounding the tomb is a plastered and red painted parapet, ending in a row of stones with a diameter of 6.5 metres. Two complete skeletons lay in the centre extended on their backs with legs detached after death and bent out of position. One of these skeletons, belonging to an adult male, was partly covered, partly propped up with stones and was facing towards the snowy peak of Mt Hermon (pl. 2). An earlier burial had been unceremoniously pushed aside when the tomb was used for a second time; the person buried wore a *dentalium*-shell head-dress and may have been a woman. Two skulls of previous occupants had been removed and buried with her, the one put on her feet, the other near her right shoulder. The skeletons were then covered with earth and paved over with stones on which a hearth was constructed. Near this hearth, about 1 m. square, another skull was deposited and the whole covered with earth, over which again there was laid a circular pavement, 2.5 m. in diameter, surrounded by a low wall. In the middle of the pavement lay three great stones surrounded by smaller ones.

The discoveries at Eynan have thus revealed the hitherto unsuspected importance attached to the burial of a Natufian chieftain—as well as the antiquity of certain funerary rituals which in the Pre-Pottery cultures of Jericho, lasted on for another two thousand years or so.

The Karim Shahir Culture

We come now to the second of the Near Eastern Mesolithic cultures, the Karim Shahir culture. This is represented by three open sites: Karim Shahir itself, Gird Chai on the Great Zab and Zawi Chemi near Shanidar on the same river. Oval and circular stone structures with a flimsy superstructure and hearths are reported from Zawi Chemi, but at the other two sites hearths and storage pits are the only signs of habitation, which may have been of a seasonal nature. There is no actual evidence for agriculture, but millstones, querns and a fair number of chipped and ground stone hoes, as well as the storage pits, may indicate its beginnings *(fig.3)*. Sickle blades are much less common than in the Natufian culture, but at Karim Shahir sheep, goats, cattle, dogs and horses could, except for the latter, have been domesticated, since many of their bones have been found.

Most of the small finds consisted of stone, either chipped or chipped and ground, and a large proportion of the flint industry was of microlithic type. At Gird Chai obsidian appears for the first time, showing contacts with the north, where the obsidian deposits cluster around Lake Van. At Karim Shahir some finer ground stone objects were found, including beads, pendants, rings, bracelets and a possible mace-head. Both here and at Zawi Chemi we find the first chipped stone celts (small axes) with polished cutting edges. Querns and pounders for the crushing of red ochre were common. Red ochre, a grinding stone and a necklace of small shell beads were found with the flexed burial of a young woman in a rough grave in the Shanidar cave, but otherwise no burials are known in the Karim Shahir culture. Bone pins, awls and worked bone and shell and some unbaked clay figurines, probably of animals, are the only other objects that have been found from this culture, which is probably roughly contemporary with the Natufian. None of the Karim Shahir sites excavated so far can be regarded as permanent villages for all three have yielded evidence of only a single occupation stratum. The same probably applies to most of the Natufian sites so far known, with the exception of Jericho and Eynan, and these may therefore rightly be called the earliest village sites yet found in the world.

Tools, weapons and articles of adornment of the Natufian culture of Palestine. In the third row from the left is the sickle handle from El Wad shaped like a fawn. (fig. 2)

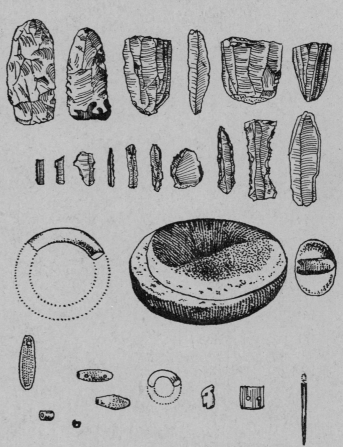

Characteristic tools and objects of the Karim Shahir culture in North Iraq. They include stone rings, beads and bracelets, ground stone querns and a grooved polisher. (fig.3)

Jericho

The next period certainly saw the beginnings of settled village life, though again we are not sure whether agriculture and animal domestication were really practised on any scale. Unfortunately the information for the beginning of this period is very scanty (pl. 3).

Directly overlying the burnt Natufian shrine at Jericho is a deposit of rather simple occupation material, called proto-neolithic by the excavator, which preceded the first fortified town of the Pre-Pottery Neolithic A period. Few details are available about this phase, but it is said to be characterized by a flint industry of Natufian type combined with settled occupation. Its date should fall somewhere in the 8th millennium BC, probably in its first half. It may be contemporary with the developed phases of the Natufian as known from the Carmel caves.

This was followed by the first fortified town yet found in the Near East, Jericho of the Pre-Pottery Neolithic A period. This seems to have developed from the proto-neolithic village and had an extraordinarily long life. No less than twenty-two architectural phases could be established, from one of which—I understand one of the later ones—two C 14 dates, giving an average of c. 6800 BC (c. 6770 and 6850) were obtained. Assuming that it had been occupied for a fairly long time before this level, the beginning of the town must go back to the second half of the 8th millennium BC. Its end may have come some time around the middle of the 7th millennium.

The fortifications of this town, which may have occupied about eight acres, are only partly known. A huge stone tower (pl. 8) 8.5 m. in diameter and still standing 6.5 m. high, contains a stairway of 28 stone steps descending about twenty feet at an angle of 30⁰. The steps are made of single slabs of stone over three feet wide and the roof, of the same large masonry, slopes obliquely. At the bottom, a horizontal passage, about twelve feet long, runs eastward to where there must have been a door giving access to the tower. Up against the tower ran a city wall, built of stone, 1.5 m. wide, freestanding and preserved up to a height of 3.55 m. Against the tower on the north side within the wall was a series of thin mud-brick walled and plastered enclosures, interpreted by the excavator as water cisterns. A channel from the top of the tower led towards them and it is thought that the water must have been stored for irrigation purposes. The tower was in use for a long time, during which two successive coats of masonry were added to it, associated with the building of two later town walls, which succeeded the original wall. Both later walls were no longer freestanding, but retained the gradually rising levels of building debris around the tower, where the water tanks were repeatedly rebuilt.

The latest of these three town walls is an enormous structure, standing on the truncated remains of the middle wall. Together they reach a height of over 5 m. and once carried a mud-brick superstructure of 'hogbacked bricks', long narrow bricks with tapering ends and a rounded top. In front of the wall a great rock-cut ditch (pl. 12) was found, 8.5 m. wide and 2.10 m. deep, a prodigious labour, for there is no evidence that picks or hoes were used. To remove the rock, stone pounders must have been employed no doubt in conjunction with the age-old device of splitting by fire and water, exactly in the same way as, much later, the ancient Egyptians quarried their hardest rocks.

South of the tower and at another point at the northern end of the mound mud-brick houses were found of circular or elongated oval plan, some consisting of a single room, others of as many as three rooms. The floors of these rooms were sunk below the level of the surrounding area and wooden steps flanked by wooden doorposts led down into them. Walls and floors were plastered with mud and the inward curve of the brick walls suggest a dome-like superstructure in wattle and daub.

Burials were found beneath the houses in graves about 1 m. deep. Bodies were contracted and in one case it looks as if the house was simply pulled down after its master's burial. Groups of skulls without skeletons were found elsewhere on the site and in one case a baby's body and a group of baby skulls were found under a bath-like structure, an arrangement that strongly suggests human sacrifice.

Little is as yet known of the artifacts made by these people. They had a flourishing bone industry, but the stone industry is quite different from that of its successor in the Pre-Pottery Neolithic B or 'plaster floor' phase. No finely worked stone bowls were found and the characteristic querns of the later phase are equally conspicuous by their absence.

A period during which the site was abandoned followed the collapse of the defences and possibly a gap existed before newcomers settled on

the site. The fact that Jericho was fortified from the very beginning of the Pre-Pottery Neolithic A period and the steady repair of the fortifications clearly shows that some redoubtable enemy lived not very far away, for defences of this nature are hardly raised against marauding bands of nomads. This enemy might have been the ancestors of the Tahunians of the Pre-pottery Neolithic B phase. Excavations at the Oren Valley site give some support to this view. Here, on top of the Natufian level, a Tahunian Pre-pottery settlement was found with stone bowls, grooved stones, elongated mortars, hatchets of Tahunian type, sickle blades, arrowheads, and saws. The flint objects were unpolished. The architecture, in two building levels, consisted of stone round and oval buildings with hearths and clay floors. Above it was another pre-pottery stratum with rectangular buildings, polished stone implements and imported material like obsidian and jade.

M'Lefaat

Possibly contemporary with the Pre-Pottery Neolithic A of Jericho is M'Lefaat on the River Khazir, twenty miles east of Mosul in N. Iraq. It is a village site with at least 1.5 m. of deposit containing several building levels. It had stone walls. The heavy stone tools that have been found (celts, hoes, pounders, mortars and querns) are better made than in mesolithic Karim Shahir, but its microlithic flint industry closely resembles it. There was no obsidian, so characteristic of the Jarmo culture, nor was any decorative stonework discovered. Clay figurines were found; these were rare at Karim Shahir, but are very common at Jarmo (see page 59). Sheep or goats, and medium-sized cattle, probably not yet fully domesticated, far outnumber wild animals, such as deer. There is little evidence for hunting at M'Lefaat. This site is typologically closer to Karim Shahir than to Jarmo and it is possible that they were in some way connected.

From Pre-Pottery to Pottery Cultures

The period now to be dealt with covers roughly the thousand years between the middle of the 7th and the middle of the 6th millennium BC. By this time all sites are of a permanent nature, mostly villages, but some, such as Jericho and the newly discovered Çatal Hüyük in the Konya plain on the South Anatolian plateau, are definitely of town size. Khirokitia in Cyprus is also extensive enough to be regarded as a small town rather than a village.

Although agriculture and the domestication of animals are by now virtually certain, the evidence available is still ambiguous. Even at Jericho we are not certain that grain, though certainly reaped, was sown and stored, and only at Jarmo, in Iraqi Kurdistan, and Otzaki in Thessaly has actual grain been found. As for animal domestication, the evidence is not much better. Only the dog and goat are definitely known to have been domesticated at this period at Jericho and Jarmo, and at Jericho the main meat supply came from hunted gazelles. Perhaps the domesticated goat was kept only for its milk. In the Pre-Sesklo culture of Thessaly on the other hand, domesticated sheep and goats formed the main meat supply, and as the animals are not native to Greece and were probably imported from Anatolia, it is likely that the same was the case there. This also applies to agriculture. Only from Jarmo have we more ample evidence of the varieties of food eaten. There are wild pigs, gazelles, sheep, goat, cattle, red deer, roe deer, onager (doubtfully identified), wolves and foxes, snails, fish, fresh water crabs, acorns, pistachio nuts, lentils and peas, and most important of all, *Emmer* and *Einkorn* wheat, as well as a primitive two-row barley. Only five per cent of the animal bones are those of wild animals.

Having briefly sketched the economy of the period, we must now review the variations in material culture. We may take first three late Pre-Pottery cultures; Jericho, Khirokitia (Cyprus) and Jarmo (Kurdistan), all descendants of a local mesolithic tradition, and then the first Pottery Neolithic cultures further north, in Southern Anatolia and Greece, which represent the beginning of a new tradition.

Jericho

Jericho at this period, (the 'plaster-floor' phase, or Pre-Pottery Neolithic B), was still a walled town, occupying about eight acres, which, if closely packed with buildings, on modern analogy, would have housed about 3,000 people. Streets have not been found; houses communicated with each other through courtyards and open spaces. The architecture is almost stereotyped; it arrived fully developed on the site and apparently did not change during the twenty-one phases recorded. The houses consisted of several rectangular rooms, communicating with one another through wide open doorways, the jambs of which are carefully rounded. Both walls and floors are covered with fine gypsum plaster, stained with red ochre and highly burnished. The walls, built of long cigar-shaped bricks, thumb-impressed on top, stand on stone foundations. Several buildings appear to have served cult purposes *(fig. 4)*. A small rectangular shrine was entered by a door at the narrow side (pl. 13). Facing the worshipper stood a polished

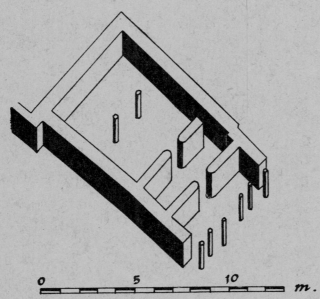

Plan of a shrine at Jericho from the 'plaster-floor' phase. The doorways with rounded jambs copy the forms of domestic architecture. (fig. 4)

flattened stone in a carefully plastered niche. Another building, perhaps a temple, had a rectangular room, at least 6 m. long and over 4 m. wide with an excellent floor of burnished plaster, in the middle of which a plastered rectangular basin filled with white ashes was sunk. On either side of this room, balancing annexes of curvilinear plan were built up against it.

Rush mats, round or rectangular, covered the floors. In one room thirty-one bodies were found dismembered below the floor, probably the result of a massacre, after which the town was again rebuilt. In the house beneath which the bodies lay, a group of skulls was found, with the features restored in painted plaster and eyes inlaid with cowrie shells (pl. 9). Whether these were trophies or the heads of revered ancestors, whose bodies were found below the floor, has not yet been decided, but analogous practices in the Natufian culture of Eynan rather lends support to the latter supposition. Most of the skeletons from the Pre-Pottery Neolithic B levels at Jericho belonged to the same slender Mediterranean race as the Natufians, from which they were probably descended. These remarkable pieces of modelling from Jericho give one a vivid impression of what these people looked like. One of the painted skulls shows a moustache, but most are clean-shaven.

Pottery was still completely unknown, but its place was supplied by finely carved limestone bowls and no doubt by other vessels in such perishable form as baskets, skins and gourds. Querns of elongated shape are characteristic of this culture and so is the Tahunian flint industry. Arrow and javelin heads, made in pale yellow or pink flint

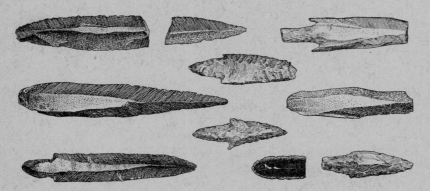

A typical 'Tahunian' javelin, arrowheads and sickle blades from Jericho Pre-Pottery Neolithic B (c. 6500–5500 BC). (fig. 5)

(fig. 5), with delicate tangs are as characteristic as the long sickle blades, which often show the siliceous sheen from cutting reeds, grain or grass. It should be noted that there is no trace left of a microlithic element in the flint industry. Little is known about the religious beliefs of these people, other than funerary rites. They carefully made small clay figurines of the 'Mother Goddess' type *(fig. 6)*, and of animals, which everywhere in the Near East are associated with a fertility cult.

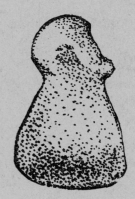

'Mother-goddess' figurine in baked clay from Jericho Pre-Pottery Neolithic B. (fig. 6)

The origin of this culture is not yet known, but it is suspected to have come from the north. The Pre-Pottery culture of Jericho, in particular the curious funerary habits, strike one as a local development from the Mesolithic Natufian, but as long as equally early sites in the Orontes valley of Syria remain to be found and excavated, it would be premature to stress the uniqueness of Jericho too much.

KHIROKITIA

Nothing so early has yet been found in Syria, but an extremely interesting little township of this period has been excavated at Khirokitia in Southern Cyprus. The Khirokitia Pre-Pottery Neolithic culture is the earliest known in the island: a C 14 date of c. 5500 BC has recently been obtained for this phase. The site covers a hill, approximately 250 m. in diameter, situated within a bend of the river Maroniou and commands a view down to the south coast. A main road running for about 200 m. through the settlement was traced leading up the hill from the river and 48 round houses of tholos type (i.e. with domed roof) were excavated. Their total number may have approached the thousand mark, implying a population of several thousand souls (cf. Jarmo; estimate about 25 houses, population about 150). Domesticated sheep and goat and possibly pig were found and agriculture was probably practised, although the evidence rests again on sickle blades, querns and grinding stones. The flint industry is peculiar and possibly a descendant of Upper Palaeolithic. Central Anatolian obsidian was imported in fair quantities and to that same source the clumsy attempts at making pottery, discovered in the bottom level—soon abandoned for the use of stone vessels—may be attributed, for Southern Anatolia at this period was already making quite advanced pottery.

The polished stone industry of the Khirokitia culture is with the architecture its most characteristic feature. A Khirokitia spouted stone bowl was found (in the Amuq A period of N. Syria) contemporary with Pottery-Neolithic Mersin. Spouted stone bowls (pl. 6,7) and dishes of round, square or roughly rectangular shapes are the most common forms. These are mostly plain, but many of the finer are decorated with plastic bands, knobs, etc. Among the finer vessels are shallow round dishes, reminiscent of the Natufian of Eynan and the late Pre-Pottery of Jericho, possibly lamps, some animal-shaped vessels and some with human heads. Engraved pebbles of uncertain use are common. Stone figurines of humans occur and there is one female head in clay.

Garments were fastened with bone pins and articles of personal ornament include stone beads, pendants, bracelets, necklaces made of carnelian and pikrite (a form of grey-green chrysolite ; pl. 5), often in combination with *dentalium* shells, so characteristic of the Natufian. Weaving is attested by the presence of spindle-whorls. Handles of flint tools, awls, pins and needles were made of bone. Maces were used as weapons.

The Khirokitians were a round-headed (brachycephalic) group of unknown affinity, but it is suspected that the extreme brachycephaly was the result of widespread cranial deformation. They practised burial among the houses, like the Natufians and the Pre-Pottery people of Jericho. Contracted single burial below the floors of the houses appears to have been the rule. Objects were buried with the dead, especially stone bowls, often ceremonially broken. Stone bowls and necklaces were usually buried with women, and pins etc. with men and children. Women appear to have played a great part in this culture. There are possible cases of human sacrifice and libations to the dead.

The houses were round, bearing a domed mud-brick or pisé super-structure on a stone wall, which was often double. Hearths, platforms for sleeping, pits in the floor and an upper floor in part of the tholos are common. Windows and cupboards in the wall or in the stone pillars which supported the upper floor are well preserved. Several compounds were found consisting of one large beehive house and several others used as kitchens or workshops for grinding corn; court-yards were often paved with stone and stone ramps led down from the main artery of the settlement. Some stone tables found in passages and courts show where the meals were eaten. Khirokitia gives one the impression of a well organized community, in many respects remi-niscent of Natufian Eynan and Pre-Pottery Jericho, which may have its origin in a Cypriot Mesolithic still to be discovered. Three phases of the culture have been identified; in the third painted pottery, a completely new element, appears together with some long-headed newcomers and the culture declines.

Jarmo

The third late Pre-Pottery culture of this period to be described is that of Qal'at Jarmo in the Chemchemal district of Iraqi Kurdistan. This was a permanent village, with an estimated duration of about 250 years (probably an underestimate), about 25 houses, occupying two-thirds of its total area of 3-4 acres, and a population of 150 souls. As no burials were found, nothing is known of the physical type of the Jarmo people. Seven metres of debris contained about 15 building levels, the top five with primitive pottery, some of it unbaked, and some Hassuna archaic ware towards the end, whereas the lower ten are without pottery. Finely carved stone vessels and clay basins or hearths set in the floor and baked in situ were found instead. No doubt there were also baskets and skins, for reed matting formed a basis for the soft mud floors. Fair-sized houses were characteristic, each with several rectangular rooms, which were in the later phases pro-vided with ovens and chimneys, and built of pisé (i.e. clay and gravel) or 'touf'. Mud-brick as a building material was unknown in Mesopot-amia until much later. Roofs were made of mud laid on reeds.

Some of these houses had stone foundations, stone being easily procurable in this hilly country and among the artifacts, those in stone predominate. Ground stone types include querns, mortars, pounders, finely carved stone bowls and dishes for eating, axes and celts; mace-heads were used as weapons and perforated disks, bracelets and beads as personal ornaments. Palettes are found for ochre-grinding and pins, awls, spoons, bangles and pendants are made of bone. The chipped stone industry is predominately in flint and consists mainly of blades for composite tools, knives and sickle blades. Microliths still account for about 40% of the total. The flint was local, but side by side with it obsidian was used, imported from Eastern Anatolia, the nearest source over three hundred miles away. Obsidian tools are nearly all micro-lithic at Jarmo, adding another 30% to the total of microlithic tools at Jarmo. Not all obsidian was microlithic, however, for a magnificent obsidian dagger over 0.35 m. long was found in the Jarmo period levels at Tell Shemshara. This is the biggest obsidian tool yet found in the Near East. Among the more interesting finds from Jarmo, a curved sickle with wooden haft must be mentioned, in which four simple unretouched flint blades were set end to end and fastened with natural pitch or bitumen.

Very common at Jarmo were unbaked clay figurines *(fig. 7)*, mainly sheep and dogs, but including a fair number of sitting pregnant women of 'Mother Goddess' type. The animals may have been toys, but the female figures obviously are not. The appearance of pottery towards the end of the period is probably a local invention.

So far we have described the three best known late Pre-Pottery cultures of the Near East. There is some evidence for others, e.g. at Ras Shamra (Ugarit) on the North Syrian coast, and at Gremnos Maghoula and Sesklo in Thessaly. The latter culture, which may be as early as the middle Pre-Pottery period, has yielded microliths, flint and obsidian, bone tools, ground stone bowls and even grain. Other Pre-Pottery Neolithic cultures will eventually, no doubt, be discovered in Southern Anatolia, Syria and Iran.

Characteristic objects of the Jarmo Pre-Pottery culture. Below, left: earliest pottery from the upper levels. (fig. 7)

Anatolia and Greece

We come now to the Pottery cultures of Anatolia and Mainland Greece, which are contemporary with the Pre-Pottery cultures just described. The emergence of agricultural economies here appears to be relatively late in comparison with Palestine and North Iraq, but perhaps only because research in these countries has lagged far behind that in the Fertile Crescent. The most important characteristic of these South Anatolian cultures and their counterpart in Mainland Greece (but not the Cyclades or Crete) is the presence from the very begin-ning of a well-made pottery associated with a flourishing obsidian industry. How old the use of pottery is in South Anatolia is not yet known, for at not a single site has a Pre-Pottery stratum been reached, even though it can be traced into the second half of the 7th millen-nium BC. At Beldibi near Antalya in S.W. Anatolia, primitive pottery has just been found stratified in the last level of a Mesolithic culture with Natufian affinities.

The distribution of the Neolithic Pottery cultures of Southern Anatolia, as known at present, is shown in *fig. 8*, and it must be emphasized that the present distribution looks as if these cultures originated on the South Anatolian plateau and not in Cilicia, as was hitherto thought. Not enough is yet known of the earliest Greek Neolithic pottery, the so-called Rainbow ware of Southern and Central Greece and the Pre-Sesklo cultures of Thessaly, to say whether they are an independent and spontaneous development or derived from Anatolia. The latter is by no means unlikely, for both agriculture and animal domestication in Thessaly in the Pre-Pottery levels there are undoubtedly of Anatolian origin and there is evidence that certain contacts were maintained with the mother-country throughout the Neolithic as well as the early Chalcolithic period.

The Neolithic cultures of Southern Anatolia can be traced in a continuous belt from the edge of the West Anatolian plateau to the plains of Cilicia and the Amuq. The eastern and northern limits of these Neolithic cultures are still unknown. Three main cultures can

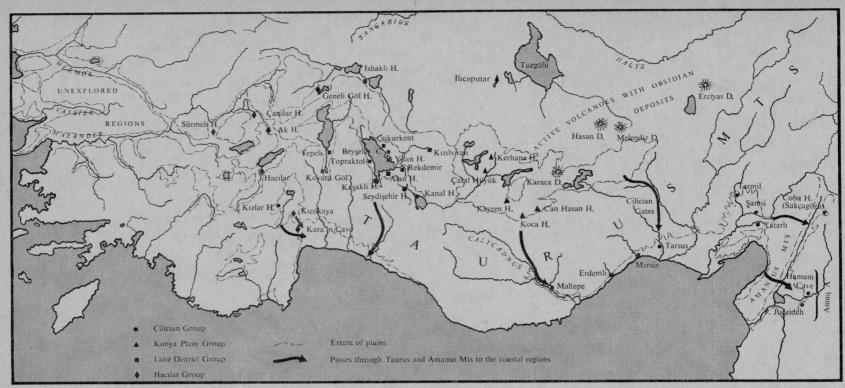

Distribution of the Neolithic cultures in Southern Anatolia. (fig. 8)

be distinguished: a Neolithic of Cilicia and Amuq plains, type-site Mersin; a Neolithic in the Konya Plain and the Pisidian Lake District, type sites Çatal Hüyük and Çukurkent; and a Neolithic in S. W. Anatolia represented by Kızılkaya in its earlier and by Hacılar in its better known later phases. The regions between this area and the west coast are still unexplored, but certain finds from Aghio Gala in Chios point to the existence of probably another Neolithic culture in this region. Beyond the Aegean the early neolithic sites are mostly near the east coast, a distribution which suggests that the bearers of that culture arrived by sea. Two main provinces are found, one comprising Thessaly and another which includes Central Greece and the Eastern Peloponnese.

Most of the Anatolian and Greek sites of this period appear to have been villages, some small, some large like Mersin and Çukurkent. At Çatal Hüyük in the Konya plain, however, we have a neolithic town site, about 500 m. long, 150 m. wide and over 15 m. high, more than twice the size of late Pre-Pottery Jericho, with which it is roughly contemporary. On the surface of the mound rectangular houses built in mud-brick on stone foundations are everywhere visible. Such houses, some quite substantial, were also found at Mersin (the only excavated neolithic site in Anatolia). A sounding at Mersin produced about 8–9 building levels with twice that number of floors, but excavation on a more extensive scale would no doubt have greatly increased that number. Virgin soil was not reached because of the rise of the water table, not only at Mersin, but also at Tarsus and at Tell Judeideh in the Amuq. Red painted plaster floors, reminiscent of contemporary Jericho, were found in the Amuq, at Tarsus and at Alan Hüyük on Lake Beyşehir recently. Gypsum plaster floors have also been found in Hacılar VIII and VI, but have not yet been reported from Greece.

A characteristic of the Cilician and the Konya Plain Neolithic is the presence of pressure-flaked obsidian tanged lances and arrowheads, usually worked on both sides. Short sickle blades, notched and backed blades are the only other forms in use. The source of obsidian was the then active Central Anatolian volcanoes (Hasan, Melendiz, Mekke and Erciyas) and it seems to have been transported over considerable distances; the nearest known workshop to the volcanic area is Ilıca-pınar, 100 miles away! A recent survey in the Central Anatolian region failed to locate any other workshop sites, though from Mersin we know that the raw material was brought down to Cilicia to be worked locally. This seems to have been the case everywhere; at Çatal Hüyük obsidian can be picked up in huge quantities and many tools are unfinished. (A group of the best is illustrated in *fig. 9*.) The excellence of the pressure-flaked lanceheads suggests long practice in obsidian working but only excavation of the site could reveal this. Micro-liths are not found in these cultures, just as in the Tahunian. Apart from obsidian, a small amount of flint and chert was used.

The ground stone industry is well developed; greenstone axes and miniature jade celts, set in antler sleeves and bone sockets respectively (cf. later pl. 21), are common all over the South Anatolian neolithic province as well as in Greece, but there adzes are also common. Not a single adze has so far been found in neolithic Anatolia. In the later Neolithic of Hacılar, the stone industry is on the wane; blades and blade cores are the only chipped obsidian, chert and flint tools found and obsidian is less common. The stratified evidence from Mersin supports the conclusion that in the late Neolithic the obsidian industry declines. Fragments of polished stone bowls, usually marble or white limestone with pink veins, are found on all neolithic sites and the same variety of stones are used for making female figurines (pl. 11), stamp seals (Mersin, Amuq; cf. later pl. 21), pins with human or animal heads, beads and pendants.

Female figurines were also made of baked clay, and sometimes a stone head was set in a clay body (Çukurkent). In the late Neolithic of Hacılar tall standing clay figurines were made in a variety of forms (pl. 15). Heads were extremely well modelled and their pigtails are incised. Another small figurine was cut out of mother-of-pearl (pl. 11). Animal figurines are rare, but an animal head was used to

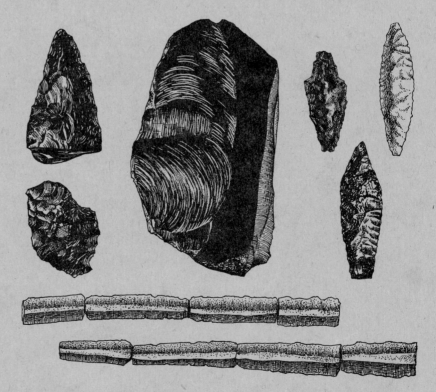

Çatal Hüyük: pressure-flaked lance and arrowheads in black obsidian, and core, 7th millennium BC. Bottom row: sickle blades like those in fig. 2. (fig. 9)

decorate a spoon handle from Hacılar and stylized bulls' head lugs are found on the neolithic pottery there (cf. later pighead, pl. 20). The earliest Greek figurines are either naturalistic or clumsy pear-shaped clay idols with coarse incision.

A characteristic of the earliest pottery in use in these south Anatolian and Greek cultures is its high technical quality, from the very beginning. Here there are no crumbly or unwashable wares (as at Jarmo), but firm hardfired fabrics, often remarkably thin. Small grits form the normal *degraissant*, and only in the coarse ware of Cilicia and the Amuq is straw admixture found. A slip is occasionally used, but a real characteristic of these wares is a good overall burnish, which towards the end of the period may give way to a brilliant polish, as can be seen in the colour photographs (pl. 16). Variations in colour are both regional, the result of firing different clays, and chronological. Although the Cilician and Amuq A wares are generally dark in colour, black, dark grey, brown and red-brown, those of the Konya Plain and the Lake District are on the whole lighter—blackish grey, grey, brown, reddish brown, and buff (pl. 16, top), and the earliest Hacılar ware (level IX) is predominantly cream-coloured or light grey (pl. 16, middle). In the late Neolithic at Mersin finer clays are imported (Mersin XXVI and XXV) and light grey, jet-black, red slipped and buff wares appear.

The earliest pottery from Greece is often mottled or black inside and red, brown or buff outside, like that of Hacılar IX–VII, hence its name 'rainbow' or variegated (pl. 14). Some of the finer fabrics from the Konya Plain to Greece are porcelain-white in colour, undoubtedly in imitation of marble. Shapes are on the whole very simple; bag-shaped hole-mouth jars and bowls predominate in Cilicia, Amuq A and the Konya Plain in the earlier neolithic levels. In Cilicia and the Amuq they tend to be rather shallow, but deeper forms seem to be more common in the Konya Plain, and the Lake District, and both occur in Greece. Whereas handles are absent everywhere, even lugs are a rarity in Cilicia, though they are common on the Anatolian Plateau. There they are horizontally placed like ledge handles, whereas in Greece they are set vertically.

Decoration other than burnish is rare. In Cilicia excised design is succeeded by shell-impressed rocker incision; in the Konya Plain this does not exist, but incised lines, chevrons and ribbed plastic bands are used instead (pl. 16, top). The earliest pottery of Greece is not ornamented. The late neolithic of Hacılar shows many links with that of the Konya Plain and Lake District, but possesses a series of shapes, including oval cups with four vertical tubular lugs, not found there. Oval shapes and tubular lugs are however a feature of the Aghio Gala and the Fikirtepe culture. There is one other important innovation all over the area in the late Neolithic, and that is the invention of painted pottery. The use of a red wash on cream-coloured wares led to the development of designs. Such early designs occur at Mersin XXVI, Çatal Hüyük and Çukurkent and from the very beginning at Hacılar (pl. 16, middle), where by level VII a highly imaginative series of patterns is in full use (pl. 16, bottom). Similarly early painted wares are found at Otzaki in Thessaly and at Lerna in the Peloponnese. The idea of painting pottery must have spread fast, for from the very beginning of the next period we find painted pottery in use in the greater part of the Near East, even in areas where no pottery at all had been in use before (pl. 19).

The Early Chalcolithic Period

This period, which began about the middle of the 6th millennium BC, might be called that of the red-on-cream painted pottery cultures, were it not for the fact that in Anatolia and Iran the presence of the first metal objects has already led to the introduction of the term 'Early Chalcolithic', (i. e. copper and stone). Both paint and slip of course show variations; to mention one, in Southern Iraq and Iran, the red paint may be brown or black and the surface, though often cream, may shade to red in the second half of the period. All these painted wares are accompanied by burnished red, buff or black wares and there are as usual poorer wares for kitchen use.

Though the greater part of the Near East from the Balkans to S.W. Iran was now producing painted pottery (pl. 14, 16–19) there are areas where this was not the case. One such is the Syro-Palestinian coast and the Orontes Valley south of the Amuq. Here black and brown burnished wares (pl. 24), combed, scored or incised, were used, without a trace of any painted pottery. The first painted pottery in the Southern Jordan Valley, at Jericho and at Ghrubba, seems to have been intro-

duced by nomads from the north. A black and grey burnished ware is found with painted pottery north of the Amuq plain (e.g. Sakçagözü and perhaps Carchemish), and without it east of the Euphrates (e.g. bottom levels at Chagar Bazar). The map (pl. 19) and illustrations show the spread of the technique and the styles of painted pottery, the rough distribution of each culture, and a typical pot for each of these cultures, clearly illustrating the diversity of shapes, designs and style. The chronological table shows their relation in time, for some are later than others.

It was during this period that the flat southern lands of Iraq and Khuzistan were first occupied. The settlers belonged to the Hassuna culture of N. Iraq, and the most important new sites are Samarra on the Tigris and Baghuz on the Euphrates. They probably came first to the well-watered land along the foothills of the Zagros in Susiana, and later went in search of new lands in what afterwards became Sumer. One of the new settlements was at Eridu, where an elementary knowledge of irrigation was a pre-requisite, since the annual winter rainfall is not likely to have been sufficient to ensure an adequate cereal crop. Such knowledge could have been gained in their earlier home, the southern part of the Hassuna culture area.

The date of the earliest Eridu settlement could be late Samarra, but the technique of the Eridu pottery (pl. 19) does not appear to be derived from there *(fig. 10)*. The spread of painted pottery traditions over the vast area from the Balkans to S.W. Iran is perhaps best explained as the result of the movements of nomadic or semi-nomadic tribes. The obsidian trade, which continued during this period, may also have been in their hands. Moving over considerable distances during the course of a year, they had the maximum opportunity and interest in diffusing new ideas. The spread of painted pottery was certainly not the result of great invasions.

Certain general features may be noted in these earliest painted pottery cultures. In those of Anatolia and Greece generally, the vessels were usually coated in a cream slip and burnished, before or after painting, a tradition derived from the earlier unpainted pottery. The earliest painted pottery in N. Iraq (Hassuna archaic ware) and in Palestine (Jericho Pottery Neolithic A) observe the same tradition. Elsewhere, matt painted pottery is more common, especially in Iran, Mesopotamia, North Syria, at Ghrubba and even to some extent in

Painted pottery bowl from Samarra, one of the earliest cultures to show animal representation on painted ware. (fig. 10)

Cilicia. Straw admixtures in the clay do not seem to be common west of the Amuq. Another general characteristic is that the ornament, whether linear or solid (e.g. Hacılar and Jericho Neolithic A) is always geometric. Only in Mesopotamia and Iran, and then only in the second half of the period, do animal and human representations occur (in the Samarra, Tepe Jarri B (late), Tepe Siyalk II and Chasma Ali cultures). In later periods, Iran and Iranian influence seems to have been the main source for animals on painted pottery.

Little else can be found which serves as a general characterization of this period, except such generalities as settled village and town life, based on mixed farming, supplemented by hunting and fishing; a fertility cult, involving the manufacture of figurines of the fertility goddess; the use of sling and mace in preference to the bow and arrow (except in Cyprus, Syria and Palestine, where old traditions had not yet died out).

Burial customs varied: burial in the house in Cyprus, at Byblos and in Iran; burial (probably in cemeteries, except for infants) outside

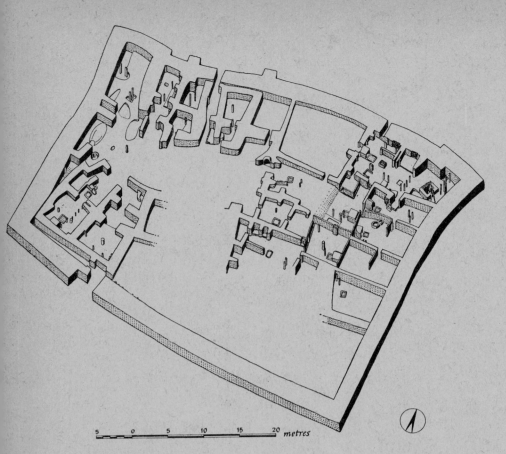

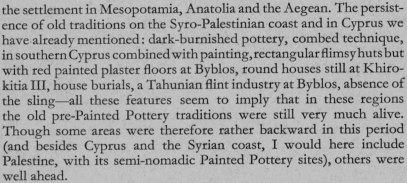

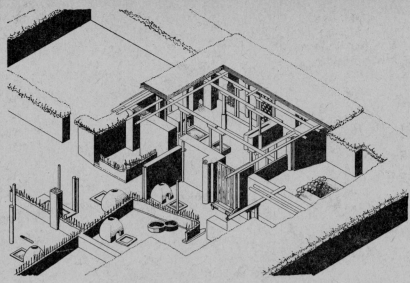

Hacılar II: isometric plan (left) of the settlement, showing the houses arranged round courtyards. In the centre are the two workshops illustrated in pl. 30. In the north-east corner is an elaborately constructed house which was provided with a well and with its own doorway through the wall. The reconstruction above shows that there were niches in the back wall and a standing stone recalling that of Jericho (see pl. 13). This, together with the presence of a group of burials under the floor—the only ones to be found at Hacılar—suggests that this building was some sort of shrine. (fig. 11, 12)

the settlement in Mesopotamia, Anatolia and the Aegean. The persistence of old traditions on the Syro-Palestinian coast and in Cyprus we have already mentioned: dark-burnished pottery, combed technique, in southern Cyprus combined with painting, rectangular flimsy huts but with red painted plaster floors at Byblos, round houses still at Khirokitia III, house burials, a Tahunian flint industry at Byblos, absence of the sling—all these features seem to imply that in these regions the old pre-Painted Pottery traditions were still very much alive. Though some areas were therefore rather backward in this period (and besides Cyprus and the Syrian coast, I would here include Palestine, with its semi-nomadic Painted Pottery sites), others were well ahead.

A momentous invention of the Highland zone, Anatolia and Iran, was that of metallurgy. This is the only region of the Near East where the necessary metals are found. As early as level XXIII at Mersin, copper pins appear, and towards the end of Siyalk I and in II, hammered copper awls and pins have been discovered. Copper is also said to have been found at Samarra but its exact date is disputed. Most tools are, however, still in flint or ground stone (pl. 21). Several pottery shapes in the Çatal Hüyük, Hacılar and Sesklo cultures are strongly metallic, an indication of the rare, but treasured, use of metal. One natural result of the new invention was a decline in the chipped stone industry, although luxury goods such as stone vessels (pl. 22), figurines, and articles of personal adornment were still produced in stone.

Other domestic industries underwent little change but of the crafts in perishable materials such as weaving and basketry only patterns borrowed by the potter survive. Modelling in clay reached a high degree of artistic craftsmanship in the beautiful figurines of the Hacılar and Sesklo cultures (pl. 23, 26), which excel all others known in their size and naturalism.

Buildings of this period have been found at Hassuna, Matarrah, Baghuz and Eridu in Mesopotamia and at Siyalk in Iran. Pisé walls without stone foundations are the rule in both countries, the first mud bricks marked with thumb-prints appearing only in the shrine at Eridu XV and at Siyalk II (where they are used for foundations). With the exception of a round building in Hassuna I, all houses are of rectangular plan, containing several rooms, passages and courtyards and are provided with bread-ovens and at Hassuna with sunk grain bins, gypsum-lined and coated with bitumen. In Cilicia, South Anatolia and Greece, the technique of mud-brick on stone foundation (rarely omitted) continues from the previous period. House plans were rectangular, consisting of one or more large rooms and courtyards. A characteristic of the Hacılar and Sesklo cultures is the frequent use of internal buttresses to support the heavy flat roof. Bread ovens are frequent and grain was stored in domed pits at Mersin and in clay bins

at Hacılar. There is evidence that Hacılar II was surrounded by a defensive wall. A reconstruction of the 'potters' shops' of Hacılar II with their beautiful and often fantastic painted pottery (pl. 27-29) is seen in pl. 30. Hacılar I was heavily fortified and was probably the seat of a local ruler, rather than a fortified village. The extraordinary amount of fine painted pottery with its infinite variety of design and its unparalleled shapes makes one think that it must have been a centre for the production of luxury ware. (fig. 11, 12)

The stretch of fortifications uncovered at Hacılar consists of a heavy outer wall, 7–10 feet wide, behind which shelter several rows of rooms, many of which were accessible only from the upper storey, constructed of light materials and probably only inhabited in summer. An entrance passage—the prototype of a gate—consisted of a small open area, narrowed appreciably at either end by cross walls which left an easily defended opening of not more than three feet. This is the earliest fortress known in Anatolia, but others will no doubt be discovered in the future. A later development of the same plan with a proper gate flanked by two towers, was found in Mersin XVI and belongs to the end of the Middle Chalcolithic (Halaf) period, c. 4250 BC (C 14 gives a date of c. 4125 BC for the beginning of the next [Al-'Ubaid] period).

At the end of the Early Chalcolithic period, then, let us say c. 5000 BC, we find that throughout the greater part of the Near East all the requirements for the birth of civilization were present. Villages, market towns, e.g. Çatal Hüyük West (over 1,300 feet in diameter!) in the Konya Plain and possibly Mersin, and the castles of local rulers (e.g. Hacılar) dotted the more fertile parts of the countries. Everywhere life was based on mixed farming, supplemented by hunting and fishing. Goods and raw materials were traded over great distances, often no doubt through the agency of nomadic tribes during their annual migrations. Obsidian, copper, though still rare, marble and other attractive stones, such as carnelian, nephrite and rock crystal, sea-shell and perishable substances like fabrics and the contents of vessels—for pots after all would have been largely traded for their contents!—rank among the main articles of trade. Metallurgy in its infancy was practised in certain highland areas (pl. 31), but only the rulers would be in a position to possess metal vessels, copied in pottery by their subjects. Shrines, such as at Eridu, and stone and clay figurines of the female deity expressed man's belief in higher powers.

Failure to Advance

Nevertheless, the expected birth of civilization did not take place. It was delayed for nearly another millennium and a half and when it did come it was not in the areas which had hitherto been most prominent, but in the dismally flat lands of S. Iraq and a little later in Egypt, areas which until then had been of little or no importance. Why was this so? The subject is too complex to go into here in detail, but it seems true to say that before further economic or technical progress could take place, certain political improvements were necessary—a complex social hierarchy (either royal as in Egypt or theocratic as in Sumer); systematic urbanization; strong political control and adequate concentration of economic resources—and these do not seem to have developed until the later centuries of the 4th millennium BC, and then only in Sumer and Egypt.

The fifth and most of the fourth millennium BC witnessed the growth of other cultures in hitherto comparatively unimportant—or rather archaeologically little known—regions. Of these the Halaf culture in Northern Mesopotamia and the Hajji Muhammad culture, closely followed by its descendant the 'Ubaid culture in Southern Mesopotamia are the most outstanding. Both are generally judged to be of extra-Mesopotamian origin; the first is thought to have originated in unexplored Tur al Abdin, Diyarbakır area and the Southern Taurus, the second in what later became Elam in and along the foothills of the Southern Zagros but this is not certain.

For the first time we see mountain tribes take over from the plainsmen, a pattern which can be observed in the Near East to the present day. Characteristic of these secondary painted pottery cultures is the much greater extent of their distribution and influence (map, *fig. 15*), gradually breaking down a series of previously separate cultures, though it would be an exaggeration to think of the Halaf and later the 'Ubaid cultures which spread to the Mediterranean, as culturally homogeneous.

The northern Halaf culture is best known for its tholoi-like shrines (*fig. 13*), incorporating the Mesolithic round house element, its magnificent (though late) polychrome pottery (pl. 34) and its typical well-carved obsidian beads, stamp-seals and amulets (pl. 33). Its skilful use of obsidian, worked into vessels and necklaces, is matched by the pottery which betrays unmistakable metal prototypes, showing the great ascendancy metal vessels were acquiring in this northern area. This splendid culture was wiped out by the arrival of the 'Ubaid culture from the south, which is noted not so much for its ubiquitous rather dull pottery (though not always), as for its high development of religious architecture at Eridu and Tepe Gawrah (*fig. 14*).

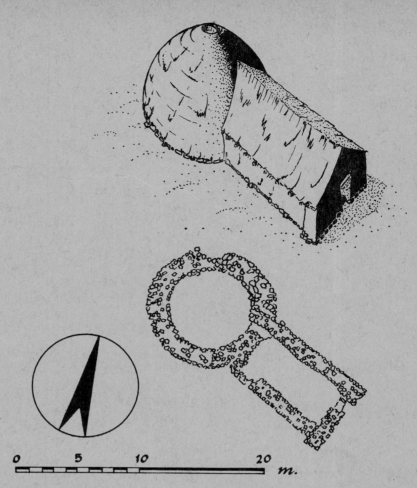

Reconstruction and plan of a tholos-like shrine of the Halaf culture, from Arpachiyah, middle Chalcolithic period. (fig. 13)

Reconstruction of the 'Ubaid temples at Tepe Gawrah, Level XIII (Chalcolithic period). (fig. 14)

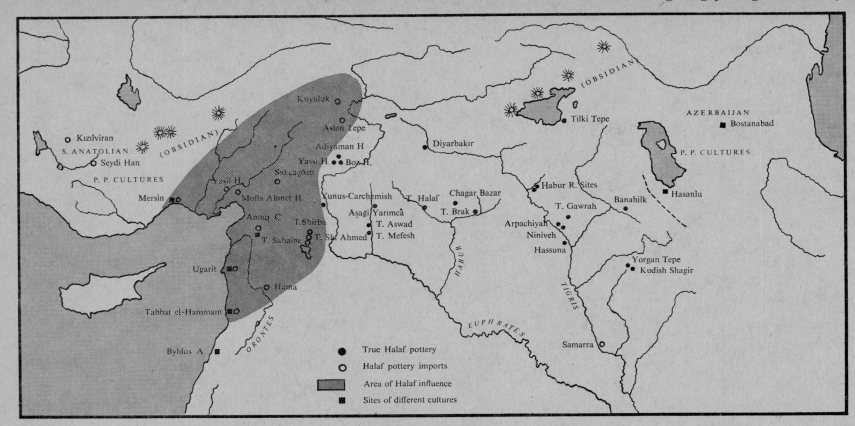

Distribution of the Halaf and other cultures of the middle Chalcolithic in the 'Fertile Crescent'. (fig. 15)

Mud-brick only now becomes common in Mesopotamia. In many respects the 'Ubaid culture set the standard for Mesopotamian religious architecture.

When these developments were taking place in Iraq, the first village communities arose in Egypt, probably as the result of an extension of the Yarmukian/Jericho Pottery-Neolithic B culture of Palestine.

In the Highland zone, one culture after another, mostly with painted pottery, is found in Iran, Cyprus, Anatolia and Greece. In Western Anatolia, however, a late Chalcolithic with white-painted, red, buff, brown and black burnished wares succeeded Hacılar and somewhat later a similar culture extinguished the painted pottery culture of the Konya Plain and Cilicia. The earliest culture found in Crete belongs to this same family of dark burnished wares, but lacks the white paint, and others spread over Greece, the southern Balkans and northern Anatolia. Eventually c. 3500 the Uruk culture, with predominantly red and grey burnished ware, long thought to have been of Anatolian, but far more likely actually of East Iranian origin, extended over Mesopotamia and put an end to the last native painted pottery culture there. Out of the amalgamation of the Uruk people with the earlier population there sprang towards the end of the Uruk period the first Mesopotamian civilization.

III THE BIRTH OF WRITTEN HISTORY

Civilized life begins: Mesopotamia and Iran

M. E. L. MALLOWAN

Chronology. The relation in time of the archaeological levels of some of the major sites in Mesopotamia and Iran (after Le Breton). The dates mentioned in the chapter which follows are based on the system originally proposed by Professor Sidney Smith whose longer chronology, as opposed to the various shorter schemes offered by other authorities, has been increasingly strengthened by recent evidence. We have therefore adopted the following dates: Hammurabi *acc.* 1792 BC, Sargon of Agade *acc.* c. 2370 BC. Before that time we have to reckon in round numbers, and in our opinion the weight of the archaeological as well as of historical evidence, early synchronisms with Egypt, and the high dating for prehistoric material which has been obtained from C 14 analyses, tend to support the relatively high dates which we have proposed. It will however be some years before we can obtain a sufficient number of C 14 samples from both Early Dynastic sites in Mesopotamia and Bronze Age settlements in Iran to enable us to arrive at a conclusive chronology.

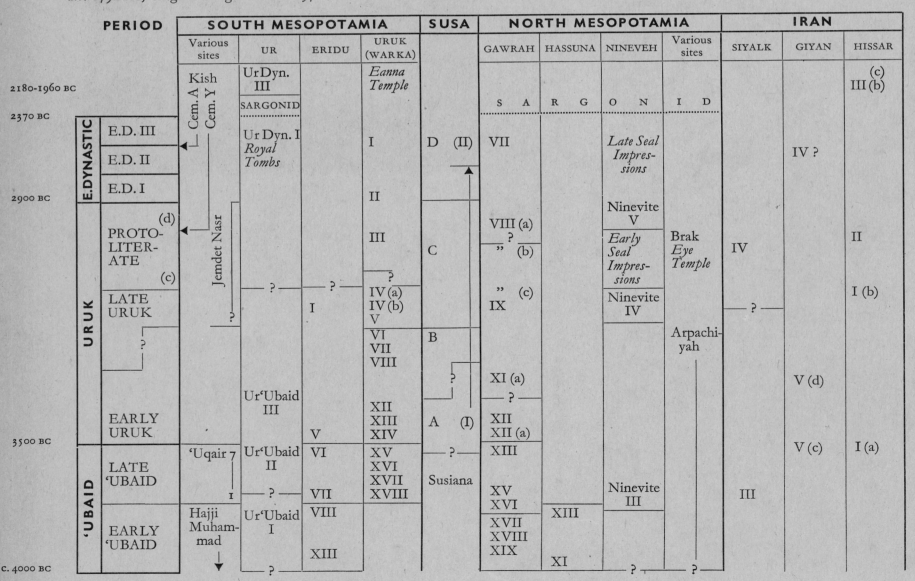

The first light of civilization dawned in the fertile valleys of the Tigris and the Euphrates, in the centuries around 4000 BC. The rich agricultural plains of the south produced an abundance of food—wheat and barley, meat, fish and wild fowl were plentiful. In such conditions and in the light of his growing skill as a farmer, man no longer had to move from exhausted land. He could live for generation after generation in the same place, feed his family and provide for others as well. The earth gave him a surplus which was to change his life.

For the population multiplied, villages grew into towns and towns into cities: as early as 4000 BC a city such as Eridu must have numbered several thousands of souls. In a community of this size, men got together to produce such necessities as clothing and housing; craftsmen began to work full time; traders grew up who specialized in bringing the new raw materials from abroad, and officials arose to control the organization of labour and to supervize the distribution of food.

To protect themselves from the wrath of their gods, the people paid tribute to a powerful priesthood; their temples became institutions which combined cathedral chapter and civil service, university and court of justice, and within them were worked out not only their relationship to the universe and the gods but also the problems of administering human communities. As the material outcome of this intellectual and spiritual development, we see simple building raised to the status of monumental architecture, and craftsmanship turning to produce some of the earliest works of conscious art.

Most significant of all was an invention which was destined to spread over the entire world—namely the art of writing. The memory of man is fallible and, when disputes arise, needs a permanent witness. In this respect as an aid to a title of ownership and property rights, visible records soon become indispensible and the birth of writing is a natural outcome in a complex society. And from *writing* stems history itself.

The oldest known picture-writing is contained on the two sides of the limestone tablet shown right, found at Kish and dated c. 3500 BC. On it appear signs for head, hand and foot, for a threshing sledge and for numerals. (1, 2)

Far back in the pre-history of Sumer, about 3500 BC, a temple was built at Eridu which was to be the classic prototype for the monumental architecture to come. All that remains of it today is the gypsumplastered limestone platform, but this reconstruction shows the mudbrick superstructure, with buttresses, columns and portico; an arrangement that set the standard for many later buildings. It was however not the first sanctuary on the site. The god of the temple was considered to be landlord and owner in perpetuity of the ground which had been consecrated to him. It was therefore the practice to fill in the temple periodically and bury it, sometimes with statuary and amulets, also the property of the god. Over the buried temple, the new one was built, and such were the accumulated remains at Eridu that the new temple towered above the surrounding plain. (3)

Delicately made vessels, as the one above, were found at Bakun (c. 3500 BC), with designs abstracted from nature, such as ibex, horned birds, swimming ducks, fish or running water. (5)

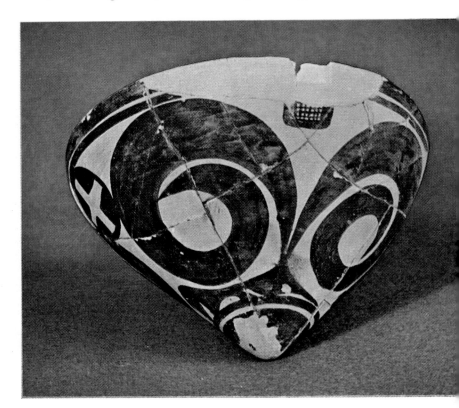

The tall tumblers of Susa are typical of the brilliant work of the Iranian potters around 3500 BC. The example above has a design based upon a stylized ibex with extended horns. At the top is a band of long-necked water-birds. (4)

Designs sensitively adapted to the form of the vessel are character-istic of the Iranian ware of c. 3500 BC. On the bowl above, found at Persepolis, the design is built up from four interlinked ibex whose exaggerated horns fill the main surface. (6)

The complex architecture which appeared on the plains,
the growth of the cities and the spread of writing were not reflected in the upland valleys and on the high fertile plateau of Iran. For the people of Iran, endowed with mountain pastures and with minerals immediately to hand, lacked the stimuli which induce small commu-nities to grow and coalesce. But, artists to their finger-tips, they were producing painted pottery in 3500 BC, which was in sharp contrast to the monochrome utility ware which was to be pro-duced in Mesopotamia for some centuries. The delicate and ele-gantly painted pottery which has been found in the graves of Susa is a brilliant achievement—the wide open bowls and tall tum-blers, sometimes of egg-shell thinness, are outstandingly beautiful. Wholly satisfying in its proportions, the pottery carries patterns which, whether geometric or abstractions from nature, show a sensitive understanding of the relation of design to space which is unexcelled by any other prehistoric potter.

The beautiful Susa ware of Iran has not been found in Mesopo-tamia proper but some centuries later a polychrome pottery became fashionable there. About 3200–3100 BC, vessels were being made in the Diyala valley, for instance, with designs in scarlet, black, dark brown and buff, at first with geometric patterns but also with stylized human and animal figures and plant motifs.

Elaborate red and dark brown geometrical designs appear on the restored shoulder (above) of a vase found at Khafajah, Diyala valley, and dated c. 3200 BC. (7)

During the next three or four centuries painted pottery continued to be produced in Mesopotamia. The four restored vases above, found at Khafajah, show the development in design and shape, from 'Jemdet Nasr ware' before c. 3100 BC (top left) through the various stages of the later 'Scarlet Ware'. (8)

The striking 'Scarlet Ware' vase shown above is restored from sherds found at Tell Agrab, Diyala valley, and is dated c. 3100 BC. The central design, extended above, includes figures with female bodies but beaky animal-horned heads, a tethered bull, birds on the wing and rayed suns. (9)

The distant people of the Indus valley must have established trade with Mesopotamia by 2500 BC, overland through Baluchistan and possibly by sea between the Euphrates and the Indus. This stone bowl made of dark grey steatite, has an intricate scene in relief with features strongly suggesting Indian influence. On the left, an Indian bull is prominent, with a male figure with long locks of hair. He grasps two sinuous objects in either hand, apparently representing running water which flows in a continuous stream from under the animals' mouths. Further round the bowl (right), a second male figure with scalloped skirt stands on the rumps of two lionesses, grasping a serpent in either hand. On another portion of the design (not shown), a vulture and a lion attack a prostrate bull. Other objects include a star, a scorpion and ears of corn. It has been suggested that the connection of water, bulls, snakes and vegetation points to a rainmaking ritual.

The whole is Indian in character, the bull being reminiscent of the principal motifs of Indian seals. The male figure is not typically Mesopotamian and this kind of stone, of a quality also familiar in Baluchistan, was used for the fashioning of various vessels in the Royal Cemetery of Ur.

A fragment of a green stone vase decorated with comparable mythological figures was found in one of the Sin Temples at Tell Asmar. Both this and the bowl date from c. 2500-2700 BC. (10, 11)

69

The highest achievement of the sculptors of Uruk is represented by the white marble head above. Its simple treatment of planes and economy of modelling conform with the artistic standards of the end of the Uruk period (3200-3100 BC); the sensitive rendering of the cheeks, mouth and chin shows a skill which is not repeated for many centuries. (12)

modern Warka, has given its name to the stage of prehistory in Mesopotamia from 3500-3000 BC, because the discoveries on its site, more than on any other, illustrate the development which eventually became characteristic of the whole region. It was far ahead of Iran, being especially marked by its accomplished temple architecture, which rose to a golden age of achievement about 3200 BC when there was a glorious array of temples laid out on a magnificent scale. Buildings had been placed on stone foundations for some time and brilliant colour effects must have been achieved by the ornamentation of the façades—by mosaics made of hundreds of thousands of clay cones, their heads painted black, red and sometimes white.

Coinciding with these great temples, we find the earliest abundant evidence of writing upon clay tablets. Five or six hundred tablets, or fragments of tablets, have been found. Most are economic, and almost invariably they contain numerals—one is a memorandum of the delivery of bread and beer for one day to a number of individuals, whose names are given. Lists of commodities appear, supplied to or delivered by officials of the temples—dairy products, milk and cattle, wheat and barley and above all herds of sheep. At one time there appear to have been no less than thirty-one signs to represent the word *udu*, sheep; in a century or so this number was reduced to two.

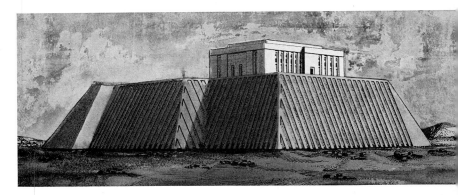

The White Temple of Uruk was built on a site dedicated to the sky-god Anu, as important to the Sumerians as Zeus was to the Greeks. For more than a thousand years sanctuaries had been built on this consecrated ground; after serving its time each was filled in with brickwork to become a foundation for the next. When the White Temple was begun this base (called the 'temple tower' or 'Ziggurat') was forty feet high.

The temple was approached from the ground by a steep flight of stairs and a ramp, and further staircases in the side chambers led to the roof, where prayers were said at sunrise. The building followed the classic model set far back in prehistory at Eridu; it was of mud-brick with whitewashed walls; the façade was decorated with elaborate buttresses and recesses; the double entrance was at the end opposite to the altar, the main exit a wide side door, with a further door to the right of the altar. The corners of the building point north, south, east and west.

The White Temple, reconstructed in the drawing above, was built at the extreme end of the Uruk period; a round date for its erection would be 3200-3100 BC. (13)

The crude but expressive carving on the left is in high relief on a boulder of black basalt, part of a *stele* that was probably once set up in a temple. It was found at Uruk, and its style is that of the early Uruk period. The carving shows huntsmen spearing and shooting lions, the archer using a recurved bow.

The carving is especially interesting because the costume of the man with turban, long coat and waistband, typical of Mesopotamia, can be matched on the famous knife handle found at Gebel el-Arak in Upper Egypt. Also a similar type of recurved bow recurs on a palette from predynastic Egypt, showing a lion hunt. It is inferred that there were travellers between Sumer and Egypt more than 5000 years ago. (14)

Eight hundred miles upstream from Uruk, in North Syria, was the 'Eye Temple' of Tell Brak. In a tunnel beneath it, made by plunderers, the yellowish white alabaster head (left) was found. The carving is crude but forceful, with roughly done eyes and ears, and simplified mouth—more in the style of modelling in clay. But there are already signs of facial modelling and an understanding of proportion which achieve a feeling for personality and character. The back of the head is flat and grooved, and the figure is wearing a kind of *tarbush*. It is one of the earliest known examples of North Syrian sculpture, c. 3200 BC. (15)

'Every living creature that moveth' is depicted in the amulets found at or near Tell Brak—polished miniatures many of them a delight to handle. Below are included an ivory duck, a ram's head, a frog, and, at the foot, a small carnelian bead engraved with a stag. This art was widespread in Sumer. (16)

The altar of the Eye Temple is reconstructed below, surmounted by an idol based on those which have been found at other sites as well as Brak, for example Ur, Mari, Lagash. These are sometimes much larger, occasionally made of terracotta, and have a pair of open loops. They have been called spectacle-idols. (17)

Thousands of these eye-idols (below) were found in the temple mound at Tell Brak. They are in alabaster, black or white, with thin biscuit-like body and 'eyes' once tinted with malachite paint. Their interpretation is uncertain; perhaps they were dedications to the god of the temple; the idol bottom right may be a mother and children. (18)

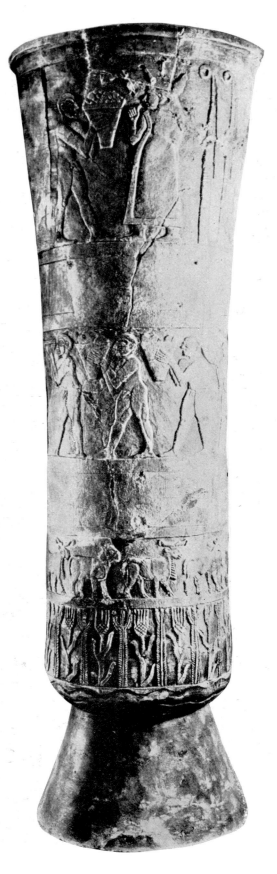

The Gods of Sumer,

on whose favour the people considered their prosperity depended, no doubt required regular tribute. Their mortal representatives, the priests, sustained by the produce from ecclesiastical land, were therefore able to apply themselves to the maintenance and administration of the temples.

Seasonal festivals brought joy to the people and the wealth acquired from tribute enhanced the splendour. The organized life of the community centred about the activities of the temporal power which was vested in the king and his court, and in their service the scribes learnt the skill of writing and to their patronage flocked the leading artistic talent and craftsmanship of the country.

A monument from Uruk of supreme interest is the massive alabaster vase on the left, which, with its pedestal base, is more than a yard high. The design which runs round it depicts the presentation of the first fruits of the land, animal and vegetable, to a goddess, doubtless Innana, who is shown at the top, in front of her two reed standards. Behind her (not shown) are two lesser divinities mounted on pedestals which rest on the back of a ram (the mounting of divinities on animals was to persist for many centuries).

A priest in ritual nudity advances to meet the goddess, presenting to her a magnificent bowl of fruits. Behind him (not shown) appear the feet and long skirt of a figure which probably represented the king (the vase is fragmentary at this point) whose tasselled train was carried by a servant in a short tunic. In the centre of the vase appear nude priests, their heads shaven and shorn, carrying vessels laden with food and jugs of wine, and at the foot are rams and ewes and representations of wheat and the date-palm growing near running water. It would seem that here we have one of the earliest pictures of the Spring Festivals, later known to the Sumerians as *akîtu*.

The vase was found in a stratum of the Jemdet Nasr period (3200–3100 BC) but probably originated earlier. It was repaired in antiquity with copper rivets. (19)

The famous Blau Monuments, shown on this page and at the foot of the previous page, were once condemned as forgeries, but are now universally recognized as genuine products of the later Uruk period, probably made before 3200 BC—it will be seen that the human figures cut in relief upon them are in the style of those on the alabaster vase (pl. 19) and on the basalt *stele* from Uruk (pl. 14). They are in a dark shale, and their shape is clear evidence that they were models of craftsmen's tools.

The crescent-shaped relief is probably a copy of a pottery scraper (an actual scraper from Ur is shown for comparison). On one side (bottom left) of the relief a bearded figure is presenting a pedestal vase or statue (with perhaps a lion's head at the top) as a temple offering. He is accompanied by a woman. On the reverse (below right), an overseer inspects craftsmen at work on some kind of anvil.

The pointed tool (centre and right) probably represents a craftsman's chisel (a copper chisel from the Royal Cemetery at Ur is also illustrated). At the top, a standing figure again carries an offering, this time a lamb, and below a kneeling craftsman is at work. On the reverse appear archaic Sumerian signs, both pictographic and stylized, the meaning of which is still obscure. But they include numerals, various receptacles and possibly the sign for fat or oil and for field. We may therefore guess that it is a record of property, or gifts presented or dedicated to the temple by craftsmen attached to it. (20-25)

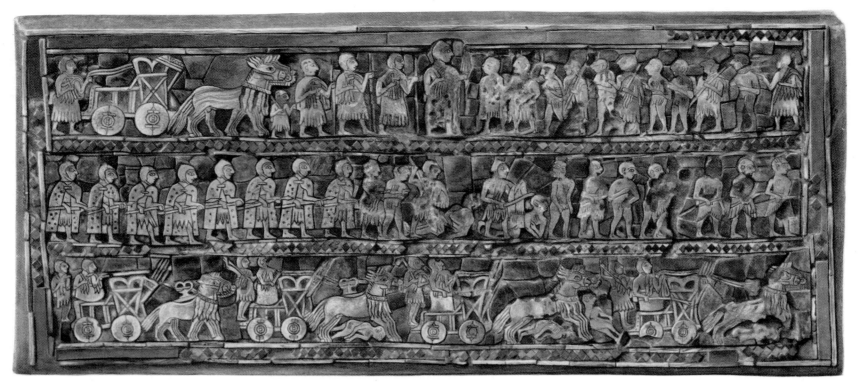

The 'Royal Standard' of Ur illustrates well the activities centring round the seat of temporal power: the king and his court. It is an oblong box about one and a half feet long, with ends tapering towards the top, decorated with figures composed of shell and some limestone pieces against a background of lapis lazuli fastened on to the wood by means of bitumen. It was found in a plundered corbel-vaulted stone tomb, one of the earliest in the Royal Cemetery of Ur; the wooden backing had decayed, but the panels were skilfully lifted as found by Sir Leonard Woolley and subsequently reset with a minimum of restoration.

The two long panels in this drawing of it, each in three rows, represent respectively scenes of War and of Peace. According to the Sumerian convention the narrative on each has to be read from the bottom upwards. In the bottom row, heavy chariots with solid wheels, drawn by wild asses or 'onagers', are seen giving the *coup de*

grâce to a defeated enemy. In the middle row, bound prisoners are being driven by the king's heavy shock troops—a 'phalanx' equipped with short spears, felt cloaks and helmets (perhaps of leather). At the top, the king, who is the largest of the figures in the procession, has alighted from his chariot and reviews captives who are led in by his light troops.

In the 'Peace' panel, at the bottom, servants lead onagers; others carry heavy burdens strapped round their heads in the manner of Kurdish porters. The middle row depicts bullocks, fleecy rams, an oryx (?) and fish. Finally, at the top, the court

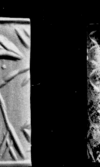

c. 3300 BC (or earlier). Standards of the goddess Innana and sheep with long ears; also a king or priest holding sacred rosettes. (30)

c. 2300 BC. A group is arranged in heraldic style. Bull-man and bull-hero each hold a rampant bull by the tail and despatch it with a dagger. The sacred tree surmounts a mountain-symbol. (35)

c. 3200 BC. Continuous frieze of a horned antelope amid vegetation.
c. 3000 BC. 'Brocade' style seal showing ibex, eagle, stars. (31, 32)

c. 2100-2000 BC. A presentation scene. Note the monkey and dwarf behind the throne. c. 2050 BC. Two goddesses in high, horned hats lead a worshipper before a bearded king. (36, 37)

banquet is in progress, the king and his court quaff wine to the accompaniment of music. The bull-headed lyre is similar to instruments found in other tombs at Ur.

The short ends (left) contain scenes which include mythological animals.

It seems most probable that this box was not a standard, for which there is no parallel in Sumerian art, but rather the sounding box of a musical instrument, for it resembles in shape the lyres from other royal tombs; the strings and cross pieces, overlaid with precious metal, were doubtless removed by robbers. The box may perhaps be dated c. 2700 BC. (26–29)

The ten cylinder seals below are typical of the marks of personal property and ownership which were used in the Uruk period and for centuries afterwards for the registration of documents. The engraving of the seals shows a brilliant formal art which by 3300 BC had attained a remarkable ability in the representation of animals, verging on realism, a fine sense of spacing and proportion and a vivid convention in scenes connected with the worship of the gods and the dedication of men and animals to the temples. The next two centuries showed a tendency to scamp the older, generously spaced designs and to indulge in a kind of conventionalized shorthand, but the art was to reassert itself in succeeding periods. The seals were made of limestone, gypsum, dark grey scapolite, aragonite, greenstone, black haematite, green schist and other stones. Nos. 30, 31 belong to the Jemdet Nasr period; 32–34 are Early Dynastic; 35 is Akkadian; 36, 37 Ur III; and 38, 39 Isin-Larsa. Each is shown with an impression.

c. 3000 BC. Resting antelopes with horns extended for the purposes of the design, and stylized representation of vegetation. (33)

c. 2000-1900 BC. A black haematite seal showing a presentation scene. A worshipper, presented by a goddess, is greeted by the god from his throne. A flaw runs across the figure of the god. (38)

c. 2800 BC. A bearded hero wearing a ball-headed comb holds a pair of rampant bulls by the neck; a bull-man grasps lions. (34)

c. 2000-1900 BC. A goddess, preceded by a dwarf, presents a worshipper. In front of the god is the crescent symbol of the moon-god Sin. Note the squat figures and indifferent engraving. (39)

The civilization of the south

spread over the whole of Mesopotamia during the flourishing Uruk period, and influenced cities altogether outside the domain of Sumer. It was to continue under the rule of Sargon, who was the first king to establish control over the greater part of this area, and his successors, and during the brilliant revival which followed the destruction of the dynasty by the barbarian Guti from the mountains of western Iran. The revival began at Lagash, and was brilliantly maintained under the third dynasty of Ur.

The king of Lagash, Gudea, or his son Ur-Ningirsu, is depicted by the mottled-green diorite statue below (the inscription is partly broken away and effaced by some conqueror, doubtless at the time when the city was sacked). The beautifully poised hands and the head, rather large for the body, are characteristic of the period. The assured style of the modelling, the gentle folds of the cloak, enhance the vitality of the powerfully rendered head and torso. It is dated c. 2200 BC and is one of the finest statues of the Sumerian revival. (40)

One of the most remarkable works is the electrum wolf's head above, found at Gawrah, east of the Tigris, not far from Nineveh. It has gold wire teeth, and the ears, lower jaw and teeth are separately attached by copper and electrum pins. The inside of the head and the eye-sockets are filled with bitumen. It is dated within the Uruk period, possibly c. 3200 BC. (41)

The kneeling king, or priest, below, is from the 'Square Temple' at Tell Asmar. It is in semi-translucent alabaster, dark amber in colour, and is dated c. 2750 BC. (42)

A gold rosette used as a head ornament or on clothing. It was found in a tomb at Gawrah and is dated after 3000 BC. (43)

The great stele of Naram-Sin, over two yards high, commemorates a victory of the fourth monarch of the dynasty founded by Sargon. He defeated a West Iranian chieftain of the Lullubi in a woody mountainous district near Sulaimaniyah. The king leads his warriors to the top of a high wooded mountain; armed with spears, bows and arrows and socketed axes, they look like loose-limbed athletes on the move. The sense of movement, soft and easy flow of line, cleverly contrived spacing and bold sense of composition make it a notable artistic achievement. It was found at Susa, is in sandstone and is dated c. 2250 BC. (44)

The finest monument of the Sumerian revival is the great Ziggurrat of Ur, a magnificent building which was an early prototype of the staged tower of Babel. It reached the appearance of the reconstruction below after many periods of alteration which incorporated much older structures within it. A triple staircase led up to a sanctuary on the top where the king performed the sacred marriage rites with the high priestess of Ur. The casing of perfectly fired square burnt-bricks is chiefly the work of Ur Nammu (c. 2100 BC) whose name is stamped on them; others inscribed by his grandson show that the building had to be underpinned later on. The 'weeper' holes in the burnt-brick casing must have been designed to prevent it from splitting during the rainy season, when the massive mud-brick core became saturated with water.

The walls rise with a pronounced backward slope, accentuated by the fact that the wall face itself is built on a curve—apparently intended to give an appearance of greater strength to a containing wall holding up so massive a superstructure.

The tower was still venerated and maintained by Babylonian rulers, particularly Nabonidus, as late as the sixth century BC. (45)

The copper goddess, above, was found in a wooden box which had formed the base for a limestone statue—together with a whetstone, perhaps a craftsman's dedication. The goddess has the horns of divinity, metal rings round her neck and long tresses of hair; her dress is flounced and pleated. The arms, separately made, are missing. She is dated c. 2100–2000 BC. (46)

The great Ziggurrat of Ur, photographed during excavation. The ramps which supported the triple staircases are clearly visible. A great courtyard and temple lay at the foot of the building which was built within a sacred enclosure. (47)

The great period of sculpture during the Sumerian revival, elsewhere best represented by the workshops at Lagash, is illustrated also by this vigorous carving of a woman's head. The engraved modulations of the hair, elaborate bun at the back of the head, and fillet round the forehead are an admirable setting for the face. The head is in diorite and was found in the Nin-Gal temple at Ur. It is dated c. 2150 BC. (48)

The conferment of kingship by the gods is commemorated by the *stele* of Ur Nammu (right), a monument in white limestone about five feet across by ten feet high, dated c. 2100 BC. At the top are the sun and the crescent moon; the king, larger than any other of the human figures, salutes an enthroned goddess, now fragmentary but probably Nin-Gal. She carries a child in her arms, perhaps symbolizing the king's divine nurture. Streams of flowing water pour down from above.

In the second row the king is introduced (right) to the moon god Nanna, who confers upon him the rod and line symbolic of justice and right, appropriately in the form of the masons' primary implements. On the left he salutes the goddess Nin-Gal. Each of the gods is enthroned on a stepped platform at the edge of which stands a palm-tree with fruit hanging over the lip of a pedestal vase.

In the next row the king carries an axe, an adze and other building instruments, the weight of which is relieved by an attendant who eases them from the king's shoulder. The ladder below is perhaps for building the Ziggurrat—but most of the lower portion of the *stele* is missing. The *stele* was discovered at Ur. (49)

A glorious abundance in metallurgy and the fine arts is evident *before* the decline of Sumerian authority after 2500 BC. The richest source of the work of the craftsmen of Ur has been the Royal Cemetery. The electrum helmet (left), found in one of the latest graves (c. 2500 BC) was accompanied by a rich panoply of weapons and a large collection of jewellery. The gold is 15 carat and the helmet was hammered from a single sheet of metal, with the features in relief and the details chased. The interior was fitted with a quilted cap, traces of which were found; the cloth was brought up over the outside of the helmet to protect the wearer's skin from the sharp edge of the metal, and held by laces passed through the small holes round the rim.

It was the helmet of Prince Mes-kalam-shar; his skull inside was well enough preserved to determine that he was left-handed. (50)

Gold, silver, lapis lazuli, shell and red limestone were used to make the statue (left) of a he-goat and its pedestal, one of two confronting each other. Its forelegs are hobbled to the branches of a golden tree; the white shell fleece was fixed to a wooden body with bitumen. It was found in the great death pit of the Royal Cemetery of Ur. (51)

The mighty Sargon of Agade, the founder in about 2370 BC of a dynasty and an empire controlled for the first time by kings who spoke not Sumerian but the Semitic Akkadian language, is represented by this almost life-size bronze head. It is cast, with portions of the beard and parts of the head-dress chased (compare the hairdressing with that of the electrum wig of Mes-kalam-shar opposite). The head is very solid and heavy though partly hollow; it was found at Nineveh.

Sargon would pass as a typical Semitic sheikh of the desert, long-headed, with high cheek-bones, slightly aquiline nose, fleshy lips and downy moustache. (52)

The great death-pit of Ur, the 'King's Grave' in the Royal Cemetery, was rich in treasure because of the uneconomic and no doubt unpopular practice of human sacrifices on a large scale which accompanied the burial of a king—together with every kind of endowment from the possessions of the court. Up to seventy-four persons were buried in the death-pit; the reconstruction on the right is based upon Sir Leonard Woolley's findings in the grave. A part only of the assembly is shown, some of the ritual victims who must accompany their sovereign on his last journey. The burial chamber itself (top left) already houses the royal coffin, in which also the bodies of three or four of the king's personal attendants have just been placed. The assembly in the tomb comprises members of the court, soldiers, men-servants and women dressed in all their finery, and with them musicians bearing harps or lyres, cymbals and systra. The four-wheeled waggons are harnessed to their draught oxen, with the drivers in the cars, the grooms holding the animals' heads. Every man and woman will receive a little cup of clay, stone or metal: it contains a potion which each will drink as a final act of homage. Thereafter someone will come down and despatch the animals, and perhaps arrange the drugged victims. Finally, earth will be cast upon them, and the grave-shaft filled in. (53)

Work of the later Ur craftsmen is illustrated by the terracotta plaque (left) of a nude bearded hero, with curled hair and moustache, carrying a vase from which water pours to overflowing on either side. It is dated c. 2100 BC. (54)

A woman musician is depicted in the terracotta plaque above. She has long tresses of curled hair and is playing the cymbals. The plaque is dated from the Sumerian revival c. 2000-1900 BC. (55)

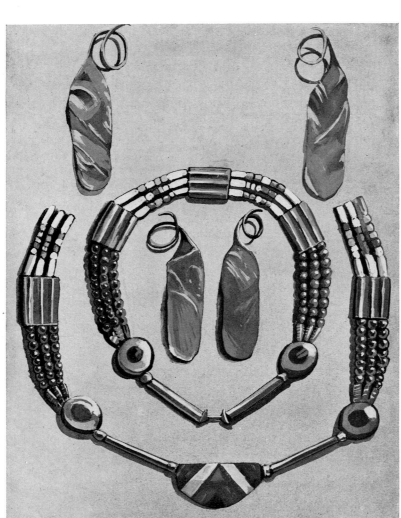

On the road to Badakhshan and further east the trading post of Tepe Hissar in northern Iran was a caravan halt for many centuries. From it, abundant evidence of the transit trade with Mesopotamia has been recovered, especially in the much prized lapis lazuli. In the last phases of its lifetime, perhaps around 2000 BC, it was an extremely rich centre, well equipped with all those kinds of goods which were coveted as the fruits of civilization. On the left is a selection of gold hair ornaments and necklaces of agate and carnelian beads from this period, found at Hissar. (56)

Civilized life begins:
Mesopotamia and Iran

M. E. L. MALLOWAN

Geography and Natural Resources

AT THE STAGE which is known as the Uruk period cities began to multiply and to expand in many distant parts of Western Asia. This process was already well advanced in about 3500 BC and the most spectacular evidence of it comes from the city of Uruk (Erech of the Old Testament) *(fig. 3)*. The site lay on an arm of the southern Euphrates in Sumer, a great tract of territory which after 2000 BC was called Babylonia. Here in the middle of the fourth millennium BC art and architecture, many different kinds of technology, and eventually metallurgy, began to display unprecedented developments. Elaborately buttressed walls, lofty temples and public buildings, their façades decorated with a polychrome mosaic of clay cones, greeted the traveller as he passed through the town gates. This was but one of many Mesopotamian townships; Ur, Eridu, Lagash, and Nippur must have presented a similar appearance, and far up the Euphrates places such as Mari and beyond it Brak in the Habur valley showed how far this particular form of urban life had spread.

Such complex organisations were unable to exist without access to many different kinds of raw materials, mostly imported from abroad. Trade, the organisation of labour, sustenance of the people, cultivation of the land, required an elaborate social organisation and a bureaucracy capable of maintaining records of its transactions. The necessity of establishing title to property, close supervision over the distribution of goods, the care of rations for all kinds of workers employed by the state, could not have been systematically organised in these expanded communities without the aid of written records. The invention of writing was therefore indispensable to the concentration of life in cities, and this accomplishment, which most men regard as fundamental to civilization, was achieved at this period. The city of Kish has yielded what is probably the oldest pictographic tablet (pl. 1, 2) and at Uruk itself in the stratum known as Uruk IV we have the earliest collection of writing on clay, at first pictorial, then gradually evolving towards a wedge-shaped (cuneiform) script.

Mesopotamia, which we define as the tract of territory controlled by the Euphrates and Tigris rivers, was a cradle geographically constructed for the growth of urban life. Towards the southern end of these valleys there were broad expanses of flat agricultural plains with no natural obstacles to movement, capable of producing an abundance of food. An assured supply of wheat and barley, meat, fish and wild fowl from the southern lagoons had already in the early prehistoric period known as 'Ubaid (see chapter II) caused the population to multiply. Seasonal leisure between one harvest and another; a desire for security; co-operation for the production of necessities such as clothing and housing; the natural gregariousness of family life, had in a city such as Eridu even before 4000 BC attracted a concentration which must have numbered several thousands of souls. The care of souls required temples for the well-being of the gods as well as of men. These developments which came to maturity in the Uruk period fostered the multiplication of what we may call luxuries. Man had discovered that he does not live by bread alone.

The most striking symptom of luxury is an elaborate architecture, nowhere better illustrated than in the cities of the Uruk and immediately succeeding periods. In examining the transmission and development of architectural design we may see the extent to which industrial enterprise was diffused by direct contact between the most distant communities, especially in Mesopotamia. This comparative study will also serve to stress the different pace of development in Iran which, in spite of many artistic and technological achievements, lagged behind its western neighbour owing to its geographical disunity.

The contrast between the two countries may at once be appreciated, even from a perfunctory glance at their respective geographies. The great mountain systems of Iran which encompass, especially in the centre, vast and inhospitable desert have encouraged a straggling disunity of ribbon development in the piedmont, and isolated pocket communities on the fertile hill plateau. There is no trunk river to unite one end of the country with the other. Streams flowing down from the mountains die a quick death on the desiccated salt-plains; the distribution of the larger rivers has tended to concentrate homogeneous developments within restricted areas. Moreover, in the mountains and in the foothills intersected by fertile valleys an adequate supply of water from the melting of the snows, from springs and streams, has usually sufficed for the sustenance of relatively small communities with a limited number of mouths to feed. In addition the mountains of Iran are rich in minerals, in stone and in metals. Iranian smiths and stonemasons have had no need to travel far abroad.

In Mesopotamia the geography is entirely different. Here are two great rivers, Euphrates and Tigris, respectively about 1800 and 1200 miles in length from their sources in Armenia down to the Persian Gulf. Both rivers have always attracted traffic, more especially along their banks, and apart from the flood season, upon their streams. But of the two it is the Euphrates with its lower banks, less violent floods, facilities for navigation and for irrigation which has had the greater effect in distributing and unifying the products of civilization. One of the most striking proofs of this tendency is, as we shall see below, the remarkable similarities in the art and architecture of Brak with that of Uruk eight hundred miles downstream; well before 3000 BC these two cities must have been in close touch with one another, whilst on the middle reaches of the same river the city of Mari shared in all the technological accomplishments of Sumer. The Euphrates thoroughfare has indeed been the very life-line of Mesopotamia and its ancient name Uruttu or Urudu, 'copper' river, signifies its function both as transmitter of the raw material from the northern hills of Asia Minor, and as the valley in which the earliest Sumerian smiths worked that commodity and gained a profitable livelihood from it. This was a trade route along which from the earliest times goods travelled on their way back and forth from the Persian Gulf to the Mediterranean Sea.

The Tigris on the other hand, swift as an arrow, as the ancient name Idiglat implies, is a more violent, less predictable river and has tended to disrupt rather than to unite communications, so that settlements along its upper reaches show different influences from those farther south. A settlement such as Tepe Gawrah in the eastern valley of the upper Tigris has displayed a very different prehistoric pattern from that familiar in Sumer. But even the Tigris has been subject to the levelling influence of the Mesopotamian plains, for there is a point in the Babylonian bottle-neck at which the two rivers flow no more than thirty miles apart and traffic has crossed and recrossed from one river back to the other. This reach, known from about 2400 BC onwards as Akkad, has often attracted important urban installations, their rulers well aware of its importance as a nodal point for control of north as well as south. Moreover the conformation of the land further to the north has also provided natural facilities for trans-Mesopotamian traffic which, already in the Uruk period, may well have bifurcated from Nineveh-on-Tigris overland across to Erbil and Arrapha (Kirkuk) in order to join the Diyala valley route to Akkad. When, as not infrequently happened in prehistoric as in historic times, there was a dichotomy between north and south it was the lower Zab which acted as the upper boundary to a no-man's-land between it and Sumer or Babylonia.

Thus whilst there have been different stresses in geography making in one direction for unity, in another for disunity, it is on the whole the former that has prevailed, in contrast to what we have observed in Iran. Furthermore the deficiency of raw materials in Sumer which forced its cities to seek stone and metal elsewhere could in the end only be satisfactorily relieved by a co-operative effort in which the several cities, despite intermittent warfare, had to collaborate alike for the collection, for the manufacture, and for the distribution of the goods which they required.

It is true that the wars between the city states and the shifting of authority from one dynasty to another as recorded in the ancient

Sumerian King List might seem to provide a contrary argument. But the fact that the Sumerians from the earliest times believed that the kingship over the country had to be authorised by the holy city of Nippur is sufficient proof that the importance of an established central authority was recognised. Further, if we follow the course of history we find increasing evidence of the assertion by single city states, Ur, Uruk and the like, of an imperial power which sought to embrace even wider tracts of territory within their orbit. This process culminated in the twenty-fourth century BC under the rule of the Agade dynasty which for about a century appears to have been dominant over a large part of Mesopotamia whence it exercised a forceful control on the more important trade routes to Syria, Anatolia, and Iran.

The preoccupation with the task of acquiring raw materials from abroad entailed continuous contact with countries on the other side of the mountains. Already in the Uruk period cities we find abundant evidence of imported limestone, basalt, timber, semi-precious stones such as lapis lazuli and carnelian, all obtainable from Iran. We have a record in the literature of the heroic age of a dispute between Enmerkar, a King of Sumer, the legendary builder of Uruk, and the lord of Aratta, a city in the Elamite mountains of Iran. The story makes it perfectly clear that the Iranians were trading semi-precious stones against Sumerian wheat and barley, and a dangerous quarrel arose from the failure to negotiate a trade agreement acceptable to both parties.

This very difficult document, which is still not fully understood, is couched in a style much favoured in Sumerian literature; it illustrates a contest of wits between the two parties, each capping the other with a conundrum well in keeping with the quizzical character and strange humour of the Sumerians. However that may be, this early literary reference to grain is of special interest, for ground research has now proved that wheat was cultivated, no doubt in very considerable quantities, in the 'Ubaid as well as the Uruk period, but that later in Early Dynastic times production of that cereal declined owing to excessive irrigation, lack of drainage and consequent salination of the land. Thereafter production of barley increased sharply in proportion to that of wheat because the former crop has a much greater resistance to salt.

Trade between Mesopotamia and Iran had to seek difficult and narrow passes through the mountains. But these were successfully negotiated from the earliest times. The smaller mountain passes in the north were used for trade with Azerbaijan through the district of Amadia, Rowanduz, or Sulaimaniyah. The prehistoric painted pottery known as Ninevite V *(fig. 1)* was, as we shall see, probably introduced from northern Iran to prehistoric Assyria about 3000 BC and was dispersed along these routes. The main highway however was along the famous pass which led up from the Diyala valley through Bisutun, Kermanshah, Hamadan, and on to prehistoric Rhages which lay at the entrance to the way across the Elburz to the sea through the Caspian Gates.

Ninevite V pottery, with rich painted decoration, probably introduced from northern Iran c. 3000 BC. (fig. 1)

Contact with Iran was also maintained through the river valleys tributary to the Tigris, especially the Zabs and the Diyala. The upper Zab was also an instrument for the diffusion of Ninevite V pottery between Iraq and Iran, and similarly the Diyala for that of 'Scarlet Ware' which has been found at sites such as Moussian and Tepe Ali Abad in Early Dynastic I-II, c. 2800 BC and later.

At the southern end of Sumer the extension of the Zagros hills fans outwards in a yet more easterly direction, and this has allowed room for a broad expanse of plain with an uninterrupted run into Susiana. This district of Iran is therefore geographically indistinguishable from the adjacent tract of territory in southern Iraq, and already in the Uruk period there is a striking rapprochement between the arts and crafts of the Sumerian capital cities and those of Susa—markedly noticeable in the types of stamp and cylinder seals sometimes identically engraved.

Thus there were many channels for communication with Iran which has from the beginning of prehistory seen the invasion and transit of tribes on their way from Central Asia and from India seeking fresh pastures elsewhere. Most important as illustrating this movement is the trans-Caspian route which has intermittently linked the Oxus with the Tigris. The easier way was along the south side of the Elburz Mountains, for sand, swamp and forest impede progress along the South Caspian shore. Archaeological evidence for early caravan trade along this route has come from the excavations at Tepe Hissar where the discovery of large quantities of beads, especially of lapis lazuli, makes it possible to infer that this district must have been a thoroughfare for traffic which passed from the lapis mines of Badakhshan (N. Afghanistan) to the Tigris valley. This trade which may have begun at the end of the Uruk period, in what is known as the Jemdet Nasr phase, continued to thrive throughout Early Dynastic times. Evidence for the reception of lapis lazuli in Mesopotamia has been abundantly provided by discoveries at Tepe Gawrah on the upper Tigris and in the lower Euphrates valley. Hissar itself seems also to have been in touch with Baluchistan where the pottery of Rhana Ghundai reveals a ceramic connection. In this part of southern Iran we also find evidence of a transit trade between S. Mesopotamia and the Indus valley, a process which must already have been established at the end of the Early Dynastic period (c. 2500 BC), and in the course of the next five centuries increased in momentum, seaborne through the Persian Gulf.

The evidence for the links between Mesopotamia and India through Iran is still tenuous, but decorated stone vessels (pl. 10, 11), 'Scarlet Ware' pottery (pl. 9), glazed steatite 'Indianesque' seals, as well as copper seals and spiral-headed pins provide undeniable proof of contact. The most distant tracts of overland territory are involved, and such contact implies movement along routes that ran parallel with the Elburz mountains of northern Iran, bifurcating southwards into Baluchistan, as well as trade by sea between the Euphrates and the Indus rivers. In about 2000 BC the island of Bahrein in the Persian Gulf seems to have been an important entrepot for commerce between Mesopotamia and India.

The sharp contrast between the physical geography of Mesopotamia and Iran explains the different pace of development in the two countries. Whereas the former was always in need of the raw materials which are indispensable to urban life, and had to adapt its political institutions to its economic needs, the latter, endowed with mountain pastures and with a sufficiency of minerals, lacked the stimuli which induce small communities to coalesce into larger groupings. It follows therefore that especially in architectural progress Mesopotamia took the lead, and that here literacy was more widespread. The mountaineers of Iran, artists to their finger-tips, remained unrivalled in their archaic adherence to colourful design and the humble embellishments of daily life, as is everywhere revealed by their painted potteries, which were a reflection of their tapestries and carpets. It was only in the last stages of the period which we are considering that dynasties from Iran began to aspire to a control of the elaborate and wealthy political structure which had evolved in Mesopotamia.

The Chronology of the Uruk Period

We may now turn to consider the broad achievements of man in this part of the world from the Uruk period onwards, and here we may immediately perceive how far ahead Mesopotamia was, compared with contemporary Iran. Uruk, modern Warka, has given its name to this stage of prehistory because that site more than any other illustrates a development which eventually became characteristic of the whole region. It is marked by an accomplished architecture and by certain forms of ornamentation which are exceptionally easy to recognise.

The subdivisions of that long period which was probably already in its maturity in about 3500 BC are of interest only to professional archaeologists concerned with its minutiae. The Uruk site consists of eighteen levels, differentiated by pottery styles. The material succession has been defined by the evidence obtained from a deep sounding in the precincts of the sacred area called E-anna. This pit, about 20 metres in depth, contained within it the accumulated debris of the long period of occupation beginning with the 'Ubaid. Levels XVIII-XIV are marked especially by a characteristic hand-made pottery with dark geometric designs on a light ground. Thereafter this ware began to die out and was succeeded mainly by a monochrome ceramic, wheel-turned, plain drab or buff coloured, and by an increasing number of black, grey and red pots. This corresponds to levels XIV-V. Uruk ware reached its full development in the period known as Uruk IV which coincided with the climax of architectural development.

Uruk pottery is widespread, especially its latest products, in the southern as well as the northern half of the country, and has been found in abundance both at Carchemish on the upper Euphrates and at Nineveh on the upper Tigris. As time goes on its sharp and angular pottery betrays increasing influence of the metal types which must have served as models for the less expensive clay, and in the next period Uruk III, usually known as 'Jemdet Nasr', there is abundant evidence of metal throughout the country and also of a polychrome red and black ware which however was less widely diffused.

Different labels have been used for the Uruk-Jemdet Nasr succession which is referred to by some archaeologists as 'protoliterate'. But it would be more satisfactory to denominate the whole of this long period as 'Uruk', since that site, so far as we know, contains a homogeneous series of material. This period is sharply differentiated from the Early Dynastic which begins in about 3000 BC and can readily be distinguished from the intervening Jemdet Nasr, the end product of 'Uruk'.

Uruk Pottery

Our knowledge of the earlier stages of the Uruk period is defective and may remain so until subsequent expeditions to Warka are able to uncover the architectural remains which lie most deeply buried there. None the less there are certain articles which are hallmarks of the period, notably very roughly hand-made bowls with bevelled rims which the Germans describe as *Glockentöpfe* (bell-shaped pots). They appear to persist throughout all the Uruk phases, become increasingly common towards the end (Jemdet Nasr) and are ubiquitous, for the type occurs not only throughout Sumer and Akkad, Kish, Ur, Lagash (Telloh), Nippur, 'Uqair, but also in the Diyala valley; at Nineveh, at Carchemish, and Hama in Syria, at Susa in Iran, and even at Abydos in Egypt. At Nineveh these vessels were deposited in hundreds; they were usually turned upside down in the soil and contained vegetable matter and are thought to have been used to consecrate the soil under building sites. If that hypothesis is correct they served the same purpose as the inscribed Mandaean and Hebrew incantation bowls which in the eighth to tenth centuries AD were prophylactic against demons. Delougaz has however pointed out that these and other vessels fashioned from a soft semi-liquid paste were deliberately manufactured to achieve the maximum of porosity, and that they would have been perfectly adapted for some such domestic purpose as the separation of curds from whey. Even so they could still have provided an appropriate offering to the devil.

Also characteristically Uruk-Jemdet Nasr are cups sometimes with twisted cord-like strap handles, and vessels which in modern oriental fashion had long tubular spouts which the drinker inserted into his mouth. Towards the end of the period the spouts were conveniently made to droop in order to make drinking easier. Tab and lug handles, often perforated, were also common. The rarity of painted decoration was compensated for by finer vessels with hard slips, sometimes purple, sometimes of a sealing-wax red.

The predominantly monochrome wares of the Uruk period *(fig. 2)* in Mesopotamia are in sharp contrast to the gaily painted fabrics of Iran where a natural conservatism made for a perpetuation of painted designs. In that country the delicate and elegantly painted pottery of Susa, known as Susa A, is a brilliant achievement (pl. 4, 6). It was predom-

inantly a funerary ware deposited with inhumation graves in a cemetery which contained over 2000 burials outside the walls: Susa was already a populous city. Among the rather restricted varieties of shapes, wide open bowls and tall tumblers, sometimes of an almost egg-shell thinness, are outstandingly beautiful products. For whilst the proportions of the vessels are wholly satisfying, the designs, either purely geometric, or geometric abstractions from nature, representing plants and birds, are perfectly distributed over the surface of the vessel and adapted to the form. The broad and confident sweep of the painter's brush displays a remarkable dexterity of hand and a sensitive adaptation of design to space unexcelled by any other prehistoric potter. Reeds growing in the marshes and drawings of aquatic birds and turtles remind us of the wet and soggy country in which the city was founded. One picture shows a hunter with his bow: hunting dogs, ibex, a member of the horse family, and birds on the wing are portrayed, but always as abstractions from nature, in keeping with the predominantly rectilinear and curvilinear patterns on most of the vessels. Sometimes the designs are organically related to prototypes in basketry or leather; their skeuomorphic character (copying the features appropriate to one substance in another) was long ago stressed by J. L. Myres.

Perhaps the most interesting deduction to be drawn from a study of these designs is that they must also reflect a preoccupation with textiles, and it is safe to conclude that side by side with the pots there must have been Persian carpets ancestral to those of the present day. The contemporaneity of this pottery with the earlier phase of the Uruk period is proved by its association with stamp seals or seal amulets often animal in form, and that it occurs relatively early in the period has been proved by stratified discoveries at other sites in Susiana where it is intermediate between the preceding 'Ubaid and succeeding undecorated pottery of late Uruk type. It is also important that open cast copper chisels and mirrors were associated with this pottery and that a flat axe was bound in linen, thus attesting the working of flax at this early period. The well-made metal objects are the earliest of their kind in Susiana, though elsewhere, at Siyalk in Central Iran and at Tepe Hissar, there is evidence of an earlier metallurgy.

Other Iranian sites of the period can also display fine examples of painted ceramic. Second only to Susa comes Bakun in the province of Fars where again we may see a series of delicately made vessels including fine goblets and other types where the painter makes skilful play with counterchanged designs (pl. 5). Once more the artist is constantly abstracting from nature: at Bakun a set of ibex horns is sufficient to indicate the beast itself; horned birds, fish, grotesquely drawn demons, suns, a triangular standard on a pedestal, plants, swimming ducks, running water are amongst the painter's repertoire. Some well made stone vessels in calcite and alabaster, stamp seals, and evidence of a simple flint blade industry were also discovered.

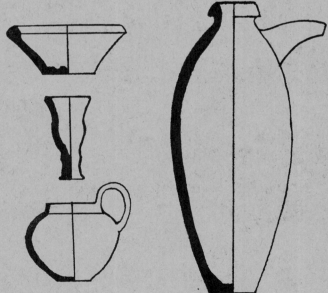

Monochrome slipped and burnished ware of the Jemdet Nasr period, c. 3000 BC. (fig. 2)

Villages: Bakun, Tepe Hissar and Siyalk

Bakun was a simple village site which consisted of a series of mud-walled houses roughly rectangular in plan. Twelve dwellings could be distinguished with one to seven rooms in each; some rooms were spacious—up to 8.5 by 11.5 metres. The village gives the impression of being an ill-planned agglomeration, a sort of cellular beehive with neighbours living in the closest proximity. There is little evidence of architectural sense here. Hearths, cooking utensils, rubbing-stones and fire-dogs were found: the basic apparatus of a community living on a primitive agriculture. There were two kilns with separate firing chambers, furnaces and vertical flues for the baking of pottery. However simple the community, it included craftsmen who were highly skilled potters, and at least one of their vessels is closely related in design and technique to the ware of Susa A. Models of painted oxen remind us that these villagers were raising cattle. Little clay models of painted goddesses with prominent breasts, tattooed with swastikas, must have been used in magic or worship. Finally evidence for the storage of food, probably cereals, comes from a number of clay sealings which would seem to have been attached to sacks with string.

In other Iranian settlements which may be contemporary with the early stages of the Uruk period we find the same contrast between the squalor of the houses and the elaborate elegance of the pottery. This can be well demonstrated at Tepe Hissar on the southern piedmont of the Elburz Mountains. Irregularly planned and small disjointed rooms bespeak a primitive village, whilst the pottery first hand-made, then wheel-turned, displays the same technological change-over which occurred in the course of the Uruk period in Mesopotamia: the associated circular button seals and square amulets show that there was a certain community of fashion in the cutting of seals throughout northern Mesopotamia and Iran at the same time. Whereas pottery always tended to display strong regional characteristics, the art of the stone-cutter tended to be comparatively uniform.

Similar observations apply to the site of Siyalk in central Iran, one stage of which (towards the end of Siyalk III) is probably contemporary with Uruk. Here again, whilst the pottery is well formed and decorated with attractive designs of ibex and leopard, the architecture is disappointing. Nevertheless the buildings are sufficiently solid to suggest that eventually some other Iranian site may reveal a more imposing prehistoric architecture. Indeed there is evidence of heavily buttressed walls which are sometimes niched; another decorative feature is the use of a red ochre wash on wall surfaces: in Siyalk III we find the earliest known Iranian example of a large circular column. The artisans of Siyalk and Hissar, like those of Susa, were already producing simple cast copper tools, daggers, pins, chisels, gravers and the like, which prove that metal, though still rare, was being produced in sufficient quantity.

Temple Architecture at Uruk

When we return to consider contemporary urban developments in Mesopotamia the higher level of achievement as compared with Iran is remarkable. At Uruk itself (VI-V) we find the first evidence of buildings on stone foundations. Temple plans were based on those of the preceding Al 'Ubaid period and display a building tradition already of a high antiquity. The golden age of architectural development, however, comes in Uruk IV when there is a glorious array of temples laid out on magnificent scale.

The normal plan is an oblong building with central nave, aisles on either side, and podium or altar at the far short end of the sanctuary. Similar buildings have been found at 'Uqair, at Khafajah in the Diyala, and at Brak in the Habur valley. The ornamentation of the façades is most striking. It consists, especially in Sumer, of a mosaic of coloured cones, clay nails, their heads painted black, red and sometimes white, arranged in patterns on the wall plaster. Hundreds of thousands of such cones were used in the adornment of a single building, a most expensive form of decoration which as excavations have shown, were constantly liable to collapse. The polychrome effect must have been very brilliant, and the patterns used seem sometimes to have been copied from matting. It is possible that the technique originally arose from the use of wooden nails which fastened wooden planking to the walls, traces of which have been found on a temple façade at Uruk. The imprint of a wooden stockade was found at Warka on the façade of the north front of the White Temple *(fig. 4)*, and of wooden panelling in the niches. An essential part of the temple décor was an elaborate system of niches and reveals which appear to have been a mark of religious as opposed to secular architecture: this form of decoration, inappropriate to mud-brick because constantly liable to damage, may well have derived from a wooden prototype such as one might expect in more hilly country. Access to the buildings was some-

Contour plan of the walled city of Uruk (Warka), one of the most important centres of Sumerian civilization. (fig. 3)

times through the long side, sometimes through double doors at the short end opposite the altar.

One of the most remarkable buildings of this age is the great complex known as the 'Pillar Temple' *(fig. 5)* at Uruk (Warka). Here the approach is up two flights of steps which confront a raised platform entirely decorated with cone mosaic. After ascending, one then passed through a columned hall in which a double row of free-standing mosaic columns, eight in all, formed an outer portico to the inner building. In addition there were engaged columns in one of the side walls. The diameter of these columns is as much as 2.62 metres and is

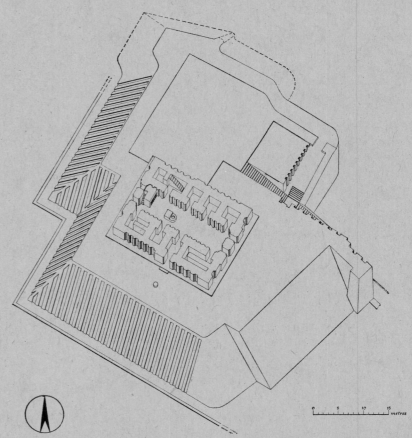

The White Temple at Uruk, showing how the sanctuary was placed on the terrace of the ziggurat (temple tower). (fig. 4)

The hall of the Pillar Temple at Uruk, which represents the climax of Mesopotamian temple building in the Uruk period. (fig. 5)

the earliest known instance of columnar architecture on a grand scale. In conception and execution this marks the climax of Urukian architecture: the building is not as yet completely excavated and we are therefore still uncertain as to its plan behind the columned portico.

Many other buildings were erected at Uruk in the course of the same period (Uruk IV); the vast scale of the lay-out at this time is illustrated by a successor to the Pillar Temple known as Temple C, the dimensions of which were over 54 × 22 metres, built with small prismatic '*Riemchen*' bricks 16 × 6 cm. square, a characteristic unit of brickwork which was abandoned in Early Dynastic times. Temple C exhibits the familiar tripartite plan in unusually complicated form, for it appears to be a double temple on a long and a short axis, the two parts at right angles to one another.

The long continuity of this type of architecture at Uruk is illustrated in another part of the site dedicated to the sky-god Anu whose primacy for the Sumerians may be compared to that of Zeus for the Greeks. A building known as the 'White Temple' (pl. 13) perched on the summit of a ziggurat forty feet above ground level, was approached by a steep flight of stairs and a ramp which gave access to the top of the terrace and finally to the temple gates *(fig. 4)*. Here we have the classic form of Sumerian tripartite temple, the prototype of which was first exemplified far back in the 'Ubaid period at Eridu (pl. 3). The building is of mud-brick with whitewashed walls; the façade and the nave are decorated with the elaborate buttresses and recesses appropriate to a Sumerian temple. There is a double entrance at the end of the aisle facing the stepped altar or podium opposite. A table for burnt offerings stood in the centre of the aisle and the visitor could leave the temple either at the opposite end to his point of entry, leaving the stepped podium on his right, or else through a wide side door. The large chambers on either side of the nave must have been used by the priests both as treasuries and for the storage of ceremonial equipment. There were staircases in the side chambers which gave access to the roof whereon Sumerian ritual prescribed the saying of prayers at sunrise and at other times.

The White Temple was built in the Jemdet Nasr period, that is to say at the extreme end of the vast scale of the Uruk period immediately preceding the Early Dynastic. A round date of about 3100-3200 BC may be assigned to its erection. The so-called Ziggurat or temple tower on which it was set had risen gradually in the course of more than a millennium, for in fact beneath the White Temple the tower incorporated within it a series of much earlier sanctuaries which after serving their time had been filled solid with brickwork and became terraces for later constructions.

The practice of burying the temple and erecting another on the top of it is altogether in accord with the Sumerian concept of the god as landlord and as owner in perpetuity of the ground which had been consecrated to him. Indeed on other sites such as Tell Asmar and Brak, statuary and amulets, the property of the god, were buried in his abandoned temple, doubtless because they were considered to be his eternal possessions. This attitude of mind is corroborated in Sumerian liturgy which prescribed the pouring of libations, milk and honey over the foundations of an older temple before its successor

was built, and explains also the remarkable architectural conservation which on sacrosanct plots of ground preserved the essential features of the ground plan for periods as long as two thousand years.

Other Temple Sites

Many buildings approximately contemporary with the White Temple have also been found on other Mesopotamian sites. A temple at 'Uqair not far from Babylon is partly similar in lay-out and of especial interest, because the temple podium was decorated with polychrome murals depicting the lion and the leopard, animals which seem to have been closely associated with divine worship. Indeed under one corner of the more or less contemporary White Temple at Uruk the skeletons of a leopard and a young lion were found buried in a mud-brick box.

The end phase of the Uruk period through Jemdet Nasr has also been well illustrated by the series of five 'Sin Temples' at Tell Asmar in the Diyala valley. Here, as at Uruk, each building was filled up solid when abandoned. The nave had a podium at one end and in some cases an offering table in the middle. Whilst there is a strict conservatism in the lay-out of the sanctuary, in the course of time, as the gods' domains became richer, the building grew very considerably in size so that the last in the series had three courtyards, outbuildings, kitchens and ovens commensurate with the greater number of ministrants. As is to be expected, there are many differences in the plan from the more standardised forms of the Uruk temples: especially noticeable is a long room at the end of the building usually serving as a staircase, and finally falling into disuse. In course of time therefore the sanctuary, which had once been a central nave, came to be situated at the extreme end of the building and the god became less accessible than he had been before. This tendency towards inaccessibility which coincides with the growth and complexity of social organisation is doubtless inevitable both in divine and in human affairs.

It must however be remembered that in addition to the more complex temples there were others of a simpler type, devoted to less important divinities, more in keeping with rustic worship, and these were widespread in Mesopotamia, for example at Nuzi and at Mari. One of the most interesting of these is the earliest shrine of the Abu Temple at Tell Asmar *(fig. 6)* obviously accommodated to fit in a

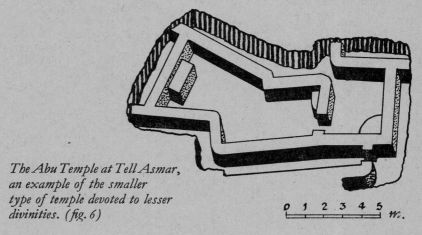

The Abu Temple at Tell Asmar, an example of the smaller type of temple devoted to lesser divinities. (fig. 6)

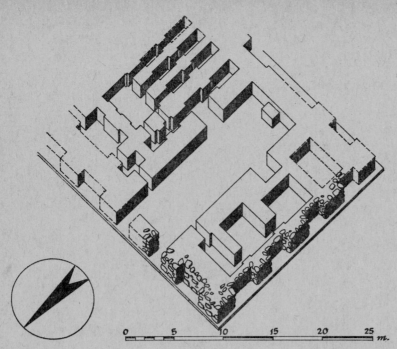

The Eye Temple at Brak, showing the cruciform nave, with the podium or altar at the far end. (fig. 7)

An impression of the Eye Temple at Brak, looking up the nave towards the altar on which stands the eye-idol. (fig. 8)

restricted space among other buildings. It is flanked by a curved alley and has a bent entrance. A small anteroom leads into an oblong sanctuary with re-entrant walls: the altar or podium was placed at the far end against the short wall.

As a last illustration of Jemdet Nasr period architecture we may turn to the Eye Temple *(fig. 7, 8)* at Tell Brak, in the Habur valley, 800 miles upstream from Uruk. Here in spite of considerable local differences we have in essence the basic features of a Sumerian temple plan. The building is tripartite with a great central nave, podium at the short end, double entrance opposite to it. West of the nave are large storage and service chambers; east of it, a subsidiary sanctuary with narrow and deeply oblong dependent rooms. Large basalt and limestone boulders as well as sun-dried bricks were used in the construction of the walls.

A most interesting feature is the cruciform plan towards the end of the nave, a very early anticipation of Christian practice, perhaps so designed for liturgical purposes. Nowhere has the former brilliance of these sanctuaries been more dramatically illustrated, for adhering to the three sides of the podium against the back wall was the polychrome façade, composed of gold and of corrugated blue and white limestone (pl. 17). The empanelled front of the podium had been fastened to a wooden backing by means of gold-headed nails with silver stems. The podium itself, three feet high, consisted of miniature prismatic *Riemchen* bricks. The walls of the sanctuary were white-washed and decorated with copper panelling upon which was a repoussé eye-design, the symbol proper to the divinity worshipped at Brak. When the building was finally abandoned it was filled solid with brickwork to make way for yet another temple, the plano-convex bricks of which indicate that it should be assigned not to the Jemdet Nasr but to the Early Dynastic phase.

The Brak Eye Temple exhibited the brilliant polychromy of the Jemdet Nasr period, for the outer face of the north wall was decorated with a coloured cone mosaic and the inner with rosettes of white marble, black shale and red limestone. That the architects of the time were working to certain accepted proportions is proved by the fact that the nave (18 × 6 metres) is exactly three times as long as it is broad, a canon of measurement which was also used in the temple at 'Uqair and in Sin Temple VI at Tell Asmar.

Cult Objects and Religious Art

Deep down in the artificial platform on which the Brak Eye Temple was set was a series of four older buildings which no doubt conformed to the basic plan of the latest one. Associated with these earlier temples were abundant remains of the treasures dedicated to them. Unique amongst the many thousands of objects discovered in these lower levels are the 'eye-idols' in black and white alabaster (pl. 18) of which there are thousands of examples. They consist normally of a thin biscuit-like body surmounted by a pair of eyes in human form once tinted with malachite paint. Most probably they represent dedications by every member of the populace to an all-seeing god who watched over the fortunes of the city. There were moreover many different varieties of idol, including figures with three eyes, pairs with four eyes, and pairs with engravings of smaller idols on the front of the body which were possibly family dedications. More important members of the hierarchy were perhaps represented by figures wearing crowns, one form of which is an attribute of the god Enlil on the much later Kassite boundary stones. A single idol is engraved with a stag, symbol of the Sumerian goddess of childbirth Nin-har-sag. Its interpretation, like that of the others, must in the absence of written records remain uncertain, and indeed the enigma of these unique objects is one that has long exercised the ingenuity of scholars. There is some satisfaction in reflecting that the true answer may never be known.

It seems likely that these unique idols are to be connected with a simpler form which has been found at other sites, for example Ur, Mari, Lagash, as well as at Brak. These, sometimes much larger in size and occasionally made of terracotta, have the same biscuit-like body surmounted by a pair of open loops: they have been called spectacle-idols. There is also another type with infilled loops intermediate between these and the eye-idols proper, and this is the reason for seeing a connection between them. In the reconstruction of the Eye Temple sanctuary shown in pl. 17, the open-looped spectacle idol has been placed on top of the podium, a reasonable assumption suggested by a small model in soapstone.

The amulets discovered at Brak in association with the Eye Temples display another achievement of the same period: a high degree of artistry and skill in the cutting of stone, particularly in the miniature representation of animals (pl. 16). The soft stones such as serpentine, limestone and gypsum, as well as bone and more rarely ivory were most favoured and in them the artists of Brak carved the typical fauna of the country; the animals that roamed both in the plains and in the hills. Lions and other felines, bears, stags, gazelles, monkeys, foxes, hedgehogs and scorpions were the most popular wild animals. In addition there were models of sheep of the domestic and wild variety, goats, pigs, frogs, eagles and ducks. Usually these amulets were almost in the round, the underside flat and engraved with combinations of birds, snakes and various cryptic signs. Thus was depicted 'every living creature that moveth', to quote the words of the Old Testament account of the Creation in Genesis; and their likenesses were deposited in the temple, doubtless in recognition of the dependence of the animal as of the human world on the god's procreative powers. Many of these polished miniatures are, like Chinese jades, a delight to handle. Sometimes the artists made play with the graining of variegated stone and whilst observing a restrained economy of form, contrived to imprison in the stone the living image of the animal. This art was widespread at Uruk where models of wild and domestic sheep, the divine flocks, were numerous: every capital city of Sumer can display miniatures of the kind, which are also common at the site of Susa in Iran, in association with Susa A pottery. But that this is a peculiarly Mesopotamian and not Iranian form of artistry is proved by the fact that on no other Iranian site do any of these models occur.

Sculpture

In larger sculpture too, and in the representation of the human form, the Uruk-Jemdet Nasr artists were already showing considerable ability. The sculptured heads from Brak are amongst the earliest examples of this sculpture. The carving is severely stylised; eyes and ears are primitive in technique, but there is already a sensitivity of facial modelling and an understanding of proportion which achieves a feeling for personality and character (pl. 15). These stone heads were perhaps parts of composite statues the rest of which were of wood, and it may be that the stone models of laced shoes with turned-up toes also belonged to them. It is remarkable that the same type of shoe is still worn by North Syrian peasants today.

The highest achievement of this art is however represented by a white marble head from Uruk which in its simple treatment of planes and economy of modelling displays exactly the same technique as that used on the animal amulets, and although unique is altogether in conformity with the artistic standards of the Jemdet Nasr period (pl. 12). The sensitive rendering of the cheeks, mouth, and chin is admirable and we have to pass through many centuries of the Early Dynastic period to witness the same skill again.

Two other stone monuments from Uruk possibly even more ancient than this celebrated head may have been executed in Uruk IV and are also landmarks in the history of sculpture. The first is a large boulder of basalt rock, crudely but expressively carved and no doubt once used as a *stele* in a temple (pl. 14). It illustrates a hunting scene in which a spearman and archer with recurved bow are shooting down lions. The subject is of especial interest because of certain parallelisms with the art of predynastic Egypt. The costume of the man with turban, long coat and waistband typically Babylonian can be matched on the famous Gebel el-Arak knife handle on which foreign boats also appear as on Uruk seals; a similar type of recurved bow occurs on a predynastic Egyptian lion hunt palette now in the British Museum. The inference that there was some contact between Egypt and Sumer at the time is confirmed by the presence in Egypt of Jemdet-Nasr type cylinder seals, and indeed towards the end of the period the façades of the first dynasty tombs excavated at Saqqara suggest technical inspiration from the buttressed temples of Mesopotamia where the tradition of niches and reveals was of a much higher antiquity.

A second monument from Uruk is of supreme interest; it is a massive pedestal-based alabaster vase (pl. 19), the surface decorated with a series of registers depicting offerings of cattle and the first fruits of the land to a supreme goddess, doubtless Innana who is depicted at the summit in front of her two reed standards. Behind her are two lesser divinities mounted on pedestals which rest on the back of a ram: the mounting of divinities on animals was a feature of the much later divine iconography at Yazılıkaya in Asia Minor and on many monuments in Assyria, a practice which perhaps ultimately derives from this much more ancient Mesopotamian precedent.

Advancing to meet the goddess is a nude priest who presents to her a magnificent *corbeille de fruits*. Unfortunately the vase is fragmentary at this point, but behind him we can still see the feet and long skirt of a figure which probably represented the king whose tasselled train was carried by a servant. In the other registers the nude priests who carry vessels laden with offerings and jugs of wine, the rams, ewes and representations of wheat and the date-palm would seem to indicate that here we have one of the earliest known pictures of the Spring Festival, later on known to the Sumerians as *akîtu* and no doubt already celebrated at Uruk in the fourth millennium BC.

The Invention of Writing

Architecture, town-planning and the fine arts, the many pictures on stone monuments and on seals of the gods' shrines and of the offerings devoted to them are in themselves sufficient proof of the complex organisation of urban life throughout Mesopotamia in the Uruk-Jemdet Nasr period. It is therefore hardly surprising that this was the period during which the art of writing was invented. Coinciding with the great temples of Uruk IV we find the earliest abundant evidence of writing upon clay tablets. The signs were at first pictures of the objects, animate and inanimate, which played a principal part in the life of the community. Sheep and cows, cereals, milk-pails, agricultural implements, the façade of a temple, a cattle byre, the human head, the act of eating or drinking, the human foot, the act of walking or going, even the reed standard of the goddess Innana were obvious pictograms, either isolated or combined, the meaning of which was self-evident. But even in Uruk IV only a limited number of signs is in a true sense pictorial and the significance of many is still unknown. Writing therefore must have begun earlier still and indeed a stone tablet from Kish, purely pictographic, appears to illustrate the first stages of this art (pl. 1, 2). It is also interesting to reflect that the pictorial concepts which eventually found expression in writing as well as the methods applied were deeply rooted in a prehistoric past. The signs used for star, god, heaven ✳, for water ≈, for earth ⬬, for heaven and the deep ▨, had long been represented on the painted pottery of Mesopotamia and Iran, and were no doubt already invested with magical prophylactic meaning.

Prehistoric artists had long understood the art of making a part of the object stand for the whole, the principle of *pars pro toto* fundamental to the earliest pictograms and applied for example in the fifth millennium BC by Halaf potters when they designed the *bucranium* with a variety of devolutions to stand for an ox: *(fig. 9)*.

A succession of pictograms used by the Mesopotamian potters of five thousand years ago to signify 'ox'. (fig. 9)

It may also be observed that on pottery this same design was at first represented vertically, just as the earliest scribes tended to favour writing in vertical columns. Later on, when the *bucranium* became a purely geometric stylisation it was made to run horizontally round the bowl: similarly the scribe as he drew away from the pictogram towards a developed cuneiform arranged his script in horizontal instead of vertical columns. Since on the earliest texts the scribe began his vertical inscriptions on the right-hand side this change over to horizontal writing had a practical advantage in that subsequent lines were no longer obscured or smudged by the movement of his hand.

Thus the reed which the painter had used for the adornment of his pots was cut anew to serve as a stylus for the scribe. Both conceptually and technically therefore, the development of writing in Mesopotamia presents some interesting analogies with that of painting. On the earliest documents moreover, the arrangement of the signs does not appear to follow any specific or logical order, but seems rather to have been left to the caprice of the writer who, like the pot painter, thus had freedom of choice in the disposition of his subject. It was the tradition of painting, we suspect, that gave the impetus to writing when social conditions required it, and an ingrained habit of mind which stimulated its development. The genius of the Sumerians has the rightful claim to priority for this invention which precedes the different hieroglyphic system used by the Egyptians.

The ideas first expressed in picture writing however were of limited range, and very soon the need was felt and the means found to express more complex messages. To this purpose the monosyllabic tonal Sumerian language readily lent itself; for example the sign TI (∀) which depicted an arrow was also the word for life. Consequently on the Jemdet-Nasr tablets this sign which had once been a pure pictogram was used as a phonogram in the expression EN.LIL.TI: (may the god) Enlil grant life. Furthermore TI, life, was made to do duty as a syllable in a compound word. In texts from Fara, a stage of writing which followed Jemdet Nasr, the two first phonetically written words were MA.NA, *maneh*, a measure of weight, and DAM.GAR, merchant. Nevertheless the Sumerians, as Professor Driver has remarked, only took the first halting steps in that direction because their script had been designed to represent their own names for the objects in daily use. Moreover Sumerian words were in the main monosyllabic and were not altered through inflexion, but by prefixed and suffixed syllabic values for which comparatively few signs sufficed. The final development of a syllabic script was in fact only achieved by the Babylonians a thousand years later. The syllabic system was a real convenience to them because theirs, unlike Sumerian, was an inflected language; they were unencumbered by any primitive sign values of their own, and Sumerian monosyllables could therefore be perfectly adapted for this purpose.

Sumerian writing, however, by an ingenious turning of pictures to sound soon achieved a great capacity for expression. The pictogram which originally denoted a concrete object became a symbol for an abstract concept. Thus ✳, an eight-pointed star, was made to signify AN, heaven, sky, and DINGIR, god; it also stood for 'high'. Similarly ⌈, DU, leg, was conscripted to serve as several verbs; GUB, to stand; GIN, to go; and TUM, to carry off. Such writing was therefore liable to many ambiguities since while in the instances quoted one sign had many sounds (polyphones) there were also conversely homophones such as *sig* which had the same sound and many meanings. In speech the latter difficulty could be overcome if, as we assume, Sumerian like Chinese was a tonal language. In the practice of writing these ambiguities were alleviated by the addition of determinative signs inserted as prefixes and phonetic complements as suffixes, but often only the context can give a clue to the meaning.

Other devices were also used by the early scribes to extend the meanings of their signs. We have already observed the principle by which ≈, a pictogram, Sumerian A, water, also stood for the preposition 'in', which was represented in speech by the same sound A. The Sumerians also had signs for three other vowels: e, i and u. Furthermore ☿, the picture of the *mons Veneris* conjoined with the sign for mountains, SAL+KUR, maid of the mountains, was used to signify *geme*, slave-girl, because the Sumerians often abducted their slaves from the mountains. Associated ideas such as LU, man + GAL, great, became LUGAL, king, in the Fara texts which were written just before the beginning of the Early Dynastic period.

The five or six hundred clay tablets, or fragments of tablets, mostly from Uruk IV, a lesser number from III and a few from II are so far the largest and earliest stratified collection of writing known. It is therefore of singular interest to examine their contents in so far as the often obscure combinations of pictograms and semi-pictograms will allow. The majority of the documents are economic and almost invariably contain numerals which relate to the persons or things recorded in them. Some are ration lists, one in Uruk III is a memorandum of the delivery of bread and beer for one day to each of a number of individuals whose names are mentioned, one in each compartment of the tablet. As a rule however it is not possible to offer any specific translation for the agglomeration of signs, but it is clear that they were for the most part lists of commodities supplied to or delivered by officials and others concerned with the administration of the temples. The complexity of administration in 3500 BC required such memoranda and token receipts especially for dairy products, milk and cattle, wheat and barley, and above all for the herds of sheep which must have been one of the most profitable sources of revenue. Indeed in Uruk IV there appear to be no less than thirty-one signs to represent the word UDU, sheep; these no doubt denominated many different breeds, including wool-bearing and fat-tailed, the latter under the sign ⊕. The tendency to reduce and organise these many variations is shown by the fact that in Uruk III only three and in II only two sets of signs were used for sheep.

Daily Life at Uruk

It is obvious from these lists that fish was an important article of diet; the date palm and the vine also occur. Amongst the domesticated animals we have frequent occurrences of ox, cow, calf, goat, and pig, whilst the wild animals include lion, mouflon and deer. There is also a sign for the hound.

Amongst the objects of daily life we find signs for many different kinds of vessels, vases with and without handles, spouted drinking pots; seed-ploughs, nails, possibly also ploughshares and harrow; weapons include socketed axe, throwing spear, dagger, bow and arrow. There is a sign for a musical instrument: harp or lyre. Boats and carts, four-wheelers and two-wheelers, are common.

Most interesting is the fact that the sign for copper, *urudu*, is already of frequent occurrence in Uruk IV; it is represented in the form of an ingot (⊿). Nearly all of the above-mentioned basic commodities have assumed the standard forms which were in current use during the Early Dynastic period and occur for example as deposits in the Royal Cemetery of Ur, more than five centuries later. These lists of

material objects therefore show that the Sumerian pattern of domestic life had been well established in the Uruk period.

The Uruk lists also contain the names of certain specialised professions. Notable is the NAG.GAR, carpenter, artisan, perhaps one of the oldest craftsmen's names in existence, for it survives today in the Arabic *najjar*. We find priest, SANGA; chief smith, SIMUG-GAL; chief herdsman, SAB-GAL. Of the gods only Innana is mentioned; EN.LIL occurs at Jemdet Nasr.

A remarkable set of carved stone documents known as the Blau Monuments (pl. 20-25), once condemned as forgeries, have been rehabilitated through the discoveries at Uruk. They are made of a dark (?) shale inscribed with archaic signs both pictographic and stylised, and as the human figures cut in relief upon them are in the style of those on an alabaster pedestal vase and on the basalt *stele* from Uruk they may be securely assigned to the period Uruk III-IV. The shape in which the two objects are cut is clear evidence that they are a copy of craftmen's tools. One of them is a reproduction of a chisel, a type familiar in the Early Dynastic period in the Royal Cemetery of Ur. The other, a crescentic object, is perhaps a copy of a pottery-scraper, for similar tools have been found in terracotta. Moreover, both instruments illustrate craftsmen apparently engaged in making objects on some kind of anvil. On the obverse of the scraper we see a bearded figure in the act of presenting a statue (?) or a pedestal vase, doubtless as a temple offering. The character of the object is uncertain but the top of it may terminate in a lion's head. On the chisel, a standing figure is carrying another offering, this time a lamb. Unfortunately it is impossible to be certain of the meaning of the inscription, but since it includes numerals, various receptacles, possibly the sign for fat or oil and for field, we may hazard a guess that it is a record of property or gifts presented or dedicated to the temple by craftsmen attached to it.

Methods of Calculation: Lexical Documents

One of the most marked characteristics of Sumerian civilization is the use of a sexagesimal metric system, evidence for which is abundant both at Uruk and at Jemdet Nasr. Calculations were based on the figure 60, a most practical mathematical standard, because it is exactly divisible by 30, 20, 15, 10, 6, 5, 4, 3, and 2. The number 60 is especially useful as a multiple of the dozen which again is exactly divisible by 4, 3, and 2, and thus invaluable for domestic allocations of commodities, and for subdivisions of land. It is curious that side by side with the sexagesimal, a decimal system was also used, but at Jemdet Nasr it seems that the latter was particularly applied to the measurement of barley: its similar application at Uruk is therefore probable, and it is perhaps a legitimate inference that its suitability for cereal measurement was dependent on the tithe as a tenth part of the produce being payable to the state, that is to the god who in the Uruk period must have been the supreme landlord. The Uruk texts also display familiarity with fractions which include $^3/_4$, $^1/_2$, $^1/_4$, $^1/_{16}$, $^1/_{32}$, and $^1/_{64}$.

Thus the early sign lists were made to record an agricultural and pastoral economy which was based mainly on the temple's services and requirements. It is however probable that a considerable volume of private business was already conducted side by side with that of the state, and indeed both at Fara and at Ur many documents were found in private houses.

There is lastly some further remarkable evidence to be gleaned from the texts. A few of them are not commercial but literary, more especially lexical—lists of signs and their values. One from Uruk III is a list of names of fish; another a list of dogs indicated by the sign for UR, comparable to a list of animals from Fara where such lexical texts and sign lists were common. The practice of compiling learned lexical documents, the purpose of which was to organise and systematise every branch of knowledge, is another marked characteristic of Sumerian civilization and it led to as high a degree of accomplishment in the sciences as was possible without using the inductive method, an attainment first accomplished by the Greeks. At all events the discovery of these few documents in Uruk IV is surprising proof that the scientific content of the earliest tablets is directly related to the literary achievements which became widespread throughout the Sumerian capitals from the Fara stage onwards, throughout the third millennium BC. Moreover, as soon as writing was invented the profession of the pedagogue was established, together with all those tedious exercises inseparable from a literary education. Behind every modern schoolmaster lies the shade of his first precursor at Uruk.

The Spread of Writing to Iran

The invention of writing was too valuable to remain the monopoly of Sumer and before very long it spread to Iran. Nevertheless, as we have previously explained, the more isolated and self-sufficing character of society in that country did not encourage the diffusion of this art. It was therefore to be expected that the first evidence of a script should appear in Susiana, a land which is geographically an extension of Sumer. At Susa itself at first we have evidence of numerals on clay *bullae* to be followed shortly afterwards by clay tablets inscribed with proto-Elamite writing, which is still undeciphered. The signs were pictograms more or less stylised, distinct from Mesopotamian and expressed a distinct language.

The limited use of these early scripts in Iran did not begin before the Jemdet Nasr period (Uruk III) and indeed these archaic forms probably survived into the early part of the third millennium BC contemporary with the Early Dynastic of Mesopotamia. The same time-lag in Iran is also apparent in the greater longevity of Mesopotamian forms of design both on stamp and cylinder seals, which, it is true, show many varieties independent of the west, but nonetheless are often closely comparable to types current in the Tigris-Euphrates valley. The tablets discovered at Siyalk in central Iran are associated with levels which contain pot types familiar in the Tigris-Euphrates valley in Sumer, and others of Ninevite V variety in Assyria at the turn of the Jemdet Nasr to Early Dynastic. Thereafter in Iran the development of writing, for which the evidence is so far almost exclusively confined to Susiana, followed that of Mesopotamia.

The Sumerians

At this stage of our enquiry we may well ask the question: when did the Sumerians who played so large a part in laying the foundations of civilization first appear as an identifiable ethnic group? That they were well established in the Jemdet Nasr period we know for certain, since the language of the documents and their methods of calculation are well established as Sumerian. Moreover, since the beginnings of writing in the preceding stage known as Uruk IV are so closely related to that of Jemdet Nasr, it may be taken as virtually certain that they were present in S. Babylonia at this stage also. But the question of their identification in this country prior to that must remain doubtful and there is no general agreement about the answer.

If we follow the pattern of architectural development at Eridu where the basic form of temple plan can be traced back to the very early stages of the 'Ubaid period, we may surmise that the Sumerians were present in the country long before they can first be attested by their written documents. On the other hand if we consider the striking innovations of the Uruk period: the use of polychrome cone mosaic in the walls; the sudden increase of metallurgy; and the marked changes in the character of the pottery as well as some changes in burial customs, we may be tempted to attribute such innovations to the entry of a new people: to the Sumerians themselves, whose characteristic appearance on the monuments, robust, fleshy, with beaky noses, is first apparent on the Uruk vase and contemporary cylinder seals. But their broad-headed appearance when represented as shaven and shorn is strangely at variance with evidence from the actual skulls which are predominantly dolicocephalic (long-headed).

So far the examination of skeletal remains has not been decisive, for there is a long-headed type from the beginning with some broad heads at Kish. At Ur in the Early Dynastic period when Sumerians were dominant there was evidence of a long and narrow-headed type. Two of the royal skeletons were said to have been the remains of persons of fine physique and rich brain endowment. With the advent of dynasties speaking a Semitic language (Akkadian) about the middle of the third millennium BC we find in art a striking bronze head, perhaps Sargon of Agade himself, who would pass as a typical Semitic sheikh of the desert, apparently long-headed, with high cheek-bones, slightly aquiline nose, fleshy lips and downy moustache (pl. 52). In Iran the evidence from Siyalk, Hissar and other sites is that in the early periods long heads were dominant, although some moderately broad-headed types were already present at Siyalk long before the Early Dynastic period.

On the whole it is likely that the ancestors of the Sumerians, together with other types of peoples speaking Semitic languages, were present

from the very beginning; that they came to maturity in the Uruk period about 3500 BC and that they were politically in the ascendant for a thousand years thereafter in Babylonia.

With the Sumerian period of hegemony we may associate an acute sense of personal property and ownership, the traces of which are manifest in the use of the cylinder seal for registering documents (pl. 30-39). In the engravings of those seals we find a brilliant formal art which in Uruk IV had attained a remarkable ability in the representation of animals, verging on realism, a fine sense of spacing and proportion and a vivid convention in the representation of scenes connected with the worship of the gods, the dedication of men and animals to the temples. In the Jemdet Nasr period there was a tendency on the seals to scamp the older generously spaced designs and to indulge in a kind of conventionalised shorthand, a degeneration from the free bounty of the older style. This glyptic art was to reassert itself however in the succeeding periods and perhaps attained its apogee in the third Early Dynastic and Sargonid age. In Iran, which favoured the stamp seal rather than the cylinder, a more restricted spacing had favoured a shorthand style from the beginning and the successive changes in glyptic are less violently apparent, except at sites such as Susa where there was often close contact with Sumer.

Architecture outside Sumer: Tepe Gawrah

We may now consider architecture in places outside the range of direct Sumerian influence. Some interesting variations occur at a site such as Tepe Gawrah fourteen miles east of the Tigris, not far from Nineveh. Here in the Uruk-Jemdet Nasr periods we find, it is true, the tripartite temple plan with central nave and façade ornamented with niches and reveals comparable to the architecture of Eridu. But at Gawrah there is one different feature which perhaps betrays influences from the hill country of Mesopotamia and Iranian Kurdistan: it is the layout of a deep porch at the entrance to the temple in the short side, well-illustrated for example in Gawrah VIII c *(fig. 10)*, an architectural form which seems to make its first appearance in a preceding stratum (XI) probably contemporary with an early Uruk phase.

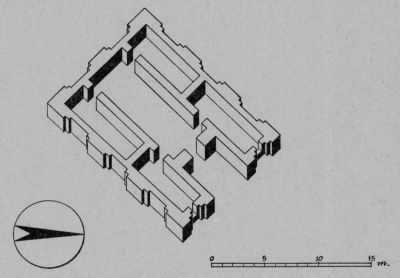

Tepe Gawrah: Temple VIII c, showing the deep porch at the entrance. Probably built before 3200 BC. (fig. 10)

Earlier still we have another architectural form which in northern Mesopotamia has enjoyed an extraordinary continuity, namely the round house as at Gawrah XI a *(fig. 11)* centrally placed and dominating the site. This was clearly the headman's house; it contained a spacious central hall 13×2.6 metres in dimensions, with a long clay partition running down the middle of the room; one of the smaller rooms (E) with inner buttresses originally built with a niche in the end wall may have been used as a sanctuary. The round house had a very solidly built perimeter and was approached by a steep ramp; it was clearly designed with an eye to defence. Around it were smaller irregularly built rectangular houses, ill-planned.

The Uruk-Jemdet Nasr period at Gawrah was an extraordinarily prosperous one and the evidence shows that the whole of Mesopotamia, including cities altogether outside the domain of Sumer, were flourishing at the time. This age of technological progress had made for widespread material wealth, abundantly illustrated by the rich deposits in graves found under the houses on the citadel; stone as

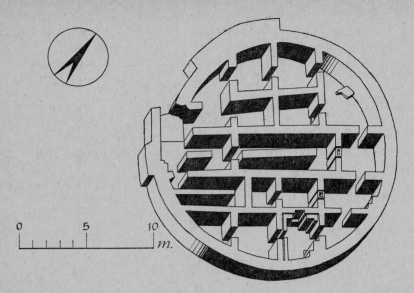

0   5   10
|.........|.........|_____ *m.*

The headman's round house at Tepe Gawrah dating from the Uruk period, c. 3500 BC. It was clearly designed to withstand assault. (fig. 11)

well as mud-brick and timber was used in their construction, some of the vaults were corbelled. The dead were buried within the walls, for apparently the inhabitants lived in fear of attack and it was desirable for the wealthier dead to be under the protection of the living. Their tombs would have been well worth rifling.

Jewellery and Ornaments

Perhaps the most extraordinary feature of the deposits assigned to the dead is the quantity of beads. One tomb contained 3000; another included 750 cowries which must ultimately have come from the Indian Ocean, perhaps through the Persian Gulf. Among the materials used for beads and amulets there was lapis lazuli, ivory, turquoise, jadeite, carnelian, haematite, obsidian, quartz, diorite and faience. Many of the stones must have been imported from Persia, others may have come from Armenia. The 450 lapis lazuli beads in one of the graves no doubt originated in distant Badakhshan. It seems probable that Tepe Hissar, a piedmont site in northern Iran, was a station on the transit route for the lapis trade, since lapis lazuli beads appear there from about the end of the Jemdet Nasr period and subsequently. This much prized stone was exported to Ur and deposited in great quantities in graves of the second and third Early Dynastic periods, after which time the richer veins may have been worked out, for the supply decreased thereafter.

Bead deposits in enormous quantities have been discovered also at Nineveh, Brak, and Uruk in the Uruk-Jemdet Nasr sequence; faience beads at Brak were associated with the early Eye-temples by the hundred thousand; indeed they were puddled into the mud-bricks of the temples. We are indeed reminded that originally the necklace must have been regarded as a most powerful charm against the forces of evil. Beautifully made amulets and stone vessels were also features of the time: in metal one of the most remarkable is an electrum wolf's head with open mouth and gold wire teeth from Gawrah (pl. 41). Gold, silver and electrum were also abundantly worked, and at Gawrah clothing was adorned with gold rosettes (pl. 43), buttons and beads.

Examples of pottery from Chagar Bazar. Top: incised pots, in greenish clay (right) and bound with a fine strand of silver wire (left). Bottom: Ninevite V ware (see also fig. 1); two painted pots flanking an unpainted pedestal vase. (fig. 12)

Pottery

At the turn of the Jemdet Nasr to Early Dynastic period fine specimens of incised grey and black pottery of a type known as Ninevite V were sometimes bound with strands of silver wire, and indeed some of these vessels were probably substitutes for the more expensive silver. Good specimens of such pots have been found in the Habur valley at Chagar Bazar, at Nineveh and elsewhere *(fig. 12)*. Associated

with this incised ware is a painted variety of Ninevite V which includes bowls and vessels with high pedestals; the latter are often decorated with horned animals which have long giraffe-like necks and remind us of the strange beasts which occasionally figure on contemporary protodynastic Egyptian stone palettes. This pottery, often executed in a violet, almost plum-red paint, is the northern equivalent of the southern Jemdet Nasr ware. But this variety of Ninevite V abundant in the Khosr valley of prehistoric Assyria must have been introduced from Persia, probably through Azerbaijan where it has been found, for example on the site of Hasanlu. Varieties of the ware also appear at other Persian sites, notably Hissar and Siyalk where its early context and derivation from even more ancient ceramic proves its ultimate Iranian origin. When it appears in N. Mesopotamia and in Assyria it is closely associated with a good quality of metal work, especially with copper tools such as chisels apparently cast in an open mould.

The Early Dynastic Period

Enough has been said and illustrated to demonstrate that the foundations of civilization had been well and truly laid in the Uruk-Jemdet Nasr period, and to show how large a part the Sumerians played in that achievement which in time spread over wide tracts of North Mesopotamia, Syria, and Iran far beyond their primary orbit. It would require yet another even longer chapter to show how the superstructure was built upon those foundations; but a few landmarks may suffice to indicate the trends of development and to illustrate the importance of recent evidence in the assessment of chronology.

ARCHITECTURE
In architecture the most characteristic criterion of the Early Dynastic period is the use of the cushion-shaped plano-convex brick. In the northern tract of Mesopotamia however the plano-convex brick was more rarely used. It occurs at Brak in the upper Habur valley, but is not at home on the upper Tigris. During the earliest stage of the Early Dynastic there are Early Dynastic I buildings in which the older *Riemchen* are used in conjunction with the newer cushion-shaped bricks, e.g. in the shrine of the Abu Temple at Asmar contemporary with Uruk I. Why this inconvenient unit of building was employed is unknown; some authorities believe that it was a transition to mud-brick by new peoples accustomed to building in stone. In fact there is a precedent in Sumer itself where cushion-shaped cement bricks have been found at a much earlier period. It may be that some convention dictated by religious authority was responsible for the perpetuation of this inconvenience in Early Dynastic times.

The Early Dynastic sequence has been divided into three stages, I-III, and is best illustrated at the site of Khafajah in the Diyala valley where five consecutively built 'Sin Temples' (VI-X) have revealed a remarkable continuity in the architecture. Here was a series of enormous mud-brick temples defended by powerful walls which still incorporated within them the established form of oblong sanctuary. All the necessary service rooms were grouped around a vast squarish courtyard which had now assumed the form that became characteristic in Babylonia after 2000 BC. This stratified evidence is of special importance because of the great depth of accumulated debris embraced by these sequent buildings, each of which was powerfully built and capable of lasting for a long space of time. The many changes of style in the objects associated with them must also imply protracted stages of development. In our opinion a span of rather more than 500 years from about 3000-2450 BC is a modest computation for the length of the whole period, and accords better with the long chronologies which C14 is now indicating for previous prehistoric stages than any of the reductions proposed by authorities who favour the scaling down of Early Dynastic and historic dates.

Our knowledge of Early Dynastic period I is relatively defective in comparison with the abundant evidence for the two succeeding stages, II-III, and it is probable that this was the shortest of the three. It is however certain that the architectural developments characteristic of II-III were already fully established in Early Dynastic I and this is nowhere better illustrated than in the spacious and elaborately built Sin Temples VI-VII.

From evidence at Tell Asmar in the Diyala valley it would also seem that the type of private house characteristic of Babylonia after 2000 BC was already defined at least in embryo a thousand years earlier. The pivotal feature was a central room with flat roof to which the remaining apartments were subsidiary: it was only in the later

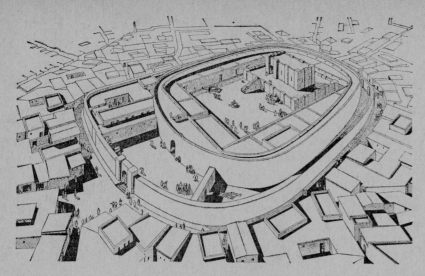

The 'Temple Oval' at Khafajah, after a drawing by H. D. Darby. The sanctuary is set on an elevated platform, the priest's house between the outer and inner perimeters. (fig. 13)

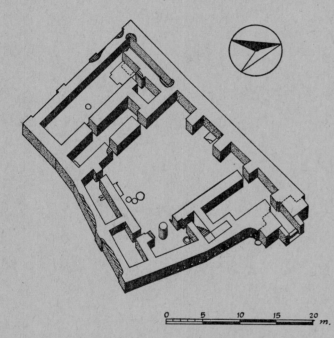

Sin Temple VIII, one of five Sumerian temples of the Early Dynastic period built consecutively at Khafajah, and dating from c. 2800 BC. (fig. 14)

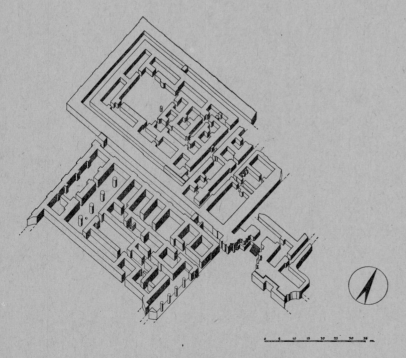

Early Dynastic palace at Kish, one of the earliest royal residences in Sumer and comparable to the Sin Temple VIII at Khafajah. (fig. 15)

Akkadian period that this developed into an open courtyard. The houses had only a single storey; small squarish open windows perhaps protected with wooden grilles were already known; they could be blocked with bricks in case of inclement weather. Cylinder seals with designs in what is termed the 'brocade' style (pl. 32) are the best criterion of Early Dynastic I and some examples were found in the Sin Temples VI-VII.

At Khafajah the most impressive monument of the Early Dynastic II-III period is a sacred perimeter known as the 'Temple Oval' *(fig. 13)* secluding the temple itself from the simple houses which cluster around it. This was a self-sufficient unit which covered an area of more than three hectares including enclosure walls, huge courtyard, workshops and magazines, sanctuary at one end, priest's house at the other.

Very important in the Early Dynastic series is a building at Khafajah known as Sin Temple VIII (Early Dynastic II) *(fig. 14)*, because of its architectural similarity to a great palace at Kish: plano-convex bricks were the standard unit of construction in each case. The stepped approach flanked by towers; the niches in the façade; and the use of the column in both buildings prove that they cannot be very far removed in time, while the objects found in Sin VIII indicate that it is perhaps contemporary with the earlier part of the Royal Cemetery of Ur. This contemporaneity is also suggested by the fact that a cemetery known as Kish A (E.D. III) was dug into the ruins of the (E.D. II) Kish Palace when it was abandoned, and that the contents of Kish A match many of those at Ur in E.D. III. The earlier sequence is demonstrated by the discovery of an older inscribed tablet embedded in a bench within the Kish palace, of the Fara type (immediately post-Jemdet Nasr) while the earliest graves of the Ur Royal Cemetery similarly were dug into houses which contained Fara type tablets.

The Kish Palace *(fig. 15)* and another spacious building at Eridu also probably of Early Dynastic II are in fact the earliest examples known to us of a royal residence set apart for the king. And it is indeed remarkable that in the long history of Sumerian architectural development there is no decisive evidence before that period of a separate palace. In fact the architectural evidence accords with that of the texts, namely that originally the king and the chief priest were one. The old Sumerian title *ensi* probably meant the lord who established the foundation of a temple, and it was the temple which originally owned all the land.

The king as priest had special quarters in the temple, the GIG.PAR, and a building recently excavated at Nippur perhaps illustrates separate domestic quarters within the temple complex. Enmerkar, the king who built Erech, received emissaries from Iran in the *gu-en-na*, the throne-room of the temple. We have to wait for a prince of Lagash named Entemena c. 2400 BC (end of Early Dynastic III) to find a deed of sale which records that 'in those days Entemena was prince of the city of Lagash and Enentarzi was priest of Ningirsu'. This would appear to be the first written evidence of separation between church and state.

Two generations later, Urukagina was engaged in correcting the abuses which had arisen from the increasingly bureaucratic state with its tempting opportunities for peculation in land, oppressive dues and taxes, and exorbitant burial fees.

When we are able to observe a well defined example of a palace we may assume that the king was the *lu-gal* (great man) and that he lived in the *e-gal* (great house): as head of the state he was still the *ensi*.

Moreover, Sidney Smith has rightly called attention to the fact that since the late Babylonian equivalent of this word was applied to the holders of allotments of state territory won by conquest, it may be deduced that the original meaning implied that the *ensi* was the tenant farmer of the god. And this in effect the earliest rulers of Uruk must have been, as we may judge from the predominantly agricultural and pastoral economy to which so many of its monuments and remains bear witness.

ART, EARLY DYNASTIC II-III

The Early Dynastic II-III period is not only abundantly attested by the architecture, but also by the contents of the remarkable tombs of the Kish cemeteries and that known as the Royal Cemetery of Ur where up to 74 persons were buried in order to accompany the deceased king (pl. 51, 53). It is significant that the chariot burials which are a feature of the period at Kish and at Ur have also been discovered at Susa in Iran. The practice of sending retainers to their death with the king has now been noted in a cuneiform tablet entitled 'The Death of Gilgamesh'.

At Ur the Early Dynastic graves are, apart from their contents, interesting architecturally, for they illustrate the use of stone, of the dome, of corbelling and the barrel vault for the construction of which stone, kiln-fired burnt bricks, as well as mud-brick were used.

Metallurgy and the fine arts now spread in glorious abundance, much of it immobilised below ground in deference to the extravagant concepts, more congenial to the Egyptian than to the Mesopotamian mind, which demanded every kind of endowment for the deceased king. The abandonment of this uneconomic and no doubt unpopular practice of human sacrifices on a large scale seems to have coincided with a decline in Sumerian authority after 2500 BC.

Early Dynastic stone statuary more rarely reached the high level of metallurgical achievement. At Mari however on the middle Euphrates there are some splendid calcite and alabaster statues of the gods, rulers and priests. At Tell Asmar we are confronted by the work of a provincial workshop, the merits of which have been much exaggerated (pl. 42).

The Sumerian tradition of stone carving both of human and animal figures is well reflected in Iran: at Susa carved plaques, and statuary in the style of Early Dynastic III as well as stone vases, cylinder seals, metal vessels, tools and weapons betray a close relationship with S. Mesopotamia. At Susa pedestal vases decorated with designs of humped bulls in relief already betray a connection with carvings characteristic of the Indus valley, and we may admit with some confidence that trade relationship with Harappan cities were already established at that time, c. 2500 BC (see chapter VIII).

Assur

The widespread influence of Sumer at the end of the Early Dynastic period is also well demonstrated far up the river Tigris at the city of Assur which after 2000 BC was to become the religious capital of Assyria. Temple G which is thought to have been dedicated to a goddess, probably Ishtar, was laid out in a simple type of ground plan, with oblong sanctuary and side chambers, as in many other Mesopotamian cities such as Mari and Nuzi. At Assur there were benches against the walls upon which statues in Sumerian form, depicted as clothed in fleecy skins, were dedicated to the god. Models of pedestalled houses, perhaps shrines, decorated with doves and snakes, were also associated. The most remarkable discovery however was a painted gypsum plaque apparently depicting the goddess lying on her bed. She was accoutred with jewellery and choker such as were found on Queen Shubad and her attendants in the Royal Cemetery of Ur, and is thus unmistakably reminiscent of Sumerian religious practice. The city of Assur would seem to represent the most northerly penetration of direct Sumerian rule at this time (Early Dynastic III) though objects of Sumerian manufacture have been found in even more distant places such as Byblos on the west coast of the Lebanon.

The Agade Period

In about 2370 BC history records the ascent to the throne of the founder of the Agade dynasty, Sargon, who for the first time established political control over a large part of Mesopotamia under a Semitic as opposed to a Sumerian regime; that is to say the language of the rulers was Semitic Akkadian. A bronze head discovered at Nineveh, already mentioned, perhaps depicts that monarch himself. In style the hairdressing is closely comparable to a slightly earlier electrum helmet which belonged to Mes-kalam-shar, a prince buried with a rich panoply of deposits in one of the late Early Dynastic graves in the Royal Cemetery at Ur (pl. 50).

Sargon and his successors took over their Sumerian heritage and earned their acquisitions both by the might of arms and by their high development of the arts. Statuary and seals of the period may be ranked amongst the finest monuments ever produced on Mesopotamian soil. The great *stele* of Naram-Sin, fourth monarch of the dynasty, illustrates his victory over a west Iranian chief and is a notable artistic achievement. The king is depicted leading his warriors to the top of a high, wooded mountain: an impression of movement, soft and easy flow of line, cleverly contrived spacing and bold sense of composition are characteristic of the period. This monument (pl. 44) is executed in the grand manner and can be matched in miniature by the superbly carved cylinder seals which are another and no less brilliant achievement.

The largest known building of the Agade period is a palace discovered at Tell Brak in the Habur region of N. Syria with a frontage of over 100 metres (fig. 16). The inscribed bricks record the name of the same king, Naram-Sin, who clearly established it as a fortress and blockhouse to guard his lines of communication with Anatolia where, as we know from much later texts, his ancestor Sargon had promoted trade and supported merchants who had appealed to him for help. No doubt the motive for his interest in N. Syria was to secure the rich metal ores of eastern Asia Minor. It can hardly be a coincidence that contemporary metal work discovered in treasure troves at Brak can in part match the treasure found in the second city of Troy which during the Agade period must have been in touch, probably by the sea route, with the cities of N. Syria and Mesopotamia.

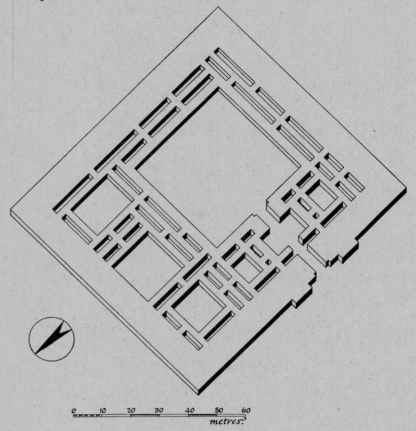

The palace of Naram-Sin, King of Agade, at Tell Brak. A similar type of fortified palace was discovered at Assur. (fig. 16)

Ur

The capital city of the dynasty, Agade itself, has yet to be found, probably in the neighbourhood of Babylon, and a great prize may await its discoverer. The dynasty was brought to an end by barbarous hordes called the Guti who reflect the relative backwardness of W. Iranian mountaineers at the time. There was however one more brilliant Neo-Sumerian revival, first at Lagash under Gudea whose black diorite statues (pl. 40) and long Sumerian inscriptions record another period of prosperity. But the climax of this period of revival was achieved by the Third Dynasty of Ur whose first two rulers, Ur Nammu (pl. 49) and Shulgi, made Ur and Uruk glorious cities, rebuilt the sacred enclosure, the *temenos*, and wherever possible substituted kiln-fired burnt-bricks of the finest quality for the traditional mud-brick which so frequently required repair. The noblest monument of the time is the great Ziggurat of Ur, a staged tower approached by triple staircases (pl. 45, 47). These monarchs also established direct authority over Assur and were supreme at Susa in Iran where some rich treasures, statuary and jewellery of gold and other metals, were deposited by them.

The authority of the Neo-Sumerian dynasty of Ur even so far north as Assyria is well exemplified by the Ishtar Temple E, conventional in plan, approached by a stepped entrance flanked by towers, laid out with oblong sanctuary, a room at each end and two others to one side; the corners of the building face approximately the cardinal points of the compass (fig. 17). A votive plaque recorded that the temple was erected by one Zariqu who proclaimed himself viceroy of Amar-Suen (once known as Bur-Sin) the third king of the Third Dynasty of Ur (2037-2028 BC). At Assur graves of this period were sometimes lavishly endowed with offerings, and one of them which contained a gold frontlet impressed with concentric circles, gold lunate earrings, etched

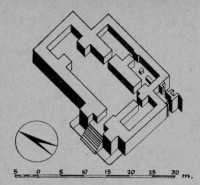

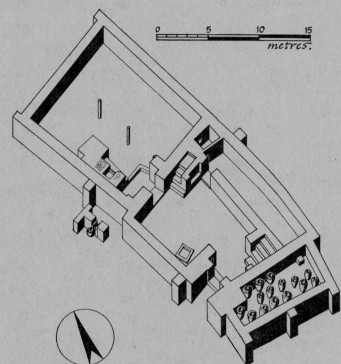

Temple E at Assur dedicated to Ishtar. It illustrates the influence of Sumerian architecture in Assyria. (fig. 17)

The 'Burnt Building' at Tepe Hissar. Analogies with the Ishtar Temple at Assur (fig. 17) may reflect contemporary Mesopotamian influence on Iranian architecture. (fig. 18)

carnelian beads and a lapis lazuli seal in the Cappadocian style, is of particular interest. The quality of its jewellery is to some extent comparable to rich deposits found at Tepe Hissar in northern Iran, in the last period of its occupation (IIIb and IIIc), with a likely date, as we shall see, of about 2000 BC. Elsewhere in Sumer, at Uruk, there is also similar evidence in the shape of a magnificent collar composed of carnelian, gold filigree surrounding agate, silver and turquoise beads, all threaded on silver wires. The turquoise was no doubt imported from Iran. This set of jewellery was made for a priestess of Shu Sin, the King of Ur (2028–2003 BC); such ornaments would not have been out of place at Hissar.

Tepe Hissar III

Since much material associated with the Third Dynasty of Ur appears to be comparable with discoveries in northern Iran it is interesting that we are at last able to point to an Iranian building which has some analogies to one in Mesopotamia. We have noticed above the plan of a temple dedicated to Ishtar at Assur, and with this we may compare that of the 'Burnt Building' at Tepe Hissar IIIb *(fig. 18)*. Both are oblong buildings with a single entrance defended by towers; each is divided into three parts with a store-room at one end and flanking chambers. Moreover the lengths, though not the proportions, of the two buildings are approximately similar: about 26 metres at Hissar, 29 metres at Assur. It is possible, though not certain, that the end room at Hissar contained a shrine within it. At all events here for the first time we have two architectural units in Iraq and Iran which, however remotely, may be the result of a common technological development at a time when the two countries were increasingly in touch with one another. We need not press the similarity too closely, but it would not be surprising if the two buildings had been built not very far apart in time, for as we shall see, this was a period of great prosperity at Hissar, and that must have been largely due to a transcontinental trade.

The mud-brick building at Hissar was richly endowed with gold

daggers, gold, silver and copper vessels and expensive jewellery; millet was found in the store-rooms. The place fell in dramatic circumstances to enemy attack. Signs of a desperate battle were evident from many ovate flint arrowheads in the precincts of the building which was finally devastated by fire. About a dozen charred skeletons of men, women and children were found within it. Communal graves elsewhere on the site may have been the result of defeat at the hands of more powerful cities on the other side of the mountains, Shah Tepe or Tureng Tepe for instance, where there appear to be later traces of occupation.

In the last phases of its lifetime (III b–c), Tepe Hissar seems to have been an extremely rich centre, well equipped with all those kinds of goods which were coveted as the fruits of civilization. Apart from an abundance of gold, variegated jewellery (pl. 56), copper and silver vessels, there were alabaster, calcite and veined stone vases of exceptional beauty and elegance. Pedestal vases in stone were much favoured. There were many varieties of beads, among them much lapis lazuli, and it may well be that Hissar was an entrepot in the profitable trade which must have resulted through the export of that stone from the mines of Badakhshan to other parts of Iran as well as to Mesopotamia. There is sufficient continuity of style between the objects of the last two periods of Hissar III b–c to make it certain that both were in a continuous development, not separated by any length of time. But in spite of the great variety of material goods it is still impossible to be certain about the date of these Iranian phases of civilization owing to the absence of written records.

On the basis of developments in style and in technology dates have been proposed by various authorities, some as early as 2300 BC, others as late as 1500 BC. None has used convincing arguments. Since many of the metal and stone vessels, as well as the weapons, are in the Early Dynastic tradition of the Royal Cemetery of Ur there is a case for arguing the earlier of the two dates mentioned. The case for proposing a date some time after 2000 BC depends largely on the use of the axe-adze and of certain types of well developed spears with medial rib and ridge-stopped tangs *(fig. 19)*. But in fact there are parallels for the

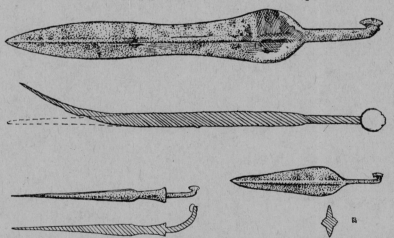

Examples of spears found at Tepe Hissar. Note the medial rib on the two larger blades, and the ridge-stopped tangs. (fig. 19)

latter from Carchemish and Ugarit in North Syria which may well be dated at least a century before 2000 BC, and Hissar is situated geographically in just the region where one would expect smiths to adapt and combine axe and adze to form a single tool *(fig. 20)*. There are

Adze-axe found in the 'Burnt Building' at Tepe Hissar. It is one of the earliest known implements of this type. (fig. 20)

excellent parallels for this rather rare type of instrument as late as the reign of Shalmaneser III, c. 850 BC, but that alone would be an inadequate reason for arguing that this instrument was unknown in Assyria where it had not yet appeared in an earlier context before that time.

In the absence of conclusive evidence there are in fact stronger reasons for dating Hissar IIIb a little before 2000 BC and IIIc a little after it, or indeed at about that time. In general the extravagantly long-spouted, sometimes trough-spouted vessels from Hissar *(fig. 21)*, in silver as well as in stone, recall certain types used in the *karum* at Kültepe in Cappadocia, as also do stone vessels decorated with concentric circles which can be compared with others used at Susa during the Third Dynasty of Ur. The latter is a period which can also offer parallels for the many types of elaborately decorated copper maceheads *(fig. 22)* that are also a feature of Hissar III. Lastly the use of lead

Alabaster trough-spouted vase from Level III c at Tepe Hissar. (fig. 21)

Hissar III: copper macehead, and stylised alabaster mother-goddess figurine (cf. fig. 24) with copper rings in the head. (fig. 22)

vessels is also suggestive of the interest in that commodity at Kültepe c. 1900 BC, whilst the modelling of faience amulets, including frogs, at Shah Tepe which appears to have outlived Hissar affords parallels with the Larsa period in Mesopotamia at approximately the same date.

There is other evidence to illustrate the widespread contact between Hissar and distant cities at this period. Certain types of compartmented copper seals have been found here, at Shahi Tump in Baluchistan, at Anau III in Turkestan, and one decorated with an eagle can be matched at Susa. The alleged presence of amber may imply an even more distant trade and one cylinder seal carries the design of an Indian humped bull.

Finally it is worthy of notice that in Hissar III b the skull of a horse was found and furthermore the horse is alleged to have been domesticated at Shah Tepe, much earlier still, thus long anticipating the first appearance of it at Boghazköy in Central Asia Minor in the early Hittite period. An analysis of some 250 skeletal remains in Hissar III revealed the fact that females to males were in the ratio of two to one and that 87 per cent of the persons examined had died before the age of 40, a very sharp contrast to modern average figures for longevity in America and in Europe.

The extraordinary wealth accumulated from trans-Caspian trade is also most strikingly shown by a celebrated hoard known as the Asterabad Treasure *(fig. 24)* which included gold, metal vessels, a gold ibex head, axe-adzes, copper spears and other implements. Amongst them two golden signal horns or trumpets closely matched similar instruments from Hissar IIIc and were obviously contemporary *(fig. 23)*.

The Rise of New Empires

The widespread contact between distant parts of the civilized world at that time implied a desire to share in the wealth available to man, and a determination to compete for it if it were withheld. It is no surprise that in about 2000 BC, after a millennium and a half of Sumerian dominance in Mesopotamia, new forces both there and in Iran were ready to take over for themselves the authority of government.

We have already seen that the monarchs of Agade had assumed authority in the twenty-fourth century BC, and in so doing had for

the first time established rule by speakers of a Semitic language. In due course they were supplanted by the Third Dynasty of Ur, the last Sumerian line of rulers, whose last king Ibbi-Suen was shortly after 2000 BC carried captive to Iran. Afterwards, although the Sumerian language was long used by learned scribes for religious and magical literature, the Sumerians themselves ceased to be important. Their great heritage was however taken over and organised by new Semitic

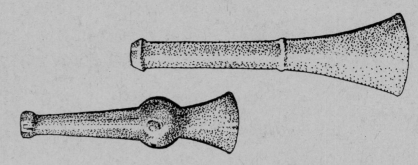

Two silver trumpets from Hissar. The lower one is noticeably similar to the two gold signal horns from the Asterabad Treasure shown in fig. 24. (fig. 23)

dynasties, Amorites and others, who swarmed eastwards across Syria into the fertile valleys of Tigris and Euphrates. New capitals aspired to imperial control: first Isin, then Larsa, then Babylon, occasionally admitting elements from western Iran within the government. In about 2000 BC we may discern a turning point between these newer forces and the old; it was a period at which Mesopotamia was reorganising itself and Iran was awaiting the emergence of a vigorous agricultural tribe, the Kassites, who were later on to play a powerful part on the Near Eastern stage.

Part of the celebrated Asterabad Treasure, a hoard whose whereabouts are no longer known (from a 19th-century engraving). (fig. 24)

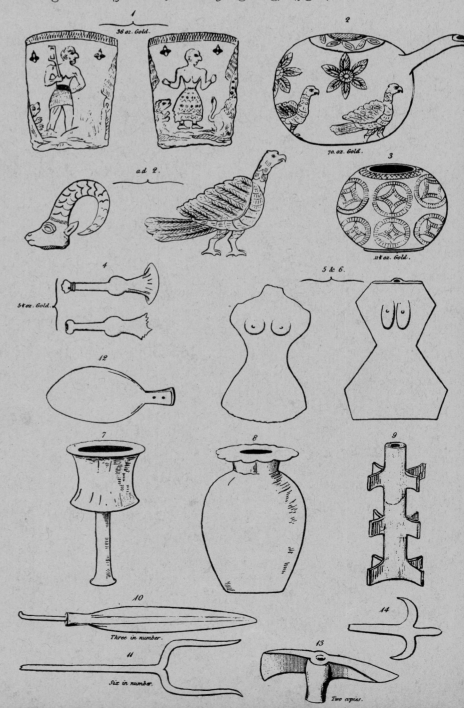

IV THE RISE OF THE GOD-KINGS

The first flowering in Ancient Egypt

CYRIL ALDRED

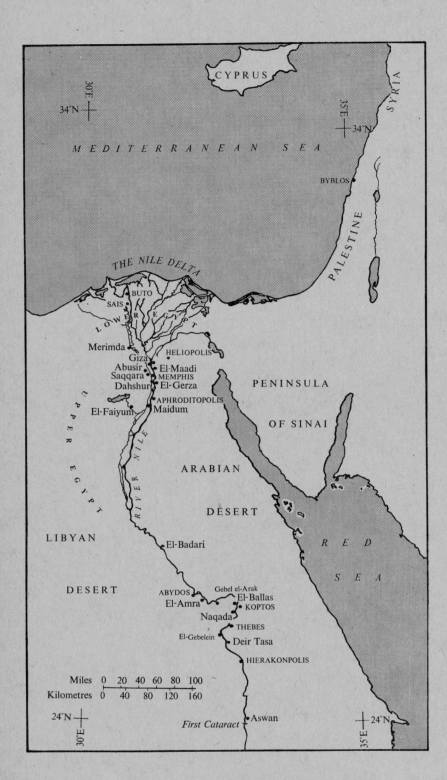

Date BC	Period	Culture Lower E.	Upper E.	Main Sites
c. 5000	Neolithic	Faiyum 'A'		Faiyum depression
			Tasian	Deir Tasa Mostagedda
c. 4000	Chalcolithic	Merimda	Badarian	El-Badari Merimda Beni-Salama
	Early Predynastic		Amratian	El-Amra El-Ballas Hu Abydos Mahasna
c. 3600	Middle Predynastic	Maadi	Early Gerzean	El-Maadi
c. 3400	Late Predynastic		Late Gerzean	El-Gerza Haraga

c. 3200 *At this time the union was achieved of Upper and Lower Egypt under one king. This is the beginning of the Historic Period, the main sites of discovery being Hierakonpolis, Memphis and Abydos.*

HISTORIC

Date BC	Period	Dynasties and Principal Kings		
c. 3200	Archaic	Dynasty I		
		Narmer	(Menes)	
		Hor-aha	(Ity)	
		Djer	(Iteti)	19+years
		Wadjy	(Ity)	
		Wedymu	(Khasety)	
		Adjib	(Merpaba)	20+years
		Shepses ?	(Semerkhet)	9 years
		Ka-aa	(Senmu)	
c. 2980		Dynasty II		
		Hotep-sekhemwy	(Neterbau)	
		Nebre	(Kakau?)	
		Ni-neter		22+years
		Peribsen		
		Kha-sekhem		
		Kha-sekhemwy		17 years
c. 2780	The Old Kingdom	Dynasty III		
		Sa-nakht		
		Djoser	(Neter-khet)	19 years
		Sekhem-khet		5? years
		Kha-ba		12+years
		Neb-ka		
		Huny		24 years
c. 2680		Dynasty IV		
		Sneferu		24 years
		Kheops	(Khufu)	23 years
		Djedefre		8 years
		Khephren	(Khafre)	25–30 years
		Mykerinus	(Menkaure)	21–28 years
		Shepses-kaf		5 years
c. 2560		Dynasty V		
		Weser-kaf		7 years
		Sahu-re		14 years
		Nefer-ir-ka-re		7 years
		Shepses-ka-re		7 years
		Nefer-ef-re		4? years
		Ni-weser-re		34? years
		Men-kau-hor		8 years
		Djed-ka-re	(Isesy)	28 years
		Wenis		30 years
c. 2420		Dynasty VI		
		Tety		12 years
		Pepy I		45 years
		Mery-en-re I		14 years
		Pepy II		94 years
		Mery-en-re II		1 year
c. 2200		Fall of the Old Kingdom		

Chronology

In his *History of Egypt* compiled c. 280 BC, which has been preserved only in extracts from other classical writers, the Graeco-Egyptian priest Manetho grouped the reigns of the various kings into thirty-one dynasties. This system is still employed by Egyptologists who further arrange the dynasties into longer periods, such as the Old, Middle and New Kingdoms, each characterized by a homogeneous culture and divided from each other by intervals of political confusion.

The prehistoric ages are also grouped into certain broad periods named after various sites in Egypt where a distinct culture has been identified. The dating of such sequences has been determined by archaeological evidence, but has recently been controlled by C 14 analyses.

Six thousand years ago

the seeds of Egyptian civilization were sown, in the valley of the river Nile. It was here, in the narrow strip of fertile land, watered by the annual inundations, that man and beast concentrated, after the gradual drying-up of North Africa had made the rest of the country uninhabitable. It was here that the roaming hunters first squatted, then settled, tilling the soil, domesticating the animals, harnessing the river, building huts, forming communities. It is here, strung out on both river banks, as the map shows, that the earliest traces of their life have been found. The oldest of them dates back to about 5000 BC and between them they embrace the eighteen hundred years of the prehistory of Egypt of which anything is known.

This prehistoric age falls into four periods, named after the sites where distinct cultures have been found: Deir Tasa (Tasian), El-Badari (Badarian), El-Amra (Amratian), El-Gerza (Gerzean).

Almost nothing is left of the Tasians, except a little pottery. Of the Badarians we know that they grew wheat and barley, raised sheep, goats and pigs, possessed hoe and plough, used copper and baked bread. The Amratians were the first to make stone vases; the Gerzeans the first to use glaze and gold. Common to them all was pottery, shaped entirely by hand, each period developing its characteristic shapes.

The Nile meant life to these peoples—a beneficent Nile which annually overran its banks and left refreshed, fertile earth behind it as it receded. The early squatters, finding they hardly needed to till and manure their fields, were encouraged to stay put and rely more on cereals and less on the products of the hunt for their food. They had leisure in which to specialize, as in the raising and breeding of domestic animals; they were pressed by their increasing numbers to tame the annual inundations by irrigation works—and this was best done on a large scale by co-operative effort which led to the emergence of local political organizations to control such enterprises. Their culture at this time can have differed little from that of the pagan tribes of the Upper Nile today.

But they were hemmed in by deserts and the sea, and although the great Uruk civilization nine hundred miles away was far advanced by this time, it was not until towards the end of the prehistoric age that new ideas and techniques began to infiltrate from abroad. The foreign 'know-how' was quickly seized upon: building in mud-brick began, the first hieroglyphic writing appeared on slate palettes, and, as will be seen from the pages which follow, crafts such as carving in low relief reached a high degree of decorative skill.

By 4000 BC the people of El-Badari were making tools and utensils like these. They ground their cosmetics on stone palettes, used ivory spoons and knives chipped from a flint-like quartz. Their pottery was no longer coarse and ill-fired; the jar in the centre has fine, thin walls and a polished surface. The pottery figurine had perhaps a magical purpose—to serve the dead. (1, above)

Four hundred years later, the people of El-Amra hollowed lug-handled jars out of stone—the forerunners of one of the most characteristic products of Ancient Egypt. They made black-topped jars in various shapes, and red burnished pottery with white-slip decoration. A fish-tail lance-head is shown, and two cosmetic palettes, one fish-shaped and the other with its round rubbing-stone. (2, above)

A distinct culture, some three hundred years later (c. 3300 BC), emerges from a study of deposits at El-Gerza and other sites in the North. In the South it has been found permeating and superseding the Amratian; notably at the vast cemeteries of Naqada and El-Ballas. Its pottery is decorated with red designs on a buff ground: ship-like forms (which should be compared with the designs on the textile overleaf), conventionalized water and hills, and spirals resembling

the veins in the conglomerate of which stone jars were made. The stone jars (one is shown right) have now become common, probably because the invention of a cranked brace with weights acting as a fly-wheel, and flint borers which could be discarded when worn, made the hollowing out of the vessels much less arduous. A cosmetic palette and rubber are also shown, and a slate chest-ornament in the form of a bird. (3)

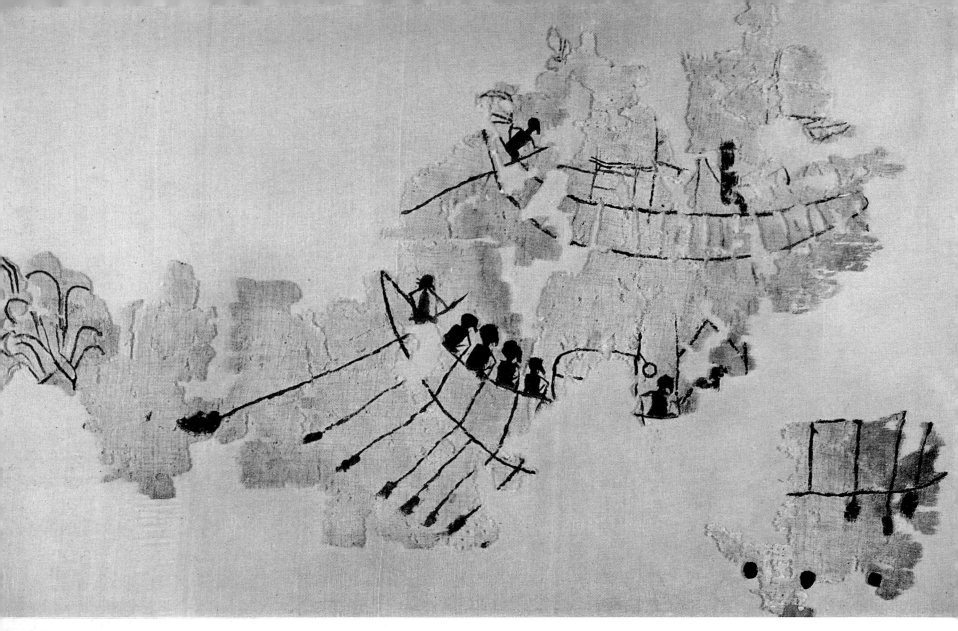

Boats of the prehistoric Nile are shown in this ragged fragment of a painted textile, found in the cemetery at El-Gebelein (above). The fabric is linen with a very fine thread: the delicate task of reassembling it took four years. Both vessels have a double cabin amidships, both a steersman in the stern. Unlike most representations of human figures from prehistoric Egypt, Mesopotamia and the Mediterranean area, these are not 'beak-nosed' and wear beards. Compare the design of the ships with the decoration on the pottery in pl. 3. (4)

'Wavy-handled jars' showing the change from a foreign prehistoric form to the native style perhaps two hundred years later. The plastic decoration resembles that on vessels found in Palestine; the red criss-cross lines are meant to suggest a net sling. (5)

In the beginning of civilization, a settlement in Upper Egypt was something like the drawing opposite, which is reconstructed from archaeological evidence of Amratian times, c. 3800 BC. On the river, men in papyrus skiffs can be seen hunting hippopotami with harpoons. The 'beehive' huts of the villagers are woven of grass and reeds; the chief's house is larger and rectangular in plan, as is also the shrine of the local god. This is distinguished by the poles with streamers attached that stand before the threshold, and by the fenced-off sacred enclosure containing offerings to the gods.

A woman squats before a horizontal loom pegged to the ground. A patch of drying mud left by the retreating Nile after the annual inundation is being sown with barley; women and children are turning in the seed with wooden hoes, followed by a man who drags a log across the ground to smooth it down.

A party of hunters have returned with their kill—ibex, gazelle and desert hare; the choicest portion is reserved for the chief by the leader, who has been wounded in the chase. The chief, whose distinguishing features are a skin cloak and ostrich feather, and who wears an ivory amulet, is at once medicine-man and rain-maker. He squats on a low stool and gives advice. (6)

Joinery for everyday use was understood: the compartmented box above, found in the same tomb as the seat below, was probably for holding gaming pieces. (7)

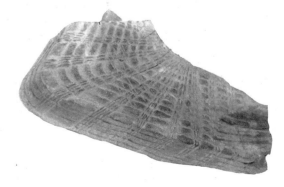

Carving in wood by Egyptian craftsmen reached high technical proficiency by the beginning of written history (about 3000 BC). Designs were copied from those worked out in rush or basketry: the fragment of a seat from an ebony chair (above), found in a tomb of the period, shows a pattern imitating rush-work. (8)

Rippled like ribbed sea sand, the thin flint-blade of the knife on the opposite page is an example of the perfection reached by the flint-knappers of prehistory. But it is the carved ivory handle which makes the knife one of the most celebrated discoveries of Gerzean Egypt. On the reverse (this page) a hero subdues two lions, resembling the Mesopotamian 'Lord of the Beasts', Gilgamesh. (The same unusual theme appears in a wall painting on a Late Gerzean shrine at Hierakonpolis.) Below the hero stand two hunting-dogs, and beneath these are ibexes, one of which is being attacked by a lion—a scene which suggests links with Libya.

On the obverse of the handle (opposite page) appears a water-battle, with boats which, although traditionally Egyptian, have vertical prows and sterns rather like the *belems* of the Tigris. The two contending sides wear different costumes.

These early evidences of foreign influence on prehistoric Egypt suggest that the more advanced civilization of Mesopotamia was already extending its influence, and perhaps its trade, from the north up the Nile. It has been suggested that sea-going boats had by this time been developed for coastal trade in the timber-growing region of Byblos in Syria.

This beautiful example of the growth of relief carving was found at Gebel el-Arak in Upper Egypt and is now in the Louvre. (9, 10)

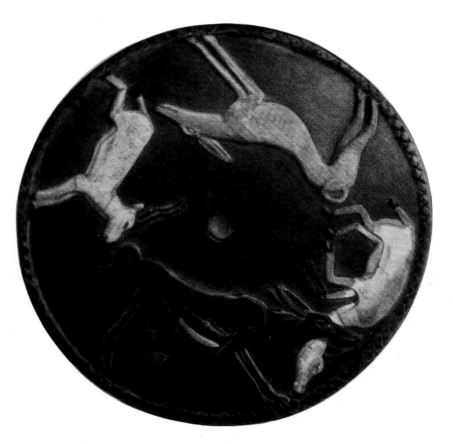

The lively disk above, used in a table game, has survived almost in its original condition. It is carved in low relief from black steatite, with pink-stained alabaster let in to the surface. It shows two hunting-dogs attacking two gazelles, with fine craftsmanship displaying all the features of the best later relief work. The artist has arranged the animals to square the circle, with a feeling for space confined within strict rectangular or cubic outlines which is a characteristic of all dynastic art in Ancient Egypt. (11)

Carved from a solid block of schist, a rock which splits in thin irregular plates, the remarkable dish above possibly imitates a form originally made in metal. It was found in the tomb of Sabu, about 3100 BC. (12)

The coming of the god-kings

was signalled by the rise of Narmer (c. 3200 BC), first king of all Egypt and identified as the semi-legendary Menes, first of the Pharaohs. The settlements of prehistory centred around a village, under the leadership of a chieftain and with its local version of one of the universal deities. But towards the end of prehistory we can detect already the beginning of a pattern which was to be repeated again and again in Egyptian history—the striving of Southern princes towards control of ever larger tracts of the valley of the Nile, until the anarchy was reduced to unity and one kingdom arose out of many districts.

But the country was still known to the Egyptians themselves as the Two Lands: the North, which was the more culturally developed, and the South, which was more politically disciplined. Not until 3200 BC was unification of the whole country achieved for the first time. It was King Scorpion (page 106), perhaps Narmer's immediate predecessor, who vigorously expanded the South, leaving his successor the power and wealth necessary for the conquest of the North.

The result was a typically African solution to the problems of government, for the early monuments clearly show that the king was regarded as a god rather than the human agent of a god. While Mesopotamia

remained still a congeries of rival city-states, Egypt was to develop the political machinery of centralized rule under which all kinds of communal enterprises such as irrigation and reclamation of land could thrive.

The prehistoric chieftain, a rain-maker and medicine man with magic power over the weather and therefore able to keep his people in health and prosperity, has become the Pharaoh, a divine being with command over the Nile and able to sustain and protect the nation. A kingship so identified with the welfare of the land, and reinforced by the Osirian myth of divine succession, formed an ideology powerful enough to dominate the lives of the Egyptian people for three thousand years.

A vivid record of King Narmer survives in this beautifully carved palette recovered from a site at Hierakonpolis in Upper Egypt. It is regarded as celebrating the victory of the Southern king over the North. At the top, in the centre, appears the name of the king within a palace building. At each side is the head of the mother goddess Hathor, with the face of a woman and the ears and horns of a cow— we can see in the emerging woman's face the manifestation of the

gods in human form which seems to come simultaneously with the rise of the god-kings.

Beneath the king's name, on the obverse of the palette (left), are three pictorial strips. The king, wearing the Red Crown of the Delta cities of Buto and Sais, approaches in procession two rows of corpses of native rebels, with bound arms, and severed heads laid between their feet. Behind the monarch is his sandal-bearer and foot-washer, in front of him his priest and four standard bearers carrying fetishes. The glyphs above the bodies define Buto as the place of slaughter.

The central strip contains a circular depression around which are disposed two fabulous serpo-pards with their bearded attendants. This intertwining device appears not only on other Egyptian objects but also on old Babylonian cylinder seals. It has been suggested that the design symbolizes the union of Upper and Lower Egypt. At the bottom of the palette the king as a strong bull breaks down a township, with a large palace or temple and smaller houses within, and tramples upon a vanquished foe, probably a Libyan.

On the reverse of the palette (right), Narmer wears the White Crown of Aphroditopolis, which was to become the Pharaoh's emblematic headgear as King of Upper Egypt. He strikes down an enemy held by the hair, and above his victim a rebus seems to read 'Pharaoh the incarnation of the hawk-god Horus, with his strong right arm leads captive the Marsh-dwellers'. The king is attended by his sandal-bearer. At the foot of the palette are the spread-eagled corpses of two foreigners.

The palette was used for religious purposes, dedicated probably to Hathor. It clearly records the climax in the movement towards political unity in Ancient Egypt, but a deeper significance can be deduced from the commanding size in which the king is depicted compared with that of his subjects and enemies. It is the *divine* might of Narmer which dominates the scenes. The hieroglyphic labels, although they are not properly understood, make the palette one of the first documents in the written history of Egypt and emphasize that we now have to do with a civilized state.

The palette is another striking example of the growth of sculpture in relief. In his composition of the king who holds a conquered enemy by the hair, and in his perception of the human form—head, hips and legs shown in profile, eye and thorax from the front—the artist is using elements which were to be considered adequate as long as Pharaonic Art endured. (13, 14)

The annual miracle of the Nile, for the recurrence of which the divine king is surety, is illustrated in this reconstruction based on the mace-head of King Scorpion, perhaps the immediate predecessor of King Narmer. The floods have receded and the earth is free; soil must be cleared from the silted-up irrigation channels and spread to fertilize the fields. A high official kneels before the king to receive the first basketful; the king wears the white crown and ceremonial dress and carries a hoe or pick; behind him stand his fan-bearers, his foot-washer and sandal-bearer (wearing an amulet), his bodyguard with bow and arrows and his priest. Four fetishes are carried on tall poles to symbolize the divine attributes of the king. The peasants, in charge of the scribe with arm raised, wait to take over; beyond them stand the mud-brick walls of the royal residence. It is a solemn fertility rite, to bless the urgent work of cultivation that must now be done. (15)

Carving in ivory at this time is illustrated by the statuette of an early king above, wearing the white crown and patterned cloak which were the traditional costume of the jubilee ceremonies. (17)

The mace-head of King Scorpion (right), found at Hierakonpolis and dated c. 3250 BC. The king, already appearing in divine size, wears the White Crown and an animal tail and carries a hoe or pick; his symbol is to the right of his head. Behind him are his fan-bearers, and above are the royal standards with, hanging from them, lapwings and (not visible) bows. The reconstructed mace-head (in the Ashmolean Museum, Oxford) is carved in low relief from limestone.(16)

Eleven wood reliefs from eleven niches were found inside the tomb, wonderfully fresh and delicate in their execution. They show Hesy-re, a leading official of Djoser's time and 'scribe and acquaintance of the king'. In the one reproduced here (below), his hair is dressed in courtly style, he has a short moustache and carries his batons of office, the scribe's palette, water bottle and penholder. (19)

The next four hundred years

after the rise of King Narmer (c. 3200 BC) are still comparatively unknown to us, but it is clear that the economic and cultural progress continued which was made possible by the unification under one king. The arts and sciences flourished. Writing must have advanced, helped by the invention of a flexible paper made from the pith of papyrus, and 'scribe' became a proud title. An elaborate system of taxation was established, standard measures of length and capacity came into use, astronomy, elementary surveying and practical mathematics were necessary. Copper working developed rapidly in skill and applications, and there is evidence of carving in wood, ivory and stone (pl. 8, 9, 10, 11) and working in gold and jewellery. The period gives the impression of problems tackled by a questing spirit with assurance and bold experiment.

This promise flowered finally with the reign of King Djoser and the rise of one of the great geniuses of the ancient world: the vizier Imhotep. In later ages this remarkable man, a Newton or an Einstein of his time, was celebrated as an architect, astronomer, priest, writer, sage, and above all as a physician, being eventually deified as the god of medicine. His greatest memorial, however, is the astonishing 'house of eternity' he built to hold the body of his king: the Step Pyramid of Saqqara.

King Djoser himself is preserved in jubilee costume in the limestone statue above, found in a vault of the Step Pyramid. His face has been damaged by thieves who, afraid of the wrath of the god, gouged out his inlaid eyes. He wears an early version of the *nemes* wig-cover, with pointed lappets. (18)

The wonder of the age was undoubtedly the Step Pyramid at Saqqara. Nothing like it had appeared on earth before. As the first use of stone in a building of any size it was a superb achievement. The model (right) is so posed and lighted as to look as the original must have seemed to the Egyptian peasant pausing in his labours in the Saqqara fields: 'white, mysterious and silent upon the skyline'—perpetual and convincing evidence that he was ruled by true gods.

The massive enclosing wall had a perimeter of over a mile and a height of more than thirty-three feet. The six rectangular stages of the tomb itself reached a height of over two hundred feet. Within the tomb was a maze of galleries and surrounding it, inside the wall, courts and buildings in duplicate, simulating the structures used at coronation and jubilees with appropriate insignia for the rites performed by the king, once as ruler of Upper Egypt and again as king of Lower Egypt in different dress and surroundings.

It was a city not for the living but for the dead, to serve its purpose by magic. Most of the buildings are a façade only; of fourteen great gateways in the wall, only one is a true entrance. But the elegant proportions and firm treatment of plant motifs are evidence of a sensitive taste with little parallel in later times. (20)

Statues and reliefs of the king himself are among the mass of objects found in the chambers. In the relief from the South Tomb shown right, Djoser strides round the Ceremonial Circuit—a perambulation of a courtyard defined by six hoof-shaped boundary marks, perhaps symbolizing the domain over which he ruled. Such a ritual formed part of the celebrations during the periodical jubilee festivals. He is holding the 'flail' of a primitive pastoral king and a small leather portfolio probably containing the title deeds to his domains. In front of him is one of the royal standards; above him hovers the divine falcon with a symbol of life; behind appear symbols of life and dominion bearing fans. His Horus name is immediately in front of his head. The relief is set in a faience border. (21)

Much used in decoration were glazed tiles of rich blue faience. The decorated chamber of the South Tomb (below) is reconstructed in this painting to show how they must have looked. (22)

A tomb that would last for ever,
an eternal dwelling for the god-king, was a paramount necessity of
the cult of the dead, an essential safeguard of the well-being of the
people. In the hundred years from 2650 to 2550 BC the human and
material wealth of the nation must have been expended in large
measure on this single purpose. To build the great pyramid of Kheops
required well over two million large blocks of limestone, some of
them weighing as much as fifteen tons. The stone for the core was
hewn on the spot, but the facing blocks, of finer limestone, were
quarried across the river, to be floated and dragged to the site. While
the figure of 100,000 workers supplied to the Greek historian Herodotus by the interpreters of the day is now thought to be greatly
exaggerated, the assembly of skilled craftsmen continually at work
must have been considerable and the provision of the labour a remarkable feat of organization. The astronomical setting of the pyramids,
to meet the requirements of the cult of the sun-god, Re, the fulfilment
of the design of the building and the masonry of the individual stones,
especially in the corridors and chambers within, were accomplished
with astonishing accuracy.

How these great monuments were built is not known. The most
acceptable suggestion is that illustrated by the model below of the
building of the smaller pyramid for Mykerinus: four rubble and mud-
brick ramps were built, one starting from each corner, against the
undressed outer surface of the casing-stones. Each emerged at the top
and each was extended course by course as the pyramid rose. Up three
of them the stones were dragged on sledges; the men descended by
the fourth with sledges empty. Once the capstone was in place, the
casing blocks would be smoothed progressively as the ramps were
removed. The pyramid painted in the background is Khephren's. (23)

In the view from the air of the cemetery near Giza (left), the great pyramid of Kheops is above, that of his son, Khephren, second and the smaller, later pyramid of Mykerinus below. Each tomb complex consisted of a group of four buildings: a gate or valley temple near the limits of the Nile, a covered passage to the girdle wall, the mortuary temple in front of the pyramid, and lastly the pyramid itself as the monumental climax. To east and west of the Great Pyramid can be seen the mound tombs of the king's relations and officials of the court. The Sphinx lies off the picture, at one side of the beginning of the passage from the Khephren valley temple. (24)

Twenty-three statues of King Khephren, hewn in green diorite, alabaster and grey schist, decorated the long hall of his valley temple, bathed in a diffused light from oblique openings in the wall above. It is shown, right, as it is today and in an artist's reconstruction; one of the most impressive interiors bequeathed to us from this time. The temple is built in massive local limestone faced inside and out with slabs of polished red granite. It is a complete realization in stone of the mortuary concept, built for the final funeral ceremonies of a god-king. (25, 26)

The massive size of the pyramids is not easily grasped. The figure towards the top of the de-surfaced strip of the Khephren pyramid (below) gives some impression. The Kheops pyramid, in the distance, had sides 250 yards long, was 158 yards high. Casing-stones were removed by Arab conquerors in later centuries, leaving the stepped effect of today. (27)

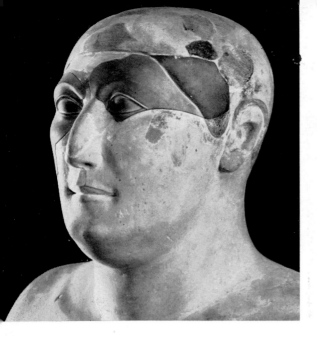

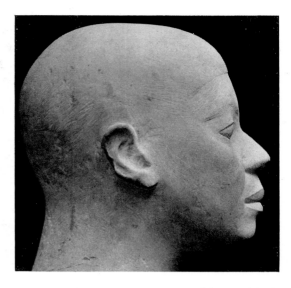

The resourceful architect and engineer, the vizier Hemon, King's Master of Works, was massive and powerful like the Great Pyramid he built. The monumental character of the impressive statue from his tomb at Giza, of which the head is shown above, reveals the same intellectual approach, the same ruthless exploration of form of which the geometrical perfection of the pyramid is the architectural counterpart. The statue is in unpainted limestone, with an inscription inlaid with coloured pastes. The inlaid eyes were gouged out by tomb robbers and have been replaced in plaster. (28)

In the 'reserve heads' above, the same uncompromising spirit is dominant as in the head of Hemon (left). Such heads as these, which are probably of a son of Kheops and his wife, perhaps a Nubian, are not tomb statues but were put in the actual burial chamber, perhaps to serve as substitutes should the bodies themselves be destroyed. The heads are of limestone, c. 2640 BC. (30, 31)

The lonely majesty of the god-kings is superbly expressed in this statue of Khephren (right) which once stood with its twenty-two companions in the long hall of his valley temple. Carved from a hard igneous stone, it achieves a complete statement of the monumental: the pose of the hands follows that of the statue of Hemon—the left flat on the thigh, the right clenched as if holding a sceptre—and establishes a balance which is without conflict. It was to be copied, especially by royal sculptors, for many generations. The high-backed throne is surmounted by the falcon-god Horus, its open wings protecting the king. The heraldic plants beneath the throne symbolize the union between Upper and Lower Egypt under the king. (29)

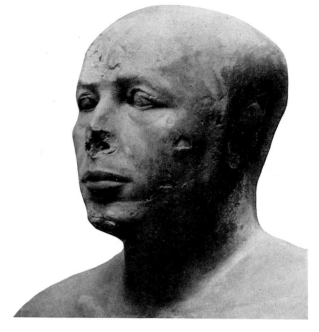

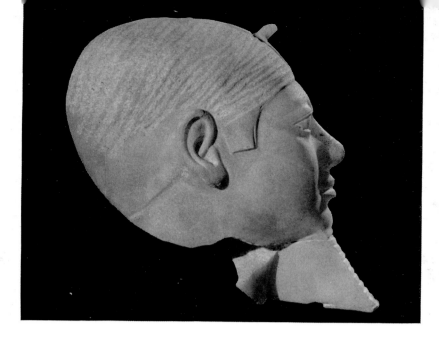

A warmer and more naturalistic feeling appears in the next generation in the bust of Ankh-haf above (c. 2600 BC). With its curiously modern appearance, this bust is unique in the Old Kingdom. The limestone has been coated with a skin of plaster, varying in thickness and painted light red—a treatment which has encouraged a more sympathetic handling of the surfaces. As vizier, Ankh-haf was undoubtedly able to commission a royal master-sculptor. (32)

The growing humanity of the Pharaoh is particularly evident in the head of the later statue (above) believed to be of Shepses-kaf (c. 2560 BC). The translucency of the alabaster softens the contours and imparts a life-like glow to the modelling. The head represents the climax of the Old Kingdom sculptural style: what has survived in royal statuary from the rest of the period, though often highly competent, shows a certain formalism. (35)

Husband and wife, composed as a group in the limestone relief below, contrast with the lonely divinity of Khephren and the separate treatment of Re-hotep and Nofret on the next page. Prince Khufu-kaf, a son of Kheops, supported by his wife, receives funerary offerings. The wife wears bracelets similar to those found in the re-burial of Hetep-heres I and a choker with spacer beads. The relief is in the austere, restrained style of the period, making its effect by purity of line. It is one of the earliest representations of such a group, from a mastaba chapel at Giza, c. 2630 BC. (33)

The god-king becomes more human. In the slate statue of My-kerinus and his wife (right) the divine, solitary majesty of the earlier statues is subtly transformed into the essential humanity of husband and wife. The simple and appealing embrace is less austere than that of the earlier relief (above); the robust, watchful features of the king contrast notably with the serenity of his wife. The work, found in the king's valley temple at Giza, c. 2565 BC, lacks its final polishing. (34)

The magnificent furniture of Queen Hetep-heres I, the mother of Kheops, was part of the wealth of work by the best artistic talent in the country which has been found in the pyramid complexes. This gold-sheathed bed furniture (above, left), at once opulent and austere, is from her re-burial at Giza (c. 2600 BC). Fine linen hangings probably served as a mosquito net; Herodotus, writing of 5th-century Egypt, mentions fish-nets being used as such. (36)

The first confident statement of the Egyptian sculptor which has survived is the double statue shown on the left, of Prince Re-hotep and Princess Nofret (c. 2660 BC). Re-hotep was probably a son of King Sneferu and the statue was found in a tomb chapel of a pyramid cemetery of the king. Husband and wife are not composed as a group, but are meant to be regarded as a pair. The sculpture shows a restrained naturalism, in the painted surfaces and inlaid eyes, but monumental tendencies in the simplified planes and underlying masses. Comparison with the later developments on the previous two pages is rewarding.

As high-priest of Heliopolis and army commander, Re-hotep occupied some of the highest offices. His wife Nofret (her name can mean either 'the good' or 'the beautiful') was a member of the court. The contrast between the brown of the man's skin and the creamy yellow of the woman's is typical. The group, found intact, gives a good idea of what a complete Egyptian statue should look like. (37)

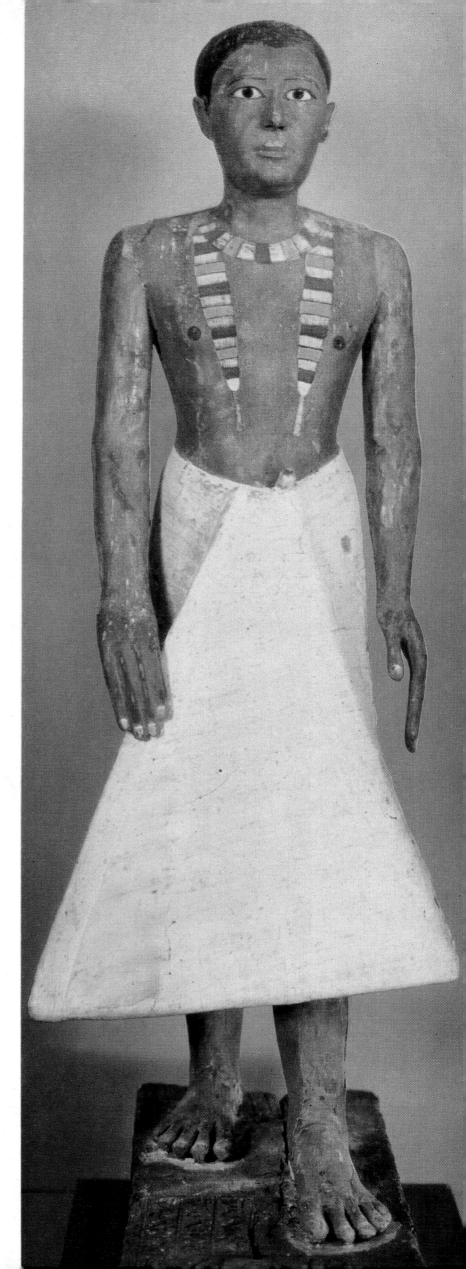

◄ **Prince Ka-wab,** son of Kheops and father of Queen Meresankh III, is shown (left) in practical costume and pose, in part of a relief from Queen Meresankh's tomb. (38)

Some of the divine size and aloof dignity of Khephren is preserved in the scene above from the reliefs found in the tomb of Queen Meresankh III at Giza (c. 2575 BC). Queen Hetep-heres II and her daughter Meresankh III, richly adorned, are shown in a skiff or punt, pulling papyrus heads. (39)

Few statues in wood have survived so complete and in their original paint as that on the right, of the Overseer of the King's Tenants, Methethy. Although dated about 2440 BC, the costume notably resembles that of Prince Ka-wab in the relief above (left), about 135 years earlier. (40)

A shadowy existence in eternity seems to have been the reward of faithful service to the god-king. Clustered round his pyramid were the tombs of his relatives, officials and priests, equipped on a more modest scale with sculpture and appointments. In later years more examples have survived of such private sculpture and of presentations to officials from the royal workshops. On this page are three, in limestone, from about 2500 BC.

An educated man, his learning shown by representing him as a scribe. His left hand holds the papyrus scroll, the other is ready to write. The body is orange-brown, the hair black, the eyes inlaid, of crystal, alabaster and bronze. The restrained, questioning expression is of great psychological charm, and the work of high artistic value. (41, below)

The steward Memy-sabu and his wife (above) contrast with the aristocratic monumentality of pl. 43. The sculptor, helped by the traditions that the wife should be smaller, has achieved a natural pose and an expression of an unaffected, personal relationship. The peasant faces, modest perhaps and somewhat coarse, suggest the beginnings of a vital *genre* style. (42)

The Overseer of the Granary, Iruka-Ptah, is represented (above) in the old tradition, with his wife and child on much smaller scale. (43)

The glory of the sculpture
of the period around 2500 BC lies in the reliefs that decorated the walls
of the royal temples. A few fragments only have survived, but in these
the astonishing delicacy and minuteness of the carving and the sensitive drawing give an impression of supreme technical and artistic
mastery.

The public life of the king was recorded in a series of scenes
which decorated in limestone the walls of the funerary temple of
King Sahu-re at Abusir, c. 2540 BC. Here the king is shown (below)
shooting with bow and arrow. Above is a detail of the intricate
patterning of the king's pleated kilt from another relief. (45, 46)

The royal hunt scene, a fragment of which is shown above, is
from the funerary temple of King Weser-kaf at Saqqara, c. 2560 BC.
Birds fly and perch among the papyrus of the marshes. (44)

Alert with intelligence, the profile of King Pepy I above is from a life-size statue of the king and his son. It is copper-sheathed, the only surviving example of copper sculpture from this period and too corroded, perhaps, to give a reliable impression. The king's crown, probably of gold or gilded metal, is missing. The eyes are inlaid. (47)

A god-king kneels. In the earliest known example of its kind (c. 2360 BC), King Pepy I makes libation offerings to another god. The slate statuette is exceptional for its lively realism—arms and legs have been completely freed from stone fillings and the splayed-out toes and grasping hands have carefully finished nails. The alert, lively expression of the face is enhanced by the inlaid eyes. The hole in the headdress was for the insertion of a guardian cobra, probably of gold but now missing. (48, right)

The tremendous human effort

and expenditure of material resources required for the building of the Giza pyramids were not repeated for the tombs of later kings. The successors of Kheops, Khephren and Mykerinus, whose pyramids were built at Abusir and Saqqara, abandoned the grandiose conception and giant masonry of their predecessors. This decline in size of the Pharaoh's tomb coincided with a decrease in the divine stature of the Pharaoh himself and a rise in importance of the worship of the sun-god Re and of its centre at Heliopolis. The Pharaoh was now thought to be son of the sun-god—according to a myth of the time—by the wife of a priest of Heliopolis.

The pyramid field at Abusir

is reconstructed in the model on the left. It contains, from left to right, the pyramids of Nefer-ir-ka-re, Ni-weser-re and Sahu-re. Approaching them, from the river's edge, run elevated, covered stone causeways, by which the body of the king could be conveyed from a valley temple at the landing-stage. (49)

To worship the sun-god,

the kings of this period erected sun-temples, after the model of the sanctuary at Heliopolis. The best preserved of them is that of Ni-weser-re at Abu Gurob (c. 2500 BC). It can be seen in the distance, in the pyramid field (pl. 49), and is reconstructed in the model on this page. The architect has made use of the rising ground to build a temple group on two levels, linked by a sloping causeway. The sanctuary, on the lower level, consists of a walled enclosure, 330 feet long and 250 feet wide, containing store-rooms and corridors with finely sculptured scenes. The ritual of the sun-cult was practised in the courts of the upper level, dominated by the squat obelisk on its tall base. As a bizarre feature, but a practical interpretation of the myth, there stands outside the temple walls a mud-brick barque, waiting to carry Re on his journey across the heavens. (50)

A king was a ruler from birth.

The child, though on its mother's knee, is shown as a miniature adult, regarded as a king from birth. It is King Pepy II, nursed by Queen Ankhnes-mery-re, c. 2350 BC, and is in alabaster. (51)

The teeming, busy life of the people

continued throughout the exotic first flowering of Egyptian civilization we have seen in these pages. While the giant tombs were planned and constructed, while the king's workshops were busy with sculptures which would rest in them, while the priests were practising and developing the religion of the god-kings and the cult of the dead, the eternal Egyptian peasant was at work—forever toiling in the fields, never far from sudden plague and famine, driven by hunger and superstition.

The private tombs of the period around 2400 BC were decorated with complete scenes that have been preserved, carved in relief and painted in bright colours. They give us a vivid and intimate picture of the pastoral life of the day—the work of a settled agricultural civilization, sowing and reaping its crops, tending its animals on the farm, growing its fruits, grinding its corn and preparing its food and drink.

They show us also that the Ancient Egyptians could play and live the good life of the country, enjoying field sports in marsh and stream, country crafts, music, dancing and games. They illustrate manners and customs which—while his superiors sought the benefits of eternity, were vanquished and arose again, wrote precepts of conduct, struggled for power—have brought the people virtually unscathed through five thousand years of changing history.

The work in the fields is richly illustrated in this relief in colour from the tomb of the City Governor, Mereruka, at Saqqara (c. 2360 BC), where some of the finest reliefs of this period have been found. On the extreme left of all three rows, facing left, are offering-bearers carrying the first-fruits of the field. In the top row, asses are being assembled and loaded with panniers for carrying sheaves of corn ('Gee up!' is the meaning of some of the glyphs above, 'Ho-ho you slow coach!'); on the right the ass, after showing its characteristic reluctance, is finally driven off. In the centre row (left) flax is harvested and bound; on the right, corn reapers work in time to a vertical flute ('Oh, folks, hurry up!' they say, and 'This barley is very fine, O thou fellow-worker'). A fat quail is on the ground. In the bottom row, the owner and his sandal-bearer watch the sheaves of corn being thrown into a stack; labourers with pitchforks toss the sheaves on to the threshing floor, where the corn is trodden out by goats, asses and oxen. A caption reads: 'Make a going around with them!' (52)

Attendants minister to the dead Queen Nebet, wife of Wenis (c. 2430 BC), in the relief below. A dwarf handmaiden has charge of the Queen's sandals. (53)

Youth at play is shown in these sketches (left) from reliefs also in Mereruka's tomb. Above, girls play 'the vine'—a swinging game, and learn to dance with mirrors and castanets. In the centre, boys play a kind of pick-a-back, a tug-of-war and a kind of leap-frog. Below are shown endurance games, one of which, involving kicking, is practised in the Faiyum to this day. (54)

The fruits of the earth were still supplied symbolically for the comfort of the dead. In the relief (below, left) from the tomb of the Vizier Ptah-hotep at Saqqara (c. 2450 BC), girls representing his several estates bring offerings in kind. (55)

Bird trapping and the grape harvest are illustrated by reliefs (opposite, left, and below, right) from the tomb of Nefer-her-en-Ptah at Saqqara, c. 2450 BC. The birds, rising in alarm, make a lively scene; the grapes are picked from a pergola into the baskets. (56, 57)

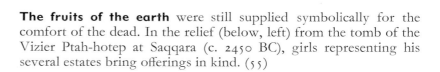

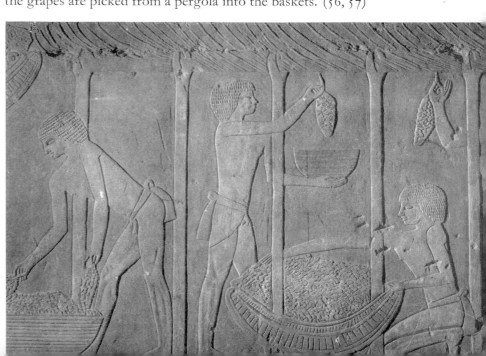

The craftsmen were skilled workers in copper, as well as in stone. This group of copper vessels, and the offering table, are from the tomb of Idi, c. 2300 BC. The libation vessels with spouts recall some of the forms from the Royal Cemetery at Ur, while the flat rectangular dishes may be intended as symbolic food. (58)

A porter carrying a trussed gazelle, modelled in terracotta, probably about 2360 BC. It is reproduced (right) for the first time. (59)

'Good speech is more hidden' said a sage of the time, 'than the green gem, yet one finds it in maids among the millstones.' This limestone statuette (below) of a maidservant grinding corn dates from about 2500 BC. (60)

Servants at their daily tasks, carved in stone and set in the tombs, served by magic the needs of their dead masters—and are evidence of the spreading downwards of the patronage which began as gifts from the king to a favoured courtier. The grant of a share in the after-life, or at least of a kind of memorial, was an encouragement of some substance to faithful service. But in the carving of these minor though lively works of art, the artist was released from the social and religious conventions which produced the athletic and well-nourished élite facing eternity with such composure. A slightly sardonic attitude accompanies these glimpses into a humbler world.

The potter of Ne-inpu-kau is a masterpiece of almost brutal realism. The undernourished figure of the potter as he squats before his wheel, with his large extremities, his gaunt face, his bony knees and the ribs sticking out under his chin, is far removed from the representations of the aristocracy. Limestone, c. 2400 BC. (61)

The first flowering in Ancient Egypt

CYRIL ALDRED

The Beginnings of Human Settlement

THE RETREAT of the northern ice-cap, and with it the Atlantic rain-storms in the later phases of the Old Stone Age, produced a progressive desiccation over the Eastern Mediterranean. The park and grass lands of North Africa were transformed into shrinking regions of scrub and pasturage around failing water courses and scattered oases. This process continued well into historic times assisted by man-made devastation, by the overgrazing of thin pastures by herds of goats, and later by the camel, until a complete aridity had crept northwards to reach the shores of the Mediterranean.

With this climatic change, there came an alteration in the habits of the ancient nomads who had roved at will over the region, hunting the game that abounded in the forests and savannahs. They have left traces of their passage in the worked flints of characteristic palaeolithic types that can be picked up on what is now high desert; and some hint of their hunting life may be gleaned from the rock drawings of food animals such as the antelope, elephant and Barbary sheep that they scratched in wadis all over the region (fig. 1). In their search for dwindling water-supplies, both animals and man were now forced into a closer proximity until the greatest concentration was reached on the verges of swamps and alluvium in the valley of the Nile, and it was at such a point of time that the first steps must have been taken in the domestication of some animals such as the pig, dog and long-horned cattle.

This natural process of corralling men from a wide area into a shrunken river valley produced a mixed race at a very early stage so that Hamites, Berbers and Semites mingled their blood and speech before the dawn of history, though the Egyptian race was to be reinforced in historic times by infiltrations and migrations of these same components from the Sudan, Libya and the Levant.

The transition from a food-hunting to a food-producing economy in this region cannot have been any sudden event. In prehistoric times the Nile Valley wore a very different appearance from what it has today and one would now need to go very far south in the Sudan to find similar conditions and a comparable flora and fauna. The early settlers found a valley full of swamps and pools left by the uncontrolled inundation of the Nile every year, in which vast thickets of reeds and sedge grew over a man's height and acted as cover to every kind of pond fowl and freshwater fish, besides hippopotami and less desirable creatures such as crocodiles. The elephant, lion, ass, ibex, Barbary sheep, antelope, wild ox and smaller desert game frequented the wadis that flanked the river, since up to late historic times these ancient water courses still resembled parkland with low shrubs and flowering meadows. Even today infrequent rainstorms far out over the desert can flood these same dried valleys, producing in a short time an abundant ephemeral flora with its attendant insect and animal life. It is probable therefore that there was not much compulsion on these first settlers to change their way of life radically, and they doubtless enjoyed a mixed economy, trapping birds and fish among the pools, hunting for game in the wadis and exploiting such marsh vegetation as papyrus and the wild Abyssinian banana (*Musa ensete*), and such catch crops as barley or emmer wheat dibbled crudely into chance-flooded ground after rainstorms, in much the same manner as that employed by the primitive Hadendowa and Abebdeh of the Sudan in recent times. While such a crop was growing the family would be obliged to squat in the vicinity and adapt its pastoral and hunting life to more settled conditions.

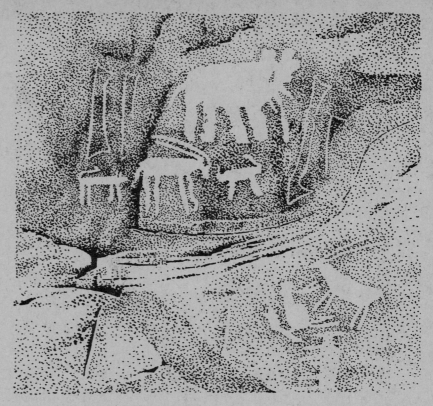

Predynastic rock-drawing of food animals from Upper Egypt. (fig. 1)

The Change from Hunting to Farming

At some stage in this misty past a group of these squatters must have taken the momentous step of deciding to stay put and to grow these cereals as a main food crop. Perhaps over-exploitation of the marsh plants caused a local shortage of such food. The papyrus and the *ensete* would certainly be eradicated by the draining of swamps in order to grow wheat and barley. Such food-grains and the techniques of raising and harvesting them were almost certainly introduced into Egypt from an Asiatic, perhaps Natufian, source. What was novel in their cultivation in Egypt was that there only the most primitive equipment was sufficient to grow bumper crops. The inundations of the wayward Nile, not yet confined by a stable climate and irrigation works into a more or less predictable channel, would devastate tracts of land leaving behind a rich mud on which grain needed merely to be scattered and trodden in by foot or hooves in order to grow. The Nile flood rises in July with the melting of the snows in the Abyssinian uplands and subsides in November when seeds can germinate and ripen in the gentle heat of winter and spring. The first Egyptian farmers therefore hardly needed to till and manure their fields; such work was done for them by a beneficent Nile.

The growing of cereals on a larger scale was the first stage in a revolution that was to replace a food-gathering nomadic existence by an urban civilization based on agriculture, for grain could not only be grown by man at his will and without great effort, it could also be readily stored on the dry desert margins. Not only need there be no immediate shortage of food, but more food could be produced than the local community required for its needs. By upsetting the balance of nature, Man was momentarily relieved from the constant search for the means of subsistence and had leisure in which to specialize in various skills. It enabled him, for instance, to develop that complementary branch of agriculture, the raising and breeding of domestic animals.

But this new and artificial mode of life did not solve all the problems of Man's existence; it merely altered the rhythm of their occurrence. More food encouraged the production of more people and their animals. More land had to be cultivated to grow more grain and a start was made on a spiralling process that still continues today. The annual inundation of the Nile had to be tamed, its prodigality distributed over wider tracts of ground by irrigation works, and its fertilizing silt spread on fields newly won from the desert. The draining, clearing and irrigating of land in the Nile Valley was most effective when done on a large scale, and co-operative effort in such work would become inevitable as the settlements on the banks of the Nile increased in size and numbers. This co-operative effort would be particularly needed at the critical moments when the floods began to rise and fall and hard and extensive labour had to be exercised within a short space of time. The transformation of the destructive power of the inundation into a beneficent force accustomed the Egyptians to an organized way of life and led to the emergence of local political institutions to direct such enterprises and ensure their success. The logical outcome of this process was the unification of the entire country under a single government as small families of settlers gradually grew into village communities and these in turn grouped themselves into larger districts as the exploitation of the Valley became more intensive.

The first steps in harnessing the Nile Flood, in developing a thriving agriculture and creating a political system to ensure the persistence of the artificial conditions thus secured, were all taken by the prehistoric Egyptians.

The Early Predynastic Period

The various stages in this long struggle towards civilization can be traced at different places in Upper and Lower Egypt, where excavations have revealed cultures of distinctive types which may be grouped into two broad categories. An earlier phase has been identified covering much of the material remains as found at the neolithic sites of Deir Tasa in the South, and Faiyum 'A' and Merimda in the North, and extending through the Chalcolithic cultures of El-Badari and El-Amra, again in the South. The later manifestations of this prehistoric culture are sometimes referred to as the Early Predynastic Period. To the Middle and Late Predynastic Periods belongs the second category of material which has been excavated at sites near El-Gerza in Lower Egypt and notably at Naqada in Upper Egypt. The name 'Late Gerzean' has been applied to a common version of this culture which extended over both Upper and Lower Egypt just before the historic period.

From the material remains of this first phase of prehistoric cultures, we are able to build up a picture of the early Egyptians, and to see how they gradually adapted themselves to a settled agricultural way of life which at the end of the period, towards 3600 BC, can have differed little from the culture of the pagan tribes of the Upper Nile today. They appear to have been a slight race of medium height with long narrow skulls, brown skin and dark wavy hair, though their physical remains are scanty except in the South. We find them camping at first on the verges of the marshes under the protection of reed shelters or windbreaks; but at Merimda in the North there was a huddle of low oval structures each built of lumps of mud with a pot let into the rammed earth floor to collect the rain that leaked from the thatch. This primitive village with its rudimentary houses and a communal granary consisting of mat-lined pits suggests a distinct social advance even if its standard of comfort was not high. The remains from Faiyum 'A' date from c. 5000 BC.

Both wheat and barley were grown from Neolithic times. Wooden sickles, set with flint teeth, and a flail for threshing have survived from the Faiyum 'A' sites where storage pits were also found lined with mats. Querns and mealing-stones from all sites show that milling was a household industry. Basketry was practised as early as the Faiyum 'A' period, where besides platters, a notable boat-shaped container has come to light *(fig. 3)*. Mats were woven of grasses and rushes and used for lining both grave and grain pits. Another textile, a coarse kind of linen found also among the Faiyum 'A' deposits, shows that the growing and processing of flax was understood even from the earliest days, and this pre-supposes that spindle whorls and looms also existed, though the latter have not been recovered.

The technique of weaving linen improves steadily throughout the period. Garments were also made from animal skins sewn together by means of bone needles, and skill in softening and tanning hides is evident at Badari. A remarkable improvement in objects of luxury and personal adornment can also be traced from the perforated stone and shell disk beads of Faiyum 'A' and the stone bead necklaces and girdles of the Badarians. Bracelets of ivory and shell are also common. Eye paint made from green malachite is found at all predynastic periods and the stone palettes on which the cosmetic was ground with a stone muller becomes standard equipment for nearly every burial of note. The wild castor plant furnished oil for cleansing and softening the skin. Combs were made from bone or ivory and in Amratian times are decorated with figures of birds or animals *(fig. 2)*.

(fig. 2)

Tools and weapons were almost exclusively of stone and flint. Arrows were tipped with bone or flint points. The throw-stick was

known in a form that persisted almost unchanged into Pharaonic times, and was probably employed, as then, for fowling. A mace with a disk-shaped stone head is common in the South after the unwarlike Badarian period, but begins to be replaced by the northern pear-shaped head at the end of the Amratian period. A fish-tailed lance-head is characteristic of the deposits of Amratian times, but cannot have been particularly effective as a weapon and may have been an amulet (pl. 2).

At this period, food appears to have been fairly plentiful. Dogs, goats, sheep, oxen, geese, and in the North, pigs, had been domesticated, and game, fish and fowl abounded. It has been suggested that grain was boiled for porridge as well as baked for bread. Cooking vessels and food containers were made of pottery and this industry shows a steady advance from the coarse clay cups and bowls of Faiyum 'A' and the ill-fired ware of Deir Tasa, through the fine thin-walled bowls of Badari with their combed and polished surfaces (pl. 1) to the red burnished pottery of the Amratians, notable for their predilection for fanciful shapes and white slip decoration or carbonized surface

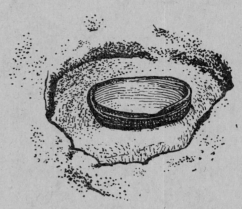

Boatshaped basket found in a storage pit in the Faiyum (c. 5000 BC). (fig. 3)

variegation (pl. 2). In Amratian times also there first appear in the South vases hollowed out of stone, though archetypes are known from the earlier northern site of Merimda. These are the forerunners of one of the most characteristic products of Ancient Egypt at all periods of her history.

Among these objects of utility should also be included a number of ivory statuettes mostly of women and doubtless included in burial deposits to serve magically the needs of the deceased. The earliest of such figurines comes from Badari and even at this remote period, a dimple above each buttock is represented by a shallow drill-hole in precisely the same fashion as was employed on much more sophisticated examples of three thousand years later *(fig. 4)*.

The intellectual and spiritual life of these early dwellers on the Nile can never be known to us. That they believed in a kind of hereafter for some members of the community is evident from the many burials that have been found on hut sites and in the later cemeteries at the various centres. The body is usually crouched on its side as though in sleep or awaiting re-birth and the presence of worldly goods shows that the after-life was not expected to differ greatly from the one that had been pursued on earth. Some of their beliefs may be glimpsed as a tenuous thread in the warp of later Pharaonic religion. The earliest Egyptians, dependent upon the rains for their existence, appear to have worshipped sky and star deities. Their leaders were doubtless rainmakers and, as in the Sudan in recent times, were probably killed ceremonially, perhaps by drowning or dismemberment, when their powers began to wane. Vague references to such ideas and similar primitive concepts may be found in the later pyramid texts where they constitute some of the wilder poetry of that compendium of ancient beliefs.

The political system under which these people lived must also be surmised. Probably communities were small, self-supporting and comparatively isolated around village centres: but the presence of copper pins and glazed steatite beads (steatite is a kind of greyish-green soapstone) in Badarian and Amratian times suggests that trade was carried on with more advanced cultures elsewhere.

The Later Predynastic Period

The essentially African culture of the Early Predynastic Period might have remained sterile at this level, as it did apparently in the Sudan, where a Badarian type of culture persisted for a much longer time, if it had not been fertilized by contacts with a different civilization coming from Asia. During this period, some significant changes were introduced from without. The use of copper becomes more widespread, suggesting closer connections by trade or expansion with Sinai where copper ore was mined. Henceforth that metal becomes commonplace for tools and weapons, though flint continued to be employed in Egypt for a very long time for such specialized purposes as the grinding of stone vessels, the carving of ivory and the reaping of grain.

But there is also evidence for influences from further abroad. Three Mesopotamian cylinder seals of the Late Uruk or 'Proto-literate' Period have been found in Egypt, one definitely in a Gerzean grave at Naqada, and from now on the imprinting of clay seals by rolling incised cylinders over them becomes the normal Egyptian practice until the introduction of the stamp seal 1500 years later. Certain fantastic animal motifs in contemporary Mesopotamian art also creep into Egyptian decoration such as the device of two intertwined serpopards, the winged griffin and the interlaced snakes (pl. 13). Such ideas were alien to the Egyptian imagination which was sober and more logical in its creative utterances, and the innovations had a relatively short life; but their very adoption shows the force of their impact.

The most celebrated of such foreign-inspired objects is the ivory handle of a flint knife found at Gebel el-Arak and now in the Louvre (pl. 9, 10). This is carved on one side with the figure of a Mesopotamian type of hero subduing two lions. The same unusual theme appears in a wall painting on a Late Gerzean shrine at Hierakonpolis which is one of the earliest brick-built structures in the South. The reverse side of the ivory shows ships with characteristically vertical prows and sterns rather like the *belems* of the Tigris.

Another and rather less transient influence is to be seen in Late Gerzean times with the introduction of a monumental style of building based upon mud-brick. Architecture gradually abandons a form of construction in perishable vegetable materials such as reeds, papyrus stalks, palm branches and rush matting, and adopts instead a purely

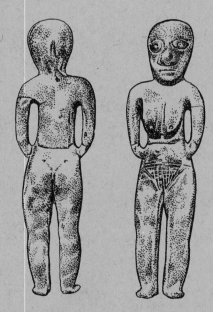

Badarian ivory figurine of a woman (c. 4000 BC). The dimple above each buttock, represented by a shallow drill-hole, can still be seen in more sophisticated work of three thousand years later. (fig. 4)

tectonic form determined by the use of sun-dried mud-brick struck from rectangular wooden moulds. This technique with its emphasis upon the pilaster and the recessed panel has some affinities with that employed in Mesopotamia where a long tradition of building in brick had existed.

Even more important is the apparently sudden emergence of a graphic method of recording speech which is beyond a merely pictographic stage. Hieroglyphic writing, which first appears on the slate palettes in Late Gerzean times, already uses ideograms and phonograms, concepts which had developed in Mesopotamia from a more rudimentary system.

The introduction of writing in Egypt coincides with a strengthening of the Semitic element in its culture at the expense of its Hamitic and Berber components. Perhaps the two phenomena were interdependent, the Semitic aspects of the literary language becoming

more dominant because the system of writing in origin had been devised to record a Semitic manner of speech. Nevertheless, there is a southward drift of people into the southern culture zones at this period which affected the physical character of the population, the long-headed Hamitic type being modified by a broader-headed mountain people perhaps from Anatolia or Syria.

All these innovations, however, have no appearance of being imposed by conquest. The Gerzean culture in the South is a development of the Amratian with its predominantly African character. There was not so much the imposition of foreign forms, as the infiltration of new ideas and techniques. The Gebel el-Arak knife-handle has a distinctly alien appearance, yet traditional Egyptian types of boat and animals also appear on it. The cylinder seal as employed in Egypt was of wood as well as stone and is incised with inscriptions rather than decorative designs. Similarly, the hieroglyphs are pictures of objects seen with Egyptian eyes and rendered with the characteristic observation of the Egyptian who could reduce a natural form to a heraldic device better than most ancient peoples. In short, what now permeated the native cultures were principles and ideas rather more than style. A foreign 'know-how' was quickly seized upon and enthusiastically adapted to Egyptian conditions by a people ripe for change.

All the evidence is that this spread of foreign influence came from the North, but our knowledge of conditions in the Delta at this period is lamentably scanty. It may be that the innovations came through an intensification of trading in the Eastern Mediterranean with the development of the sea-going ship. This invention was doubtless made in a large timber area, which Egypt was not, and it has been plausibly suggested that Byblos in the Lebanon was the most likely region where boats able to sail on the coastal waters of the Levant were developed. Wherever the sea-going ship may have been invented, the Egyptians were as quick to adapt it to their own uses as they were at a much later date to exploit the possibilities of the horse-drawn chariot, another foreign importation. The opening up of the Eastern Mediterranean by shipping must have increased considerably the number of contacts between various peoples in the area and may have stimulated the almost coeval flowering of the civilizations of Crete and Egypt.

The Gerzean Culture

The character of the Gerzean culture of Lower Egypt has emerged from the study of deposits at Gerza and other sites in the Faiyum, and its southern version has been found permeating and superseding the Amratian culture at the vast cemeteries of Naqada and Ballas near Koptos. The transition to the early dynastic style of historic Egypt is thereafter progressive (pl. 3).

The Gerzeans are generally similar in their Mediterranean racial type to their predecessors but their skulls are broader and their faces longer. Their pottery includes wavy-handled jars, similar to those found in Palestine, and a light coloured ware, usually pink or buff, painted with linear decorations in red (pl. 5). The motifs include triangular hills, flamingoes, ibexes, the *ensete* plant and human figures *(fig. 5)*. Some pots

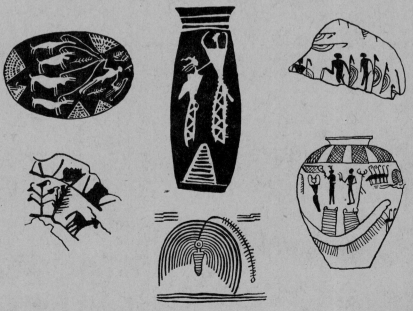

Plant and figurine motifs from Gerzean pots (c. 3400 BC). The motifs include triangular hills, ibexes, the ensete *plant (bottom row, centre), ships, a hunter with his dogs on leash, and warriors. (fig. 5)*

(fig. 6)

are decorated with designs that Petrie has interpreted as shrine-like cabins and emblems representing deities, but other authorities reject this explanation. Clearer evidence for the design of prehistoric boats comes from a fragment of textile from Gebelein now in Turin (pl. 4) where ships with rowers and steersmen as well as cabins are depicted. Other Gerzean pots are shaped and decorated to simulate the stone jars and vases that now become common, probably because the introduction of a cranked brace with weights acting as a fly-wheel and able to take expendable flint borers made the hollowing-out of such vessels much less arduous. *Fig. 6* shows this tool, the *hem*, as a hieroglyph. The knapping of flint implements achieved an unrivalled perfection and is particularly evident in the curved knives of thin section with regularly chipped blades rippled like ribbed sea sand (pl. 9, 10).

An alkaline vitreous glaze which had been used sporadically in Badarian times to coat small trade objects such as beads is now made use of to produce a unique material, Egyptian faience, which had an unfading popularity until Arabic times. This substance was apparently invented and developed by a people living on the western borders of the Delta and was named after them.

In the later phases of the Gerzean period from about 3400 to 3200 BC there are signs of a more intensive political activity and it is supposed that during this period a struggle for predominance arose between the rulers of Upper and Lower Egypt. It is at this stage that the geographical differences between Upper and Lower Egypt become important historically—Upper Egypt consisting of the narrow valley that stretched northwards from the rocky barrier of the First Cataract in the south, and Lower Egypt comprising the Delta in the north.

The Physical Environment

(fig. 7)

Upper Egypt, confined to the strip of land bordering the Nile for most of its length between cliffs, presented a rather less hospitable environment than the broader horizons of the Delta and the Faiyum depression. The Upper Egyptian could see the hostile desert hemming in the cultivation on both sides and knew that only his unrelenting toil kept the red sands from swallowing the black fertile land he had so strenuously won. His work of irrigating and draining these verges was most effective when performed communally and he early learnt to co-operate with his neighbours in this task. The Nile waterway that flowed through the entire region assisted the process of cohesion in another way: it provided an easy means of communication with every part of the area.

(fig. 8)

Lower Egypt, on the other hand, was a broad extent of rivulets, creeks, and marshes isolating tracts of meadowlands and the wider pastures on the eastern and western borders where flocks of goats and sheep grazed and cattle were bred. Its Mediterranean climate was wetter and less harsh. It was a lush region of vineyards and gardens: fish and fowl were plentiful and deposits of salt for preserving them were near at hand. The broad stream of the Nile which unified Upper Egypt, by dividing anciently into twelve branches and innumerable rivulets, parcelled Lower Egypt into a number of principalities clustered around individual village or town centres. While Upper Egypt looked northwards to its neighbour, Lower Egypt faced the Mediterranean. Its seaports had contacts with the lands of the Levant and the Aegean. Its population was more cosmopolitan, with Libyans on the west and Semites on the east. In early days it seems to have been culturally more advanced than the rustic South; in historic times it maintained its lead as the centre of the arts and crafts, probably attracting skilled workers from near and far. Unfortunately much of its past is lost beneath vast accumulations of Nile silt and we are obliged to assess its achievement not so much by the forms that have come down to us, as by the outline of the gaps that their absence has made.

It would, however, be wrong to exaggerate the differences between the two regions. They shared a common language and the same material and spiritual culture. Certain fundamental religious concepts, such as that a divine power was immanent in certain men and animals, were accepted by both, even though the exact form of deity varied somewhat from place to place. The underlying unity of thought and feeling in all Egyptians is evident from the way the civilization of the whole land blossomed profusely as soon as the two parts were rejoined in vigour and purpose after periods of schism.

Nevertheless, there is a kind of antithesis between Upper and Lower Egypt, which the Egyptians themselves recognized by referring to their country as the Two Lands, an antithesis which particularly appealed to them since they saw the world as essentially a duality.

While the North was the cultural leader, it was the South that provided the disciplined political direction. The basic unit of government in both regions was the community centred around a village with its local version of one of the universal deities, and under the leadership of some chieftain. These districts or *nomes* were the smallest particles into which the country split in times of disorder. But we can detect, even in Late Gerzean times, the emergence of a pattern that was to be repeated again and again in Egyptian history: it was the ambition of Southern princes that led them to extend their sway over ever larger tracts of the Valley until they had created a unity out of the former anarchy, one kingdom out of a conglomeration of rival districts. It is the character of these conquests in historic periods that may enable us to understand how this unification was achieved at this time.

The Transition to the Dynastic Age

Vivid evidence for the political activity that created Dynastic Egypt comes from a number of votive palettes and mace-heads which have been recovered from various sites, notably from Hierakonpolis, the ancient Southern capital. The most significant of these carved objects, in fact one of the most important monuments to have survived from Ancient Egypt since it shows in embryo nearly all the characteristics of Pharaonic art, is the slate palette of King Narmer (or perhaps Meri-nar) (pl. 13, 14). On each side, at the top, the name of the king may be read within a palace building: certain other explanatory hieroglyphic labels also appear which though obscure in meaning render this one of the first documents in the written history of Egypt and emphasize that we now have to do with a civilized state. The king's name is flanked by heads of Hathor, a primeval cow and mother goddess, at whose shrine this palette was probably dedicated; and we can see in the woman's face emerging from the cow's head the epiphany of the gods in human form that seems to come simultaneously with the appearance of these early kings.

On the obverse of the palette, the larger-than-life figure of Narmer is shown wearing the *deshret*, the Red Crown of the Delta cities of Buto and Sais, later the characteristic headgear of the Pharaoh as King of Lower Egypt. (The Red and the White Crowns are shown as hieroglyphs in *fig. 7* and *8*.) He is preceded by his priest and four standard-bearers carrying fetishes: his sandal-bearer and foot-washer brings up the rear of the procession which is inspecting rows of corpses whose bound arms and severed heads proclaim them to be native rebels. The place of slaughter has been identified from the glyphs above the bodies as Buto. The central register of this highly organized design shows a circular depression around which are disposed two serpo-pards and their attendants. This enigmatic foreign-inspired device has been explained as representing the theme of union. At the bottom of the palette the king as a strong bull breaks down a township, with a large palace or temple and smaller houses within, and tramples upon a foreign rebel, probably a Libyan.

The reverse shows Narmer, accompanied by his sandal-bearer, wearing the White Crown of Aphroditopolis, the *hedjet*, which was to become the emblematic headgear of the Pharaoh as King of Upper Egypt, clubbing a submissive enemy in a composition that now enters the repertoire of dynastic art and persists for the next three millennia. Above the victim a rebus seems to read 'Pharaoh the incarnation of the hawk-god Horus, with his strong right arm leads captive the Marsh-dwellers (Hau Nebut).' In the lower register two spread-eagled corpses of foreigners are distinguished by glyphs which probably represent the rectangular buttressed fortress of western Palestine and the 'Kite' sanctuaries of Transjordania. This palette is usually regarded as commemorating the victory of the Southern king over the North and the uniting of the two lands under one ruler. Since Narmer appears here as the King of both Upper and Lower Egypt, he has been identified as the semi-legendary Menes, the first Pharaoh.

This palette, however, has a rather deeper significance. If it commemorates anything at all, it is the divine might of Narmer himself who dominates the scenes, either as man, hawk or bull. He triumphs over rebellious subjects, as well as the foreigners on the borders of Egypt, over Asiatics, Marsh-dwellers, and Libyans.

The Ascendancy of the Pharaoh

Precisely the same theme is expressed in rather a different fashion on a votive mace-head belonging to Scorpion, perhaps the immediate predecessor of Narmer, who vigorously expanded the Southern

Kingdom (pl. 16). This object, also found at Hierakonpolis, shows the king at an agricultural rite. In the background are the royal standards with, hanging from them, lapwings and bows. In its fully developed form we meet this same idea as early as a statue-base of Djoser of Dynasty III where the king is shown treading upon nine bows symbolizing the foreign neighbours of Egypt and being worshipped by docile lapwings representing the populace of Egypt. At this early stage there is no distinction between the people of Egypt and foreigners who are both shown regarding the Pharaoh as their lord and subjugator.

In the past there has been perhaps too great a readiness to emphasize the isolation of Egyptian civilization as though it were out of the main-stream of Eastern Mediterranean culture; but it is doubtful whether future research will be able to sustain such an attitude. In more documented times we can see that the Pharaoh exercised a profound influence over adjacent lands. At his accession and jubilees he received Magi-like gifts from foreign ambassadors who begged from him the gift of life that he was supposed to bestow upon their peoples. The early dynastic monuments suggest that this relationship existed from the very first, probably as a legacy of Asiatic contacts in Gerzean times, and perhaps we should not be far wrong in regarding Ancient Egyptian civilization as a specialized branch of a common culture in the Eastern Mediterranean during the Bronze Age.

The size and importance of the king upon these early monuments clearly show that he was regarded as a god rather than the human agent of a god, and it is in this that Egypt presents us with a typically African solution to problems of government. Civilizations had arisen in river valleys elsewhere in the Near East and enjoyed economies based on agriculture. They too had unifying systems of communication and knew the art of writing and keeping records. Yet they remained a congeries of rival city-states, each jockeying for an uneasy supremacy, while Egypt displayed a national conformity under the leadership of a deity. For the Pharaoh is the classic example of the god incarnate as king. The concept comes from that layer in Egyptian culture that belongs to Africa where similar rulers still exist. A tangible god whose sole authority could produce results by the exercise of the divine attributes of 'creative utterance', 'understanding' and 'justice' appealed particularly to the Egyptian psyche.

The prehistoric rain-maker chieftain who was thought to keep his people, their crops and their cattle, in health and prosperity by exercising a magic power over the weather, is thus transformed into the Pharaoh, able to sustain and protect the nation and having command over the Nile in a rainless land. The never-failing inundations of the river were more predictable in their occurrences, though not in their volume, and therefore more amenable to control than the weather. If the environment in which the Egyptian lived was therefore largely constant and determinable, it is small wonder that his conception of reality should be so essentially static.

It would seem that the organization necessary for undertaking large-scale land reclamation and irrigation could not come into being until the political machinery of centralized rule under a sole king had been devised. Menes was traditionally accredited with the damming of the Nile to control flood-waters. It is probable that the unification of Egypt and the dramatic change it brought about in co-ordinating and accelerating all kinds of communal enterprises, seemed in retrospect miraculous. The kingship and the welfare of the land would then be regarded as indivisible.

The precedents created by Narmer were followed thereafter by his successors, not as a recipe for success but as part of the cosmic order. The tradition was reinforced by the Osirian myth which taught that an ancient divine king suffered death and dismemberment, but arose from the dead to become king and judge in the Underworld, while his son Horus ruled in his stead on earth. When each Pharaoh, who during his lifetime was regarded as the incarnation of Horus, died and mingled with his ancestors to become Osiris, it was his son, the new Horus, who stood in his place. The Egyptian world was created anew in the old pattern with each change of king.

Thus Egyptian society was itself like a pyramid, thrusting its gilded capstone into the sky, and we shall find during the Old Kingdom that nearly all the manifestations of culture are concerned with the cult of the living and the dead king on whom the welfare of the people was thought to rest. This is the explanation for the enormous works and the tremendous economic activity which the entire nation undertook for what would otherwise appear as the sole benefit of their rulers.

The Archaic Period—Dynasties I and II

The first unification of Egypt was the work of the traditional Menes, perhaps Narmer, who recognized the existence of two Egypts, the North and the South, and made himself the king of both, thus joining in his own person two opposing forces. By an act of re-organization rather than conquest, he produced order out of a warring duality. The pattern he invented had such a sanctified authority that his successors never had any inclination to change it. We can see, for instance, that the perceptual representation of the human form evident in the relief on the Narmer palette—the head, hips and legs shown in profile, the eye and thorax from the front—was regarded as adequate thereafter for drawing, painting and relief as long as Pharaonic art lasted.

But while many of the institutions of kingship remained frozen at the moment of their creation, not every form of expression could receive such final utterance in a rapidly developing world. It was the achievement of the first four dynasties that they worked out many of the most valid forms of Pharaonic culture at a time when the whole of the Near East seems to have been in a kind of ferment as the different civilizations explored the fuller possibilities of the brave new world of the Bronze Age. The early dynasties in Egypt give us an impression of a restless questing spirit tackling problems with assurance and boldly experimenting with new forms to achieve a perfection within each. As soon as a solution had been sanctioned, however, there was no further development; a new convention had been added to the stockpile of acceptable traditions.

THE CULTURAL BACKGROUND

The archaic period covered by the first two dynasties is largely unknown to us. We have the names of kings as listed by Manetho (see chronology on page 98). We also have certain archaeological evidence mostly from the plundered tombs or cenotaphs at Abydos and Saqqara which are thought to be of these rulers and their families and retainers. Literary remains are almost entirely lacking and those that do exist are difficult to interpret. Nevertheless from a comparison of what precedes and what follows, we can see that the economic and cultural leaven introduced by unification continues unabated. The Residence which Narmer had founded at Memphis, the point of balance between Upper and Lower Egypt, remained the centre of this stirring world, and indeed was the metropolis where the arts and sciences flourished throughout the Old Kingdom under the patronage of its creator-god Ptah *(fig. 9)*.

(fig. 9)

Writing too must have made considerable progress from the ambiguous stammerings of the monumental inscriptions on the slate palettes. A flexible paper manufactured from the pith of the papyrus plant is known from the time of Dynasty I at least, and this Egyptian invention must have made the keeping and duplicating of records, memoranda and literary compositions very much easier and more compact. A rapid and cursive form of writing with pen and ink may also be traced back to this period. A convenient instrument for organizing and documenting the work of a centralized state thus existed in Egypt right from the start, and during the Old Kingdom we shall find that officials were proud to have themselves represented as scribes (pl. 41).

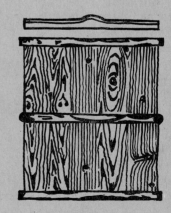

Wooden tub and striker for measuring corn. From a painting on the wall of the tomb-chapel of Hesy-Re. (fig. 10)

As part of this public administration, an elaborate system of taxation appears to have been developed at an early stage. Standard measures of capacity for assessing the amount of the corn harvest, for instance, certainly exist by the time of Dynasty III, when a set of wooden tubs and strikers was painted on the walls of the tomb-chapel of Hesy-re *(fig. 10)*. Linear measure like that of medieval Europe was based upon the human arm, forearm, finger, palm and so forth. The inundation of the Nile yearly erased the petty boundaries between fields and estates so that a system of accurate survey and mensuration had to be devised to re-establish the old limits. While there was thus every stimulus for the Egyptian to develop the science of mathematics his approach to the subject was never more than pragmatic. A decimal system had existed before dynastic times. Later treatises deal with practical mathematical problems which all required to be solved in the building of mastabas (the long, low, rectangular mound with sloping sides built over the tomb of a private person during the Old Kingdom) and pyramids during the first four dynasties, but it was not studied theoretically as an end in itself.

Similar progress in astronomy was stimulated by the necessity of forecasting the annual rise of the Nile. A sighting instrument for making observations of the stars was invented during this period and enabled the correct time for the celebration of calendrical feasts to be accurately determined *(fig. 11)*. In an unscientific society the proper moment for the observation of a religious rite was of vital importance. Astronomy was also employed in providing fixed points by which buildings could be properly aligned according to ideas of dogma. Much of this science flourished at Heliopolis, the centre of a sun-cult, the ritual of which was largely concerned with time-measurement and the study of the sky and the movement of heavenly bodies. The accurate orientation of pyramids and their geometrical precision may have owed much to the influence of architects of Heliopolitan origin. It was during this period that the old agricultural lunar calendar which had existed in Egypt since Predynastic days was supplemented for secular purposes by the introduction of a more accurate calendar based upon twelve months each of thirty days with five extra feast days, though this system too had to be further improved a little later by the use of a third calendar.

The Material Culture

The material remains from the greatly devastated sites at Abydos and Saqqara give tantalizing glimpses of a culture at once primitive and sophisticated, traditional and experimental. We can see that such crafts as the manufacture of stone vessels continued in vigour, exploiting natural formations in banded stones, and even developing a daring virtuosity. Pottery on the other hand declined in artistry and settled down to a drab utility. The introduction of the potter's wheel at the beginning of the period probably hastened the process. In contrast, copper working shows a rich development. Very many tools, weapons, and ingots of copper have been found in an important tomb of Dynasty I; and also from this same deposit came scores of bowls, ewers, and vases raised by hammering sheets of copper. These are the ancestors of a long line of such metal vessels in Egypt (pl. 58). From the end of the Old Kingdom have survived two greatly corroded statues of Pepy I and his son made by hammering copper plates over a wooden core, which seem to be in a tradition that goes back to the beginning of the period, since an inscription exists mentioning copper statues made by a king of Dynasty II. It is clear that the goldsmith and jeweller did not lag behind in the techniques of working gold and electrum but unhappily very little of these precious metals has escaped the clutches of the tomb robber and we have practically no representative material from this period.

The fragments of worked wood and ivory that have been recovered from the tombs of Dynasty I reveal that the joiner was disposed to copy faithfully decorative forms that belonged to work in rush or basketry (pl. 8). The carving is highly accomplished with that unmatched technical proficiency of the Egyptian craftsman at his best. A compartmented box from the same source, however, displays a full appreciation of the functional possibilities of construction in wood (pl. 7). Ivory carries on an inheritance from prehistoric times though only the figurine of a king wrapped in his Jubilee robe as he strides forward in a pacing ceremony is complete enough to give a full idea of its quality (pl. 17). Among these scanty remains particular mention must be made of an object from a game which has survived almost in its pristine condition (pl. 11). It consists of a black steatite disk carved in low relief on one side with the figures of two hounds attacking two gazelles, both of which are formed from pieces of pink alabaster let into the surface, as is one of the dogs. Not only does this disk show in its fine drawing and craftsmanship all the features of the best later relief sculpture, but the way in which the artist has disposed the elements in his design, arranging the animals so as to square the circle,

(fig. 11)

reveals a fundamental feature of all dynastic art in Egypt—a feeling for space defined within strict rectangular or cubic outlines.

All this is in marked contrast to the malformed signs and inept carving of the inscriptions on contemporary ebony and ivory labels, probably because these were from the hands of maladroit scribes better at wielding a pen than a chisel *(fig. 12)*. Two literary works surviving in versions of a later period are thought from internal evidence to date to Dynasty I. One of these is a treatise upon surgery, especially upon fractures, which is remarkable for its empirical approach to the subject. The other is a work on theology, ascribing the creation of the universe to Ptah of Memphis, in which an entirely unusual search for first principles is evident. Some scholars have been inclined therefore to detect at this period of extreme activity in so many fields of endeavour, a novel if tentative groping towards a scientific attitude on the part of the Egyptian to the universe around him. It is, however, so hesitant as to be barely perceptible and the approach once made is soon abandoned and never afterwards followed.

Ivory label of King Wedymu (c. 3100 BC). The clumsiness of the inscription contrasts with the boldness and technical mastery of contemporary stone-carving. (fig. 12)

The Old Kingdom—Dynasties III-VI

The promise of the first two dynasties was achieved in the next two. In the absence of nearly all historical and literary documents, we are obliged to assess the achievement of the civilization of the Old Kingdom from the funerary monuments around the great sites near Memphis—the architecture and sculpture that have survived in a ruinous condition at the cemeteries near Giza, Saqqara, Abusir and Dahshur.

There must have been in the prehistoric ages unknown geniuses of the order of a Newton or an Einstein, whose thought and imagination reached out beyond their time and transformed the life of mankind. We are fortunate, however, in knowing a little about one of the earliest of such men in historic times, Imhotep, trained in the learning of Heliopolis, the vizier of Djoser, an early king of Dynasty III. In later ages Imhotep was celebrated as an architect, astronomer, priest, writer and sage, and above all, as a physician, being eventually deified as the god of medicine. His greatest memorial however is the funerary monument that he erected for Djoser at Saqqara, to which the name of the Step Pyramid or Step Mastaba is now given (pl. 19-22).

Building in early dynastic times had progressed beyond the mud hovels and reed shelters of prehistoric days, though these were still in use among the peasantry. The introduction of mud-brick and massive structural timber imported from the Lebanon encouraged a change in the type and size of the more important buildings such as palaces and temples, though many decorative features derived from building in flimsy vegetable materials plastered with mud were copied in the new medium. This was the architecture of the living which was also employed for the superstructure of the 'houses of eternity' of the dead *(fig. 13)*. The development of architecture during the early Old Kingdom is largely concerned with the search for more permanent materials, wood and mud-brick replacing lashed bundles of papyrus stalks, rush mat-work, palm-thatch and wattle and daub. Stone begins to be used for parts of the house subjected to hard wear such as lintels, thresholds and doorposts; but the next step of building entirely in stone was never taken for the living, even the most exalted, but for the dead. The urge towards a monumental conception of architecture arose from the need to house the dead king in a tomb that would last for ever. While there is an inscriptional reference to a stone temple in the reign of Djoser's father, the art of building in stone was traditionally accredited to Imhotep, and certainly his Step Pyramid is the earliest known stone structure of any size.

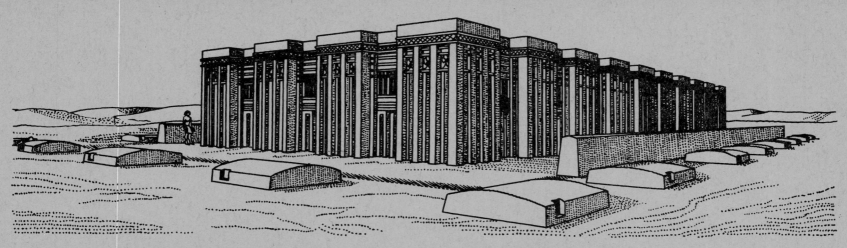

Reconstruction of the superstructure of a royal tomb at Saqqara, probably that of Queen Merneith, Archaic Period, Dynasty I, c. 3100 BC. (fig. 13)

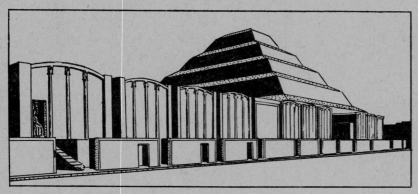

Reconstruction of the Chapels and Jubilee court of the Step Pyramid of Djoser at Saqqara. Dynasty III, c. 2750 BC. (fig. 14)

Imitation in stone of a stake fence, barring access to the mortuary buildings of Djoser at Saqqara. (fig. 15)

The actual tomb of Djoser was in a maze of galleries beneath a stone erection consisting of six superimposed rectangular stages with sloping sides diminishing in size as they reach skywards to a height of over two hundred feet. This stepped pyramid dominates a complex of buildings surrounded by a massive bastioned enclosure wall with a perimeter of over a mile, and a height of more than thirty-three feet (pl. 20). Within this vast compound were courts and edifices which were presumably modelled upon those used by Djoser during his life-time. Apart from a mortuary temple and serdab (a kind of oubliette from which a statue of the deceased could look out onto the offerings in the offering-chamber of his tomb) containing a statue of the dead king, these buildings are in duplicate and simulate light structures used at coronation and jubilee ceremonies when the king performed every rite once as ruler of Upper Egypt with appropriate insignia in a characteristic Upper Egyptian shrine, and again as king of Lower Egypt in different dress and surroundings. It is a unique feature of these mortuary buildings, however, that they serve their purpose by magic not actuality. Most of them present a mere façade in front of

a solid rubble core. Of the fourteen great gateways that interrupt the rhythm of the bastions on the enclosure wall, only one is a true entrance. Similarly, stone imitations of wooden doors standing open were carved where approach was permitted: at other points representations of stake fences barred access *(fig. 15)*. The dummy nature of many structural features rather encourages the view that the architect and masons were feeling their way in an entirely new medium. The quarrying and handling of large stones had not been perfected and the small-block masonry shows a translation into more permanent material of construction proper to mud-brick and vegetable products. This, the elegant proportions and the emphatic carving of plant forms such as papyrus stalks, pendant leaf capitals and fasciculated columns lend an air of naturalism and vitality to the buildings which is rather in conflict with their mortuary purposes.

Nevertheless, at the time of its completion, this monument must have been the wonder of the age, as indeed it remained for subsequent generations in Egypt. Nothing like it had appeared on earth before. It enshrined within its chambers a mass of objects almost as novel as itself, wall panels decorated in blue-glazed tiles in imitation of the coloured reed mats hung on interiors (pl. 22), large statues of the king in seated and standing poses, stelae in delicate low relief in which the athletic figure of Djoser performing the ritual of some eternal jubilee is accompanied by hieroglyphic inscriptions of coherent assurance (pl. 21), the coffin of an infant made in six-ply wood, and the tens of thousands of handsome vessels in alabaster, breccia, rock crystal, serpentine and 'every costly stone'. All this treasure was in addition to that greater store that must have been plundered from it long ago. The Egyptian peasant pausing from his muddy labour in the Saqqara fields to look up at it could never know what lay behind its single entrance port, but the sight of that vast monument standing white, mysterious and silent upon the skyline must have convinced him that he was ruled by veritable gods.

The Giza Pyramids

The style set by Djoser's Step Pyramid was evidently copied by his immediate successors who, however, were unable to finish their undertakings. But the recently discovered complex of King Sekhem-Khet near by already shows a more massive form of building using large stone blocks without reference to mud-brick. This megalithic type of construction was exploited particularly by the kings of the next dynasty who at Dahshur, Maidum and Giza evolved funerary monuments in the form of a stone pyramid, doubtless under the increasing influence of Heliopolis where a pyramidal stone was of great significance in the cult of the sun-god Re. The climax of this development came early with the building of the Great Pyramid of King Kheops (Khufu) at Giza (pl. 24). The vizier Hemon, a cousin of Kheops, was the King's Master of Works and evidently responsible for this mighty monument built to an astonishing degree of accuracy by the simplest of means. The impressive statue of Hemon, from his tomb at Giza, gives a brilliant portrait of this resourceful architect and engineer (pl. 28).

The construction of the pyramid took well over two million large blocks of limestone, some of them weighing as much as fifteen tons. The stone for the core was hewn on the spot, but the facing blocks were of finer limestone and quarried at Tura across the river. There have been many suggestions as to how the pyramids were built. The most plausible has recently been made by the American scholar Dows Dunham as a result of excavations in which he assisted at Giza. He has postulated that four rubble and mud ramps starting at each corner of the pyramid base were built on the undressed outer surface of the casing-stones and extended at the upper end as the pyramid rose course by course (pl. 23). Three of the ramps were used for hauling blocks and other materials to the course under construction: the fourth was reserved for men descending with empty sledges. Dunham's calculation is that 2,500 workmen only could have operated effectively at the working face, and in the later stages of the building doubtless even fewer could have been accommodated. Many more men would have been employed in the quarries and in transport work, but he considers that the figure of 100,000 supplied to the Greek traveller Herodotus by the interpreters of the day, is a gross exaggeration. Petrie has also pointed out that organization of labour would be more important than mere numbers of workmen, and it is probable that while the task of quarrying, assembling and fitting the blocks occupied skilled craftsmen continuously, the labour of hauling the stone into position was seasonal, being performed by field labourers thrown out of work by the Nile inundation.

When the capstone of the pyramid had been put into place the work of smoothing the rough casing-blocks would proceed as the ramps were removed. Around the pyramid proper was built a girdle wall enclosing subsidiary buildings, including the mortuary temple connected by a causeway to a temple near the limits of the Nile. The best preserved of these structures at Giza is the Valley Temple of the Second Pyramid built for Khephren (Khafre) a successor of Kheops (pl. 27). It is constructed in massive local limestone faced inside and out with slabs of polished red granite. Such temples may be stone versions of a light pavilion in matting and reeds in which the corpse of the early kings underwent purification and embalmment, the fluids used in the latter process doubtless being returned to the near-by Nile for the greater fertility of Egypt. In the T-shaped hall of this Valley Temple the final funeral ceremonies were conducted before the coffined corpse of the king was taken along the covered causeway to the pyramid precincts. This hall is one of the most impressive interiors that the Old Kingdom architects have bequeathed to us, with its granite ceiling and unadorned square piers, also of red granite (pl. 26, 27). Light was admitted by oblique openings cut in the tops of the walls where they met the roof, and fell upon the polished alabaster floor, casting a diffused glow upon the twenty-three statues of the king, hewn from green diorites, alabasters and grey schists, that stood at intervals along the walls. This temple is a complete realization in stone of the mortuary concept. It is designed and executed in that same uncompromising and austere spirit that raised the pyramids of Giza in all their accuracy and integrity and did not scruple to use the hardest of stones, polished basalts, granites and diorites, as well as alabasters and limestones in their construction. These pyramid complexes, too, contained closed repositories of statuary, reliefs, furniture and appointments on which the best of the artistic talent in the country was concentrated; and we are indeed fortunate that so much from this brilliant and classic period in Egypt should have survived. In particular mention must be made of the magnificent furniture of Queen Hetepheres, the mother of Kheops (pl. 36). The superb workmanship and design of these gold-sheathed chairs, boxes, bed and canopy with their coloured inlays in faience and carnelian (a reddish stone like chalcedony) reveal a taste at once opulent and austere, restrained and brilliant in the traditions of the age.

THE LATER BUILDINGS

It is clear, however, that the tremendous demands upon human and material resources which the building of the Giza pyramids made were not considered desirable or possible for the tombs of later kings. Even the third pyramid at Giza, that of Mykerinus (Menkaure), is appreciably smaller than its two rivals. The successors of the kings of Dynasty IV built their pyramids at Abusir and Saqqara (pl. 49) and abandoned the grandiose proportions and megalithic masonry of the Giza group. This decline in the size of the Pharaoh's tomb coincides with a decrease in the stature of the Pharaoh and a rise in the importance of Heliopolis where the sun-god Re was worshipped. The Pharaoh was now thought to be the son of the sun-god and this idea which appears as early as Khephren is particularly in evidence after the middle of

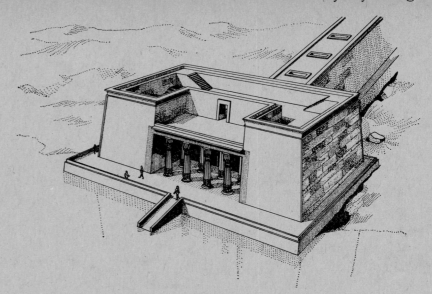

Reconstruction of the Valley Temple of Ni-weser-re, with the causeway leading from the Nile to the main pyramid complex. c. 2500 BC. (fig. 16)

Dynasty V. According to a folk-story which probably originated at this time, the first three kings of Dynasty V were the sons of Re by the wife of a priest of Heliopolis. An innovation of the reigns of these kings is the sun-temple that each of them erected after the model of the sanctuary at Heliopolis and which differs fundamentally from other temples of the Old Kingdom. The best preserved of them is that of a later king of the Dynasty, Ni-weser-re, at Abu Gurob where the architect has made ingenious use of the configuration of the ground to produce a temple complex on two levels linked by an oblique sloping causeway (pl. 50). The sanctuary consists of a walled enclosure, 330 feet long and 250 feet wide, containing store-rooms and corridors with finely sculptured scenes. The ritual of the sun-cult was observed before altars in two open courts dominated by a squat obelisk, the cult image of the sun religion, which arose from a tall podium. A bizarre feature of the temple architecture, taking on more of the quality of a sculptural adjunct, was a large representation of one of the two barques in which Re was thought to travel across the heavens. This was built of mud-brick a short distance south of the enclosure wall.

In both the sun-temples and mortuary buildings of this dynasty great use is made of red granite columns in the form of date palms and clusters of papyrus *(fig. 17)* and these features give a delicate and more vital appearance to the architecture, perhaps under the influence of the earlier style of the Djoser complex near which two of the pyramids of this dynasty were built. The choice of polished granite, basalts and smooth alabaster blocks for the construction, however,

Reconstruction cut-away of the Court of the Pyramid Temple of Sahu-re, showing date-palm columns. Dynasty V, c. 2550 BC. (fig. 17)

continues the tradition of Dynasty IV. The advent of the VIth Dynasty saw no violent change in the character of such architecture so far as can be judged from the little that has been excavated. The last great monument of the age, the pyramid complex of Pepy II, fully maintains the fine standard of craftsmanship of the Old Kingdom and despite a tendency towards formalism in its relief decoration remained a source of inspiration to later generations anxious to recapture a little of their past grandeur.

The Old Kingdom—Dynasties III-VI

THE EARLIER SCULPTURE

The ruins of the pyramid complexes have preserved some meagre traces of the statuary and reliefs that once formed part of their decoration and equipment, and it is from this sculpture above all that we are accustomed to measure the full achievement of Old Kingdom civilization. Clustered around the pyramid of the king were the mastaba tombs of his relatives, officials and mortuary priests, expressing in death a relationship in which they had stood in life to their dead lord, as though they thereby received a little of his immortality. For while the king was believed to rule after death among the gods much as he had done on earth, it is less clear what sort of after-life was reserved for his subjects. Several different beliefs existed together, but at this period it would seem that for private persons some kind of shadowy existence in their 'houses of eternity' was all they could expect, subsisting upon the offerings brought by pious relatives or magically materialized for them by the recitation of certain prayers. Originally much of the cult of the dead seems to have centred around the partaking of a funeral meal at the tomb, in which communion the deceased was supposed to join, but this rite early found graphic expression in a representation of the tomb-owner seated at table. Such scenes carved on wooden or stone slabs were let into a niche in the mastaba wall, and from this was elaborated, as the age advanced in prosperity and skill, a stone-lined chamber with painted reliefs, and serdabs containing statuary. Thus the sculptural furnishings of the pyramids were copied on a more modest scale for the mastabas of kings' children, ministers and courtiers.

It is customary to regard artistic fashions as having been set by the king's craftsmen and followed more or less faithfully by his subjects both in style and iconography. The picture seems true in its general outlines but so little of the royal sculpture has survived that it is hazardous to be too categorical. There are, moreover, certain Pharaonic themes such as the symbolical slaughter of the traditional foes, or the Jubilee Rites, which were quite inappropriate for representation in the tombs of private persons. On the other hand, the pilgrimage by boat to the 'Goodly West' (i.e. the hereafter) which enters the repertoire of subjects for decoration in mastaba chapels towards the end of the Old Kingdom does not seem to have been depicted in pyramid temples. Certain scenes, such as the assembly of personified districts, or *nomes*, offering their produce to the king at his accession or jubilee, are translated into the procession of personified estates making funerary offerings to their non-royal overlord (pl. 55).

Fragments of wood and ivory suggest that the carving of statues in these transient media had reached a fair competence by dynastic times, as is revealed by the almost complete ivory figurine of a king in his Jubilee robe (pl. 17). There is evident in sculpture as in architecture, however, the same impulse towards achieving a mastery in eternal stone and it is in such hard rocks as diorite and basalt that the finest expression of the Old Kingdom sculptor is achieved. But throughout the period, limestone remains the proper medium for relief, the only notable exception being the wooden panels of Hesy-re, a contemporary of Djoser (pl. 19). Limestone, too, is the material from which the bulk of private statuary was carved, and in which the first confident statement of the Egyptian sculptor has survived (pl. 36). These statues of Re-hotep and Nofret belong to the earliest years of Dynasty IV. In their restrained naturalism, with their painted surfaces and inlaid eyes, they seem to be at the end of a development which is lost to us, representing a lively vital intention, the equivalent in sculpture of the architecture of Djoser. There is something of the same irresolution between the lifelike surfaces and the monumental tendencies evident in the simplified planes and underlying masses. This conflict is composed in the slightly later statue of Hemon (pl. 28) which is unpainted, though the inscription is inlaid with coloured pastes. The portraiture of the body is as individual as that of the face, and the arms are now arranged in a pose that so satisfied the subconscious desire of the Egyptian for a perfect equipoise of rival forces that it is repeated with minor variations until the end of Pharaonic art. The monumental character of this striking statue reveals the same intellectual approach, the same uncompromising and ruthless exploration of form, of which the geometrical perfection of the Great Pyramid is the architectural counterpart. This spirit is particularly dominant in the so-called 'reserve heads' made in unpainted limestone to be placed in the burial chambers of some of Kheops' relatives and retainers (pl. 30, 31). In the next generation a transfusion of this style by a warmer and more naturalistic feeling is to be seen in the bust of Ankh-haf where a coating of plaster laid over the limestone has encouraged a more plastic handling of the surfaces (pl. 32). These heads, and the statues of Re-hotep and Nofret with their highly personal portraiture, must be regarded as products of the royal workshops and made at the king's command. The most impressive of such pieces is the diorite statue of Khephren which once stood with its twenty-two companions in the hall of his Valley Temple (pl. 29). More than any other statue to have survived from Egypt, this superb specimen in a hard igneous stone expresses the apotheosis of kingship. In the same sculptural tradition, though quite different in its inner statement, is the unfinished pair statue of Mykerinus and his Queen (pl. 34). The lonely, god-like majesty of the earlier statues of the dynasty has been subtly transformed into the essential humanity of the royal pair shown as husband and wife on an equal footing. The same feeling pervades the triads from the Mykerinus Valley Temple where the goddesses are shown with the features of the Queen, as is usual in Egypt. These groups are but elaborate three-dimensional versions of a theme which appears a little earlier in relief showing personifications of the various districts of Egypt bringing their tribute to the reigning king. The dyad of Mykerinus supported by his Queen is really a development of the statues made separately but meant to be regarded as a pair, as for example those of Re-hotep and Nofret. Husband and wife are now shown in a simple and appealing embrace, a pose which appears in contemporary relief (pl. 33). Often the embrace is mutual as in certain private sculptures which quickly adopted the idea (pl. 42). An earlier style, however, which represents the wife and children on a much smaller scale than the master of the household, is not superseded and the two exist side by side without conflict (pl. 43).

The humanization of the Pharaoh which may be sensed in the dyad and triads of Mykerinus is particularly evident in the head of a statue believed to be of Shepses-kaf where the translucency of the alabaster softens the contours and imparts a life-like glow to the modelling (pl. 35). This head represents the climax of the Old Kingdom sculptural style which virtually spans the period of Dynasty IV. What has survived in royal statuary from the rest of the period, though often highly competent, shows a certain formalism.

The reliefs from the pyramid temples of the dynasty exist in mere tantalizing scraps, which however reveal the same assured yet precise drawing and masterly technique that are evident in the statuary, though they also suggest a striving rather than an achievement. One of the best preserved examples of this restrained style are the reliefs from the mastaba chapel of one of the sons of Kheops, Khufu-kaf and his wife receiving funerary offerings (pl. 33). The painted reliefs of the end of the dynasty show a decline from this high standard, largely because they are carved in a coarse limestone which had to be supplemented with plaster. Their bright colours, however, anticipate the lively scenes in the private chapels of the next dynasty when the many craftsmen trained on the enormous funeral monuments at Giza were free to undertake commissions for court officials at Saqqara (pl. 40–43).

THE LATER SCULPTURE

While the more modest tombs of the kings of Dynasty V made less demands upon the reserve of artistic talent, it is clear that the standard of craftsmanship in the palace workshops is well maintained particularly at the beginning of the dynasty.

Royal statuary is rather rare, the few examples being of unequal quality, and suggesting that the triumphs of the Dynasty IV sculptors had now been reduced to a successful formula, which however was less effective the further it moved from its fount of inspiration. The royal sculptures of Dynasty VI are also scanty. The copper-sheathed statues of Pepy I and his son are too corroded to give a reliable impression (pl. 47), but the votive statuettes in the Brooklyn Museum show that new forms may have been developed during the later Old Kingdom, when we find the divine Pharaoh deigns to kneel to the gods (pl. 48). In private sculpture more variety is apparent owing to the greater wealth of examples. One new type of statue is that of the owner as a scribe writing or reading (pl. 41). Such compositions have not so far been found among royal sculptures, though the Pyramid Texts speak of the king as acting as the secretary of the gods. Much of this private statuary is of wood which was designed to be covered with a skin of painted gesso (plaster and glue), though few of these carvings now survive in anything like their pristine condition (pl. 40). Often such funeral furnishings were the gift of the king to a favoured courtier and with the increasing diversion of wealth into private hands as the period advanced such patronage was spread downwards. There appears, for instance, a number of named statuettes of servants in the tombs of their masters who thus secured for them a kind of memorial (pl. 59–61). The prime intention, however, was that such statues should show the servant at his daily tasks serving by magic the needs of his dead master. In the carving of these minor though lively works of art, a rather sardonic attitude on the part of the artist towards his subject is often apparent, as though the sanctions that applied in representing his betters had for the moment been lifted. For an instant we have a glimpse into a humbler world than that of the athletic and well-nourished élite who face eternity with such composure.

The glory of the sculpture of this later period, however, are the reliefs that decorated the walls of the royal temples during early Dynasty V. The astonishing delicacy and minuteness of the carving and the sensitive drawing give an impression of supreme technical and artistic mastery, even in the wretched fragments which are all that have survived (pl. 44-46). The iconography of these scenes is expanded to include a number of novel subjects apparently introduced by the sun-cult of this dynasty with its interest in the calendar and time-measurement. In addition to the representation of Nile gods and district gods bringing the riches of Egypt to the king, there appear personifications of the three seasons, each being accompanied by characteristic animals and plants. The complete cycle of work in the fields was shown as a sort of visual hymn of praise to the sun-god for all his bounty (pl. 52). While only fragments of this classic art remain, complete extracts from the same scenes are better preserved in the versions carved in private tombs during Dynasties V and VI, although the quality is poorer. It is from these coloured reliefs that we gain so vivid and intimate a picture of country life in Ancient Egypt during the Old Kingdom, a teeming busy life observed with kindliness and humour—the field sports in marsh and wadi, the incidents of pastoral life, the boating on the Nile, the country crafts, the good life on the estate, music, games and dancing (pl. 54).

The Civilization of the Old Kingdom

In the earliest dynasties, it would appear that the king ruled the whole of Egypt as his private estate. As late as Dynasty IV the Palace with its adjoining official buildings was the 'Great House' (the Per-ao, whence the Hebrew 'Pharaoh', a circumlocution used much later to refer to the king himself) where the government of the country was conducted by chosen officials to whom the royal authority had been delegated. Many of them were sons or near relatives of the king who sponsored their upbringing and education, granted them property during their lifetimes and saw to the provision of their tombs and funerary endowments after death. This highly centralized state began gradually to split up from the later years of Dynasty IV when provincial governorships and other offices came to be regarded as hereditary appointments. The resources of the state treasury were eroded by gifts of land, exemptions from taxation, often in perpetuity, and alienation of income or property mostly for the benefit of the occupants of vast cities of the dead around the silent pyramids of their former rulers. On the other hand, the provincial governors, now fast becoming feudal potentates, no longer sought burial near the tomb of their overlord, but made their own cemeteries in the district capital, and clearly regarded themselves as little inferior to so many minor kings. After the long rule of Pepy II, when the succession fell into confusion, the central authority had become too weak to hold back the rising tide of anarchy, and the civilization of the Old Kingdom collapsed with the political system that had created it.

Under the divine authority of the Pharaoh, Egypt during the Old Kingdom achieved a vigorous, characteristic and self-assured culture, untroubled by doubts and unfaltering in its belief that material success depended upon completing a practical education, doing right for the king, respecting superiors, and exercising moderation in all things. The ideal of the golden mean is as much in evidence in the calm and disciplined art as in the books of precepts which the sages wrote for their posterity. Such a civilization is essentially aristocratic. At first only the king mattered, but as his divinity came to be shared to some degree by his children and descendants, his exclusive powers, like the centralized authority of the state, began to disperse among a ramified privileged class who boasted of their acquaintance with the king and partook in some degree of his immortality. It was for them that all the economic and artistic activities were created. It was they whose hopes of eternity were satisfied with tombs and endowments. They formed, however, no idle court nobility. Included in this élite were the architects, designers, writers, thinkers, theologians and master craftsmen of the day. The second king of Dynasty I was a noted anatomist; besides Imhotep, Prince Hardjedef, the son of Kheops, was celebrated long after his lifetime as a sage; Weni and Harkhuf were the first among a distinguished line of African explorers; the Viziers Ka-gem-ni and Ptah-hotep were moralists whose sayings were long handed down as literature. All this achievement was the exotic flower upon a plant whose root was the eternal Egyptian peasant, forever toiling in the fields, living with his animals for the moment only, never far from sudden plague and famine, hedged around by grosser superstitions than those of his masters, but able unlike them to escape the inhibitions of polite society, and preserving intact the same sardonic gusto, the same manners and customs that have brought him virtually unscathed through five thousand years of changing history.

V THE FIRST MERCHANT VENTURERS

The sea peoples of the Levant

WILLIAM CULICAN

Areas of Phoenician settlement

Areas of Phoenician trade and influence

Miles 0 50 150 250
Kilometres 0 200 400

		CYPRUS & ASIA MINOR	SYRO-PALESTINIAN COAST & N. SYRIA	CENTRAL PALESTINE	EGYPT	MESOPOTAMIA
						HISTORICAL LINKS
BC 3000					2700 Contacts with Byblos	
	EARLY		BYBLOS	GEZER JERICHO MEGIDDO AI		2680 Gudea of Lagash imports Lebanese cedar
					2650 Pharaoh Sneferu imports Lebanese cedar	
			SMALL CITY STATES OF WESTERN SEMITES			2450 Akkadian mention of 'Amurru'
1900			NOMADIC SEMITES FILTER INTO EGYPT ⟶		1900 Nomad Semites pictured at Beni Hasan	
	MIDDLE	Rise of the Hittites	1900-1788 Cultural centres of Byblos & Ras Shamra Exchanges with Egypt	The Patriarchal Age of Abraham, Isaac & Jacob		
			c. 1730 HURRIAN STATES in N. Syria			1730-1700 Archives at Mari show existence of Amorite kingdoms
			HYKSOS INVASION			
1550		INTENSIVE	TRADE OPENS BETWEEN	CYPRUS, PALESTINE AND	EGYPT ⟶	KASSITE DYNASTIES
			Rise of the MITANNI KINGDOMS	1500 Cultural focus shifts to Central Palestine		
			Penetration to Euphrates ◁		1525 Campaigns of Tuthmosis I against Hyksos	
	LATE		Capture of Arvad ◁	Siege of Megiddo 1468 ◁	1483-1463 Campaigns of Tuthmosis III in Palestine and Syria	
		Hittites intervene in Syro-Palestinian affairs	15th cent. King Idrimi of Alalakh	TELL EL-AMARNA LETTERS	1440-1358 Amenhotep II, III, IV dominate	
		Rise of ENKOMI			Syrian tribute to Egypt	
			SPREAD OF MYCENAEAN INFLUENCE IN THE ENTIRE		LEVANT	
		Close contacts between Cyprus & Ugarit	1400-1250 Flourishing of Ras Shamra. Ugaritic Epics	Reciprocal Canaanite-Egyptian influences in Art and Religion		
		Hittite influence at Ugarit and interference in Syro-Palestinian affairs		Beginning of the Israelite settlement of Canaan		
			1308, 1206 Battles at Kadesh ◁		Seti I & Rameses II	
1250	I	1200 INVASION OF	THE SEA PEOPLES	⟶	Repulsed by Rameses III	
				PHILISTINES SETTLE on S. Palestinian coast		
				1200-930 Subjugation of Canaan by Israelites		
		Rise of SYRO-HITTITE KINGDOMS		Saul, David & Solomon		1094 Tiglath-Pileser I in Syria
			Rise of the Monarchy of Tyre ◀			
930			ARAMAEAN STATES IN N. SYRIA ◀			884-859 Ashurnasirpal
		Phoenician rule at Citium in Cyprus	814 Carthage founded?	Divided Monarchy in Israel		
				684 Jerusalem attacked ◀		Sennacherib
			666 Tyre reduced ◀			Ashurbanipal
	II	Greek trade with Levant introduces oriental taste to the West	700-600 Phoenician expansion in West Mediterranean			
			609 Phoenician circum-navigation of Africa			
				586 Jerusalem destroyed ◀		Nebuchadnezzar II

(Left vertical labels: BRONZE AGE; IRON AGE. Vertical note: EGYPTIAN INFLUENCE FALLS OFF / EGYPT'S EMPIRE)

The ancient communities of Palestine and Syria never came together into a larger political entity, with its own consistently developing culture, as did Egypt or Sumer. From the beginning of recorded history two ill-distinguished groups of peoples—the Canaanites (South and East) and the Amorites (North and West)—lived here: peoples of the same Semitic stock, speaking much the same language, and differing in little besides their names. The Amorites came mainly under the influence of the Sumerians and the Hurrians of North Syria, while the Canaanites were strongly influenced by Egyptian ways of thought and expression. Both groups formed small independent kingdoms, exposed to sudden raids or gradual infiltrations from north, south and east, and falling under the successive influence of neighbouring powers, which never considered them important enough to merit colonization. In addition, the physical diversity of the region made political unity difficult, if not impossible. The dry steppes of North Syria attracted invaders from the north; the fertile strip of the Lebanese coast made for the development of self-sufficient trading and farming communities; and in the low hills of Jordania, more fertile then than now, small peasant kingdoms arose such as that of Jericho, with patches of plain guarded by fortified towns. All these disunited communities and city-states, though individual genius could flourish here and there, were continually open to attack and domination by stronger and more cohesive neighbours. Their main importance in the history of civilization is not as originators but as transmitters. They were the sailors, the traders and the colonists. And it is in the Levant that we find the first traces of a written alphabet.

Amorite rather than Egyptian in style is the ivory-handled dagger from the temple of Byblos (2nd millennium BC) shown below. The gold-foil scabbard covering shows a peasant herding, with two assistants, an unlikely flock of a goat, lion, baboon, dog and fish. (1)

Technical mastery of goldsmithing can be seen in the crescent-shaped Syrian axe below. The shaft is covered with gold foil and decorated with applied wire and granulation work. Axes of this type are typically Syrian, and this elaborate example might have been carried by a cult statue of the Byblos temple (c. 1800 BC). (2)

Inlaid with lapis-lazuli, the vase below, of beaten gold, is the only surviving example of the elaborate metal vessels carried by the tall, bearded, white-clad Syrian and Lebanese tribute-bearers we see in Egyptian wall-paintings of the 2nd millennium BC. It was found in a temple deposit at Byblos. (3)

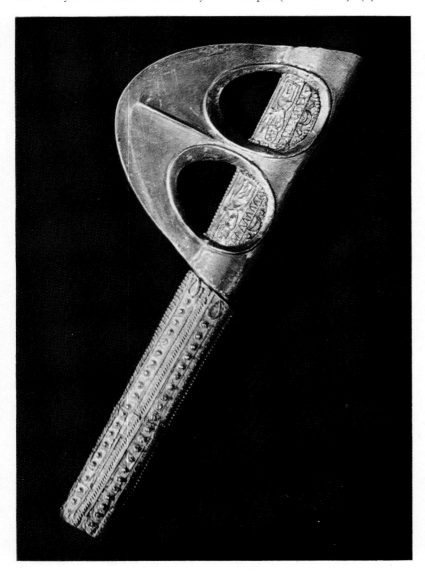

Collar of beaten gold from a royal tomb at Byblos (2nd millennium BC, when the kings were vassals of Egypt). The Horus-hawk design is a well-known Egyptian type, but the treatment of the feathers and the action of the bird point to local craftsmanship. The egg-and-tongue border is a device which becomes peculiarly Phoenician in later times, and hence passed into the art of Greece. (4)

Dedicated to the sun, like those of Egypt, the obelisks of the 2nd millennium BC temple at Byblos in the Lebanon probably had reflecting caps of gold, as similar temples in Egypt had. Here, however, the obelisks were erected in two rows in a rectangular enclosure—a quite different arrangement from any that has been found on the Nile. (5)

The Shepherd Kings of Egypt or the Hyksos, a race of Asiatic herdsmen-warriors, swept over Syria and Palestine and had imposed their rule on Egypt by c. 1700 BC. Coming mainly from the north, possibly from beyond the Caspian Sea, they brought with them knowledge of metallurgy, iron weapons, and in particular the domesticated horse, and thus the use of the horse-drawn vehicle as a new and unassailable weapon of war. In their wake came other Indo-Europeanized peoples, the Hurrians and the Mitannians, to invade and dominate the North Syrian desert and seaboard. The grip of Egypt was still strong, however, and the Mitannian overlords were themselves subject to the Hyksos kings of Egypt.

Wide-eyed and mournful, King Idrimi of Alalakh (in the Turkish Hatay, north of Syria), in the white magnesite statue above, wears the conical hat and rolled-border cloak of the Mitanni kings. In fact, however, he was only a vassal of the Mitanni kings, at a time when they were gaining in influence, temporarily, at the expense of the Pharaohs (15th century BC). The whole of the front of this statue, from the chin to the skirt of the cloak, is covered with 104 lines of a cuneiform inscription giving the royal autobiography. (7)

A vassal of Egypt, the Mitannian king whose bronze statuette (above) was found in Egypt symbolized the relationship by wearing the conical Egyptian crown and the rolled-border cloak of the Mitannians. (6)

Purple-robed Phoenician traders from the Lebanese coast had brought their merchandise to the Nile Delta ever since the cedar trade of the early years of the 2nd millennium. The Canaanite merchants in the scene reconstructed above (c. 1400 BC) are having their goods weighed on the dockside. Their single-masted ships, with the lateen rig still used in the Mediterranean today, had a tall vertical prow and stern as can be seen in Egyptian wall-paintings. Their cargoes, checked by the official buyer and recorded by his tally clerk, included fruit, wine in conical amphorae, ivory carvings and humped Syrian bulls. In the background can be seen a chattering group of Phoenician women in flounced white frocks, their hair worn loose. Among other things exported by these early Levantine traders would be cloths, flasks of oil, ready-made lightly-framed chariots, and cargoes of the shellfish *murex*, from which was obtained the purple dye that patterns the robes of the merchants in the illustration. These merchants would have come with their ships from Byblos, or perhaps from Ugarit (modern Ras Shamra), which cornered the foreign markets in the middle of the 2nd millennium BC and became the first great international seaport, a cosmopolitan centre of the export trade comparable to Beirut today. (8)

Vessels just like these above can be seen on Egyptian wall paintings, borne by Syrians bringing tribute to the Pharaohs (see below). The red 'spindle bottle' is of a type found in Syria and Cyprus in the 15th century BC and the small black flask, of about the same date, is Cypriot. The oil-horn has a duck-bill stopper, and an ivory base-plate inlaid with a 'Syrian star' in ebony. (10)

Syrian tribute-bearers bringing gifts to Tuthmosis IV (about 1400 BC), from a mural in a tomb at Thebes (right). Their purple-fringed, white garments and their bushy hair bound by a slender fillet are typical of the northern coastal regions. Their gifts include leather quivers, an oil-horn (cf. pl. 10 above), a metal cup in the shape of a griffin's head, gold vases and a naked child slave. (9)

139

What were the religious beliefs of the Hurrians and their Mitannian overlords about 1500 BC? Very little is known about them, but we do know that the latter worshipped Indo-European gods such as Varuna, and Indra the war-god. The use of the Egyptian *ankh*, or breath-of-life symbol, on cylinder seals suggests that the aristocracy adopted foreign religious concepts. Their Canaanite subjects worshipped, among other deities, a moon god, symbolized by a disk and crescent.

In the 'Holy of Holies' of a small Canaanite shrine of the 13th century BC, found at Hazor near the Sea of Galilee, was a row of stones of the type in which the Canaanites thought the deity dwelt. Among them the small central stele (right) shows a pair of outstretched hands reaching upwards to the disk and crescent of the Canaanite moon god. (11)

The squatting stone figure (below) from the same shrine, is probably a god. He is holding a bowl into which offerings were poured to evaporate. Beside him is a pottery bowl for the pouring ceremony, left upside-down to drain. The stele in pl. 11 is just to the right of those shown here. (12)

Ritual basalt bowl from the Canaanite temple at Hazor (right), decorated with a running spiral in relief, a motif common to both Canaan and the Aegean. Probably both it and the pottery urn behind were used to store water for cleansing the altars. The plan of the temple in which these vessels were found is the closest yet discovered to the plan of Solomon's temple in Jerusalem. This part of the sanctuary contained figurines and a cultic bronze bull. (13)

Bronze figure of Teshub, the North Syrian god (above). Such small 'baals' in local Canaanite shrines were the abomination of the Israelites in the promised land. (14)

Found in an Egyptian tomb, this 14th-century wooden cup (right) was made by a Levantine carver, probably at Ras Shamra. The tall hat is Mycenaean, but the hair style N. Syrian. It appears to be copied from faience cups produced at Ras Shamra or Enkomi. (15)

An attempt at portraiture is hinted at in this lid of a Phoenician limestone sarcophagus from Beirut (above). Its date is not known, but it might be as early as the 10th or 9th century BC, to judge from its archaic style. The deceased, obviously a nobleman, wears a crown and holds an Egyptian-type sceptre. Sarcophagus lids with stylized human heads were used by the Phoenicians from the 6th to 4th centuries, and have been found in Palermo and Cadiz. (16)

The mingling of artistic styles and traditions in the period roughly from the 14th to the 12th century BC was a natural result of the increased commercial intercourse between Levantines, Egyptians and Aegeans. The Levant made a symposium of the Mesopotamian, Egyptian and Mycenaean styles, but added its distinctive contribution, not only artistically but also in its wealth of imaginative religious mythology, which greatly influenced Egypt and Cyprus.

A wounded bull stands at bay while towards and past him gallop horses, hounds and bucking steers. There is vivid artistry and a fine feeling for spatial arrangement in this carved ivory game box (below) from Enkomi, Cyprus (12th century BC). Gone is the static formality of much of the earlier ivory carving; instead, Levantine art of this period tended towards scenes of dynamic action, or to more formal pieces enlivened by vivacity or humorous touches such as the Egyptians could never produce. The mirror handles below are c. 1300 BC and bear a mixture of Canaanite and Mycenaean motifs; the one on the right shows a warrior killing a griffin-vulture. (17)

The flying gallop of the horses (above) on this gold bowl from Ras Shamra is a theme common to Aegean and Levantine art in the 14th century BC. The scene shows a Canaanite prince in his chariot, hunting a bull. (18)

The quest for ivory in Tarshish shows the importance of this material for Phoenician artists of the 8th-9th centuries. The superb plaque on the right, of ivory inlaid with glass pastes and in part covered with gold foil, comes from the Assyrian city of Nimrûd, and is probably of the 8th century BC. It shows a lioness attacking and devouring a slave boy, who has close-cropped, curly hair like a negro's. Negroid characteristics are well marked in Phoenician and Punic male figures, and confirm Phoenician contacts with Africa. (19)

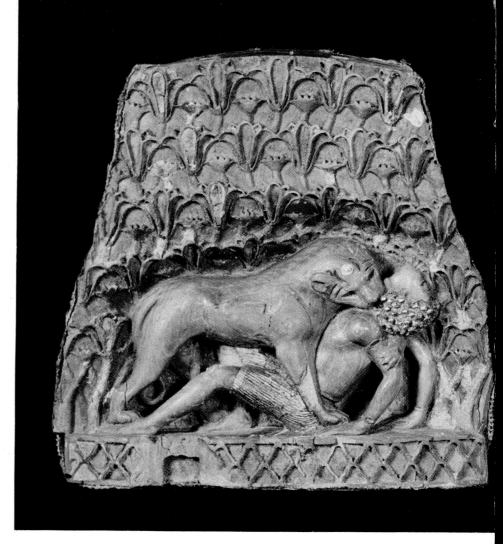

A gold sceptre, inlaid with blue and white pastes (below), from Curium in Cyprus. Though superficially it resembles Egyptian work, it is not Egyptian in detail, and may have been made by the skilled Cypriot jewellers of the 12th–11th centuries BC. (20)

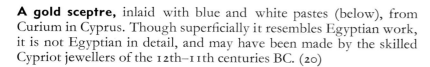

The delicate simplicity of Phoenician ivory. The openwork panel below, from Nimrûd, c. 8th century BC, shows a lion guarding a sacred tree, and wearing the headdress and breastplate of Hathor. The influence is Egyptian but the craftsmanship is Phoenician. (21)

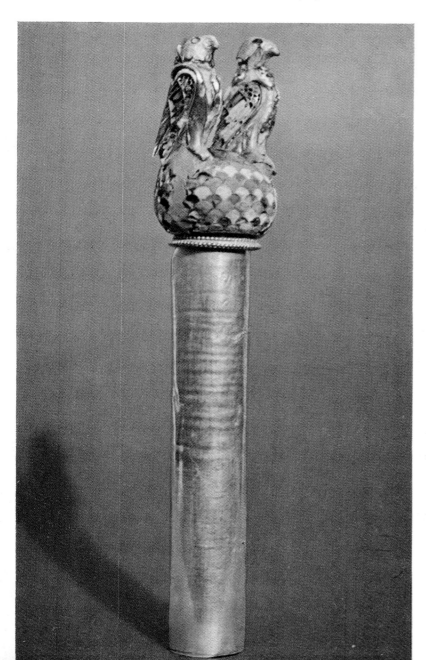

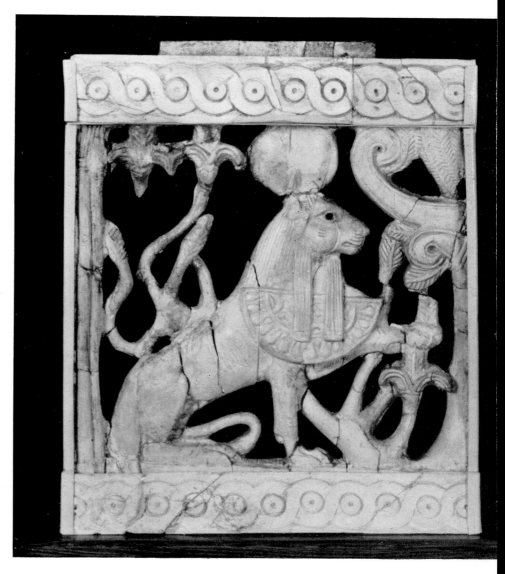

In face, dress and posture the figures on this ivory panel (above) from Nimrûd, capital of the Assyrian kings, are strongly Egyptian but the workmanship is Phoenician of the late 8th or early 7th century BC. The feather-crowned cartouche, which the two divine attendants are saluting with upraised hands, contains the name of an unknown prince. (22)

Grasping the ornate 'tree of life' and dressed in an elaborately embroidered tunic is a man who may represent the god Tammuz (right). This is one of an opposing pair of ivory panels found at Nimrûd (c. 700 BC). Tammuz was the symbol of vegetation and his roots lay in the Syrian rites of the annual renewal of life. Of Phoenician workmanship, it shows Syrian rather than Egyptian influence. The kilt topped by an open fringed surcoat was worn by wealthy Phoenicians, and can be seen in pl. 33. (23)

The vigorous, snarling lion is a typical theme of 8th-century BC Syro-Hittite art, admired and copied by later Greek artists. The grey steatite spoon from Carchemish (above) was used by altar-servers to place incense on the altar without burning their fingers. This was originally an Egyptian idea, adopted and embellished by Syrian and Canaanite craftsmen. (24)

Two religions meet in one figure from another ivory plaque in the same group as pl. 22. The priestess-attendant bears the horns and disk of the Egyptian goddess Hathor, while the wings folded round her body are an attribute of the Phoenician version of Isis-Astarte. Her clothes and the papyrus flower in her left hand were decorated with coloured glass. (25)

Cypriot fantasy was brought into extravagant blossom by the cross-fertilization of Mycenaean and Phoenician culture between the 8th and 6th centuries BC. The 8th-century painted jug from Citium, above, is divided into panels by stylized versions of the Phoenician sacred tree. Around them deer play, and exotic birds, perhaps peacocks, which the Phoenicians brought, along with apes and ivory, from 'distant Ophir' or the equally problematical Tarshish. (26)

In the arts of personal adornment Cyprus led the Levant for three centuries. This terracotta statuette of a Cypriot woman of c. 650 BC (left) shows some elaborate jewellery (compare pl. 28 opposite) and a headdress or perhaps a wig apparently made of feathers. (27)

A Cypro-Phoenician princess at her toilet, c. 700 BC (opposite). She would wear masses of jewellery, like the terracotta statuette on this page, and her slave-girl would help her make up her face with harsh-coloured cosmetics. Details of the background are taken from still extant tomb structures, which were built to resemble the houses of the time; many details, such as the pottery designs, and the wide wooden capital bearing the weight of three wooden beams, are still a living part of Cypriot tradition. In spite of her jewellery and her make-up, the princess is still of an age to keep her pottery toys (on the chest by the window) and to amuse herself with pet partridges. The pendant seal at her waist was a Phoenician custom, and this one is copied from an actual seal found in Etruria. Windows with carved upright bars are shown on Phoenician ivories and the 'proto-Ionic' capital by the door was an invention of Iron Age Palestine. The small ape-shaped scent bottle on the table is a product of Phoenician faience workshops on Rhodes. (28)

The exotic birds and flowers on the Cypriot jugs (below, left) show Phoenician influence (c. 7th century BC). Figures on the right-hand jug wear the royal Phoenician costume. The red burnished juglet is a ware typical of coastal Phoenicia, and bears the owner's name in the Phoenician alphabetic script. (29)

The glass scent bottle below copies the shape of an Eastern Greek amphora. It is made of Phoenician glass, inlaid with threads of a different colour, c. 5th-4th century BC. (30)

carried their merchandise, including the productions of their artists and craftsmen, from the coastal strip of their homeland to the end of the Mediterranean. They founded colonies, such as Carthage, and these in turn took the parent influence further. The spread of this trade can be clearly charted today by the help of objects found all over the Western Mediterranean and beyond the Straits of Gibraltar.

Both shape and decoration are Phoenician in the golden belt above, found at Aliseda in Spain (c. 650 BC). In the main bands of relief a hero—forerunner of the classical Hercules and the biblical Samson—wrestles with a lion. The decorative borders are of Phoenician 'dish-palmettes', derived from water-lilies. The tubular hinges and the terminal binding of plaited wire are typically Phoenician techniques. (31)

A pride of golden lions. Excavated Etruscan tombs at Praeneste (Palestrina) in Latium have yielded many sumptuous objects whose workmanship was inspired by Phoenician craftsmen. Below is part of a large shoulder-clasp from a cloak such as was worn in Etruria in the 7th century BC. The miniature lions with their filigree ornamentation are typical of the 'orientalizing' period of Etruscan art. (32)

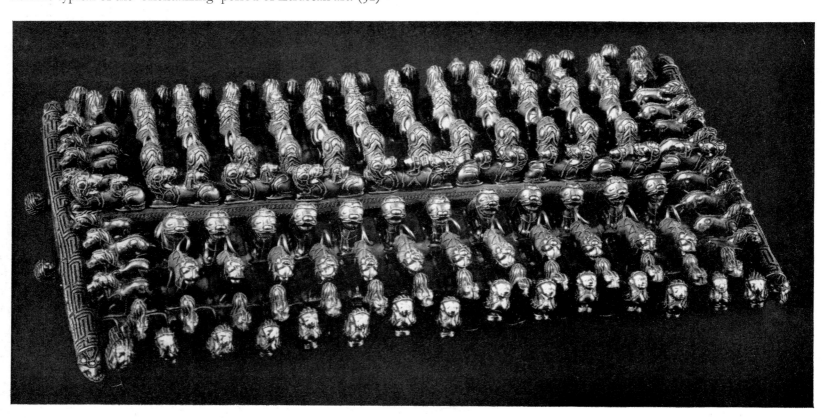

Silver drinking bowl of Phoenician design found in the tomb of a 7th-century BC Etruscan prince. In the outer frieze, which is Assyrian in style, the prince is seen leaving the palace gates in his chariot, hunting deer, picnicking at midday, being attacked by hairy giants (perhaps inspired by gorillas, which the Phoenicians discovered), and rescued by Astarte, patroness of chariots. After this eventful day he returns peacefully home. The centre and the inner frieze are copied from Egyptian themes. Compare this bowl with pl. 18, the Ras Shamra bowl, a stylistic ancestor. (33)

Probably made in Carthage, these two objects were found in tombs at Carmona, Southern Spain, and date from about 600 BC. The bone comb (above) and the ivory panel (right), which probably decorated a box, are obviously of Phoenician inspiration, though no precise parallels to this art style have been found. (34,35)

To avert sickness, the Phoenician settlers of Tharros, in western Sardinia, hung this type of grotesque mask (left) on their house walls. (36)

Coinage came late to Carthage. This gold coin of the 3rd century BC follows the Greek style, the female head being copied from coins of Syracuse. On the reverse is the horse that was on all Punic coins—an allusion to Carthaginian horse-breeding. (37)

The bones of children cremated in sacrifice to the goddess Tanit, the Carthaginian Astarte, were buried in urns in the precinct of her temple (below). The urns sometimes had dedicatory altars and stelae built above them; some of these can be seen in the background. (38)

The sea peoples of the Levant

WILLIAM CULICAN

Emergence

THE STORY OF the ancient communities of the Levant is broken in both the geographical and the historical sense, making it difficult for us to perceive any consistent patterns of culture common to them as a whole. Throughout their history the cities of Palestine and Syria remained the centres of small and independent kingdoms under petty rulers, whose allegiances were divided between Egypt, Babylonia and the great Hittite Empire. In such city-states, while individual genius might be fostered, the culture as a whole could not take on that characteristic form that we see for instance in the great kingdoms of oriental antiquity.

Two main factors were responsible for this situation. Firstly, all the great powers looked upon Syria, and Palestine, its southern extension, merely as a sphere of influence, never important enough to merit colonization or colonial development. Secondly, the Levantine region is itself one of great physical diversity. It was natural that the arid steppes which cross North Syria to the foothills of Kurdistan should attract incursions of Northern peoples seeking *Lebensraum*, and that the narrow strip of fertile coastal land, cut off from the desert by the mountain ranges of Lebanon, should foster the growth of peaceful cities absorbed in market gardening and sea-borne trade. In the low hills of Jordania, settled in since the dawn of the use of metals, and more fertile in antiquity than today, yet different communities arose, ancient peasant kingdoms such as that on the site of Jericho, with strong fortified cities governing patches of plain. These communities were highly vulnerable from the south-western desert through which both Egyptian and Israelite conquerors came, just as the coastal cities were vulnerable to attack from the strong communities settled thickly in north-west Syria, in the foothills of the Amanus and the Amuq plain.

At the beginning of recorded history in the late third millennium BC, we find two ill-distinguished groups of peoples—Amorites and Canaanites—in possession of the Syro-Palestinian area, the former northerly and westerly, the latter southerly and easterly, but belonging to the same Semitic stock, speaking basically the same language, and differing in little besides name. There were, however, cultural differences, which stem from the fact that the Amorite group ('westerners' as their name, given them by the Sumerians, means) assimilated Sumerian and North Syrian Hurrian elements, whilst the Canaanite 'lowlanders' (or perhaps 'purple-dyers') assimilated Mediterranean elements on the coast and became strongly influenced by Egyptian ways of thought and expression.

Byblos

The most important excavated Amorite cities are Byblos on the Mediterranean coast and Mari on the Euphrates—the last being a Sumerian foundation, but with a strong Amorite element in the population. Of such cities as Tyre and Sidon, both possible Amorite foundations, material of the Bronze Age is not known.

Byblos is the first to enter the pages of written history. The city, and the cedars that its inhabitants traded from the slopes of Mt Lebanon, are noted in Egyptian records about 2700 BC when the Pharaoh Sneferu (4th Dynasty) imported forty shiploads of cedar logs for shipbuilding. Well-preserved cedar beams were found propping up his burial chamber entrance in the southern pyramid at Dahshur, and in 1954, beside the Great Pyramid of Giza, the funerary boat of his successor, Kheops, was discovered intact with its cedarwood fittings still retaining, it is said, some of their original odour. Fragments of alabaster vases bearing royal cartouches (the oval figures that enclose royal or divine names) found at Byblos are dated even earlier, to Egypt's Second Dynasty; it is, therefore, possible that Egypt's contact with Byblos goes back to the dawn of Egyptian history.

In the 6th Dynasty, the trade with Byblos was put on a surer footing and Egyptian texts begin to record special Byblos ships constructed for trade with the port. Whether Byblians or Egyptians manned these ships is not certain, but the recorded facts suggest that Egypt was the prime financier in this trade and led the Mediterranean shipping of the period.

In Byblos herself, evidence from monuments suggests that it was in the strong 12th Dynasty (from c. 1990 BC) that relationships with Egypt were especially close. Royal tombs built into the cliffs on the shore of Byblos have been found with their treasures intact, and objects from rifled tombs have found their way to museums in Paris and Beirut. Amongst the intact tombs are those of Abishemou (Abi-is-my-father) and his son Ibshemouabi (my-father's-name-is-good), contemporaries of Pharaohs Amun-em-het III and IV (c. 1840–1785 BC). An obsidian ointment jar bearing the cartouche of Amun-em-het III was found in Abishemou's tomb and a gift box of incense from Amun-em-het IV in the tomb of his son; whilst to unnamed kings had been sent golden pectorals, other pieces of jewellery and jars of salve.

Although themselves Semites, the kings of Byblos are invested with such Egyptian titles as 'prince', 'count', or 'sheikh of sheikhs'. Their precise political standing in relation to Egypt is unknown, but they were probably vassal kings or high commissioners controlling a local population subject to Egypt. Foreign place-names in lists of Amun-em-het III's reign, which covered the second half of the nineteenth century BC, show that the entire coast as far north as the Nahr el-Kebir was included in the Egyptian political sphere as well as the inland plain of the Beqa'a. It has been suggested that the gift jars presented to the Byblian kings might have contained the very chrism (consecrated oil and balm) of investiture which the pharaohs of a later period sent to their Syrian allies, and that the gold-inlaid curved sceptres found in the tombs are symbols of temporal power from the hand of Egypt.

Some of the objects found in the royal tombs of Byblos (e.g. tridents with elongated central spike like those described in chapter XI) may be of Caucasian origin, but the majority naturally show the influence of Egypt. Alongside this influence, however, there is a recognizable local style. A golden pectoral, for instance, depicting the Hathor cow suckling Amun-em-het III and a scallop-shaped pendant from the tomb of Ibshemouabi might have passed in an Egyptian bazaar, but any Egyptian jeweller would have noticed innovations and inaccuracies in design. Collars of gold-foil with a beaten design of the Horus-hawk (pl. 4) copy a well-known Egyptian type, but again the treatment of the feathers and the action of the bird are un-Egyptian, whilst the egg-and-tongue design on the outer border is a device which becomes peculiarly Phoenician in later times and hence passed into the art of Greece.

Objects found in the temple, as distinct from the royal tombs, at Byblos are more characteristic of local Amorite craftsmanship. A gold foil, once the cover of a scabbard, shows a peasant mounted on a donkey herding with the help of two assistants the incongruous flock of a goat, lion, baboon, dog and fish (pl. 1, *fig. 1*). The features of the peasants are reminiscent of the famous painting in an Egyptian tomb at Beni Hasan, of the family of the Asiatic 'Abisha' people arriving in Egypt with their goods mounted on donkeys. The men, stubby and black-bearded, have the same bird-like faces with hooked nose. The Beni Hasan painting fills in further details of these semi-nomadic peasants, dressed in long multicoloured tunics and the clanswomen in gaily patterned dresses (no two alike) and red leather boots. Their weapons are the spear and throwing stick, and their music that of the

Drawing of the embossed design on the dagger sheath in pl. 1. The art probably owes more to Amorite than to purely Canaanite sources. (fig. 1)

harp. In the painting we see them bringing eye-paint and two fine desert gazelle for the prince buried here in about the year 1890 BC.

A dagger-handle sheath from Byblos *(fig.2)* shows even better than the scabbard local Amorite artistic ideas, with the characteristic elongation and the symmetrical positioning of the two goats, whilst objects of greater luxury from the temple show a technical mastery of goldsmithing equal to that of Egypt. Gold foils from crescentic Syrian axes (pl. 2) bear granulated designs of religious scenes, whilst a circular pendant and a fine gold vase are not only granulated but elaborately inlaid with lapis-lazuli and other stones. In this vase (pl. 3) we have the only surviving example of those elaborate metal vessels borne in the hands of the tall bearded and white-clad Syrian and Lebanese tribute bearers depicted in Egyptian mural paintings from the 12th to the 18th Dynasties (1990–1314 BC).

Very little is at present known of the other coastal cities, such as Tyre and Sidon, in the early part of the second millennium, nor, as also in the case of Byblos, with their relations, political and ethnical, with the inhabitants of the Lebanese mountains. A remarkable series of copper statuettes found mainly on both slopes of the Lebanon range and dated by a few associated objects to the Middle Bronze Age (c. 1700 BC), tell us something of the physical type of the people dwelling in the mountains. They were short and stocky, wide of eye and pronounced of chin. Their trim beards, and swept-back plaited hair are found on contemporary work in the north Syrian city of Mari on the Euphrates, and in later times in the Hurrian town of Tell Halaf in northern Syria. The racial type portrayed in the Lebanese statuettes is pronouncedly North Syrian, and indeed related statuettes occur in the Turkish Hatay and further into Anatolia. The male statuettes are dressed in a manner eminently suitable to mountain herdsmen, with a short kilt fitted with a broad brace or belt, probably of leather laced in front with a tasselled cord.

It can be concluded from material found in tombs at Lebea, Kafer-Djarra and elsewhere that besides settling in the coastal cities, attested at Byblos and Sidon, the Middle Bronze Age population, archaeologically characterized by pottery including elegant 'button-

Drawing of the design on the dagger handle in pl. 1. (fig. 2)

based' jars, extended a considerable distance into the hills. It is probable that in the immediate Lebanon area the Canaanite population was limited to the fertile coastal strip and, as recent excavations have shown, to the plain of the Beqa'a, leaving the older population stratum of the hills unmolested or employing them perhaps as porters of goods to Palestine beyond, whose population at this period, although given the archaeologically unsatisfactory name of 'Canaanite', was probably predominantly of the more northerly Amorite stock.

The royal archives of the Amorite centre of Mari on the Middle Euphrates, written in the cuneiform script (see page 159), show that in the early part of the second millennium BC the Amorites were essentially nomadic in their way of life. One of the loosely affiliated Semitic tribes in the Mari region bore the name Habiru, a name also found in later Egyptian texts. Now although there is insufficient philological evidence directly to connect this name with that of the later Hebrews, accounts in the Mari archives, and in the legal tablets from Nuzi in N.E. Mesopotamia relating to the Habiru tribes, introduce us to political and legal habits with which the patriarchal history in the Bible makes us familiar. It is probable that it was from some such tribe that Abraham's 'wandering Aramaean' father came. It was as the husband of a woman of such a tribe that the homesick Egyptian traveller Sinuhe found himself in the twentieth century BC. In his account of his adventures he describes vividly the Bedouin life and the country: 'Figs there were in it and grapes. It had more wine than water. Plentiful its honey, abundant its olives. Its trees bore every

fruit. Barley was there and wheat. There was no limit to the kind of cattle.' Even so, Sinuhe could not bear to stay, die and be buried, 'with but a sheepskin for a shroud', in a strange land, and 'gave up the sand to them who are in it'.

The Hyksos

From other details of Sinuhe's story it appears that Asiatic nomadic tribes were already beginning to make incursions into Egypt soon after 2000 BC. After the Middle Kingdom, by about 1750 BC, the Hyksos, a group of Asiatic herdsmen kings, swept over Syria and Palestine and imposed a foreign Dynasty on Egypt. It is possible that in the southern aspect of this mass folk-movement the conquering element was Canaanite or Amorite. Some of the earliest Hyksos kings bore Canaanite names and the deities whose worship was introduced to Egypt by the Hyksos kings were largely Canaanite ones. The weight of the Hyksos incursion came, however, from the more northerly Hurrian region and brought with it superiority in metallurgy and weapons and, above all, the use of the horse, domesticated beyond the Caspian by Indo-European peoples, as we see in chapter XI, and the horse-drawn chariot as a new and unassailable weapon of war.

The Hyksos migration ushers in a century of obscurity in the history of the Levant. Presumably the old Canaanite aristocracy of merchants and business men was now replaced by alien feudal chariot knights installed as a ruling class over the native population. When Egyptian records recommence we find besides the establishment of the Hyksos in Egypt, a new Indo-European knighthood in North Syria, that of the Mitannians dominating from their capital, Waššuggani, on the upper Habur River, the peoples of that territory and the Northern Seaboard. It was a southward movement of the Indo-Europeanized peoples, first the Hurrians, and later their Mitannian overlords from the upper Habur region into the North Syrian desert, which probably pushed the Southern peoples into Egypt.

Egyptian Domination of the Levant

It was Ahmosis I, founder of the 18th Dynasty, who in 1570 BC crushed the Hyksos Dynasty, which since the late eighteenth century had been maintained by superiority of arms in the capital of Avaris in the Nile Delta. During this period the so-called Hyksos scarabs with their delicate spiral designs were widely traded and are found on all sites between Syria and the Nile, associated often in coastal sites with the Tell Yahudiyeh ware, a class of elegant black pottery with white dot ornamentation. But at no site is the advent of the Hyksos domination strongly marked, although the fortification of the Palestinian farming towns such as Jericho, now at its height, was now carried out with wide-sloping ramparts especially designed to combat chariot warfare (naturally already adopted by the Egyptians), and besides scarabs, horse-bits occasionally appear. At Gaza in South Palestine the unique phenomenon of the burial of soldiers with their horses, a custom of Indo-European origin, has been found during excavation.

The Asiatic campaigns of Ahmosis are little known although, towards 1525 apparently, Tuthmosis I continued them as far as the Euphrates. It was Tuthmosis III, of whose campaigns we are graphically informed by the reliefs carved on the walls of the temple at Karnak, who finally came to grips with the Canaanites and Hurrians in their homelands (1483–1463). Under the threat of these campaigns the defences of the Palestinian farming towns were greatly strengthened. With three hundred princes and their *mar-janni* (charioteer knights) shut up within her, Megiddo stood siege for seven months. The presence of these charioteer knights in the plain of Sharon provides another indication of the dominance of Hurrian elements in Palestine at this period.

A keypoint in the fifth Syrian campaign of Tuthmosis III was the capture of the Northern Canaanite island city of Arwad (Aradus) situated in a strategic position a mile and a half from the mainland, which features now for the first time as a city of great wealth. Along with Aradus the pharaoh gained possession of the Syrian coast towns of Simyra and Ullaza and a stretch of the north Lebanese–south Syrian coast called Djahi in Egyptian texts. Obviously it was harvest time: the large booty exacted by Tuthmosis, and recorded in the triumphal narrative at Karnak, included the grain being ground on the threshing floors as well as horses, silver dishes, lead, copper, lapis-lazuli (not a local product), green feldspar (a crystalline mineral), incense, oil, jars of honey, and 6,428 jars of wine. 'Behold', says the official communiqué: 'the army of His Majesty was drunk'.

The precise nature of what Tuthmosis and his successor Amenophis II hoped to achieve by these campaigns is doubtful, but it can be surmised that the accounts of these campaigns written on the walls of the temple at Karnak are somewhat exaggerated and that the elaborate 'booty' must on occasions have been gifts from these prosperous commercial towns to avert the costly catering for an unwelcome Egyptian visit. Kadesh on the Orontes, the fountainhead of Hyksos disturbance, was however completely destroyed, and the prestige of Egypt was felt in this area until the decline of the New Kingdom.

Despite the ravaging of the Mitanni lands, the destruction of the Mitannian army was not achieved. But such was the lack of unity between the southern city-states and the great northern powers, and the impact of the friendly overtures made by the prince of Alasia and the great king of Hatti to the pharaoh, that the rebellious Hurrian in the North Syrian plains evidently acquiesced in the establishment of an Egyptian protectorate over Syria and Canaan. Each city-state in these regions maintained independent relationships with Egypt, giving rise to a complicated diplomacy. In the Canaanite cities some sort of supervisory Egyptian government was set up and mobile seaborne squadrons of Egyptian soldiers were at readiness to maintain peace.

This subjection imposed on Canaan conditions unlikely to foster the development of national enterprise in any direction except that of trade; but the Mitannian kingdom, now with its western capital at Alalakh in the Orontes valley, held more of its own. Its relations with Egypt were cemented by dynastic marriages between the royal families. The mother of Amenophis III (about 1401–1362) was a Mitannian princess. His son Amenophis IV also included amongst his royal brides a daughter of the Mitannian king Tusratta, well-known from Egyptian records of this period.

The Mitannians

Very little is yet known of the artistic, religious and other cultural traditions of the Hurrians and their Mitannian overlords. These latter worshipped Indo-European gods like Varuna and Indra and their adoption on cylinder seals (*fig. 3*) of the 'ankh' (breath of life) symbol

Drawing from a seal showing a Mitannian king in high hat and rolled-border cloak greeting his goddess, the Babylonian Ishtar. The Egyptian life-symbol between their heads is often found on N. Syrian seals of about 1700 to 1500 BC. (fig. 3)

and the winged disk of the sun from Egyptian sources suggests the currency among the aristocracy of religious concepts other than those current in Canaan. Perhaps even the chariot racing and lion hunting, those first sports of kings, to which they were addicted, had a religious symbolical meaning which enhanced their popularity as a sport. Mythological subjects on Mitannian seals are largely derived from the Babylonian repertoire, but ritual or symbolical scenes abound and a particular fondness is shown for the sacred tree and heraldically placed animals. Some of these symbolical seals with ox-heads and griffins show some influence of Cretan art forms, as indeed do those of Kassite Babylonia. The pottery too, delicate black-and-white ware, is for instance at Alalakh painted with copied Minoan designs and provides us with our earliest evidence of 'Western' trade with the Syrian coast. The chalice-shaped vases with narrow feet surpass in proportion and refinement any created up to that time in the Oriental world.

The inscribed statue of King Idrimi (15th century) from Alalakh (pl. 7) and a few copper statuettes as well as seal representations illustrate Mitannian kings of the middle second millennium clad in a tall 'mitre' and wearing the thickly bordered mantle peculiar to the Hurrian-Mitannian area. A particularly fine statuette from Egypt shows a Mitannian prince, perhaps a member of the Pharaoh's court, affecting the Egyptian crown (pl. 6).

Trade

In Egyptian wall-paintings of about this time the purple-robed Phoenicians of the Lebanese coast appear bringing their merchandise. The purple dye, for which the Phoenician coast became famous in later times, is first named in a cuneiform text from Ras Shamra (Ugarit) showing that a certain quantity of raw wool had been delivered amongst weavers who were responsible for the distribution of the dyed cloth. Although the shell-fish *(murex)* from which the dye could be made has a wide distribution in the Mediterranean it is in the region of Tyre and Sidon that the best varieties occur.

In the 18th Dynasty (1570–1314 BC) we have our first reference to the native shipping which carried these wares to the Delta. Such ships, in no way comparable with the large vessels built at the command of Queen Hatshepsut in about 1500 BC, can be seen in a wall-painting (now destroyed) from a Theban tomb. The form of the vessel (pl. 8), though basically Egyptian, has a high vertical prow and stern, and sides which appear to be made of wicker. A large paddle acts as a rudder. It is not now the cedar wood which is the chief item of commerce, but wine jars, cloths, flasks of oil and cattle. Buyers weigh the wares and a good deal of bartering and sampling animates the scene. The wine jars, the circular flasks, and the tall-necked jugs are all recognizably Canaanite, and the bulls of the humped variety native to Syria. Of the merchants themselves, some wear the purple-patterned garments of the coastal cities, others the simpler white Syrian dress, whilst the women are dressed in a frilled white frock and wear their hair loose. Arriving in full sail with the hold so full that a temporary deck can be lashed across it, the ships are soon unloaded by kilted slaves and the sails furled by a host of clambering boys. Other Syrians featured in the wall-paintings, some from Mitannian centres in the Orontes valley. Amongst other articles, they trade ready-made chariots of a lightly-framed type similar to that surviving in the tomb of Amenophis III, now in Florence. Egyptian accounts leave no doubt that the ash, hornbeam and willow woods needed for chariot construction were all native to the Mitannian hill lands.

Colonies of Canaanite and Syrian traders were certainly settled in Egypt from the reign of Amenophis II (1440–1415 BC). In his tomb inscribed sherds of pottery recording the names of foreigners, and objects of foreign design were found. Consequently it was during his reign that the worship of Canaanite deities entered Egypt and trade on a large scale between Egypt and Syria by way of Alasia (Cyprus) was opened up. This perhaps explains the appearance in 18th-Dynasty Egypt of Syrianizing elements in Egyptian decoration. In the magnificent Tut-ankh-amun tomb they become in fact dominating. The themes are not initially predominantly Aegean. The motif of rams feeding at a stylized sacred tree is probably of Mesopotamian or North Syrian origin transmitted by Canaanites.

Although Byblos still continued as an important port in the mid-second millennium, Ras Shamra ('Fennel-head' in Arabic), situated on a coastal bluff between Iskenderun and Latakia, cornered the foreign markets. The ancient name of the port was Ugarit, a name already known before its archaeological discovery in the 1920's from Hittite documents and the so-called Tell el-Amarna Letters, an archive of cuneiform tablets containing the correspondence of princes of Syria and Palestine with Amenophis III and IV and discovered in Upper Egypt.

Ras Shamra (Ugarit)

Ugarit was probably the first great international port in history. Her cosmopolitan urbanity, diplomacy, suavity and adaptability anticipate the character of modern Levantine life and her mixed cultural status must have been something like that of present-day Beirut.

Many of the buildings and objects found at Ugarit agree considerably with the cultural status of other cities in N. Syria in the 2nd millennium, but its importance in the history of Levantine civilization is that western influence is unparalleled at any other site. During the period 1800–1600 BC Minoan pottery was being imported. Cretan pottery has been found in other cities of Syria and Egypt and it was imitated in the Orontes town of Atchana; but nowhere as in Ugarit did Minoans form a trading colony with separate living quarters in the harbour and in the 'ghetto' of the town. Beneath their stately homes in the harbour region they buried their dead in chambered tombs of careful construction under the house floors. After 400 years of service these chambers became filled to capacity with bones and pottery, and thus no attempt could be made to preserve the careful burial rites of their Aegean homelands.

After relations between Ugarit and Minoan Crete had for some time been broken, the Mycenaeans in their turn formed a substantial colony and must have been a considerable element in the Ugaritic population during the city's most flourishing period from 1500–1200 BC. The tombs in the port area (Minet el-Beida) were still used, and thousands of Mycenaean pots were found in them. Much of the more ordinary pottery can be shown to come from Rhodes, but some are undoubtedly 'Cypro-Mycenaean', for by this time the Mycenaean colonies had gained a grip on Cyprus.

One of the outstanding results of the recent excavations has been to demonstrate the deep penetration of Mycenaean trade into the Levant. Whilst Near Eastern imports into Mycenaean tombs in Greece are as yet limited to a few scattered wine jars of a type of which hundreds have been found stacked in the Ugaritic warehouses, Mycenae was exporting on a large scale to the Lebanese coast, to Canaanite cities such as Hazor in Galilee and to the Orontes region. Much of this trade probably passed through Ugaritic hands, though Cypriot 'milk-bowl ware' is found in the southern region of the coast and might indicate a Cypriot origin, for Mycenaean Cyprus was strongly drawn into the Ugaritic orbit of trade.

The important cuneiform texts discovered in the royal library at Ugarit tell us something of the city's western policies. Naturally relations with Cyprus were strong, for Ugarit lay opposite the eastern tip of the island, and possibly her kings founded a new dynasty in Cyprus, which was rich in copper. In the excavations of 1931 a silver bowl was found with remains of a script which resembles at once Cretan Linear B and ancient Cypriot Linear script, but identical with neither. More of this script has now been found and although it cannot be deciphered, we can be certain from those remains that an Aegean language was spoken at Ugarit, or at least written for the purposes of keeping trade records. Records in the same language have been found in the city of Enkomi on the opposite shore of Cyprus.

Ivory carvings

A number of interesting ivories have been found in Syria and Palestine, notably at Megiddo and Ugarit, which show affinities with both Mycenaean and Aegean styles (13th and 14th centuries BC). It is, however, often difficult to decide whether they signify the influence of Mycenae on Canaan or vice-versa. Motifs such as the 'sacral ivy' on the Megiddo plaques are Mycenaean, but others, like the drooping palm on a box from Tell Farah, are Canaanite. The one distinctive beast in the animal repertoire, the winged and plumed griffin, which was enthusiastically adopted by Egyptian art of these centuries, can be shown to have a slight Canaanite antecedence.

Other ivories from the Syro-Palestinian area are of a straightforward Egyptianizing type. Quite elaborate scenes were borrowed from Egypt, as those on the Tell Farah casket showing swamp and banquet scenes and, in addition to these distinctive themes, items of furniture and dress are also Egyptian. Slightly more Canaanite in detail is an ivory scabbard-plaque from Megiddo showing a knight leading naked prisoners before an enthroned king. The layout of the scene is Egyptian, but the throne and garments Canaanite, whilst a general vivacity about the scene and a humorous touch added by the birds picking up the crumbs by the royal throne show a typically Canaanite addition to a set pattern.

In contrast to such genre scenes, are motifs on the recently discovered bed-stead fittings in the palace at Ras Shamra (Ugarit). Here we find repeated the official royal Egyptian themes of smiting a kneeling enemy. The delicate modelling undoubtedly owes something to the graceful relief style of the time of Amenophis III. Yet even here the errant hand of a Canaanite craftsman has drawn some garments incorrectly. The most interesting panel from the bed shows the goddess Hathor facing frontally and feeding two youths at her breasts. Not only in this plaque are details wrongly drawn but the whole motif is a violent misuse of an Egyptian one showing the unique relationship of a prince with his goddess. Between the horns of the goddess appears the Hittite royal emblem, a hint of the growing influence of this northern power upon the Ugaritic royal family.

The Hittites

Hittite power in S.E. Anatolia reached its zenith under Suppiluliumas (1380–1355). It was he who attacked and conquered the Mitannians, and the firm foothold he gained over North Syria brought him face to face with the Egyptian power. The Ugaritic king Niqmeda

paid tribute to him in the 14th century and throughout the 13th century the dynasty of Ugarit was subservient to the Hittites. The palace archives reveal the intervention of the 'great kings' and 'great queens' of the Hittites in the affairs of the city.

Hittite influence counted for little in artistic circles in Canaan and few of the ivories show anything of the heavy Hittite style. Specimens of beaten metal work produced at Ugarit in the fourteenth century illustrate Syro-Canaanite art in its best phase of syncretism, or combinations of divergent artistic traditions and styles, with an animal style and filling ornaments which find remarkable parallels in objects from the tomb of Tut-ankh-amun. The figures on a shallow golden bowl from Ras Shamra: winged bulls, eagle-griffins, lions attacking their prey, and vultures flying overhead, as well as a close combat scene between a hero and a lion, whatever their diverse origins, were to become the stock-in-trade of later Phoenician goldsmiths. A second golden bowl from Ras Shamra is embossed with a connected scene of a chariot hunt for bulls (pl. 18). Though cursorily rendered, the scene is one of great action only to be compared with the Enkomi game-box mentioned below. These were the bowls referred to in the Ugaritic Baal epic : 'bowls for a god, whereon the like of wild beasts of Yemen and wild oxen up to ten thousand are their decoration'.

No objects of comparable luxury come from the Syro-Hittite region, although a glimpse at beaten metalwork of a more northerly style is given by a gold embossed disk found at Izmir in Western Turkey. On this feature horned demons holding up a sun disk of Hittite form but in a manner typically Hurrian. The beasts and the palm trees, however, compare, except for differences of technique, with those of the more elaborate Ras Shamra bowl, and the piece might be a product of that colony of Hurrian workmen known to be established at Ugarit.

The widespread trade relations of Ugarit had a partly political basis. The palace archives unveil for us a political episode linking the city with Cyprus. Two princes of Ugarit, Hishmi-Sharruma and Arad-Sharruma, because of a fault committed against King Ammistamru II, a close relation, merited banishment to the Isle of Alasia. Tablets recording this judgement were made out by the Dowager Queen Anatmilku in the presence of Hittite and Mitannian royalty. To such dynastic history may be added the official request for the presence of Egyptian workmen in Ugarit made by Niqmeda II.

One of the products that illustrates the keenness of Ugaritic adaptability and helps us to trace her trade is pale blue faience, an Egyptian invention copied at Ugarit and Enkomi. At this latter site Mycenaean stirrup vases and an Egyptian duck-shaped toilet bowl are copied in this material, and faience goblets in the form of the heads of curly-haired women wearing black hats of a type found at Ras Shamra also occur at Assur, Mari, Ur and Tell Abu Hawan, the forerunner of the modern port of Haifa (pl. 15).

'Sea Raiders'

From about 1200 BC we have historical and archaeological evidence for a great invasion of peoples by sea into these closely related states of Syria, Canaan, Cyprus and Egypt: the effects are difficult to assess. One of the tribes involved in this folk-movement (which is thought to have overthrown the Hittite Empire about 1200 BC and then turned southwards against the Egypt of Rameses III), bore the name of Danaana and appears again as 'Danuniyim', settled in Cilicia in the eighth century BC. At this later period the Danuniyim seem to have adopted Phoenician as a language by choice. Inscriptions in one of their strongholds at Karatepe in the Cilician hills are written bilingually in Hittite and Phoenician, and it is possible that there was a proto-Phoenician or Canaanite element in the Sea Peoples by the time they descended on the Egyptian Delta. It is these Sea Peoples who are thought to have destroyed Ugarit, and they never resettled it or any other part of the coast from Tyre northwards.

It is indeed curious that amongst the names of the various ethnic groups composing the Sea Peoples preserved in Egyptian sources, some seem to be connected with the languages of peoples who in the first millennium appear in West Mediterranean lands. Such are the Shrdn, tall bearded men with horned helmets (as the Egyptians depicted them) linked perhaps with the later Sardinians; the Tshkr, with whom the prehistoric Sikels of Sicily have been connected, and the Trshw in their tight fitting caps, perhaps ancestral to the Etruscans of Italy, whom the Greeks called 'Turshenoi'. If these linguistic connections are correct, then we must see amongst the Sea Peoples groups ancestral to western peoples still in a migratory stage before their settlement in western lands, for archaeologically these peoples cannot be identified at this early date.

The Philistines

The Philistines were a group of these Sea Peoples and the only one that gained permanent settlement in Palestine apart from the small colony of Tshkr, on the coast south of Haifa. They occupied the coastal strip between the Carmel peninsula and Gaza and, so the Bible affirms, came from Caphtor or Crete. Sweeping into Canaan and into Egypt, attacking the coasts from their high-prowed boats and landing their women and children in ox-drawn carts—so are they pictured about 1175 BC in reliefs on the walls of the Medinet Habu temple built by Rameses III to celebrate his victory over them in the Nile Delta. Although they gained a deep footing in the Gaza region their expansion into the Negev was checked by the Israelites, now gaining possession of the land in S. Palestine by a slow infiltration culminating in direct combat with the Philistines at the battle of Ebenezer (I Samuel, 4).

The theory of the Aegean origin of the Philistines is amply supported by archaeological data. Their pottery found in many southern Palestinian sites forms a large and homogeneous group deriving from late Mycenaean wares. The exact predecessors of this pottery are however difficult to determine: its equivalent, not found in Crete, has so far only been found at Sindara in Cyprus, a site near to Enkomi, where also the passage of Philistines is illustrated by graffiti and seals. The Philistine custom of burial in pottery coffins was perhaps developed during a brief sojourn in Egypt, although the practice of covering the mouth and face of a rich man's corpse with gold foil is found earlier in the shaft-graves at Mycenae and again in Mycenaean Cyprus.

In the Biblical account the Philistines appear to have had the monopoly of iron working in Canaan and their huge round shields and short stout swords obviously impressed the designer of the Medinet Habu reliefs. Not until the appearance of the Philistines in Palestine does iron become common as a metal for everyday use. The Hittites had used the metal on the shores of the Black Sea before 1300 BC, but its use in the period of the Tell el-Amarna Letters was still novel, and an iron dagger and iron rings covered with gold foil sent by king Tusratta of the Mitannians to Amenophis III were regarded as a precious curiosity. There can be little doubt of the tradition implied in the Bible that it was from Philistines that the Hebrews learned the use of iron. The Hebrew words for 'knife' and 'helmet' came from a Philistine or other Aegean source.

Albeit impoverished by the depredations of the Sea Peoples, the coastal cities maintained their trade. Carved ivories from Paphos in Western Cyprus date from the eleventh-twelfth centuries and one of the best ivories artistically, the game box from Enkomi, now in the British Museum, belongs to the twelfth century. The long sides of the game box show a local Cypro-Canaanite prince hunting bulls from a chariot. Gone is the static formality of much of the earlier ivory carving. Instead here is a scene of dynamic action admirably suited to the shape of the box, and probably to the game it was meant to house. The flying gallop of horses and slinking of hounds, the leaping cows and bucking steers, the old bull, shot in the shoulder, making a stubborn stand—all this adds up to a scene of vivacity unattained by any other product of Levantine art. The prince's footman wears the tufted head-dress peculiar to the Philistines (pl. 17).

The half-mythical, half-historical travelogue of the Egyptian Wen-Amun, written about 1070 BC, gives some account of the conditions of trade at that period such as the banding together of impoverished individuals or states to form trade syndicates. In one of these syndicates Sidon is mentioned for the first time, the 'Fisher Town' which gradually rose to power in the first millennium and in the period reflected by the compositions of Homer had entirely eclipsed Byblos, which in the time of Wen-Amun's visit still held some form of dominance over the other coastal towns. To Homer, however, Sidon and the Sidonians became synonymous with all that was 'Phoenician', the name given by the Greeks to the people of the modern Lebanese seaboard.

The Phoenicians

Before the rise of the city of Sidon, and little over a century after Wen-Amun's visit, Tyre, called Sidon's daughter in the book of Isaiah, had risen to maritime prominence and was probably head of the carrying trade. The main part of the city with its royal palace, the temple of the god Melkart, and splendid bazaars, was built on a majestic scale on an islet off-shore. So impressed was Solomon with Tyre's Melkart temple that he invited his close ally King Hiram of Tyre to build his temple in Jerusalem in Phoenician style and to furnish it with ivories and bronzes of types which have survived. The Book of Kings and Chapter XXVII of Ezekiel acquaint us with that far-flung trade of Tyre in the ninth and eighth centuries which reached Egypt and Arabia and even beyond. Hiram of Tyre was able with Solomon's assistance to launch an expedition from Ezion-geber, 'King Solomon's Mines' discovered on the shores of the gulf of Aqaba, to Ophir. The main object of these expeditions was to obtain gold, but precious woods and diamonds were also brought back. From the recent discovery at Tell Qasile near Jaffa of a storage jar inscribed in cursive Phoenician script 'Gold of Ophir', historical substance is given to a land hitherto thought to be legendary.

The name of another land to which Hiram and Solomon sent joint expeditions, Tarshish, is also problematical. The similarity of the name to the Assyrian name for Tarsus in Cilicia perhaps led to some further confusion in the vague geographical world of ancient writers; but the fact that expeditions were mounted to it every three years only, and the nature of the cargo brought back (gold, silver, ivory, apes and peacocks), which could certainly not be obtained in Cilicia, show that it was much further afield. Traditionally Tarshish has been connected with the realm of Tartessos in South Spain known principally from the sixth-century Greek logbook *Ora Maritima* of Festus Avienus, and thought to have been in the Guadalquivir valley. The names of its kings are known, the most famous of which was Arganthonios who died about 550 BC. The gold, silver, copper and tin of this region were certainly exploited by prehistoric peoples, but no evidence of Phoenician presence in the region early in the first millennium has been unearthed. The rich treasure of goldwork found at Aliseda, Càcares, and a recent find of embossed golden jewellery near Seville, whilst both markedly Iberian in certain aspects of style, bear a strong influence of Phoenician jewellery techniques. Neither of these 'Tartessian' treasures however can be shown to date earlier than the eighth century, whilst that of Aliseda probably belongs to the second half of the seventh. Two magnificent bronze jugs in Phoenician style, one from Huelva the other from Badajoz, show Phoenician presence in that region there at that date, by which time Greeks too had begun to frequent the Guadalquivir valley.

Phoenician Ivories

The quest for ivory in Tarshish illustrates the importance of this material for Phoenician artists in the eighth and ninth centuries. Not until the ferment caused by the incursions of the Philistines from the West and the Hebrews and Aramaeans from the East had settled was the Syro-Palestinian region able to revive its late first millennium tradition in carving. Most of these ivories share a common style but it is impossible to name the place of origin of any particular piece. Some of them from Assyrian sites belong to the Assyrian orbit, while others—notably those from the royal palace at Nimrûd itself—fall loosely into two groups, characterized by their 'Syrian' or 'Phoenician' details. But in spite of this mixed inspiration and artistic tradition, their carvers managed to achieve a synthesis which is itself creative, and to express a refined, and typically Phoenician, taste.

Excellent ivories from Nimrûd, here illustrated (pl. 19-21), retain remains of coloured inlay and gold with which parts of the ivories, particularly the clothing, were covered. Some of them, even in their present fragmentary state, are masterpieces; such as the ivory scene of the lion devouring the curly-haired boy in a thicket of reeds (pl. 19). Other pieces, such as those in openwork showing designs of hinds browsing on lilies or comely maidens gathering flowers, have a delicate simplicity often compared with verses from the Book of Psalms, whose imagery they could sometimes well illustrate. Even the 'Soliciting Astarte', a fertility theme in which a female face stares through a half-open window, is treated without crudity.

For the history of art the ivories have an importance which reaches beyond the Levantine world. The cultured tyrants of the Aegean, the Bacchiads of Corinth and Polycrates of Samos, respected Phoenician refinement and bought its products. Phoenician ivories found in Samos, Crete and Rhodes are probably examples of that seventh-century love of exotic oriental objects which began in Greece that period known as 'orientalizing', which, through classical art, has left its legacy to our own times.

But besides purchasing objects from Phoenician merchants, the Greeks had themselves by the late eighth century established trading colonies on the Levantine coast. One of these was Al Mina, situated at the mouth of the Orontes at the western end of a caravan route across the Syrian desert. Other colonies were probably planted to the south, perhaps at Jebley and at Tell er-Soukas between Latakia and Tripoli. There is abundant evidence provided by potsherds of a type known from the Cycladic islands that in the eighth and possibly the late ninth centuries the Greeks were familiar with the North Syrian region and with the area of the Danuniyim in Cilicia, which played a considerable part in Greek mythological history.

Hittite States in Syria

After the break-up of the great Hittite Empire in the late second millennium, a number of small city-states had grown up in the Çeyhan valley, the Marash plain, the upper Euphrates valley with Syrian extensions in the Amuq plain and about Aleppo. Of these the chief was Carchemish, a stronghold of the Empire on the Euphrates which maintained much of its Hittite character. Other cities however in which the basic Hittite population had been gradually outnumbered by immigrant Aramaeans (a surviving branch of the old Amorite groups), were strongly Semitic, and for a period the official language at Sinjerli as at Karatepe was Phoenician. In other cities such as Marash, Aleppo and Tell Tainat, the Anatolian element predominated and Hittite was spoken. As these city-states were buffers between Assyria and the central Anatolian kingdoms, Assyrian influence was varyingly felt.

The artistic expression of these Syro-Hittite cities was somewhat unified by the practice they adopted of decorating their royal palaces with dados carved in low relief as can be seen on the façade of the Temple Palace of Tell Halaf in N. Syria. Tell Halaf was the capital of the Assyrian-dominated province of Guzana. The Temple Palace (a building that combined secular with religious functions) was rebuilt and decorated with a sculptured dado by King Kaparu in the second half of the 9th century, and his name, and those of his father and grandfather, are given in cuneiform on the skirt of the woman and

12th-century bronze cauldron stand from Curium, showing a man bearing a copper ingot in the shape of an ox-hide, such as have been found in Cyprus and in examples in the E. and W. Mediterranean. (fig. 4)

the left shoulders of the two men who form the pillars supporting the architrave. Like the Phoenician ivories, it contains a mixture of motifs, as do also the sculptures from Sinjerli and Carchemish, which are especially valuable for their wealth of detail in dress and accoutrements. The daily life of a people mixed in origin yet remarkably homogeneous in their material culture is here more fully illustrated than anywhere else in the Levant in the early first millennium. Scenes of hunting from chariot and on foot, fowling and trapping, the royal banquet, a girls' band, a party for two, and a school lesson are examples of the repertoire. An important feature of Syro-Hittite art is its interest in carved lions, vigorous snarling beasts which were admired and copied by Greek artists of the seventh century.

The influence of the style can be seen in a set of bronze shields from Mount Ida in Crete. From a late ninth-century grave from the Kerameikos cemetery in Athens comes a beaten bronze bowl which has both Syro-Hittite and Cypriot characteristics. Other bronze bowls

Reconstruction of the façade of the Temple Palace at Tell Halaf, a Hurrian city of north Syria, which was the capital of the Assyrian-dominated province of Guzana. Buildings of this portico-ed type with long parallel rooms placed at right angles to the entrance appear to have been evolved in north Syria in the late 2nd millennium BC. Their purpose was both religious and secular. This drawing shows the building as reconstructed and ornamented by King Kaparu in the second half of the 9th century BC. Sculptures which decorate the dado, whilst related to Assyrian and Syro-Hittite sculptures in style, include motifs which occur in Persian, Elamite and Urartian art and are probably of Hurrian origin. On the skirt of the woman and left shoulders of the two men who form the pillars supporting the architrave is a cuneiform inscription giving Kaparu's name and those of his father and grandfather. (fig. 5)

found in Greece at Delphi and Olympia have a Phoenician repertoire of lions and skirted sphinxes executed in a rather Assyrian manner. These examples should be assigned to the mid-eighth century, whilst a fragmentary bowl of similar style from a grave at Fortetsa in Crete and of a more distinctively Phoenician decoration cannot be closely dated from its context. In addition, a number of bronze and golden bowls are known from Cyprus. These as a rule employ deep incision alongside beaten technique and dispose the decoration, rich in mythological content, in three friezes round the circumference. The Cypriot bowls, the style of which allows us to imagine more clearly the work of Phoenician coastal workshops in the eighth century, are lineal descendants of the fourteenth-century Ras Shamra bowls (pl. 33). The Delphi and Olympia bowls on the other hand probably represent the metalworking tradition of a Syrian centre influenced by late Egyptian works. Other Phoenician metalwork, metal attachments for harness, come from Cyprus, Rhodes and Samos and to some extent copy earlier ivory trappings found at Nimrûd.

Phoenicians and their Colonies

The rise of Tyre as a major maritime power had important consequences in the Mediterranean basin. After Mycenae, Tyre became the second colonial power in the Levant, colonizing the isle of Cyprus and by the foundation of Utica, Cadiz and Carthage establishing permanent colonies in the West Mediterranean.

It is generally assumed that the Phoenicians arrived in Cyprus some time after the Mycenaeans, but at Enkomi at least by the thirteenth century BC a permanent colony of Ugarit, manufacturing specifically Canaanite objects, seems to have been established. Political stories in the Ugaritic archives suggest the setting up of banished Ugaritic dynasties there. Canaanite interest in the 'copper isle' of Alasia and its bull's-hide-shaped ingots goes back at least to the twelfth century and is perhaps earlier, but direct evidence for the permanent establishment of Phoenician colonies is lacking before the eighth century BC unless we except an inscribed tombstone dated on the grounds of its inscription to the first half of the ninth. This tombstone merely records the burial of a Phoenician in the unknown locality of Cape Eshmun, but an inscription on an 8th-century bronze bowl found near Amathus reads: 'Governor of Kartihadesht, servant of Hiram, King of the Sidonians'.

Cyprus

It seems that the tributary kingdoms of Cyprus were already in existence in the late eighth century. Indeed the Jewish historian Josephus takes us back almost thus far when he records that Citium broke away in revolt from Elulaius of Tyre, who we are told successfully withstood the attack of Shalmaneser V about 727 BC.

In later times Phoenician dynasties are thought to have reigned also in Idalion, Citium and Curium. Archaeologically these sites are fairly well known but it is impossible from the pottery record to make clear distinctions between what is Phoenician and what is native Cypriot. This difficulty is increased by our very scanty knowledge of the native Phoenician settlements on the coast during the ninth and eighth centuries BC. What little is known of Phoenician pottery of this period shows its strong dependence upon Cypriot styles and is difficult to distinguish from it. Eighth-century Phoenician burials at Athlit and Ezzib (Achzib) south of Tyre and in the immediate Tyrian region contain red burnished (pl. 29) and black-on-red painted wares known from many sites in Eastern Cyprus. The former of these wares might be of non-Cypriot origin (it is found in quantity at Al Mina) whilst the latter was certainly manufactured on the Phoenician coast but perhaps not exclusively there. The date of these wares seems to extend from the late tenth to the early eighth century BC. A further characteristic of the graves is the use of cremation alongside (i.e. in the same tomb in cases) extended inhumation burial. Close parallels to these eighth-century mainland tombs have so far only been recorded in the Larnaka district of Cyprus near the site of ancient Citium.

The cross-fertilization of Greek and Phoenician culture in Cyprus between the eighth and sixth centuries caused the latent Cypriot flower of fantasy to break into extravagant bloom. Comical painted birds, singing strings of Z's (the earliest known attempt at recording musical notes) appear on the bichrome pottery along with capering goats, human-headed sheep and a fantastic arboretum of curly palm trees (pl. 26). The painting tradition is a development of late Cypro-Mycenaean tradition, but the palms and dish-palmettes, goats and sphinxes

Coloured glass beads of Phoenician workmanship (8th–5th century BC). The wolf was found at Ezzib on the coast of Israel, the other three heads at Carthage. The Phoenicians did a considerable trade in such beads. (fig. 6)

are of Phoenician origin and the scenes chosen to decorate shallow dishes and plates show a close acquaintance with Phoenician beaten metal work.

Whilst of the homeland Phoenicians we have few surviving monuments, of the Cypro-Phoenician culture we have a wealth of detail bequeathed in painting, terracotta modelling and statuary. It is difficult to say how much of this exotic culture was typical of Phoenicia herself although its preoccupation with details gives it an intimate femininity more Phoenician than Greek.

In the terracotta models, some of which are genre scenes of daily life such as women baking bread or having a bath or washing at a communal laundry, and from the limestone sculptures we obtain an idea of rich racial diversity in features and types of dress, varying from the cunning-faced Cypro-Greeks to those of the bland Cypro-Phoenicians. Other statues, found near Arsos, depict a fat-faced group which fit into neither category. Enough real treasure has survived from Cypriot tombs to show that in the arts of cosmetic and jewellery, for both men and women, Cyprus led the Levant for three centuries: many details of male and female dress and jewellery can be reconstructed from vase paintings and terracottas (pl. 27) and although no buildings survive, a number of built limestone tombs preserved mouldings and other details employed in better-class Phoenician domestic architecture.

The Western Phoenicians

By Greek tradition, which is untrustworthy since it tended to exaggerate the importance of the Phoenicians as forerunners of their own colonies, the foundation of the far-western cities was placed very early; 1104 BC in the case of Cadiz, 1100 for Utica. Archaeological proof for these early dates is entirely lacking, but evidence of Phoenician activities at a date early in the first millennium has recently been sought in the epigraphy of a stone found at Nora, on Cape Pula in South Sardinia, but there has been considerable disagreement over this.

The date of 814 claimed by the Sicilian historian Timaeus (who ought to have known) for the foundation of Carthage must be taken into serious consideration. In spite of the total destruction of the city by the Romans, a considerable amount of material has been recovered from Punic tombs and from a group of votive deposits of children's bones made in a graveyard dedicated to the Carthaginian goddess Tanit (pl.38). Unfortunately the only dateable objects in this material are imported Greek vases in the Protocorinthian style, which made their appearance in the West Mediterranean at the earliest at the end of the eighth century. One of these vases was found in a tomb containing an inscription in letters of a style corresponding to that of the Nora Stone in Sardinia. Even a group of pottery with geometric ornament (*fig. 7*) found below the deposits in the Tanit precinct cannot be shown to be earlier than the third quarter of the eighth century. Thus, because of the 'lost century' between the traditional foundation date and the beginning of the archaeological record, many are inclined to place the foundation of Carthage during that period in the late eighth century when both Greek and Phoenician were active in the West Mediterranean and established themselves in Sicily. The archaeological records of Phoenicians at Motya is almost as early as that of

Cinerary urn (behind) and pottery with painted decoration, from the earliest pottery deposit at Carthage. The decorative elements date to about 720 BC, although no exactly similar pottery is known. (fig. 7)

Carthage, whilst evidence for Phoenician establishment in Malta is found in the early seventh century.

Carthage seems to have been founded by Tyre in the period of upheaval following upon the year 700 when the city was solicited on both sides by Esarhaddon and the pharaohs of the Twenty-fifth Dynasty. In 673 BC Tyre was brought to the critical choice of losing herself to Egypt or making a new foundation overseas. In fact Tyre was completely overcome by the Assyrians in 666 and was reduced to the status of an Assyrian tributary power. Baalu, King of Tyre, escaped with his two daughters Dido and Anna, sailed, and founded Carthage. Dido and Anna we know as the heroines of Virgil's *Aeneid* which still preserves the tradition of their father's name as Belus (Baalu).

From this must be separated another tradition mixed with the Dido-legend of the foundation of Carthage by Pygmalion, an earlier king of Tyre, and his sister Elissa, whose name probably stems from Alasia, Cyprus. It is possible that this earlier legend applied to the Kartihad-esht (Carthage) in Cyprus, already mentioned, which became prominent in the early eighth century.

Whatever the case there is no doubt that it was in the middle of the seventh century that Phoenician activity in the West Mediterranean reached its height. Motya, the island city near Marsala in Western Sicily, was a flourishing entrepot between Carthage and Etruria by that date, and by the end of the century Tharros had been founded on the gulf of Oristano in Sardinia and had trade contact with the peoples of that island whose resources in bronze and wool were of great value. A settlement on the Balearic island of Ibiza was also made, according to the traditional date, in the middle of this century, although no material earlier than the fifth century has yet been found on the island. Trade between Ibiza and the nearby Greek colony of Emporion (Ampurias) was brisk, and apart from the importance of the raw materials of Ibiza it was probably in rivalry to the 'Greek corner' of the North-West Mediterranean that Ibiza found its role.

It cannot be said that the civilization of the Western Mediterranean owes much artistically to the foundation of these colonies. The second quarter of the seventh century was the heyday of orientalizing trade in Etruria to which date must be assigned the gilded silver vessels with Phoenician design found in the rich tombs of Cerveteri and Praeneste (Palestrina) (pl. 33) and small faience juglets in human shape and amulets probably made by Phoenicians resident in Rhodes. The bowls appear to be either of Cypriot origin or to be copies of Cypriot work made by Etruscan artists. The use of the madonna lily as a marker on some of these bowls is a particularly Cypriot device *(fig. 8)*. Both Phoenicians and Ionian Greeks had a hand in this trade in objects from the east. The presence in earlier contexts of provincial Assyrian metalwork and copies of Cretan work, the former of which probably reached Greece and Etruria alike from some Ionian source, suggests

that there were channels for the dispersal of orientalizing objects other than those opened by the Phoenicians. At any rate, none of these pieces of Phoenician or Assyrian metalwork appears to have reached Carthage.

Recent archaeological work has filled out the picture of Carthaginian expansion in the Mediterranean. Whilst nothing is known of Cadiz, excavated material in Utica, traditionally the oldest foundation, is not older than the seventh century. New sites at Rachgoun, an offshore island near Oran, and Mersa Madakh, on the nearby coast, are apparently of the early sixth century and work on the Spanish Moroccan sites of Lixus and Tamuda indicates a growth in the communities of that region in the fourth century, at which date the rock of Gibraltar was held by Carthaginians.

All ancient authorities are agreed that the Atlantic was a Phoenician preserve, giving access not only to the fabulous 'Tarshish' but to the unlocated 'Tin Isles' or Kassiterides. There is no evidence that Carthaginians reached Galicia (let alone Britain) before the second century BC, but their activities on the west coast of Africa are attested at a number of points. On the island site of Mogador off the coast of French Morocco, which is perhaps the 'Karikon Teichos' founded by the Carthaginian general Hannon in 525, have been found sherds with graffiti in sixth-century Punic whilst a tomb found at Cape Spartel must be fourth century.

It seems safe to accept the foundation of Carthage in the second half of the eighth century BC, contemporaneous with or only slightly earlier than the Greek settlement in the west and the foundation of Ischia, Cumae, Syracuse etc., for it is with these earlier settlements that Carthage shares the same Egyptianizing objects (faience and jewellery in particular) in the earlier levels of grave material. After Carthage and Utica, whose high antiquity archaeology has not vindicated, great cities are few. Motya rose to wealth by her proximity to the Sicilo-Greek sphere of trade and doubtless by a mixture of Greek cunning and Phoenician enterprise; but we do not know the cause of the prosperity of Sardinian Tharros. Otherwise, a few small towns like Ibiza and Nora and Rusadir (Melilla in Spanish Morocco) were almost certainly primarily concerned with the exploitation of raw materials in their immediate hinterlands. For the rest, we meet but a collection of trading stations and minor ports, mainly established in the 4th century at the earliest, whose miserable architectural remains speak of a very low cultural level. Into this category fall Mersa Madakh, Cap Bon, Sidi Absalem in Spanish Morocco, Olbia in Sardinia, and various sites on the Levant coast of Spain.

Commerce, for which the sea was a highroad rather than a barrier, alone determined the mechanism of this expansion. In no case can any Phoenician penetration of the hinterland for commercial purposes be demonstrated: it was by the provision of markets rather than in exploitation that this commercial Empire flourished. When Carthage lost the Tartessos market to the Samians in 650 or 630 BC, and Spain had become the chief source of silver for the Ionian cities in the sixth century, Carthage was still able to maintain herself by the command of the ivory and metals of the North African interior, as well as her own handicrafts in carpentry, cushion-making and fine fabrics and upholstery, to the quality of which ancient authors testify. Exploitation of raw materials such as the pine-pitch and timber of Ibiza and the lead of Sardinian Sulcis as well as the exploitation of the esparto grass of the Valencian coast, and other raw materials of which there is no archaeological record must have provided for the basic economy of the lesser towns. The smaller coastal stations, besides providing the frequent harbourage necessary to a coastal carrying trade, most probably exploited local fisheries as a source of income. Pliny tells us how lagoon fishing with nets slung from stakes set up in shallow water was a particular practice of the Phoenicians and doubtless they introduced present-day lagoon fishing methods to the West Mediterranean. Cagliari, Olbia, Motya are all situated near lagoons and it is astonishing to see how many Punic settlements (Ibiza, Cadiz, Alcudia de Elche, Sidi Absalem, Cagliari and Olbia) are situated on the edge of natural salt pans where material was at hand for the preservation of fish. Ibiza, at least, according to Athenaeus, was famous for her kippers, and the large cigar-shaped amphorae with wide mouths found in almost all Punic establishments were doubtless used for the trading of salt or salt-fish. One such amphora was found at Motya full of fish bones, and offerings of cooked fish were often placed in the tombs where their backbones are still found adhering to the curious little plates with partitions to receive the gravy. Whether the Phoenicians carried

The frieze of a Phoenician engraved silver cup (7th century BC). The chari-oteers are Assyrian in appearance, the hoplites more Egyptian. The madonna lilies and club-like cypress trees are motifs used by the Phoenician silversmiths in Etruria, where the cup was probably found. (fig. 8)

their fishing enterprises into deep waters is difficult to decide. Certainly large fish hooks and small harpoons have been found in several of the sites, and a number of fish hooks found with the Punic pottery in Gorham's Cave, Gibraltar, leave little doubt as to the occupation of these cave dwellers. Perhaps the tunny was fished as off the Sardinian west coast in historical times: tunny fish feature on the earliest coinage issues of Cadiz, Rusadir and Cartagena, and in combination with the murex purple shell on the earliest issue of Tyre itself.

How did the Phoenicians of the narrow coastal strip of Palestine with their poor resources, political disunity, and restricted man-power manage to settle this network of small communities? The genius of the Carthaginians, like that of the Tyrians and the Cypriots, consisted in planting but small numbers of colonials and allowing them to mix freely with the local populations. To the Greeks these bastard communities were known as the Libyphoenices of Africa, and the Bastulophoenices of South-East Spain.

Conclusions

It is difficult to assess the part of the Levant in the history of material civilization, in which it played the role of transmitter rather that of originator. The Canaanite role in literary history, however, is now beginning to be realized. Long after Sidon had been destroyed by Esarhaddon in 675 and Ashurbanipal had finally come down upon Tyre 'like the wolf on the fold' in 666 and extinguished her last breath, names such as Zeno, the philosopher-founder of Stoicism (333–261), born in Citium, and the philosophers Boethus of Sidon and Antipater of Tyre, though all belonging to strongly Hellenized communities, were still regarded by the Greeks as continuing the Phoenician tradition of acumen. Philo of Byblos (64–181 AD) in the composition of his work on Phoenician religion claimed as his authority a sixth-century (or perhaps earlier) Phoenician historian Sanchuniaton. The existence of this Phoenician source has long been disputed but correspondences between his statements and the fresh mythological documents found at Ugarit are striking and leave little doubt of his authenticity.

The discovery at Ras Shamra (Ugarit) of clay tablets written in a Canaanite dialect in an alphabetic cuneiform script has revealed a wide selection of literary epics and religious poems. Most of Canaanite literature was written on papyrus and hence has perished but the tablets do contain a fragment of it, and they shed light not only on the religious beliefs of the Canaanites, but also to some extent on the literary forms, different from those of Mesopotamia and Egypt, current on the Levantine seaboard in the second half of the second millennium BC.

The material is mostly of a ritual kind connected with that promotion of seasonal fertility so vital to a gardening and farming community. The theme of the dying and rising god is here told more fully than elsewhere in the Near East: Mot, the spirit of death, banishes Ba'al, the lord of vegetation, as is appropriate in a land where summer drought puts an end to vegetation, but with the renewal of the rain in autumn Ba'al renews his victory over Mot and in a divine marriage with Anath, the fertility goddess, fecundates the earth. Such tales, told in elaborate detail and intended certainly for recitation if not dramatic acting, contain the germ of Greek drama. Close parallels also exist in language and thought with that of the Bible. The Hebrew idea of the kingship of Jahweh was probably derived from that of El as described in the texts and biblical passages, particularly in the Book of Job, copy Ugaritic ideas. Phrases, for instance in Psalms 88 and 89, attributed in their headings to authors with Canaanite names, seem to be directly taken from the Ba'al Epic of Ugarit.

There appears firm foundation for the view that the Ugaritic poems contain part of a set of mythological themes which had spread over the East Mediterranean and which influenced the literature of ancient Greece. The theme of the warlike expedition for the winning or recovery of a beautiful bride for instance, is found in the Ugaritic Epic of King Keret, who conquered the land of Udum in order to marry the king's daughter Hurriya 'whose eyeballs are gems of sapphires, whose eyelids alabaster cups' and this immediately recalls the expedition of the *Iliad* undertaken for the recovery of the fair Helen by Menelaus.

Other Homeric themes, as has long been recognized, are paralleled in biblical history. Not only is there the same romantic interest in women and marriage, which occasioned the wrath of both Achilles and Samson as well as the love of battling heroes (David and Goliath, Achilles and Hector) but also Homeric heroes are given the same skill in music and song attributed to David.

An important link in the connection between the archaic Greek and the biblical literatures might have been the literature of the Philistines, completely lost. It is demonstrable that the Aegean Philistines exerted a great material influence on the Israelite world. It was with the help of Philistine mercenaries that King David was able to establish himself on the throne of Judah and expand the Israelite influence to the Euphrates. He belonged to a tradition which held music and poetry in high esteem and it is permissible to suppose that the folk-tales of the Philistines, whose 'exodus' from Egypt might have provided a parallel to that of Israel herself, inspired his music.

The great gulf which separates the literature of Canaan, on the one hand, and that of the Greeks and Hebrews on the other, necessitates some such intermediary. Although the Ugaritic stories imply the observance of social obligations, these are never raised by philosophic reflection to the level of morally binding obligations. They were preoccupied with ritual and symbolic situations and hence with only idealized relationships in personal and political matters. Nowhere do they deal with personal actions morally judged by an accepted code; and nowhere are the symbolical actions applied personally: the Canaanites did not for instance apply the theory of the dying and rising god to a personal ideology as did the Greeks from the similar cult of Adonis, or the Egyptians from the mystery cult of Osiris.

The Ugaritic poems accept the world as ready made, do not moralize upon its significance, or preoccupy themselves with theology or ethics or conceptions of life after death. Notions of that humanism which magnifies the literature of Greece and the Bible and had already on a small scale been attempted by Sumerian proverbs and wisdom literature, were absent. For its essentially amoral character the Hebrews condemned it.

Writing

It was not, however, only in the invention and elaboration of ideas, but also in the simple mechanism that they invented for their transmission that our debt to the Canaanites is great; for the system of alphabetic writing was invented in the Syro-Palestinian area. Invention itself was the last stage of a long process of evolution beginning with what does not yet merit the name of writing but is pictography. Mesopotamian peoples developed such a system and also invented a phonetic system in which signs stand for various syllables; it is in this way that the cuneiform languages of Mesopotamia are written. Egyptian hieroglyphic writing developed in a similar manner but went further by its use of what is called acrophony, or the restriction of phonetic value of certain signs to their initial consonants only. This produced a kind of alphabetic writing first employed in the second millennium amongst the Semitic workers in the Egyptian turquoise mines at Serabit el-Khedem in the Sinai peninsula. These Sinaitic inscriptions (formerly dated about 2000 but now believed considerably later) employ signs derived from Egyptian hieroglyphics and others which do not belong to any Egyptian system of writing. Some of the non-Egyptian signs relate to the earliest known alphabetic inscription from Phoenicia, written in the tenth century on the stone coffin of Ahiram, King of Byblos.

159

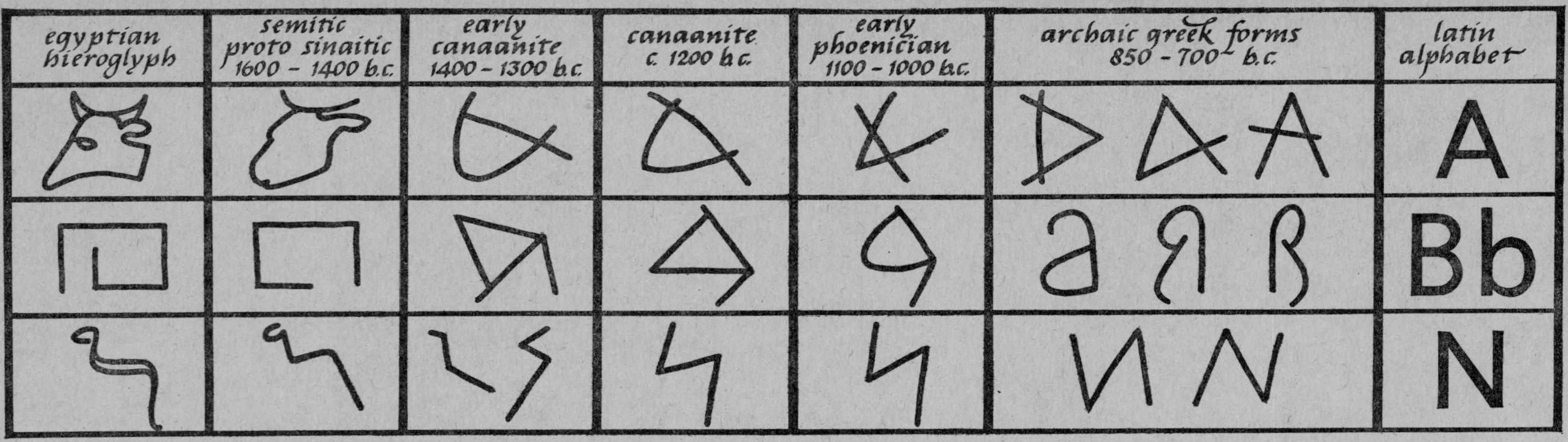

egyptian hieroglyph	semitic proto sinaitic 1600 - 1400 b.c.	early canaanite 1400 - 1300 b.c.	canaanite c. 1200 b.c.	early phoenician 1100 - 1000 b.c.	archaic greek forms 850 - 700 b.c.	latin alphabet
						A
						Bb
						N

The development of the alphabet: the diagram shows how aleph, *an ox,* beth, *a house and* nun *or* nahas, *a snake, evolved into the letters A, B, N of our alphabet. (fig. 9)*

Before this date, however, writing more removed from Egyptian hieroglyphics is found painted on potsherds in the South Palestinian area; at Shechem, Gaza and Lachish. These are obviously alphabetic, although their interpretation is controversial: upon archaeological evidence they date from slightly before 1500 BC. The discovery of inscribed javelin heads dating from about the eleventh century, and also of more late thirteenth-century inscribed swords, makes it now easier to fill in the general lines of evolution of this Proto-Canaanite script from the sixteenth to tenth centuries. One of the remarkable features of this evolution is that between the fifteenth and thirteenth centuries the change from vertical to horizontal script turns the signs ninety degrees so that the finished product, whilst looking more like the letters of the Phoenician alphabet of the first millennium, looks less like Egyptian hieroglyphic. The Ugaritic texts are written in alphabetic script of modified cuneiform characters, whilst at Byblos pseudo-hieroglyphic inscriptions contemporary with the Egyptian Middle Kingdom (2100–1700 BC) conceal a hitherto undeciphered language probably alphabetically written.

It is not known from which Phoenician centre the Greeks learned the alphabet. The lack of consistency in the direction in which the Greeks wrote gives to early Greek writing a great variety of forms, but archaic inscriptions from Thera and Rhodes for instance have forms tolerably close to those of the Ahiram sarcophagus. The date at which the Greeks began alphabetic writing was probably in the early eighth century BC: by the end of that century such inscribed late geometric Greek vases as have now been found in the graves of the early Greek settlers on Ischia near Naples transmitted alphabetic forms to Italy.

Although the alphabet is the greatest of Levantine legacies, we are now beginning to realize the cultural and religious debt which ancient Greece, and hence we ourselves, owe to the ancient Levantine world. Further discoveries will surely reveal a cultural continuity between the ancient Levant and archaic Greece which was hitherto unsuspected.

Meanwhile let us summarize the character of ancient Levantine civilization under one of its most cherished symbols, *malum punicum*, the pomegranate, which the Phoenicians planted throughout the Mediterranean. Luscious but hard of skin, wholesome but fragmentary, vivid but shallow, seedy but ever-refreshing, ripe but enduring, and if not the most palatable, at least the most shapely fruit.

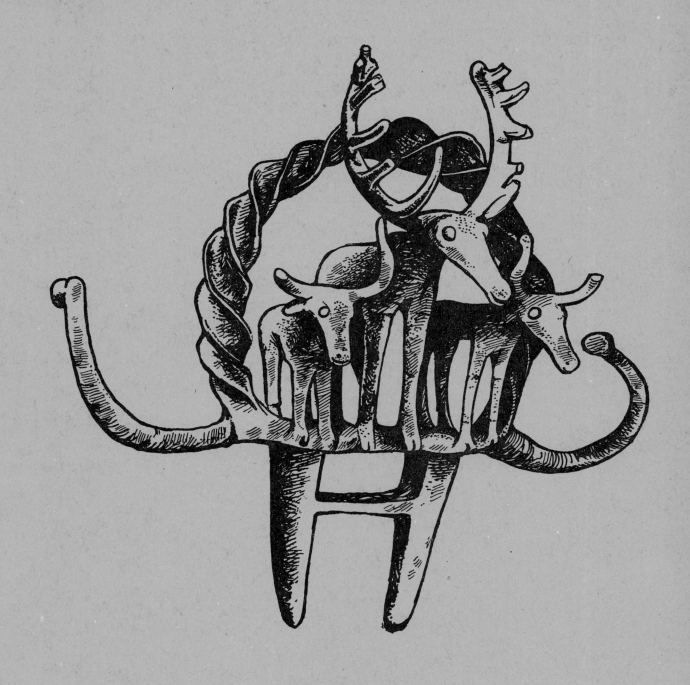

VI MELTING POT OF PEOPLES

The early settlement of Anatolia

SETON LLOYD

Anatolian Cultures in the Late Bronze Age (approx. 14th and 13th centuries BC). The shaded areas represent archaeological provinces, as defined by surface exploration in recent years. Superimposed on these are the names of the states mentioned in the Hittite records, as we now think them to be distributed. As in all such maps the boundaries of distribution are only provisional.

Map legend:

Central Anatolian type pottery:
- × Modern Towns
- C. Anatolian
- Cilician
- Konya Plain
- 'Inner Phrygia'
- N. Central Anatolian

W. Anatolian type culture:
- N.W. Anatolian Troy VI–VII
- S.W. Anatolian Beycesultan III–II
- S. W. Anatolian – Eastern Variant
- Mycenaean – Greeks

B.C.	PERIOD	WEST ANATOLIA	SOUTH ANATOLIA	CENTRAL PLATEAU	LAKE VAN	HISTORICAL
550	IRON AGE	G R E E K S		Boghazköy	Toprak-kale	585 Destruction of Urartu
700			Karatepe	Gordium I		695 Fall of Phrygian Empire
			Carchemish			716 Sargon II of Assyria subjugates Syro-Hittites
			Malatya	Boghazköy II Alishar IVC	URARTU	
1000		Troy VIIA	SYRO-HITTITES	I PHRYGIANS		1094 Tiglath-Pileser I in Syria
1200			E. Greeks			1192 Sack of 'Homeric' Troy
	LATE BRONZE AGE		Mersin VII City	Beyce-sultan III II		1300 Beycesultan destroyed, ? by Hittites
				'Hattusas' (1400) HITTITES		
1600		Troy VI		Alaca II Boghazköy IV		
	MIDDLE BRONZE AGE			V Kültepe Karum II		
1900		Troy V		Beyce-sultan VI		
2000	EARLY BRONZE AGE III	Troy IV		Alishar III		c.1960 Ibi-Sin King of Ur
		Troy III	Mersin XI Cists	Horoztepe Boghazköy V		
2300		Troy IIG (Poliochni V)		Alaca HüyükIII Royal Tombs		Widespread destruction in West
	EARLY BRONZE AGE II	Dorak	Mersin XI?			Egypt: Sahu-re King
2600	E.B.A. I	Troy II	Mersin XIIA	Alishar I		
2900	CHALCOLITHIC	Troy I (Thermi)	Mersin XVI	Tarsus		
3000		Fikirtepe Kumtepe		XXII		

The historical bridge between Europe and Asia,

a natural route of passage in ancient times for migrant peoples and invading armies alike, lies to the south of the Black Sea thrusting westward towards the Balkans. This is Turkey-in-Asia, now known by its medieval name, Anatolia. Its central part consists of a high plateau, bounded to the north and south by mountain ridges which separate it from the coastal plains beyond. From the highlands in the east, Tigris and Euphrates draw their water; to the west, minor ranges project like fingers into the Aegean Sea, reappearing as islands in the Greek archipelago.

Remote enough in early times to be safe from the threat of Egyptian and Babylonian militarism, Anatolia was nevertheless subjected to an almost unbroken sequence of migrations and conquests by peoples moving westwards from Central Asia or arriving by sea from western Europe. But these seem hardly to have modified the character of the indigenous population, now reconstructed as a result of archaeological research. The picture with which it presents us is one of sturdy peasants, among the first of the world's peoples to settle to farming and stock-breeding, distinguished among themselves only by the diverse geographical circumstances of the various provinces which they occupied. Cultural changes in their lives were mostly imposed upon them by alien aristocracies who succeeded one another as rulers of their country, occasionally raising some part of it to the status and dignity of an imperial power and correspondingly improving the lot of its inhabitants. Their empires have long since vanished, but the Anatolian peasant of today has much in common with his ancestors.

Writing came late to Anatolia, a thousand years or more after its invention in the cities of Mesopotamia. But the increasing archaeological evidence, although it does not reveal a continuous thread of development towards civilization, has contributed greatly towards our knowledge of the country's prehistory.

Between 2400 and 2200 BC, the people of the Bronze Age city at Alaca Hüyük, in the great bend of the Halys River on the central plateau, buried their ruling families in a series of tombs, of which thirteen have been found. It was a rewarding discovery to the Turkish archaeologists at work on the site, for after many investigations of village settlements they were here suddenly confronted by evidence of city life, of advanced technology, fine craftsmanship and symptoms of aesthetic discrimination. The complicated pattern of ritual burial clearly suggested a capacity for abstract thought.

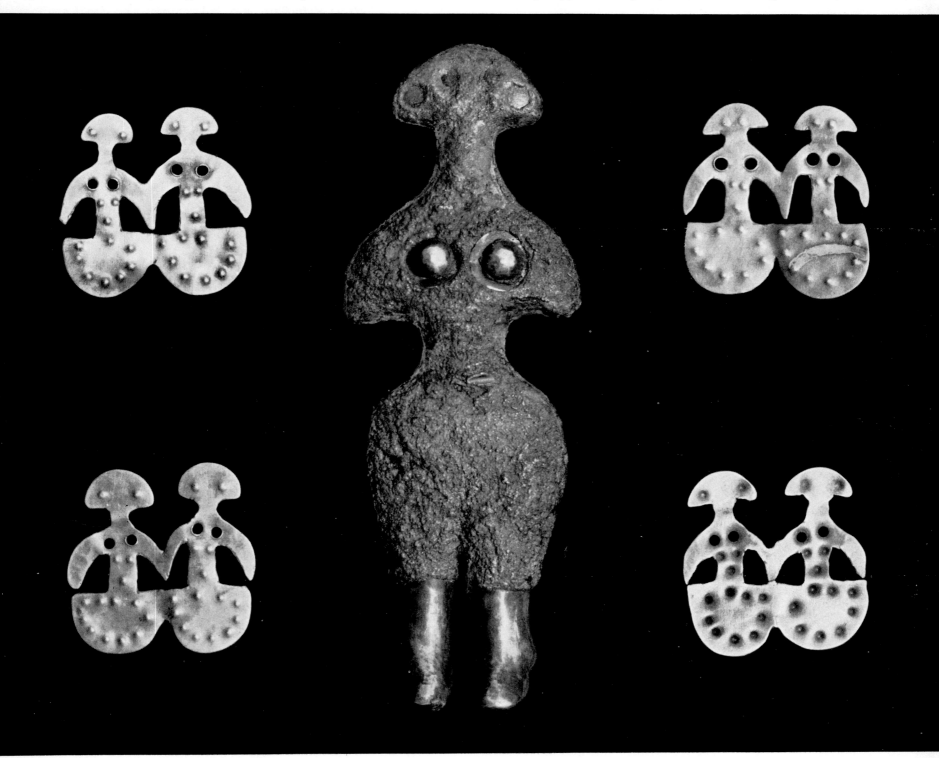

Some of the strangest among the many gold, silver and bronze objects found in the tombs at Alaca Hüyük were the figurines above (c. 2400–2200 BC). The twin symbols are cut in gold foil, the central figure is in bronze, with boots and breasts overlaid in gold. (1)

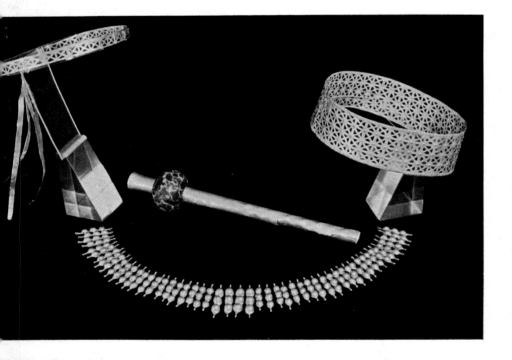

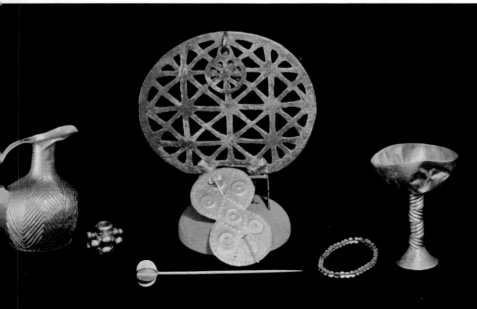

The treasure in the tombs of Alaca Hüyük included many religious symbols and private possessions of the royal dead. Men were accompanied by their weapons, women by their ornaments or toilet articles and both by vessels for food and drink, mostly made of gold, silver or bronze. On the left (top) is one of the strange ornaments which have been called 'standards', because they were probably mounted at the head of a pole. It is in copper, and shows the figures of a stag and two steers; animal symbols are not uncommon in Anatolian ritual of this period.

Centre (left) are two diadems in open-work gold, one with a tassel of gold ribbons; a gold necklace and a mace with a head of veined stone and a handle covered in gold foil.

Below (left) are a gold flagon and chalice, a pin, brooch and bracelet in gold, a gold ornament and a copper 'sun-disc', used perhaps decoratively (as in the reconstruction above). (2, 3, 4)

A royal burial more than 4000 years ago is reconstructed above from the discoveries at Alaca Hüyük (c. 2400–2200 BC). The king is to join his dead queen, who lies in the re-opened tomb, decked in jewellery, and surrounded by gold and silver vessels (like those discovered, left) and red burnished pottery. The bier on which the king lies with the body of his dog beside him is decorated with figurines and stag ornaments; he wears a diadem, necklace and brooch; a battle axe and a mace—and, most precious of all, a dagger with a crescent-shaped gold handle and a blade of *iron*—will be buried with him. The canopy is decorated with 'sun-discs'.

When the timber roofing is again lowered over the tomb the skulls of oxen will be replaced on top, and the waiting cattle will be slaughtered to accompany them. (The sketch, right, of an actual tomb shows cattle skulls and hooves *in situ* and sun-discs laid in the tomb.) The cemetery is on the edge of the town, whose buildings

are seen in the background. These, and the costumes, are based on somewhat later Hittite material. The burial rite and animal ornaments have many points of similarity with contemporary Caucasian tombs (cf. chap. XI, p. 320-1). (5, 6)

Nearer to the Black Sea at Horoztepe north-east of Alaca Hüyük, another group of royal tombs has been discovered, dated c. 2200 BC. In one of these, the bronze figurine of a woman (left) was found. She is suckling a child and wears her hair in a chignon, secured by a clasp behind her right ear. The empty sockets of her eyes must originally have been filled with inlay. (7)

The bronze rattle (below, centre) is also from Horoztepe. A lion follows two ibex up each side of the frame; on top are a stag and three hinds. (8)

Buried near the figurine at Horoztepe was the pole-mounting of a bull in bronze (below, right). Its muzzle, triangular forehead marking and horns are enriched with an alloy of gold and silver. (9)

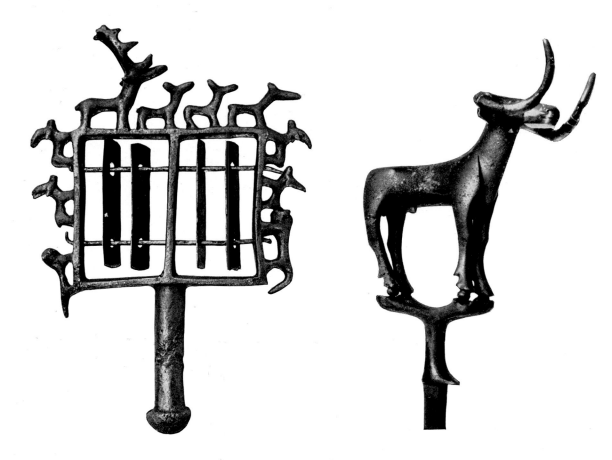

The discovery by peasants of a tomb at Mahmutlar yielded more objects from the Early Bronze Age. They included the crushed remains of a gold jug (below) very similar to those from Alaca Hüyük and a series of bronze axes (left) of an Anatolian type ancestral to those of the later Bronze Age in east central Europe. (10, 11)

It was in the royal residence of Early Bronze Age Troy that Schliemann found the deposits of gold jewellery and precious objects which he fancifully named 'Priam's treasure'. He has described how, in order to prevent his workmen learning of the discovery, his wife Sophia stood at his side, 'ready to pack the things I cut out in her shawl and to carry them away'. Above is an engraving of c. 1873 in which Sophia wears some of the jewellery. Actual pendants from the treasure—much of which is now lost—are illustrated alongside, with (below) a gold bracelet whose double-spiral ornament was afterwards adopted by the earliest European metal-workers. (12–15)

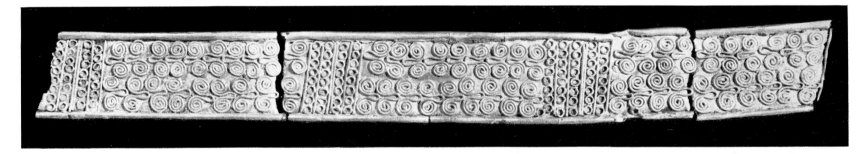

Famous in the literature of antiquity

Troy stood upon a shoulder of rock commanding the western approach to the Dardanelles. At the time of the Alaca tombs (c. 2400 BC), Troy was a flourishing fortress, enclosed in walls with great towered gateways. Its great *megaron* hall occupied a central enclosure, the main public building or assembly hall of the community. Round it clustered lesser buildings, including the residential quarters of the royal family.

When Schliemann dug down into the ruins of this period, he found fallen walls, baked and vitrified into solid masses among the calcined rubble of their stone foundations. For the buildings were of timber framework, even the protective outer walls being plentifully reinforced with wooden beams. Like Jacobean London in the Great Fire, this second City of Troy burnt furiously. As at Poliochni, hastily buried treasure and wholesale destruction mark the end of a kingdom which must have controlled this north western province of Anatolia and the seaways of the north Aegean.

The city was to rise again, and burn again, repeatedly in the centuries to come, and would be immortalised by Homer's epic poem. Today its ruins sleep beneath this mound of earth. (16)

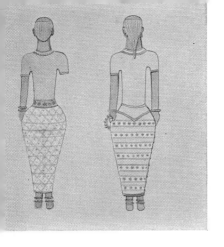
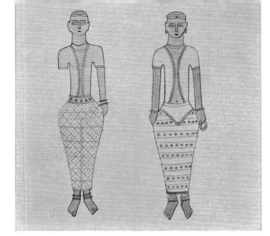

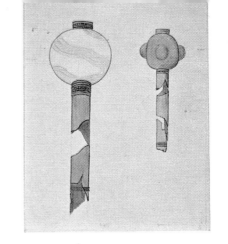

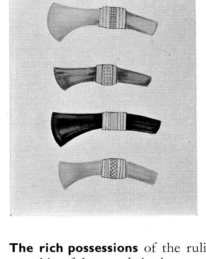
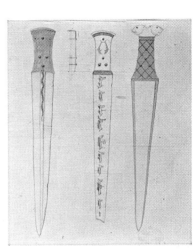

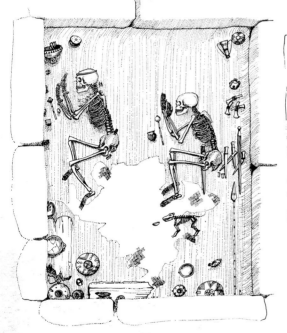
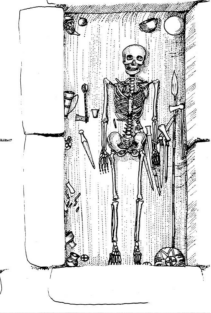

The rich possessions of the ruling families and the skilled craftsmanship of the people in the country around Troy are well illustrated by discoveries in two tombs at Dorak, near the Marmara coast. It is possible to date the tombs closely, for in one was found the remains of a wooden throne, its legs once encased in gold foil. On one fragment appear the cartouche and titles of the Pharaoh Sahu-re, who reigned from 2553 to 2539 BC. It is the first piece of evidence, also, of contact between Egypt and the sea-going people of north-west Anatolia.

The illustrations are drawings by James Mellaart, from the objects themselves and photographs taken at the time of discovery. There were two main tombs, one of a king alone (right), the other of a king and his queen (here drawn to a smaller scale, left). In the single tomb was found an *iron* sword with a hilt of two leopards carved in black obsidian and inlaid with gold and amber spots (top right). With it was found (second row, right) a silver blade engraved with sailing ships, almost the earliest known outside Egypt. Near the point of the weapon a dolphin appears and two more in gold ornament the hilt.

With the king in the double tomb was buried a dog (as at Alaca Hüyük) and beside him lay a sceptre of pink-veined marble (top, centre), its wooden handle encased in a sheath of embossed gold. The queen's sceptre has a knobbed amber head and silver-cased handle. Behind the king were four ceremonial axe-heads (second row, centre), in nephrite, lapis lazuli, obsidian and amber, the shaft-holes bound with gold and silver, related perhaps to weapons of the late Neolithic battle-axe groups of Central and Northern Europe (see chap. XII p. 351, *fig. 5*). (17–22)

A goddess and her handmaidens are probably represented by the figurines shown on the left above. The goddess (with long hair and fringed belt) is in electrum; her close attendant, in silver, carries a rod with which perhaps to strike music from the instrument in her right hand. The figurines above, in bronze with silver garments and ornaments in gold are probably priestesses or worshippers, wearing the normal dress of the ruling class. The jewellery is exactly paralleled by that found with the queen in the double tomb, although the figurines are not certainly from the tombs and may be later. All are about 6 ins. high, and were cast in a two-piece mould. (23–26)

Pottery from graves at Yortan, to the south-east of Troy, had parallels at Troy itself (the second settlement, c. 2600 BC). Among the vessels from Yortan on the left are two beak-spouted jugs on short feet and a 'face-urn' with human features. (27)

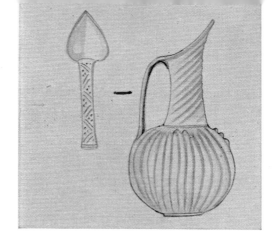

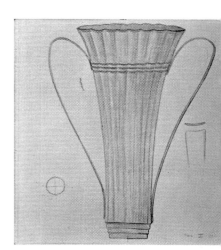

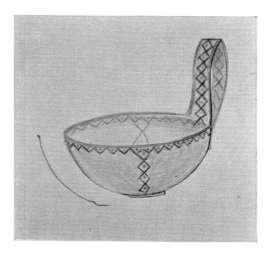

A woven floor-covering, the oldest 'carpet' ever discovered, lay beneath the king in the single tomb opposite. Its pattern, texture and colouring could easily be reconstructed from the woollen fragments which survived. The queen also probably lay on a rug, and her skeleton was still covered with scraps of textile. (28)

The queen's household treasure, found in the double tomb opposite, included a beak-spouted vase in fluted silver, the handle shown separately in plan (top left), a gold jug with cutaway spout and embossed decoration (top, right), and a high-handled bowl. In another vessel was a necklace of about 20 gold beads in the form of double spirals, such as have been found at Ur, Troy, Poliochni and Brak. From the single tomb came the beautiful two-handled drinking vessel in fluted gold, a shape always identified with the *depas amphikypellon* mentioned by Homer.

In this group of objects from the tombs at Dorak, the taste and craftsmanship rivals that of Egypt and Crete. The precious materials are unusually varied and great discrimination is apparent in the blending of colours and contrasting textures. They recall the climate of the Aegean world, and though typologically connected with Alaca and elsewhere, they have a distinctive character of their own. (29–32)

Temples of this time took the form of rectangular shrine-chambers arranged in pairs (perhaps because they were dedicated respectively to male and female deities). One such double sanctuary was excavated at Beycesultan, near the headwaters of the Maeander river. Its larger shrine is here shown right, with a reconstruction: offerings were passed between twin *stelae*, over an altar resembling the 'horns of consecration' in Cretan buildings of a later age. In front are offering jars; behind, a screen separates the sacrificial area from the priest's inner sanctum. It is a 'male' shrine, the wooden post again recalling the 'pillar-cult' of Crete. (33, 34)

In the east a lively trade developed

with the expanding kingdom of Assyria, whose capital was at Assur on the Tigris. The Assyrians had taken control of the trade-route which brought metal ores and other Anatolian products to Mesopotamia, and with the agreement of the native princes they had established half a dozen or more trading posts at strategic points in the interior. By the nineteenth century BC, the most central and important of these was outside the city walls of Kanesh (or Kültepe), in the Upper Land of the Central Plateau. There, in their suburb, the Assyrian merchants seem to have lived on excellent terms with their Anatolian neighbours, with whom they frequently inter-married. And in it archaeologists have discovered many beautiful objects, both Anatolian and Mesopotamian in character, and large numbers of tablets. Often neatly stacked on wooden shelves or in earthenware vessels, sometimes in clay envelopes bearing the impression of the merchant's seal, these were inscribed with the the records of business transacted.

The mound of Kanesh (Kültepe), within which lie the remains of a thriving Bronze Age city. It is drawn (above) in birds'eye view from the south-east and beyond it lies the modern Turkish village of Karahüyük. Among the trees on the extreme right are the excavations of the Assyrian trading post or *karum*. For many years this site eluded the archaeologists, who in vain had searched the mound itself for tablets such as had been found and sold by the peasants to local antique dealers. At last in 1925 a third expedition under Professor Hrozny challenged the reticence of the villagers. 'This time the peasants' luck did not hold. In addition to his great ability as a philologist, Hrozny was a good linguist and spoke excellent Turkish. Two of his employees were natives of Kayseri, where the situation at Kültepe had long been a standing joke, and by cross-questioning them he eventually arrived at the truth. The meadow to which they led him was hardly more than 100 yards distant from the foot of the main mound, but screened from it by a line of trees, and he could immediately see that its surface was disturbed by traces, only half-heartedly concealed, of amateur excavations on a considerable scale. His own labourers were at once directed to the locality, and during the weeks which followed his perseverance was rewarded by the recovery of more than a thousand 'Cappadocian' tablets and much valuable information regarding the setting in which they lay.' (Seton Lloyd: *Early Anatolia*, Penguin Books, 1956). (35)

The Anatolian mother goddess is probably represented by the ivory statuette above. Probably the 'household god' of some family, it was found in the trading post at Kanesh and dates from the nineteenth century BC. (37)

The red terracotta ram's head (right) found in the trading post at Kanesh, was perhaps a decorative addition to a red burnished Anatolian drinking-cup. (36)

A steatite mould from which a terracotta plaque could be made. It shows a group of deities, god, goddess and two children, whose dress and equipment are characteristic of the native Anatolian religious tradition at Kanesh. (38)

Vessels in animal form for drinking or pouring liquids were common at all periods in Anatolia. This grotesque lion is skilfully painted and modelled in the tradition of the Kanesh potters. (39)

The empire of the Hittites, a formidable product of ancient militarism, was born in the central plateau of Anatolia. Its capital, strategically placed within the great bend of the river Halys, was Hattusas, known today as Boghazköy. Two miles to the east, and some 600 feet above the plain, a natural spring at the foot of limestone cliffs created a setting for a sacred grove: the precinct now called Yazılıkaya. On the terrace in front (the foreground of the photograph on the right) are traces of a complex group of buildings guarding the approach. Worshippers would pass through this to find themselves in a rock sanctuary of great natural beauty. As they entered its shadowy interior the silence was complete. On each side, at eye level, a pageant of divine and human figures could be seen carved in relief on the face of the rock. It is shown in the drawing above: the eye follows the procession to an isolated centre-piece where god and goddess confront each other. On the right of this chamber a cleft in the rock leads to a narrow inner sanctuary, also dramatically decorated with significant reliefs. One is shown above: the 'young god 'Sharma holds the king a in protective embrace. Beyond, where a royal statue must have stood, his name appears in hieroglyphs on an otherwise empty wall-face.

The buildings are reconstructed in the drawing on the right. A procession of priests and worshippers approaches a portico leading directly to the inner sanctuary through a rock-cleft now blocked by fallen stones. (48–51)

The tablets of Adud-Sululi. The business archives of this merchant of the *karum* included the four typical tablets in envelopes above. They were impressed in soft clay with cuneiform writing and signed by rolling cylinder seals over them. They were then baked hard and covered with clay envelopes, also inscribed (part of one tablet is visible).

Thousands of such tablets have now been found at Kanesh, trading agreements, records and business correspondence. One bore the seal of Ibi-Sin of Ur, c. 1960 BC (possibly used by a less exalted individual after the king's death); another mentioned Puzur-Ashur, son of Sargon I of Agade, giving a year a little after 1800 BC. Between these dates, which are still controversial, the lifetime of the colony at Kanesh probably covered the greater part of the nineteenth century BC. (40–43)

The meeting-place of merchants, the Assyrian trading-post or *karum* at Kanesh, is reconstructed in the painting opposite. A caravan of 'black' Cappadocian donkeys is reaching the entrance to the settlement and halts at the control point inside the gateway. It has come from the 'palace' in the walled city beyond, where its goods were offered first for purchase by the ruling prince after paying taxes. The donkeys carry bales of Assyrian cloth, which are being checked from a pile of clay tablets in the foreground and may then be stored in the warehouse behind. On the left a merchant sits on the flat roof (commonly used for such purposes today) and inscribes a letter on a clay tablet; below on the right other tablets are to be hardened in a courtyard kiln. Standing in groups are pottery vessels with the burnished red or cream finish popular at the time.

The walls are built of brick reinforced by timber on a base of stone. The buildings are of typical Anatolian construction; the upper floors are used both for business and residence. The road is paved and its stones are rutted by wagon wheels.

Typical of the Cappadocian landscape is the snow-covered peak of Mt Argaeus, an extinct volcano. (44)

The beautiful pottery vessels of Central Anatolia in the nineteenth century BC are represented in the finds from the *karum* at Kanesh. On the right (above) are examples of the earlier 'Cappadocian Painted Wares', black on red or cream, and (below) of the later graceful burnished ware, also found at Alaca Hüyük and Alishar. (45, 46)

A great fire destroyed the karum and the Assyrian trading colonies came to a sudden end. What brought this about is uncertain, but it is perhaps significant that, dated about the same time (c. 1800 BC), there has been found in the actual city mound of Kanesh the bronze spearhead below, inscribed with the words 'Palace of Anittas.' It was to Anittas and his father Pithanas that later tradition ascribed the beginnings of the Hittite dynasty, destined to become rulers of a great empire. (47)

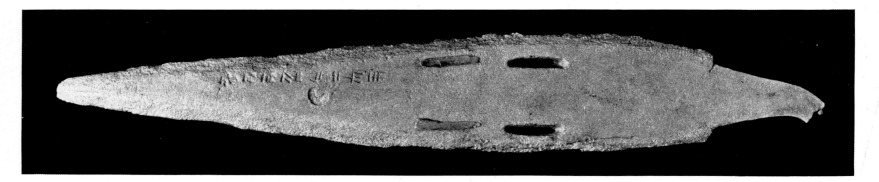

The dagger god, cut in the wall of the inner sanctuary at Yazılıkaya, is to the left of Sharma and the king. The carving represents a sword, its hilt composed of four crouching lions, two facing to the point of the sword, two facing outwards, back to back. Above is a human head with the conical head-dress of a deity. The gods represented in the sanctuary seem to belong to the Hurrian rather than the Hittite pantheon, introduced perhaps by Puduhepa, the Hurrian wife of Hattusilis III, who after her husband's death became for a time (c. 1250 BC) co-regent with Tudhaliyas IV, the king whose figure appears in the reliefs. (52)

The king himself, Tudhaliyas IV, is shown (below) in the procession in the outer chamber. He bears his pictographic insignia on his right hand. (53)

The royal archives of the Hittites were found in long store rooms in the high citadel. The thousands of clay tablets inscribed in cuneiform (part of one is shown above) provide rich historical material, complete with kings' names and dates of battles and treaties, as well as much information on social structure, economics, law and religion. (56)

The 'Lion' Gate at Boghazköy (above) was built of closely fitted masonry without regular courses. The guardian figures are primitive, but they anticipate such features in Assyrian buildings by many centuries (and those at Persepolis by a thousand years). (57)

The seat of the Hittite kings Hattusas, spread out on each side of a deep rocky gorge and looked northward over a wide cultivated valley. The city was founded by Hattusilis I, c. 1500 BC, and was at first about 400 yards long, mounting up to a high citadel. At the height of its greatness it was extended, perhaps under Suppiluliumas, by a tremendous crescent of fortifications flung up over the hillside to the south, making an enclosure four miles in circumference. The walls themselves were a prodigious feat of engineering for so early a period. A great rampart of earth, in part faced with a revetment of dressed stone, supported the masonry substructure of a double wall about thirty feet high, completed above in brickwork (which has now disappeared). There were chambered towers at short intervals.

Sculpture is to be found only in the gateways at Boghazköy. At the King's Gate appears the warrior figure above, primitive but curiously impressive. He wears a belted kilt, and a helmet with an extension down the back; his battle-axe recalls weapons found in the Persian province of Luristan; his sword, with its crescent-shaped hilt and curved scabbard, finds parallels in Palestine and reappears in Bronze Age Europe. (54)

The 'Sphinx' Gate at Alaca Hüyük, in the Hittite city built over the Early Bronze Age cemetery, is one of the rare attempts at sculpture in the round, possibly under the influence of Syrian craftsmen. There is a Spinx gate also at Boghazköy. (55)

The downfall of the Hittite Empire

began soon after 1200 BC. In an eastward thrust of peoples from Thrace and Macedonia, Phrygians swept the country as far as the north-western slopes of the Taurus mountains and destroyed the imperial strongholds on the Halys. But the expulsion of its people from their homeland did not end the history of the Hittite nation, for they descended through the Anti-Taurus into the valley of the Upper Euphrates and swept on further into the plains of North Syria. This new environment was not strange to them; local rulers had long been vassals of the Hittite kings and the cities had paid tribute to the imperial treasury.

The centuries which followed were an insecure and unstable time. The grafting of migrant Hittites upon Aramaeans and Hurrians, and the armed interventions of the Assyrians from the east, produced a constellation of small and disunited city-states, in which first one element and then another gained ascendancy. But the archaeological heritage from the cities, such as Carchemish, Sinjerli, Marash, and Malatya on the fringe of the plateau, and from reliefs such as those at Ivriz and Karatepe, is far greater than from the imperial regime itself.

At Ivriz, in the Taurus, the famous relief above is sculptured on a vertical face of rock. Its inscription has been translated: King Urpallu is paying homage to his fertility god, Tarhundas. Urpallu was one of the princes of Tabal, a province which included Cappadocia and Lycaonia; he was defeated by the Assyrian Tiglath-Pileser III in 738 BC. The god is dressed in Hittite costume, with horned cap, but the pose of both figures is unusual and the decoration of Urpallu's costume is of a type which can be traced as far west as Ephesus. It may be that here is an early example of Phrygian influence, as the invaders mingled with the people of Tabal. (58)

The carving of the relief at Ivriz is reconstructed in the painting above. At the point chosen a torrent gushes out of the cliff side and the water tumbles down through a built-up rock basin to form a river below; it is already a sacred spot. Workmen are busy on the rock face with chisel and mallet, supported by a rough scaffolding of pine logs.

King Urpallu has driven over to inspect the work and greets the master mason. His light chariot is of wood, its wheels reinforced with metal. His bodyguard are helmetted and carry spears and shields. Behind them is a wooden bridge over the torrent, from which the road winds away along the cliff face. (59)

The lion hunt opposite is from the 'Lion' Gate at Malatya, which was the site of the kingdom of Milid, established soon after the fall of Hattusas. Such reliefs are now plentifully annotated with hieroglyphic inscriptions. (60)

The old pictographic writing which the Hittites had inherited from an earlier stage in their cultural history. It was the original vehicle for one of the Indo-European dialects from which the Hittite language was composed. The example above is one of many found at Carchemish, dating from the time of Luhas (c. 1960 BC) to the annexation of the city by Sargon II in 716 BC. (61)

The grotesque seated god above was found at Carchemish. His throne was square, shaped like an armchair; his fists, resting upon his knees, held a mace and a double axe. He was bearded and wore a horned head-dress. The base consists of two lions held by a relief-figure of a mythical hybrid.

During the years following its discovery (by Sir Leonard Woolley) the statue itself completely disappeared; the head of one of the lions is in the British Museum, the base, in part reconstructed, in the museum at Ankara. (62)

The face of the sphinx, left, is from Karatepe in Cilicia; the carving is shown from the side in the picture opposite. The embroidered cloth covering the front legs is a form of ornament also used by the Phoenicians.

In the eighth century BC, a princeling bearing the Anatolian name of Asitawad built himself a fortified country palace at Karatepe. It was in a very beautiful and also very remote recess of the hills on the banks of the river Ceyhan, where it breaks down through a rocky valley into the Cicilian plain. In the fashion of the time he ornamented the two gateways with sculptured reliefs, his builders, it seems, working against time; for some slabs are unfinished, some are well done, others unskilled, and the whole shows an extraordinary mixture of styles, with influences from Hittite Anatolia, from Assyria and from Egypt through the medium of Phoenician art. Only here and there has a master hand touched the work with some feeling for modelling and suggestion of movement. Nevertheless the remains of this palace at Karatepe are of immense archaeological interest. (63)

The influence of Egypt at Karatepe, through Phoenician art, is seen in this relief (above), representing the Egyptian god Bes, with monkeys squatting on either shoulder. But the inscription is in the old Hittite pictographic writing. The suckling goddess of Karatepe, (right) feeding a standing boy under a palm tree, is perhaps a local interpretation of the Egyptian Isis and Horus. (64, 66)

The major importance of Karatepe lies in the recovery from the gateway of duplicate inscriptions, one in Hittite hieroglyphs the other in what has been described as 'the purest known Phoenician'. It is expected that these bilingual slabs will assist greatly the translation of the many Hittite hieroglyphic texts not yet fully understood.

The king at table, though supported by throne and footstool, takes food from a dish at nose-level, while retainers bring more food and drink or carry fly-whisks. Beneath the table, a monkey waits for scraps. In the relief below, a calf is coaxed to the slaughter and a servant carries a kid on his shoulder. The scenes are from the southwest gate of Asitawad's palace at Karatepe, eighth century BC. (65)

The inscriptions record Asitawad's foundation of the fortress and describe him as ruler of a kingdom which includes the plain of Adana. In the final invocation of the gods, Baal of the Old Testament is mentioned. The reliefs have been preserved *in situ* and some are shown below. (67)

The Malatya colossus, over three and a half yards high and carved in the round from a single block of limestone, was found in the portico of the 'Lion' Gate at Malatya, on the eastern edge of the Hittite homeland. It is the statue of a king, dressed in a pleated over-mantle, one corner of which returns over his right shoulder and is held by his left hand. The rosettes on his head band may also be seen in sculptures from Sakçagözü and Nimrûd in Assyria. They suggest a date in the late eighth century BC.

The statue had fallen from its base, face downwards on the stone pavement, losing its right arm and nose. But pious hands had rolled it over and built round it a sarcophagus of stone slabs, as though it lay in a tomb. The nose was found by excavators, but was mislaid again during the journey to Ankara. The statue now stands in Ankara Museum, restored from photographs. (68)

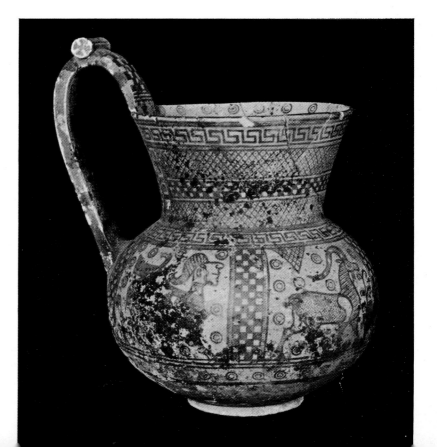

The Phrygian invaders from the West

established their capital at Gordium, on the river Sangarius (Sakarya) in western Anatolia, and adopted the surrounding territory as their 'homeland'. A spur of the hills adjoining the city mound is covered with tumuli beneath which the ruling families of Gordium seem to have been interred. Dominating the whole burial ground is a single tumulus rising to the immense height of over 150 feet and locally known as the 'Tomb of Midas'.

The Phrygians spread east across the central plateau, displacing the Hittites from their capital at Boghazköy. There they also settled, dominating Anatolia until, early in the seventh century BC, weakened by invaders from beyond the Caucasus, their authority was usurped by the kingdom of Lydia.

Some of the finest Phrygian pottery was found in a wooden chamber beneath one of the tumuli at Gordium known as the 'Child's Tomb', because the only human remains were a few teeth of a child 4–5 years old. Examples of the pottery, dated in the late 8th century, are shown opposite. (69, 70, 71)

The striking terracotta panel above is one of several found in a settlement at Pazarlı, near Boghazköy. Painted and glazed reliefs such as these were evidently a characteristic ornament of Phrygian buildings. The striding warriors, with their circular shields and plumed helmets, and other panels with domestic or wild animals (below) recall certain elements of archaic Greek art. (72, 73)

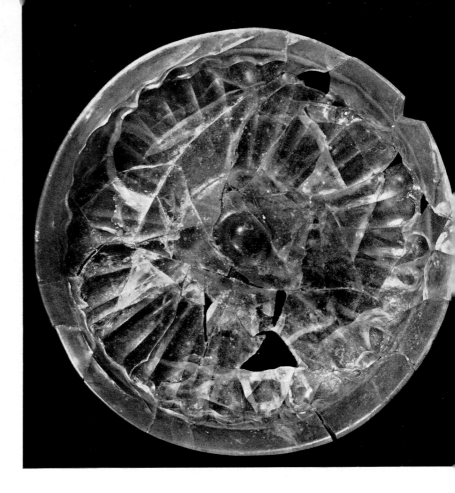

In the 'Tomb of Midas' at Gordium was found the bronze 'situla' above. It is in the form of a lion's head, its eyes inlaid with white paste and blue stone; with it was another in the form of a ram. Very similar examples can be seen in the reliefs of Sargon II's palace at Khorsabad.

It is surprising in view of the well-known legend, that in the 'Tomb of Midas' much bronze was found, but neither gold nor silver. The occupant of the tomb may equally have been some other king. (74)

The bowl of clear moulded glass on the right was found in the 'Child's Tomb' at Gordium. It was inside a bronze vessel very similar to examples found in Assyria (9th–7th centuries BC). The material was easily identified by the minute bubbles which distinguish it from rock crystal and is an unique find at so early a period. (75)

A strange by-way of Anatolian history is associated with the province surrounding Lake Van in the extreme east of Anatolia. A nation called Urartu flourished there at the time of Phrygian Gordium; an Urartian prince fought against the Assyrians side-by-side with the ruler of Karatepe. Urartian cities were distinguished by their rock citadels, ponderous architecture, remarkable engineering and a very high level of craftsmanship, especially in metal.

The bronze ritual cauldron (left) was found at Altıntepe, near Erzinjan. It stands on a tripod with bull's feet, is ornamented with bull's heads and inscribed in 'Vannic' cuneiform. The influence of Urartian metalwork is thought to have reached as far as Etruria and cauldrons similarly ornamented appear even in the Celtic world. (76)

A Vannic fortress in miniature is portrayed by the fragment of a model in bronze shown below. It presents an almost unique record of Urartian architecture, since it shows the treatment of towers and battlements, doors and windows—information which is rarely provided by surviving remains. (77)

The early settlement of Anatolia

SETON LLOYD

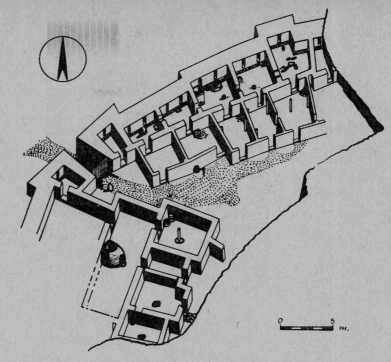

Part of the chalcolithic fortress at Mersin. To the north are the garrison's quarters, in the foreground the commander's house with its baking oven. The fortress wall is pierced by slit-windows; c. 3700 BC. (fig. 1)

ANATOLIA is a modern name applied to Asiatic Turkey: to the great peninsula of Asia Minor, thrust out from the main continent towards south-east Europe. The name is taken from the Turkish form, *Anadolu*, but at no time until the present had Asia Minor been thought of as a single political or geographical unit. The structure of the country is dominated by the great Anatolian Plateau, bounded on north and south by mountain ridges which sever it from the coastal plains, where climate and altitude combine to produce distinctively different territories. To the west, the Plateau descends more gently to the Aegean and the Sea of Marmara.

This geographical diversity is reflected in the prehistory and early history of Anatolia, which shows no continuous thread of development such as that which can be perceived in Egypt or in Mesopotamia, but instead a series of diverse cultures reacting one upon another, and invariably affected by the fact that Anatolia is a great natural route of passage, joining the Asiatic to the European world of antiquity. In considering its ancient history therefore, we must try to bring together these separate and individual strains of Anatolian culture into a coherent pattern before we can assess the contribution made by them to early civilization as a whole.

Like every region of Western Asia, the story of early Anatolia divides into two phases, that before the use of writing in the peninsula and that after. In the former phase, we are dealing with prehistory constructed wholly from archaeological evidence, whereas once written documents are available, we move into a period of ancient history in which archaeological and historical evidence are used in concert. Anatolia comes comparatively late into the field of literacy, for our first written documents are hardly earlier than 2000 BC, a millennium or so after the invention of writing in Mesopotamia and Egypt. It appears, too, not as an indigenous development, but as a remote extension of Mesopotamian culture itself, and as a result of the setting up of Assyrian trading colonies in Asia Minor. The earliest documents in Anatolia are in fact those written by Assyrian merchants in their commercial centre of Kanesh, the modern Kültepe, in Cappadocia, around 1900 BC, in their own cuneiform script, which was adopted by the contemporary Anatolian rulers of the city for their own purposes (pl. 40–43). But this early business correspondence—accounts, bills of lading and so on—gives us little precise historical information, and true historical documents, with references to political and military events, begin some five hundred years later when the Hittite kings, still using the cuneiform script borrowed from Mesopotamia, record their achievements.

Our knowledge of all that happened in Anatolia before this period must accordingly depend exclusively on the results of archaeological research, which, in our own time has fortunately been able to make a very considerable contribution. It has carried back the story of human endeavour in this area at least another three thousand years and introduced us to peoples who were, and would otherwise have remained, completely unknown to us. But, as peoples, they do remain without exception anonymous; so that in discussing the sequence of developments in these earlier periods, we are compelled to fall back on the rather arbitrary terminology by which archaeology identifies the chronological epochs to which they belong. Here in Anatolia, as elsewhere, the 'Neolithic Revolution' which ended the Stone Age is separated from the beginning of the Bronze Age proper by a 'Chalcolithic' period. The Bronze Age is divided into 'Early', 'Middle' and 'Late' phases, the first occupying in time the greater part of the third

millennium BC, the second covering the period of the Assyrian colonies in the first half of the second millennium and the third corresponding to the centuries illuminated by the Hittite records, which ended with the destruction of the Hittite Empire in about 1200 BC.

The clear historical character of this later period, the evidence of political development and religious thought, the sequence of royal names and the battles or treaties associated with them, all serve by contrast to emphasise the drab impersonality of the 'archaeological' ages which preceded it, where the biography of a nation can be written only in terms of broken pottery and the discarded belongings of its most humble artisans. Yet, even in this obscure half-light of 'material cultures' and 'racial criteria', where some great national disaster must be envisaged from a layer of burnt debris or a vast migration inferred from the shape of a corroded bronze implement, brief moments of illumination do intermittently occur. For, at remote intervals and in diverse geographical settings, chance archaeological discoveries have unexpectedly parted the veil, bringing suddenly into sharp focus some isolated episode in the drama of cultural evolution, where the movement of domestic routine or public performance is momentarily arrested in a characteristic tableau.

Two such discoveries are related to an age so remote that they do not fall strictly within the scope of this essay. The first, at Hacılar, near Burdur has already been described in a different context (chapter II). The second, at Mersin in Cilicia, presents us with the fascinating spectacle of a miniature chalcolithic fortress of about 3700 BC; almost the first example of deliberately planned military architecture in the history of the world *(fig. 1)*. With others dating from later periods we must presently concern ourselves in detail.

The Bronze Age in Anatolia

During the third millennium BC we find the country already divided into six or seven fairly clearly defined cultural provinces, distinguished by slight disparities in their material remains; and these correspond closely to the most natural geographical divisions of the country *(fig. 2)*. There is (1) the north-western province, which includes both the site of Troy and the productive Yortan cemeteries. Excavations at the former and much illicit digging among the latter has revealed its character in considerable detail. Next, a large part of the Plateau proper, including the famous Halys Bend, falls within what has come to be called (2) the Central Anatolian province, and here too the local peculiarities of the Early Bronze (or as some prefer to call it, the 'Copper') Age civilization have already become familiar to us through excavations. The rather mixed culture of (3) Cilicia at this time has also been a subject of much study, and something is known about a remote (4) north-eastern province, typified among other finds by a rather outlandish assemblage of material from Karaz, near Erzerum,

Map showing the Early Bronze Age cultures of Anatolia. (fig. 2)

which seems to have Caucasian affinities. But there is also (5) a south-western province centred around the sources of the river Maeander, very recently revealed by the Beycesultan exavations, and another apparently confined to (6) the Konya Plain, whose limits can only be defined by inferences made from the pottery found on the surface of its early Bronze Age mounds.

Much that we know of these Early Bronze provinces is necessarily derived from the study of small-town or village communities and their legacy of broken pottery. The picture created is one of sturdy and rather unimaginative Anatolian peasants, leading a life very little different from those of their modern counterparts. Their houses were made of mud-brick, the walls being reinforced with timber beams and standing on stone foundations; and the flat mud roofs with squat chimneys had, no doubt, storks' nests in the early summer. The villages must have presented very much the same appearance as the remoter hamlets today, where the use of cement and corrugated iron is still mercifully rare. The people kept sheep, goats and large cattle, which they guarded with the help of dogs, and hunted wild pigs or stags. They broke the ground with light wooden ploughs, harvested with copper sickles, threshed probably with flint-toothed wooden sledges and winnowed in the wind: then they ground their flour with basalt querns and baked bread in a conical clay oven. In their homes lamps burned before tiny domestic shrines, and their dead were buried outside the houses in simple pit-graves or stone-lined cists. For many centuries they remained conservative and even intransigent in their ways. Any symptoms of change or progress during this period in fact seem due rather to the substitution of one alien aristocracy for another than to any migratory upheaval among the peasants themselves.

Alaca Hüyük

Turkish archaeologists excavating in the deeper levels of the Hittite city-mound at Alaca Hüyük discovered a group of thirteen tombs, perhaps those of a local ruling family in the early Bronze Age, buried among the rich paraphernalia of funerary ritual and accompanied by their private possessions. After having been compelled for so long to content themselves with the limited testimony of 'vernacular' horizons, the excavators were here suddenly and most gratifyingly confronted with the *metropolitan* aspect of contemporary civilization; and they were amazed at the evidence of advanced technology, fine craftsmanship and capacity for aesthetic discrimination which the

discovery provided. Added to this were clear and significant indications of abstract thought governing the complicated pattern of funerary ritual (pl. 1–6).

The interments had evidently been made at long intervals, over several generations. Some were single tombs; others contained both a man and a women, buried on different occasions, which suggest that when the first interment was made the location of the tomb must have been marked on the surface. Men were accompanied by their weapons; women by their ornaments or toilet articles and both by domestic vessels and utensils, mostly made of precious metals (pl. 3). Notable among the weapons was a dagger with a crescent-shaped gold handle and a blade of iron—a metal known to have been far more valuable than gold at this time—and among the personal ornaments, a gold filigree diadem with a tassel of gold ribbons (pl. 4). Then there was a wide variety of objects of religious significance connected with the funerary ritual—strange openwork grilles of bronze, sometimes adorned with the figures of animals (pl. 2), which have been called 'standards' because they were probably mounted at the head of a pole, and ornaments of a similar function in the form of single animals, finely wrought in bronze and inlaid with silver. There were also strange metal figurines, one of which was of bronze with boots and breasts enriched with gold (pl. 1). The tombs themselves were rectangular pits lined with rough stone walling and covered in with a ceiling of wooden beams (pl. 5–6). Laid above this were the skulls and hooves of beasts (sometimes including a dog), sacrificed as part of the funeral ritual, and the debris of a religious feast. The tombs have been dated between 2400 and 2200 BC. They give us much valuable information of the metal and stones available in Central Anatolia at that time and also of the known metallurgical processes, which included smelting and hammering, soldering, *repoussé* relief, sheathing and inlay. Gold could also be drawn into wire or polished with sand, and alloys were used in welding gold and silver together.

Another such cemetery is located at Horoztepe (pl. 7–9), near Tokat, where the shallow tombs of Early Bronze Age royalty are apparently covered by a modern burial ground. They seem a little later than the tombs at Alaca Hüyük—perhaps 2200 BC.

Early Bronze Age architecture and building construction varies very little from district to district. Stone foundations are used and an upper structure, either of stone or of mud-brick inserted as panels of filling in a framework of timber posts and beams. The upright posts which occur at intervals of two to three feet in the walls are attached to the ends of roof-beams above, giving a form of stability which is intentionally kept slightly elastic as a precaution against earthquakes.

As for the forms of private dwelling houses, at Beycesultan these most usually approximated to the 'hall-and-porch' plan, commonly known as a *megaron*. Nor was this apparently a fashion peculiar to south-western Anatolia in the Early Bronze Age, for, in ruins of the native city at Kanesh, a small palace with a 'megaron-hall' was recently discovered *(fig. 4)*, having a huge raised circular hearth in the centre and four columns supporting the roof, exactly as is found in the Mycenaean palaces of Greece. The fact that this example was dated a thousand years earlier has begun to suggest that this architectural form originated in Anatolia.

Temples (pl. 33, 34, *fig. 3*) took the form of rectangular shrine-chambers arranged in pairs (perhaps because they were dedicated to separate male and female deities), and each had an 'altar', surrounded by *ex voto* objects consisting of twin *stelae* between which the offerings were passed, over a built-in structure resembling the 'horns of consecration' in Cretan buildings of a later age. A feature of the 'male' shrine was an isolated wooden post reminiscent of the 'tree' or 'pillar' cults of Crete.

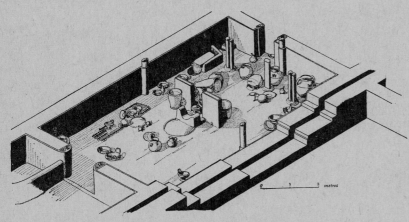

Partial reconstruction of the 'female' shrine at Beycesultan; (the corresponding 'male' shrine is shown in plates 33 and 34). Fragments of matting and offering-jars lie as they were excavated. (fig. 3)

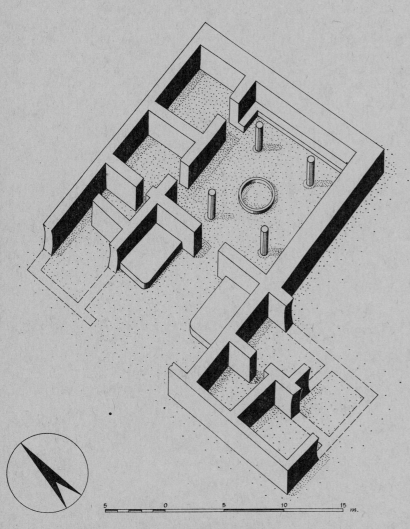

Early Bronze Age megaron *at Kültepe. Such halls, with porch and central circular hearth, can be paralleled in the second city of Troy (see fig. 5) and, complete with columns, at Tiryns in Greece a thousand years later. (fig. 4)*

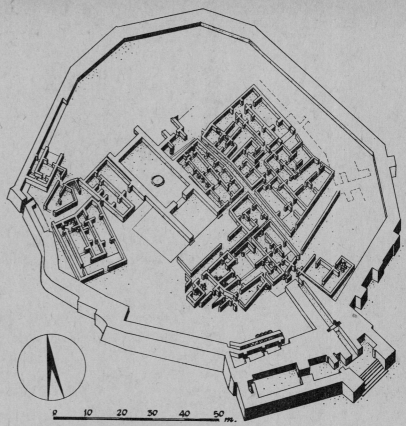

Troy: the Early Bronze Age fortress (Level IIG). The largest building is the megaron. *The gateway, with its long narrow entrance, projects as a tower and there is a postern gate in the west. Date: c. 2300 BC. (fig. 5)*

Troy 'II G'

But for the more general lay-out and composition of a city at this time one must turn to the north-western province. Perhaps the most representative early Bronze Age settlement here is Troy at the level known as 'II G' *(fig. 5)*. The vast *megaron* hall, occupying a central enclosure in the fortress, and standing among the network of more normal sized buildings which surround it, had a roof span of 30 feet, and can easily be recognized for what it was—the main public building or assembly-hall of the community. The actual residential quarters of the ruling family are easy to identify in a complex of less pretentious buildings to the west of them. The city walls with their great towered gateways (once more of brick and timber on a stone substructure), do not seem disproportionately substantial in comparison with the number of buildings which they enclose.

One aspect of these ruins by which no one could have failed to be impressed was evidence showing the manner of the city's destruction. Everywhere Schliemann found fallen walls, baked and vitrified into solid masses among the calcined rubble of their stone foundations. To the system of building we have already referred, and it must greatly have contributed to the ferocity of the fire, which in a few hours reduced the fortress to a waste of smouldering ashes. Even the protective outer walls with their powerfully buttressed sub-structures, were plentifully reinforced with wooden beams, while the houses themselves probably had upper storeys lightly built of plaster in a framework of timber. Closely clustering together over narrow alley-ways, they must have resembled the 'half-timber' slums of Jacobean London and have burnt as easily. Troy stands upon a projecting shoulder of rock, where Gallipoli and the island of Imbros are dimly visible. Fishermen in their boats watched the destruction of the Second City of Troy and saw the flames reflected in the 'wasting springs' of Scamander; but they could not know how often in centuries to come Ilium must burn again (pl. 16).

It was in the settlement of this period at Troy that Schliemann also discovered the treasures of gold jewellery and precious objects which he affectionately (and of course wrongly) associated with the name of Priam (pl. 12–15, *fig. 6*). Among these there are minor typological parallels with metal objects from the Alaca tombs: but more basic differences, both in design and technique serve to emphasise the geographical and perhaps ethnological disparity between the Early Bronze Age provinces represented by the two discoveries. Pottery and weapons from the Yortan graves (pl. 27), supplemented by others from Troy itself, indicate the character of these north-western people.

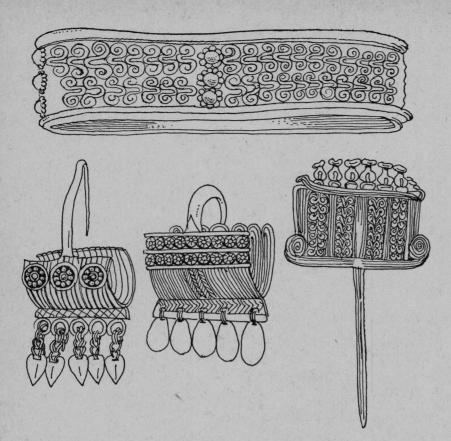

A bracelet from Troy, similar to that shown in plate 15, with two earrings and a pin; based on Schliemann's original drawings. (fig. 6)

Dorak

On a small rock promontory overlooking a lake near Bursa several graves have been found which vividly reveal the nature and predilections of the prehistoric inhabitants of the region (pl. 17–22). A large cist-grave contains the bodies of a local ruler and his wife: a smaller one has a single male burial and nearby 'pithos' burials (burials in large pottery jars) are perhaps those of servants. Once more, the men are buried with their weapons; the woman with her ornaments and personal belongings. One man has the body of his dog with him and there are figurines—perhaps of the 'dancing-girl' or 'concubine' type, whose dress and appearance are meticulously reproduced (pl. 23–26). The tombs are dated not only by domestic vessels in gold and silver (pl. 29–32), but also, almost miraculously, by an imported fragment of gold foil bearing an inscription in Egyptian hieroglyphs which includes the name of Sahu-re, the second king of the Fifth Dynasty of Old Kingdom Egypt. Finally there are the remains of a woven floor-covering in which both the pattern and the colours of the thread are still distinguishable (pl. 28).

But it is above all the design and workmanship of the objects which reveals both the character and the material wealth of this Troadic people in about 2500 BC. The modelling of organic and other decorative forms is almost Egyptian in its excellence. The precious materials are unusually varied and great discrimination has been exercised in blending colours and contrasting textures. Not only do the figurines reveal a minor aspect of contemporary dress, but there are clues to environmental reaction. Today, almost within sight of the tombs, fishing boats pass and dolphins play among the waters of Marmara. And here are the Early Bronze Age ships engraved upon the blade of a dagger, while its point is decorated with the shape of a dolphin. One is conscious, among these relics, of the Aegean world, to an extent which alone would totally distinguish them from those of Alaca Hüyük.

Migrations and Trade

The final centuries of the third millennium BC were a time of major migrations. It has been suggested that an Indo-European people speaking a dialect known as Luvian spread themselves over southwestern Anatolia and perhaps beyond the Aegean. At Beycesultan the arrival of newcomers identified as Luvians is indicated by the first break in the site's continuous occupation by indigenous peoples. These peoples, it is further suggested, were later joined by refugees from the Troad into which a second wave of immigrants, this time speaking Greek, had followed in their wake. Meanwhile a third

group of Indo-Europeans, the Hittites, were moving into Central Anatolia from the direction of the Caucasus.

The nineteenth century BC, the beginning of the Middle Bronze Age, found the commercial colony at Kanesh well established. The expanding Assyrian Kingdom with its capital at Assur on the Tigris had taken control of the trade-route which brought metal ores and other Anatolian products to Mesopotamia, and they had established half a dozen or more trading posts *(karum)* at strategic points in the interior with the agreement of native princes. Kanesh was evidently the most central and important of these. The *karum* there resembled a 'chamber of commerce', through the authority of which prices could be fixed, debts settled and transport arranged. Goods exported from Assyria included cloths and fabrics of widely varying qualities, some of them very costly, which were exchanged against copper and other minerals including carnelian and amber, and a little iron which at that time commanded five times the price of gold. Silver was used only as currency. The goods were carried by the then-famous 'black' donkeys of Cappadocia in caravans. These were led or organised by men called 'transport factors' who took responsibility for delivery of the goods and payments. They were often accompanied by official messengers carrying the equivalent of 'royal mail'. Something is known of the route they took, which passed by Sinjar to the crossroads city of Harran, then followed the 'Royal Road' of later times, crossing the Euphrates at Birejik and mounting to the plateau by way of Marash and Elbistan. No case is recorded in the tablets of a caravan being interfered with on the way.

In their suburb at the foot of the Kanesh mound (pl. 35, 44), the merchants seem to have lived on excellent terms with their Anatolian neighbours, with whom they frequently inter-married. Every consignment of goods, before delivery to the *karum*, had to pass through the 'palace' of the native ruler in the Anatolian city above, which exercised an option to buy and otherwise levied taxes. But this was done in an equitable and orderly manner and the colonists were otherwise left unmolested to live according to their own customs, as the excavation of the *karum* has shown. Unlike their Anatolian neighbours, for instance, the Assyrians buried their dead beneath the floors of their houses, and these graves have been most fruitful of works of art mainly of a Mesopotamian character.

The houses themselves on the other hand followed the old Anatolian tradition; a 'half-timber' construction on a stone foundation *(fig. 7, 8)*. Certain rooms on the ground floor were used for storing tablets, and the whole business archive of a single family has sometimes been recovered from the ruins of a single house (pl. 40–43). When the tablets were found in place, they were often neatly stacked on wooden shelves or in earthenware vessels, and their clay envelopes were often found intact, bearing the impression of the merchant's seal (pl. 38). Other rooms on the ground floor were kitchens or domestic offices and here, in orderly arrangement, were found the beautiful pottery vessels characteristic of this period in Central Anatolia; the polychrome of 'Cappadocian Painted Wares' in the earlier levels (pl. 45) and the wonderfully graceful shapes of the later red or cream burnished vessels (pl. 46), together with others, fantastically shaped, with excrescences in the form of birds or animals (pl. 36), which seem peculiar to the site. The upper floor seems to have been used both for residential and business purposes.

The Hittites

In the time of Sargon I of Agade, the Cappadocian tablets begin to supply a little information about her neighbouring Anatolian peoples, loosely designated by the term 'Hatti'. The names are given of other cities which have kings or at least boast of 'palaces' and so suggest the dignity of a local ruler; and one state, Burushattum, is singled out for special distinction, since its ruler is dignified with the name of 'Great King'. Innumerable names of private individuals also appear and some of these have a special significance, since they already suggest the presence of a new element in the population. Two Indo-European dialects, Kaneshite and Luvian, can be distinguished in their composition, and though neither of these is the true ancestor of the Hittite language, it is possible to conclude that the racial material from which the Hittite nation was later to consolidate itself is already present. But in the end, the most important historical evidence comes from a few documents, found in the actual city mound at Kanesh and derived from the archives of the local ruler, for they mentioned the names of a prince called Pithanas and his son Anittas.

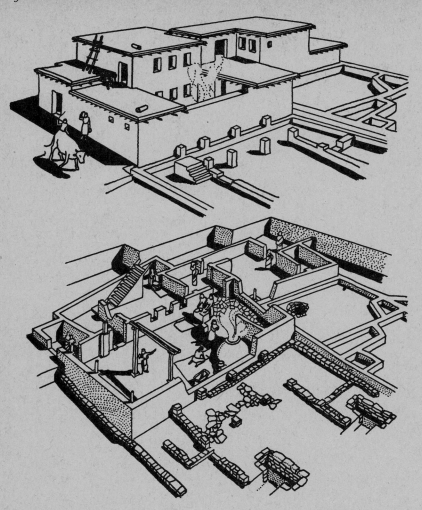

Kültepe: a typical house in the karum. *Rooms are asymmetrically grouped round a courtyard, which in this case contains an oven for baking tablets.* (fig. 7)

The interior of one of the houses of the karum. *The construction is of brick with a framework of beams. Corn-grinding and bread-baking are in progress.* (fig. 8)

Now it is from these two half-legendary individuals that Hittite royalty in later times claimed its descent, and a Hittite recopying of an ancient document concerning them gives some interesting details about events in their lifetime. Pithanas was ruler of a city called Kussara, and the document gives an impressive list of neighbouring cities which he conquered. One interesting point is that it includes the name Nesa. This city supplies the term 'Nesite' for the Indo-European dialect which crystallised into a distinctive language spoken by the newly arrived Hittites, and possibly in Nesa these Hittites had already begun to concentrate their forces. Pithanas in any case treated the conquered city with notable lenience, having perhaps understood the advantage to be gained from an alliance with this new and virile element in the population. His son Anittas actually transferred his residence from Kussara to Nesa, and it may well have been with the support of Hittite chariots and horses that he afterwards completed his father's conquests, by capturing Burushattum and thereby acquiring for himself the title of 'Great King'. The discovery in a public building at Kültepe of a bronze spearhead bearing the simple inscription, 'Palace of Anittas', naturally made all this sound more real (pl. 47). It is clear in any case that during the early decades of the seventeenth century BC, the Hittites gradually displaced the indigenous Hatti and the history of Anatolia in the centuries which followed becomes primarily concerned with the fortunes of this remarkable people.

One of the few cities listed in the conquests of Anittas whose later identity can be recognised is Hattusas, now known as Boghazköy. Its situation in the centre of the province enclosed by the curve of the Halys river must have been a strategic one, for an early Hittite king moved his capital thither from Kussara. Hattusas from then onwards became the dynastic seat of the Hittite king-emperors and focal centre of their civilization. Excavation of Boghazköy resulted in the discovery of their official archives (pl. 56), and from these the shape of Hittite history and civilization have since been reconstructed. The information emerging from the archives would today provide sufficient material for a history-book, complete with kings' names, numbered campaigns and dates of individual battles or treaties, as well as chapters on such subjects as social structure, economics, law and religion. This great volume of information is impossible to summarize usefully, and we shall therefore confine ourselves to assessing the cultural status of the Hittites among contemporary nations and their contribution to world civilization.

No historian would today be deceived by the magniloquent phraseology and extravagant claims with which the Hittite kings themselves adorned their records. Yet in the same records, minor episodes or incidental circumstances are occasionally mentioned, with no apparent intention of impressing posterity, which nevertheless serve toconvince one of the respect engendered by Hittite military prowess and political authority among the other powers of the contemporary scene. Even during the earlier phase of their history—the 'Old Kingdom'—there is the unquestionably authentic episode when Mursilis I, in a campaign whose success must have exceeded his wildest expectations, penetrated into Mesopotamia as far as the walls of Babylon and, finding its defences unprepared, entered the city and slew its Amorite King. Suddenly to find themselves masters in the Mesopotamian capital, amid the pomp and luxury associated with so great a centre of world civilization, must have astonished Mursilis and his simple highlanders almost to the point of embarrassment for they soon withdrew to a more familiar climate. Later, in the time of the 'Empire', there is also the attractive picture of Suppiluliumas, the greatest of Hittite conquerors, receiving the Egyptian envoys while encamped before Kadesh, and his almost incredulous bewilderment on understanding that they brought with them a request from their Queen, the widow of Tut-ankh-amun, that one of his sons should become her husband. Such a marriage actually took place after the famous treaty made between the two kingdoms in 1269 BC, though in this case between a Hittite princess and an Egyptian Pharaoh.

Boghazköy

But perhaps the most effective testimony of all to the undoubted stature and ability of this Anatolian nation at the height of its political ascendancy and wordly aggrandisement, is to be found in a different quarter altogether. A visit to the actual remains of the Hittite capital at Boghazköy, with its ruined palaces and temples, monumental sculptures and the four-mile circuit of its ponderously constructed

Reconstruction of a section of the walls of Boghazköy. A rampart of earth is faced in part by a stone revetment, while the walls form a double shell with rubble filled chambers between. The postern is in the centre foreground. (fig. 9)

Reconstruction of the outer face of the 'Lion' Gate at Boghazköy (plate 57 shows the inner face and stone sub-structure.) The upper parts were of mud-brick and timber (fig. 10)

walls, cannot fail to leave one with the conviction that this city has been the cradle and home of a great imperial people.

The city spreads itself out on either side of a deep rocky gorge and looks northwards over a wide cultivated valley. The older part of the town is a mere four hundred yards long, mounting up to a high citadel. Here was the seat of government and in long store-rooms, at some time destroyed by fire, the thousands of tablets composing the royal archive were brought to light. In 'Imperial' times the old city became inadequate and a vast extension was planned. Perhaps in the time of Suppiluliumas, a tremendous crescent of fortifications was flung up over the hillside to the south, making an enclosure which must have a total area of well over three hundred acres. Here the walls themselves present a prodigious feat of engineering for so early a period (fourteenth century BC). Their foundations are raised to a consistent level by a great rampart of earth, partly faced with a sloping wall of dressed stone *(fig. 9)*. Above this the sub-structure of the double wall which stands about thirty feet high, is built of enormous stones, not laid in regular courses but meticulously joined. The brick structure above this has of course disappeared. There are chambered towers at short intervals, and in certain places outer 'apron' walls to prevent a direct attack. A postern or sally-port is created at one point by a stone vaulted tunnel passing beneath the rampart. There are five main gates with flanking towers, three of which have been named from the sculptures which adorn them—'Sphinx', 'Lion' (pl. 57, *fig. 10*) and 'King's Gate'.

Four buildings in the extended town have been identified as temples. One of them is an enormous limestone building with a colonnade facing onto a wide central court, and stands in a sacred enclosure or *temenos* enclosing an immense number of store-chambers and other subsidiary accommodation. In such buildings the actual sanctuary, which contained a cult-statue, is built of granite. It has an indirect approach and projects a little beyond the main façade in order to obtain lateral lighting for the statue.

The cult-figures themselves were missing from these temples, and elsewhere very few examples were found by the excavators of carving or modelling: so that our knowledge of Hittite art of this period is for the most part derived from two other sources, namely the portal

sculptures adorning the city gates and from rock-reliefs in the neighbouring shrine at Yazılıkaya. The most famous of the former is the 'warrior' from the King's Gate, now in the Ankara Museum (pl. 54). The figure is curiously impressive, though its importance consists more in the archaeological evidence which it presents of dress, weapons, etc., than in actual artistic merit. The lion and sphinx figures too are primitive work and the interest of the latter lies mainly in the fact that the dual sculptures anticipate such features in Assyrian buildings by many centuries (and those at Persepolis by a thousand years).

Yazılıkaya and Hittite Religion

By far the most interesting sculptures both from an artistic and a religious point of view, are the reliefs at Yazılıkaya (pl. 48–53). This beautiful shrine is situated outside the city at a point where a spring of fresh water must once have discharged into a small valley shaded by trees. Deep clefts in the limestone, open to the sky and carpeted with grass and flowers, make a setting for the cult and the reliefs are carved on the vertical sides of two main recesses or 'chambers'. Outside them can be seen the ruins of an elaborately constructed entrance-gate, or propylon, through which they were approached *(fig. 11)*. The outer

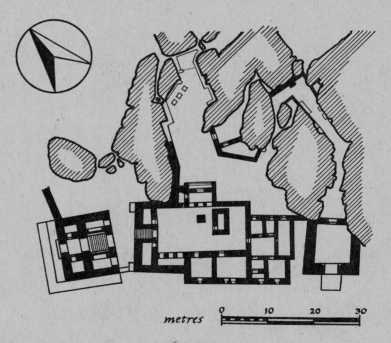

Yazılıkaya: entrance was from the S.W. ('propylon' block); the large area further E. is the courtyard containing the temple-shrine; and a porticoed building N. of this leads to the rock-galleries. (fig. 11)

chamber, which has traces of an altar-platform and was perhaps used for ceremonies such as the ratification of treaties, is decorated with a pageant of deities, some standing on their appropriate cult-animal or identified by a group of hieroglyphs (pl. 49). These figures are carved with no more than average proficiency; but those in the inner sanctuary are animated and infused with a religious emotion which craftsmanship alone could not have made articulate. The figure of a young king (identified as Tudhaliyas IV), in the protective embrace of a god (pl. 48) is hardly less impressive than the symbolism of a huge dagger which appears thrust into the rock before him (pl. 52).

The Hittites were a practical, intellectually unpretentious people, devoid of the finer graces which adorned some other Near Eastern countries in their time. But they were born soldiers with great men to lead them and they were governed in peacetime by statesmen with a well-developed imperial policy. Also, religion seems to have played an important part in the conduct of their lives, and their beliefs were based on some curious concepts. One of the most remarkable scenes in the history of ceremonial ritual must have been enacted during their periodical festivals, when the priests and celebrants, surrounded by helmeted guards and a throng of bullet-headed townsmen, issued from the austerely monumental public buildings of Hattusas and converged on the causeways leading up the adjoining valley to their mysterious shrine. Life in their fortified mountain-gorge had made them intuitively conscious of a mystery inherent in the natural rocks which surrounded them; and it was perhaps among the clefts and caverns of Yazılıkaya that their sluggish emotions responded most easily to ritual stimulation.

The Hittites and their Neighbours

Rock reliefs of a similar character are to be found in other parts of Anatolia. But this raises the question of political geography in Hittite times. A good deal is known from the Boghazköy records about neighbouring states, against which the Hittite kings waged war, or with whom they had more peaceful connections; and in the map on p. 162 their location, inferred from the textual evidence, is shown in such a way as to be comparable with the rather less equivocal division of the country into cultural provinces delimited by archaeological research. Some controversy still persists in regard to the placing of Ahhiyawa, because this name was applied by the Hittites to a people who in the past have often been identified with the Achaeans of Homeric legend. But archaeologists, finding that the Ahhiyawa homeland can be located on the Anatolian mainland without violating any logical inference from the texts, have recently begun to favour a new theory regarding this north-western province. It may, they consider, have been from here that the first true Greeks crossed the Aegean to colonise the European mainland at the beginning of the second millennium BC. According to this theory, the Ahhiyawans were themselves recent arrivals, having appeared from the west simultaneously with the arrival of the Hittites from the east. By this process of reasoning, the Ahhiyawans would have been a proto-Greek people who remained on the Anatolian mainland during the centuries in which their own colonists were creating the Mycenaean *commune* in the Aegean. This would explain the close ties between the Mycenaean merchants and the Trojans of the sixth settlement—a facility not enjoyed by the Assuwans of the central Aegean coast who were an Anatolian people and perhaps distrustful of the Greeks.

At this point we should perhaps remind ourselves that, by the time the Achaean Greeks organised the expedition against the city of Troy described by Homer, the events mentioned in the Hittite records were already becoming historical. The best known date, computed by the Greek chronologists of later times, for the fall of Troy, (and one which archaeologists find most easy to accept), is 1192 BC. By that time, if any reliance is to be placed on Homer's list of Priam's allies, the political scene in the Troad and its hinterland was in the process of fairly rapid change. The area we have tentatively identified as the Late Bronze Age state of Ahhiyawa, could hardly have remained unaffected by the eastward migrations across the straits, which were now beginning to take place at regular intervals. Nevertheless, the survival of an Ahhiyawan element in the population of Priam's Troy would explain the cultural affinity which Homer envisages between the Trojans and Greeks. It is a pity that no light was thrown on this subject by the excavations of the Homeric settlement at Troy itself (settlement VII A), whose remains had been largely destroyed by the foundations of later buildings.

Turning to Arzawa, a state with which the Hittite kings seemed to have been continually at war without effecting any permanent conquest, there is evidence from the excavations at Beycesultan to show that the city there partially excavated may, during the Middle Bronze Age have had the dignity of a state-capital. Amongst other buildings dating from this period (1900–1750), a remarkably large palace was brought to light *(fig. 12, 13)*, planned in a way which partly resembled those of Minoan Crete and elaborately constructed of brick and timber on a stone foundation. Its unusual amenities included a system of sub-pavement passages, presumably for circulating hot air in

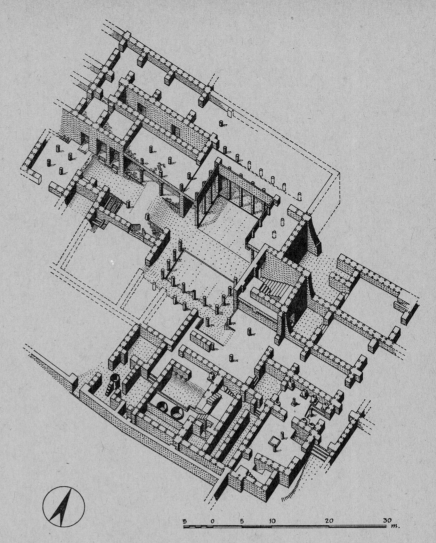

Partial reconstruction of the Arzawan palace at Beycesultan; half-timbering on a foundation of tree-trunks. The central courtyard, with its galleries and long columned upper-storey, the monumental entrance and the grand staircase recall later Minoan palaces. The date is between 1900–1750 BC. (fig. 12)

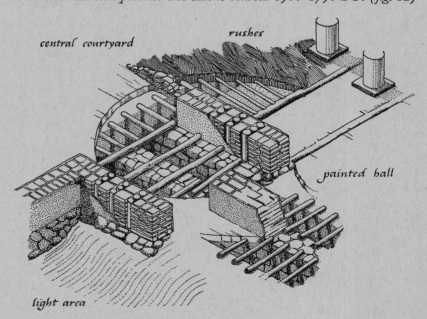

Schematic drawing of sub-pavement passages of the Beycesultan palace, perhaps indicating a system of heating or ventilation. (fig. 13)

the winter; and though the destruction of the building by fire after looting, perhaps during one of the early Hittite wars, has destroyed much other valuable evidence, one gains the impression that the Arzawans were a people of wealth and dignity. There was also a walled enclosure full of large administrative buildings of a sort which would have justified the expectation of written archives. The fact that no inscribed material was found, though there is reason to believe that Arzawa at this time fell within the area inhabited by an Indo-European people, speaking and writing the Luvian dialect, has led to some speculation regarding the use of writing materials other than clay tablets, which might have perished.

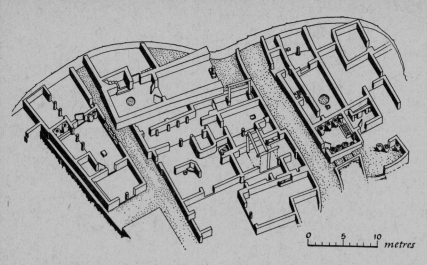

Plan of the Late Bronze Age compound at Beycesultan. Two of the main streets are shown, flanked by megara, *stabling, food store and private wine-shop. The distinctive pottery used at this period (c. 1250 BC), with its lustrous forms in imitation of metal, is now considered characteristically Arzawan. (fig. 14)*

In the Late Bronze Age, the city at Beycesultan lost its importance and became the seat of a small feudal prince. His palace compound *(fig. 14)* which was partly excavated contained residences in the form of *megara* and elaborate stabling accommodation for horses. Elsewhere a religious shrine with a 'horned' altar once more recalled Minoan symbolism. *(fig. 15)*

Other states appearing on the map, apart from the so-called Upper and Lower Lands which fall both historically and archaeologically within the sphere of direct Hittite influence, include Kizzuwatna, over which the Hittite kings usually maintained a fairly tight control since it covered their lines of communication for campaigns in Syria. At the end of the Early Bronze Age, a people called Hurri, coming from the neighbourhood of Lake Urmia, had established themselves as a ruling class in this area, and it was the Hurrian wife of King Tudhaliyas IV who had been responsible for introducing an alien element into the pantheon depicted in the reliefs at Yazılıkaya. An offshoot from Hurrian stock had also at this time created the important state of Mitanni, whose territory extended into northern Assyria. Apart from these, the most active though historically obscure people were the barbaric Kaskaeans of Pontus and Paphlagonia, who seemed perpetually to be creating a 'second front' in the Hittite wars.

Reconstruction of a Late Bronze Age shrine at Beycesultan, showing the 'horned' altar and ritual hearth, again recalling Minoan symbolism. The pottery shows the influence of metal-work. (fig. 15)

Southward Migration of the Hittites

The Hittite Empire came to an end almost simultaneously with the fall of Troy and the beginning of the Iron Age. In the opening years of the first millennium BC, Phrygians from Thrace swept the country as far as the north-western slopes of Taurus and destroyed the imperial strongholds on the Halys.

The political history of the Hittite nation did not end with the destruction of Hattusas and the expulsion of its people from their homeland in Anatolia. Driven southward from the cities and pasturelands of the plateau, they descended through Anti-Taurus into the valley of the upper Euphrates and pressed on further into the plains of North Syria. These were familiar lands to them; for their rulers had long been vassals of the Hittite kings and the cities had paid tribute to the imperial treasury. Several national elements now composed their population: Aramaeans from the tribal lands in the south, families of Hurrians and expatriate Hittites, once concerned with imperial administration and trade. These latter now gained political ascendancy and the cities, particularly the old provincial capitals such as Carchemish (pl. 62) and Sinjerli, soon resumed the semblance of Hittite principalities, though the non-Hittite element in their internal composition preserved for each its individual and independent character. So the imperial regime was succeeded in the Early Iron Age by a strange historical aftermath, during which the Hittite world became no more than a constellation of small and disunited city-states, striving by miscellaneous alliances to maintain their independence on the periphery of the Assyrian Empire.

Curiously enough this period of five centuries, during which the cities in fact often became vassals of the Assyrians or were subjected to non-Hittite rule when the Aramaean element in their population got the upper hand, has bequeathed to us a far greater heritage of archaeological remains than the imperial regime which preceded it. The whole accumulation from this source creates a curious picture of a hybrid civilization, spreading over a wide geographical area, which does not conform to any conventionally defined province in later times. The linguistic diversity of the inscriptions and the complex evidence of foreign influence on sculptural style, provide a clue to political insecurity and unstable fortunes of the states themselves.

Hittite Picture-Writing

The period is sometimes known as 'Neo-Hittite' or 'Syro-Hittite'; and the cities not already mentioned include Marash, Sakçagözü and, on the fringe of the plateau, Malatya (pl. 60, 68). Some of them have been partially excavated and their public buildings have yielded, in addition to statues, large quantities of stone slabs, sculptured in relief in a style showing much foreign influence. The content of the pictures and that of rock reliefs dating from this period, like the one at Ivriz (pl. 58–59), is often supplemented by inscriptions in a form of pictographic writing which the Hittites had inherited from an earlier stage in their cultural history (pl. 61). It was in fact the original vehicle for one of the Indo-European dialects from which the Hittite language was composed, but when these excavations took place it had not yet been deciphered. But inscriptions in Aramaic and Phoenician do also occasionally occur alongside the hieroglyphs, and it was the discovery of a bi-lingual text of this sort in 1947 which eventually made the decipherment of the pictographs possible. The discovery was made at a place called Karatepe (pl. 63–67) on the banks of the Ceyhan river, where it breaks down through a rocky valley into the plain of Cilicia. An eighth century princeling, describing himself as a vassal of the king of Adana, had here built himself a fortified country palace with formally designed gateways which, in the fashion of the time, he ornamented with sculptured reliefs. The sculptures (whose preservation *in situ* the Turkish government has contrived), show a conspicuously low standard of workmanship and a most perplexing confusion of styles; but there is a long and informative inscription, repeated on either side of the main entrances, first in Hittite hieroglyphs and then in Phoenician. Since the Phoenician script is already well understood, the 'crib' which is thus conveniently provided to the hieroglyphs has been welcomed, like the Rosetta Stone or the Behistun inscriptions in an earlier generation, as a linguistic key which may give access to a whole new literature. But one must hasten to add that this hope has not yet altogether been fulfilled. It often takes a very long time for philologists to decipher a script, even after all the necessary evidence has been collected. Meanwhile, our knowledge of Syro-Hittite history continues to depend for the most part on the dim reflection of events and personalities which are to be found in the Assyrian annals. But also something is to be learnt from them about those of Urartu: and this brings us to a strange by-way of Anatolian history.

Urartu

Near the modern city of Van and overlooking the beautiful lake from which it takes its name, stands a great citadel rock, upon the vertical faces of which are inscribed in neat cuneiform writing the fragmentary annals of a dynasty which ruled in these parts during the early centuries of the first millennium BC. When the 'Vannic' language of the inscriptions was deciphered in 1890, it became possible to identify these kings as rulers of a nation called Urartu (or Ararat) with whom the Assyrians were known from their own records to have been in contact from the ninth to the seventh centuries BC. Its capital was at Van itself but its frontiers extended beyond the eastern provinces of modern Turkey to Lake Urmia and the Araxes. Over this area its fortress cities are scattered. Built usually on a strategic hill-top or mountain site with a strong citadel on the summit and a residential walled city on the slopes beneath, they give an interesting clue to the character of the Urartians. One notices their mountaineer's preference for high places, the ponderous monumentality of their architecture, remarkable feats of engineering and preoccupation with military security (pl. 77). One also recognises many characteristics matching those of their neighbours the Assyrians; but, remembering that the north Mesopotamians built for the most part on flat sites, using mudbrick exclusively as a material, one is led to speculate whether this

were not how their cities would have looked, had they been sited on the summits and flanks of mountains. Urartian art also reached a very high standard of excellence, to judge from the antiquities excavated in the citadel at Van in the last century. Their metal-workers in particular (pl. 76), being within easy reach of copper mines, made and ornamented large vessels for which the demand extended as far as Phrygian Anatolia, to which we must now finally turn.

The Phrygians

The Early Iron Age in Phrygian Anatolia is represented by rock-cut tombs and 'water-cult' shrines sculptured to resemble the façades of buildings, and also by the capital city at Gordium on the Sangarius river (Sakarya) which is now being revealed by excavations. At Gordium too a wealth of bronze-work, some of it Urartian, and of inlaid wooden furniture came to light in 1957 when a royal tomb was opened in the largest of the many tumuli which surround the ancient city.

This vast mound of earth, originally almost two hundred feet high, makes a conspicuous landmark in the valley of the Sakarya river, and has for long been traditionally known as the 'Tomb of Midas' *(fig. 16)*. Archaeologists from the University of Pennsylvania located the actual tomb-chamber by drilling vertically into the tumulus, and then drove a tunnel towards it at plain level. But the chamber was covered by an inner mound of stone rubble, held in by a retaining wall, and when this was breached, the greater part of the rubble had to be drawn off leaving a huge empty dome, with little to support the great weight of earth above. It was therefore with some trepidation that an opening

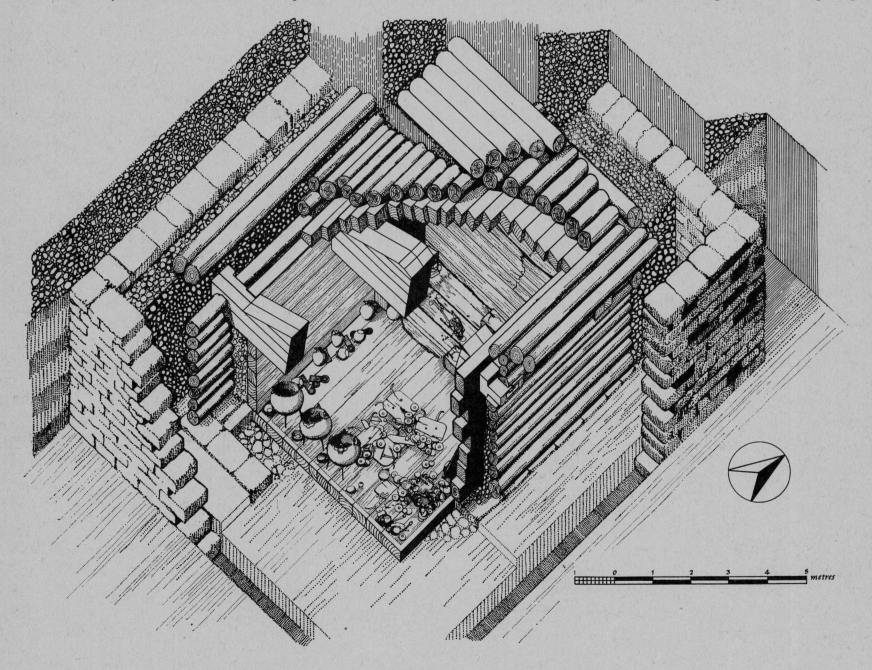

Reconstruction of the 'Tomb of Midas', the largest of the Gordium tombs. On the N. side lay the skeleton of a man about 60 years old, on a bed covered

with about 20 layers of linen and wool coverlets. Cauldrons, pottery, a large number of brooches, tables and other furniture were also found. (fig. 16)

was eventually cut in the wall of the chamber, a structure built from baulks of juniper two feet thick. The courage of the excavators was rewarded when flood-lamps were brought and the interior of the tomb illuminated.

Directly beneath the opening, the skeleton of a Phrygian king lay upon a huge collapsed bed among the decaying remains of no less than twenty rich coverlets. Behind, against the further wall, were the remains of elaborate furniture, inlaid with rare woods in intricate patterns. One piece had consisted of shelves on which rested many scores of bronze vessels (pl. 74). Its collapse spilled out a cascade of metal over the floor, where it now lay filling the whole chamber with the brilliant peacock blue of patinated bronze. Against the side walls stood gigantic copper cauldrons on iron tripods, which had contained food and drink; these were ornamented at their rims with the busts of bearded men or with female figures of the type known later in Greece as 'sirens'. Strange devices of embossed leather which had decorated the walls also covered the floor. Some of the bronze vessels bore inscriptions incised in wax, which should help to throw new light on a Phrygian script today still imperfectly understood. But the most puzzling aspect of this tomb, in view of the Midas legend, was the total absence of gold and silver or weapons enriched with precious stones. The only personal ornaments with which the king was provided consisted of more than seventy bronze 'safety pins' *(fibulae)* contained in a linen bag.

There can be no doubt about the high standard of culture which these and other finds represent: but there is already something European in the background of Phrygian art. And when, after the Cimmerian invasions in 680 BC the Phrygian dynasty came to an end and its dominion was usurped by a Lydian kingdom with its capital at Sardis, Anatolian culture began rapidly to lose its individual character and to assimilate itself to that of the Greek cities now flourishing along its coasts.

VII THE HOME OF THE HEROES

The Aegean before the Greeks

M. S. F. HOOD

BC		TROY		CRETE		ISLANDS		MAINLAND			EGYPT	BC
1000												1000
1100	LATE B.A.	VIIB/VIII		SUB-MINOAN				SUB-MYCENAEAN			XXI	1100
1200			LATE MINOAN	IIIB2				IIIC		NEW KINGDOM	XX	1200
1300		VIIA		IIIB1				IIIB	*Linear B*		XIX *Akhenaten*	1300
1400				IIIA	*Linear B*			IIIA	? Gla			1400
1500		VI		II		MID. CYC.		II	*Tholos Tombs*		XVIII *Tuthmosis* III	1500
1600	EARLIER BRONZE AGE	V	MIDDLE MINOAN	IB IA IIIB			? Trianda (Rhodes)	I	*Shaft Graves*		*The Hyksos*	1600
1700		IV		IIIA IIB					Mycenae Tiryns Pylos	MIDDLE KINGDOM	XIII	1700
1800		III		IIA							XII *Amun-em-het* II	1800
1900		II		IB		EARLY CYCLADIC	? Chalandriani (Syros)		Orchomenos Rafina Lerna Asine		XI	1900
2000				*Palace of Minos* *Palace*	Apeso kari							2000
2100		I	EARLY MINOAN	III IA II			*Tholos Tombs*	EARLY HELLADIC MID-HEL.			VII–X	2100
2200				I	Mallia Gournia Vasiliki							2200
2300									Dimini		VI	2300
2400										OLD KINGDOM	V	2400
2500		?	NEOLITHIC					NEOLITHIC			IV	2500
2600	NEOLITHIC				Phaistos						III	2600
2700									Sesklo		II	2700
2800											I	2800
2900				Knossos							?	2900
3000				?								3000

It should be noted that this chronology differs in certain respects from that usually followed

196

A paradise of sea-indented lands and sea-girt islands
welcomed the stone-using farmers when they arrived in the Aegean, some time before 3000 BC. There were few other humans, the climate was genial, water was more plentiful and the soil more fertile than it is today. Vines and olives probably grew wild, the sea was abounding with fish, while deer and goats roamed the forests—as well as the more formidable beasts, bears, wolves, boars and lions which play such a prominent part in the legends of this region.

The settlers almost certainly came from the Near East. They knew how to grind stone for axes and adzes, how to make and decorate pottery, and they may have brought with them the wheat which they grew and the sheep, cows and pigs they tended for food. They left rich traces of their occupation in the plains of Thessaly.

They traded with their neighbours both by sea and by land and it is perhaps from these contacts, perhaps from new immigrants or invaders, that they learned to work in bronze. This was perhaps about 2500 BC, the beginning of an age in which a high civilization was to arise in the Aegean, starting in Crete.

On the plains of Thessaly, at Dimini, archaeologists discovered the Late Neolithic settlement reconstructed in the drawing above. Its maze-like walls may have been for defence, though they were narrow and could not have stood very high. Piles of stones which were found along the walls suggest the defender shown, armed with a sling against marauders. The chieftain's house, or 'megaron', so similar in plan to that of the Palace of Troy II (chapter VI *fig.* 5), stands in the centre compound. (1)

Superb pottery, with vigorous painted designs, was discovered at Dimini. The vase on the left was found in the chieftain's house. Its decoration is in black and red and the basic pattern is typical of the Late Neolithic of the whole Balkans; the spiral which appears here recurs again and again in the art of the Aegean. (2)

In Crete at the beginning of the Bronze Age (c. 2400 BC), the women probably used the three little lidded bowls below to hold cosmetics, and spouted vessels characteristic of the period in the Aegean had already appeared. The form was also at home in Anatolia.

The 'House of the Tiles' at Lerna, on the Mainland of Greece, may date from c. 2000 BC. It is shown excavated (right); baked clay tiles covered the roofs, and a defending wall (which ran where the workmen are digging) was necessary. The seal-stamped fragment of clay (above) found in the house was probably used to mark property; the spider in the centre appears also on Cretan seals of the time. 'Sauce-boats', so-called, like this one from Lerna (above left) were common on the Mainland; in fact they were drinking vessels, with the spout shaped to fit the mouth. (4, 5, 6)

of the southern Aegean, so close that on a clear day a mariner sailing from one side to the other need never lose sight of land, is illustrated by many finds. The people were naturally seafarers, their culture influenced by visits to the Mainland and to Crete.

The giant marble idol, left, over five feet high, was found on Amorgos. Figures with crossed arms are frequent, but no other so large is known. Such figures may represent the Nature Goddess, the 'Great Mother' worshipped by early man in many parts of the world. (7)

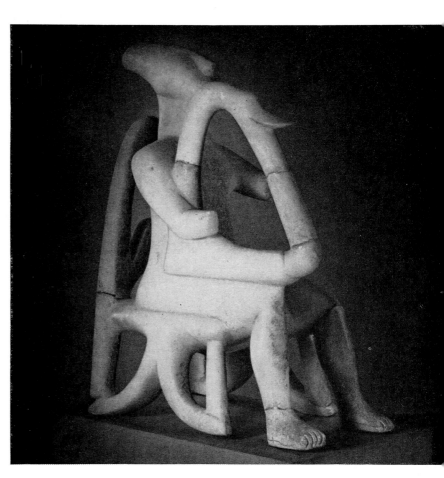

The man with the harp, above, was found on Keros, and may date from the earlier Bronze Age. With a similar marble figure from Amorgos, it is among the first pieces of evidence for the use of stringed instruments in the Aegean. (8)

The high-prowed ship above, recalling those painted on Egyptian Predynastic vases (chapter IV, pl. 3), is scratched on a clay utensil found on Syros. On the prow is a fish emblem, the keel projects behind and oars seem to be shown, but no mast. The utensil is shaped like a frying-pan and might have been used as a lid; or containing water it could have been used as a mirror. Much play is made with spirals. (9)

Little clay figures of men and women, and also of animals, have been found in large numbers in Crete. The one below is of a man, wearing a dagger and the 'Libyan sheath'; it was found in the hilltop sanctuary of Petsofa at Palaikastro in East Crete and dates from c. 1750 BC or earlier. The human figures probably represent worshippers and the animals cheap substitutes for sacrifice. (10)

The 'frying-pan' shape appears also in the clay vase below, found on Syros. The 'chip' decoration, reminiscent of woodwork, is seen also in pl. 9; it may be that wooden vessels decorated in this way were made in the islands. These 'frying-pans' are traditionally assigned to the Early Cycladic period, but some at least may be quite late, contemporary with the mature Middle Minoan in Crete (after 1800 BC). (12)

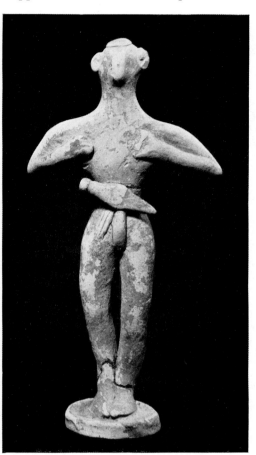

Fighting weapons included spear and dagger blades in bronze, in the islands with slots for binding them to the wooden handles. The one above (centre) was found on Amorgos and may date from c. 1750; similar blades have been found in Cyprus, in Troy and even in the Danube basin. (11)

The interlocking spirals appear once more on this stone model of a building from Melos, used perhaps for votive purposes. The circular chambers in two rows suggest that the building was a granary. What seems to be similar provision for the storage of grain and oil has been found at Mallia and Knossos on Crete. (14)

Vases shaped like animals and birds were made in the Aegean, and further east, in all periods of the Bronze Age. This amusing example, a bear (?) drinking from a bowl, comes from Syros. (13)

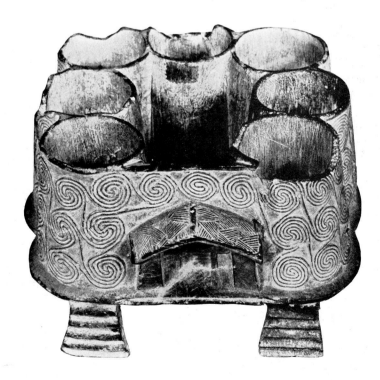

The high civilization in Crete

began to flower soon after 2000 BC. Secure in their island isolation, protected perhaps by strong sea power, the cities grew and great palaces arose within them. In magnificent surroundings, backed by high mountains, the citizens of Phaistos, Mallia, Gournia and, most extensive and magnificent of all, Knossos, lived an abundant life. Processions and dances, gladiatorial fights and bull-leapings are depicted in the wall paintings. Large areas of the palaces were reserved for magical or religious ceremonies under the guidance of the priest-kings and queens. A form of writing was in use, craftsmen worked in gold, silver and bronze and the potters produced some of the finest work ever made in Greek lands. It was a civilization comparable with that of Mesopotamia or of Egypt under the great Twelfth Dynasty.

At Mallia now giant storage jars stand amid the ruins of the palace. In the view on the left, we are looking north towards the sea. (15)

A city that was destroyed about 1450 BC lies fully excavated after three and a half thousand years. Gournia, in eastern Crete, was a town of flat-topped houses, sometimes three storeys high, packed along narrow streets. The palace occupied the high ground in the rear centre; to its right, steps led up from the main street to a shrine. (16)

The sea has receded from Agia Triada, once probably the harbour town of Phaistos. This view (on the left) is from the ruins of the palace and looks north across the town to the distant Mount Ida. (17)

The ruins of Phaistos still retain something of their grandeur in the romantic Cretan setting. Here we look over the excavated central court of the palace, north towards Mount Ida. The great sacred cave of Kamares lies just below the saddle between the twin peaks on the extreme right. (18)

A distinctive style of Cretan pottery is shown in the 'Kamares ware' cup from Phaistos in the centre. Its design is in red and white on a lustrous black ground. The cup is datable to c. 1700 BC. The jug on the right, with the fine grass design, is Cretan ware of the beginning of the Late Bronze Age, c. 1500–1450 BC. (19, 20)

Round-bellied birds were found on jugs in the Temple Repositories of that palace at Knossos which was destroyed about 1600 BC. Such jugs were imported from Melos, where the example above was found. (21)

The great staircase in the palace of Phaistos leads from the West Court to the upper floor. The ground floor was occupied by storerooms as at Knossos. The large and fertile plain which Phaistos controlled stretches away into the distance. (22)

The houses in which the Cretans lived were normally built to a certain height of rough stone (rubble) with mud or mud-brick above. But for outside walls carefully squared masonry was also used, as the little plaques above demonstrate. The left-hand one, of faience partly restored, depicting the façade of a house two storeys high, was found in the palace at Knossos by Arthur Evans, who dated it to about 1750 BC. The right-hand one, found on the Royal Road west of the palace, is of ivory. It was in a deposit of rubbish dating from about 1400 BC or not much later. Such plaques were probably used as inlays for wooden boxes or chests. (23, 24)

The two superb gold cups from a royal tomb at Vaphio, south of Sparta on the Mainland, are certainly the work of a Cretan artist of about 1600 BC. The scenes in relief depict methods of capturing wild bulls, perhaps for the sport of bull-leaping. On the cup above appears a fine impression of the strength of a charging bull; an attempt to snare it in nets has ended in disaster.

On the right is the design on the second cup; a tame cow is used as a decoy and (opposite) a man hobbles with a rope the hind leg of a captured bull (meant perhaps to represent the one under decoy). The rocks at the top, shown in conventional form, are meant to be considered as seen from above. (25, 26, 27)

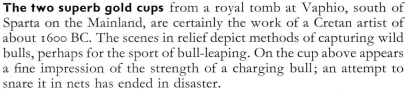

The double-axe, used both as a tool and weapon and as an offering to the gods or as a symbol of divinity, played an important part in the lives of the early Cretan people. Bronze double-axes were already being made probably by the beginning of the 2nd millennium BC in Crete and the picture above shows a stone mould of the kind used in the process (the axe is reproduced in plaster), found in the Bronze Age palace at Mallia. On the right is a gold votive double-axe from a sacred cave at Arkalochori, south of Knossos, dating from c. 1500 BC. The cave contained several such model axes in gold and silver, as well as many bronze sword blades, all of which were left as offerings to the gods. (28, 29)

The painted Cretan coffin from a tomb at Agia Triada, bearing the religious scenes depicted above, is exceptional in that, although shaped like many clay examples, it is carved out of limestone. The whole outer surface was coated with white plaster to serve as a ground for the paintings. One of the long sides (left) shows men bringing offerings—a boat and two young bulls—to the tomb, before which stands the deceased. On the left (against a white background) are two women, painted white in contrast to the brown of the men, one of whom is pouring libations into a vase set between two stands, which carry sacred double-axes surmounted by birds. Behind them, a man plays the lyre.

The other long side (not shown) depicts a sacrifice, with a player on the double pipe and five women. On a table-like altar a bull lies trussed; it has been stabbed in the neck, so that the blood flows into a vase on the ground, where other animals wait their turn for sacrifice.

One of the ends shows the scene above (right). A woman and another figure (perhaps the deceased) ride in a chariot drawn by griffins, while a strange bird hovers above them. The painting on the other end is also a chariot scene. (30, 31)

Exquisite workmanship marks the ritual vases used for pouring libations, which took many forms in the early Aegean. In the example on the left we encounter the Cretan bull motif again; it was found in the 'Little Palace' at Knossos and is carved from soft black stone (steatite); large parts of the vase and the golden horns have been restored. It was probably made about 1550 BC. A bull's-head vase, resembling this one, is being carried by one of the Cretan envoys painted on the walls of the tomb of User-amun, vizier of Egypt in the time of the Pharaoh Tuthmosis III (*acc* c. 1490 BC). (32)

The famous palace at Knossos,
not far from Heraklion on the northern coast of Crete, was excavated
during the first decade of this century by Arthur Evans, who christened it the 'Palace of Minos'. It is at once the largest and best preserved of the great Bronze Age palaces on the island. The ruins show
that there were several phases of building and re-building from perhaps before 2000 BC onwards, the earlier structures having been
partially destroyed, by earthquakes or other disasters, at various
times throughout the centuries until c. 1400 BC or later, when the
Palace site was finally abandoned.

'La Parisienne' is the name which has been given to the large-eyed
head of a girl on the right. She appears as part of a fresco on the walls
of the palace at Knossos. She wears a kind of scarf, gathered up
behind and tied into a 'sacral knot', which was a religious emblem;
she may therefore be a priestess. The fresco is believed to date from
about 1500 BC, which would make it contemporary with the vases
below. (33)

Sea-creatures inspire the designs on the 'marine style' vases of
this time (c. 1500–1450 BC). The slim libation vase below, with its
elegant whorl-shells, star-fish and sea-weed, was found at Zakro in
eastern Crete. The two-handled flask (below, right) painted with the
staring eyes and waving tentacles of an octopus, is from Palaikastro
and dates from about the same time. (34, 35)

205

The 'Snake-goddess', the little faience statuette below, found in the Temple Repositories of that palace at Knossos that was destroyed c. 1600 BC, bears a certain resemblance to the girl on the fresco over-leaf, but is of earlier date. It shows a goddess wearing a leopard crown and a long flounced dress with an apron over it, held in place beneath the bared breasts by a wide belt. (36)

A dance of worshippers in a field of lilies is the scene on the engraved bezel of a gold signet ring, below. The tiny figure is probably the goddess coming in answer to their prayers, and the large central figure may be the same goddess after appearing among them. In the background are what appear to be snakes, an ear of corn and a human eye (from a tomb near Knossos, c. 1500 BC). (37)

The 'Throne of Minos' stands against the wall in the 'Throne Room' of the palace at Knossos (below). The frescoes with wingless griffins are copies of the originals, which were still in position up to the top of the throne when the room was excavated. The upper part of the walls, and the roof, are wholly restored. (38)

The ruins of the Palace of Minos, looking east from the Middle Minoan cemetery on Mount Ailias, with the snow-capped peaks of Mount Ida in the distance. The Bronze Age city extended up and down the valley, beyond the limits of the picture to right and left. The reconstructed south propylon and Grand Staircase can be seen in the centre, while on the right are the three pillars before the throne room. For a plan see p. 222. (39)

The rise of Mycenae

was delayed perhaps by disturbances on the Mainland sometime
between 2000 and 1700 BC, when many of the earlier settlements
were destroyed by fire. With the coming of conquering invaders
from Anatolia a marked change and temporary decline is discernible
in the material culture of the people. But soon the influence of the
flourishing Minoan civilization is felt again and by about 1550 BC
pottery, gold and silver ware and weapons in the Cretan style were
treasured possessions of the ruling classes. To this time belong the
royal shaft graves of Mycenae, whose dramatic contents were first
uncovered by Schliemann nearly a hundred years ago, as he sought
for evidence to support the legends of Homer.

The head of a warrior (right) on an ivory plaque from Mycenae,
c. 1400 BC shows a helmet plated with rows of boars' tusks, very
like one described in the Iliad some seven hundred years later. Compare it with the bronze helmet of about the same time from Knossos.
In this, the knob at the top is rivetted in place and has a hole to take
a plume. The cheek-pieces are separate: perforations allow for fastening a padded base. Similar helmets are found in the Early Bronze Age
of Central Europe. (43, 44)

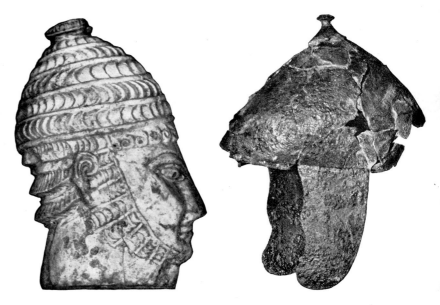

209

Seals with distinctive designs began to be used in Crete early in the Bronze Age. Their purpose was to identify and protect property: a bale or box or door was fastened with string and a lump of wet clay was then placed over the string like sealing-wax and stamped with a seal. The seals were carved on stone, bone or ivory, or even metal, and many examples of clay sealings have survived. In the picture on the right are shown some of the many Cretan seal-stones in Heraklion museum. The two capped with gold (centre, and bottom left) are of lapis lazuli, imported perhaps from as far away as Afghanistan. The round one shows a man with an immense dog or lion.

The carnelian cylinder has a picture of lions hunting and the bottom right seal shows a lion attacking a bull. The little green stone (c. 1600 BC) bears a ship with two masts. The carnelian cylinder was found, with other seals, in a warrior's grave at Knossos, dating from the period of the 'Last Palace', c. 1400 BC. (42)

A sacred dance in progress in the great central courtyard of the
palace at Knossos. In this reconstruction we are looking towards the
western façade. To the left can be seen a sacred shrine, decorated
with numerous 'Horns of Consecration'; golden double-axes adorn
the tops of the columns of the upper storey, which taper downwards
in the characteristic Minoan manner. The great central stairway with
its huge wooden column is flanked with frescoes showing a procession
of watching women such as are here seen sitting in the first-floor
balcony on the right. The attitudes and dress of the dancing women
are vouched for by fresco paintings. The architectural details are
based partly on excavation, partly on the frescoes. (40)

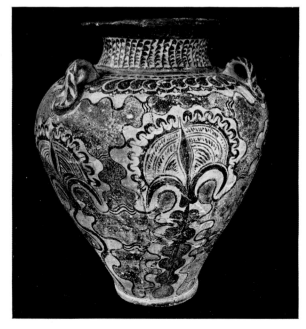

The influence of Egypt may perhaps be discerned in the design of
stylized papyrus flowers on the large 'Palace Style' vase on the right.
This highly ornate style of decoration, which dates from the 'Last
Palace' period (c. 1450–1400 BC), was confined to the more important
centres and must represent luxury ware. (41)

old
ut ▶

The citadel of Mycenae in its last phase in the 13th century BC looked down over its massive walls upon the 'tholos' tombs which surrounded it. The reconstruction above, which views the citadel from the northwest, shows warriors making their way up the causeway leading through the town; they wear protective clothing of leather and carry kidney-shaped shields of hide reinforced with metal. They are armed with long swords and leaf-shaped spears; their plumed helmets are of leather studded with metal discs and carry boars' tusks (compare the design on pl. 59, the 'Warrior Vase'). The two-horse chariot is based on clay models and frescoes of the time; on the left are two of the 'tholos' graves. (45)

my excavations in the Acropolis of Mycenae first view

Digging in progress in one of the shaft graves at Mycenae. The area is that of grave circle A, at an early stage in the excavation; the entrance to the circle can be seen in the background to the right. Schliemann's Greek wife Sophia stands in the foreground. (46)

The famous Lion Gate at Mycenae, from the outside. The circle of shaft graves excavated by Schliemann lies behind the bastion on the right. Each lion rests its forepaws on one of a pair of altars of the traditional Cretan type surmounted by a sacred column, symbol of the Divinity on whom the lions attend (the sacred column is a frequent motif of contemporary seal engravings). The relief is of limestone, but the lions' heads—now missing—were apparently of some other material (perhaps white marble, alabaster or wood coated with bronze) jointed into the limestone. The Lion Gate, which was set in position perhaps in the 14th century BC, is one of the curiously few examples found of monumental sculpture from the Aegean Late Bronze Age. (47)

Tombstones decorated with carving were set on top of the shaft graves at Mycenae. The one shown below is of grey limestone almost a yard and a half high; it surmounted shaft grave 5 of grave circle A. The low relief depicts a king armed with a short sword with 'horned' shoulders, resembling many found here and elsewhere throughout the Aegean world at the time (c. 1600–1500 BC). He pursues an enemy carrying a short sword or broken spear. Once again we encounter the linked spiral, which is no less common in the contemporary Bronze Age of Hungary and the north, and it is on these tombstones that we find the earliest pictures of chariots in the Aegean. (48)

The six shaft graves of circle A were surrounded by the circular enclosure wall shown in the drawing and photograph below. The wall was built of parallel rows of large slabs of limestone and horizontal cover slabs (one of these can be seen restored to its original position near the entrance, centre right of the photograph). Wooden tie-beams were used to hold the uprights together and to help support the cover-slabs. The space within the double-wall was filled with earth. One of the shaft graves is visible just to the left of the entrance; behind are the ruins of a house (the so-called 'granary'), built against the inside face of the massive defence wall; the inside of the Lion Gate is hidden by this house in the drawing. The 'Warrior Vase' (pl. 59) was found in the house immediately behind the great wall in the foreground. Grave-circle B, some distance away, is of earlier date. (49, 50)

Huge vaulted chambers, built of stone and known as *tholoi*, replaced the shaft graves for the burial of members of the ruling families. The change took place during the 15th century BC, when Mycenae reached the height of its prosperity and splendour. (It was in 1400 BC that the palace at Knossos was destroyed by fire, perhaps by enemies.) These vast tombs were half underground and were approached by a long passage *(dromos)*; a characteristic feature was the tall rectangular doorway with its sharp-pointed gable. The picture on the left shows the entrance to the so-called 'Tomb of Clytemnestra', wife of Agamemnon. This doorway, like that of the 'Treasury of Atreus' (see opposite) had an impressive façade, in this case flanked by fluted half-columns. The right-hand picture shows the underground stairway leading to the covered well outside the ring walls of the citadel. Both the massive corbelled roof and the sides of the stairway were originally entirely covered with plaster. (51, 52)

Pottery in a great variety of shapes of all phases of the late Bronze Age has been found at Mycenae and other Mainland sites, much of it clearly copied from metal vessels. The four examples (left) all date from soon after 1400 BC: a 'stirrup-jar' with a false spout between the handles, a two-handled flask with long neck, a squat *alabastron*, used for oil or ointment and a drinking jug. (55)

The 'Treasury of Atreus' at Mycenae is the largest of the great *tholos* tombs of the Mainland and is among the most astonishing architectural masterpieces of its time anywhere in the world. The picture on the right gives a vivid impression not only of its size but of the fine corbelled vaulting. Bronze pins found in the stonework indicate

that some form of surface decoration was formerly attached. The entrance from the *dromos* is on the right, the other doorway leads to a side chamber. An idea of the elaborate nature of this tomb's entrance façade is given by the drawing above, a reconstruction by the Greek prehistorian Spyridon Marinatos. Cretan influence is suggested by the bull theme and by the 'Horns of Consecration' surmounting the lintel, while the linked spiral is once again in evidence. The extant portions of the façade, which was made of green and red stone, are now divided between Athens and London. (53, 54)

The gold cup with high-swung handles (right), from the fourth shaft grave at Mycenae, was a form much copied in clay between c. 1700 and 1500 BC. The high-stemmed clay goblet *(kylix)* is a characteristic Late Bronze Age type and goes back to a form first introduced c. 1400 BC; this example is datable to c. 1250, and its highly stylised decoration is ultimately derived from a flower design. (56,̦57)

The rich treasures of the shaft graves of Mycenae, buried with the dead kings and their wives and companions, date from the 16th century BC. They show a striking mixture of the barbaric and the civilized, of old and new traditions brought together: vases of clay or metal (bronze, silver and gold), gold masks upon the faces of the dead, crowns and diadems, gold and silver jewellery and gold-mounted weapons. Many are Cretan, or the work of Cretan craftsmen on the Mainland, some again appear to be native, while some of the metal-work reflects the art styles of the Caucasus or of the northern nomads of the steppes.

The later royal and princely tombs, in spite of plundering, have also produced many beautiful things. In the art of metal-working, as in those of gem-engraving and vase-painting, the Aegean of the Late Bronze Age probably led the civilized world.

The nearly life-size head on the left, found at Mycenae, is in limestone, with a surface of white plaster and detail painted in red and blue. It may be the head of a sphinx, the lion with a woman's head, the strange beast whose history goes back to the early Orient and of course appears in Egypt. The head is one of the very few examples known of large sculpture in the round in Creto-Mycenaean art. (58)

The 'Warrior Vase' was found by Schliemann in a house next to grave-circle A at Mycenae, although it dates from much later, towards the end of the Mycenaean period (c. 1200 BC). On it is painted the design below: a procession of soldiers march off to battle. They carry kidney-shaped shields and wear corselets and greaves; their helmets, probably of leather, are fitted with horns and strengthened with metal discs; the 'balloons' on their spears are probably wine sacks or bags containing provender. A woman waves them goodbye. Compare this design with the terracotta painted relief of striding Phrygian warriors (chap. VI, pl. 72) found at Pazarlı, near Boghazköy and dating from something like five hundred years later. (59)

'I have looked upon the face of Agamemnon!' telegraphed the excited Schliemann when he found this mask of beaten gold. It was in shaft grave 5 at Mycenae, covering the face of one of the dead, and although a find of the greatest interest it is not the mask of Homer's king, who lived several centuries later. Another find by Schliemann at Mycenae was the 'Lion Hunt' dagger below. It is of bronze inlaid with gold and silver set in black niello; the decoration depicts men in combat with lions; they are armed with bows and throwing spears and protected by huge rectangular and figure-of-eight shields made of bull's hide. They wear shorts held in place by a belt round the narrow waist in the Cretan manner—though no such inlaid daggers have yet been found in Crete. (60, 61)

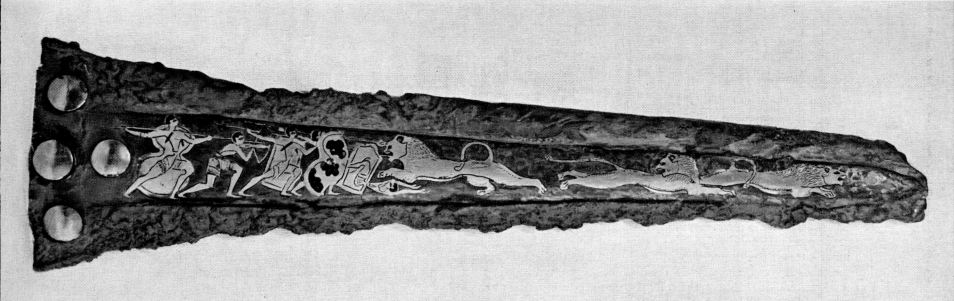

Curious signs reminiscent of letters, carved on stones from the Palace of Minos, attracted Arthur Evans to start his excavations at Knossos. In 1900, the first year, he came upon Late Bronze Age clay tablets with writing incised on them. Eventually it became clear that various systems of writing had been used on the island in different phases of the Bronze Age. The examples found were none of them plentiful enough to offer hopes of decipherment, except the latest, of which there was a large amount preserved. Evans called this latest script Linear B.

In 1939 an archive room was discovered in a Late Bronze Age palace at Pylos, on the Mainland, with exactly similar tablets, and many more have been recovered since. In 1952 Michael Ventris claimed that the language of Linear B was Greek; his solution of the problem is still debated, but it is clear that each sign represents a syllable and that the tablets are business memoranda in which a simple numeral system can be understood.

The 'Tripod Tablet' found in the 'Palace of Nestor' at Pylos, in the south-west Peloponnese, carried the Linear B inscription drawn above. It lists types of vases, including cooking vessels with three legs, and may date from as late as c. 1200 BC. (62)

The tablet in Linear B above was found by Arthur Evans at Knossos and dates from the 'Last Palace', c. 1400 BC. Words are divided by vertical strokes, and each figure stands for a whole syllable. Many of the signs are ideograms or pictures of the things discussed in the tablets.

The tablets were normally made of unbaked clay, which stands small chance of survival. It is to the enemies of the Minoans and Mycenaeans, earthquakes perhaps, or marauding invaders, who burnt the palaces that we owe the fire-hardened records that have now been found. (63)

Among the great Mainland citadels of the later Bronze Age was the one at Tiryns, not far from Mycenae. During the 14th century BC it was fortified with massive stone walls. In the left-hand picture above is seen what is left of the main gate leading from the outer to the inner citadel; the palace was above the wall to the left. Beyond lies the east gate (to the right) and the plain of Argos, with Mycenae in the distance. The right-hand picture shows the continuation of the ramparts of the citadel and the east gate. On the opposite page is a

view of the 'Great Casemate' at Tiryns, looking south; the sheer bulk of the stone blocks used in the construction of the ramparts is vividly conveyed. Note the characteristic corbelling of the passage-way, which we have already encountered in the *tholoi* at Mycenae.

The fortress and palace appear to have been overwhelmed towards the end of the 13th century: the skeletons of some of the last defenders, fallen or thrown from the battlements, were found lying beneath piles of burnt debris at the foot of the walls. (64, 65, 66)

Some ancient rite at which we can only guess is symbolised by the gold signet ring (top) found in the lower town outside the Acropolis at Tiryns. It was apparently part of a tomb-robber's hoard buried at the very end of Mycenaean times. The goddess sits on a folding-chair, her feet on a footstool, and holds a cup; behind her is a bird like a falcon, before her an incense-burner. Four demons with jugs approach her, whilst in the heavens are sun and moon, four ears of corn.

It is interesting to compare the design at the bottom of the bezel of this ring with the fragment of a stone architectural frieze from Knossos in the picture below it, dating from c. 1600 BC. (67, 68)

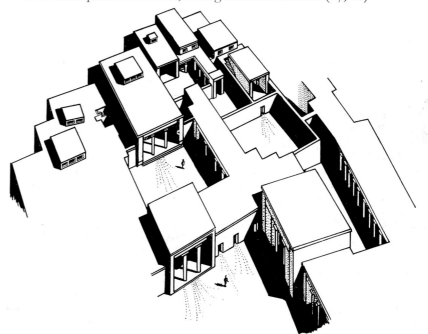

Within the citadel of Tiryns, in legend held by the princes of Mycenae only 10 miles distant, and of whose colossal fortifications the travel-writer and historian Pausanias spoke in tones of awe, stands the palace here reconstructed in a bird's eye view from the south. Approached by a pillared *propylon* (bottom left) and courtyard, is the main *megaron* with its hearth and throne. The floor and walls were painted, the latter with scenes of a boar-hunt and life-size figures of women. (69)

The famous 'Aegina Treasure' was said to have been found in a Mycenaean tomb on the island of Aegina, but it is now believed to be Cretan, plundered perhaps during the 19th century from the Chrysolakkos burial enclosure at Mallia, and dating from c. 1600 BC. The treasure includes head-bands or diadems (top and bottom), pendants and necklaces (centre), earrings (the four plain circles towards the bottom), and finger rings (five in all shown here). The four gold bosses on either side are probably dress or belt ornaments; they have little holes round the edges for sewing them to fabric. The materials used, apart from gold, include carnelian, amethyst and lapis lazuli. (70)

This clay bath-tub from Pachyammos in northern Crete dates from c. 1350 BC. Appropriately, it has fish painted on the inside. Though made for domestic use, such tubs were often employed as coffins in Crete, and sometimes also on the Mainland. (71)

The Aegean before the Greeks

M. S. F. HOOD

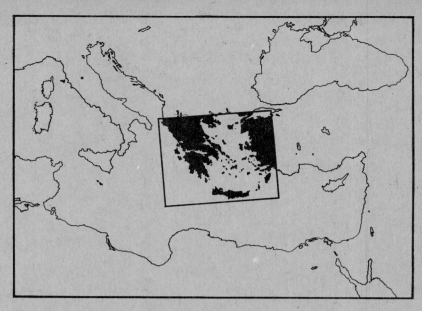

The position of Crete and Greece in relation to the Near East and the West. The boxed area is that of the map on page 196. (fig. 1)

Neolithic Settlers in the Aegean

WHEN THE FIRST stone-using agriculturalists reached the shores of the Aegean, some time between the end of the 6th and the beginning of the 4th millennium BC, they found territory which must have offered a particularly attractive environment in which to live. Here was a kind of water-linked paradise, where the climate was genial; the heats of summer being tempered by cool winds, while the winters were relatively mild owing to the effect of the surrounding sea. The land was fertile enough, with little plains divided by mountains, ideal for the support of the first small communities. Vines and olives probably grew wild in early times, while deer and goats roamed in the forests of oak, fir and cypress, which covered the mountains and most of the plains. But there were also more dangerous beasts—bears, wolves and boars, and great oxen and lions, the memory of which survived in legend; like the Cretan bull, or the Nemean lion and boar of Erymanthus whose pursuit formed some of the labours of Herakles.

Water was more plentiful than it is now, when many ancient springs are dry and the forests that retained the ground water and encouraged rainfall have largely disappeared owing to the activities of generations of men and goats. The sea, abounding with fish, provided an easy means of communication, even for primitive boats; the islands make the Aegean more like a series of lakes, with land on a clear day never out of sight in sailing from one side of it to the other, and everywhere inlet among the rocky coasts little bays with sandy beaches ideal for hauling boats ashore, as Odysseus and his crew do each night in Homer. Flint, that basic raw material of early man, is rare; but obsidian, a volcanic glass easily chipped into sharp flakes and blades, is found in the islands of Melos and Yali near Kos. Emery, useful in grinding stone for axes or bowls, is peculiar to the island of Naxos. When metal was wanted there was copper, gold and silver, in sufficient quantities scattered throughout the islands and on the mainland.

The earliest neolithic cultures in the Aegean were almost certainly due to immigrants coming from the east, and it seems that they found lands empty or nearly empty of other human inhabitants. Until the last war no certain traces of occupation during palaeolithic or mesolithic times had been recognised in Greece, but in 1941 stone implements of a very late phase of the Palaeolithic were recovered on the south shores of the former Lake Copais near Haliartos in Boeotia in a deposit beneath the debris of a neolithic settlement. This remained an isolated discovery until 1958 when palaeolithic industries both of a Mousterian and of an Aurignacian type (*cf.* chap. I) were found in separate levels along the River Peneios in Central Thessaly.

The neolithic settlers no doubt brought with them knowledge of how to grind stone for axes and adzes, and of how to make pots with shapes and styles of decoration comparable with those of the other early pottery-using cultures of the Near East (described in chap. II). They may have introduced, not only the art of farming, but also probably the actual crops in the case of wheat, and some at any rate of the animals—cows, sheep and goats, and swine—which they domesticated. To islands like Crete, and possibly to the mainland of Greece as well, they came by sea.

From what immediate region or regions did these neolithic settlers arrive in the Aegean? From West Anatolia perhaps, or along the south coasts of Anatolia from Cilicia, or from still further afield in Syria or Palestine or North Africa. Almost certainly they did not all come from one narrow area and at one time. The changes of fashion in the shaping and decorating of pots, which succeed one another in the early Neolithic and Chalcolithic cultures of Mesopotamia and adjacent regions, appear to be reflected (although perhaps only after an interval of time) in the Neolithic cultures of mainland Greece. But this is not necessarily proof that successive waves of immigrants were reaching Greece from the Near East.

On the mainland of Greece plain hand-made pottery occurs in the very earliest stages of the Neolithic; but throughout most of the Neolithic period there the finer vases have painted decoration with designs in red or black on a white or yellow ground. The main early phase of the mainland Neolithic with this painted pottery is called Sesklo, and one of the later phases Dimini, after two sites in South Thessaly. Now the recent excavations at Otzaki Magoula near Larissa in Central Thessaly have distinguished three separate phases (Pre-Sesklo, Proto-Sesklo and Early Pottery Neolithic) before the Sesklo. Moreover at the very bottom of the settlement mounds at Otzaki and at Sesklo itself have been found deposits left by neolithic people who apparently did not yet make pottery (Pre-Pottery Neolithic, as at Jericho and elsewhere, as described in chap. II).

Sesklo and Dimini

The area of Thessaly, with its great extent of inland plain so different from the rest of Greece, is extremely rich in neolithic remains, and most of the excavations of neolithic sites in Greek territory have been done there. This may be because Thessaly was the region most favoured by the earliest neolithic settlers; but it may also mean that it remained comparatively backward, with Neolithic cultures surviving there after the use of bronze had begun in other parts of Greece. In the Sesklo phase of the Mainland Neolithic the pottery is often of high quality and is painted with simple linear designs, but that of the later Dimini phase is often decorated with spirals and meanders, and the designs on the same vase may be in two colours (polychrome) instead of only one as earlier (pl. 2). These Dimini designs are remarkably like those on the painted pottery of some of the early Neolithic cultures in the Balkans to the north, related to those of Tripolye described in chap. XI. They might therefore reflect the appearance in Greece of northern invaders; but alternatively this style of vase decoration may have developed in Thessaly, and spread to the north through the influence of trade and similar contacts.

Dimini itself is the only neolithic settlement in Greece that has been completely excavated (pl. 1). It lies not far from the sea on the western edge of a fertile plain opposite the modern city of Volos (ancient Iolkos). Here on a low hill at the foot of the mountain a small village clustered round a two-roomed building which was evidently the chief's house. This was entered through a porch from a large open court; an arrangement which in conjunction with the plan of the house itself is very reminiscent both of the 'Palace' buildings of Bronze Age Troy (chap. VI) and of the still later Bronze Age palaces of Mainland Greece. A series of ring walls round the settlement with houses in the spaces between them may have been defensive in character, although they are in most places hardly wide enough to offer a platform on which defenders could stand. These feeble ring walls, built of rough undressed stone, could not in any case have stood very high. The whole settlement from outside must have looked very much like a large sheep-fold of the kind still often seen in the mountains of Greece.

In the earlier (Sesklo) phase of the Mainland Neolithic a typical form of house was rectangular, almost square, with buttresses projecting from the walls inside and a row of posts down the centre. Such houses, like those of Dimini later, may have had pitched rather than flat roofs, but this is not certain. The roofs were made by laying reeds across the rafter-beams and piling mud thickly above them. The walls were normally built of mud or mud-brick upon low foundations of rough stone, and upright wooden posts might be incorporated in them. The materials and the methods of construction were basically the same as those still being used in the remoter villages of Greece today. But no village today makes the superb pottery of Sesklo or Dimini with its vigorous painted designs.

Ground stone axes and (notably in Thessaly) adzes were used throughout the Neolithic everywhere in the Aegean area. Domestic animals included cattle, sheep and goats, and pigs. Hunting for food was perhaps little practised; in Thessaly, where the bones of animals found in the settlements have been well studied, very few remains of wild beasts have been identified among them. Barley was certainly grown during the period of the Sesklo culture in Thessaly, and for the Dimini phase, wheat, figs, pears and peas are attested.

Weapons in Thessaly included the sling, since many sling bolts of fired clay have been recovered. But arrowheads of flint and obsidian are also found in the Neolithic of the Mainland, so the bow was also in use. Obsidian was imported, apparently from the earliest times, both to the Mainland and to Crete. Since the nearest sources of it are in the Aegean islands like Melos, this implies contacts of some kind by sea. Bracelets of stone and *spondylus* shell (a mussel native to the Aegean and the Black Sea) from Thessaly, comparable with those of the earliest Neolithic cultures of the Danube basin, indicate rudimentary trade overland.

Neolithic Crete

The Neolithic of the great island of Crete on the south edge of the Aegean differs in many ways from that of the Mainland. It appears to develop without interruption from its beginnings until the Bronze Age. The earliest pottery is remarkably like some of the early (chalcolithic) pottery of Palestine. The clay vases are normally burnished, with dark brown or black surfaces, sometimes bearing incised decoration which may be filled with white paste. During the middle phases of the Cretan Neolithic some of the finest of this burnished pottery has a delicately rippled surface which is very distinctive and attractive. The most important site is at Knossos, where the Bronze Age 'Palace of Minos' was built on top of a neolithic settlement mound with deposits about ten metres deep formed by the collapse or destruction of successive mud-walled houses. In the later stages at any rate these houses may consist of several rooms with compartments for animals: their roofs were probably flat as in the Bronze Age in Crete. In the Aegean islands apart from Crete few if any traces of neolithic occupation have yet been recognised.

Religion is reflected in the clay female figurines, perhaps goddesses, which in one form or another are characteristic of all the Neolithic cultures of Greece. Not much is known about neolithic burial customs either on the Mainland or in Crete. In Crete caves may have been used for inhumations by whole villages or families. Some cremation burials in pits were found in a cave at Prosymna near Mycenae on the Mainland. Cremation burials in jars of a later phase of the Neolithic have recently been identified in Thessaly.

The Discovery and Dating of the Ancient Aegean Civilizations

Bronze-using cultures in the Aegean cover a period of some fifteen hundred years or more, from about 2500 BC to 1000 BC. The serious study of the Greek Bronze Age began less than a hundred years ago. In 1866 an eruption on the island of Thera (modern Santorin) led to the discovery of Bronze Age settlements overwhelmed by some ancient explosion of the volcano there, and two years later tombs with characteristic Late Bronze Age (or 'Mycenaean' as it came to be called) pottery were excavated on behalf of the British Museum

at Ialysos, in Rhodes. Then in 1876 Schliemann opened the first circle (A) of royal shaft graves at Mycenae itself (pl. 46). His claim to have found the graves of the legendary king Agamemnon and his companions murdered by Clytemnestra on their return from Troy riveted attention. This led to intensive exploration and study of Bronze Age remains in Greece; and controversy began to crystallise round the twin problems of how far the Bronze Age civilization of Greece can be regarded as truly Greek, and how far the legends and traditions that appear to refer to it are historical.

In 1900 Arthur Evans began to explore the most famous legendary site of the island of Crete, Knossos. The discovery there of a civilization, at once more refined and considerably older than the 'Mycenaean' of the Mainland and other islands, gave a fresh impetus to Aegean prehistoric studies. This Cretan civilization was clearly in some ways ancestral to the Late Bronze Age 'Mycenaean'. Was the Mycenaean civilization then merely the latest form of the Cretan, spread perhaps by conquest and colonisation throughout the Aegean area? Or was it essentially an independent creation, influenced by Cretan civilization, but reflecting the genius of the people of the Mainland? And in that case did the Mainlanders who were responsible for the Mycenaean civilization already speak the Greek language? When, if they did, was the Greek language introduced to Greece, and when did people of Greek speech first begin to settle in Crete? These questions still occupy the field of debate in Aegean prehistoric studies.

In the first year of his excavations at Knossos in 1900 Evans came upon Late Bronze Age clay tablets with writing incised on them (pl. 63, *fig.* 2). It was in fact his interest in early writing and the hope of finding evidence for it that had first impelled him to excavate there.

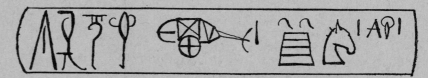

Inscribed clay tablet, with writing in Linear B script from Knossos. It appears to list the equipment issued to a chariot warrior and provides the earliest Cretan evidence for the war chariot. (fig. 2)

For curious signs carved on some of the stones of the Palace were reminiscent of letters; and similar signs were found on a class of early sealstones peculiar to Crete. It eventually became clear that various systems of writing had been used in different phases of the Bronze Age in the island. But only the latest of these, called by Evans the Linear B script, seemed to offer any hopes of decipherment owing to the comparatively large number of clay tablets written in it which had survived at Knossos.

No similar tablets, however, were found at any other site, either in Crete or on the Mainland, until 1939. In that year an archive room was discovered in a Late Bronze Age palace at Pylos, the legendary capital of Homer's Nestor, with clay tablets exactly like those found by Evans at Knossos some forty years earlier (pl. 62). Since the war many more Linear B tablets have been recovered at Pylos, and from 1952 onwards at Mycenae also. Meanwhile in 1952, Michael Ventris in England came forward with the claim that the language of these tablets was Greek. His decipherment has won acceptance from many authorities, although it is seriously challenged by others. The solution of this controversy is perhaps the most important single issue in Aegean prehistoric studies at the moment.

Both on the mainland of Greece and in Crete and the Aegean islands the main sequence of cultures throughout the Neolithic and Bronze Ages is reasonably clear. But there are considerable difficulties when it comes to correlating these sequences with one another. Evans devised a system of periods for the Cretan Bronze Age based in the first instance upon changes in the shapes and styles of decoration of the pottery. He called the Cretan civilization Minoan (after Minos, the legendary king of Knossos) and split it into early, middle and late phases, each with three sub-divisions. In 1918 separate systems were proposed for the Mainland of Greece (Helladic) and for the Aegean islands (Cycladic). These three systems in their last phase are almost parallel, since from the beginning of the Late Bronze Age (about 1550 BC) the material culture of the whole Aegean area is more or less uniform. The Late Helladic and Late Cycladic periods are usually called together 'Mycenaean' after Mycenae, the most important city of the period on the Greek Mainland.

The chronology of the early part at least of the Aegean Late Bronze Age is relatively well fixed by connections with Egypt and the Near East. Pottery vessels imported from the Aegean have been found in Egypt and Syria; over 1300 fragments of them for example were recovered by Petrie from the rubbish dumps of the palace of the heretic King Akhenaten at El Amarna, datable between about 1370–1352 BC. There is also good evidence for connections between Crete and Egypt during the time of the powerful Egyptian Twelfth Dynasty (about 2000–1785 BC), and this allows reasonably close dating for the Middle Minoan periods in Crete. The early part of the Bronze Age in Crete (Early Minoan) seems roughly to correspond with the end of the Old Kingdom (Sixth Dynasty) and the First Intermediary period in Egypt. It must have begun, therefore, about 2500 BC. The dating of the earlier part of the Bronze Age in the Cycladic islands and on the Mainland of Greece is far less well-established, and opinions about the dates for the Early and Middle Cycladic and Helladic phases vary by several centuries. The later range of possible dates are those preferred by the author.

The Earlier Bronze Age in the Aegean
(c. 2500 to 1500 BC)

In spite of some local differences, the civilization of the Aegean as a whole from the beginning of the Bronze Age is marked by a certain uniformity of character. This is seen for instance in the new types of pottery which now come into fashion throughout the area. The most striking among these is the handled jug with a spout for pouring liquids (pl. 3, centre), and this and other shapes of vase characteristic of the early Bronze Age in the Aegean are also at home in Anatolia. It is therefore often assumed that the changes throughout the Aegean at the beginning of the Bronze Age reflect the arrival of new peoples from that direction. A further argument for this view is based upon the evidence of language. In later times over Greece and large parts of Anatolia are found distributed certain types of non-Greek place-names, including names of rivers and mountains (notably those ending in –ss or –nt like Knossos, or Tiryns, near Mycenae, with the genitive in classical Greek *Tirynthos*). It therefore seems that once, before the Greek language was spoken in Greece, peoples sharing the same non-Greek language (or closely related languages) lived both in Anatolia and in the Aegean area; and it is inferred that this non-Greek language was introduced by immigrants from Anatolia at the beginning of the Bronze Age. But on the other hand these non-Greek names may reflect the pattern of immigration in still earlier (Neolithic) times, and it is not impossible that the Early Bronze Age civilizations of the Aegean were largely developed by the peoples already settled there.

In Crete, however, similarities in dress, in religion, and in aspects of material culture such as seal stones and amulets (notably amulets shaped like a human leg) found in the tombs of the earlier Bronze Age, suggest that actual immigrants may have been reaching the island from the direction of Egypt, and perhaps also from North Mesopotamia or Syria. The comparable Egyptian seals and amulets appear to date from the end of the Old Kingdom (Dynasty VI) or from the period of its collapse, the First Intermediary Period (c. 2300–2100 BC). It is about this time that a mass of invaders from some region of Central or West Anatolia seem to have swept southwards into Syria and Palestine, destroying the towns of the comparatively civilized peoples that they found there and settling themselves. These invaders may have helped directly or indirectly to bring about the fall of the Old Kingdom in Egypt, and at a time of such disturbance refugees might well have found their way by sea from the coasts of the East Mediterranean to the Aegean.

Ships with oars and sails often appear engraved on sealstones of the earlier Bronze Age in Crete (pl. 42, bottom centre), or incised on pottery objects in the Cycladic island of Syros (pl. 9). These are shaped like frying-pans, and may have been mirrors, water being placed in the pan to give a reflection. Only in the Late Bronze Age (c. 1550 BC onwards) do polished bronze mirrors, long used in Egypt, come into fashion in the Aegean. The island ships in particular are remarkably like some painted on Egyptian Predynastic vases. There was no doubt trade between Egypt and the Aegean from a very remote period (*fig. 13*); several Egyptian stone bowls of Early Dynastic types have been found at Knossos in Crete, and emery from Naxos may have been exported to Egypt for help in grinding stone vases there even before 3000 BC. Certainly by the beginning of the

Twelfth Dynasty (c. 2000–1785 BC) connections between Egypt and Crete had become extremely close. Egyptian scarab seal stones were brought to Crete and imitated there, while Cretan pottery found its way to Egypt. The spiral, a favourite motive of decoration in Crete and throughout the Aegean from early in the Bronze Age, becomes very popular in Egypt at this time. This may be owing to the influence of Aegean fashions in Egypt or perhaps (though on present evidence this appears less likely) of Egyptian on the Aegean. An Egyptian statue of the Twelfth or Thirteenth Dynasty was recovered from a deposit of about 1650 BC in the Palace at Knossos.

Cylinder seals from Mesopotamia (chap. III) were reaching Crete by the time of Hammurabi (c. 1700 BC) if not earlier. A clay vase of the very beginning of the Middle Minoan Period (c. 2000 BC) and several early daggers of types characteristic of Crete have been found in Cyprus, and fragments of Middle Minoan pottery at Ras Shamra (Ugarit) and Byblos in Syria and Palestine. But the main exports of Crete were probably things like wine, oil from olives, cypress wood, and woven stuffs which might be dyed with purple made from shell fish (*murex*), as in the Levant (chap. V).

There is also evidence for contacts between the Aegean and adjoining regions to the north and west. Perhaps as we have seen, the fashion for spiral decoration reached the Aegean from the Balkans, the basin of the Danube or Transylvania, where spirals appear to be much at home in the earliest Neolithic cultures. Curious embossed bone plaques, which may be idols of some kind, are found at Troy and turn up in Greece (at Lerna) and in south Italy, Sicily and Malta. Similarly clay hooks and double hooked 'anchor ornaments' occur throughout the same area from Troy though Macedonia and the rest of Mainland Greece as far as the Aeolian islands (north of Sicily) and Malta. Daggers of a type recovered from early tombs in the Mesara plain of south Crete also appear in Italy. And, by the 16th century BC at least, liparite (a kind of obsidian or volcanic glass flecked with white pumice) was being imported from the Aeolian islands to be manufactured into stone bowls at Knossos.

Metal, copper and bronze for tools and weapons, as well as gold and silver for vases and ornaments, by then was in use throughout the Aegean area. A flat copper axe was lying on the floor of a house of the latest phase of the Neolithic at Knossos, and it appears that copper tools and gold ornaments were already available before the end of the Neolithic period on the Mainland. But in the Bronze Age for the first time actual moulds for casting tools (pl. 28), weapons and ornaments, are found, together with furnaces for smelting ore as in the Early Helladic settlement at Rafina near Athens and in the palace at Phaistos in Crete. Distinctive types of tool or weapon are characteristic of different areas: the double axe (pl. 29), and its variety with one blade set as an adze (axe-adze), are at home in Crete, together with spear and dagger blades having rivets to grip their wooden shafts or handles; in the Aegean islands the equivalent weapons have flat or hooked tangs and slots through the blades for binding them to their shafts (pl. 11). Later, socketed spear-heads are found in Crete, and daggers there develop into long rapier swords with tangs for the wooden hiltplates. Bows and arrows were presumably used throughout the Aegean; but arrowheads of metal, flint or obsidian, are curiously rare in Crete, where however bows appear in representations on sealstones. The most characteristic arm of defence in Crete was a great shield of cow-hide, shaped like a figure-of-eight and covering a man from head to foot (pl. 61): conical helmets are worn by warriors who appear to be attacking a town in a mosaic of faience plaques, the inlay of some kind of wooden chest, found at Knossos (c. 1700 BC). Such helmets may have been armed with metal as they sometimes were in the later Bronze Age. Little chopper-like instruments resembling early Egyptian razors, and tweezers also apparently used for removing hair, together with stone palettes for grinding paint for the face and eyes, are common throughout the Aegean world from the beginning of the Bronze Age. Bronze fish hooks, large circular earrings, and diadems of gold or silver are found in Crete and elsewhere in the islands and on the Mainland at this time.

Crete in the early part of the second millennium becomes the seat of a high civilization comparable with the civilizations of contemporary Egypt under the great Twelfth Dynasty and of Mesopotamia. This civilization is characterised by the manufacture of exceedingly beautiful pottery, including some of the finest ever made in Greek lands. The vases are gaily decorated with elaborate writhing designs in white, or in several different colous (polychrome)—white, yellow, orange and red—on a shining black lustrous ground (pl. 19). The shapes of most of the finer vessels are clearly copied from metal originals, and they are often, especially the drinking cups, of an egg-shell thinness like the gold and silver originals they imitate. Very few metal vases of this period have survived in Crete; but a hoard of over 150 silver cups (with one of gold), which may be imports from Crete, was recovered from a foundation deposit in a temple at Tod in Upper Egypt presented by the Twelfth Dynasty King Amun-em-het II (c. 1927–1893 BC).

On the Mainland even during the Neolithic period some of the pottery appears to be copies, although perhaps remote and indirect copies, of metal vessels. To the beginning of the Bronze Age belong some actual examples of gold vases, like the superb 'sauce-boat' in the Louvre. This type of spouted bowl on a low foot, named from its resemblance to a modern sauce-boat, but actually a drinking cup, is very characteristic of the Mainland Early Helladic culture (pl. 5).

Settlements throughout the Aegean now attain the size of regular villages or even towns. These may be defended by massive fortifications with towers and gates on the Mainland (as at Lerna, pl. 6, and Rafina near Athens) and in the Cycladic islands (Chalandriani in Syros); but in Crete scarcely any certain example of a fortified town is known until after the end of the Bronze Age. Perhaps the isolation of the island, and some degree of political unity, combined with superiority in civilization and in sea power, made fortifications seem unnecessary, as in Egypt.

The Palace at Knossos

Great palaces now began to be built in the chief cities of Crete such as Knossos, Phaistos (pl. 18, 22) and Mallia (pl. 15). None of the existing remains of these can be securely dated much before 2000 BC; but there may have been earlier palaces. Perhaps the large and imposing building assigned to the very beginning of the Bronze Age at Vasiliki in East Crete was one. But the most extensive and magnificent of all the Cretan palaces was the famous Palace of Minos (as Evans christened it) at Knossos. The ruins visible on the site today are mainly those of the palace destroyed in the first part of the Late Bronze Age about 1400 BC, but the plan appears to have been essentially similar during the earlier stages of its history, and in spite of a good deal of variation in detail the arrangements of the other great Cretan palaces were much the same.

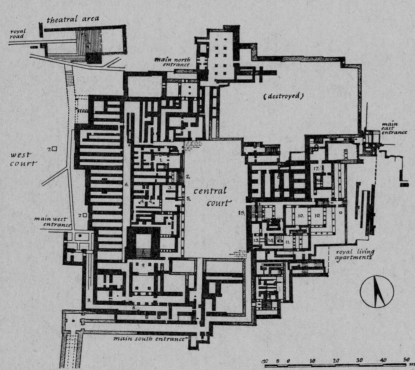

Knossos: plan of the Palace of Minos as it was c. 1400 BC. (1) throne room; (2) main staircase to first floor; (3) Temple Repositories of earlier palace, destroyed c. 1600 BC; (4) pillar basements; (5) triple shrine facing central court; (6) corridor with storage rooms to the west; (7) altars; (8) Corridor of the Procession; (9) stair from corridor to first floor; (10) Hall of the Double Axes; (11) bedroom; (12) bathroom; (13) room with lavatory; (14) private store or treasure-room; (15) grand staircase to royal living apartments; (16) stone-carver's store-room with lumps of 'lapis lacedaemonius'; (17) 'schoolroom'. (fig. 3)

The palace at Knossos (pl. 39, 40, *fig. 3*) was roughly square, measuring about 150 metres each way. In the centre was a large rectangular open court. A main entrance on the north facing towards the sea led directly into this central court from outside; and there were three other entrances into the Palace building, on the west, south and east. The ground floor along the west side of the central court was occupied by a series of rooms devoted to religious rites and ceremonies. The most famous of these, the 'Throne Room', built in its surviving form shortly before 1400 BC, has a stone chair flanked by stone benches with guardian griffins painted on the walls above (pl. 38). Facing the throne are steps leading down into a sunk rectangular pit, which was probably used for ritual anointings or lustrations of some kind. For the kings (and their queens; indeed it may have been the queen, not the king, who sat on the ritual throne in the 'Throne Room') were evidently priest kings, and the Palace was a sanctuary as well as containing the living quarters for the king and queen and their retainers, and the government offices together with store chambers for the taxes paid in kind. Behind these cult rooms on the west side of the central court ran a long corridor with rows of store-rooms filled with large jars to hold corn or oil. Sunk in the floors of both corridor and store-rooms were stone-built chests, lined with stone slabs, and in some cases originally with an inner lining of lead as well for clothes and other valuables. The whole of the storey above this west wing of the palace appears to have been occupied by the state apartments, richly decorated with fresco paintings on the walls (pl. 33) and approached by monumental flights of steps both from the central court and at the south end from a wide passage (the 'Corridor of the Procession', so named from the frescoes of life-sized figures walking in some great religious procession which adorned its walls) that led round to the west entrance.

On the east side of the Palace, built into a cutting in the side of the hill (really the debris of the old neolithic settlement) on top of which lay the central court, were the actual living quarters of the king and his family. These were entered from the central court down a remarkable flight of stone stairs, surviving intact for a height of three storeys at the time they were cleared by Evans in 1901. On the ground floor was a suite (for the king?) consisting of a bedroom, with attached bathroom and lavatory, and an enclosed treasure chamber or storeroom; while beyond, approached through a winding corridor, were spacious day rooms or audience chambers. Light came through windows, opening onto little yards (light wells) left in the centre of the building. This suite of rooms was apparently duplicated (for the queen?) on the floor above, and a private staircase led from one suite to the other. To the north of the block with the royal apartments were the workshops of the skilled craftsmen, like engravers of sealstones and makers of stone bowls. Here also may have been the school room where the scribes learnt to write. At Phaistos an open court with a great furnace for metal working occupied an equivalent part of the palace.

Other Sites

Round the palaces in Crete lay extensive cities. The only Bronze Age town in the Aegean that has been entirely cleared by excavation is Gournia in East Crete (pl. 16, *fig. 4*). The ruins visible there today are for the most part those of the town destroyed at the beginning of the Late Bronze Age (c. 1450 BC), but the plan was probably much the same during the earlier period. In the centre of the town stood the little palace of the local king or governor. The houses, each with several rooms, were packed along narrow streets. At Knossos some idea of the appearance of the houses, often two or three storeys high with flat roofs, is given by the little plaques of faience which had evidently served as inlays in some wooden chest or box (pl. 23). A similar plaque, but in ivory and somewhat larger, was found there in 1957 (pl. 24). The façades of the palaces and great houses might be constructed of carefully squared masonry as these plaques indicate. But normally house walls were built to a certain height of rough stone (rubble) with mud or mud-brick above; and even the palaces like Knossos had upper storeys of mud brick. Timber was used, at least in the palaces and great houses, to make an interlacing framework or 'half-timbered' construction tying the whole structure of the walls together. This would have given a welcome strength against the earthquakes to which the island is such a victim.

On the Mainland a building like the Early Helladic 'House of the Tiles' at Lerna, with several rooms and apparently two storeys high,

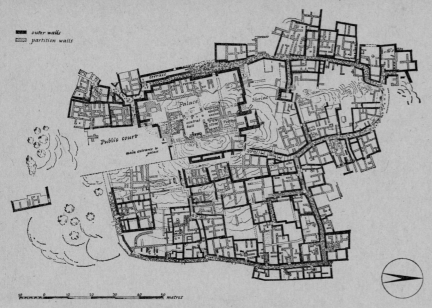

outer walls
partition walls

Above: Gournia at the beginning of the Late Minoan period, c. 1500 BC. The Palace occupies a large part of the town area. Compare this with the view shown in pl. 16, where the north is also to the right. Below: the 'House of the Tiles' at Lerna, Early Helladic, c. 2000 BC; pl. 6. (figs. 4, 5)

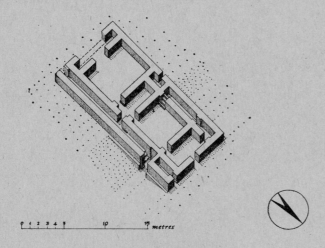

may have been a palace or chief's house (pl. 6, *fig. 5*). It is so named from the baked clay tiles, which had evidently covered the low-pitched roof; such tiles are peculiar to the Early Helladic culture of the Mainland, and are perhaps the earliest clay roof tiles in the world. An immense circular building, of which a part was exposed in the lowest Early Helladic levels beneath the Late Bronze Age palace at Tiryns not far from Lerna, may also have been a palace. But smaller round buildings in the Early Helladic settlement at Orchomenos near Thebes might have been granaries, like the circular chambers in the Middle Minoan palaces at Mallia and Knossos in Crete. A stone model from the island of Melos (pl. 14) shows a building, perhaps such a granary, with circular chambers arranged in two rows as at Mallia.

Writing and Seals

In Crete from an early phase of the Bronze Age there is evidence for some system of syllabic writing (with signs for each syllable as in the contemporary systems of Egypt and Mesopotamia). At first the signs were pictures like the hieroglyphics of Egypt; but by 1600 BC a system with more stylised signs was in use. The signs of this later system were easily scratched on clay tablets or written in ink. The examples of writing which survive are mostly lists and inventories on clay tablets, or short inscriptions on seals or stone ritual vases. But it seems clear that a good deal of writing was done in ink on some kind of paper, made from papyrus as in Egypt, or (according to one tradition) from palm leaves; palms may have grown wild in Crete at this time. Words in ink survive on some clay cups from Knossos dated to about 1650 BC. The evidence for writing during the earlier part of the Bronze Age on the Mainland and in the Aegean islands is more uncertain. But isolated marks scratched on clay vases certainly resemble signs of a script.

With the knowledge of writing in early times there often went the practice of using seals to protect and identify property. A bale or box or door was fastened with string, and a lump of wet clay was then placed over the string like sealing-wax and stamped with a seal. Seals carved on stone, bone or ivory, or even metal, are found dating from every phase of the Bronze Age in Crete (pl. 42), and many examples of clay sealings have also survived there. On the Mainland, however, seals are extremely rare until the Late Bronze Age, in the 16th century BC and onwards, and when they turn up in earlier contexts they look as if they had been brought from Crete or were rough imitations of Cretan seals. But in some Early Helladic sea-port towns, like Asine and Lerna, numbers of clay lumps with seal impressions on them have been recovered (pl. 4). These might have sealed merchandise imported from Crete if the seals that made them were Cretan. But some of the impressions may have been from seals manufactured locally, even if following Cretan models. If these seals were of wood instead of stone, ivory or metal, they would have perished, and this might explain why so few actual examples of early seals have been found on the Mainland.

Also rare on the Mainland until the Late Bronze Age, but common at all periods in Crete, are stone vases. In Crete there is an extraordinary variety both in the shapes of these vases and in the range of many-coloured stones from which they were fashioned. Stone vases were also common from early times in the Cycladic islands, where however they were usually made out of the fine white marble so abundant there.

Beliefs and Customs

In Crete there is a great deal of evidence for religious beliefs and practices from the beginning of the Bronze Age onwards. The kings and queens were priests, if not actually divine, like the kings of the other nations of the Near East at the time. Large areas of the palaces were reserved for the performance of magical or religious ceremonies. One of the surviving scenes painted on the walls of the Palace at Knossos seems to depict some great religious ceremony which is evidently taking place in the central court there (pl. 40). The women in their long flounced dresses dance before serried masses of spectators. But there were also sanctuaries in caves, and in open-air enclosures (often 'peak sanctuaries' on the tops of mountains and high hills), which might contain small shrine buildings and altars. In the Late Bronze Age at least there were separate shrine buildings in towns like Gournia, or associated with palaces as at Agia Triada (pl. 17) and Mallia in Crete, and perhaps at Eleusis on the Mainland. But great temples like those of Egypt and Mesopotamia have not been recognised in the Bronze Age anywhere in the Aegean. Sacred trees and pillars of stone and wood stood in the sanctuaries in Crete; and there were pillar basements for cult in the palaces of the kings and in the ordinary houses. Processions and dances, gladiatorial fights and bull-leapings, are depicted in the wall paintings or engraved on stone vases and sealstones, and were probably religious or magical in their intention. Methods of capturing the bulls used for the bull leapings are vividly represented in relief on two superb gold cups dating from about 1600 BC found in a royal tomb at Vaphio near Sparta but almost certainly of Cretan work (pl. 25–27). Special vases *(rhytons)*, shaped like long funnels (pl. 34) or in the form of some animal or of its head (pl. 32), were evidently used for pouring drink offerings. The chief deity was a goddess, a Nature Goddess under various aspects, ancestress of the Demeters and Athenes of later Greek times, and a young god, the equivalent perhaps of the dying Adonis, Atys or Osiris, of Anatolia, Syria and Egypt, also appears but in a subordinate rôle. Snakes, birds and other animals, including imaginary griffins and sphinxes (pl. 31, 58), are seen as manifestations or guardians of divinity. Double axes (pl. 29), horns of consecration, and the great figure-of-eight body shields used in hunting and war (pl. 61), are among the objects consistently associated with cult.

There may have been large statues of the goddess in human form; but if so, they were presumably of wood and have not survived. From the Cyclades however come remarkable figures of marble, usually female (pl. 7), but also of men playing the harp or pipe (pl. 8). In the islands they are mostly found in graves, and they were exported both to Crete and to the Mainland; little clay figures of men, women and animals, are common enough in Crete, and large numbers have been found in 'peak sanctuaries' like that of Petsofa at Palaikastro (pl. 10). Most of these no doubt represent worshippers and their offerings of animals for sacrifice, perhaps cheap substitutes for them. But a faience figure from Knossos dating from about 1600 BC seems to depict the goddess herself crowned and entwined with snakes (pl. 36).

These figures, and especially the clay figurines of worshippers, provide interesting evidence for fashions in dress in Crete at the time. The men seem normally to wear a short loin cloth, which may (in the court dress of the Palaces at least) be held in place by a broad belt of material or even metal. Women have long flounced skirts (although a skirt which only reached to the knees is also worn), with short-sleeved jackets that leave the breasts bare. Cloaks were evidently used by men and women during the winter. Small bronze pins, apparently designed for fastening the dress, are found in Crete and elsewhere in the Aegean. On the Mainland and in the islands there is little evidence for dress apart from such pins until the beginning of the Late Bronze Age in the 16th century BC, when the fashions are virtually indistinguishable from those of Crete.

During the earlier part of the Bronze Age the normal way of burial in Crete was in collective tombs. These are true houses of the dead, which often preserve a memory of types of dwellings which had long gone out of fashion for the living. Caves were much used as tombs at the beginning of the period, and later artificial cavelike chambers might be excavated in soft rock, as at Knossos. The bodies were sometimes squeezed into large jars before being placed in such tombs; and ordinary cemeteries of jar burials in holes in the ground also occur. Where the rock was hard, rooms or compartments might be built of stone above ground as at Palaikastro and Mochlos. In the Mesara plain of south Crete the early built tombs are circular. Some of these circular, or 'tholos' tombs as they are called, are impressively large; one at Platanos measures over 13 metres in diameter across the inside, and has walls nearly 2.50 metres thick. None of these tombs survives intact, but the thickness of their walls and the inward lean that can often be observed in them suggest that the chambers were domed; some of the smaller almost certainly by corbelling in stone, the larger perhaps with mud or mud-brick.

These communal graves in Crete were evidently the scene of elaborate funerary rites. Dozens of vases of stone and clay, doubtless containing offerings of food and drink for the dead, have been found placed outside the tombs at Mochlos and the 'tholos' tombs of the Mesara. For example, in front of the door into the circular chamber of the small 'tholos' tomb at Apesokari (*fig. 6*) was a complex of cult rooms including a 'pillar room' and a little shrine with an altar. Outside the entrance to this complex was another altar surrounded by a pavement strewn with remains of clay vases.

The most elaborate of all these communal tombs is a great rectangular building, about 40 metres long by 30 metres wide and divided into many compartments, which stood just outside the city of Mallia. This was known by the local people as Chrysolakkos, 'gold-hole', because of the amount of gold objects plundered from it before it

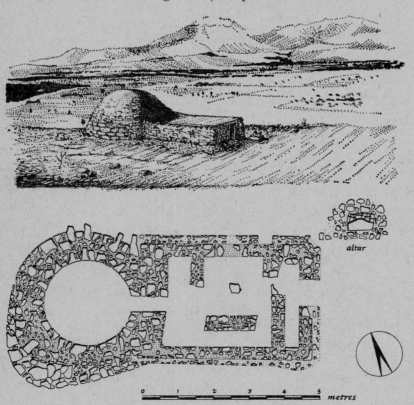

Apesokari: reconstruction and plan of early tholos tomb, c. 2000 BC. View looking north across the Mesara plain, Crete. (fig. 6)

altar

was systematically excavated. A famous treasure of gold jewellery which may possibly have come from this tomb is now in the British Museum (c. 1600 BC) (pl. 70).

On the Cycladic islands during this period burial was usually in small stone-built graves with one or two skeletons at most. From these has come a rich harvest of marble bowls and figurines, and of crude hand-made clay vases with distinctive incised ornament. The Early Helladic tombs of the Mainland are of various kinds, both single graves and small family tombs, built or cut in the rock.

The civilization of Crete continued to develop without a break throughout the earlier part of the Bronze Age. This even picture is only interrupted by the earthquakes to which the central parts of the island in particular are from time to time subject. One of the most devastating of these earthquakes appears to have taken place about 1600 BC, when the Palace at Knossos was entirely destroyed. Many of the finest treasures recovered by Evans during his excavations came from the ruins of this palace, which was however almost immediately rebuilt, although not perhaps on so magnificent or vast a scale as before.

Mainland Cultures

The Early Helladic civilisation of the Mainland gives place to the Middle Helladic at some point variously dated between 2000 and 1700 BC. Many of the Early Helladic settlements are destroyed by fire, and when they are re-occupied a marked change is discernible in the material culture. There is now a new type of pottery, often made on the fast wheel (already in use for some time, it seems, in Crete), either painted with decoration in dull (matt) colours, or alternatively with a plain burnished grey surface imitating both in shape and colour metal vases of silver. Pottery of a similar kind is found especially in the central parts of Anatolia. The houses of the Mainland during the Middle Helladic period are normally long and narrow, often with a porch in front and a semi circular (apsidal) end at the back; and this type of house is also traditional in Anatolia. The most significant change, however, is in the burial customs: burial in tombs *outside* the settlement is now largely (though not entirely) replaced by burial in single graves below the roads or even underneath the floors of the houses *inside* the settlement. In Central Anatolia a similar custom was established from an early date. There may therefore have been a regular invasion or immigration into the Aegean area from Anatolia at this time. In addition there is slight evidence to suggest that people from the Balkans, related to the Corded Ware and Battle Axe folk of Central Europe (chap. XII), had begun to enter the northern parts of Mainland Greece.

The disturbances at the beginning of the Middle Helladic period may have somewhat arrested the development of civilization on the Mainland. But soon at any rate the influence of Crete began again to be felt, leading to the virtual 'Minoanization' of the whole Aegean area before the end of the 15th century BC. Islands, like Melos and Thera, perhaps also Kythera in the South Aegean, have what is in effect a provincial form of Minoan civilization, while at Trianda in Rhodes an actual colony of Cretans has been identified from the remains of the vases they made. The exact character and degree of the Minoanization of the rest of Greece is a matter of controversy, whether it was the result of influences through trade and other contacts, or the effect of conquest of the Mainland by Cretans, or (at any rate eventually) of Crete by people from the Mainland. Towards the end of the Middle Minoan period (c. 1700 BC onwards) the very distinctive style of decoration of the Cretan pottery, with its red and white designs upon a black surface (pl. 19), begins to be imitated by the potters of Mainland coastal towns like Lerna. But it is not until the Late Bronze Age (from about 1550 BC), when a new fashion for designs in black or brown on a light yellowish ground develops in Crete, that Cretan influence really becomes dominant abroad. It is to the beginning of this period that the royal shaft graves at Mycenae seem to belong. In some of these a few vases decorated in the earliest Late Minoan style from Crete have been found.

There are two groups of these graves at Mycenae; they lie about 150 metres apart in what appears to be an earlier extensive cemetery of the Middle Helladic period (pl. 49, 50). Either at the time when the burials were being made or afterwards each group of graves was surrounded by a circular wall. The six tombs of circle A, the first discovered, by Schliemann in 1876, are in general later than those of circle B excavated since the war (1951-4). Each tomb consisted of a rectangular pit or shaft of varying depth cut in the soft rock, lined with stone to form a burial chamber at the bottom. When the burials had been made this chamber was roofed with the help of wooden beams and the shaft was filled above it. On the top of the grave was set a tomb-stone *(stele)*, which might be carved with spiral designs or with a picture of the dead man riding in his chariot to war or to the hunt (pl. 48). The idea of a roofed chamber at the bottom of a shaft was probably derived from the type of royal grave, a stone-built vault in a deep pit, long used in Mesopotamia and adjacent areas of the Near East. Tombs like those of Mycenae but earlier in date have been found at Alaca Hüyük in Central Anatolia (chap. VI), and may also have been employed in Crete during Middle Minoan times to judge from a recent discovery at Knossos. The dead kings and their wives and companions in the shaft graves at Mycenae were buried with a rich array of vases of clay or metal (bronze, gold and silver, pl. 56), with gold masks upon their faces (pl. 60), and crowns and diadems, gold and silver jewellery, and gold-mounted weapons (pl. 61). Very many of the gold and silver vases, and of the weapons and other objects, appear to be Cretan; either imported or plundered from Crete, or made by Cretan craftsmen, whether captives or free, working for the native kings. Some objects are more likely to be the product of native craftsmen imitating the Cretan style of work. Others again are purely native in style, or brought from Anatolia or elsewhere.

The shaft graves show a striking mixture of the barbaric and the civilized, of new and old traditions brought together in the treasures buried with the members of the ruling dynasties at Mycenae. The fine painted pottery is Cretan, or copied from Cretan styles; so too as we have seen many of the fine metal-work objects, of bronze or silver or gold, must have come from Minoan workshops either in Crete, or established under patronage on the Mainland. But from outside the Aegean world comes the horse and the chariot while some of the metal-work reflects the art styles of the Caucasian region or of the steppes: the art of the Northern Nomads which we encounter again in chapter XI. And from even more remote sources must come the amber necklaces mentioned again below, for here we have evidence of trade contacts with North-West Europe and, as we shall see in chapter XII, with the remote British Isles themselves.

Later Phases of the Bronze Age, c. 1500-1000 BC: The Greeks

Minoan influence upon the Mainland of Greece and the Cycladic islands reached its height towards the turn of the 15th century BC, and a civilization more or less uniform in character spread throughout the Aegean area. This uniformity is very marked for instance in the pottery: by about 1400 BC the fine vases being made in different parts of the Aegean are apt to be indistinguishable in shape and decoration. While the original influence is admittedly Cretan, there is disagreement as to how far various elements of this civilization were really contributed by the people of the Mainland or the islands. This problem is considerably involved with the question of when the Greeks arrived in Greece.

It is clear that Greek was not always spoken in the Aegean area, and the language must therefore have been introduced from outside. Even in classical times, in the fifth century BC and later, there were groups of people in the Aegean 'Greek' in civilization but knowing strange un-Greek languages of one kind or another, like the so-called Eteo-Cretans (true Cretans) in the eastern part of Crete. Moreover the Greek language itself has many words borrowed from some earlier and unrelated language, and the names of many rivers and mountains, and of cities famous in legend, appear to belong to this, as we saw earlier in this chapter. The Greek language was presumably therefore brought by invading peoples who, to judge from the different dialects of Greek existing in later times, had arrived in two or three successive waves at distinct intervals.

The archaeological evidence suggests that there were only two occasions when a large invasion of the kind that might have first brought the Greek language into Greece could reasonably have taken place, at the beginning of the Middle Bronze Age (between 2000 and 1700 BC), or towards the end of the Bronze Age after 1300 BC. If the Greeks entered in the earlier of these periods, either they might have come bringing with them the distinctive Middle Helladic culture from Anatolia, or they might have arrived as nomads leaving little trace from somewhere in the Balkans to the north.

If the claim that the Late Bronze Age Linear B script of Crete and the Mainland represented an early form of Greek were right, it would prove that the Greek language was already dominant in the Aegean by the fifteenth century BC. But the decipherment is disputed, and in the author's opinion at least it is highly improbable that the language of the Linear B tablets is in fact Greek.

Leaving aside the actual language in which the Linear B tablets were written, it can be seen even without reading a syllable the type of document with which we are dealing (pl. 62, 63). The tablets are obviously business memoranda, largely in the form of lists, in which the simple numeral system can be understood, and the type of object listed is in most instances recognisable by means of a pictograph, or conventionalized little sketch of, for instance, men or women, weapons, and chariots or their wheels, and so on. As such, they must be the product of an efficient bureaucratic system in which such matters were recorded in a manner comparable with the tablets of accounts and other details which were found as an outcome of the temple bureaucracy of Ancient Mesopotamia. In other words, the tablets are not the records of an imaginative literature (as in so many other early Mesopotamian documents, or those of Ugarit described in chapter V; such records in the Aegean were presumably written, as we have seen, on some perishable material like papyrus as in Egypt), but they deal with the hard dry facts of business life, and the organization of state resources, in goods and in manpower. Some seem to have been labels for stores, others 'index cards' to a file of tablets itself. Many more must have existed than can ever be recovered by excavation, since they were made of unbaked clay which stands a small chance of survival in Aegean soil unless it is accidentally burnt and hardened. It is the enemies of the Minoans and Mycenaeans, earthquakes and the marauding war-bands, which have, by sheer arson, preserved the records of the people who suffered from their onslaughts.

During the century before 1400 BC the evidence from the destruction of cities and the decline or abandonment of other great palaces like Phaistos or Mallia in Crete suggests that Knossos had there imposed some sort of highly centralised government which may have extended (as the legends about King Minos hint) over some of the islands as well. The Palace at Knossos was overthrown and burnt about 1400 BC, but whether by enemies or earthquake is uncertain. It seems to have been afterwards restored and re-occupied as a palace, although on a very much simpler scale. But in the fourteenth century BC Mycenae reached the height of its prosperity and splendour, and was probably the centre of a far reaching political domination. It was then for instance that the largest of the royal tholos tombs like the Treasury of Atreus was built.

These circular stone vaulted chambers *(tholoi)*, usually half underground and approached by long entrance passages *(dromoi)*, from about 1450 BC onwards take the place of shaft-graves for the burial of kings and princes at Mycenae and elsewhere on the Mainland. The so-called 'Treasury of Atreus', a legendary king of Mycenae, father of Agamemnon, (pl. 53, 54) is among the most astonishing architectural masterpieces of its time anywhere in the world. About 14.50 m. in diameter and 13.20 m. in height inside, this great corbel-vaulted tomb is throughout constructed of carefully squared and fitted blocks of stone; and the walls were originally decorated with bronze plaques, perhaps rosettes, the bronze nails for affixing which are still visible. The monumental entrance, over five metres high, was roofed by two huge lintel blocks, the inner eight metres long, five metres wide and 1.20 metres thick, and weighing well over 100 tons. A triangular space was left open above the entrance in order to relieve the weight on the lintel; but this space was originally concealed from view on the outer façade by a screen of slabs of different coloured stones, some red, some green, with spiral and other designs in relief; while the doorway was flanked by elaborately carved green half-columns now in the British Museum. The circular chamber was built in a cutting in the rock, but the upper part of the dome projected above ground and was covered by a mound, which may have been coated with white clay; the base of the mound being kept in position by a substantial stone wall (*fig.7*).

Unlike the earlier shaft graves, only one of these royal tombs of the Late Bronze Age (at Dendra near Mycenae) has been found more or less unplundered. Even here the chamber had been ransacked; but the burials of the king and of two women, a queen perhaps and a princess or servant who may have been forced to kill themselves and enter the tomb at the same time with him (suttee), were lying undisturbed in pits below the floor with a great wealth of gold and silver cups, gold-mounted swords and jewellery. There had evidently been

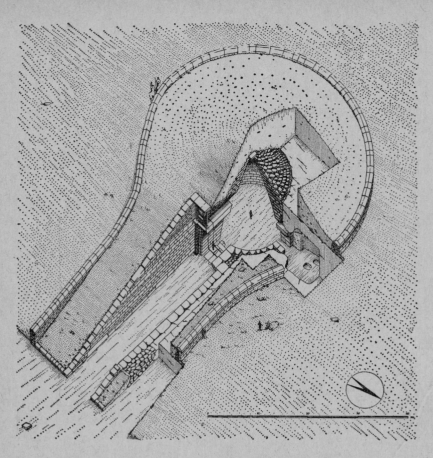

The 'Treasury of Atreus', Mycenae. Axonometric reconstruction, showing entrance, vault and retaining wall round the base of the mound. See reconstruction of façade, pl. 53. (fig. 7)

an elaborate funerary ritual: the tomb was clearly built for the king during his life time, and when he died his grave-pit was dug through the floor of the tholos chamber. At the same time another pit was dug just inside the door of the chamber and a pyre of logs erected over it.

We may reconstruct the scene in some detail. The funerary procession comes down the long dromos into the chamber. The king is lowered into his grave with his treasures, cups of gold and silver, rings and sealstones, and weapons. Then his followers throw other treasures at his feet as a last token of respect, as flowers are thrown nowadays into a grave. More perishable things, wooden chests with mountings of gold and bronze and inlaid with ivory and glass-paste, filled perhaps with gold-adorned materials, together with offerings of food and drink in clay vases, are piled upon the pyre inside the entrance of the chamber, and there burnt.

'One of the dead man's kinsmen', writes the excavator Persson, 'takes a large vessel of wine . . . and shatters it against the logs of the pyre, so that the contents are poured out. The upper part of the shattered vessel falls into the fire; he stands there with the bottom in his hands, he throws it down to the dead man in the grave—so we found the fragments . . . The pyre gradually burns down—it is piled just by the entrance and thanks to the pit under the logs there is a good draught. It collapses and the remains disappear into the pit—half charred bits of wood, burnt gold and bronze mountings, burnt ivory, bits of glass and broken vessels filled the greater part of the pit. Then the King's companions, his servant, his dog and possibly his wife, are laid in their places . . . ' The dead are covered with earth, and large stone slabs are placed over the filled pits. Lastly the doorway of the chamber is blocked with stones, and the deep dromos filled with earth to the surface.

Burial now except for kings and princes throughout the Aegean world was normally in rock-cut chambers, square, round or semi-circular in shape, approached by long descending passages (dromoi) like the tholos tombs. These may be family vaults as at Mycenae, or single graves or graves with only a few burials, as usually at Knossos and elsewhere in Crete, but also on the Mainland. Rectangular stone tombs or slab-lined cist-graves were built in some areas, at Eleusis for instance near Athens, where the hard rock discouraged the excavation of chambers.

The early part of the Late Bronze Age (16th–15th centuries BC) is the period of the greatest splendour, if not the highest artistic achieve-

ment, of the Aegean civilization. The treasures of the Mycenae shaft graves date from the beginning of this time. But the later royal and princely tombs, in spite of plundering, produce many beautiful things, especially jewellery, and seals of fine stones like amethyst, agate and carnelian. Furniture, chairs and boxes are adorned with ivory, and round ivory caskets are carved from sections of elephants' tusks with elaborate scenes in relief. Figurines in ivory or bronze may represent worshippers, or the gods and goddesses themselves.

Copper or bronze is now freely employed for the ordinary vessels of household use—lamps, jugs and basins of various kinds, including pots on three legs for cooking over a fire (*fig. 8*), and huge cauldrons like some from Tylissos in Crete more than a metre in diameter (*fig. 9*). The table vases, especially drinking cups, of the great might be of gold or silver, richly embossed (pl. 56). The finer clay vases imitate those of metal in their shapes (pl. 55); they have a yellowish surface decorated in black, brown or red paint, with a variety of designs taken from the plant or marine world, including grass, lily and papyrus, and octopus or argonaut motifs (pl. 35). Characteristic is a handled cup on a high stem *(kylix)* (pl. 57).

Among the many bronze tools of the period are huge saws (perhaps for cutting cypress) from Crete, over a metre and a half long. Weapons are beautifully shaped and adorned, the spear-heads often with finely moulded channels and ridges along their shafts, the swords with gold-mounted handles and large pommels of ivory, agate or rock-crystal. Daggers, like some already from the Mycenae shaft-graves, may have blades with gold and silver inlays against a background of black niello (pl. 61); and cups with similar inlays are also made.

In the art of metal-working, as in those of gem-engraving (pl. 37, fig. 10) and vase-painting, the Aegean in the Late Bronze Age probably led the civilized world. But of monumental sculpture in stone there is curiously little trace. A noble exception is the famous limestone relief above the Lion Gate at Mycenae, set in position there probably in the

'Tomb of the Tripod Hearth' near Knossos: group of Late Minoan bronze vessels, c. 1300 BC; movable plaster hearth in the foreground; three-legged cooking pot at the back recalls those in the 'Tripod Tablet', pl. 62. (fig. 8)

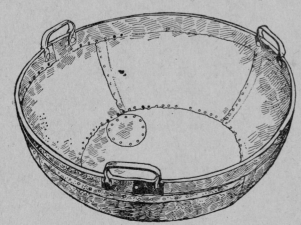

Tylissos, Crete: great bronze cauldron, one of several from a Late Minoan house, c. 1450 BC. The largest of these cauldrons measure over four feet across. (fig. 9)

14th century BC (pl. 47). The heads of the lions are missing; they were made separately, perhaps of some other material like marble or alabaster. Inscriptions of the kind that contemporary kings of Egypt and Mesopotamia delighted to cut on their temples, or rock carvings like those of the Hittites, are entirely absent in the Aegean.

Wheeled vehicles of some kind were being used in Crete from early in the Bronze Age to judge from a model of a four-wheeled cart found at Palaikastro. Horses are first attested during the Middle Helladic period on the Mainland. They may have been brought to the Aegean, together perhaps with the light two-wheeled chariot, from the civilized Near East, or by invaders from the north or from Anatolia. The earliest pictures of chariots in the Aegean are on the tomb stones *(stelae)* set above the shaft graves at Mycenae (pl. 48). They also appear on gems and painted on the walls of the palaces on the Mainland and (as a recently discovered fragment of fresco shows) at Knossos in Crete. Clay tablets from Knossos of about 1400 BC list chariots among equipment issued to warriors, and parts of chariots which were stocked in the Palace armouries. Perhaps in connection with chariot warfare, a smaller round shield replaced the great eight-shaped body shield of earlier times, and body armour and helmets of metal or armed with metal plates or, in the case of helmets (pl. 43, 44) with boars' tusks are now in use.

Differences between Crete and the Mainland

The great tholos tombs of the Mainland in the Late Bronze Age may be descended in some way from the early circular communal tombs of Crete. But while many of these tholos tombs are known on the

Knossos: clay impression, doubtless made by a gold signet ring, c. 1400 BC. A goddess in long flounced skirt stands on top of a mountain; on the right a worshipper. (fig. 10)

Mainland, they are rare in Crete, where, however, there exist other varieties of built tomb, square or rectangular inside with corbelled domes (like tholos tombs) or keel-vaults *(fig. 11)*. In several other ways the civilization of the Mainland differs from that of Crete. Clay coffins, for instance, are much used for burials in Crete, but hardly occur on the Mainland; while little clay female figurines of a distinctive type, toys or votives, very common in the later Bronze Age on the Mainland, are extremely rare in Crete. More important however are the differences between the palaces of Crete and those of the Mainland.

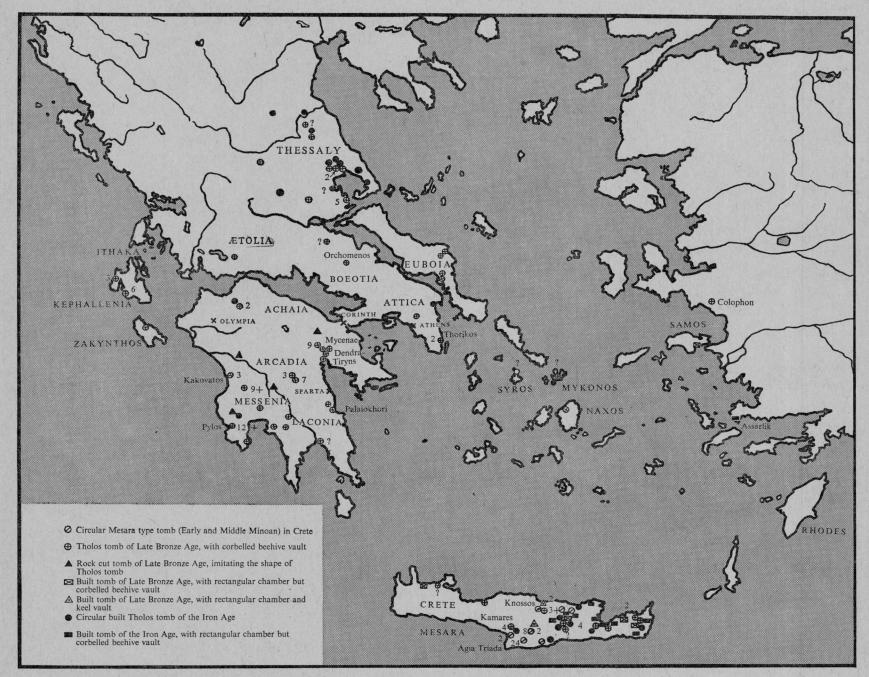

The distribution of 'tholos' and allied types of tomb. Where there is more than one Mesara type or other Bronze Age tomb at a site, the number is given.

Rock-cut tombs are not numbered, nor are the Iron Age tombs, which often occur in large numbers in regular cemeteries. (fig. 11)

In the great Mainland palaces, at Mycenae, Tiryns and Pylos (*fig. 12*), the methods of construction involving the use of squared limestone masonry for important façades, and a frame-work of wooden timbers to hold the walls together, are essentially Cretan in their origin; as are the fresco paintings and the stone mouldings (pl. 68) that adorn the main rooms. But whereas the Cretan palaces are centred upon a large open court, those of the Mainland cluster round the 'megaron', a great room, so-called because in its arrangements it is reminiscent of the halls *(megara)* of the kings that Homer describes. This is squarish, having a roof supported on four pillars and a vast circular hearth in the middle; it is normally approached from an open court-yard through a columned porch and ante-room (*fig. 12*). This plan, so foreign to Crete, is really an elaborate version of a type of building already of great antiquity in Anatolia, and seen in neolithic Dimini.

There are signs that the Minoan civilization was very much on the surface on the Mainland. Sealstones, for instance, are not nearly as common there as they are in Crete, and those that are found on the Mainland are normally the fine seals of kings and great men; while the cheap crude seals used by ordinary people, abundant in Crete, are rare. On the other hand writing was certainly known and practised in the capital cities there: the palace at Pylos, and great houses at Mycenae, destroyed towards the end of the 13th century BC, have produced clay tablets written in the Linear B script of Knossos (pl. 62). In addition to the tablets there are clay store jars from the

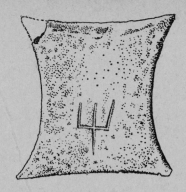

Trade in Crete. Left: Cartouche of Tuthmosis III (1484–1430 BC) on an Egyptian alabaster vase found at Katsambas, the port of Knossos. Right: Copper ingot in the shape of a bull's hide from Agia Triada, inscribed with the Cretan sign of a trident, c. 1500 BC. (see chap. V, p. 157) (figs. 13, 14)

beads were found in them and in 'tholos' tombs at Kakovatos and Pylos on the west coast of the Peloponnese. Built 'tholos' tombs and rock cut tombs as far away as south Spain seem to precede Aegean models, however (cf. chap. XII, p. 349).

The Decline of the Aegean Bronze Age

The history of the decline of this Aegean Bronze Age civilization is not entirely clear. The interpretation of the archaeological evidence is linked with that of the legends and traditions which seem to refer to events at this time. The last wave of Greek invaders, the Dorians, are traditionally supposed to have entered Southern Greece about 1100 BC. But long before then impoverishment is visible in the style and execution of the arts of gem engraving, fresco painting and vase decoration. In the latter a growing provincialism is reflected in the development of local styles.

On the Mainland during the 14th century BC strong 'Cyclopean' walls built with huge rough stones begin to transform palaces into castles as at Tiryns (pl. 64–66, 69), or towns into fortresses like Mycenae and the Acropolis at Athens. At Athens and Mycenae remarkable covered passages descend to underground springs outside the walls. About this time a great wall appears to have been erected across the Isthmus of Corinth, to defend the Peloponnese from the north.

In the following century (the 13th century BC) the palaces were burnt to the ground and never rebuilt. The most northern, like the 'Palace of Cadmus' at Thebes, may have been the first to suffer. On the island of Gla in Lake Copais not far from Thebes a vast 'Cyclopean' wall, the largest defence circuit of the Bronze Age known in Greece, was begun but never completed; and the palace there was consumed by fire almost before it had been inhabited. At Mycenae the building of royal 'tholos' tombs ceased; and towards the end of the 13th century BC a large part of the city was destroyed by fire, after which much of the area with houses outside the walls was abandoned. The fortress and palace at Tiryns also appear to have been overwhelmed about this time: the skeletons of some of the last defenders, fallen or thrown from the battlements, were found lying beneath piles of burnt debris at the foot of the walls. The palace at Pylos was wrecked now or not much later, about 1200 BC. Only at Mycenae is there evidence for a second great destruction, involving the citadel inside the 'Cyclopean' walls, during the very latest phase of the Bronze Age about 1100 BC.

In Crete there is the same picture of decline and disaster. No more royal or princely tombs are built at Knossos. The city there shrinks in size, and the re-occupied palace is destroyed or deserted. In the final stages the old inhabitants of the island, where the Dorians are now settling, escape abroad (perhaps to settle in the Levant as the Philistines), or flee to the hills of the interior; their villages, with iron tools and weapons, but with pottery still Minoan in character, appear on the summits of high and inaccessible peaks like Karphi in the Lasithi mountains. Outside such refugee settlements in the remoter parts of east and central Crete are found cemeteries of diminutive tholos-vaulted tombs, the feeble descendants of the great masonry tombs of the Aegean Bronze Age.

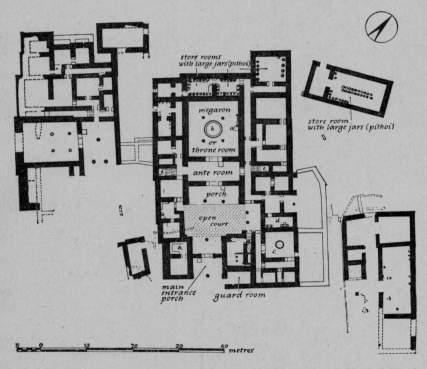

Pylos: plan of the Palace of Nestor, c. 1300 BC: (a) throne; (b) great circular hearth; (c) smaller circular hearth; (d) bathroom; (e, f, g) stairs; (h) archive room with clay tablets. (fig. 12)

'Palace of Cadmus' at Thebes, and others from Mycenae and elsewhere on the Mainland, with brief Linear B inscriptions painted on them.

During the Late Bronze Age there is every evidence that the Aegean had flourishing connections with the rest of the civilized world as well as with the barbarous West and North. At the beginning of the period peoples called by the Egyptians *Keftiu* (who appear to be Aegean, probably Cretans) are depicted in the tomb of Rekh-mi-re, vizier to Tuthmosis III (1494–1436 BC), bearing very Minoan-looking gifts to Pharaoh. Late Bronze Age pottery from the Aegean has been found at sites all round the eastern Mediterranean, in Anatolia, Syria, Palestine and Egypt; and was exported westwards to south Italy and Sicily. Sometimes the pottery from settlements is so abundant as to suggest that there were actual Aegean colonies towards the end of the Bronze Age in Cyprus for example and at Taranto in South Italy. Large ingots of copper in the shape of bulls' hides, apparently Aegean in origin, have turned up in Cyprus, South Anatolia, and Sardinia to the west (*fig. 14*). Amber was being imported from the Baltic to Mycenae as early as the period of the shaft graves. Vast necklaces of amber

VIII ANCIENT INDIA

The civilization of a sub-continent

SIR MORTIMER WHEELER

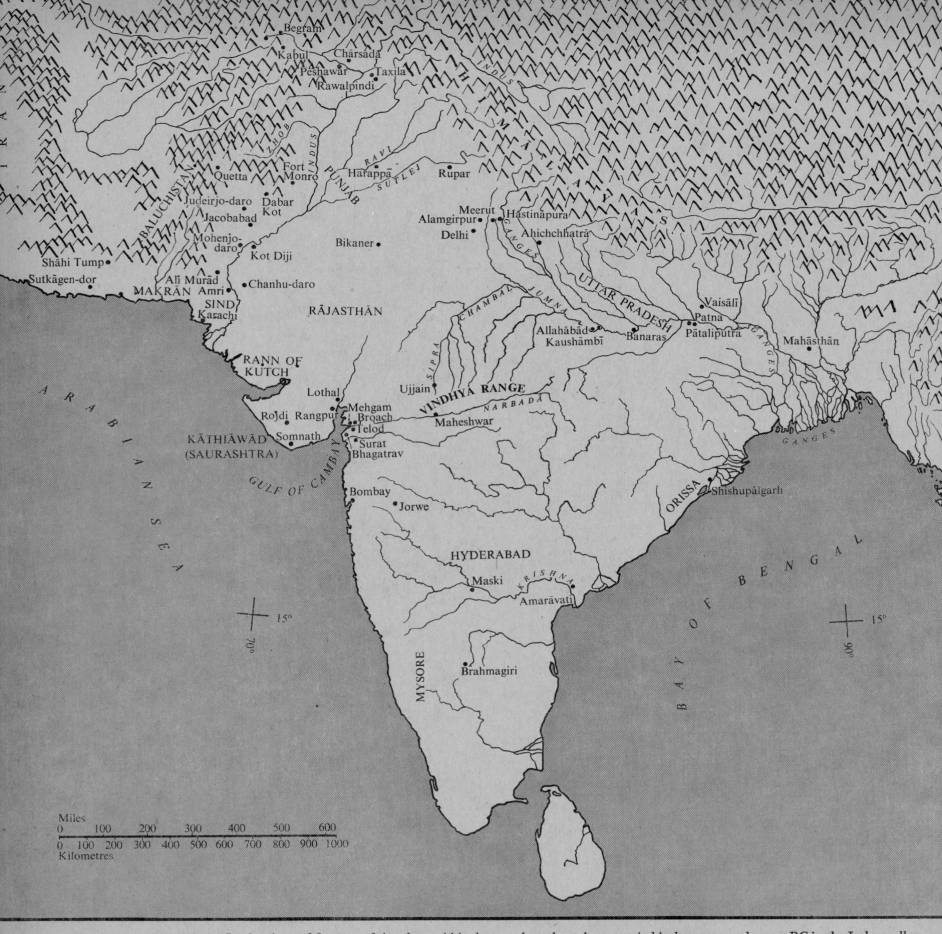

A note on chronology. In the time of Sargon of Agade or Akkad, in Mesopotamia, for whom a date about 2350 BC is now widely accepted, goods of various kinds—pottery, seals, beads, and other knick-knacks—reached the Mesopotamian cities from the Indus valley of Pakistan. In that valley a widespread civilization was then in its early prime. How long previously it had first taken shape is uncertain, but an estimated initial date about 2500 BC is supported by a recent Carbon 14 dating from the small site of Kot Diji, 25 miles east of the great Indus city of Mohenjo-daro. At Kot Diji sixteen strata have been recognized in section; the top four of them were pure or mixed 'Indus Civilization', whilst the underlying layers were of an antecedent culture. The uppermost of these twelve underlying layers, immediately beneath the Indus material, produced a Carbon 14 date of 2463 BC with a possible error of about 140 years on either side (Pennsylvania University analysis).

Subsequently the Indus Civilization had a long life which is thought to have carried it down towards 1500 BC in the Indus valley itself, though further south, in Kāthiāwād or Saurashtra, it may well have lasted somewhat longer. It there merged into various central Indian chalcolithic cultures for which a date between 1500 and 1000 BC is increasingly probable.

For the chronology of the miscellaneous cultures which anticipated or overlapped the Indus civilization in the hills of the Baluchistan border there is at present no reliable local evidence, and partial analogies from Iran or Mesopotamia are an unsafe guide.

In summary, the time-table for the early civilizations of the Indo-Pakistan sub-continent seems to run as follows:—

INDUS CIVILIZATION	c. 2500 BC to 1500 BC and later
GANGES CIVILIZATION	
Bronze or Copper Age	c. 1000 BC to 500 BC
Iron Age	c. 500 BC onwards

Two remarkable cities,

built some 4500 years ago, are the largest sites to be explored of the most widespread of the great civilizations of the ancient world. It arose, as did those of Egypt and Mesopotamia, from a farming community in the fertile valley of a great river—fertile but marsh- and jungle-ridden, infested with fevers and wild beasts and subject to treacherous and formidable flooding. To build a civilization in this exacting environment was a challenge which required genius and skill and determined and inspired leadership, and it was met by the people of the Indus with little outside help beyond the knowledge that it had been done before. These farmers grew wheat and six-

rowed barley and field-peas, and amongst their remains have been found melon seeds, sesame and date stones—and the earliest traces of cultivated cotton known anywhere in the world. They bred cattle and buffaloes, camels, horses and asses, and they traded with Afghanistan, Iran, Mesopotamia and probably with southern India. But of close cultural integration with the outside world there is little evidence: the great walled and fortified cities of Mohenjo-daro and Harappā rose from a local ancestry still imperfectly understood, to become sophisticated civic communities which were to last a thousand years.

Of sculpture in stone, little has been found; the few examples mostly represent men or gods, four or five of them in a squatting attitude. The limestone head above, ascribed to the 'Late Period' of Mohenjo-daro, shows a beard and shaven upper lip, recalling Mesopotamian heads of approximately the same time, but the owl-like Mesopotamian stare is widely different from the contemplative expressions of the Indus. The closely cropped wavy hair is held together by a fillet and the head has conventional shell-shaped ears. The artist has achieved a sensitive modelling of the lips and cheeks: 'It looks', as the excavator carefully remarked, 'as if some attempt at portraiture had been made'. (1)

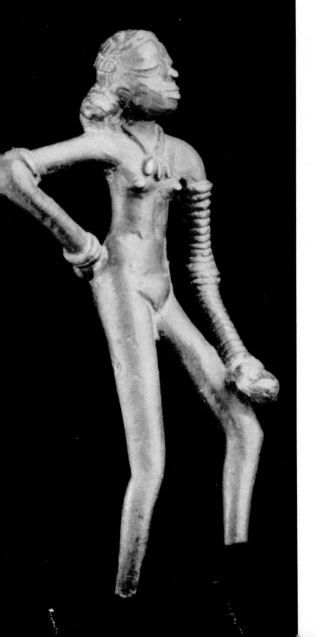

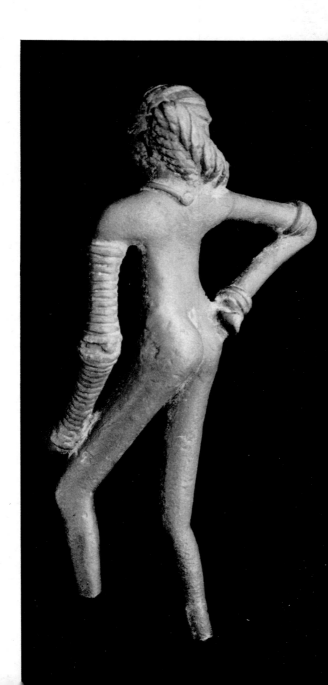

This pert and provocative dancing-girl is one of the most remarkable Indus figurines. The slim figure, naked except for her many bangles and her necklace, is in bronze, and was found in a house in the same area as the head above. The right hand rests on the hip, the left arm hangs loosely and the posture of the legs is easy. The head, expressively tilted, is a skilful impression of an 'aboriginal' type, with large eyes, flat nose and bunched curly hair, but whether it represents a Baluch native or a girl from south India is not known. (2)

The safe storage of grain was a matter of the utmost importance to the cities of the Indus Civilization. It had to be protected both against marauders and from the rising waters when the rivers burst their banks during periods of heavy rainfall. Mohenjo-daro was commanded by an artificial mound or citadel, up to 50 feet high and fortified by a baked-brick wall and solid towers. On the summit of the mound was a large-scale bath or storage tank and a big granary, built of massive timberwork and set upon a high brick base consisting of twenty-seven blocks, the criss-cross arrangement of the passages between the blocks ensuring the circulation of air beneath it.

The granary stood upon the steep verge of the citadel; half way up its northern end was an unloading-platform above a recess into which the grain wagons could be driven. The reconstruction above shows this northern frontage, with an ox-wagon drawn up before the recess and a suggestion of the means by which the sheaves were hoisted to the granary. The builders have succeeded in creating a point of access from the surrounding countryside which can also be defended readily against attack. (3)

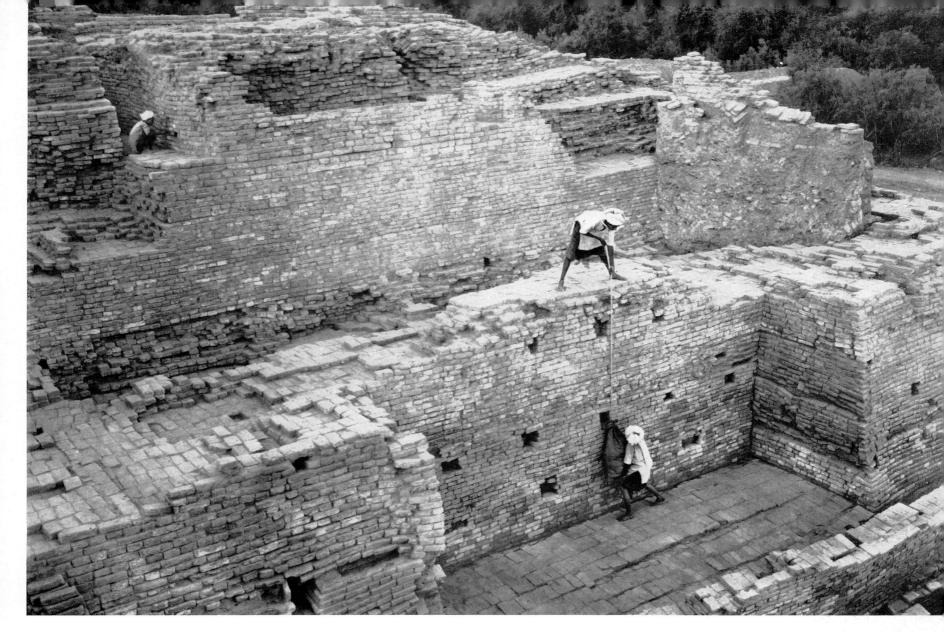

The unloading point in the baked-brick base of the granary at Mohenjo-daro, as it stands excavated today. A figure crouches (top left) in the opening of one of the ventilation channels; the reinforcing interlace of timber decayed anciently and was partially replaced by brick patches, but holes and grooves originally occupied by 5-inch square timbers are clearly visible. (4)

The two-wheeled ox-carts shown in the reconstruction opposite are based upon toys or models of which a number have been found at Mohenjo-daro. The one on the right is of terracotta; others, of two- and four-wheeled carts, are in copper or bronze. They have solid wheels and a single shaft; how little the wagons have changed over some forty-five centuries is shown by the photograph of a country cart in Sind today. (5, 6)

A great abundance of small terracotta models has been found in the Indus valley; the humped bull (left) from Mohenjo-daro shows a masterly grasp of the animal's form, with its strong neck and shoulders, its head and heavy dewlap. More than three-quarters of the models are of bulls, but whether the bull was a sacred animal as in India today cannot be judged. (7)

Small masterpieces, distinctive in kind and unique in quality, are found among the famous seals of the Indus valley. To make them, the stone, usually steatite, was cut with a saw and finished with knife and abrasive; the design, a sunk pattern, was cut with a small chisel and drills and frequently the seals were then coated with an alkali and heated to produce a white lustrous surface. Normally the seals were square, with a perforated boss at the back for handling and suspension, but round ones have been found and a few cylinder seals.

Many animals were known to the craftsmen who made the seals: elephant, tiger, rhinoceros, antelope, crocodile or gharial; the humped bull is majestically rendered, grotesque composite creatures occur, but commonest of all is an ox-like beast with a single horn, always facing a strange object on a short post. A second hidden horn may be intended behind, but it has been pointed out that both Ktesias and Aristotle described the unicorn as 'the Indian donkey'. A few human figures appear, mostly inferior, but three seated figures from Mohenjo-daro have a special interest: they recall the great Siva, god of the Hindus, not yet manifest.

With the designs are incised undeciphered pictographic symbols, and the purpose of the seals must remain uncertain until these are understood. But the seals were probably used to stamp bales and other property and it is likely that part at any rate of the inscriptions were personal names. (8)

Round seals with pierced projections at the back have recently been found on the islands of Bahrein and Failaka in the Persian Gulf. On the right below are back and front views of one of these, compared with (on the left) a round seal from Mohenjo-daro. The bull and foot pictogram also occurs on seals found at Ur—but on the whole the Indus seals are essentially individual, and these examples represent the influence of Indus traders on the commercial world of the Persian Gulf. (9)

A pattern found widely in the Ancient East is the trefoil decoration on the cloak of this bearded figure of steatite from Mohenjo-daro. It occurs also on Indus beads and on stone, pottery and wood-work from Mesopotamia, Crete and Egypt of 2300–1300 BC. As a religious symbol (the trefoil was particularly connected with the stars) it may therefore have a common meaning extending to the Indus valley, and the figure could represent a deity or priest-king. The brutal, domineering aspect of the face is enhanced by the low receding fore-head, the firm, thick lips and the long slit-like (but not Mongoloid) eyes. Note the shaven upper lip and the fillet which binds the hair; the nose was long and the ears are conventionally rendered, suggesting the cross-section of a shell; one of the eyes still held its shell-inlay when the figure was found, the trefoils were originally filled with red paste and the whole work was covered with a 'fine smooth 'slip'. A hole bored on each side of the neck may have been intended to hold a metal necklace. The highly stylized hair may possibly indi-cate a late Indus date. (10)

It was the women, it seems, for whom the clearest links with the ancient civilizations of the West were forged, for similar gold beads occur at Mohenjo-daro, in Mesopotamia about 2400–2300 BC and in Troy IIG about 2300 BC. Faience beads are numerous in the Indus and occur between 3000 and 1500 BC in northern Syria, Crete and Egypt; etched carnelian beads are identical in cities of the Indus and at Ur, Kish and Tell Asmar in Mesopotamia (about 2300 BC). Among those shown below are beads in decorated carnelian and in steatite. (11)

An as yet undeciphered script was used by the people of the Indus, both on their pottery and on their seals. The pictographs are as different from those of Mesopotamia and Egypt as these are from each other: within a short range of time and space, three great civil-izations produced three utterly divergent systems of notation. On the pottery sherds (below) appear graffiti and, on the fourth and largest, a stamp, presumably that of the owner or potter—marks which occur frequently and suggest a fair measure of literacy in the Indus popu-lation. (12)

The solid burnt-brick towers at the south-east corner of the citadel wall of Mohenjo-daro are shown excavated on the left. The earliest of them was originally reinforced like the granary with an interlace of timber—a method later abandoned. The towers seem to have been a strong-point, for about 100 baked clay missiles were found on a late platform. (13)

Below the citadel the town stretched to the Indus, which has moved some two miles eastward in more recent times. On the left, a room of one of the buildings is shown excavated. It faced the street and is one of three neatly paved with bricks set on edge; the five conical pits sunk in the floor may have been either dyeing vats or holders for jars in a public restaurant. Behind were living quarters round a courtyard; it was a large building, measuring 87 × 64½ feet. (15)

The Great Bath on the citadel of Mohenjo-daro had a floor measuring 39 × 23 feet. It is shown excavated in the centre of the opposite page. At the ends, which faced north and south, brick steps lead down to the floor, with timber treads set in bitumen or asphalt, presumably obtained from Baluchistan. Asphalt was also used for waterproofing the bath itself. Near the south-west corner was an outlet leading to a high corbel-vaulted drain, which cut across the loading-bay of the granary, indicating that the bath was of later date. Verandahs enclosed the bath and at the back of three of them were rooms, one of which contained a large double-lined well, possibly the source for the bath. Further north was a group of cells with private baths, maybe for some priestly order. In modern Hindu ritual (as indeed in other religions) ceremonial cleansings are an important feature; it is in such a context that we might view the Great Bath, ancestor to the baths or tanks which abound throughout India today. (14)

The Indus figurines were often crudely done. Compare the three terracottas from Mohenjo-daro on these pages with the dancing girl of pl. 2 or the humped bull of pl. 7. On the right is a common 'mother-goddess' idol, with wide girdle, loincloth and necklace and grotesque pannier-like headdress—the features are built of lumps of clay, without any attempt at true modelling. Above is a squatting monkey, and on the left a more lively 'Flook'-like creature. (16, 17, 18)

Harappā, the second great city

of the Indus Civilization, some 400 miles north-east of Mohenjo-daro, was plundered more than a century ago. It, too, had a citadel, the general outlines of which it has been possible to reconstruct from the ruins since excavated. As at the sister-city, its buildings had been raised on a platform of mud and mud-brick contained on all sides by massive defences, along which were large rectangular bastions at regular intervals. The double range of granaries on a revetted platform supplied with ventilation ducts, and the double range of barrack-like dwellings which formed a workmen's settlement, together with the general siting close to the former river (the Ravi, which now flows six miles farther north), indicate that the collection and storage of grain was municipally organized and closely controlled.

In the reconstruction above, we are looking from the bank of the river towards the north face of the great citadel. Beyond it lie the two cemeteries, the more southerly of which (R. 37) was contemporary with the Indus Civilization. On the right are the granaries, while between them and the citadel can be seen the workmen's quarters. The shape of the boat in the foreground is based on designs scratched on contemporary pottery, as well as on present-day river craft. (19)

This painted jar of the finest Indus type came from cemetery R. 37 at Harappā. Note the group of peacocks in addition to the various leaf motifs. The colours range from buff to pink, red and black. (20)

The method of pounding grain four thousand years ago recalls that used in Kashmir today. The circular brick platform below—one of a group of at least seventeen found at Harappā—has a hole in the centre which could have served as a mortar for a long wooden pestle. In one of the hollows were found fragments of straw, burnt wheat and husked barley. (21)

Cemetery R. 37 yielded nearly 60 skeletons, each accompanied by 15–20 pots in the most mature Indus style. Trinkets too were recovered, but on the whole the grave goods were poor: it was the burial place of the average citizens rather than the nobles. The grave shown below is unique in that it was outlined with mud-bricks, like those of the Nal Culture of southern Baluchistan. (22)

The once teeming life of the lower town at Mohenjo-daro can perhaps be imagined when we look at this photograph of the excavated main street filled with Indians, mules and ox-carts. The unpaved and dusty roads were supplied with brick drains, whilst brick-built manholes were sited at intervals, to be cleared from time to time by the municipal sanitary squads who occasionally left their debris in a convenient heap for later discovery. (23)

Sudden death came to Mohenjo-daro about the middle of the 2nd millennium BC, when the city was sacked by raiders. The inhabitants were massacred in the streets and houses, and left to rot where they lay. In one room alone in the lower city the skeletons of some 13 adults and a child, some wearing bracelets, rings and beads, were found in attitudes suggesting fierce and unrelenting slaughter. Two of the skulls bore cuts which have all the appearances of a sword slash, one being 'a straight cut 146 mm. in length'. The city was subsequently deserted, save for the intrusion of a few Buddhist monks nearly 2000 years later. (24)

Who were the attackers who sacked the declining Mohenjo-daro about 1500 BC and scattered the civilization centred on the two cities? We shall not know, but it was roughly at that time that there appeared in northern India the Indo-European Aryans, whose war-god Indra was the 'fort-destroyer', who 'rends forts as age consumes a garment'. In a late level at Mohenjo-daro was found the copper axe-adze opposite, with shaft hole rare on the Indus but similar to Caucasian and Persian work of c. 2000 BC. (26)

One of the great sites of India is that of Kaushāmbī. Its ramparts (above) recall those of Harappā; they consisted of a mud bank faced externally with a backward-sloping baked-brick wall which, beside the eastern gate, still remains to a heigh of 154 courses. Near the base, the wall had begun to bulge and weep-holes had been cut through it to relieve the pressure. Within the defences were well-built brick houses and a famous Buddhist monastery, ascribed to the century of the Buddha's death. Kaushāmbī dates from before 500 BC and a mass of material has been recovered—it was a wealthy city. (25)

The 'Lotus City', Chārsada near Peshāwar, owed its prosperity to a later conquest—by the Achaemenid Kings of Persia in the 6th century BC. They brought security to the trade routes from the north-west and wealth to towns along them. Chārsada was overcome by Alexander: its great mound (right) rises high from the plain today. (27)

The Ganges Civilization

was the second great phase of Indian development. It arose in the river country formed by the basins of the Ganges and the Jumna. Signs of the Indus Civilization have been found on its fringes, but it was not until after 1000 BC that life in towns began. Between then and 500 BC there appeared in fertile river clearings the towns and cities which are the background of the Indian epics: Hastināpura on the upper Ganges, the epic capital of the Kaurava kings; Ahichchhatrā in Uttar Pradesh, also mentioned in the Mahābhārata; Kaushāmbī, beside the Jumna 30 miles from Allahābād; Vaisātī, capital of the tribe which produced the Buddha—it was a great burgeoning of civic life. The earliest occupation is not yet associated with buildings, but copper weapons (rarely bronze) seem to have been in use. In the first urban period, painted grey pottery was distinctive and copper (very rarely iron) was used for tools and weapons. Iron arrived finally towards the end of the 6th century, doubtless introduced by the conquering Persians, who were responsible also for the introduction of money, struck at first on the Persian standard. Now, too, a glossy black pottery replaced the Painted Grey Ware, and baked bricks, as well as mud-bricks, were used in building.

The soak-pits which were to have a long life in the civic history of Indian towns began to appear after 500 BC. Those on the left are from Hastināpura, made up alternatively of superimposed jars with perforated bases and superimposed terracotta rings. (28)

The ancestors of the Indus Civilization are not yet known. The Nal style pottery below was recovered from a hill village culture one of a group in south Baluchistan which pre-dates Indus ware. It shows a certain relationship with Persian wares such as that from Siyalk III (chapter II/p. 54). But it does not anticipate the pottery of the Indus Civilization. (29)

The Persians brought trade also to Taxila, near Rawalpindi, although it was a rambling conglomeration of poorly-built houses, as the photograph of the excavated mound shows (below). Sophisticated jewellery has been found there, but it is dated after the visit of Alexander in 326 BC. (30)

A sharp cultural cleavage occurred in peninsular India around the beginning of the third century BC. The primitive stone-using culture became a richly equipped Iron Age, characterised by the erection of megalithic cists or monuments and the use of iron and a black-and-red pottery which had spread from the north. It can perhaps be associated with the southward extension of the Mauryan Empire by Bindusāra, father of Ashoka.

The megalithic cist (left) is at Tiruvelangadu, Chittoor district: it has a 'dog-kennel' opening at the present ground level and remains of an overlying cairn can be seen on the capstone. It is one of a group of such dolmen-type graves. (31)

The earliest known Bengal famine and the measures taken by the local authority to combat it (by the issue of paddy from reserve stocks) are recorded on the limestone slab from Mahāsthān, above. Both alphabet and language resemble those of Ashoka's pillar-edicts of about 250 BC, and the slab probably dates after the powerfully organized Mauryan regime had thrust eastwards in the 3rd century BC and, in place of the small neolithic societies persisting there, had established townships such as Mahāsthān. (32)

One of the sacred cities of India, Ujjain, was an early offshoot of the Ganges Civilization. It dominated the trunk-route from the Ganges-Jumna basin to the Arabian Sea and present evidence suggests that civilization came to it suddenly. Its massive mud rampart was reinforced by timber breakwaters (above) set diagonally to the stream of the river. Iron was found in the lowest of the related strata, suggesting a date of c. 500 BC for the first phase of the fortifications. (33)

The civilization of a sub-continent

SIR MORTIMER WHEELER

The Beginnings

CIVILIZATION, in a minimum sense of the term, is the art of living in towns, with all that the condition implies in respect of social skills and discipline. At the time of writing, the oldest known town, girt with a defensive wall and rock-cut ditch, is Jericho which, on the available Carbon 14 datings, was a going concern in the 8th millennium BC. Jericho has been described in chapter II; it occupied 8–10 acres of a covetable oasis in the arid Jordan valley, where settled inhabitants might early find a need for the jealous guarding of their precious water-supply and their closely circumscribed economy. Future research will amplify the picture, but Jericho, carried back, as it now is, even beyond its civic state to an underlying mesolithic village, is likely to retain a high measure of significance in the story of social evolution.

On a wider landscape, too, the hint offered by Jericho is reasonable enough. The principal food-grains (except rice, not known much before 1000 BC) and the principal herd-animals subsist or subsisted in a wild state in western Asia, between the Himālayas and the Mediterranean. It is a corollary that large-scale food-production was first practised in that region; and the first towns, with their primary dependence upon food-production, are the natural sequel. In other words, food-production and town-life began in western Asia, and not later than the 8th millennium BC.

In common usage, however, 'civilization' implies a certain maturity of citizenship, somewhat in excess of the attainment at present ascribable to early Jericho. More particularly, it is held to include a systematic method of accounting, so that revenue and wages may be adequately registered, and orderly government ensured. *Writing*, in some form or other, is on this view a presupposition. There is perhaps a tendency on the part of the modern mind to overestimate the value of literacy; certain it is that the unscribbled brain is capable of remarkable feats of retention and calculation. But let it go—the somewhat arbitrary addition of writing to the qualifications of citizenship makes at least an easy yard-stick and may lend precision to our thinking.

On this basis, civilization may still be claimed to have emerged first in Mesopotamia where, in the latter half of the 4th millennium (Uruk Period), temple accounts were first kept in pictorial and other signs inscribed on clay tablets. In space and time it is alike proper that Mesopotamia remain our main reference-point in any review of the birth of civilization south of the Himālayas.

The Indus Civilization (c. 2500-1500 BC)

There, beneath the Himālayas, arose the first phase of evolved city-life, named from the location of its first and largest sites the Indus Valley Civilization. Discoveries by Sir John Marshall and his colleagues after 1921 gave to India an additional thousand years or more of rich prehistory, and to the world the largest of its three most ancient civilizations. Current exploration both in India and Pakistan is still adding materially to our understanding of the Civilization, and I propose in the following pages to integrate the new with the old without excessive particularization. The results will be a somewhat modified and indeed extended view of the subject, covering roughly the 3rd and 2nd millennia BC.

As to the immediate ancestry of the Indus Civilization there is indeed comparatively little (in 1960) that is new, although the old evidence has from time to time been flogged into a somewhat unreal semblance of life. The general nature of that evidence is tolerably clear whilst its details remain elusive. Briefly the position is this.

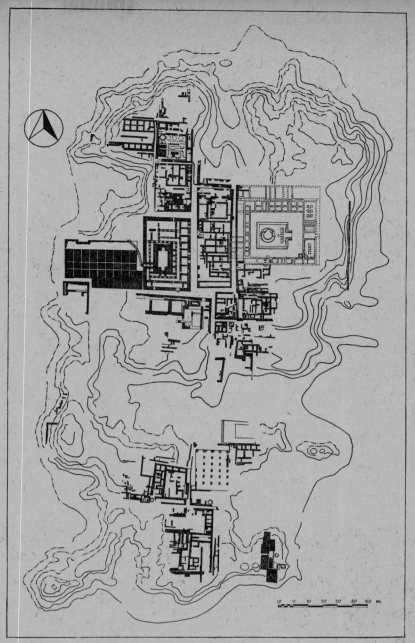

Mohenjo-daro: the citadel. The building on the left, marked in black, is the granary. On its right is the Great Bath, and further east again (in lighter shading) are the ruins of a later Buddhist monastery. (fig. 1)

In the 4th and 3rd millennia, the Iranian plateau, riven by sharp uplands and tumbling steeply to the flanking riverine plains of the Tigris-Euphrates and the Indus, was the home of a multitude of disparate societies, essentially neolithic but verging gradually upon a stone-bronze (or chalcolithic) technology. Fed by animal husbandry and a little agriculture, their villages were sufficiently durable to develop into mounds or *tells*, though some degree of nomadism may be suspected as in similar communities today.

To this widespread village-society it has been customary to trace the primary urban development of Mesopotamia. There the 'Ubaid culture, on the eve of the mature Babylonian civilization, has been traced eastwards, possibly through Susa, and ascribed to 'some sort of expansive force and internal readjustment' affecting the tribal communities of southern and central Persia. Basic differences, of which more will be said, between the Indus and Mesopotamian civilizations bar the possibility of any direct colonization of the former from the latter; and at the same time our knowledge of the Ganges and central Indian cultures is sufficient to preclude an origin further east or south. We are left with the Baluch or Iranian borderland as the immediate source of the Indus Civilization, at any rate in its more material aspects. Less material but equally significant facets may reflect a somewhat different story.

Mohenjo-daro and Harappā

First, however, something must be said of the shape and substance of the Indus Civilization itself. It is at present best known from its two largest cities, Mohenjo-daro beside the river Indus in Sind, and Harappā, beside a former course of the tributary Ravi, nearly 400 miles to the north-east in the Punjab. Both cities were upwards of three miles in circuit, and both seem to have conformed with certain distinctive and evolved principles of urban planning. Mohenjo-daro was

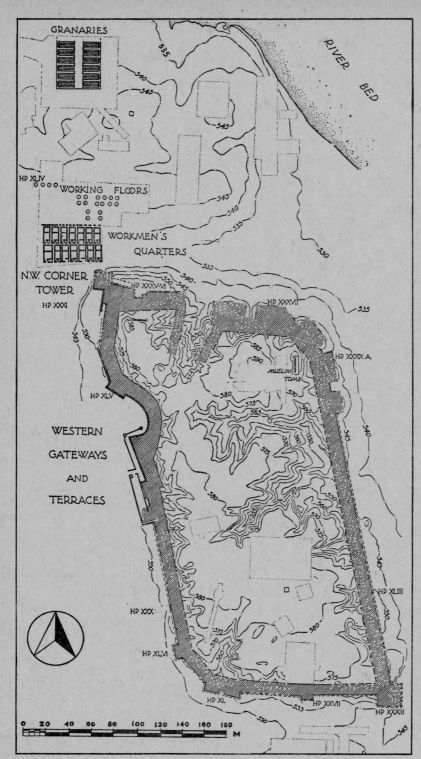

Harappā: the citadel, showing the thick walls revetted with mud-brick. In the extreme north are the granaries reconstructed in fig. 7. Within the citadel, no recognizable buildings have survived. (fig. 2)

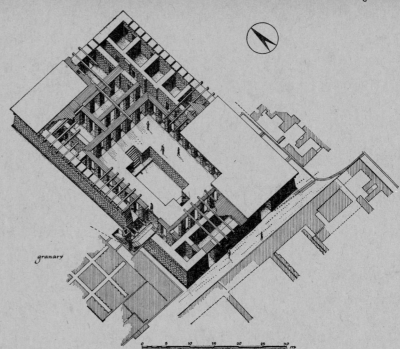

Mohenjo-daro: axonometric reconstruction of the Great Bath. The bath itself is approached north and south by brick steps with timber treads. Further north are rooms with private baths, perhaps for priests. (fig. 3)

Amongst other buildings on the mound were two pillared halls, a series of cells and baths (presumably for priests) beside the Great Bath, and a long building (230 × 78 ft) which was identified by its excavator as 'the residence of a very high official, possibly the high priest himself, or perhaps a college of priests'. One guess is as good as another, but certainly this was no ordinary house. Much work remains to be done by future excavators, but enough has been cleared to show that the citadel was both a religious and a secular headquarters: with the prototype of the ritual tanks of medieval and modern India, halls of assembly, and the State Granary which, in the economics of those times, may be equated with a modern State Bank. The general indication of combined kingly and priestly rule fits the habit of the 3rd millennium.

Below the citadel the town *(fig. 5)* stretched in orderly array to the Indus, which has moved some two miles eastward in more recent times. The main blocks, of which six have been identified and others

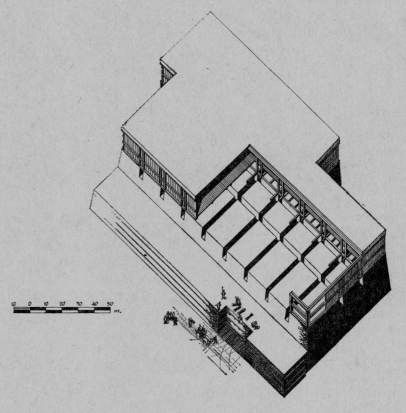

Mohenjo-daro: axonometric reconstruction of the granary. It is built on a podium with ventilation passages, and originally consisted of 27 blocks of brick-work, with a criss-cross lay-out of passages. See also plates 3, 4. (fig. 4)

commanded by an artificial mound or citadel, up to 50 feet high *(fig. 1)*, which occupied a flanking unit in a chessboard lay-out consisting of oblong blocks, each about 200 by 400 yards and divided by broad thoroughfares (pl. 23, *fig. 5*). At Harappā, a corresponding mound has been identified, and presumably overlooked a similar street-plan in that much-disturbed site *(fig. 2)*. The citadel at Mohenjo-daro was fortified by a baked-brick wall and solid towers (pl. 13), of which the earliest in a group excavated at the south-eastern corner had had built-in timbering. On the summit of the mound, the known structures included a carefully constructed bath or tank, jacketed with bitumen (pl. 14, *fig. 3*); and, beside it on the steep verge of the citadel, a high brick podium or substructure which had carried a large timber granary above intersecting ventilation channels. Half way up one end of the granary was a loading-platform above a recess into which the grain-wagons could be driven from the adjacent countryside (pl. 3, 4, *fig. 4*). Like the south-eastern tower, the podium had been inadvisedly reinforced by timbers which had decayed anciently and had been partially replaced by brick patches. Nevertheless, the tall solid structure, necessarily accessible and marginal by right of its primary function, must have constituted also a substantial strong-point in the citadel's defences.

MOHENJO-DARO
HR. AREA

Mohenjo-daro: plan of part of the residential quarter. The basic lay-out was that of a grid-iron, with blocks of buildings of roughly equal size. Main streets were about 15 metres wide, and the houses were divided by narrow lanes (sometimes 'dog-legged' to break the impact of the wind). The houses, with windowless outside walls, opened their doors on to these alleys rather than on to the main streets. The house in fig. 6 is in the extreme N. E. corner. (fig. 5)

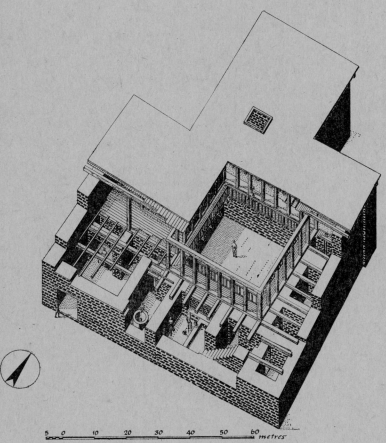

Mohenjo-daro: axonometric reconstruction of a typical house in the HR Area. The doorway leads into an entrance-room with a tiny porter's lodge; through this lies the courtyard, with the household rooms opening off it. (fig. 6)

may be presumed, were subdivided by straight lanes parallel or at right-angles to the arterial streets (pl. 23). The houses *(fig. 6)*, often substantial and sometimes of appreciable size, consisted typically of rooms round a courtyard and contained stairs to a former flat roof or upper storey, a bathroom, sometimes a well, and occasionally a privy on the ground or upper floor, similar to privies found in Mesopotamia (for example, in the Akkadian palace at Tell Asmar). Throughout, the streets and buildings are marked by the brick drains which are characteristic of the Civilization, both at Mohenjo-daro and elsewhere, and, with their trim inspection-holes, are the most elaborate of their kind in ancient Asia. In its prime, the whole city bespeaks middle-class prosperity with zealous municipal supervision.

Temples have not been clearly identified, but further examination would probably reveal two or three in the areas already excavated: notably, the so-called 'House A1' in the 'HR Area', where a small but substantial oblong structure is approached by an outer gateway

and two symmetrically disposed stairs parallel with the frontage, and has yielded fragments of two stone sculptures. Elsewhere in the same Area (in B 5) a regimented block of cells has been regarded variously as a priests' college with an adjacent temple and as a police-station! Once again, much further excavation and more analytical recording are alike necessary. Shops, including one with floor-sockets for large jars (pl. 15), can be recognized along the main streets; the private wells are supplemented by public wells, accessible from the streets and lanes; and here and there are small 'sentry boxes' for the civic watchmen. Construction is normally of baked brick in 'English bond', unbaked brick being confined almost exclusively to the internal platforms with which the builders strove to keep the floors above the rising flood-level. Most of the brickwork was originally covered with mud-plaster.

Harappā was plundered more than a century ago by railway-engineers, but the general outline of the citadel has been recovered, with a few fragments of the street-plan. The fortification of the citadel mound (pl. 19, *fig. 2*) consisted of a mud-brick rampart tapering upwards from a 40-foot base, with a similarly tapering external revetment of baked brick. In the 300 yards which intervened between the citadel and the river were barrack-like blocks of workmen's quarters, serried lines of circular brick floors for pounding grain (pl. 21), and two rows of ventilated granaries, twelve in all, marshalled on a podium *(fig. 7)*. The total floor-space of the granaries was something over 9000 square feet, approximating closely to that of the Mohenjo-daro granary before enlargement. The whole lay-out, in the

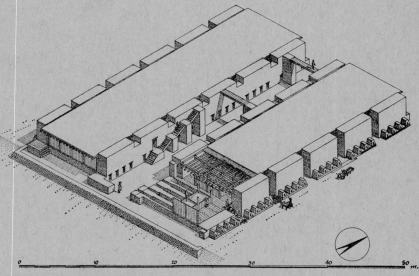

Harappā: isometric reconstruction of the granaries (north-east corner of the plan in fig. 2). See also pl. 19. Separate granaries are ranged in two rows of six, with a wide central passage. The triangular holes are ventilation flues. (fig. 7)

shadow of the citadel, suggests close administrative control of the municipal foodstocks within convenient proximity to the river-highway.

Some 80 miles south of Mohenjo-daro, the small Indus town of Chanhu-daro has produced similar evidence—drains, baked-brick houses, and mud-brick platforms built in the recurrent endeavour to surmount the rising flood-level—but lacks the citadel of the larger cities and does not materially enlarge the picture in detail. More recently, another small *tell* or town-mound has been investigated at Lothal, on the sea-plain of Kāthiāwād, 450 miles south-east of Mohenjo-daro. Here too the site of the town was raised and bolstered with mud-brick and mud, and mud-brick (perhaps in a drier climate) was used with baked brick in the structure of the houses. Drains and wells of baked brick were of normal Indus type. A substructure with criss-cross ducts between a series of mud-brick blocks, each 12 feet square, is probably the basis of a granary similar in principle to that of Mohenjo-daro. It had been accidentally burnt, and baked sealings, presumably from bales stored at one time in the overlying barn, had fallen into the ducts. Nearby, on a flank of the mound, an oblong enclosure 710 ft long and about 120 ft wide, with sides revetted in baked brick, has been identified as a dock for shipping. Further reference will be made to Lothal at a later stage.

These examples will serve to illustrate the general character of the Indus towns. Their surviving architecture is plain in the extreme, but the possibility or even likelihood of elaboration in timber, which has nowhere survived above the former ground-level, will present itself to anyone familiar with the rich Indian tradition in this material.

Customs, Social Conditions and Art

Of the Indus people themselves, little physically is known, though a growing mass of skeletal material awaits the lagging attention of Indian anthropologists. The few skulls that have been examined suggest a very mixed population. At Harappā a graveyard south of the citadel has yielded nearly 60 skeletons, normally extended with the head towards the north, and each accompanied by an average of fifteen or twenty pots representing the mature Indus culture. One of the graves had been revetted, on an oblong plan, with mud-brick (pl. 22). In another, the body had been enclosed in a coffin of which the side-walls had been of local rosewood (a scented timber) and the lid of deodar or cedar, doubtless floated down from the hills. But all the burials were manifestly those of ordinary citizens; no 'royal tomb' has yet been identified in the Indus Civilization, an omission which is no doubt due to the accidental imperfection of archaeological investigation.

More recently, at Lothal a number of burials have been discovered high up on the north-western fringe of the site, belonging in all probability, to a late sub-Indus phase rather than to the Civilization properly so-called. Three of the graves enclosed a double burial, possibly that of a man and a woman, though whether the Hindu custom of widow-sacrifice is indicated it is too early to say.

Amongst the equipment of the Indus citizens, priority must be given to their famous seals, generally of steatite, which are distinctive in kind and unique in quality (pl. 8). The normal seal was square with sides from ¾ to 1¼ in. and with a perforated boss at the back for handling and suspension. Exceptionally the seal is round (pl. 9), with or without a boss, and there are a few cylinder seals reminiscent of those of Mesopotamia; but the essential individuality of the Indus seals is emphasized by contrast with more or less remote analogies, mostly circular with a pierced boss, found in southern Mesopotamia and on Failaka and Bahrein and representing a north-westerly extension of Indus influence transmuted by the alien commercial world of the Persian Gulf.

Carved on the Indus seals with a small chisel and a drill are intaglio designs (i.e. engraved with a sunk pattern, so that the impression appears in relief) which may often be claimed as small masterpieces. They include a wide range of animals which must clearly have been at that time familiar denizens of the Indus valley: elephant, tiger, rhinoceros, antelope, crocodile or gharial. Above all, the zebu or humped bull is majestically rendered, with a monumental strength out of all proportion to the small field available. The commonest type is that of an ox-like beast seemingly with a single horn and nicknamed therefore the 'unicorn'; it may be suspected that two horns are in fact intended, one behind the other, but it has been recalled that Ctesias and Aristotle both ascribed the unicorn to India. In front of the 'unicorn' is invariably a strange object on a short post, commonly if grotesquely

named a 'standard', but possibly representing a decorative manger, or even an incense-burner. Composite grotesque animals also occur: one has the face of a man, the trunk and tusks of an elephant, the horns of a bull, the forepart of a ram, and the hindquarters of a tiger with erect tail armed with claws. Sometimes human forms are included, though the inferiority of their rendering recalls a similar disparity between the human and animal figures of the palaeolithic cave-art of western Europe. Three examples from Mohenjo-daro have a special interest in that they appear to represent a prototype of the great god Siva of the later Hindu religion.

Most of the seals bear also a short inscription in a pictographic script which, in spite of brave attempts, has not yet been interpreted. The pictographs are as different from those of Mesopotamia and Egypt as are these from each other. It is an interesting phenomenon that, within a short range of time and space, three great civilizations produced three utterly divergent systems of notation. The possible significance of this fact will be considered later.

The full function of these seals—more than 1200 of them have been

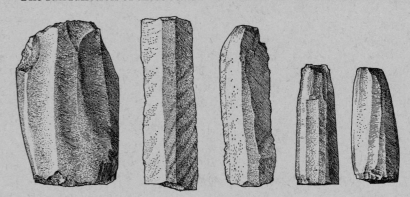

Mohenjo-daro: chert blades and polished cores. Parallel-sided chert flakes were struck from a prepared core, often without retouch. (fig. 8)

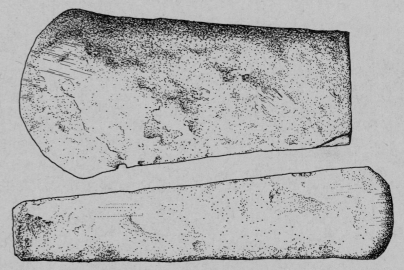

Mohenjo-daro: copper axe blades; two typical examples, one short with expanded edge, the other long and narrow with nearly parallel sides (fig. 9).

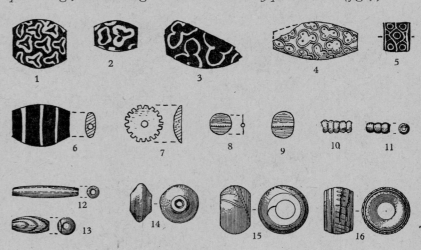

Beads from Mohenjo-daro and Harappā. 1–4, 6, 7, 10, 11, steatite paste; 5, etched carnelian; 8, gold; 9, 15, 16, faience; 12, 14, terracotta; 13, agate. (fig. 10)

found at Mohenjo-daro alone—remains uncertain until their inscriptions are understood. They were used to stamp clay sealings on bales and other commodities, and it is likely therefore that, in part at any rate, they represent personal names. The scarcity of duplicate inscriptions is a difficulty, but at least seems to rule out a religious or descriptive connotation. The boss or handle pierced for a cord implies that the seals were normally carried by their owners; and a fair measure of literacy in the Indus population is to be inferred also from the recurrence of the script as graffiti on pots or potsherds (pl. 12).

Of Indus stone sculpture, only eleven more or less fragmentary examples from Mohenjo-daro and two doubtful (possibly later) torsos from Harappā are at present known. All are of small size; save for two animals, of which one was a composite ram-elephant, they represent men or gods, four or five of them in squatting attitude. The heads (pl. 1, 10) are characterized by an extreme disharmony of the face in relation to the low receding forehead, by narrow but not Mongoloid eyes, and by the gathering of the hair in a 'bun' at the back. A beard is worn, but the upper lip is shaven, and the eyes are inlaid with shell; in these respects there is a resemblance with approximately contemporary heads from Mesopotamia (e.g. at Tell Asmar and Mari), but otherwise the owl-like stare of the Mesopotamian type is widely different from the more contemplative aspect of the Indus faces. There is indeed nothing significantly in common between the sculptures of the two regions. In bronze only a few minor works have survived: notably, a lifelike figurine of a buffalo with swept-back horns, and a statuette of a pert and provocative dancing-girl, naked except for an abundance of armlets (pl. 2). Of small terracottas there is a great abundance, including countless oxen and buffaloes (pl. 7), sometimes rendered with force and expressiveness but more often merely pedestrian trade-goods. Human terracotta figurines normally represent women wearing only abundant jewellery and, sometimes, bizarre 'pannier' headdresses (pl. 18). There are also occasional comic figures of a human or animal character (pl. 16, 17), and toy carts with solid wheels (pl. 5), usually of terracotta but rarely of copper or bronze, are common enough. Of all these products, a majority were probably toys, but some of them—female figures and perhaps bulls—may be thought to have been votive. It may be observed that bulls are represented but not cows, hens but not cocks; evidently the draught-bull and the egg-producing hen enjoyed a proper precedence, as did the mother or mother-goddess, emblem of fertility.

Important contrasts between the Indus and the Mesopotamian cultures have already been noted, but none is more striking than that exhibited by the tool-types of the two regions. Throughout the Indus Civilization the common domestic implement was a parallel-sided chert blade struck from a prepared core, more often than not without retouch (fig. 8). The cores themselves often show a high polish from their secondary use as burnishers. Stone mace-heads also occur, though examples of copper or bronze were not unknown. Copper-bronze implements include spears, knives, short swords, arrowheads, axes and fish-hooks (fig. 12). The spearheads are tanged and cannot clearly be distinguished from knives, though knives are sometimes differentiated from spears by a slightly sinuous recurved point, a peculiarity hardly ever found outside the Indus Civilization. The thinness of all these blades is remarkable, and seems to demand some special stiffening by being set well back between the split ends of the shaft or handle. The axes are flat, without shaft-hole, and were presumably hafted in a split and bound handle. Some of them are long and narrow, with nearly parallel sides; others are short and relatively wide, with boldly expanded edge (fig. 9). The obstinate retention of this primitive type long after the shaft-hole had been developed in western Asia (as early as the 'Ubaid period in Mesopotamia) is the more remarkable in that examples of this superior method of hafting did on rare occasions reach the Indus (pl. 26). Copper seems never wholeheartedly to have occupied the genius of the Indus craftsmen; as a relatively costly import, it was used with economy, although, in addition to implements, bowls, cups and dishes were sometimes made of the material. The ore may have been obtained overland from Rajasthan or from Afghanistan, but supplementary imports by sea may be suspected, and tin was almost certainly introduced in this manner.

Unlike these utile products, beads do show a few clear links with the West and help thus to mitigate the isolation of the Indus culture (pl. 11, fig. 10). Circular beads of gold with a prominent axial tube occur at Mohenjo-daro, in Mesopotamia about 2400–2300 BC, and

Typical Indus decorated sherds. The designs include purely geometrical patterns as well as stylized birds, fish and vegetation. (fig. 11)

in Troy IIG about 2300 BC, (see chapter VI) whilst faience copies from the Indus are likely to be home-made. Again, 'segmented' faience beads are numerous in the Indus and occur between 3000 and 1500 BC in northern Syria, Crete and Egypt. Etched carnelian beads are identical at Mohenjo-daro, Chanhu-daro, and in Mesopotamia at Ur, Kish, and Tell Asmar (about 2300 BC). Other types are more local, but they include a distinctive trefoil decoration which is found also on one of the Mohenjo-daro sculptures (pl. 10) and a stone base and on stone, pottery and woodwork in Mesopotamia, Crete and Egypt between 2300 and 1300 BC. The Indus Civilization provides a clear—though not the only—instance of an interchange of ornaments and charms combined with a basic technological independence.

Lastly, the pottery (fig. 11). Most of the Indus pots are wheel-turned and are of pinkish ware with a bright red slip, though a buff background is not uncommon. Decoration, mostly in black, consists either of plain horizontal lines of varying thickness, or of more pictorial motives: notably, intersecting circles, scale-patterns, chequers, pipal leaves, rosettes, lattice-work, cross-hatching, and occasional peacocks and fish (pl. 20). Human forms are very rare and are relatively crude. Shapes include 'dish on stand' or fruit-dish (an Asian type widespread in time and space), small vessels bearing a knobbed decoration, large slenderfooted bowls or containers, cylindrical perforated strainers, and cream-coloured goblets with pointed foot. The last are sometimes stamped, presumably with the potter's name, and are confined to the late period in the Indus valley itself; the more southerly extensions of the Civilization in Kāthiāwād (or Saurashtra) do not seem to have used it, and on the other hand it is absent from pre- or non-Indus settlements in the Indus and neighbouring regions.

(fig. 12)

Pre-Indus Cultures

Before any attempt is made to build up these and other *minutiae* of the Indus Civilization into a composite whole, something must be said of the Civilization's cultural environment. What was its material ancestry? What its ultimate fate?

For its material ancestry a systematic search is still necessary and would not indeed be difficult to organize. Thus the high mound of Dabar Kot in the Zhob valley of northern Baluchistan exhibits in its sides the Indus Culture bracketed above and below by other cultures, and would amply reward a single season's excavation carried out with skill and purpose. Or the considerable Indus site of Judeirjo-daro recently noted on the plain 18 miles north of Jacobabad in Sind, with its superficial hint of a relatively early date, would doubtless provide a new and valuable introductory phase to our problem. Meanwhile, three sites may be singled out as of special interest in this context.

The first is Amrī, south of Mohenjo-daro in Sind. There a group of mounds was briefly explored in 1929 and showed two successive chalcolithic cultures: a later one of normal Indus type and an earlier (underlying) one marked by a similar technology but by a totally distinct pottery. This is of buff, cream or pink colour, usually with a plain band of reddish brown at the neck and with geometric design in black or chocolate giving a polychrome effect to the whole. The patterns, painted apparently after firing, include panels of chequer-work or hatching, chevrons, lozenges and zigzags or 'sigmas'. Small beakers are a characteristic form, and the ware is, on the average, of good quality. In no significant respect does this pottery anticipate that of the Indus Civilization, but equally there is no hint that it long preceded it. Its distribution lies primarily between the Indus river and the southern Baluch hills, but it is related to variant cultures in the hills themselves, between Quetta and the sea (pl. 29).

The second of the three sites is Harappā itself. There in 1946 slight traces of a pre-Indus culture were found beneath the citadel-defences, which here marked the arrival of the Indus Civilization. These traces are restricted to potsherds of a fine dark purple-red ware decorated, particularly round the rim, with carefully ruled horizontal black bands. This ware recalls other non-Indus wares in northern Baluchistan but has no close affinity with those of the mature Indus Civilization.

The third site is the most striking of the three. At Kot Diji, 25 miles east of Mohenjo-daro, recent exploration has revealed a fortified village—or small town with a fortified citadel—under an open Indus settlement. The site showed sixteen successive layers of occupation of which the last three were typical of the Indus Civilization, the fourth was 'mixed', and the remainder represented an antecedent culture that has been called 'Kot Dijian'. A central Carbon 14 dating for the uppermost Kot Dijian stratum (Layer 5 from the top) is understood to be in the neighbourhood of 2400 BC and for Layer 14 (the lowest but two) about 2700 BC. This is sufficiently consistent with the hypothetical initial date of c. 2500 BC previously attributed on other grounds to the beginning of the mature Indus Civilization.

The open settlement of the top three layers is marked by characteristic Indus pottery, including pierced strainers and sherds showing intersecting-circle, pipal-leaf, comb, and scale decoration, in black on red. Between it and the under-lying Kot Dijian was a burnt layer, thought to represent the destruction of the earlier settlement with its fortification of mud-brick on stone foundations. The house-walls throughout were similarly built of mud-brick on lower courses of stone; baked bricks do not seem to have been used at all. Copper or bronze occurred in the uppermost (Indus) levels but were absent from the Kot Dijian occupation, which produced chert blades and cores and leaf-shaped chert arrowheads such as are otherwise rare in the Baluch-Indus region. The Kot Dijian pottery is wheel-turned, light and thin, is pinkish to red in colour, and is commonly decorated in black with straight horizontal lines or sometimes with waves and loops; it bears a marked similarity to the pre-citadel Harappān and to some of the Amrī wares. But in two respects this Kot Dijian culture anticipates or overlaps that of the Indus Civilization. First, its pottery already includes vessels decorated with the peculiarly Indus scale-pattern; and secondly, it also contains some of the strange triangular terracotta 'cakes' (1½ to 4 inches across) which are not otherwise known outside the Indus Civilization *(fig. 13)*. These 'cakes' have been vaguely regarded as ritual objects, but their frequent occurence in drains suggests a toilet use. Be that as it may, a link between the Kot Dijians and the Indus folk is indicated, though the significance of that link remains in doubt. As a whole, the Kot Dijian culture can scarely claim to have been in any direct sense parental to that of the Indus cities. Rather would it appear to have been a partially antecedent, partially overlapping provincial culture which was eventually brought sharply within the orbit of Mohenjo-daro.

Without further argument, then, it may be affirmed that the immediate material origins of the Indus Civilization in the narrower aspects

So-called terracotta 'cake' from Mohenjo-daro. The purpose of these objects remains obscure; perhaps they had a toilet use. (fig. 13)

of art and craftsmanship cannot at present be pin-pointed. But what of the wider aspects of the matter? Here factors of a less material and proportionately more speculative character cannot be avoided if our essay is to be something more than a catalogue.

Early Settlers in the Indus Valley

First, let it be emphasized that to the venturous mind the wide plains of the Indus valley offered a lure and a challenge. They were at that time marsh- and jungle-ridden, the haunt of the noxious beasts which were later to adorn the Indus seals, and of the fevers which modern science is at last eliminating. But they were widely fertile, and their fertility was renewed by annual floods, whilst the great rivers, full of edible fish, were also natural highways between the mountains and the sea. With this expansive prospect, any imaginative spirit, oppressed by the claustrophobia of his mountain retreat, may well have felt the stirrings of ambition. Yet ambition alone would not carry him far. The great rivers, for all their beneficence, were at the same time treacherous and formidable enemies. If not constrained and directed by wise, large-scale and sustained effort, they were destroyers no less than fertilizers, as anyone who has seen a great river in turbulent flood will testify. A society determined to profit by the vast opportunities of the plain must needs have also the genius and the skill to master an exacting and minatory environment, *and must have it from the outset*. A civilization such as that of the Indus cannot be visualized as a slow and patient growth. Its victories, like its problems, must have been of a sudden sort; and our search therefore for a systematic material ancestry for the Indus Civilization may well be a long and subtle and perhaps not primarily important one.

Intellectually, the founders of that Civilization had one crowning advantage. Two great riverine civilizations had shortly preceded them, in Mesopotamia and in Egypt. In any physical sense, neither of these was the immediate parent; the Indus Civilization, with its individual technology and script and its alien personality, was no mere colony of the West. But ideas have wings, and in the third millennium the *idea* of civilization was in the air of western Asia. A model of civilization, however abstract, was present to the minds of the Indus founders. In their running battle against more spacious problems than had been encountered either in Mesopotamia or in Egypt, they were fortified by the consciousness that *it had been done before*. And in that consciousness, after one failure and another (Amrī and Kot Diji are merely examples), they won though.

In some such manner may be reconstructed the initial phase of the Indus Civilization: as the ultimate triumph of a village or small-town community, determined, well led and inspired by a great and mature idea. The Indus people were neither the first nor the last to fulfil themselves in this dramatic fashion; and it is a fashion not easy to reconstruct on the limited basis of conventional archaeological evidence. It is not necessarily the less objectively true for that disability, for the abstract element in its composition.

Economy and Expansion of the Indus Civilization

How did the Indus Civilization make its living? First and foremost, like the other two civilizations of the age, by farming. Wheat and six-rowed barley were grown, and field-peas; melon seeds, sesame and a few date-stones have also been found, and the earliest traces of cotton known anywhere in the world. Domestic animals included dogs and cats, humped cattle, short-horns and buffaloes, and possibly (though not certainly) pigs, camels, horses, and asses. Whether the elephant was domesticated or not is unknown, though its ivory was freely used.

The Indus merchants must also have carried on an appreciable trade, since imports included gold from southern India or Afghanistan, silver, and copper from Afghanistan or Rajasthan, lapis lazuli from Afghanistan, turquoise from Iran, and a jade-like fuchsite probably from southern India. Links with Mesopotamia have already been noted, and may be extended to include Indus pottery and inlays from Akkadian levels at Tell Asmar. But much of the traffic was presumably in perishable objects, such as cotton and certain kinds of wood which are cited on the Larsa tablets of about 1950 BC from Ur in south Mesopotamia. The tablets show that Telmun or Dilmun (probably Bahrein in the Persian Gulf) was used at this time as an intermediate market by Ur shippers, who bartered their stocks there for goods brought from 'Makkan' and 'Meluhha'; and it has been conjectured reasonably enough that Meluhha, whence copper, stone, wood, ivory objects, and certain breeds of animals were obtained, was in the Indus valley. But be it repeated that there was never any close cultural integration between the civilizations of the Tigris-Euphrates and the Indus, and that their interchange was, it seems, mostly restricted to goods of a secondary kind.

And how at length did the Indus Civilization end? Did it die violently or merely fade away? Recent research has suggested that it did both. In the central Indus its death was seemingly a violent one; further south it passed by transmutation into successor-cultures. Nor is the variation surprising if we recall the astonishing range of the Civilization at one stage or another of its career. On what may be called the Indus axis it extended for 1000 miles, from Sutkāgen-dor near the shores of the Arabian Sea, 300 miles west of Karachi, to the neighbourhood of Rupar at the foot of the Simla hills. South-east-wards along the coast recent exploration has shown that it stretched for 425 miles from Karachi, through Kāthiāwād or Saurashtra to the estuaries of the Narbadā and the Kim, on the Gulf of Cambay; and this new coastal spread has introduced new and important elements, both cultural and chronological, into the Indus problem. Nor do the new factors end there. In 1958 definite evidence was found for the first time that an Indus culture, including the characteristic triangular terracotta 'cakes', had leapt or circumvented the barriers of desert and jungle which had previously been thought to exclude the Civilization from the Jumna basin, and had reached Alamgirpur, near a tributary of the Jumna 17 miles west of Meerut and only 28 miles north-east of Delhi. A further report that Indus pottery has been found under the ancient metropolis of Kaushāmbi, much lower down the river, is not confirmed, but a fringe of Indus or sub-Indus sites must now be expected on the northern plains. The pattern of the Indus Civilization is materially enlarged and significantly changed.

The End of the Indus Civilization

For a Civilization so widely distributed, no uniform ending need be postulated. Circumstances which affected it in the sub-montane lands of the central Indus may well have differed widely from those which it encountered south or east of the Indian Desert and the watery coast-lands of the Rann of Kutch. And the evidence at present available indicates that such was indeed the case.

In the valley of the Indus, Mohenjo-daro itself is our chief witness. There the dramatic end of the city has often enough been described. It was sacked by raiders somewhere about the middle of the 2nd mil-lennium BC and, save for the intrusion of a few Buddhist monks nearly two thousand years later, has since that moment been a 'wide desert where no life is found'. The attackers left the dead lying where they fell. In one of the houses sprawled thirteen skeletons—men, women and children—some wearing bracelets, rings and beads, and two of them with sword cuts upon their skulls (pl. 24). Elsewhere lay a group of nine contorted skeletons, amongst them five children. At a public well, approached from the adjacent lane by a short flight of steps, two people, of which one if not both were women, had been struck down across the steps, and two other skeletons lay in the lane outside. Elsewhere again, yet another skeleton was found in a lane. And all these grim relics lay on the highest and latest level of the city, witnesses to its last moments.

Who were the attackers? We shall not know, though I have made a guess. The trend of the archaeological evidence is that the Indus Civilization, in the Indus valley, lasted approximately until 1500 BC, with a marginal error of perhaps a century on either side of that date. Roughly to the same period are ascribed the earlier Aryan immig-rations into India; and it is accepted that these invasions are reflected in the older books of the *Rigveda*. There the invasion constantly assumes the form of an onslaught by the nomadic invaders upon the walled cities or citadels of the aborigines—Indra, the Aryan war-god, is *puramdara*, 'fort-destroyer', who 'rends forts as age consumes a garment'. Where are, or were, these forts? The fortified citadels of Harappā and Mohenjo-daro, and defences identified at certain other Harappān sites (notably Sutkāgen-dor in Makrān and Ali Murād in Sind), are without known rivals in or near the crucial time. It may even be that the Hari-Yūpūyā of the Rigveda, scene of an Aryan victory over a non-Aryan tribe, is our Harappā. There is at least a case for equating the destroyers of Mohenjo-daro with the Aryan invaders of the north-west. But I do not press it. Evidence from other Indus sites must be awaited.

One thing is clear about the end of Mohenjo-daro: the city was already slowly dying long before the ultimate *coup de grâce*. Houses,

mounting gradually upon the ruins of their predecessors or upon artificial platforms in an incessant endeavour to out-top the Indus floods, were increasingly shoddier in construction, increasingly carved up into warrens for a swarming lower-grade population. To a height of 30 feet or more, the tall podium of the Great Granary on the fringe of the citadel was engulfed by rising structures of poorer and poorer quality. Economic decline is everywhere apparent, and, apart alto-gether from that genetic decay of racial character which is an uneasy postulate, practical and immediate reasons may be inferred. The un-tiring consumption of major vegetation implied by the firing, age after age, of millions of bricks must, even with aid from hill-timbers, have bared the land and, by reducing the transpiration of moisture, have impaired the climate. Abnormal flooding, such as is known to have occurred from time to time, must have disturbed the normal processes of irrigation. Even in a brief phase of neglect, the land, with its heavy salt-content, readily turns sour. Mohenjo-daro was indeed steadily wearing out its landscape. And trade, particularly with the markets of Mesopotamia, seems in the 2nd millennium—for reasons unknown—to have become more indirect and complicated and, no doubt, proportionately less profitable than in earlier days of direct shipment. In one way and another the standards or bases of civilization were slipping: Mohenjo-daro was declining to a fall. And its later phases are sufficiently emphatic to suggest that lesser sites on the Indus axis must, economically at least, have shared a comparable fate.

After the Indus Civilization

What was the sequel? The present evidence, unimpressive in bulk, suggests that the Indus 'empire' (if its wide expanse may justify that nickname) was followed by a long phase of cultural fragmentation, not altogether unlike that from which it sprang but including, perhaps, remoter exotic elements. At Harappā the Indus city was succeeded by a culture identified as 'Cemetery H' from the name of a burial-ground which overlay the true Harappān remains and implied a break in con-tinuity, whether long or short. The Cemetery H people produced sketchy, ill-conditioned buildings and good painted pottery which includes a few semi-Harappān elements but is essentially distinct. The culture seems to be confined to a patch of the middle Indus but has been inadequately explored. Eighty miles south of Mohenjo-daro, the little Indus town of Chanhu-daro was succeeded by two successive squatter-cultures of low grade, known respectively by the place-names 'Jhukar' and 'Jhangar'. The Jhukar villagers made coarse pottery and used round button-seals, commonly bearing radiate or compartmental patterns reminiscent of 2nd-millennium types in northern Iran and the Caucasus. Again, at Moghul Ghundai in the Zhob valley of northern Baluchistan, burial-cairns have produced a tripod-jar, horse-bells, rings and bangles which have been compared to equipment of about 1000 BC from 'Cemetery B' at Siyalk in central Iran, but may be later. Stray finds, such as the famous bronze dagger of about the 12th century BC from Fort Munro in the Sulaiman Range west of the Indus *(fig. 14)*, and a copper trunnion axe from the Kurram valley on the Afghan border *(fig. 15)*, point similarly west-wards to Iran and the Caucasus. The general sense of this very scrappy material is, as a whole, that of local poverty-stricken cultures deriving a little from a sub-Indus heritage but also drawing elements from the north-west—from the direction, in fact, of the Aryan invasions. Materially there is a notable absence of any real continuity in the Indus valley between the great Civilization and its beggarly successors.

(fig. 14)

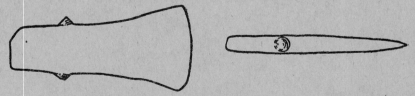

Copper trunnion axe (front and side view) from the Kurram valley. (fig. 15)

Down the coast, on the other hand, the picture is a different one. For the moment we must rest content with a preliminary note, but from the active work in progress (1960) it is already clear enough that in Kāthiāwād or Surashtra—at Lothal, Rangpur, Rojdi (south of Rajkot), Somnath and other sites—and again further south in the districts of Broach and Surat—at Mehgam and Telod on the Narbadā estuary, and at Bhagatrav on that of the Kim—the Indus culture shades off into sub-Indus and 'successor' cultures without dramatic break. This evidence is new and important.

Here a word of caution is appropriate. The process which I have just called 'shading off' from the recognized Indus culture to those which (in time or place) are peripheral to it requires watchful definition by archaeologists if confusion is to be avoided. In particular, it is necessary to review quite clearly the minimum qualifications required of a culture before the specific term 'Indus' can be applied to it. I would suggest the following as alternative or accumulative requirements: (i) Indus seals; (ii) Indus script, whether on seals or on pottery; (iii) certain distinctive decorative motifs on pottery, e.g. intersecting circles, scale-pattern, pipal-leaves, rosettes and peacocks in the Indus manner; (iv) certain distinctive ceramic forms, e.g. goblet with pointed base, cylindrical vessels with perforations (colanders), tall jars with S-shaped profile and ledged rims, and 'fruit-dishes' or 'dishes-on-stand', though these last *may* occur outside the Indus culture proper; (v) triangular terracotta 'cakes' (see *fig. 13*); (vi) kidney-shaped inlays of shell or faience; (vii) certain beads, notably discoidal with tubular piercing (see *fig. 10, nos. 8, 9*).

No doubt in time other forms or categories will be found to mark provincial or late varieties of the Indus Civilization; meanwhile, caution may again be urged in the use of the term 'Indus'.

With this proviso, it is now becoming possible in Saurashtra (Kāthiāwād) and even further south, to identify a late and developing branch of the Indus Civilization, varying perhaps locally and extending downwards in time towards 1000 BC. For this branch I propose the specific name 'Saurashtrian Indus'.

Up to date, Lothal, with its straight streets, drains, granary and platform, and with six phases of occupation, is the best-known of these Saurashtrian sites. Numerous steatite seals and some of the pottery make it impeccably 'Indus'. At the same time, its ceramic decoration tails off into friezes of birds, caprids (the goat family) and trees in an un-Indus fashion. New types also, such as a stud-handled vessel which is likely to become a 'type-fossil', occur in the later layers and begin to point towards the chalcolithic wares of the Narbadā region and central India. Above all, a constant though subordinate accompaniment of these Indus and sub-Indus fabrics is a Black-and-red ware, variegated by differential firing and sometimes simply decorated with white lines and dots. There is less and less doubt that here we have

the germ of the Black-and-Red pottery which was to be the constant accompaniment of the megalithic culture of central and southern India in the latter half of the 1st millennium BC.

Lothal is not alone in this evidence. At Rojdi, further north near Rajkot, is another sub-Indus site, the authenticity of which is established by an Indus-script graffito; and here too the Black-and-red fabric occurs alongside the sub-Indus wares. On the other hand, from what little is known of the harassed site of Rangpur, 30 miles from Lothal, it would appear that, in a continuously developing chalcolithic culture of which the earlier elements are partly 'Indus', the Black-and-red occurred after the Indus elements had vanished. But a fresh examination of Rangpur is due on more grounds than one.

Enough has been said to show the manner in which these and other Saurashtrian sites are capable of linking up the Indus Civilization with the chalcolithic cultures of central India, and, through them ultimately, with the central and southern Iron Age. Nothing has been said of other links between the centre and the north-west, but two may be mentioned. The microlithic blade industries which characterized central India in and before the earlier half of the 1st millennium BC sometimes include parallel-sided blades of a more formidable type, comparable with the chert blades of the Indus valley and Baluchistan. At Maski in Hyderabad State, for example, they run to more than 5 inches in length. Apart altogether from the fortuitous availability of material, it is difficult not to suppose that we have here a genuine intrusion from the north-west, no doubt through Saurashtra. And again the flat copper axes which occur on chalcolithic sites at Jorwe (a hoard of six), east of Bombay, and at Maheshwar on the central Narbadā are of an Indus type; and though they are of an unspecialized kind, they are consistent with a measure of cultural intercommunication between the lower Indus and the Narbadā system by way of the west coast. The evidence adds up.

Even so, the Narbadā villages of c. 1000 BC, though full of interest to the explorer of the Indian Chalcolithic, never, so far as we know, rose to such heights as would justify the term 'Narbadā Civilization'. Civilization in those parts had to wait until fresh elements came in the 5th or 4th century BC from a new direction, equipped with a new metal. That will be Section 3 of the story of civilization in India; for Section 2 we must turn aside to the Ganges basin.

The Ganges Civilization

The exploration of the two-river country, or *doāb*, of the Ganges-Jumna basin is still in a rudimentary stage, but three sites show consistently the sort of evidence that is likely to be forthcoming from many more. At Hastināpura in the upper Ganges valley the succession of cultures has been established by careful digging, and is as follows. The earliest phase, Period I, is represented by a thin layer containing rough ochre-coloured pottery of a kind which has been noted on several sites from Bikaner eastwards. It is not, as yet, associated with buildings but may possibly be related to a well-known series of copper (rarely bronze) hoards which mark the earliest, sporadic occupation of the *doāb* and may be dated, at a guess, on either side of 1000 BC. Civic life in recognizable form begins in the earlier half of the 1st millennium BC with remains of mud or mud-brick walls of unascertained plan, associated with a hard and distinctive grey painted pottery with black linear patterns, known as the Painted Grey Ware *(fig. 16)*. No microliths or other stone implements are associated with this ware, but copper (very rarely iron) was used for arrowheads and other tools and weapons. The humped bull, buffalo, sheep and pig were domesticated, and cultivated grains included rice. The date of this urban culture, with its mixed farming, was about 1000 or 800 to 500 BC. Its earlier roots have not yet been recognized, but the excellence of some of the Painted Grey Ware implies an established tradition. The ware may possibly be related, through links which have not yet been discovered, to the bowls found in secondary burials at Shāhi Tump in Baluchistan; but it is mere guesswork to suggest that its arrival in the Ganges basin may be associated with the secondary invasion of the Aryans, when, from the Punjab, they entered and Aryanized the Middle Country of the *doāb* ('two-river valley'), after picking up ideas and craftsmen from the Baluch borderland.

Later Developments from c. 500 BC

Period III at Hastināpura is marked by the arrival of iron, which may have reached the Baluch borderland some centuries earlier but had doubtless been introduced into the north-western plains of the

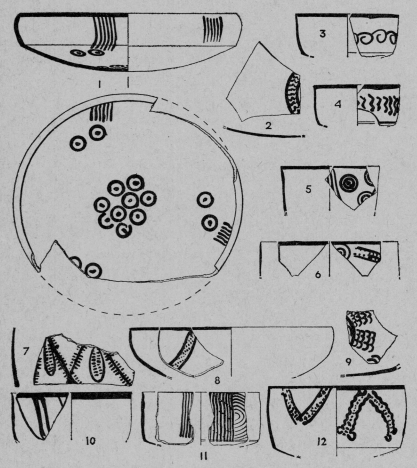

Painted Grey Ware. 1–4 from Ahichchhatrā; 5–9 from Pānipat; 10–12 from Hastināpura. The commonest decoration of this wheel-turned pottery is painted linear and dotted patterns, circles, spirals and swastikas. (fig. 16)

sub-continent by the Persians when they extended their Empire into this region in the latter part of the 6th century BC. To the same source may be traced the introduction of money which in India was struck at first on the Persian standard. And shortly after the arrival of iron a hard and distinctive glossy black ware, known as Northern Black Polished Ware *(fig. 17)*, emerged in the *doāb*, perhaps in its steel-like quality imitating the new metal. With the emergence of the Northern Black Polished Ware, the Painted Grey Ware went out of use. Baked bricks, as well as mud-bricks, were now used in the buildings, and soak-pits of superimposed jars with perforated bases or of superimposed terracotta rings now began their long life in the civic equipment of the subcontinent (pl. 28). The date of this phase must have approximated to 500–200 or 150 BC; the next phase, Period IV, produced coins of Mathurā rulers ascribed to the 2nd century BC.

On this evidence, urban life began in the *doāb* after 1000 BC, and since that time, has been continuous there. Changes in material and craftsmanship have been subordinate to a general continuity of civic consciousness and well-being. Fertile river-side clearings in the broad jungles which then covered the great plains contained the towns and cities which are the background of the Indian epics: cities such as Hastināpura itself, which was the epic capital of the Kaurava kings, or Ahichchhatrā, near Ramnagar in Uttar Pradesh, which, as capital of North Panchāla, is likewise mentioned in the *Mahābhārata*.

The ramparts of Ahichchhatrā still rise to a majestic height above the plain and are 3½ miles in circuit. Somewhat summary excavation there has produced evidence comparable with that from Hastināpura. The earthen ramparts are basically of two successive periods crowned by a baked-brick wall, and Painted Grey Ware is said to have been found in and below the earlier rampart, which should therefore not be much later than 500 BC. As at Hastināpura, coinage came into use during the succeeding Northern Black Polished Ware period, i.e. between the 5th and 2nd centuries BC. The town was rebuilt on eight or nine occasions, and lasted until it was superseded by Badaun about AD 1100. A fresh exploration of the site would be rewarding.

A no less imposing site, indeed one of the great sites of India, is that of Kaushāmbī, beside the Jumna 30 miles from Allahābād (pl. 25). The earliest defences, some 4 miles in circuit and standing to a height of over 40 feet, shortly preceded the introduction of Northern Black Polished Ware and may therefore be somewhat earlier than 500 BC. They consist of a mud bank revetted externally with a battered wall of baked brick which, beside the eastern gate, still remains to a height of 154 courses. Near the base this wall had begun to bulge dangerously, and rough weep-holes had been cut through it to relieve the pressure. It was subsequently renewed or replaced on more than one

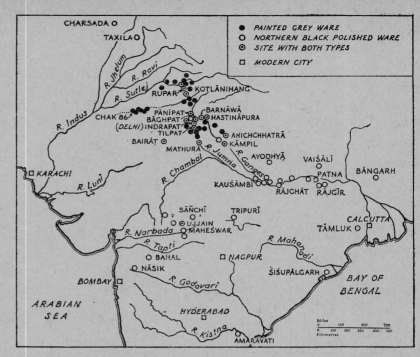

Distribution of Painted Grey and Northern Black Polished Wares. (fig. 18)

occasion, but the whole story of this very remarkable structure has not yet been worked out. Within the defences were well-built brick houses and a famous Buddhist Monastery, the Ghoshitārāma, of which the earliest phase has been ascribed to the century of the Buddha's death but may be somewhat later.

Other sites fit approximately into the same time-table. Vaisālī, in the Muzaffarpur district of Bihar, was the capital of the Lichchhavis, the tribe or principality which produced the Buddha, and recent excavation claims to have revealed the stupa built in the 5th century to enshrine a share of the relics of the Buddha immediately after his death. The city itself must go back to the 6th century BC or earlier. Again, at Banaras or Vārānasī renewed excavations at Rajghat have shown once more that the city goes back at least to c. 500 BC, and no doubt some part of it is yet earlier. Extended exploration is here prevented by the fact that the present city spreads over the site of its predecessors and owes much of its height to their underlying accumulation. In summary, year by year fresh evidence points to a great burgeoning of civic life on the northern plains by the second quarter of the 1st millennium BC.

Central and Southern India

East of Patna, where lay Pātaliputra, metropolis of the Mauryan dynasty of the 4th and 3rd centuries BC, the moderate rainfall of the plains is doubled and shortly quintupled in intensity, and close marshy jungle was a barrier to the easy advance of civilization. Here, in Bengal, is evidence of the persistence of small disarticulate societies in an essentially neolithic condition until the powerfully organized Mauryan regime thrust eastwards in the 3rd century BC and established townships such as Mahāsthān, where an inscription probably of Mauryan date declares orderly measures for combating a famine (pl. 32). Further south, in Orissa, the remarkable fortress-town of Shishupālgarh, with its four-square plan and salient gateways, is probably of the same period: as is Jaugada, in the Ganjan district of southern Orissa, where comparable evidence is forthcoming.

Meanwhile, in central India urban development had been less reluctant. Between 1500 and 500 BC the flanks of the Narbada and the adjacent rivers had been extensively occupied by busy village-communities marked by a chalcolithic technology, mostly based upon microliths supplemented by a little precious copper. The associated pottery varied regionally but was often skilful and lively, decorated not only with linear patterns but also with outlined animals and even crudely depicted human forms. Beneath the markedly local elements can sometimes be detected an affinity, a cousinship, with the chalcolithic wares of the north-west; and, like the chert or chalcedony blades and the copper flat-axes already mentioned (p. 247), the pottery is consistent with a slowly moving, intermittent connection down the west coast. And then, shortly before or after 500 BC, the developed urbanity of the Jumna-Ganges *doāb* decended upon the scene.

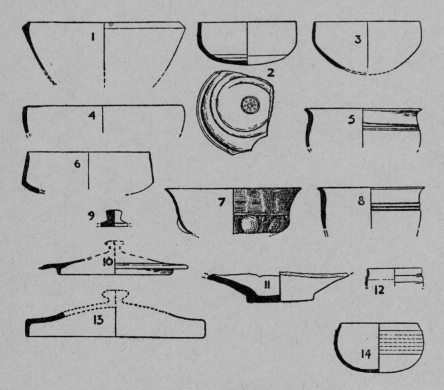

Northern Black Polished Ware. 1, 3, 5, 8, 10 from Rupar; 2 from Rājgir; 4, 9, 12 from Tripurī; 6 from Bahal; 7 from Taxila; 11, 13 from Hastināpura; 14, from Ahachchhitrā. (fig. 17)

A crucial site is that of Ujjain, where recent digging has taken place (pl. 33). Ujjain, one of the sacred cities of India and capital of the ancient kingdom of Avanti (now Mālwā), lies beside the river Sipra, a tributary of the Chambal which is itself a tributary of the Jumna. It dominated the trunk-route from the *doāb* to the Arabian Sea and, as a developed city, was an early offshoot of the Ganges Civilization. It is of a roughly pentagonal plan, with major axes of about a mile. Its massive mud rampart is 250 feet wide at the base and upwards of 40 feet high; beside the river, where it catches the full flow of the current, it was reinforced by timber breakwaters set diagonally to the stream, and there are later repairs both of mud and of baked brick. Outside the rampart, except where the river rendered additional work unnecessary, there is a formidable fosse, originally 150 feet wide at the top and 20 feet deep. From the material of the rampart were recovered the two southernmost sherds of Painted Grey Ware, but the occurrence of iron in the lowest of the related strata suggests a date little earlier than 500 BC for the first phase of the fortification, without prejudice to the possibility of previous occupation of some part of the site. Within the line of the defences were buildings of stone and baked brick, with the ring-wells or soakpits which have already been noted as characteristic of Indian towns from the latter half of the 1st millennium BC onwards. In one of the gates, the roadway had been metalled and re-metalled on numerous occasions, and bore the ruts of carts with the universal gauge of 5 ft 9 in.

On present knowledge, Ujjain suggests a relatively sudden projection of the civilization of the northern plains upon a site previously occupied, if at all, by a purely local settlement of small-town or village status. Further south, on the other hand, at Maheshwar, the evidence is clear enough. Here, where the Ujjain trunk-route crossed the Narbadā, there was a considerable and lengthy chalcolithic occupation on both banks of the river before the fully evolved technology of the Ganges Civilization was suddenly imposed upon the more northerly site, that of Maheshwar itself. There was no transition between the lower and the higher culture; the latter swept down and smothered the former with a twenty-foot accumulation of buildings, soakpits, iron implements, Northern Black Polished Ware, and organized equipment which included a sprinkling of punch-marked coins as witness to an organized commerce wholly alien to the preceding Chalcolithic. The point need not be laboured: civilization arrived in central India with a bang: it came from the Jumna-Ganges *doāb* along the traffic-lines through the Vindhya Range, and it reached the Narbadā—the east-west axis of central India—by the beginning of the 5th century BC.

The extension of civilization southwards into the heart of the Deccan and peninsular India runs parallel with that already noticed in Bengal and Orissa. There is no reason for ascribing it to a period earlier than the 3rd century BC, and, at something more than a guess, it can be associated with the southward extension of the Mauryan Empire by Bindusāra, father of Ashoka, at the beginning of that century. On two town-sites, namely Maski in Raichur district, formerly in Hyderabad State, and Brahmagiri, the ancient Isila, further south in Mysore State, the main characters of this peninsular civilization have been observed with care. At both sites there are Ashokan rock-cut edicts; at both, the advent of civilization is the advent also of iron; at both, a Black-and-Red ware which, as we have seen, has its roots in the Chalcolithic of Saurashṭra and Rājasthān now joins the main southward spread, which in some regions it had in fact anticipated; at both the rites of the dead included the erection of megalithic cists or monuments (pl. 31), the origin of which is in dispute and need not be discussed here; at both there is a sharp cultural cleavage between the richly equipped Iron Age and the semi-barbarous Chalcolithic substratum. From now on, the Peninsula was in the main stream of civilization, varied by those remarkable backwaters where, in the hills and forests, ancient tribal societies have remained to modern times as a familiar archaism in the Indian scene.

Summary

Finally, let us summarize this progressive pervasion of civilized life through the two million square miles of the great subcontinent. The story began in the middle of the 3rd millennium, when social ideas which had been elaborated in Mesopotamia fertilized certain of the lively but limited chalcolithic communities of the Baluch-Indus borderland and produced the seemingly sudden flowering of Phase I of Indian civilization, that specifically of the Indus Valley. By the early part of the 2nd millennium the Indus Civilization was colonizing the west coastlands as far south as the Gulf of Cambay and the Narbadā-Kim estuaries, either by spontaneous expansion or under increasing external pressure from the north. Certainly by the middle of that millennium, internal decay coupled with pressure from the Aryan nomads who were now arriving in the Punjab broke up the Civilization along its original axis, and some centuries of low-grade and sporadic occupation there ensued. But along the western coast, notably in Kāthiāwāḍ or Saurashtra, and, as it now seems, in the fringes of the Jumna-Ganges *doāb*, elements of the Civilization survived and were variously transmuted into a new chalcolithic small-town phase in western and central India, and into a vigorous and civilized Copper-Bronze Age in the *doāb* itself. There in the earlier half of the 1st millennium BC and in the homeland of the Indian epics flowered Phase II of Indian Civilization, to which the name Ganges Civilization may fitly be applied.

In the latter half of the 6th century BC fresh influences of a civilizing kind entered the north-western corner of the subcontinent in the train of the Achaemenid Kings of Persia, who brought security to the trade-routes thereabouts, prosperity to the towns along them—Begram near Kabul, Chārsada (pl. 27) near Peshāwar, Taxila (pl. 30) near Rawalpindi—and an improved equipment which included coinage and iron. These benefits were not slow in reaching out to the now-flourishing cities of the *doāb*. And there, perhaps in literal imitation of the new metal, the celebrated Northern Black Polished Ware, with its steel-like gloss, came into vogue as a prophetic aid to the archaeologists of the future. The new modes and techniques, however, implied no radical revolution in the life of the great plains which had already several generations of civilization behind it; rather, they confirmed and amplified the trends already at work there.

Phase III might better be described as a sub-phase of Phase II. It represents the southward thrust of the maturing Ganges Civilization towards central India; in particular, to the Narbadā valley, through which an outlet was thus secured to the harbours of the west coast. This thrust occurred not later than the 5th century BC, and may be regarded perhaps as a material aspect of that flowering of the intellect and the spirit which found expression in the outgrowth of Buddhism and Jainism from the same Gangetic homeland.

Phase IV has a more substantive quality. It was, if the evidence is read aright, essentially a product of the southerly extension of the Mauryan Empire from the Ganges at the beginning of the 3rd century BC. Over a congeries of chalcolithic cultures with a strongly microlithic bias swept the fully developed Gangetic Iron Age, represented by emissaries on a sufficiently small scale to absorb local traditions whilst imposing the (literally) iron discipline of the northern civilization. For the moment this advance petered out in northern Mysore, but it later reached the southern end of the Peninsula and, by the 1st century AD, was fully established there, with widespread contacts overseas. Starting at about the same time, that is, the 3rd century BC, it began to spread also down the coastal plains beside the eastern ghats (Ashoka's famous conquest of the Kalingas of Orissa about 264 BC is a key-point), and as far south as the famous Amarāvati on the Krishna river the Northern Black Polished Ware of the Ganges found an ultimate home. The picture of gradual pervasion from north to south is a logical and integral one. Thenceforth, Indian civilization becomes a proper and primary study for the historian, with the archaeologist now in a subordinate role.

IX A CYCLE OF CATHAY

China: the civilization of a single people

WILLIAM WATSON

The traditional sequence and chronology

The Age of the Three Sovereigns
The Age of the Five Rulers

	2852–2205 BC
The Emperor Yao	*2356–2255*
The Emperor Shun	*2255–2205*
The Hsia Dynasty	2205–1766 BC*
The Emperor Yü	*2205–2198*
The Shang or Yin Dynasty	
	1766*–1122 BC
The Chou Dynasty	1122–221 BC
The Ch'in Dynasty	221–206 BC
Empire of Shih Huang Ti	
The Han Dynasty	206 BC–AD 220

* The dates given above are those of the traditional chronology. It is now generally agreed that the defeat of the Shang by the Chou took place in the second half of the 11th century BC. Many scholars accept the year 1027 BC, as we do in this book, for that event. The dates recorded in the histories after 841 BC are accepted as accurate.

The accepted sequence of cultures and dynasties

The chart below presents in visual form the chronology generally accepted by modern scholars. The year 4000 BC has been arbitrarily chosen.

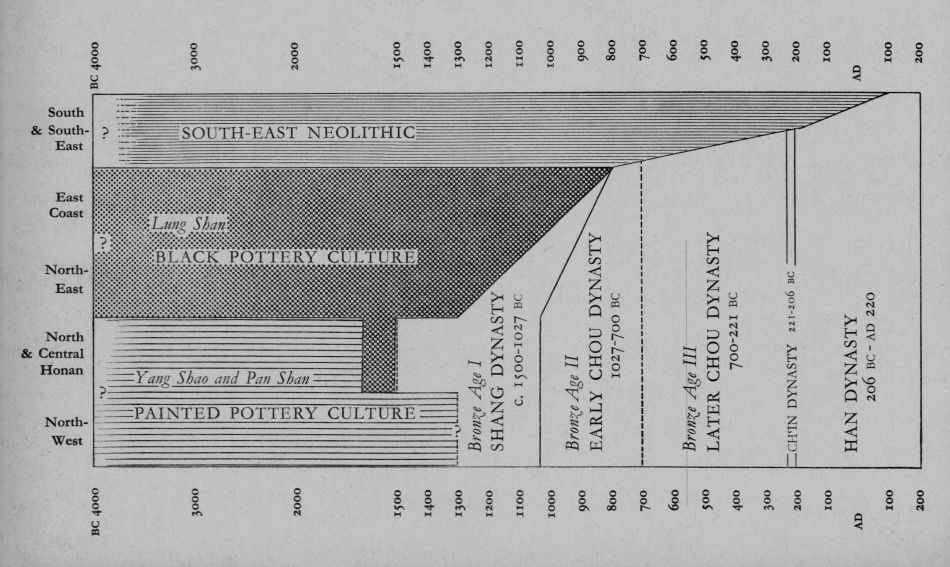

The cradle of Chinese civilization

was the great Central Plain, where the Yellow River in its lower course has spread a thick deposit of fertile alluvium, and where its uncontrollable flooding has caused terrible disasters at intervals throughout Chinese history. Over this plain, and the whole area from the Kansu and Shensi uplands to the sea, between the 35th and 40th parallels, lies the fine, compact earth called loess—the best agricultural soil in the world, which spreads in a broad belt across Asia, across the Russian steppes and the 'black earth' of the Ukraine, right up to the Baltic. Here, in the Central Plain of China, lived the Neolithic farming cultures of the north (roughly, from 4000 to 1500 BC).

Whereas the early civilizations of the West were in a perpetual state of change and development from their beginnings, Chinese culture seems to have persisted in much the same form up to the dawn of the modern world—standing aside from the main stream of history, yet ready to accept external influences and absorb them into its own distinctive pattern. But it should be remembered that between the earliest traces of man in China half a million years ago (the bones and implements of Peking Man in the caves of Chou K'ou Tien) and the first neolithic farming communities there is an archaeological gap, about which little or nothing is known.

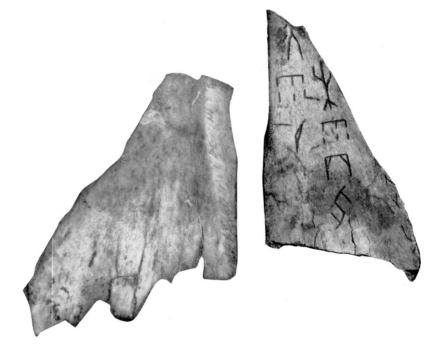

The earliest form of Chinese writing, showing no difference in principle from the script used today, can be seen on the right-hand of the two oracle bones above (c. 1500 BC). This form of oracle-taking is an important link between the Lung Shan Neolithic cultures and the Shang dynasty. Shoulder-blades of oxen, sheep and pigs were used, and sometimes turtle-shells. Shallow round or oval pits were drilled into the bone, and a heated bronze point applied to the edge of them; the resulting cracks on the other side of the bone revealed, to those who could interpret them, the oracle's answer to the question asked. Ideally, these cracks produced a main line with a small spur going off at an angle, from which shape was derived the character that means 'to divine'. The size of the small crack and its relation to the main one determined whether the answer to the question was to be favourable or unfavourable. The subject of the questions might range from the weather (as on the one shown above) to requests for advice about military campaigns; the more important of these oracle bones, with question and answer inscribed on them as on the example shown above, would be stored as a form of state archive. (1)

Funeral urn of the Pan Shan neolithic type (left). Large painted urns of this kind, found in graves and cemeteries along the river valleys of Kansu Province, resemble the Tripolye painted jars of the Caucasian Chalcolithic (see p. 303), and may be evidence of Western influence. They are burnished, and decorated with striking curvilinear patterns in black and crimson paint. (2)

The first Neolithic settlement to have been exhaustively excavated in China is at Pan P'o Ts'un, Shensi Province. The picture on the right shows a hut floor from this site, nearly fifty feet in diameter, lying only a few feet below ground-level. The huts were round or oblong in shape, the round ones being supported by four pillars placed round a central hearth (the post-holes can be seen). The roofs were probably conical, the eaves reaching almost to the ground, where they rested on small posts set closely together (holes for these posts can be seen in the upper left of the picture). The clay debris found scattered on the floors of most of the huts is believed to have been the roof covering, the timbers having perished completely. Not all of the huts uncovered can have been standing at the same time, since their floors overlapped, as do the two illustrated. (3)

The mists of legend were dramatically dispersed by the excavation of the capital of the Shang dynasty near Anyang in north Honan Province. Traditionally, Chinese history begins in a year corresponding to 2852 BC, with nine obviously legendary rulers. Then follow the Hsia, Shang and Chou dynasties. The first of these is nebulous and its existence has been doubted by some historians. With the Shang dynasty, however, we are on firm ground since the excavation of their ancient capital from 1927 to 1936 and after the war (see *fig. 2*, p. 269). Unfortunately treasure hunters (the source of the many fine bronzes of this period in museums all over the world) had been there first, and much disturbed the stratification. Many graves have been found, however, containing bronze and pottery vessels, and numerous storage pits have yielded over 10,000 inscribed oracle bones (see pl. 1). The most striking feature of the Shang dynasty is the astonishing excellence of its bronzes—the earliest bronzes found in China. They are on a level, technically, with the Late Bronze Age of central Europe, and though it is possible that a Chinese 'Early Bronze Age' may yet be unearthed, it seems more likely that the method of casting bronze came from the West. The artistry and technical skill with which the method was applied are wholly Chinese.

The Shang warrior in the reconstruction (right) needed two horses to pull his lightweight chariot. This, which is confirmed by burials of horses and chariots at Anyang (*fig. 10*, p. 273), suggests that the method of harnessing was like that of the ancient Near East, Greece and Rome, in which the weight was borne by the horse's neck, instead of the chest and shoulders—the more efficient method in use in China in the 1st century BC. The attendant carries the Shang *ko*, or halberd, and the chariot is decorated with monster-masks in bronze. The house (whose plan is based on the excavations at Anyang; see *fig. 2*, p. 269) has main timber uprights resting on bronze footings, which in turn rest on foundation stones. (4)

A holocaust of victims accompanied the burials of Shang rulers. The tomb below, excavated at Anyang, shows the central pit for the royal coffin, 14 x 12 metres, with human skeletons arranged round the edge and the skeletons of many horses beside the downward-leading ramp. For plan, see *fig. 4*, p. 270. (5)

Bronze head frontal (opposite, left), similar to those worn by the horses above, but of the early Chou dynasty (10th–7th cent. BC). (6)

The main offensive weapons until the introduction of the sword in the 5th century BC were the spear, and the *ko* halberd shown in the painting above. The bronze halberd blade opposite (centre) dates from the 10th or 9th century BC. (7)

No other country but China could have elaborated a weapon of war into the beautiful ceremonial spearhead opposite (right). Made in the Shang period (13th–12th century BC), it has a white jade blade fitted into a socket of bronze inlaid with a turquoise mosaic. (8)

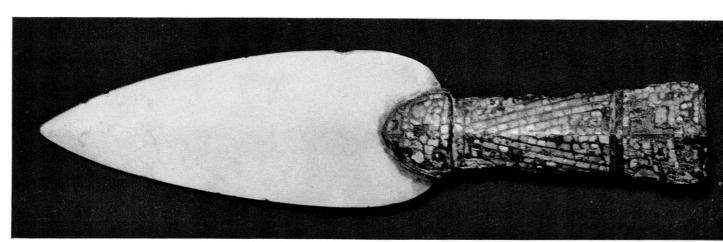

For sacrifices to gods and ancestors highly elaborate vessels were used, whose shape and ornamentation formed a tradition that persisted from the Shang dynasty right through to the Han period, and constituted one of the outstanding arts of the ancient world. Very rarely has a complete set of these vessels been found together; the set above, of early Chou dynasty date (late 11th or early 10th century BC), came from a tomb at Feng Hsiang, Shensi Province. Books composed in the 4th–3rd centuries BC set forth in detail the complicated ceremonial of public and private sacrifice—explaining which vessels were to be used for wine, or water, or food, which for preparing and which for pouring—but probably by the beginning of the Chou period the shapes were not so rigorously prescribed. (9)

Nearly two thousand years before the West mastered the technique of iron-casting, the Chinese were using it—probably from the first introduction of the metal, about 600 BC. The two-piece casting below, from Hsing Lung Hsien, Jehol Province, was used for moulding socketed bronze axe-blades similar to blades used in Late Bronze Age Siberia. (10)

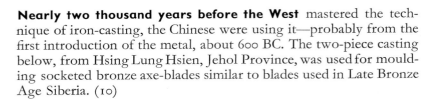

'Ghosts' recovered from the soil. In a Chou dynasty tomb at Liu Li Ko, Honan Province, a surprising discovery in 1950 was a burial (left) of nineteen chariots arranged in two rows, each chariot with its shaft resting on the box of the one in front. The bronze fittings had been removed before burial, and the timber had rotted completely away, but with consummate skill and patience the excavators traced the shape of almost every chariot from the texture and colour of the soil—a feat that calls to mind the excavation of the Sutton Hoo ship burial in England in 1939. The chariots had presumably been part of a funeral procession, and the horses which had drawn them were slaughtered, and buried in an annexe at one end of the pit. Unlike the practice in the Shang dynasty, the charioteers were spared.

Fig. 11, p. 274, shows a reconstruction of one chariot, on the basis of this find. The indications of yokes and shafts suggest that the method of harnessing had not progressed beyond the inefficient use of a neck-band (see pl. 4). (11)

Ornamented with weird animal motifs, the chariot pole fittings opposite (below) were found in a tomb near Loyang, Honan Province, which was the Chou capital. They are richly inlaid with gold and silver, and date to the 5th–4th century BC. (12)

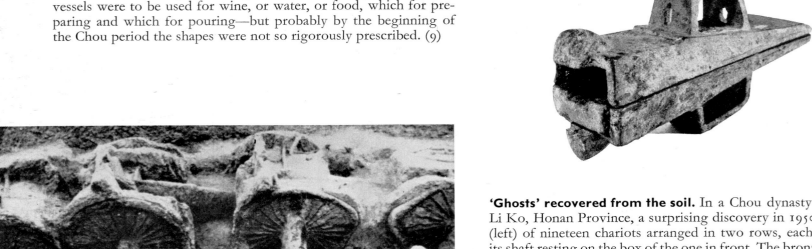

Bronze ritual vessels of late Shang dynasty date (11th century BC). Above, left, is a handled wine-holder of the type known as *yu;* that on the right is a *fang-i*, which is also a wine-vessel. The *yu* shows the monster-mask, or *t'ao t'ieh*, adapted as a motif for decoration. (13, 14)

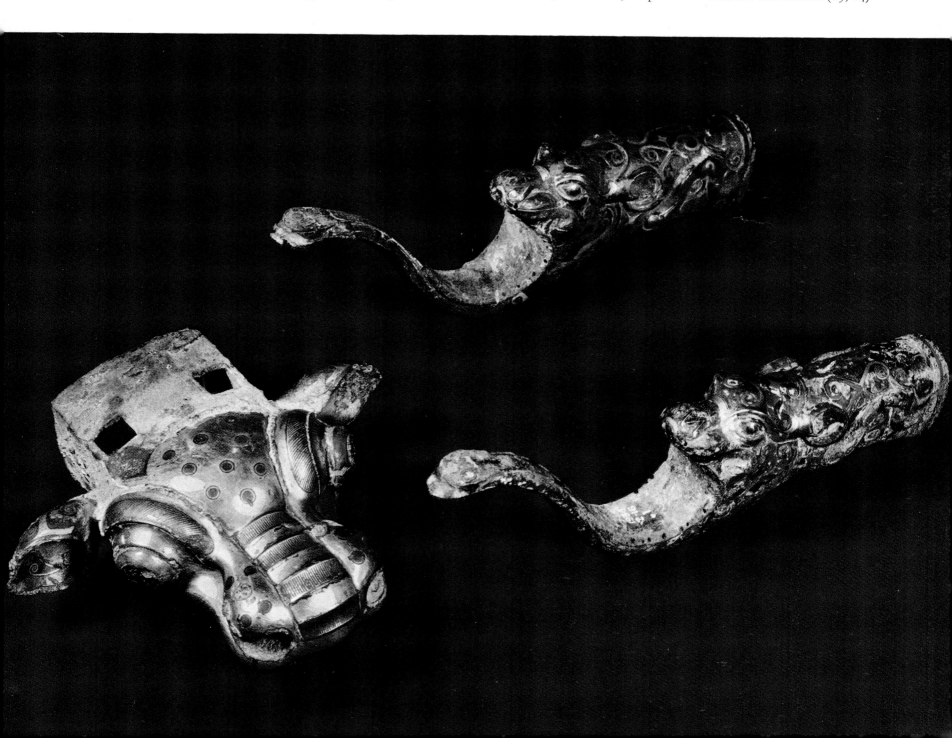

Stylized animal motifs figured largely in sacrificial vessels. The one on the right, a wine vessel of the late Shang dynasty 17 ins. in height (11th century BC), has the form of two rams back to back. (15)

In the fantastic elaboration of its ornament the bronze ritual bell, or *chung*, below must have made considerable demands on the skill of the caster. This is no longer, as in Shang dynasty art, the metal version of motifs invented in softer, carved materials, but one created for metal. Early 5th century BC; just under two feet high. (16)

The Chinese genius for powerful expression in narrowly prescribed forms is as well shown in the bronze coffin handle below as in the mirrors overleaf (pl. 22). This handle, with its intricately worked dragon mask, is 6¼ inches high and dates from the late Chou dynasty, 3rd century BC. (17)

Crude but appealing in its simplicity, this bronze figure of a serving-man (right) was made in the middle of the later Chou period (5th or early 4th century BC), at a time when representation of the human form was still rare, and had not reached a high level of artistic skill. The cylinders were probably intended to hold the stem of a lamp. Height 4¼ ins. (18)

Comparable with the art of ancient Persia, the gold open-work dagger handle below (3.8 ins. high) dates from about 400 BC. By that time, towards the end of the Chou dynasty, goldsmiths, silversmiths and jade cutters were learning, with improved methods of cutting and drilling, to render ornament as fine as any that was cast in bronze. (19)

Nomad tribesmen from the Ordos region of N.W. China made these decorative bronze plaques in the 1st century BC. (The right-hand one is 2.1 ins. high.) With their very different way of seeing things, the steppe nomads left their mark on the art of the Ordos and Hunan, and perhaps influenced the naturalism that was the most characteristic invention of Han art—the lithe tigers, the dragons, horses and crouching bears that we see in bronzes from the 1st century BC onwards. (20)

Gentlemen in conversation. The lacquered basket opposite (above) was found in a tomb at Lolang, a Chinese colony in Korea, and was probably made in the government workshops early in the 1st century AD. In its pursuit of naturalism rather than a formal geometric pattern, Han dynasty art marks the beginning of a new epoch. New conventions and new themes suggest contact with the art of steppe nomads, and possibly, indirectly, with Hellenistic art. (21)

Side by side with the beginnings of naturalism we still see the more abstract designs in Han and late Chou bronze work. Of the three bronze mirror backs opposite (centre), the one on the left, which is early 1st century AD, has a pattern of mythological animals and philosophical symbols; in the centre is a 3rd-century AD example showing the Taoist gods Hsi Wang Mu (Queen Mother of the West) and Tung Wang Kung (King Lord of the East), with a carriage and horses and a cavalry fight; and the mirror on the right is decorated with phoenixes on a background of flowers and scrolls (4th or early 3rd century BC). (22)

Salt-miners and hunters combine in a lively example of Han art (below). Salt was won in Szechwan by drilling for brine (the derrick over the well can be seen on the left), which was then dried out in pans (right foreground). Beyond, hunters are shooting game with cross-bows. Rubbing from a decorated brick, 1st or 2nd century AD. (23)

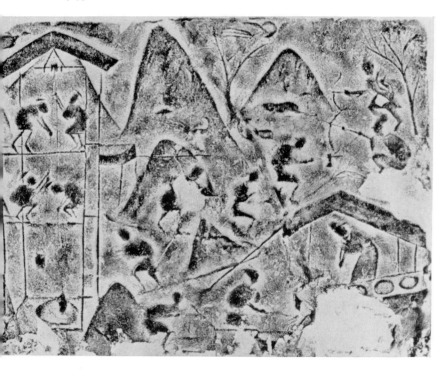

Symbol of a united China. In the 3rd century BC the Chou dynasty went out in a welter of confusion and strife—the period of 'The Warring States'. The short-lived Ch'in dynasty came to power, in the person of Shih Huang Ti ('First Emperor'), whose reign saw, for the first time, a strong and unified rule over the whole area to which Chinese culture had spread. As a defence against barbarian invasion from the north he built the Great Wall, part of which is shown above, seen through one of the postern gates. Fourteen hundred miles long, with 25,000 towers, it is a monumental expression of the Chinese faith in walls as a method of defence. (26)

Workshops controlled by the government in Han times produced lacquered articles for official use and for State gifts, many of them inheriting and adapting the designs of the later Chou bronze work. Opposite (below) are a 1st-century mirror and a lacquered toilet box and lid, the latter inlaid with a quatrefoil and animal figures in silver. Toilet boxes have been found complete with their original contents of wooden comb, hairpins and beads. Much of the lacquered ware from the government workshops has been found in an excellent state of preservation in the damp, sandy soil of Ch'ang Sha, in Hunan. (24)

Myth and legend provided favourite themes for the decorations of tombs in later Han times. The rubbing, right, is taken from stone bas-reliefs at the tomb of Wu Liang, near Chia Hsiang Hsien, Shantung Province. In the upper panel, a man wounded in the knee is shielded from his attacker with a carriage umbrella. In the centre, an attempt is made on the life of the future Emperor Shih Huang Ti. The bottom picture shows the god Fu Hsi (with set square) and his consort Nü Kua (with compasses); both they and their attendants are shown as half human, half serpentine in form. (25)

The lively feast scene on the last two pages has been pieced together from many sources in Han art. The diners, squatting on their
red carpets, recall the figures on the lacquered box of pl. 21. The
attendants, jugglers and musicians can be paralleled in pottery figurines and the stone bas-relief ornamentation of tombs. The construction of the houses in the background follows pottery models found
in Han tombs. Among the plentiful yield of grave-goods from Han
tombs are pottery vessels, figurines, models, mirrors, vessels and
ornaments of all kinds, from which a fairly complete picture can be
gained of the everyday life of the times. This picture has to be derived
mainly from the excavation of tombs, since few ancient cities were
abandoned; their remains lie beneath cities which are still inhabited
today. (27)

Playing the game of Liu Po (the rules of which have not survived)
are three figurines in green glazed pottery (right), from a grave of
the 1st or 2nd century AD. (28)

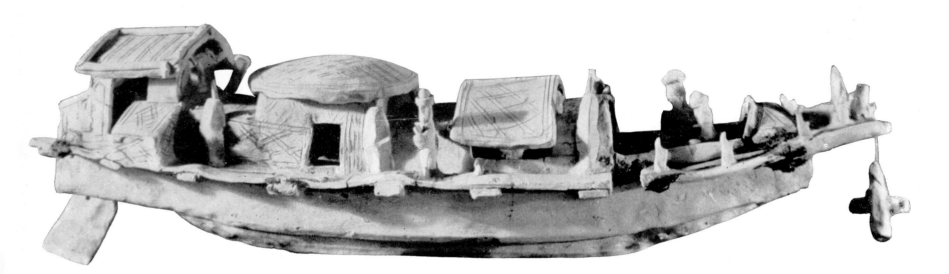

Ancestor of the sampans still to be seen on the Pearl River at Canton, this pottery model boat (above) came from a late Han tomb
(1st century AD) in the eastern suburb of Canton. Like the models
of carriages often found, it represents the conveyance of a rich citizen
or important official. The model, which is 21¼ ins. long, shows a
decked, flat-bottomed boat with deck-houses like those still in use,
roofed with matting and communicating with the 'tween-deck space.
Forward, there are three tholes a side for oars, and the steering oar is
mounted on the port side, in contrast to the starboard mounting
usual in the West. (29)

Pottery model of a farmhouse with a dog and a sheep, from a
tomb of the 1st century AD. (30)

China: the civilization of a single people

WILLIAM WATSON

THE HISTORY OF CHINA is in the main the history of a single people, using a single language and a system of writing that has not changed in principle from its beginning over three thousand years ago. No one has been impressed by the antiquity of their cultural tradition more than the Chinese themselves. Confucians claimed to base their political and moral philosophy on the character and enactments of the early kings of the Chou dynasty. The orthodox list of Chinese rulers—they are supposed to have ruled over the whole country—begins with a calendar year corresponding to 2852 BC. First come the Age of the Three Sovereigns and the Age of the Five Rulers. Many of the kings have a plainly legendary character. Impossibly long reigns are attributed to them. Their valorous deeds in flood-control and their benefactions to humanity, such as the invention of fire and of writing, mark them out as culture heroes; although scattered references to one flood hero called Kung-Kung leave us uncertain whether he started the inundation, stopped it, or aggravated it unintentionally. After the legendary rulers follow the Hsia, Shang and Chou dynasties. The first of these is nebulous and its very existence has been doubted by some historians. The historicity of the Shang was dramatically vindicated by excavation at their capital at Anyang in north Honan. The early centuries of the Chou dynasty, which reigned from 1027 BC (or 1122 BC according to the orthodox chronology), is more fully illustrated from written history, and from 842 BC its events are exactly dateable. The Former and Later Han dynasties (207 BC – AD 220) ruled over a united China almost equalling the modern territory in extent.

Geographical Background

To the West the most characteristic region of China is the great Central Plain, the creation of the Yellow River in its lower course, where it has spread a thick deposit of fertile alluvium, and where its uncontrollable flooding has caused terrible disaster at intervals throughout Chinese history. The Central Plain was the cradle of Chinese civilization. Here arose the high Bronze Age culture of the Shang period, which drew its strength from the populous communities of neolithic farmers already established throughout the plain. It was a river valley civilization, essentially comparable to the civilizations of Egypt and Mesopotamia. But the Central Plain accounts for only a small fraction of the territory we know as China. In general China is a hilly country, in which mountain ranges of great or moderate elevation and of bewildering complexity define and sometimes isolate areas of plain, uplands or plateau, all of which possess their own economic and climatic characteristics. The political and cultural development of the country from the earliest times was determined or influenced by these regional differences.

The earliest cultural exchanges affected the region of the Yellow River Valley in its broadest sense, the territory extending from the coast westward approximately between the 35th and 40th parallels. The westward limit of the Central Plain lies north and south down the middle of the first great loop of the river in its present course (until 1852 it debouched south of the Shantung peninsula). Here the T'ai Hang range, extending from the distant north, divides off the first of the parallel high valleys which constitute the present province of Shansi. Traces of early occupation have been found in these valleys, but the contrast represented historically by the rivalry of the Shang and Chou powers lies between the great plain, the domain of the Shang, and the region forming the southern part of the province of

Shensi. The latter region embraces the lower courses of valleys radiating from the elbow of the Yellow River where it turns north at Sian, and was the home of peoples who united eventually under the leadership of the Chou dynasts. A fertile plateau, grassed and well watered, lies in the lower half of the rectangle formed by the western great loop of the Yellow River. It extends north from the river Wei, bounded on the east by the Yellow River itself, on the west by the Kansu mountains, and on the north and north-west by the waterless desert of the Ordos and Ninghsia. Here millet and barley could be grown as on the great plain, but the upland character of the land suited horse and cattle raising, and to the north and north-west nomadic tribes, like the Mongols of historical times, must have based their wealth on horses, camels and sheep. South of this Shensi plateau, beginning abruptly just beyond the Wei river with the Ch'in Ling Shan, thick-set mountain chains rising intermittently to 2000 metres bar the way to the Szechwan basin, which is watered by four upper tributaries of the Yangtze. Szechwan forms another distinct territorial unit, mountain-locked on almost the whole of its perimeter. To the west lie the all but impenetrable ranges of Sikang and Yünnan which divide China from Burma and the Tibetan plateau.

South and south-west of the eastern loop of the Yellow River is a region of low hills, much dissected by streams, all of which flow into the low-lying, often marshy, valley of the river Huai. Further south, and beyond higher land, is the lower course of the Yangtze, accompanied by its strings of lakes.

Over the whole of the Kansu and Shensi uplands, the Central Plain and the north-western half of the region last defined (Honan province and the north-west of Anhui province) lies the thick deposit of fine compact earth called loess. This fertile soil, laid down it is believed by the action of the wind during the Pleistocene period, in Kansu often reaches a depth of 200 or 300 feet. There it is much eroded into narrow ravines with vertical walls, in places presenting a surface as inconvenient for agriculture as it is for travel and transport. But by its natural fertility and water-holding property the loess, where it lies in less broken expanses, provides some of the best agricultural land n the world. The distribution of the loess corresponds approximately to the areas occupied by the two neolithic traditions of the north: the painted-pottery Neolithic of the Yang Shao culture extending in its two variants from the river valleys of Kansu through south Shensi to north-west Honan, and the Lung Shan culture with its black pottery, whose primary distribution is in the great plain and the adjacent low-lying parts of the Shantung peninsula. We shall note below that similar conditions of terrain attracted the Lung Shan communities into the flat coastal plain of Kiangsu (beyond the limit of the loess) where it mingled with other neolithic traditions. But in the main the lowlands of Anhui and Kiangsu, the lower Yangtze valley and the ramifications of the Yangtze river in Hupei, preserved a distinct economy, in which a greater measure of hunting and fishing accompanied food production, and where pottery traditions were distinct from those of the north. The Neolithic of this region is however less well known, and its connection with the distinct neolithic traditions of Szechwan still needs closer definition.

The south and south-east of China beyond the Yangtze, a country of close-set, though relatively low hills, even in early times more thickly wooded than the north, presents a greater contrast with the territories so far discussed than do any of these with each other. The so-called South-East Neolithic found in the river valleys of Fukien province and in Kuangtung is characterized by stamp-decorated pottery. This is predominantly a culture of food-gatherers, who probably knew nothing of agriculture before the 1st millennium BC, and made it their staple occupation only a few centuries before the beginning of the Christian era. This vast southern tract and much of the territory to the north between the two great rivers, are regions of rice production. Ethnically and linguistically the most important division of the Chinese peoples follows broadly the boundary formed by the Yangtze. The distinctions observable at the present day seem to amount to divisions in a single great race, in which similarities preponderate over the differences. The continued existence of tribes unaffected by Chinese cultures, such as the Miao and the Lolo of the south-west, is a reminder however of a greater ethnic distinction obtaining in the past. Historical records show that peoples allied to these tribes once occupied territory far to the east of their present abode. The spread of Bronze Age culture south from its cradle in the lower Yellow River valley, and with it the influence of China, can be traced archaeologically. It reached the Huai river valley in the 7th century BC, and the Yangtze valley—the domains of the 'barbarian' state of Cu'u—a century or so later. We know little of Chinese civilization in the southern provinces before the Han period, and in so remote a region as Yünnan we can affirm that it did not make itself felt before the first century BC.

The Stone Age

The earliest traces of man in China are the stone tools and bones of *Pithecanthropus pekinensis*, or Peking Man, found in cave deposits at Chou K'ou Tien, south-west of Peking. These provide us with the first clear picture of man the tool-maker (see chap. I). A stage corresponding to the European Upper Palaeolithic is difficult to define; but in Inner Mongolia many sites are found characterized by tools made from small blades of flint and similar stones, and these suggest a parallel with the microliths of the Mesolithic cultures of Europe. The Chinese microliths are often found associated with rough reddish and grey pottery, and in these instances seem to be little if at all earlier than the full Neolithic farming cultures of the Yellow River valley.

The frequency of neolithic remains in the Great Plain and along the river valleys of the western uplands of Shansi, Shensi and Kansu indicates a density of population natural to a region so favourable for food production and comparable to that of the neolithic communities of Egypt and Mesopotamia.

The Neolithic Period: The Yang Shao Culture

This neolithic tradition centres on the middle course of the Yellow River, in Honan and South Shansi. The village site of Yang Shao, after which the culture is often named, is in Honan. The settlements, situated on low river terraces and open flat ground, are closely concentrated, some extending to an area of almost 1,000,000 sq. metres. The depth of their cultural deposits sometimes reaches 4–5 metres. The houses, best known from the village of Pan P'o (pl. 3) in southern Shensi, are founded on a round or rectangular low wall of earth surrounding a floor often slightly lower than the general ground level and supporting wooden stakes. Together with interior wooden pillars these supported a roof of thatch reinforced with clay. In some buildings the interior pillars rested on boulders (a method which is found in use in the Shang period) but the majority were sunk deep in the earth. Evidently the beam and pillar structures characteristic of later Chinese architecture had not been developed. Some floors are dressed with white clay. Inside, clay was used to form ovens, cupboards and benches. Near the huts were deep bag-shaped pits, now found filled with refuse, but having served originally as grain stores. The pottery comprises fine red and grey, and coarse sandy wares, and even a little burnished black and a white-bodied ware. Deep bowls and jars are the common forms. The painted pots, hand-made like the rest, show signs of finishing on a turn-table. Their decoration of geometric figures, painted in black (manganese) or red iron oxide (haematite), was applied on the drying clay before firing, which took place at a temperature of 1000–1400°C. The coarse ware is often decorated with simple incised patterns, or all-over combing or designs impressed from matting. There is no sign of the use of a true potter's wheel *(fig. 1)*.

In tools, chipped stone predominates, though completely polished axes and arrowheads are common enough. The burials are in rectangular earth pits, with the body laid on the back and accompanied by pots and stone tools. The chief grain was millet, traces of which have been found associated with the stone knives used in reaping it. Dogs were kept and pork was an important food. In the north-west the bones of cattle and goats have been found, but the horse was apparently not yet known either here or in the central plain.

The picture which emerges from these findings shows groups of farmers living a comparatively settled life in undefended villages, on fertile soil near to rivers, inhabiting one-roomed huts presumably in family groups, hibernating on their grain store, or supplementing it from fishing and the hunt (pl. 3). Such communities differed from comparable ones in late Neolithic times in south Russia, or late Bronze Age and Iron Age settlements in south England, chiefly by their greater size, closer agglomeration and their superior potting.

If rice was cultivated (the evidence for that is so far slight) we must imagine the close co-operation of individuals which that exacting

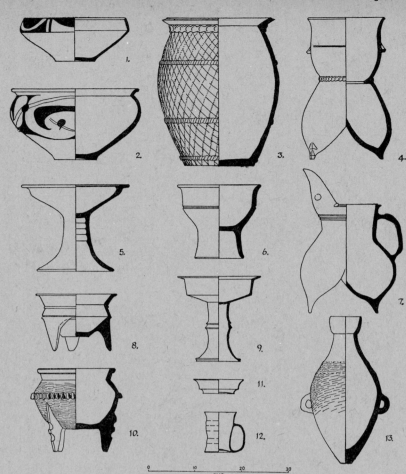

Neolithic pottery types of North China (first half of 2nd millennium BC). 1–5 and 13, Yang Shao. 1 and 2, painted black on red; 3–5 reddish and grey ware; 13, red-ware amphora as found in Shensi. 6–12, Lung Shan. 9–12, burnished black ware; 6–8, black and grey ware. (fig. 1)

labour calls for. Their weapons, at least those with imperishable parts, were the bow and arrow, and probably a sling or pellet-bow. Apart from what is implied in the simple grave-goods, we know nothing of their superstitions and customs, unless we are prepared to project backwards the suggestion of folk-songs collected at a much later date in the Book of Songs, or agree with some rather fanciful interpretations of the abstract patterns of the pot-painting as the festival equipment for ritual games and dances. The only evidences of their art are a moulded human head from the top of an urn from Kansu and the schematic paintings of a human face and of a frog-like creature on pots found at Pan P'o. Even these however show a tendency towards stylization which is a little like the later art of the Bronze Age.

Some important regional variations can be traced within the Yang Shao culture. The chief contrast is between the group of sites in the north-west, in the river basins of Kansu, and those in the central plain. Some of the most beautiful and familiar of Chinese antiquities are the great painted urns of Pan Shan and other burial sites in Kansu (pl. 2). Nothing like them occurs in central China. It was their discovery which prompted some western historians to suppose that there had been a whole cultural and ethnic invasion of China from the far west, where at such places as Anau in Turkestan and at Trialeti in the Caucasus similar painted wares are found: even more striking are the parallels between Pan Shan pottery and that from the Ukraine and Balkans, probably of the third millennium BC (cf. chapter XI, pl. 2). The resemblances are certainly very striking, suggesting some broad influence in one direction or the other, but not enough to justify us in ascribing the whole painted pottery tradition of China to foreign invasion.

The Lung Shan Neolithic Culture

Sites of the Lung Shan culture mark the first appearance of the Neolithic in east and north-east China, where the tradition of painted pottery did not penetrate. They are also numerous in the central plain, especially in Honan province. Here the stratification of deposits proves that the Lung Shan followed the Yang Shao culture, or at least survived later, and was in turn superseded by the Shang Bronze Age.

Whether these neolithic sites with black pottery are as a whole contemporary with or later than the Yang Shao culture is uncertain. There is no doubt however that the thin, hard, black-burnished pottery, made in shapes of angular profile *(fig.1)*, which archaeologists consider as the clearest hallmark of the Lung Shan culture, developed in the east. The site from which it takes its name is in Shantung. It is traced to the north-east as far as Liao-ning province, and down the east coast into Kiangsu. Its western outliers are in Shensi. Tripod vessels of the *li* and *ting* types, carinated bowls, tazzas (shallow bowls) on a high foot, and in the eastern area the strangely shaped *k'uei* are the characteristic shapes found in pottery, much of which was made on a fast-turning potter's wheel. Everywhere the fine black ware is rare; the common pottery was coarser, black, grey, red and occasionally white.

The sites are usually on knolls raised above the plain, or in the low foothills of mountains. The peasants' dwellings, which are known only from excavations in Shensi, appear to have been quite like those we have described from the Yang Shao village of Pan P'o. Dogs, pigs, sheep and cattle were bred, but like their Yang Shao neighbours, the Lung Shan farmers possessed no horses. Of their art we know nothing save the feeling for form which is seen in the elegant shapes of some of the pottery vessels. The type-site of Lung Shan (Dragon Mountain) at Ch'eng Tzǔ Yai in western Shantung which has given its name to this type of culture, is the largest which has been excavated. Here were found bones used in oracle-taking by the same method as that practised in Shang times, though without inscriptions. Potters' marks appear on some of the vessels, but there are no signs of literacy. The stone tools differ from those of Yang Shao in having a larger proportion of polished axes, and the stone sickles are crescentic, a form characteristic of north-east China and contrasting with the oblong stone knives which are the commonest type found on Yang Shao sites.

We can only guess at the duration of the neolithic phase of Chinese pre-history. If we date a Bronze Age as beginning with the introduction of metal-working in central China we may place the end of the Neolithic somewhere in the middle of the second millennium BC, although the neolithic economy of the countryside naturally lasted into later times, in the south even into the Christian era. Archaeologists have not yet succeeded in establishing clear chronological subdivisions of either the Yang Shao or Lung Shan cultures. They can, however, disprove earlier theories of major migrations into China from other and distant parts of Asia. Whatever ideas reached China from outside, in Neolithic times as much as in other periods of her history, were absorbed into the larger complex of indigenous traditions.

The archaeologists' picture of north and central China in the Neolithic period is one of populous communities sharing common traditions. Such cultural coherence can be paralleled in the river valley civilizations of the Near East rather than among the more isolated populations of prehistoric Europe, and, as in the Near East, it was the prelude to a rapid growth of high Bronze Age culture.

The Bronze and Iron Ages: Shang Dynasty to Han Dynasty

Our knowledge of the material culture of the Shang period has come until recent times chiefly from excavation on the site of the ancient capital of the dynasty near Anyang in north Honan. There the city known to its inhabitants as 'Great Shang' covered an area measuring about half a mile from north to south and a quarter of a mile from east to west, bounded to north-west, north and east by a northward loop of the river Huan. On the east the river has now encroached on the ancient precincts. A few hundred yards to the south-east is situated the village of Hsiao T'un, from which the archaeological site takes its name. The remains of the ancient occupation were mostly buried only a few feet underground and their stratification was found to be greatly disturbed by the diggings and probings of treasure hunters—the source of many of the splendid bronzes now preserved in museums all over the world. No trace of a wall or anything resembling a citadel was found, and even the foundations of houses were rarely discernible.

Excavation at Hsiao T'un laid bare a close scatter of storage pits, some carefully constructed with entrance stairways, several yards deep for the most part *(fig. 2)*. In these were found more than 10,000 specimens of inscribed animal bone used in oracle-taking. They are chiefly shoulder blades of ox and the carapaces of tortoise, the latter

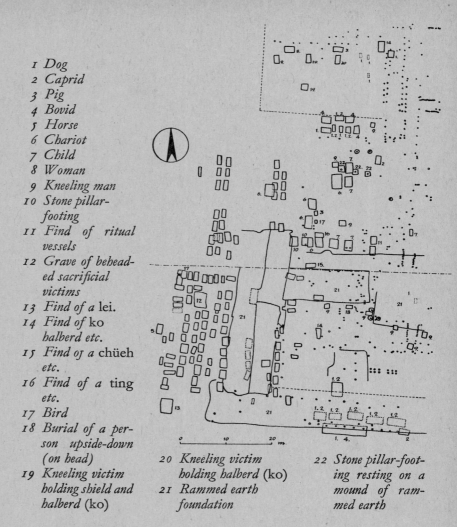

1 Dog
2 Caprid
3 Pig
4 Bovid
5 Horse
6 Chariot
7 Child
8 Woman
9 Kneeling man
10 Stone pillar-footing
11 Find of ritual vessels
12 Grave of beheaded sacrificial victims
13 Find of a lei.
14 Find of ko halberd etc.
15 Find of a chüeh etc.
16 Find of a ting etc.
17 Bird
18 Burial of a person upside-down (on head)
19 Kneeling victim holding shield and halberd (ko)
20 Kneeling victim holding halberd (ko)
21 Rammed earth foundation
22 Stone pillar-footing resting on a mound of rammed earth

Plan of Sector 'C' at Hsiao T'un, near Anyang. (fig.2)

being often distinguished by the length and complexity of their inscriptions. Many graves held bronze and pottery vessels. The most interesting group of building foundations were uncovered in the north-east sector of the site. Here the expanses of compacted earth already identified elsewhere as house flooring appeared on a larger scale, defining elongated buildings up to thirty metres in length set on three sides of a rectangular space. The positions of pillars in one hall were marked by river boulders and a shaped convex cushion of bronze that had served as their footings. More impressive however than these architectural remains were the numerous burials of victims evidently slaughtered in rites connected with the erection or function of the buildings. Men were buried outside the gates, some holding bronze vessels, others facing outwards with halberds in their hands; human victims also at intervals along much of the perimeter of the buildings; dogs singly or in groups, and no less than five burials of chariots with their charioteers in the central court *(fig. 10)*. A similar holocaust of human victims accompanied the burials in the huge cruciform pits, credibly held to be royal tombs, which lay outside the city, mostly beyond the Huan river (pl. 5, *fig. 3, 4*). The deepest part of these tombs measured about 7 metres square, with walls sloping outwards to the top. The principal occupant had been placed in a large wooden coffin lying over a small pit containing the remains of a dog. From two or from all four sides of the pit, beginning at the level of the tops of the coffins, gently sloping ramps led to the surface, each 15 or 20 metres long. On the ramps and around the coffin were laid the bodies of scores of slaughtered human victims and horses, the retinue doomed to accompany the buried king to the nether world. In some instances the human corpses had been beheaded, their bodies laid in order in one place, their heads heaped in another. These unfortunates, it is thought, were prisoners taken in war. Such remains confirm the reality of one of the emblems found cast on some of the bronze vessels: a headless human figure beneath a great axe of a form known from surviving examples.

These dramatic revelations made between 1927 and 1936 confirmed an ancient tradition which located a Shang capital among the fields lying to the north-west of Anyang. The same area had also been recognized as the source of the 'dragon bones', i.e. the ancient oracle bones which Chinese apothecaries believed to be a powerful material

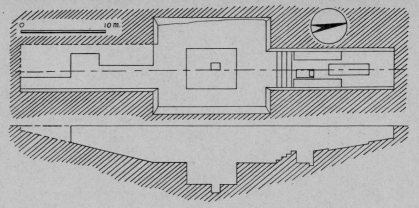

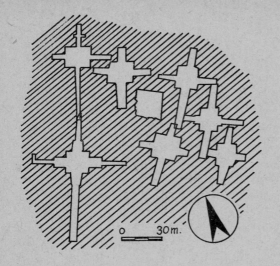

Cruciform shaft-tombs (left), and a shaft-tomb with double ramps. Both near Anyang, Honan Province; 12th–11th centuries BC. (fig. 3, 4)

of medicine. The archaeological interest of these bones was first recognized by Fan Wei-ch'ing in the last year of the 19th century, and the study of them had already reached an advanced stage before excavations were begun by the Academia Sinica. History recorded that the city at Yin Hsü ('Waste of Yin'—Yin being the name by which the Shang dynasts were known to their successors) was not the first capital of the Shang Kings. The establishment of the Shang rule in the north of Honan province followed upon a move from the eastern province of Shantung said to have been effected by P'an Keng, the 17th king. Thus the occupation of the capital at Anyang, covering the reigns of the remaining 11 kings, represents only part, possibly less than a half, of the period which tradition assigns to the dynasty.

In Honan the Shang are found to have discovered bronze and to have mastered the art of using it in a manner comparable to that of the Late Bronze Age of the Mediterranean. Herein lies a problem which is not yet fully solved. Archaeologists have long sought an earlier stage of this civilization. At Chengchou in central Honan the remains of a large Shang city have recently been discovered and are at present still being investigated. Some think that the lower levels of this site are earlier in date than the foundation of the capital at Anyang, but this has not yet been proved. The bronze vessels found at Chengchou are simpler than the majority of those unearthed at Anyang, but they nevertheless indicate considerable skill in bronze casting. Neither at Chengchou nor elsewhere in China have any of the simple tools, such as flat axes and primitive daggers, been found, which are the hallmarks of the earliest Bronze Age culture over the greater part of Asia and Europe. In China an advanced bronze technique seems to spring up unheralded by a related, more primitive stage.

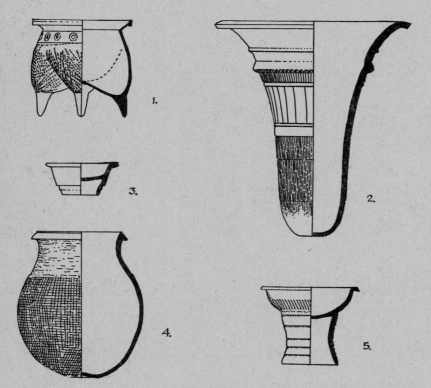

Grey pottery vessels of the Shang dynasty excavated at Chengchou, Honan Province. 1, li; 2, tsun; 3, 5, tou; 4, k'uei. (fig. 5)

Whatever the origins of the Shang dynasts and their ability to work in bronze it is clear that the population over which they ruled was descended, without any traceable foreign admixture, from the preceding neolithic inhabitants of the Central Plain. In north Honan numerous sites have shown a sequence of Yang Shao, Lung Shan and Shang potteries. At other sites the two Neolithic cultures appear intimately combined. The coarse grey-pottery tradition which is common to both survived to provide the basis of the pottery of Shang *(fig. 5)*. The *li* and *ting* tripods continued to be made in this ware and were copied in bronze. Some of the black-burnished pottery shapes of Lung Shan can be paralleled among the bronze vessels.

After the recent years of intensive archaeological reconnaissance in central and north China it is difficult to believe that a hitherto wholly unknown stage of Bronze Age culture will be unearthed. We are forced to the conclusion that the knowledge of bronze metallurgy, admittedly introduced from western Asia, spread rapidly among a people of strong cultural and artistic traditions. Almost at once the new technique was used to produce vessels of refined form and elaborate ornament. This ornament, in the rendering and in the character of the motifs, seems to be derived from carving executed in softer materials. Some surviving fragments of carved wood and ivory are treated in quite the same manner, and the decoration of the white Shang pottery can be approximately matched on the bronze vessels.

But if the groundwork of the Shang bronze-using culture was furnished by the preceding Neolithic, particularly that of the north-eastern Lung Shan tradition, there is still much left to explain apart from the discovery of bronze-casting. In spirit the art represented belongs to the great zone of flat carving in wood and gourd which in recent times has been found to embrace the whole of South-East Asia and the islands. In the presence at Anyang of bronze animal-headed knives and socketed ('bag-shaped') axes there are signs of contact with the early Bronze Age populations of South Siberia *(fig. 6)*. The socketed axes are close to east-European types, and mark the easternmost spread of a tool type invented far to the west of China. The characteristic bronze spearhead of Shang too is related to western shapes, although it may have flanges extended down the socket in a style peculiar to China, just as the socketed axe may be decorated with the *t'ao t'ieh* monster mask which is wholly Chinese.

One of the striking links between the Shang culture of Anyang and that of Lung Shan at the type-site in Shantung is the practice of divination by burning bone. At Lung Shan the shoulder-blades of cattle are found pitted and burnt so as to produce crack-lines which could be interpreted by the augur. At Anyang the process is more regular; and the bones are often inscribed with the augurs' questions, and sometimes with the answers (pl. 1). On the flat surface a small circular pit was bored, and this was sometimes overlapped with an oval pit. A heated bronze point was then applied to the edge of the pit and observations were taken from the cracking which resulted on the other side of the bone. Ideally these cracks consisted of a main line with a small spur going off at an angle, producing the shape which is used for the character 'to divine'. The relationship of angle, shape and size of the small crack to the large determined the answer, which might then be inscribed as 'favourable' or 'unfavourable' after the question. These for the most part concerned rain, the success of crops, the advisability of undertaking hunts or military campaigns or of allowing royal comings and goings of every sort. How far the king himself was looked on as a god is not clear, but the spirits of his ancestors, in a scale of descending importance as the list of them reached back to the beginning of the royal rule of Shang and beyond, were very real gods. On their favour,

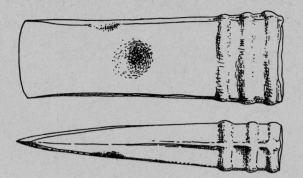

Shang dynasty bronze axe, related typologically to late Bronze Age axes of South Siberia. (fig. 6)

won by regular sacrifice, the welfare of the state depended. Important 'oracle-bones' were stored after use as a kind of state archives.

The inscriptions engraved or, more rarely, painted in black with a fine brush on the bones, are the earliest form of Chinese writing. The principles of the script do not differ from those of modern Chinese writing, though a reform in the 2nd century BC has obscured the meanings of the greater part of the older stock of symbols. Out of some 5000 ideographs in use in Shang times only about 1500 can now be clearly interpreted. Some consist of simplified or partial representations of objects, standing for the objects themselves or often for some word close in pronunciation to the name of the thing depicted; others are conventional signs. But a great part of the vocabulary consists of paired elements, their association conveying the idea, or one denoting the class of object, i.e. acting as a determinative, while the other suggests the pronunciation. This last method is the rarest in the oracle sentences, but later it predominated. It is clear that the language was in all respects the Chinese of historical times, monosyllabic, uninflected and dependent on word order for relating the parts of speech *(fig. 7)*.

The questions inscribed on the bones are brief and follow set forms, e.g.:

Day *kuei mao*, oracle examined; augur Huan; sacrifice of a dog to the ancestor *Chia*?

Kings' names are found in lists of ancestors to whom sacrifice is contemplated, the oracle being asked—as in the example quoted—to declare the appropriateness of the sacrifice. From the sentences a royal succession has been reconstructed which agrees almost completely with the king-list handed down in the histories.

The sacrifice lists also reveal that the succession was from elder to younger brother. Only in the last four generations is there any continuous succession from father to son. Consequently, although the Shang kings number 30, they represent only 18 generations. The day of sacrifice is denoted in the sentences by a combination of two symbols, the first taken from a series of ten and the second from a series of twelve (the *kuei mao* of our example). The total of combinations gave a cycle of 60 days' length. From the 2nd century BC the same symbols were to be applied to the years of the calendar. The kings were designated posthumously by one of the symbols of the series of ten (the *Chia* of our example) and sacrifice was made to them on the corresponding day of the ten-day 'week'. Such material confirmation of ancient traditions naturally invites a re-examination of the evidence for the historical existence of the Hsia dynasty which is said to have preceded the Shang. But here archaeological research has failed to help the historian. As far as excavated evidence is concerned there is nothing to contradict the possibility that the whole

concept of the Hsia dynasty was a fabrication of scholars in the 4th and 3rd centuries BC.

Ancestors were not the only spirits to whom the official sacrifices were offered. The chief deity recorded in the inscription is Ti or Shang Ti ('supreme Ti') a name which originally may have denoted merely an important sacrifice. In China as elsewhere in the ancient world we detect the tendency to turn the concept of a sacrifice into a deity. Other gods occur in the oracular sentences: Eastern Mother, Western Mother, Ruler of the Four Quarters. Sacrifices are made to East, West and South, but inexplicably, not to the North. One record of an offering of four cattle to the source of the Huan river seems to reflect more closely the animistic beliefs held by the common people, just as the augur-priest and the *shih* or 'corpse' who impersonated the deity at some functions are equivalent to the *wu* or shamans of the village. Since so many of the questions put to the oracle concerned political and military affairs, the augur-priests must have wielded considerable influence in these matters. The government of Shang was to some extent a theocracy.

Shang rule probably extended eastwards across the central plain of China to the Shantung region, and westwards to the western end of Honan province. Its influence cannot have passed to the south beyond the Yangtze, or spread far among the nomadic populations lying to the north. Sites at which the coarse grey pottery of the Shang period has been discovered do not extend far beyond the southernmost reach of the Yellow River, or westward beyond its junction with the Wei at the point where the provinces of Shansi, Shensi and Honan join. Of military organization we know nothing beyond a hint at the existence of a royal bodyguard and the practice of securing the help of provincial rulers against others of their number who had to be subjugated.

The life of the Shang population can have differed little in essentials from that of the populous city-states of Bronze Age Mesopotamia. The towns were citadels of a ruling class which enjoyed a monopoly of bronze-craft and consequently of the most efficient weapons which included the chariot. Metal was little used for tools and not at all for agricultural implements. The peasants' equipment had not advanced beyond the neolithic level; their stone reaping-knives were to persist in use until they were replaced by iron sickles half a millennium later. The fields were tilled with the digging stick and wooden spade. In the towns bronze was the material of chariot-fitments (less as structural parts than for display), of ritual vessels and other appurtenances of the official rites. As in Mesopotamia, these objects were buried with their owners, presumably for their use in a life beyond the grave, although no explicit ideas on this subject can be gleaned from the oracle sentences.

The idea that there was then a closely knit state is probably an invention of later times. The direct rule of the king can have reached only a short distance from his city walls. Beyond, an outer zone of peasant villages might be subject to overlords appointed by the king (the evidence for the beginnings of a feudal system seems to belong to the very end of the Shang rule), and farther still was an ill-defined area in which Shang rulers had from time to time to dispute their right of suzerainty with other powers.

One such power, established along the river valleys and on the uplands of Shansi and Shensi, was that of the Chou chiefs. It was their attack on Great Shang in 1027 BC that overthrew the corrupt Chao, last of the Shang kings, and founded a new dynasty.

The traditional view of Chinese historians is that the Chou rulers were primitive barbarians who were civilized by inheriting the culture of the Shang people. But it is improbable that the river valleys and highlands which were the homes of the Chou confederacy before their eastward move stood on a much lower cultural

The earliest form of Chinese writing, as found on the oracle bones, with translation and (below) modern equivalents. (fig. 7)

ox	goat, sheep	tree	moon	earth	water	tripod vessel (ting)	To show, declare	field (showing divisions)	then (man and bowl)	ancestor (phallus)	to go against, towards	heaven	to pray
	羊	木	月	土	水	鼎	示	田	就	祖	逆	天	祝

Chou dynasty pottery, showing forms typical of the 5th–4th centuries BC. The painted decoration of the tou *on the right is in black, white and red. (fig. 8)*

level at the time of the conquest than the Shang state itself. It is interesting that the oracle sentences contain no hint of an attack by Chou on Shang, but suggest on the contrary that the Shang ruler provoked attacks on Chou by other tribes, or at other times conferred the title of marquis on the Chou ruler and accepted him as a subordinate.

There are records in history and in the inscriptions cast on bronze vessels of Chou campaigns as far as the eastern seaboard. It seems that garrisons were established throughout the country under loyal commanders who in the first instance were the close associates of the Chou kings. Some hundreds of small city-states were founded, all acknowledging the suzerainty of Chou in a form of feudal hierarchy. The residence remained however at Tsung Chou in Shensi until 771 BC, when it was moved to a pre-existing Chou city near the modern Loyang. Around the new capital lay the small state directly governed by the Chou king. By now the great underlords and rulers of provinces had coalesced into some twelve major states whose allegiance to Chou was little more than formal. The king at the centre was only one factor in an uneasy balance of power. He had the duty of performing the national sacrifices to heaven and earth: his role as source of honours and material rewards for services rendered by feudal lords and ministers is commemorated in thousands of inscriptions made by the recipients on bronze vessels which were eventually deposited in their graves. Increasingly, the great feudal states engaged in internecine war.

In the western uplands of the Chou homeland horse-raising had been important probably even in Shang times. In the 9th century a Chou noble is recorded as receiving 600 horses from the 'Jung' barbarians of the north-west. It is of interest to find that the decoration of some bronzes found in the burials of chariots at Anyang, although apparently dating to the end of the Shang period, is more akin to the art of the Chou as it appears in the late 11th and 10th centuries. In these chariot graves too are found the animal-headed knives and an unexplained bow-shaped object (in our reconstruction, pl. 4, interpreted tentatively as a shield mount) which can be paralleled in the

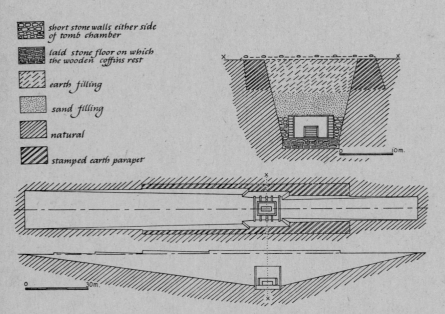

short stone walls either side of tomb chamber

laid stone floor on which the wooden coffins rest

earth filling

sand filling

natural

stamped earth parapet

Shaft tomb with double ramps at Ku Wei Ts'un, near Hui Hsien, Honan Province. The burial chamber and coffin are shown in plan and in elevation on both axes. Late 5th or 4th century BC. (fig. 9)

Bronze Age finds of the Minusinsk basin in South Siberia. Conversely, the graves of corresponding date in Minusinsk contain for the first time skulls of pronounced Chinese type. It is perhaps not surprising that the horse-raisers of north-west China should have been in touch with tribes of similar livelihood in Siberia, even across the Gobi desert. The charioteers of the Shang must have been recruited with their horses from the western provinces, and consequently display features in their equipment which have Chou rather than Shang affinities. The date of the Shang chariot graves, of the bronze parallels with South Siberia and of the appearance there of the Sinoid skulls need not be earlier than the 12th or 11th century BC *(fig. 10)*. The comparatively rare socketed axes found at Anyang also resemble closely axes from Minusinsk, although their decoration with Shang-style animal masks proves that they were made in Honan. In their Shensi river valleys the Chou tribes could benefit by cultural borrowing both from Central China and from South Siberia.

How far the inhabitants of north-west China at the time of the Chou conquest differed racially from the population of the Central Plain is quite uncertain. The theory that they were of the stock from which descended the Turkish people of later times is supported to some extent by historical tradition. Arguments based on nomenclature connect them with the supposed ancestors of the Hunnish tribes which appear in the fuller light of history from the 2nd century BC onwards. The attacks by barbarians on the northern frontier were probably caused as much by the expropriation of nomadic tribesmen by the expanding Chinese agricultural community as by organized invasion from without, at least in the earlier centuries of the Chou period. True 'steppe nomadism', the life of horse-raising, tent-dwelling tribes, despisers of tillage and harriers of the settled peasants within the area of Chinese control (eventually within the line of the Great Wall), seems not to have arisen until late in the history of Chinese expansion to the north and north-west, in the 5th – 4th century BC. Thereafter the attacks of the nomads caused unceasing trouble and expense to the Chinese.

The state religion of Chou times centred on sacrifice to Heaven and Earth. Its chief instruments were still the bronze vessels in which meats and wine were offered to cosmic and ancestral spirits. The supreme deity was 'Heaven'—T'ien—a more abstract conception than the Shang Ti of Shang times, and one related, according to some, to the heaven-worship of the ancient Turks. The royal succession was now regularly from father to son. A vast ceremonial was elaborated in which the Chou king played the leading role and on which the peace of the realm and the abundance of crops were deemed to depend. Books composed in the 4th–3rd centuries BC, the *Li Chi* and *I Li*, set forth the order of public and private sacrifice and ritual, including the mortification of filial mourning as prescribed by Confucianism, in a loving detail which smacks of the professional ritualist. *Li* which we translate by 'ritual', though as well as the outward forms it implies a whole philosophy of ordered social intercourse and hierarchic submission, was regarded as the principle on which civilization and political well-being rested. Heaven was thought to work in harmony with human affairs, reacting with disasters against misbehaviour of rulers and subjects, but particularly of the former. The king was such by the mandate of Heaven. The royal tombs no longer contained slaughtered victims.

We now know something too of the spiritual doctrine of the Chou period. After death a man was deemed to have two souls, the *hun* which departed hence and the *po* which lingered by the tomb. The *po* had to be nourished by food offerings, until it gradually faded to nothing. But these concepts, with which in his time Confucius, while not denying their existence, would no more concern himself than with the question of other gods and spirits, received little attention from the educated class. In royal as in private ritual no priests were employed, the king and the head of the family taking charge of the sacrifices. The religion of sacrifice and *Li* was the creed of the 100 Families—*pai hsing*—as the local rulers came to be called. The commonalty, the 'black-haired people' as the Chou warlords had called them from the start, preserved their old animistic beliefs. In the villages the *wu* still practised his healing and necromantic art, and the spirits of hill and stream had their due offerings.

By the 7th century BC the central Chou state, in theory controller of subordinate states, was reduced to puppet status and although maintained as a ceremonial head was held ransom to the most powerful state of the day. From the beginning of the 7th century this was Ch'i, the state occupying the rich agricultural plains and low hills of Shantung, a centre of trade in salt and in the metal ores which reached it by river from the south. In 704 BC the ruler of Ch'u, a state which embraced a huge territory extending from central Honan to the lake region on the middle Yangtze, had arrogated the title of king—*wang*—in defiance of his theoretical feudal status. The rivalry of Ch'in and Ch'i in the north, the increasing pressure of Ch'u from the south, the varying alignments of the smaller states, including Chou, as they sought protective alliances with different major powers, barbarian inroads such that of 660 when nomads devastated the north Honan state of Wei—constitute the characteristic political order and disorder of the whole of the later Chou period.

With the rise of Ch'u begins the incorporation of the south into Chinese culture, accompanying the spread of irrigation farming and bronze technology among peoples just emerging from a tribal hunting economy. In the period aptly called by Chinese historians 'The Warring States' (403 – 221 BC) the internecine warfare grew still more intensive. A new factor was the aggression of the western hill-state of Ch'in against the central states. This led to the unification of the empire in 221 BC under the Ch'in emperor Shih Huang Ti. When this emperor built his famous Great Wall he was joining stretches of pre-existing walls constructed in the 4th and 3rd centuries BC against the nomad attacks which the unsettled state of China now attracted (pl. 26). Throughout these centuries tens of thousands of soldiers (if not the hundreds of thousands spoken of in the histories) were engaged in single battles.

The states could exploit their manpower on an unprecedented scale, as in constructing the canal dug in the 5th century BC to link the basin of the lower Yangtze with that of the Yellow River, or later in the building of the Great Wall. The transport, storage and distribution of grain to the dense population crowding the valleys, which was constantly exposed to flood and famine, was already an important factor in political control. For all this vast coercion of the population by the warring lords, no regular slave system was instituted comparable to that of Italy in the early centuries of the Roman empire. In the domination of unarmed and pacific peasants it was unnecessary. Such slavery as existed was domestic, in the form which survived till recent times. Even under the Shang dynasts, despite the description of that period by present-day Chinese historians as a slave-state, there is no evidence that slave-holding was an essential feature of government or agriculture.

In these troubled times lived Confucius, whose philosophy is a system of ethics for a ruling class, formulated from ideas current in his day. To metaphysics and logic he was indifferent. Moral integrity, loyalty and fearless advocacy of just and selfless rule are the distinctive characteristics of the Chüntzŭ, the 'superior man'. Confucius' *Tao*, or 'Way', a rational cosmic order with which rulers and subjects must passively conform in the interest of peace and welfare, is akin to the old conception of a Heaven reacting to human affairs. It is enough for the ruler to attune himself to it, and take no active measures, for political order to be restored. Such harmony with the principle can only be achieved by minute attention to the rites and ceremonies collectively designated *Li*. Confucius reasserted an ancient feudal morality against the opportunism and turbulence of the rulers of his day.

Mencius (c. 372–289 BC), like Confucius a spokesman for the literati of east China, developed the Confucian philosophy towards a less exclusive humanism. He introduced the notion of 'human-heartedness' as ideally governing social relations, and stated more explicitly that the will of Heaven in the choice of a successor to the Chou paramount kingship would be declared through the voice of the 'people', i.e. of the ruling class and their clients, the literati and land-owners. He comes near to recognizing the principle asserted by later Confucian apologists of China's dynastic revolutions, that subjects have a right, even a duty, to rebel against a corrupt ruler. The theory of the command of Heaven investing a king is very different from the divine right of European monarchs.

In Motzŭ (c. 479–381 BC) we find a determined opponent of the Confucian idea: for him family affection must be extended to all mankind—universal love and pacifism are proposed as the cures for the ills of the times. At about the same period is said to have lived Laotzŭ, whose philosophy urges man to surrender his will to the cosmic process of the Tao, in a spirit far removed from the positive ethic of Confucius. The quietist and anti-rational tenor of his

philosophy has attracted an interest in the west in recent times almost comparable to that which Confucian concepts held for the French *philosophes* of the 18th century.

Weapons and Warfare

Besides bronze and pottery vessels, the tombs of Shang and Chou date preserved large numbers of weapons. Those of the Shang period are surprising for their small range of types and their relative simplicity. Bronze swords and daggers are not yet found, and bronze spearheads are comparatively rare. The principal weapon was the bow, of the so-called compound type, built with separate strips of wood furnished with bone or bronze-tipped arrows; and the halberd called *ko* (pl. 4, 7).

The latter has been compared to some long-bladed axes found in south Siberia, but the resemblance is not close. Nor does it derive very clearly, as has been argued, from a form of stone axe. With minor modifications it was retained in use as an important weapon until the Han period. Together with the spear, and like it mounted on a staff 5 or 6 feet long, it furnished the chief arm in close fighting until the general adoption of the sword in the 5th century BC.

Burial of a chariot, with charioteer and horses, found near Anyang, Honan Province. Late Shang Dynasty, 12th–11th centuries BC. (fig. 10)

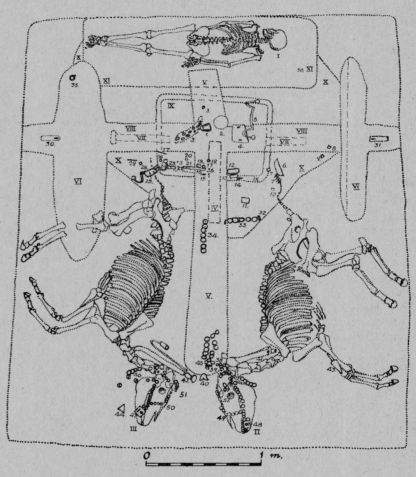

I Human skeleton. II, III Skeletons of horses. IV Trace of timber of the shaft. V Trench made to receive the shaft. VI Trenches made to receive the wheels. VII Trace of timber of the axle. VIII Trench cut to receive the axle. IX Trace of lower timbers of the box. X Traces of red lacquer paint. XI Black ashy soil.

1 Bronze bell. 2 Gold foil. 3 Cowrie shells. 4 Bronze plaque. 5 Bow-shaped object of bronze. 6 Stone blade. 7 Bronze arrowheads. 8–10 Bone tubes. 11 Bone arrowheads. 12 Socket of a bronze axe. 13 Bronze chisel. 14–15 Bronze arrowheads. 16 Bronze knife. 17 Stone point. 18 Bone tube. 19 Domed disk of mother-of-pearl. 20 Bone tube. 21 Disk of mother-of-pearl. 22 Fragments of stone point. 23 Bone ornament. 24 Bone tube. 25 Bow-shaped object of bronze. 26 Domed disk of mother-of-pearl. 27 Bone ornament. 28 Bone tube. 29 Tang of bronze arrowhead. 30–31 Bronze axle-caps. 32 Bone ornament. 33 Eight domed disks of bronze. 34 Seven domed disks of bronze. 35 Bronze ring with spur. 36 Bronze arrowhead. 37 Bone tube. 38 Bronze domed disks (about 58). 39–40 Bronze ornaments from the yoke. 43–44 Triangular plaques of bronze. 45 Bronze domed disks (17 in number). 46 Ditto (about 58). 47–48 Bronze cheek-pieces. 49–50 Bronze domed disks. 51–52 Bronze ornaments from horses' foreheads.

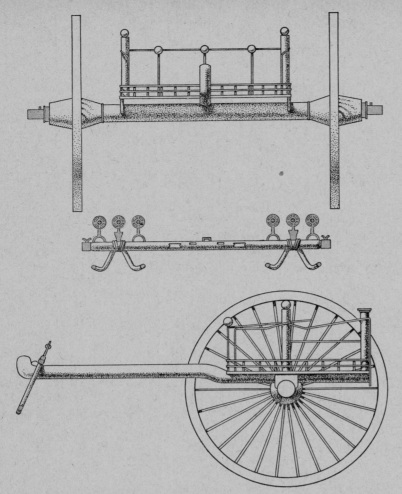

Reconstruction of a 4th century BC chariot, from traces found in the Liu Li Ko tomb of pl.11. (fig.11)

From the later part of the Shang dynasty and in the early centuries of the Chou period we must suppose however that the chariot was the determining factor in warfare. It was used, as in Greece and the Near East, mainly to convey soldiers who dismounted to fight. Over the central plain, where paths were quickly made, the mobility of the chariotry gave the Chinese decisive superiority over their chariotless enemies. In the 8th century it is recorded that the forces of the state of Ch'eng fought with chariots against the foot soldiers of the Jung tribes. The Shang chariot was constructed in all essential parts of wood: a simple rectangular frame carried, above, the floor of the box, measuring only about 4 ft by 3 ft, and, beneath, the axle beam and the shaft engaging in it at the centre. A yoke-beam rested on the necks of the two shaft-horses, which presumably exerted their pull on neck bands, as in the classical chariot of the Near East. In pulling they must have tended to choke themselves and their effort was reduced accordingly: hence sometimes the necessity of the outer pair of trace-horses—four horses in all to draw the comparatively light load of two soldiers and their weapons. The wheel rims were of wood, bound with perishable material, and encircling slender spokes (pl. 4, 11, fig. 10, 11).

The use of the fighting chariot must have declined in the 4th and 3rd centuries BC, when infantry fought the internecine battles. At the same time the nomads began to harry the northern marches with cavalry, and the Chinese had to oppose horsemen of their own. The defence of the Great Wall was chiefly in the hands of infantry, armed from Han times onward with powerful cross-bows. From Han times we have many representations of carriages for civilian use, which differ from the older chariots in an important particular: in spite of an increased load, they are drawn by only two horses, which by a new arrangement are enabled to exert their pull against a band retained against the chest and shoulders. The tendency to choke the animals is avoided, and the efficiency of the European hard horse-collar is anticipated by some eight or nine centuries.

Short bronze swords, some of them tanged for hafting, but mostly having a grip cast on, appear towards the end of the 6th century BC. At first they are little more than dirks. The typical sword of the 4th century is little different from the *akinakes* of the steppe nomads, to whom it probably owes its introduction into China. It seldom exceeds 24 ins. in length, and has a cast ribbed handle which was bound with

cord. The slight, sudden narrowing of the profile about one-third of the length from the points, as seen in many of the blades, recalls the 'carp's tongue' finesse which is a feature of some late Bronze Age swords in Europe.

Although the use of iron had been known from the 7th century BC, for long it was only cast (pl. 10). The earliest iron tools so far excavated are dated to the 5th century BC, but meantime swords and halberds, the principal armament, continued to be made of bronze. In the late 4th or the 3rd century BC iron began to be forged—the priority of casting making a strange contrast with the order of development in Europe—and long iron swords appeared for the first time. They were used by the soldiers of Ch'u, and later by the Ch'in armies.

In the later 3rd century a new type of sword appeared, apparently an enlarged version of a knife-shape also of north-western, nomad origin. The blade is single-edged, barely tapered, and terminates at the handle in an oval ring. These swords were made both of bronze and iron, and the longest of them exceed 4 feet. Double-edged blades with tangs for hafting and of equal length are also known in both metals, and apparently are contemporary with the single-edged kind. But bronze versions of the new long sword are rare; they copy the iron sword in size, but naturally they could not equal it in toughness or in hardness and thinness of the cutting edge *(fig. 12)*.

We know little yet of the economic and military effects of the introduction of iron in the early centuries of its use. It is an interesting speculation, and one which archaeologists may eventually verify, that the Ch'in armies owed their decisive might to their monopoly of the long iron swords. Shih Huang Ti is said to have melted down the bronze arms taken from his enemies to make ten human images; if his troops were armed with the iron sword, the shorter bronze sword would be of no use to them. Certainly after the unification, and in Han times, the chief weapons were regularly made of iron. An exception is the cross-bow lock, whose intricate mechanism could still be cast only in bronze. Its invention probably soon after 200 BC marks the last important advance in armament before the production of firearms. The cross-bow was as important in the stabilization of the north-west frontier as the Wall itself *(fig. 13)*.

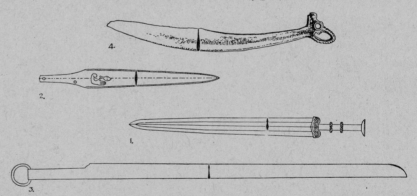

Bronze weapons. 1: Sword, 5th–4th centuries BC. 2: 'Hand and serpent' tanged sword, 6th–5th centuries BC. 3: Single-edged sword, 3rd century BC. 4: Animal-headed knife, 11th century BC. (fig.12)

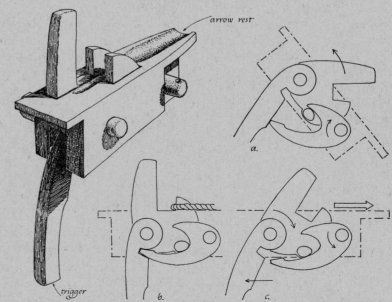

Bronze crossbow mechanism, 1st or 2nd century AD, and method of cocking. The cross-bow came into regular use in China in the 1st century BC. (fig.13)

Types of bronze sacrificial vessels of the late Shang dynasty, 13th–12th centuries BC. Nos. 1, 2, 3, 5 and 6 are for wine, 8 for water, and the remainder for food. (fig. 14)

Han dynasty pottery of the 1st century BC to the 1st century AD. (fig. 15)

The Artistic Tradition

The art of the Shang and Chou periods finds its fullest expression in the bronze vessels. They are hardly to be matched for beauty of form and decoration and skill of execution at any other time or place in the ancient world. The shapes of the vessels were no doubt derived in the first place from the pottery vessels *(fig. 5, 14)*. The *ting* and *li* descend from the characteristic pottery shapes of the north-eastern Neolithic, while the *k'uei*, which became the commonest form after the Chou conquest, copies a shape found in the grey pottery of the central plain. But shapes such as the *chüeh*, *chia* and *kuang*, specially characteristic of the Shang, are difficult to imagine in any material but bronze. In proportions and profile the best vessels show a command of plastic effect which raises them to the level of great art (pl. 9, 13, 14). The ornament is adapted to the most elaborate forms with consummate skill, enriching the surface and enhancing the relief. Yet the vessels were repetitious craft products, in which stock ornamental motifs appear in but a few combinations and variation of shape was permitted only within narrow limits. Nevertheless in the Shang period and in the earliest decades of the Chou dynasty the finest pieces show a feeling for form, rooted in but transcending utility, which can be compared with the porcelains of the Sung period. The skill displayed in adapting animal shapes to the requirements of a vessel and to the resources of ornament is repeated in the neat adaptation of ornament to ritual axes and knives, weapons and the decorative plaques which were fixed in the dashboards of chariots (pl. 4, 12, 15, 19).

From the start, in the vessels which from their comparative simplicity appear to be earlier than the bulk of material excavated at Anyang, the *cire perdue* method was used in casting. Direct casting in a pottery mould was practised also, and for rendering ornament equally fine, but the wax technique was more general. The bronze

alloy differs from that of most of the rest of the Bronze Age world in the greatly varying quantity of tin which it contains. The difficulty of bringing the ore from its source in the central and southern hills may be the cause, but even at a later period, when this region was fully controlled, the ingredients of the metal are not constant. On the other hand, the large proportion of lead included in the bronze, particularly in that of Shang date, must be a deliberate addition. By helping the flow of the molten metal and preventing gas bubbles it improved the rendering of detailed ornament. Its effect on colour was to reduce the metallic brilliance of the reddish surface: for we must picture the vessels in their original state without the beautiful green and blue patination which they have acquired in the soil and for which they are so much prized by western collectors. Chinese collectors always favoured a dark surface, and rubbed on grease to achieve it. In China the ancient vessels were treasured, to our knowledge, from Han times onwards, chiefly for their august associations as ritual vessels and for the inscriptions many of them carry.

The interest of the vessel shapes declines after the beginning of the Chou period. The basic forms of the *ting* tripod and the *hu* vase continue, and for a time the handled wine vessel called *yu*. The functions of the vessels, chiefly the cooking and presentation of food, the mixing and pouring of wine offerings, remained the same, but their shapes were clearly not so rigorously prescribed as the ritual manuals of the 4th–3rd centuries would have us believe *(fig. 8, 15)*.

The ornament of the Shang period consists principally of the monster-mask called *t'ao t'ieh* (a 'glutton'—so named in later times when it was supposed to symbolize a warning against greed; see pl. 14), various forms of dragon, other animals such as cicada, silk-worm, and birds, and geometric figures. One of the latter, a kind of square spiral resembling a Greek key-fret, forms a continuous pattern, either covering the whole surface and the other motifs, or serving as a background to the main elements. Chance resemblance to an ideograph has earned for it the name *lei-wen*—thunder pattern. This art of pattern is essentially linear, and as such foreshadows the predilection for flat, linear form which distinguishes Chinese art as a whole. It is also an 'animal art' inasmuch as it composes, resolves and recombines patterns derived from animal shapes (albeit mythical ones) and combines it with geometric figures. Thus it belongs to the Asiatic tradition known in later times from the art of the Steppes.

The relation of the Chinese tradition of animal art to the art of the steppe nomads, how far China was the recipient or the originator in an exchange of decorative themes, is an obscure problem. Where an early connection might be sought, between Shang China and the art of the Minusinsk basin in South Siberia, no intimate relationship can be traced. The animal-headed knives of 'Siberian' type found at Anyang fall out of the general artistic context of Shang, and perhaps

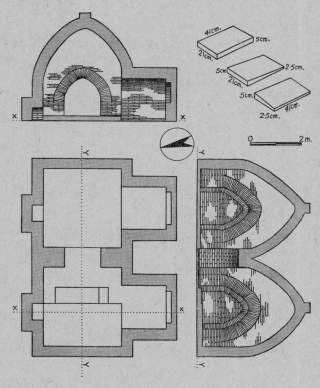

Han dynasty tomb, eastern suburb of Canton. The insert (top right) shows the shapes of the bricks used. See pl. 29 for a boat from this tomb. (fig. 16)

Bronze belt-hook (1st century BC) representing the hero Ch'ih-yu holding a sword, shield, axe and dagger, flanked by a dragon and a tiger. (fig. 17)

were imported into Honan from the north-west (cf. chapter XI, pp. 322–3). Much later, in the 2nd–1st century BC, the animal-style bronze plaques found in the Ordos region of China (pl. 20), and allied influences in Han art, mark a considerable influence of the nomad style from beyond the north-west frontier. Whether in the first instance China contributed to the genesis of the art of the eastern Steppes (as represented, for example, in the 4th–1st centuries BC, in the Pazyryk tumuli of the Altai) seems at least doubtful. The influence cannot in any case have been as direct as that of Hellenistic Greece on the art of the Scythians of South Russia (cf. chapter XI).

In the first two or three centuries of the Chou period the motifs of the bronze ornament are broader and simpler than that of Shang; bands of abstract pattern barely betray their derivation from the older dragon figures. Scale patterns and wave-shaped patterns, larger and coarser in 11th-century designs, come to predominate, and the decoration is sparser. An important change begins about the middle of the 7th century, as seen in the famous groups of vessels from Hsin Cheng in Honan and Li Yü in north Shansi. The vessel shapes are more elaborate, with a new tendency to flamboyance in the outlines; the continuous pattern of the decoration, still based on serpentine dragons, consists of smaller, tighter units, and reveals a new principle of design: interlacery, which had earlier (however much the motifs came near to the idea) been almost meticulously avoided. Influence from a Steppe tradition has been invoked to account for this change, but no Steppe material of sufficiently early date can be cited in proof. The continuous repetition of small identical motifs is repugnant to the Steppe styles as we know them later.

Other trends in the bronze decoration arose towards the middle of the 6th century and may have been the result of outside influence.

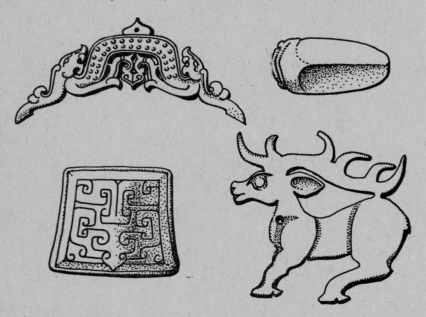

Jade ornaments of the late Chou and Han periods. Top row: pendant of dragon form, c. 350 BC; cicada, as placed in graves, 2nd century BC. Bottom row: chape from sword sheath, 3rd century BC; deer amulet, 2nd–1st centuries BC. (fig. 18)

These are the styles associated with the region of the Huai valley and the state of Ch'u. In these the small unit of the ornament has generally a spiralized circular element from which extends a narrow triangle or curled feather. The closely packed repetition of this motif enlivens the surface as never before, and makes demands on the caster's skill beyond even the intricate ornament of the Shang bronzes. The decoration is no longer, as in Shang, the metal version of motifs invented in softer, carved materials, but one created for metal.

From the 5th to the 3rd centuries BC the different styles found cast and inlaid on bronze in gold, silver and turquoise are modifications of the Huai valley style. They appear increasingly in delicately traced figures from which the 'spiral and feather' has vanished but not its dynamic quality. In the 3rd century the pattern is often organized in oblong units, which become increasingly symmetrical and heraldic in effect. Towards the end of the last century BC, however, the geometrical and abstract figures, though still present in lacquer and textiles, are yielding ground to a current of naturalism, conventionalized in a spirit that owes something to the nomad tradition. Such naturalism is the most characteristic invention of Han art: lithe tigers are pictured on bronzes in a conventionalized hilly landscape, crouching bears furnish the feet of bronze vessels, horses and a new newt-like dragon are shaped on belt-hooks *(fig. 17)*. Even in the fantasy of interlaced and contorted bodies the animal forms are instinct with new life. In some of the pottery statuettes placed in tombs we see the attempt to portray the movements of dancers. In these and in the figures of servants and others (pl. 28), in the portraits of officials which decorate the famous painted basket found at Lolang in Korea (pl. 21), and in the stone bas-reliefs on the walls of elaborate underground tombs (pl. 23, 25), the pursuit of naturalism and the abandonment of geometric pattern mark the beginning of a new epoch in Chinese art, the foundation of an artistic bias which has lasted to the present time.

What has been said of the evolution of artistic styles as seen in the sacrificial vessels might be illustrated in many smaller bronzes. In the decoration of harness trappings, belt-hooks (from the 3rd century BC), and mirrors (from the 4th century BC) the Chinese genius for powerful expression through narrowly prescribed forms is no less apparent (pl. 22, 24, *fig. 17*).

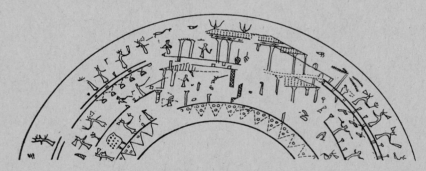

Expanded decoration on a bronze bowl from Hui Hsien, 4th century BC– the earliest known representation of buildings of the period. (fig. 19)

By the 4th century BC improved methods of cutting and drilling enabled the jade-carver to render ornament as fine as that which was cast in bronze. His craft rose to a level of perfection comparable with the gem-cutting of ancient Greece and Persia *(fig. 18)*. At about the same time lacquer began to be used for forming vessels on a base of cloth or wood. In Han times lacquer workshops controlled by the state made bowls and wine-cups decorated with geometric patterns painted gaily in black, red and yellow (pl. 24). From the Han period, on bronzes, in models and stone reliefs, come the earliest representations of wooden buildings which we recognize as characteristically Chinese (pl. 27, 30, *fig. 19*).

The rigorously centralized administration created by Shih Huang Ti after the unification of 221 BC laid the basis of a social and political order destined to survive until modern times. New laws were imposed by draconian methods at first, according to principles advocated by the Legalist philosophers of the day, and a vain attempt was made to stamp out Confucianism at a blow by a burning of books. But Confucianism had become the code of the official class, and despite the Taoist leanings of some emperors and the advent of Buddhism its position was unshakeable. In the Han period too Chinese power began to extend into Central Asia and Indo-China, where for the first time contact was made with traders of the Roman Empire.

X THE SEA-LOCKED LANDS

The diverse traditions of South East Asia

ANTHONY CHRISTIE

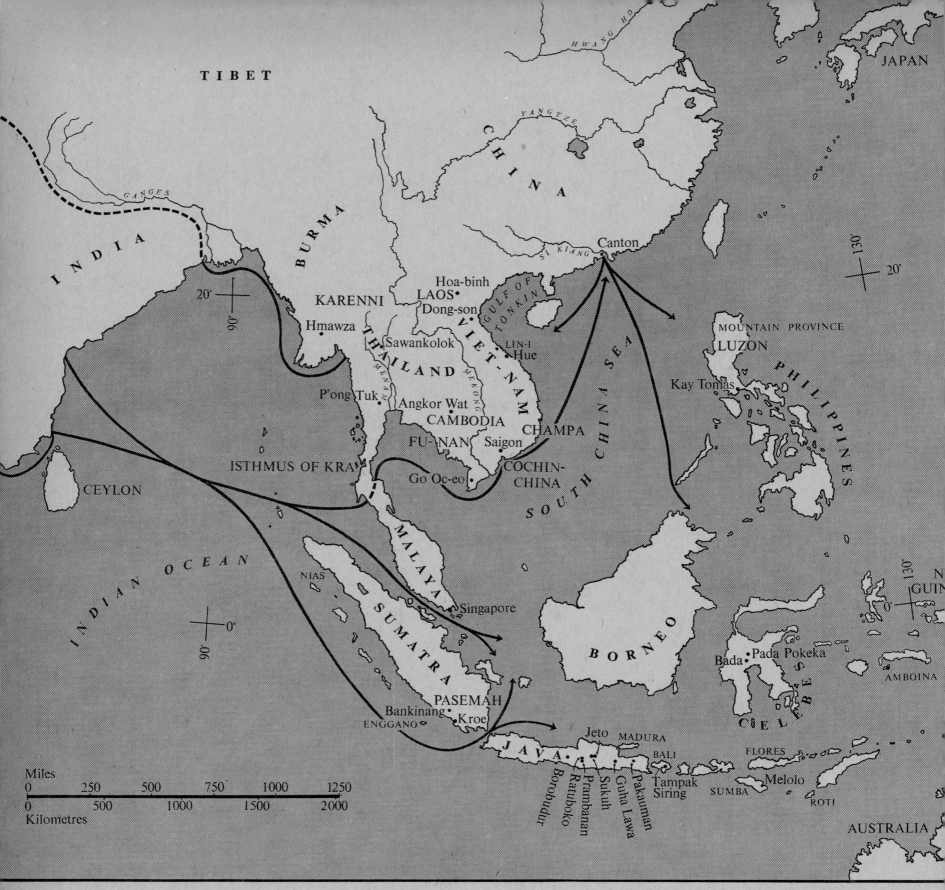

TIBET

INDIA

BURMA

KARENNI

Hmawza

THAILAND

Sawankolok

P'ong Tuk

ISTHMUS OF KRA

CEYLON

INDIAN OCEAN

NIAS

ENGGANO

Bankinang

PASEMAH

Kroe

SUMATRA

MALAYA

Singapore

JAVA

Borobudur
Ratuboko
Prambanan
Sukuh
Guha Lawa
Pakauman
Tampak
Siring

Jeto   MADURA

BALI

SUMBA

FLORES

Melolo

ROTI

AUSTRALIA

LAOS   Hoa-binh

Dong-son

VIET-NAM

LIN-I
Hue

Angkor Wat

CAMBODIA

FU-NAN   Saigon

Go Oc-eo

COCHIN-
CHINA

CHAMPA

CHINA

Canton

SI KIANG

GULF OF TONKIN

SOUTH CHINA SEA

MOUNTAIN PROVINCE

LUZON

Kay Tomas

PHILIPPINES

BORNEO

Bada ·Pada Pokeka

CELEBES

AMBOINA

GUIN

JAPAN

Miles
0   250   500   750   1000   1250
0   500   1000   1500   2000
Kilometres

South East Asia showing the main sites mentioned in the text and major early trade routes (see page 299).

A note on chronology. The chronology of South East Asian prehistory is still quite uncertain. Even the Palaeolithic, a term which strict usage confines to stone cultures of the Pleistocene Period, may be said to extend into the Holocene if we take the persistence of certain types of stone tool as a criterion. The various Neolithic cultures whose date of origin remains to be determined continue in many areas side by side with historical ones, in a few instances well into the Christian era. The peripheral area of New Guinea is still inhabited by people with Neolithic cultures. Many small groups in

the region still erect megaliths. The introduction of metal into South East Asia seems likely to have taken place *circa* 300 BC, the use of iron apparently following very closely upon that of copper and bronze. It is probable that the main 'Bronze Age' lasted until the 2nd century AD—though some features of it, in particular the manufacture of the great bronze drums, persisted into the 19th century. Nor is it wholly certain when Indian influences, and, to a lesser extent, those from China, were sufficiently established in the main areas of the region to allow us to speak of historical cultures. It has been the practice to refer this to the 2nd century AD, but evidence is accumulating to suggest that the process did not in fact become significant until two hundred years later.

East of India, south of China

is a land of rivers and a sea of islands still almost unexplored directly by the archaeologist and whose slender threads of written history reach back only to the beginning of the Christian era. But it is peopled by races whose early traditions, more extensively than anywhere else in the world, have persisted into modern times. In New Guinea today there are people living much as those of China lived 5,000 years ago. On the borders of India and Burma, in Celebes and in the islands of Nias, Flores and Sumba, giant stone monuments are still being built as their forbears raised them in 500 BC. We can therefore learn much of the advance of these peoples towards civilization from a study of their habits of living, their art and their architecture since medieval times.

Before 500 BC the mainland and the islands were inhabited by mixed racial types, some using crude pebble and flint tools, others polished stone axes, others tools in bone. Simple forms of agriculture were practised, for crude hoes have been found, and there is evidence that canoes were in use on the rivers and coastal seas. By 500 BC, bronze was in use and a little later iron, and the preoccupation of the people with life after death was leading to the erection of large stone monuments, or megaliths, to protect the spirits of the dead.

By the first centuries of the Christian era, contact by trading was established between the widely separated islands, and settlers from Indonesia had reached Madagascar; Chinese were exploring the lands which previously they had thought were occupied by men who could live happily under water, men with tails and kings who lived for ever; and Roman sea-captains from the West were writing of Chryse, the Land of Gold, and visiting the ports of Indo-China. Astride the new trade routes, secure from the barbarian hordes of Central Asia, and visited by the advanced cultures of the West and the North, the maritime peoples of the South East must already have felt the ferment of civilization.

This natural rock-shelter at Guha Lawa, East Java, yielded Neolithic objects including tools of bone—and was still occupied as late as the Bronze-Iron period towards the beginning of the Christian era. (1)

The tradition of the rock-shelter persists. This specially cut medieval hermitage is characteristic of the Hindu and Buddhist period of Java and Bali. The cult of the hermit plays an important part in Javanese tradition and literature. (2)

The hermit in his rock-cut refuge is shown in this reconstruction by Walter Spies of the royal cenotaphs at Tampak Siring, Bali. Such a hermit is probably best compared with the chantry-priest of medieval Europe, with whom he was roughly contemporary. (3)

That there was contact between the widespread territories is shown by the pre-Spanish graves at Kay Tomas on Luzon, Philippines, which contain ceramics from China, Viet-nam and Thailand. (6)

Chinese influence is clearly seen in this shapely vessel found at Sawankalok, Thailand. The kilns in which such pots were fired were probably started by immigrant Chinese, to be continued by Thai potters. By the 15th century AD wares of this type were important in trade; a Chinese report of the 13th century concerning the savage Negritos of the Philippines says: 'crawling through the jungle they shoot from ambush. If a porcelain cup is thrown towards them, they rush on it with shouts of joy, and escape with their spoils.' (4)

The cultivation of rice, which underlies the whole of South East Asian culture, is a native tradition from very early times. The rice fields of central Bali, below, are of modest dimensions compared with those of Luzon (opposite). Set amongst them, a nice blend of two cultures, are rock-cut royal cenotaphs of the period when Indian influences prevailed. (5)

The building of megaliths seems to have begun in the Stone Age. The grave (below) at Pakauman, East Java, was still in use in the 9th century AD, for Chinese vessels of that time were found in it. (7)

The dead were buried in urns—stone for the nobility, earthenware for the people. Large jars contained bodies buried whole, fully flexed, or buried as skulls with a few bones, or the charred remains of cremation. The tradition dates from megalithic times; it was adapted to meet new needs, as in the royal burial practices of the Pyu, a Tibeto-Burmese dynasty of 6th-8th centuries AD. The stone urn below was found at Hmawza, Burma. (8)

The stone statues are probably a variant upon the idea that the spirit of the dead man, or at least his power, can inhabit a megalith. This figure is from Pakauman, East Java. (9)

The new religion makes use of an old monument. At Hmawza, Burma, two stones (shown below) stand facing one another, possibly an alignment for megalithic rituals. They were carved by the Pyu of the 7th century AD with Buddhist motifs in low relief. (10)

The use and treatment of stone by the Ifugao people of Luzon, Philippines, is comparable with that of the Indonesian megalithic cultures. This picture of an Ifugao village site in Mountain Province shows the stone floor and standing pillar from a chief's house near Banaue, with the characteristic rice terraces in the background. (12)

The great rice terraces of Luzon, which run for miles along the mountainside, their earth retained by dry-stone walling up to fifteen feet high and hundreds of yards long, are achievements fully comparable with the temples of more sophisticated areas. The stones have been fetched from river valleys which may be as much as 3000 ft below; the complex irrigation system enables water to be brought in conduits which can be 12 miles long. The terraces, probably the work of 2000 years, are the most spectacular remains of the native traditions in South East Asia. (13)

This present-day wooden coffin, megalithic in design, is a striking example of the continuity of style that characterizes the countries of South East Asia. The figure carved on the coffin is shown in the flexed position in which the dead were placed in megalithic tombs. It is the work of the Ifugao tribe in Luzon, Philippines. (11)

The influence of India

began vigorously to affect the cultures of South East Asia around AD 500. There was already a flourishing trade; from before the Christian era, Indian cloth and Indonesian spices, precious stones and perfumes, medicinal products and various timbers were brought from the east along the sea and caravan routes to the great states of North Africa and the Middle East. China too was rich, a fine market for luxury goods.

With the collapse of the Roman Empire, Indian influence began to dominate; Hinduism and Buddhism were introduced, the latter especially reaching out with missionary zeal. With them the Indians brought a system of writing, a mythology and a characteristic art-style, as well as philosophical and legal systems. The result was a mixing of faiths and of styles, in which the Indian originals were modified by local variations. It is the existence of these variations that goes far to prove that the alien influence was grafted upon well developed cultures already distinct.

The massive stone image of Siva, left, has more or less completely the features of detail required by Indian religion, but it also shows clearly its affinities with the native megalithic tradition. It is from the Majapahit period (late 13th century) of East Java. (14)

Contrast the classic Indian tradition of the bronze statuette of Brahma below, from Java. (15)

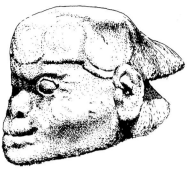

The clear continuity of tradition is seen in these two heads. The warrior (left) is from Pasemah, Sumatra, and dates from the beginning of the Christian era. The other head comes from Chandi Sukuh, Java, and was carved in the 15th century AD. (16,17)

The Goddess Incense, below left, is a representation in human form of incense itself. It is a purely local conception, illustrating the Indonesian practice of translating ideas recorded in sacred writings into human form. The bronze is medieval, from Java. (18)

A pose which could have no place in the precise rules of Indian religious art, is adopted in this medieval Javanese bronze (below right). It is a typical local variation. (19)

At the beginning of the Christian Era a Bronze Age culture flourished, named after the village of Dong-son, in North Viet-nam. The reconstruction above shows a ritual for the well-being of the rice crops across the river. Drums such as those suspended on the platform have been found buried in the rice fields. The warriors carry spears, axes and bows. Women pound rice; on the right a man plays on a mouth organ. (20)

The fine decorative work of the Dong-son people is shown in the examples opposite: a bronze dagger with hilt in human form; and one of the moulded bronze drums, richly decorated in low relief, which are a manifold source of information (boats with warriors, paddlers and helmsman can be seen on this one). The drum-head (right) has a central star and concentric decoration, which includes figures in feather robes. (21, 22, 23)

The civilizations which emerged were a synthesis of the native cultures with that of India and, to a lesser extent, with that of China. The Indian influences made their greatest impression at court level; in the villages the earlier customs and practices continued. The picture we have of pre-European South East Asia tends therefore to be biased towards the importance of Indian influence. But the medieval art of Java, for instance, shows independent characteristics in which, although the Indian elements are evident, the persistent local traditions are well represented. An interesting feature is the love of the grotesque, a strain already apparent in the Dong-son art. It finds its expression in historical times not only in extraordinary weapons for ceremonial purposes, but also in the decoration of implements with figures drawn from the more grotesque, non-Indian, characters of the *wayang* shadow theatre.

Javanese culture had matured from the Indian stage into an independent form when this relief was carved at the temple known as Chandi Sukuh (14th-15th centuries AD). It shows on the left the hero Bhima, who still serves as a model for young Javanese, learning the smith's art. It is the earliest known representation of metal-working in South East Asia, and Bhima forges his sword with an assistant at a piston bellows (right), one of the few native inventions to which South East Asia can lay claim. The bellows was the mainstay of the region's long-lived and flourishing metal industry, as also of the advanced iron industry of China. (24)

A fine medieval bronze tray from Java, which shows a characteristic treatment of flat surfaces. The Indonesian tradition in bronze-working was never wholly supplanted by Indian artistic conventions, and a clear continuation can be seen from the Bronze Age proper throughout the historical period. (25)

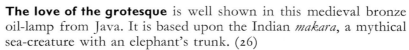

The love of the grotesque is well shown in this medieval bronze oil-lamp from Java. It is based upon the Indian *makara*, a mythical sea-creature with an elephant's trunk. (26)

Ceremonial spearhead, made of iron with gold-wire decoration. Used in parades, it shows Semar, a figure of the Javanese shadow theatre which has no counterpart in India. Probably of the 16th-17th century AD, it is an example of Indonesian work in the non-Indian tradition. (27)

Warrior on horseback, a bronze from Java of the 12th-13th century AD. Its use is not known; it may have been a toy, or it may have been used in rituals. (28)

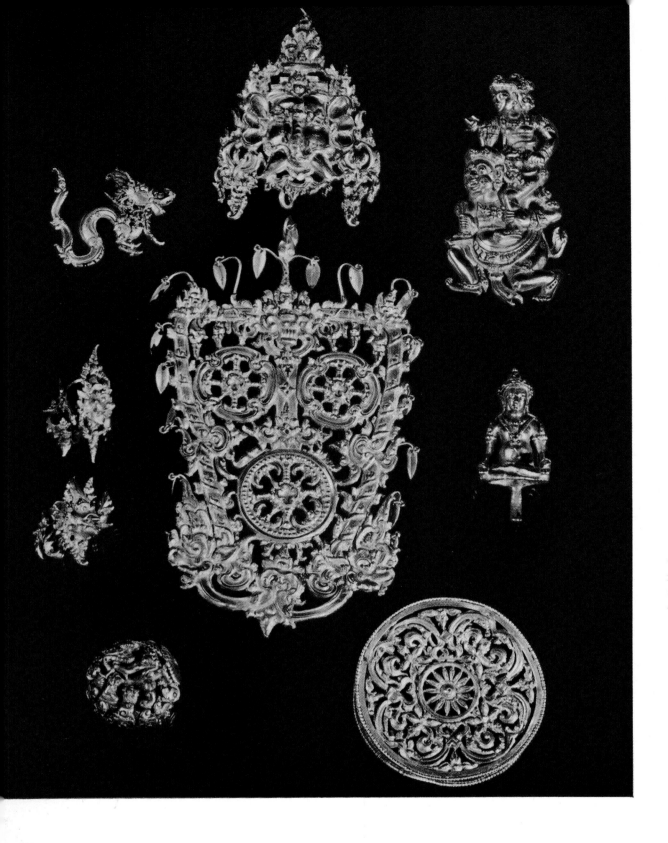

Chryse, the Land of Gold, was never found by the mariners of the West who sought it, as indeed the Conquistadors never found their El Dorado. But the rivers of South East Asia do yield gold, as do many of the world's rivers, and gold mines have long been worked in Indonesia and the Philippines. And so each court—and there were many in the various lands of South East Asia—had its golden regalia, while it was always the custom for the women to invest their wealth in jewellery for themselves and for their children. These examples of the goldsmith's art from Java are typical of the Indonesian delight in elaborate decorative forms. (29)

The island of Bali, unlike Java, never came under the influence of Islam; Hindu religious beliefs, strongly moulded by native practices, have persisted there up to the present day. A final synthesis of the two is seen in this statuette of Vishnu mounted on his Garuda. It is carved in wood and painted, and dates from the 19th century AD. (30)

That the dead live across the sea is a widespread belief in South East Asia even today and many South East Asian religious practices, especially those outside the Hindu and Buddhist systems, are concerned with communicating with them. One means of doing this is the spirit-boat, which is represented (opposite) in a textile from Kroe, Sumatra, and (right) in a wood-carving from Borneo. A striking feature of the decoration of the Dong-son drums is the boatloads of warriors (see pl. 21), which are believed to represent such spirit-boats. (31, 32)

The temple of Borobudur, in Central Java, a Buddhist foundation of the late 8th century AD, seems to have been a religious centre built by the ruling families. It contained 2,000,000 cu. ft of dressed stone, 20,000 sq. ft of low reliefs illustrating Buddhist texts, more than 500 images of Buddha and a wealth of decorative carving. The economic and administrative effort required to build it must have been supported by a flourishing trade, but may well have led to the downfall of the dynasties responsible, and to ruin and revolt in their country. (33)

For the ancient geographers, Further Asia was largely an unknown area. Theories they entertained about the closed nature of oceans led them at one time to postulate a *terra incognita* joining Asia with the southern end of Africa. This map, by Donnus Nicolaus Germanus (c. 1460), after Ptolemy's *Geography*, shows Further India as it was conceived by the Graeco-Roman world. It was not until the seventeenth century that a better practical knowledge of the area was gained. (35)

The great monument of Angkor Wat represents the culmination of Khmer culture in the first half of the 12th century AD. It appears to have served as a dynastic shrine for King Suryavarman II (AD 1113-?1150). Little is known of the civilization of the Khmers, though the influence of India is very apparent in their art. These majestic remains amid the jungles of Cambodia were discovered only about a century ago. Together with Borobudur they form the most impressive legacy in stone bequeathed to us by South East Asia. (34)

That Roman trade reached South East Asia is shown by the objects above. The disc of tin was found at Go Oc-Eo, South Viet-nam, a large town revealed by excavation which seems to have been a trading centre established at the end of the 3rd century AD. The disc is thought to be a *gryllus*, a coin with a 'joke' design on it, such as Pliny the Elder describes. The Roman lamp, of the 2nd century or possibly later, was found at P'ong Tuk in Thailand. (36, 37)

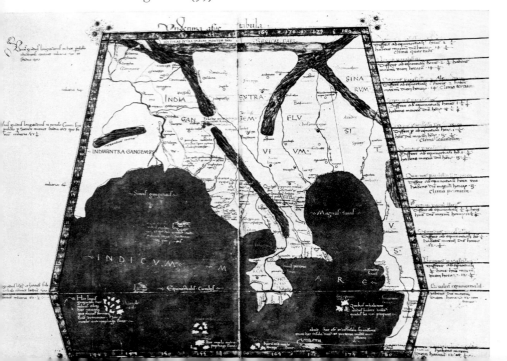

The diverse traditions of South East Asia

ANTHONY CHRISTIE

Discovery by the West and by China

'THEN THE SHIP'S course turns once more to the East, and, as one sails with the ocean always to the right and the shore to the left, Ganges city comes into view and near it Chryse, the very last land as one travels eastwards. There is a river near here which is also called Ganges, and just opposite this river there is an island in the ocean, the last part of the inhabited world towards the East, just at the place where the sun rises. It is called Chryse . . . And beyond this, in the extreme North, the ocean comes to an end in the land of This. Here, in the interior is a very great city called Thinai from which raw silk and silk thread and silk stuffs are brought overland to Barygaza, by way of Bactria, and to the Coromandel coast by the Ganges valley route. But the land of This is hard of access and they are few who come from it.'

This passing reference to Chryse, the land of Gold, in a shipping manual which was compiled towards the end of the 1st century AD, perhaps by a retired sea captain in Alexandria, is the first recorded information about South East Asia in Western sources. He had heard, it seems, that there were lands between India and China but knew no more than this and that tortoise-shell was a Chrysean export. By the next century another sea-captain, Alexander, had made a voyage to Cattigara, a port which probably lay rather to the east of Saigon, and Ptolemy drew on his report for his *Geography* (pl.35). (It is possible that Alexander took the land route across the Isthmus of Kra and did not sail around the Malay Peninsula.) In 166 AD 'the king of Rome, Antonius Marcus Aurelius, sent a mission to China which coming by way of central Viet-nam offered tribute of ivory, rhinoceros-horn and tortoise-shell. From that time dates direct intercourse between China and Rome.' The compiler of the *History of the Later Han Dynasty*, who reported this event, noted the absence of precious jewels among the gifts and wondered whether the mission was really an official one or whether the Chinese had been misinformed about the wealth and power of Rome. In fact the 'mission' was probably a party of Syrian traders who had sold their Western wares earlier in their voyage and restocked with typically South East Asian trade goods before attempting to do business in China. Perhaps they hoped to increase their standing by claiming some official status, knowing that the Chinese were not averse from treating any party of foreigners as having come to bring tribute, in recognition of China's claim to universal suzerainty.

Scattered finds of Roman objects have long been known from South East Asia. These include a Roman lamp from P'ong Tuk, Thailand and odd coins and small carved or engraved stones. At Go Oc-Eo, in the delta lands of Cochin-China, South Viet-nam, excavation has revealed a large town which seems to have been a trading centre. Here a number of objects of Mediterranean and of Near Eastern origin were discovered (pl.36, 37), as well as various Indian finds. This town probably belonged to a kingdom known to the Chinese as Fu-nan which was established towards the end of the 3rd century AD. Fu-nan, together with Lin-i, further north, in the vicinity of Hue, central Viet-nam, is one of the first kingdoms in South East Asia of considerable extent and power of which we have any real historical knowledge. Lin-i was founded towards the end of the 2nd century AD as the result of a local revolt against Chinese rule, its lands forming part of the southernmost extent of the Chinese expansion to be discussed below. There is some evidence to suggest that these kingdoms were ruled by 'Indonesians'. Further to the west, in the Menam delta, lay another kingdom, Dvaravati, which was possibly Mon. The location of all three kingdoms suggests that they arose because of their situation in estuarine areas and that their importance was due to their position as communication centres in the trading system (see map on page 278).

At much the same time as the Western traders were feeling their way into South East Asia, the Chinese had turned their attention southwards and had, in fact, occupied parts of northern Viet-nam. The reason for this was the same in each case. East-West trade had been conducted across the Eurasian land-routes, but these had been interrupted by the movements of barbarian hordes and by the intervening states whose ideas on transit dues had grown increasingly onerous. The depredation of these tribes and their interference with trade had led the Chinese to seek a way of outflanking them and to look for allies in their rear who might be prepared to join in a campaign to eliminate this threat to China's western land frontier. To begin with, Chinese knowledge of the countries to the south was little better than that available in Europe, and the accounts which have survived are little more than tales of mystery and imagination. Men who could live happily underwater, men with tails, kings who lived for ever (certain Taoist traditions had established a relationship between the South and immortality), countries where the houses, being south of the sun, must face north (a fact on which a native informant was once specifically questioned; he said that it was not true). All these ideas and many others were current in Chinese official circles. But little by little, the Chinese penetrated into South East Asia and learnt of its countries, so that their dynastic histories and other texts are precious sources of information about this region, which became known to the West and to China alike almost by accident.

For South East Asia lies upon a main east-west communication system and in a region where two monsoons meet, so that ships can sail from the Indian Ocean to China on the summer wind and current and make their return voyage in the winter. In this region, where the mainland zone is divided by north-south mountain systems into four areas and the Indonesian archipelago frames the Java and South China Seas, it is the land which divides: the sea is a unifying feature and the great rivers serve to connect the interior to the coastal ports.

The migrating peoples who came to occupy the various lands of South East Asia made use of the rivers and the sea to move into the places which they occupy today. And with one or two exceptions these were much the same at the time when the Chinese and the West discovered the region. Neither the Thai nor the Burmese had yet moved into their present positions, though Thai-speaking tribes were to be found in the Tonkin delta and its hinterland. The Viet-namese were still confined to the north of Viet-nam, as well as occupying parts of southern China. To the south of them lay the Chams who were to become a powerful coastal people occupying much of Viet-nam until they were crushed and almost destroyed by the southward expansion of the Viet-namese. The islands were already largely occupied by Indonesian speaking tribes and peoples, who were still probably powerful on parts of the mainland, especially around the Mekong delta. The Mons, who are now confined almost entirely to southern Burma and parts of Thailand, probably spread much further to the east, while the Cambodians were still to evolve the culture and power which was to become so important in the later history of pre-European South East Asia.

Migratory Movements

Our knowledge of the history of these peoples before the coming of the West and of China is fragmentary and must remain speculative until much more field archaeology has provided evidence for our study. Their movements seem to have taken the form of a steady southward drift, apparently under pressure from other peoples, of whom the last were the Chinese, moving through eastern Asia. The dates of these movements are difficult to determine, and they have not wholly finished even today, though the imposition of political frontiers has slowed them or brought them to a temporary halt. Even dating by comparison with adjacent regions is not without its hazards since South East Asia has long been a relict area in which practices and techniques have persisted long after their disappearance from less marginal regions. This fact is in itself important for the student of human cultures, both as a phenomenon in its own right and because of the survival of evidence until a much later date than elsewhere.

Little appears to have been invented in South East Asia: one or two musical instruments *(fig. 1)*, perhaps certain textile techniques, and

291

the piston-bellows which was one of the technical devices that made possible the advanced iron industry of China (pl. 24). Its importance lies in the survival of cultural traits and in its position between the two great cultural spheres of China and India, both of which have influenced its development. Nor were these adjoining regions the only ones to affect South East Asia, for the countries of the Middle East had long been in contact with it. Its position between Asia, Australasia and the Pacific Islands made it important in the transmission of cultural influences and, perhaps more surprisingly, it also contributed to the cultural history of Africa as a result of the movement of Indonesian peoples to the island of Madagascar.

The long voyage to Madagascar is proof of the maritime skill of the ancient Indonesian, and it is clear from the Chinese sources that the littoral peoples of South East Asia at the time when they first came to the notice of the Chinese about the beginning of the Christian era were very much at home in boats. There is, in the texts, a term *k'un-lun* which is used to describe people with dark skins and frizzy hair who provide ships and their crews for much of the commerce of the eastern seas. This term has a number of connotations and is difficult to define precisely, but there can be little doubt that in many contexts it must refer to maritime people who spoke Indonesian languages. These *k'un-lun* played a major rôle in the dissemination of culture throughout the countries of South East Asia and their ships carried not only foreign goods but also foreign ideas throughout the region. A curious feature of the Chinese accounts of these people is that they were at home in the water and in the mountains, but ill at ease on the plains, a statement which is, undoubtedly, of great importance, even though its exact significance is difficult to estimate. For this connection between the mountain and the shore is also to be found in the mythology of many South East Asian peoples, and it may be that this link between the maritime peoples and the mountain folk was one of the ways by which alien cultures were transmitted from the coasts to the interior of the mainland. It seems likely that the formative phase of the people who spoke Mon-Khmer languages took

Present-day mouth-organ from the Shan States, Burma. This type of instrument was known in South East Asia two thousand years ago and is still in use. (fig. 1)

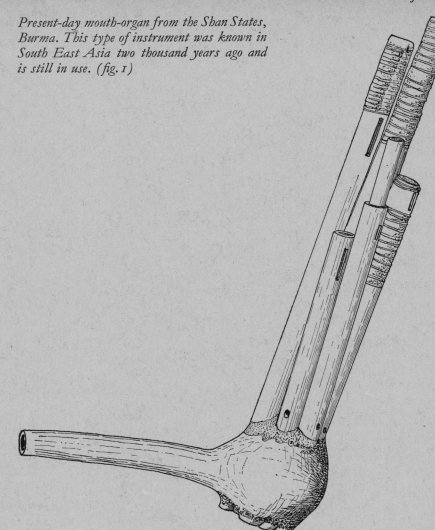

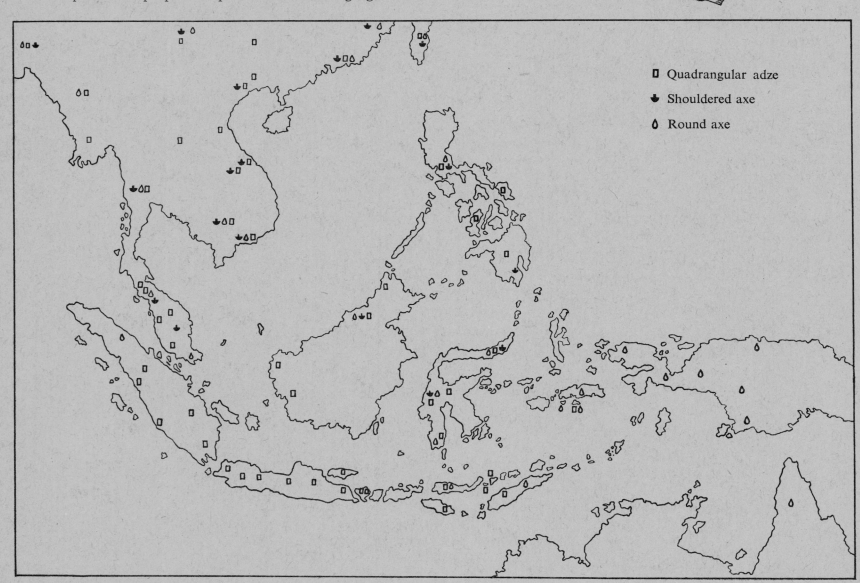

Quadrangular adze

Shouldered axe

Round axe

Map showing the distribution of Quadrangular Adzes, Round Axes, and Shouldered Axes. (fig. 2)

place at a time when these people were still located on the edge of the mountain regions of the middle Mekong valley and were susceptible to outside influences transmitted from the Viet-namese coast by way of the intervening mountain tribes.

Early Cultures

During the Pleistocene period, land-bridges had united the whole complex of islands with the Eurasiatic land mass, and it was across these that Java Man and his cognates had come (see chapter I). Later, migrating tribes crossed by boat. At the end of the Pleistocene, the region seems to have belonged to the palaeolithic industry which covered the whole of eastern Asia, including north west India, and is associated with Java and Peking Man.

The next stage is represented by three new cultures the origins of which have still to be determined. The first is known as Hoa-binhian, from the site in north Viet-nam where it was first discovered. The type tools are pebbles worked on one side only. The peoples responsible for this industry reached Indonesia by two routes, through the eastern part of the island chain and through the Malay Peninsula which has often served as a link between mainland and island South East Asia. The second culture is characterised by a flake and blade industry which seems to have been confined to the eastern part of our region. The third culture, for which the type site is an East Javanese cave, Guha Lawa, has tools and other objects in bone (pl. 1).

Skeletons from this period shows the presence in South East Asia of many different racial types—Veddoids, Melanesoids, Australoids and Mongoloids, as well as of Negritos. The Negritos are still to be found there but only in the remoter areas of the Philippines and of Malaya where they have retreated before more advanced peoples who have taken possession of their former hunting and gathering areas.

The three cultures seem to have practised a simple form of agriculture, to judge from some finds of crude hoes; and there is some evidence that they used canoes.

The Quadrangular Adze and Round Axe Cultures

At a somewhat later period, further cultural divisions can be detected, some of which are undoubtedly of foreign origin, while others may represent local developments of existing cultures. Of these, two are of major importance for the history of South East Asia. These are the Quadrangular Adze and Round Axe cultures. Their distribution is shown in *fig. 2*. It is possible that they originated certain features until then unknown in the region (e.g. the Round Axe people may have introduced the plank-built boat; the Quadrangular Adze people may have spoken an Indonesian language and used bronze) but the evidence does not allow us to be sure of this.

The quadrangular adzes, after which the first of these cultures is named, show a number of variant forms, and appear to have been made by flaking followed by grinding and polishing. They are characterised by an oblong or square shape; a single, bevelled cutting edge; a square, rectangular, quadrangular or trapezoid cross-section.

The round axe, on the other hand, has a round or lenticular (double-convex) cross-section and appears to have been made by initial flaking of the block, followed by hammer-dressing and polishing. Sometimes the last process is omitted. Both cultures include pottery, but certain special objects are associated with the Quadrangular Adze culture. These include stone rings and quoits, and also bark-cloth beaters which were employed in the preparation of the bark of trees to be used as clothing. This practice still continues in some of the remoter parts of the region and the technique seems to have spread from South East Asia into the Pacific Ocean cultures.

The distribution of one other axe-type, that known as the shouldered axe *(fig. 3)*, which is not found south of the middle of Malaya, but which extends from the Ganges Valley to Japan, has given rise to much discussion, in particular concerning its precise relationship to the Quadrangular Adze culture. The members of this culture were possibly speakers of Mon-Khmer.

The cultures so far described saw the establishment of a full neolithic economy in South East Asia with pottery and agriculture *(fig. 4)*. It is probable that cattle were also kept. There is however no doubt that, in parts of the region, hunting and food-gathering was still the normal pattern. Food-gathering, an easy procedure in the fertile parts of South East Asia, was carried on even in areas which were in other respects fully neolithic. All these cultures existed side by side, and it is impossible to define the cultural stages of South East Asia in

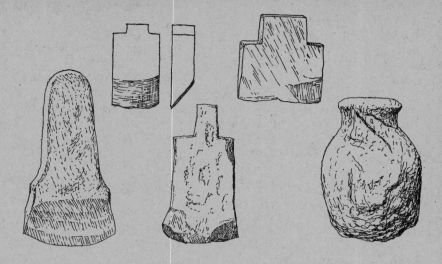

Shouldered axes from Dong-son (top right), Malaya (top left and bottom right) and Cambodia. (fig. 3)

Pottery from the neolithic site of Tengku Lembu Bukit, Perlis, northern Malaya. The pots are hand-built and are buff coloured. (fig. 4)

Stone image from Bada, Celebes. The erection of megaliths seems to be associated with hunting and fertility magic, and also with ancestor cults. (fig. 5)

conventional terms. In some areas, full neolithic cultures continued until late in the Christian era: until the 18th century in Enggano, and until today in New Guinea. The practice of building megalithic structures (about to be discussed) still flourishes in the Indo-Burmese borderlands, in Celebes and in the islands of Nias, Flores and Sumba *(fig. 5)*.

Metals and Megaliths

The use of metal and the construction of megaliths are the next two cultural traits to be noted. The date of the introduction of metal into South East Asia is uncertain, but it seems unlikely to have been before the middle of the first millennium BC. When it occurred, it seems that bronze came first, and iron followed almost immediately, though perhaps on a smaller scale. Stone tools were used side by side with metal. Geographically, the spread of bronze is significantly similar to that of the Quadrangular Adze culture, and this suggests that the metal was brought by speakers of Indonesian languages. An analysis of the types indicates, however, that there were in fact two bronze traditions in South East Asia, one of which is confined to the western part of the region. This does not develop the distinctively South East Asian forms of the eastern tradition. Similarly, there are two megalithic cultures, conventionally referred to as Older and Younger Megalithic. Where they originated, and how far they are connected with the people of the Quadrangular Adze culture remains uncertain.

The main preoccupation of the Older Megalithic people was with life after death. Those who could afford to do so, to judge from the practice of the surviving cults, erected megaliths during their lifetime in order to assure their survival in the next world. Surviving relatives might also erect stones in order to protect the souls of the dead in their post-mortem journeyings, and to ensure their safety once they had arrived at their destination. At the same time, the megaliths served as memorials to the dead and as a link between the living and the dead. By their use the living could also draw upon the experience of the dead, and it appears that the magic power of the dead man commemorated was supposed to reside in the megalith, a belief which is probably reflected in certain religious beliefs and practices of historical times.

The Older Megalithic culture is characterised by the existence of dolmens (upright stones with lintels) and menhirs (single standing stones) which are sometimes arranged in lines or in circles, perhaps to delimit areas for meeting or for dancing; by stone seats which served both for the living elders and for the spirits of the dead (these seem to have survived in Indonesia both in the form of stone coronation slabs for kings and in the 'spirit seats' of the Balinese temple on which no image of the god appears); by stone-paved tracks and platforms; by round dwellings, near which the dead were buried; and by forked sacrificial posts. These last are interesting because among the earliest surviving traces of Indian influence in South East Asia in historical times are certain inscriptions from Borneo which refer to *yupa*—sacrificial posts of Vedic rituals—which it appears had been substituted for stone pillars employed in earlier native practice. This is often the case in South East Asia.

The subject of Indian influence, particularly in the religious sphere, will be dealt with later in this chapter (page 299). At this point it is sufficient to mention that both Hinduism and Buddhism (the latter the more energetic and evangelistic) were introduced into the region at an early date, probably during the early 1st millennium AD. With them came a system of writing, a mythology and a characteristic art-style. They did not, however, entirely supersede the old faiths, but merged with them in a variety of forms. Thus there is evidence to suggest that some of the sites were kept in use by people other than those who were originally concerned with them and who, in all probability, also subscribed to 'higher', more 'sophisticated' religious systems. Finally came a re-emergence of native systems of belief and ritual, modified and developed by their contact with Indian religions, (this is notably the case in Java), and temples are to be found which clearly relate to megalithic cults at their most sophisticated, while their more primitive forms continued to exist, as they still do, in the peripheral areas.

An illustration of how an older site could be re-used in a setting of later beliefs is furnished by the group to be seen on the Yang Plateau, Argapura Mountains, East Java. The association between the megalithic cult and the volcano seems clear, an association which seems fundamental in South East Asia since the early Chinese documentary sources, and many of the remains of buildings of general Indian type point to the existence of mountains as the foci of religion. This in fact persisted into historical times and led to some considerable emphasis upon those aspects of Hinduism and Buddhism which were amenable to this concept of the mountain, whether volcanic or not, as a sacred focus. It is almost certain that the Yang Plateau site was used for cult purposes in historical times and it seems likely that the

Carving in stone of two warriors with a bronze drum, from Airpurah. The drum is of a type known as Heger I, and may be compared with that shown in plate 22. (fig. 6)

buildings at Ratuboko, Prambanan, which are associated with cults of Indian origin may have belonged in the first place to the megalithic tradition. Towards the 13th-14th century AD these traditions appear finally to have coalesced and the result is to be seen in the temple complexes of Jeto and Chandi Sukuh on the Lawu Mountains of Central Java (pl. 24). The cult here cannot be understood, nor the symbolism interpreted, without reference to purely Javanese beliefs, in addition to those of Indian origin, and there is much which must be referred to the megalithic tradition.

Some features of the Younger Megalithic culture are the same as those of the Older, especially the use of dolmens, but it has a distinctive character. Stone sarcophagi and stone cist-graves are typical (pl. 7)

Man riding a buffalo, from Pasemah, South Sumatra. This achieves an illusion of work in three dimensions, though it is really a series of two-dimensional presentations on a rock of appropriate shape. (fig. 7)

(the dead being buried in either flexed or extended positions, with multiple burials common); stone statues, probably of ancestors (pl. 9) and also menhirs which are treated as statues; glass and carnelian beads; weaving; the presence of bronze and iron tools, related to the eastern bronze culture; female figures in low relief on stone graves. The stone statues are probably a variant upon the idea that the spirit of the dead man, or at least his power inhabits, or may be called into, a megalith, and it is interesting to speculate upon the relation between this tradition and a later historical practice. In this the statues of Indian deities, either Hindu or Buddhist, or icons like the *linga* (phallus), or, finally, statues modelled upon those of Indian deities but with more or less differentiating features, were identified with kings or other notabilities and were thought to house their special power (pl. 14). These finally became more or less portrait statues and also served as memorials to the powerful dead (pl. 16, 17). It is possible that the use of rock-cut graves also belongs to this culture, though the practice of cutting these, particularly as hermitages and as shrines persisted in Java and Bali into historical times (pl. 2, 3).

An example of a Younger Megalithic site is to be seen in the extensive

Cover of a stone vat from Pada Pokekea, Behoa. The small figures may represent frogs. Large numbers of these stone vats and jars have been discovered in Central Celebes, and seem to have served as burial urns. (fig. 8)

remains at Pakauman, East Java. Here stone cist-graves are found, together with demarcated areas and megalithic statuary. That burials here continued up until at least the 9th century AD is shown by the presence of datable Chinese porcelain in the largest of the tombs. Other finds included potsherds, from both hand- and wheel-made wares, glass and earthenware beads, an iron bracelet and bark-cloth beaters, and bones, of human beings and of cattle. Cattle bones were also found elsewhere on the site and remind one of the close association between cattle sacrifice and the erection of megaliths in surviving cults of this type. The stone statues end in a cone-shaped foot and seem therefore best considered as evolved menhirs. The megaliths of this site and those from elsewhere in East Java seem to belong to a complex which extends eastwards into the Lesser Sunda Islands unrelated to the megalithic systems of Central and West Java.

At a most important megalithic area in the Pasemah region of South Sumatra there are graves of various types, stone troughs, probably used for the storage of skulls, and a wealth of statuary *(fig. 7)*. These last raise two points of considerable interest. Certain of the figures have been shown to have affinities with Chinese reliefs and sculpture of the Former Han dynasty. Other figures seem to be carrying bronze drums of a type known as Heger I *(fig. 6)*. Those we shall discuss below in connection with the eastern bronze culture. These discoveries are important for the question of the cultural relations of the South East Asian megalithic period. The second point concerns the technique of the sculptors. At first sight, the statues appear to be treated in the round, but closer inspection shows that this is not the case. In fact, the sculptor chose a stone appropriate to his theme (or this was suggested by the shape of a stone), and then proceeded to carve this in a series of relief carvings which create the illusion of sculpture in the round. A further feature of certain of the Sumatra stone cist-graves is that some of them at least were painted on the interior walls. At least two styles of painting seem to have been involved, but the records are inadequate for any detailed study of this problem. The same type of scene was depicted in paint as on the stone statuary.

In Upper Laos the megalithic remains, while extensive and complex, do not show so much evidence as in the case of Indonesia for organised and integrated arrangement. There are groups of menhirs with associated burials, often in excavated chambers covered with circular capstones. In Celebes somewhat similar capstones are found, some of which are decorated with animal figures (including frogs which are also to be found on the bronze drums to be discussed later) *(fig. 8)*. In Celebes, however, the capstones cover large stone jars similar to certain stone vessels which have also been discovered in North Sumatra.

Urn Burial Traditions

This raises the whole question of urn-burial and of urn-fields in South East Asia. In some cases these are clearly associated with megalithic cultures, but this is by no means always the case, and in at least one instance stone urns played an important part in the royal burial practices of the Pyu, the first Tibeto-Burmese dynasty in Burma of which we have any clear documentary and archaeological evidence (pl. 8). The urns in use in the prehistoric period were either of stone or of earthenware but, if we may judge from the practice of later historical times, wooden containers were also used. In Upper Laos the urns were associated with clusters of megaliths. Most of the graves had been looted, but in some, which were more or less intact, bones and human teeth showed signs of charring. A few bronze vessels, and fragments of bronze bracelets were found, together with potsherds and fragments of iron. The presence of Chinese potsherds dating from 10th-12th centuries AD points to the fact that these sites were in use over many centuries, but it is probable that some of the burials at least took place in them because they were recognised as cemeteries rather than that such burials definitely establish the persistence of a megalithic tradition.

At Melolo, Sumba Island, a large urn-field has been investigated. Here there was no indication of megalithic association. The urns were found both singly and in groups a few inches below the surface. They were of crude, hand-made pottery with straight or everted necks; *(fig. 9)*, the lids seem to have been improvised from any suitable piece of pottery. Sometimes a jar contains two or three skulls, and in the absence of any evidence for re-use it must be assumed that these were put into the urn at the same time. As decarnification (the exposure of the corpse until it was in a skeletal state) was practised, this is quite possible. Perhaps this practice was in part determined by economic considerations. Today in Bali where cremation is customary, it is common for the dead to be buried until such time as a wealthy family is in the position of having to finance the expensive ceremonials of a cremation. Then the waiting dead are exhumed and their relations take advantage of the ceremony to dispose of their own dead also without having to undertake the great expense of organising their own rituals. At Melolo the funerary gifts included shell and stone beads, shell bracelets and rings, and highly polished red or red-brown earthenware flasks. Quadrangular adzes were also found, but in view of the fact that even today neolithic tools are collected and treasured as objects of particular virtue these cannot be accepted as indicating the cultural affinities of the burials. Two finds of interest were a shell amulet in the form of a pig's head, and a jar in human shape which may be a variant of the flasks shown in *fig. 9*.

There seem to have been at least three urn-burial traditions in South East Asia. (1) Large jars were used to contain bodies in a fully flexed

Amulet and jars from an urn-field at Melolo, Sumba Island, Indonesia. Funerary offerings included beads, bracelets, rings and highly polished reddish earthenware flasks, often of an anthropomorphic type. (fig. 9)

position accompanied by funerary gifts. (2) Large jars were used to contain decarnified skulls with a few limb bones. These were also accompanied by gifts. Finally, (3) in historical times, chiefs and notabilities in some areas of Celebes were, after cremation or partial cremation, in-urned in vessels of Chinese manufacture, or of Chinese style but manufactured in the kilns of Thailand and Indo-China. These wares, like their Chinese prototypes, were widely traded in South East Asia. Many of the graves in pre-Spanish sites in the Philippines contain examples (pl. 6) while their manufacture as luxury goods became an important part of the Thai economy (pl. 4). This practice continued until the coming of Islam in the beginning of the 17th century AD.

On the basis of discoveries in the Philippines, where the evidence is much the same as that from elsewhere in South East Asia, it has been concluded that the practice of urn-burial was introduced into the region from South China. If this is so, then it must have been brought there by people moving southwards under pressure from the Chinese as these expanded from the Yellow River basin. This expansion was the source of many cultural movements into the lands to the south, and it therefore seems clear that the predominating influences in South East Asia's native cultures came from China, though not, strictly speaking, from the Chinese.

Reference has already been made to the occurrence of urn burial in historical times. We learn from Chinese sources that in the kingdom of Chen-la (Cambodia 7th century AD) the body was cremated, with Indian rituals, and the ashes gathered into a gold or silver urn which was thrown into the sea: 'the poor used earthenware urns painted in various colours'. Some apparently preferred to leave the dead for the wild beasts to destroy. In Burma, as has already been noted, the Pyu practised burial in stone urns for kings and nobility; earthenware urns were used for the people. Grave goods included gold flowers, white pebbles and iron nails. The case of the Pyu is interesting because at Hmawza in Burma, which was once a Pyu capital, there are two large monoliths facing one another and some distance apart, now carved with Buddhist motifs in low relief but which may once have formed part of a megalithic alignment (pl. 10). These, taken in conjunction with the burial urns seem to point to the continuance in the Pyu kingdom of an earlier megalithic tradition.

The use of wood as a substitute for stone and clay is yet another feature of these cultures. No evidence has survived from the early period to enable us to date this practice, but the evidence from Mountain Province, Luzon, of a wooden coffin (pl. 11) which seems to be of 'megalithic' type, is supported by other features of Ifugao villages. As an example of the 'megalithic' style in stone we may cite the stone floors and probable menhir from a chief's house near Banaue. The 'cobbles' are typical of villages in this area as are the stone-walled rice terraces. The Ifugaos, like their neighbours, were headhunters until recently, apparently another characteristic of South East Asian megalithic cultures (pl. 12).

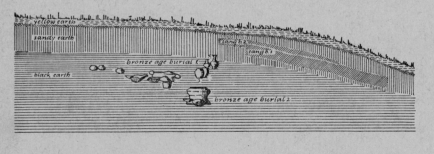

Section through the Dong-son site. Bronze Age burials underlie Chinese graves of the T'ang period which are clearly of considerably later date. (fig. 10)

The Dong-son Culture (Bronze Age)

The bronze period in South East Asia is in part contemporary with the megalithic. The first considerable knowledge of its products was due to the Dutch pastor Rumphius who sent a bronze drum, of unknown provenance, to the Grand Duke of Tuscany in the 18th century AD. In his account of the Curiosities of Amboina, (1704), Rumphius published and described a number of bronze and stone axes, which, in an explanation curiously close to that still current in many parts of South East Asia today, he thought to have fluxed out of the

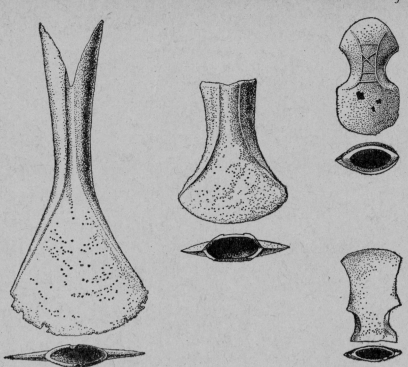

A selection of bronze axes from the western part of South East Asia, apparently not directly connected with Dong-son. Each axe is shown with its section beneath it. (fig. 11)

atmosphere by the action of lightning. It was almost two centuries before bronze objects from this region became a major topic for study, but once this began, a large body of literature soon grew up, though little was known of the sites from which the material originated. It was not until the nineteen-twenties that objects were found *in situ* at the village of Dong-son, North Viet-nam, the site which gave its name to the eastern branch of the South East Asian bronze culture, *(fig. 10)*.

The bronze objects from the western part of the region are relatively few in number and are mostly without any context. The finds consist almost entirely of socketed axes in which the blade is more or less splayed and the cutting edge asymmetrical in section. (This feature, the asymmetrical edge, seems to be a survival from the Stone Age, when it was almost universal in this region. I believe that it derives from the need to cut bamboo, the most common source of timber in the area. This type of edge seems, experimentally, to bite better into its hard slippery surface.) A selection of tools from the western group is shown in *fig. 11*.

The best known and best documented Bronze Age culture is that of Dong-son. Here objects of the South East Asian culture were found in association with objects of Chinese origin. This seems to suggest a date for the site of about 150 BC to 50 AD but there is evidence to suggest that the culture persisted until considerably later into the Christian era: the date of its origin is by no means clear but it probably dates from the early centuries BC. At present the Dong-son culture has no real 'prehistory'. It first appears in South East Asia in a fully developed form and we must assume that its technology had been evolved elsewhere although its products seem to represent local tradition and needs. In addition to these Chinese objects the finds include bronze drums, tools and weapons, vessels, ornaments and statuettes. Pottery and stone tools were also found. A distinctive feature of the copper alloy of the Dong-son culture is its high lead content (up to 25 per cent).

The weapons include daggers, axes and spear-heads. There are no swords, and arrowheads are rare, although the bow is shown on the drums. There are socketed axes which belong to a well-known Eurasiatic type and clearly enter this region from China where they are known as *pen*, but there is a second axe type which seems peculiar to this culture. It is pediform and is often decorated on the side panels. This curious weapon achieves its exotic apotheosis in Indonesia, but there can be no doubt that it was originally functional. The method of mounting, which can be seen on the drums, has survived in the Viet-namese *cai riu* and in the Laotian socketed axe. The daggers, of which the longest is 0.25 m., are manufactured with blade and handle in a single piece: there is little or no guard. One, with a ring hilt may be of Chinese origin. A Dong-son dagger from

Flores, seems to be the most easterly find from this culture. It has however been argued that the so-called *kris majapahit* is derived from a second type of Dong-son dagger with an anthropomorphic handle but there are gaps in the evidence, and the hypothesis is not very convincing. (The *kris*, of which the wavy-bladed type is late, is not illustrated on Indonesian monuments until the 13th century.) It is possible that certain bronze plates are parts of armour, a further example of influence from China where the use of body armour seems to develop at about this period. In addition to these military objects there are a number of flanged and socketed objects from Dong-son which may be shovels. They do not seem large enough for plough-shares.

There are two more types of bronze vessels at Dong-son and a third which probably belongs to the same culture, although unknown at the type site. The second type is strikingly reminiscent of certain types of woven pannier, especially from Borneo, and it is even possible that these forms, in view of some similarity of decoration, are in fact related. The third type is known from Cambodia, Sumatra and Java, and closely resembles the flask-shaped fish-basket, *kepis*, worn on the hip in parts of Indonesia, to carry live fish. A similar type of vessel is known from Yunnan where there is evidence of a bronze culture which clearly has affinities with the Dong-son culture, though the relationship is probably not very close. It is interesting to note that of these bronzes, two are close in design to containers in perishable material, a fact which suggests that these in bronze were perhaps used for ceremonials which involved the rice and fish usually carried in the more every-day plaited ones *(fig. 12)*.

Decorated vessel of bronze from Madura. In both shape and surface-pattern this recalls containers in more perishable materials. (fig. 12)

From Dong-son itself and from other bronze culture sites there are a number of representations of human figures. These occur on dagger hilts (pl. 21) on a spouted bronze vessel (the only spouted vessel found) and occasionally as free-standing objects. Of these, the most remarkable is a group consisting of a *khene* (mouth-organ) player riding pick-a-back on another figure *(fig. 13)*. The figures are treated in the same style as those on the vessel-spout. While much of the surviving bronze-work from historical times was clearly in the service of Indian religious systems, there also existed a school of 'folk-art' which produced work that is of considerable interest and charm. Thus there exist, side by side with images of Hindu and Buddhist deities (pl. 14, 15), considerable numbers of objects which clearly belong either to other, popular religious systems or to secular art (pl. 18, 19).

A certain strain of fantastication, of the grotesque, is also apparent in the Dong-son art which may well lie behind the Indonesian liking for this style. This finds its expression in historical times not only in extraordinary weapons, non-functional, unless it be thought that they had a magical power, but also in the decoration of implements with figures drawn from the more grotesque, non-Indian, characters of the *wayang* (pl. 27). The technical skill of the Dong-son craftsmen can be seen in some of their minor pieces *(fig. 14)*. It was to lead in historical times to the production of a number of fine objects, some of great size, like a Vishnu head more than one metre in height. The craftsmen of the Dong-son culture seem to have established a tradition, which still persists, of fine work with the simplest of equipment (pl. 25).

Two bronze figurines from (left) Dong-son and (right) Bangkinang, Sumatra. In the Dong-son example, the figure being carried pick-a-back is playing a mouth-organ similar to that shown in fig. 1. The other figurine illustrates a certain strain of the grotesque. (fig. 13)

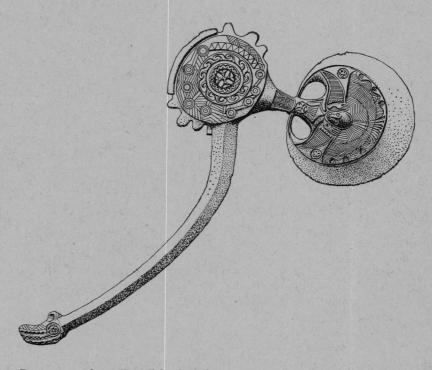

Bronze axe from Roti Island, Indonesia: a good example of the technical skill attained by the craftsmen of the Dong-son Culture. (fig. 14)

Small objects, perhaps model drums, placed in graves at Dong-son. (fig. 15)

Drums

But it was in the manufacture of bronze drums, ranging in size from miniature grave goods to specimens more than a metre across the head, that their skill is best exemplified. The basic type consists of a tympanum, a convex zone, a conical zone, and an inverted, truncated cone. Suspension lugs are arranged in two sets of pairs on opposite sides of the convex zone. The base is open *(fig. 16)*.

The larger specimens were undoubtedly made in moulds as can be detected from the seams which are easily observed, but it is possible

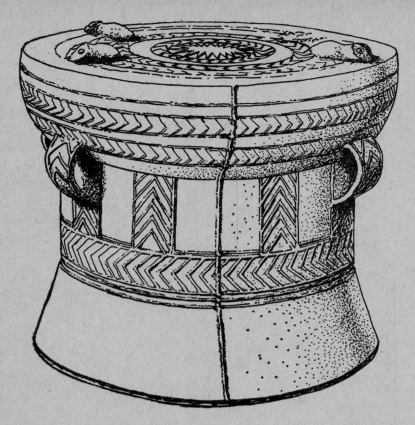

A bronze Dong-son drum: the parts consist of a tympanum, a convex zone, a conical zone and an inverted truncated cone. There are four suspension-lugs altogether. (fig. 16)

that some of the smaller models were made by the *cire perdue* technique (as was the case in Karenni, Burma, where bronze drums were still being made in this century). One of two fragments of stone moulds have, in fact, been found, and the ability to produce objects of this nature in such sizes, testifies to the skill of South East Asian metal workers some two millennia ago.

Almost the whole surface of the tympanum is decorated. At the centre is a star with an even number of points ranging from 8 to 16 in number (pl. 23). This star is enclosed in a circle running about the points and the spaces between the points are filled with designs which are probably stylised faces. Outside the central motif are a series of concentric bands of decoration. They contain human figures engaged in apparent ritual activities and decked in ceremonial feather robes. Houses and birds are often included in these scenes. Other bands are filled with processions of animals (usually deer) or of birds which generally fly counter-clockwise *(fig. 20)*. These more or less naturalistic scenes are separated by bands of geometrical designs, and the outer zone of the decoration consists of a number of such bands, beyond which is a plain undecorated band which may carry figures of frogs in the round. The convex zone, immediately below

the tympanum, is decorated with geometrical designs and also with boats which carry a helmsman, some paddlers and often a number of befeathered figures who may be warriors *(fig. 17)*. Similar scenes are also to be found on the body of the drum, in panels separated by geometrical designs. Although all the drums of this type are formally similar, it is possible to detect a distinct trend from earlier to later models in the progressive shift from naturalistic to stylistic representation of both human and animal figures *(figs. 17, 20)*.

The scenes depicted on the drums are a valuable source of information about the tribes who possessed them. From them we can determine the types of house which were constructed, and also something of the types of canoe in use. Scenes of figures pounding with long poles in mortars testify almost certainly to the use of rice *(fig. 21)*. It is possible to assert that it was the simple and not the compound Chinese bow that was used. Dancing was accompanied by castanets and the mouth-organ, and perhaps by drums of the type under discussion (pl. 20, *fig. 18*).

The function of these drums in the society to which they belonged is not easy to determine. In all probability they had a manifold purpose. At present one of their principal uses is in rainmaking ceremonies, and they may also be used at funerals to call up the spirits of the dead who are believed to appear in the form of birds. They also serve as altars. (It is by no means certain that such a usage is original: it may well be a later development among people who inherited the drum without any clear idea of its original function and adapted it to this use in view of its shape as a convenient offering platform). There is some reason to think that the drums were buried in fields as a fertility charm (they are still buried by the Lamet of Indo-China, but this is apparently a safety measure), and also as insignia of chieftainship. The Chinese say that they were placed under waterfalls to make a sound as of cavalry, but it seems to me likely that this is a misunderstood rain and fertility ceremony. It is, however, clear from Chinese accounts of campaigns in North Viet-nam at the beginning of the Christian era that these drums were of great importance to their possessors and considerable efforts were made by the Chinese to capture them.

The interpretation of the scenes depicted on them has given rise to a considerable body of literature. The most popular view is that these are concerned with mortuary ceremonies and with rites connected with ancestral spirits. In this view the canoes depicted are thought to be spirit boats, an opinion supported by the wide-spread belief in South East Asia today that the next world lies down-stream or across the sea (pl. 31, 32, *fig. 17*). This concept may be extended to include the idea of the sky as a sea. Some clues are perhaps to be found in current practices among the less sophisticated inhabitants of the region today. There seems little doubt that the 'boat' was used by the spirit-doctor in order to communicate with the realms above. This passage (preserved in oral tradition and first written down in the 19th century) from a Toraja, Celebes, priestess' incantation seems to describe a journey of the type depicted on some of the drums:

A design from a Dong-son drum, showing a boat with helmsman, paddlers and a number of befeathered figures who may be warriors. It is generally thought that these represent spirit-boats, either conveying the souls of the dead or serving as a means of communication with them. (fig. 17)

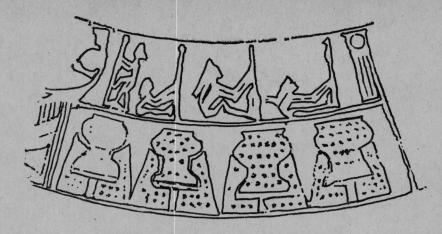

Now we are on the ridge of the roof,
We are above, on the roof . . . . .
Blow wind from the sea,
Carry us over the earth;
Blow wind from the land,
Carry us over the earth.
Row, ye birds of bright plumage:
Use the oars, ye ospreys . . . . .
The rainbow is our conveyance . . . . .
The rails of the bridge are of gold.

The meaning of this design is uncertain. Possibly drums are being cast in large stone moulds; or perhaps the figures above are meant to be striking them with poles. (fig. 19)

At first sight the reference to the rainbow introduces a new concept, and the reference to a bridge finds no place on our drums. The rainbow however, which is widely held, in South East Asia as elsewhere, to act as a bridge between the world of mortals and that above, is also thought to be associated with deer, and is thus depicted in later art. In view of the presence of deer on the drums we may therefore interpret it in this way, and conclude that the Torajas have preserved a Dong-son theme in their incantatory rites.

Trade and Communications

The arrival of the West, including India, in South East Asia seems to have been due to the activity of traders. This was essentially a matter of small pedlars and the like, petty merchants hiring spaces in ships plying on the east-west routes and often manned by crews from South East Asia. The transmission of ideas and material culture was at first incidental to this, although there can be little doubt that, after a while, ideas and experts began to be valued by the countries of South East Asia, and Indians with various skills sought their fortunes overseas. Before considering the effect which these developments had, however, it is interesting to see what trade took place. South East Asia was an entrepot and transit zone between East and West, a function which, as the history of Singapore clearly shows, not only brings wealth but is also important in the dissemination of culture. But it was also important as a producer of many objects of value in early Asian trade.

From long before the beginning of the Christian era Indian cloth and Indonesian spices, precious stones and perfumes, medicinal products and various timbers were brought from the east along the sea and caravan routes to the great states of North Africa and the Middle East. Nor did these objects travel only westwards. China was rich and well able to absorb luxury goods, so that, in the time of the first arrival of the Portuguese in this region, Corsali (an Italian trader, working on behalf of the Medici in the early 16th century) was to note that at least as much profit was to be made by loading spices for China as by hauling them over the long sea-route to the markets of Europe. By the end of the 1st century AD, pearls and precious stones, gold and rare products, silk and textiles formed part of the maritime trade of the China Sea. Tortoise-shell, gold, silver, rhinoceros horn and ivory reached China from Java in the 9th century AD. A century later Indonesian goods in the markets of Arabia included aloes, camphor, sandalwood, ivory, tin, sapanwood and spices. In the 14th century AD Indonesian shippers handled rice, salt, pepper, cotton textiles, parrots, copper coins, beads, gold, silver, betel nut, carved wooden objects, pearls, cloves, sandalwood and porcelains. Slaves too provided a profitable trade, and although these commercial activities have been characterised as 'splendid and trifling' they involved capital resources which the new East India companies, from the 16th century, the time of the arrival of the European traders, onwards, could not hope to rival.

Art and Architecture, 10th-12th Centuries

And further, they were able to supply the economic and administrative effort which was required to sustain the building of such monuments as Borobudur (pl. 33) with its 2,000,000 cu. ft. of dressed stone, 20,000 sq. ft. of narrative *bas-reliefs*, more than 500 Buddha images, and its wealth of decorative carving and pinnacles. It may well have been, however, that the strain of such works was too great, that these astonishing structures became in fact the cenotaphs of the dynasties which built them and brought their countries to economic ruin and revolt thereby.

However that may be, the monuments are a precious source of information about many aspects of South East Asian life. The reliefs with which many of them are decorated are in general occupied with

Another design from a drum. A man seems to be playing a gong-chime, with rows of gongs suspended vertically on either side. Gong-chimes have a popular place in present-day S.E.Asian music. (fig. 18)

Animals from designs on drums – on the left a deer, on the right, birds: the spirits of the dead were believed to appear in the form of birds. (fig. 20)

Design showing two figures pounding with long poles in mortars – perhaps an indication of the use of rice at this period. (fig. 21)

the narration of Indian religious texts, but the mise-en-scène is usually local and the artists modelled the settings of the stories which they were called upon to illustrate from the scenery and objects of native life. Thus the reliefs provide important evidence for the flora and fauna, the dress, the tools and weapons, the agriculture, the music, the household equipment, and the housing in perishable materials of many areas of South East Asia. Important too is the content of the illustrations for the identification of the texts in use in this region. For no manuscripts have survived from the early period and these reliefs are the best evidence for the nature of the sects and orders which established themselves in South East Asia in the formative period. In addition to texts relating experiences of the Buddha in previous existences, there are various accounts of his life and teaching and also texts which deal more specifically with points of doctrine, as well as many Hindu documents. The two Indian epics, the Ramayana and the Mahabharata are also popular and it is interesting to note that Valmiki, the author of the former, was the object of a cult in Champa, where a temple was dedicated to him, a practice which is quite unknown in his native India.

This was by no means the only innovation. In Indonesia at least, the practice of translating textual references into forms became a feature of religious art, and such things as incense were presented in anthropomorphic guise (pl. 18). As a result of this, a number of gestures and poses are found which have no place in Indian iconographical canons (pl. 19).

The Influence of India

But while East-West trade through and with South East Asia began at about the beginning of the Christian era, it probably made no significant cultural impression upon it much before 500 AD. The reasons for this are not clear, but a major factor was doubtless that Indian cultures, which are obviously the main alien influence upon this region, did not begin to play a predominant role until the waning of more westerly trade which had depended upon imperial Roman markets, by this time in collapse. The increase in direct participation by India, first, it seems, western rather than southern India, in this trade led to the wide dissemination of Indian religions, literature and architecture, as well as of Indian philosophical and legal systems. But these made their impact not upon a vacuum, but upon a region which already had well developed social and religious systems. It is not surprising therefore that the Indian originals were rapidly modified by the *genii loci* and soon develop characteristic features which differentiate them clearly. The very existence of these local variations goes far to prove that at the time when these influences became significant the pre-Indian cultures were already well developed and had become distinct. It must also be recognised that the Indian influences made their greatest impression at a court level, and that in the villages, earlier customs and practices still held sway. It is unfortunate that the remains of the court level structures have survived while humbler buildings and artefacts, made of less permanent materials, have long since disappeared. As a result the picture which we have of pre-European South East Asia is enormously biased towards the importance of Indian influence. Yet the achievement of the Ifugao of Mountain Province, Luzon, Philippines (pl. 13), who built and still build the great rice terraces, running for miles along the mountainside, their earth retained by dry-stone walling up to fifteen feet high and hundreds of yards long, is comparable with the sophisticated, court-inspired temples of more Indianised areas. The much more modest terraces of Tampak Siring, Bali, show a nice blend of the two cultures (pl. 5), but it was as the Indian ideas penetrated to the villages, and were modified and adapted to blend with the older traditions and beliefs of the area that the final synthesis was achieved, as can be seen in a 19th century Balinese representation of Vishnu on his Garuda as a Balinese deity (pl. 30).

XI THE ROYAL HORDES

The nomad peoples of the Steppes

E. D. PHILLIPS

The Neolithic and Early Metal Ages on the Eurasian Steppes before the Mounted Nomads

The Steppes and neighbouring regions during the rise of Mounted Nomadism and the Scythic Period. For the Kuban, see p. 321

Lying in a broad swathe across the face of Europe and Asia, the Northern steppes, throughout history, have been both the home of pastoral and agricultural peoples and a corridor for the passage of great migrations. From about 4000 BC, when the climate was probably moister than it is now, stone-using farmers and stockbreeders could spread over vast distances to the east. Neolithic cultures of this kind must have wandered to the northern steppes from the Near East by at least two routes: through Iran to Turkestan; and westwards to Greece, thence through the Balkans and Carpathians to South Russia. Theirs was a fairly settled existence, based on hunting and fishing, the growing of cereals, and the breeding of cattle, sheep, goats, dogs and pigs. They kept horses too (probably the first domesticated horses in history), and may have trained these natives of the steppes to carry and draw loads.

The settled farming life of the Tripolye people is shown in this reconstruction (above) based upon what has been found at a typical site, Kolomishchina in the Ukraine, dated to the third millennium BC. The corn is being cut with flint-bladed sickles set in wooden handles, each household having its own patch in the cornfield. In the background is the village of wattle and daub huts grouped in a circle, and occupying a defensive site on a spur of ground overlooking the river. Among the huts, pigs can be seen rooting among the garbage. Cattle are grazing in the distance and hunters, accompanied by large, wolf-like hunting dogs, bring in a slaughtered deer. The dress and hair-style of the women have been inferred from the many clay figurines. Though battle axes have been found, it is not likely that settled agricultural communities such as this were warlike or aggressive. (1)

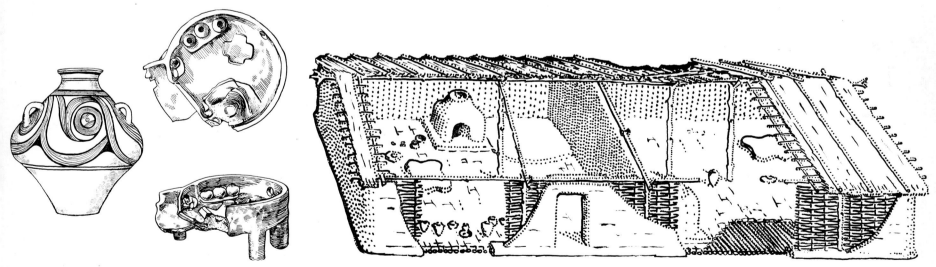

Among the advanced pottery of these neolithic farmers have been found, apart from domestic pots of a plain kind, more elaborate wares such as the 'classical' style pot above, with spiral designs painted on a yellow background, and curious clay model huts which may have had a religious or magical purpose. Complete in every detail, even to a tiny woman grinding corn, the one shown above is given a sort of porch, and appears to be standing on short legs, which suggests that huts were sometimes built on piles where the ground was marshy. It was found at Popudnia, in the Ukraine. (2)

The Tripolyans lived in clay and wattle huts which can be reconstructed from the baked clay platforms resulting from the burning and collapse of walls and floors. The cut-away drawing above shows the reconstruction of a two-room hut at Vladimirovka. Each room had a clay oven set against the wall, which would serve for heating as well as cooking. The clover-shaped platform, sometimes found adorned with paint or with engraved lines, has been interpreted as an altar. The roof would probably be of thatch, and the floor, of clay or trodden earth, rested on close-set timbers. (3)

The earliest herdsmen

began to appear on the steppes of South Russia and the Caucasus about 2300 BC, and it is from this time too that the first traces are found of those nomad peoples who may have spoken Indo-European languages. These early pastoralists made a greater use of metal, and also buried their chiefs under conspicuous mounds. It is from these burials that almost all the evidence about them comes, since, moving from place to place with their herds, they would naturally put a premium on lightness and portability. Felt tents on a light framework leave little or no trace for the archaeologist. As these pastoral societies developed, signs of rank and wealth began to appear in the burials, and the so-called 'Royal Tombs' contain luxury articles copied or imported from the Near East.

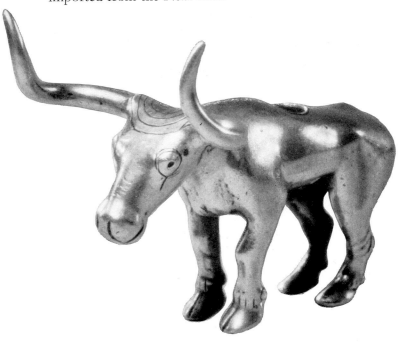

In the Royal Tomb at Maikop in the Kuban Basin this gold figure of a bull (above) was found, once part of the canopy that was held over the body of the dead chief (see *fig. 5*, p. 320). Four poles supported the canopy, and these ran down through the bull-figures, which thus rested on the hands of the bearers. (4)

At about the same time, before 2000 BC, princely burials at Alaca Hüyük, south of the Causasus, had treasures such as the stag on the right, of copper inlaid with electrum. Similarity of style implies that the Caucasian herdsmen had some contact with Asia Minor. (5)

A most complicated landscape is incised on this silver vase (below) from the Maikop burial. Against a background of jagged mountains the artist has depicted bulls, a lion with a bird of prey on its back, wild mouflon sheep and a boar. The design has affinities with Near Eastern work. (6)

The charging boar in the carved stone slab below, from Alaca Hüyük (13th century BC) foreshadows the style of Scythian animal art nearly a thousand years later, but has affinities with more or less contemporary Caucasian forms. (7)

Horse and rider, as opposed to horse and chariot, began to appear soon after the 14th century BC, originally perhaps in the north of Iran, then spreading through the mountain zone to the steppes. From Luristan, in Iran, comes this 8th-century bronze cheek-piece of a horse's bit (below); comparison with the earlier horseman on the right suggests that Cimmerian nomad horsemen may have penetrated into Iran from the steppes. (8)

The weapons of the steppe horsemen included bronze battle axes such as the one shown below (c. 1000–800 BC). Engraved, often with elaborate animal motifs, axes of this type and date, found throughout Eastern Europe, may have been made by the first speakers of Indo-European tongues. Their ornamentation shows a resemblance to Scythian weapons of nearly five hundred years later. (9)

The first mounted nomads to dominate and plunder the steppe pastoralists were the people known to classical writers as the Cimmerians, who ruled the Caucasus and the Pontic steppes from about 1200 BC until they gave way to the Scythians. This bronze cloak-pin (above) comes from Koban, N. Caucasus, and shows a mounted warrior of about 1000 BC. (10)

Chariots and horsemen painted on a terracotta sarcophagus from Klazomenai, a Greek city on the coast of Asia Minor, may be Cimmerians. This sarcophagus is dated to the sixth or fifth century BC, so these mounted warriors would be descendants of the nomad Cimmerians who invaded Asia Minor in 680–670 BC—according to Herodotus, in flight from the Scythians. (11)

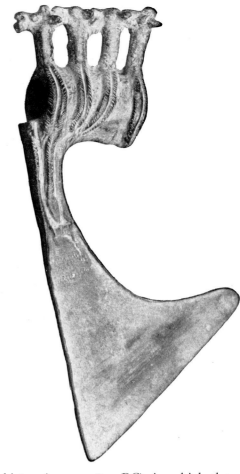

The most exciting manifestation of the steppe nomads was the individual and vigorous—at times almost abstract—art of the Scythians. The influences that made it are diverse, for it owes something to Bronze Age Anatolia, to the Hittites, to Iran, to the Assyrians, and later to the Greeks. Above, left, is a ceremonial iron battle axe,

inlaid with silver, from Uzbekistan (c. 1000–800 BC), in which the tiger attacking an ibex foreshadows Scythian modes in both theme and treatment. Elaborate animal ornament embellishes the head of a bronze ceremonial axe (above, right) from the Luristan region of Iran, of about the same date. (12, 13)

Assyrian inspiration is seen in the magnificent gold pectoral below, from Ziwiye, near Lake Urmia in Kurdistan (late 7th century BC). The Ziwiye treasure, other pieces of which are shown here, may once have belonged to the Scythian king Bartatua, who married an Assyrian princess. The stylized tree in the centre, the ibex on each

side of it, the winged human-headed bulls, are typically Assyrian; but in the corners are a running hare and a crouching animal, characteristically Scythian. Similar ones appear in pl. 19 opposite. The golden eagle below, also from Ziwiye, shows both Scythian and Assyrian influence, but is probably of Assyrian workmanship. (14, 15)

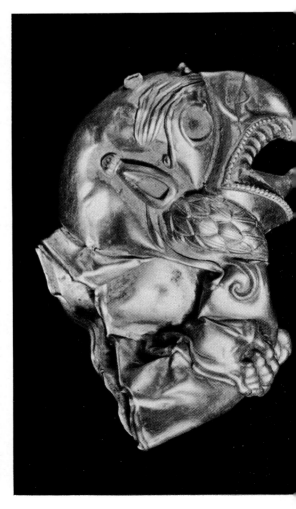

A lioness and her cub, very much in the Scythian style, decorate this Luristanian bronze axe (above). From Lake Van, c. 900 BC. (16)

Sphinxes and winged gods on the gilt and silver mirror above, from the Kuban (7th century BC) show Phoenician and Rhodian influence. It also recalls Iranian work such as the Ziwiye treasure. (18)

Gold band with crouching beasts in repoussé, inlaid with blue paste. To show the animals facing alternate ways is a typically Scythian device; compare pl. 19, on the right. From the Ziwiye treasure, late 7th century BC. (17)

One of the finest pieces in the Ziwiye treasure is this silver dish (below), about 14 inches across. It is typically Scythian in design and execution, with its concentric circles of animals facing different ways. A row of lynx-like creatures can be seen near the centre, crouching and facing left. Outside them, hares run to the right. Beyond them again, the lynxes reappear sitting up in pairs, facing each other. (19)

Gold is used in profusion in Scythian art. In the sword sheath from Kul Oba (top) a sea monster, half horse, is disposed on the hilt cover, and along the length of it are lions attacking stags. The lower scabbard, from a grave at Litoi, South Russia, excavated at the orders of Catherine the Great in 1760, shows Persian influence in its shape and

in the winged lions advancing with drawn bows. But a closer look at the wings reveals a typically Scythian trick, the 'zoomorphic juncture', by which part of one animal is turned into part or the whole of another—in this case a fish, clinging to the lion's shoulder with its teeth. (20, 21)

Achilles among the daughters of Lycomedes is probably the scene represented in this golden bow-case (below) from the Chertomlyk barrow. It is of Greek workmanship of the fourth century BC, at a time when wealthy Scythians patronized Greek artists living in the colonies on the shores of the Black Sea. (22)

The crouching stag is a favourite Scythian motif. Of the two opposite, probably shield decorations, the left-hand is from the royal tomb at Kostromskaya (7th–6th century BC), the other a Greek version from Kul Oba (5th century). The one is vivid first-hand observation, the other, by comparison, lifeless and 'cluttered'. (23, 24)

The gold brooch above is another example of Greek art within the Scythian world, having probably been made at the trading centre of Pantikapaion on the Black Sea in the 5th century BC. The sea horse should be compared with the far more lively version in pl. 20 opposite. (25)

Akin to the Scythians in their art style and their way of life, the Sarmatians from beyond the Don displaced the Royal Horde in the 4th century BC. The massive gold plaque below, now in the Hermitage Museum, Leningrad, shows a fight between a tiger and a griffin—the half natural, half supernatural combat that was such a typical theme of nomad art. (26)

Thanks to Herodotus, and the many tomb excavations that add to his account, we know more about the funeral customs of the Scythians than about any other part of their lives. The painting above gives an idea of the elaborate, frenzied mourning ceremonial at the burial of a king. The royal corpse, embalmed with wax and aromatic herbs and laid upon a bier, would be taken on a solemn procession through the dead man's territory, visiting each of his subject tribes. At the head marched men carrying ceremonial poles topped with decorative bronze terminals, or tridents tipped with rattles to scare away evil spirits. Behind the bier walked concubines, servants and grooms with saddled and bridled horses, all of whom would be sacrificed and buried with the dead king, to accompany and serve him in the hereafter. At the tail of the procession followed a growing retinue of mourners, wailing and howling, staining the ground with their blood as they gashed and mutilated themselves with knives and arrows. (27)

A first-hand picture of Scythian costume, features and weapons is given by finds such as this Greek-made electrum vase (right) from Kul Oba (4th century BC). The short, belted tunic, the trousers tucked into soft boots, are reminiscent of peasants in pre-revolutionary Russia and confirm the descriptions given by Herodotus. The scenes appear to illustrate the aftermath of a battle, for one warrior is re-stringing his bow while another, his bow-case still slung at his side, is having a mouth wound dressed by a comrade. (28, 29)

All the mounted nomads, as far as the borders of China, had something like these decorative bronze pole-terminals—which may have had a religious meaning, or perhaps were the badges of an intertribal caste of warriors. The one on the left, 7th–6th century BC from Ul in the Kuban, is typically Scythian in the involved geometric bird's-head shape and the tiny heraldic stag; the other two are Chinese, the elk being Han dynasty and the stag belonging to the later Chou dynasty. (30)

Mounted Scythian bowmen prance in frozen movement round the lid of a South Italian bronze vessel of the early fifth century BC, of Greek workmanship. This was before the invention of the metal stirrup, which makes their horsemanship seem all the more centaurlike. The Scythians fired over the shoulder, and kept their horses' manes cropped to allow themselves freedom of movement. (31)

One of the luckiest finds
in archaeology was the Pazyryk tombs in the Altai Mountains of Siberia, where nomads akin to the Scythians had buried their chiefs in barrows topped with boulders. Radio-carbon dating gives 450–400 BC for Tombs 1 and 2, and about 400 BC for Tomb 5.

Through the centuries, water had leaked into these tombs and frozen, preserving the contents in a natural deep-freeze. This process was interrupted by the incursions of grave-robbers, but still much has been preserved. Particularly noteworthy are the furs, textiles and even the bodies, which have given invaluable information for the period.

Persian influence is strongly present in these finds, but it is also clear that the Altai nomads had contact with China.

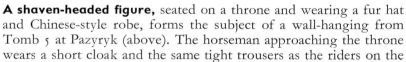

A shaven-headed figure, seated on a throne and wearing a fur hat and Chinese-style robe, forms the subject of a wall-hanging from Tomb 5 at Pazyryk (above). The horseman approaching the throne wears a short cloak and the same tight trousers as the riders on the carpet in pl. 39. The whole picture, repeated twice on a hanging some six yards by four, is carried out in felt appliqué on an off-white felt ground. The candelabra-like 'Tree of Life' suggests Mesopotamian influence; compare the gold pectoral of Ziwiye in pl. 14. (32, 33)

Griffin attacking an ibex: appliqué felt hanging from Tomb 1 at Pazyryk (left). In subject and style, especially in the impossibly twisted hindquarters of the victim, it recalls many earlier examples of nomad art: see, for instance, the Uzbek battle axe in pl. 12. (34)

Chinese influence is clear to be seen in the group of tethered swans (right), worked in appliqué felt. This formed part of the decoration of the covered funeral cart, which was taken to pieces and buried with the body. (35)

The only stringed instrument found at Pazyryk (below) was lying between the knees of the wife of the man buried in Tomb 2. Other tombs contained drums, whose main purpose perhaps was to frighten away malign spirits, but this was probably for entertainment only. It appears to be based on much the same principles as the lute. (36)

The vast, curving horns of this wooden stag (below) from Tomb 2 are made of leather. This is another example of the pole terminal so widely used on the steppes, and recalls the bronze ones from South Russia as well as the similar specimens from China. (37)

The horses buried in the Pazyryk tombs, many of them thorough-breds, were fully caparisoned, and in some cases they wore strange masks representing reindeer (below) or griffins. Made of leather and fur, these masks must have had some magical significance. (38)

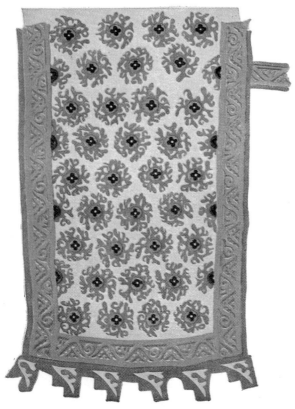

Some astonishing textiles have survived for more than two thousand years from Tomb 5 at Pazyryk. The woollen pile carpet above, which is probably of Persian workmanship, is about four square yards in extent. Around a central design of plant ornaments is disposed a procession of stags; an outer band shows a row of riders (riding in the opposite direction: compare pl. 19), dressed in hoods, tunics and tight trousers. Their horses have clipped manes and feathered headdresses. (39)

Saddle-cloths as rich as carpets were found in the Pazyryk tombs, together with ornate saddles, bridles and harness. The saddle-cloths were usually made of felt, sometimes with strips of woven material mounted on them, and with woollen tassels. (40, 41)

The nomad peoples of the Steppes

E. D. PHILLIPS

The Steppes

THE NORTHERN STEPPES, in their immense extent from Hungary to Manchuria, form a peculiar region of the world. In South Russia and Western Siberia they are more like the prairies of North America, and well suited to agriculture or to pasturage. But in other areas, particularly in central Asia and further east, they are now desert, not so different from the Sahara, Arabia and the Near East, which have also been the home of peoples with the nomadic mode of life who have made their mark on history.

The whole region between the northern forests and the great mountain zone which divides northern from southern Asia falls into two halves, a western and an eastern, which for our period have different histories.

The western half begins with the Hungarian plain between the Balkans and the Carpathians. It extends through parts of Rumania and Bulgaria to South Russia and to East Russia between the Caucasus mountains and the Ural forests. It continues through southern Siberia and the region of Kazakhstan, north of the Persian plateau, to a mountain barrier consisting of the Pamir, the western Tien Shan, the smaller ranges east of Lake Balkash, and the Altai Mountains bordering on Outer Mongolia. The eastern half beyond the Pamir can again be divided into two areas of steppe, a southern one stretching north of Tibet and south of the Tien Shan through the Tarim basin to north-west China and Mongolia, and a northern part, running north of the Tien Shan likewise to Mongolia. In Mongolia the two parts join and continue, with the Ordos desert attached on the south, through the Gobi desert between China and the eastern Altai to the Khingan mountains and to Manchuria beyond them. The eastern half is higher and harsher in climate, contains far more desert, and is sharply marked off from the mountains and from the cultivated lands of China. The northern and southern boundaries of the steppes come closest to one another in the region of Zungaria, part of northern Sinkiang, which has often been a decisive territory for the passage of nomad hordes.

East of Zungaria and far to the north and south in Eastern Asia the dominant types of man from the beginning of our period have been of the mongoloid type, as represented today by the Chinese. They originated perhaps in the Gobi region before or during the last glaciation, perhaps 50,000-20,000 years ago. In the northern forests they spread westward to the shores of the Baltic, where their presence has been traced by anthropologists (by means of characteristic skull-types) in the hunter-fisher population of the Neolithic period, about 2000 BC. But on the western half of the steppes the earliest population belonged to the white races. Mongoloids hardly appear there before the Hunnish movement into Central Asia during the last centuries BC. But white nomads were known on the north-west border of China during the first millennium BC and later left descendants among the Mongols themselves.

The course of events on the northern steppes during the period of growth of the great civilizations is a vast and vague subject, far less compact than the development of any more settled communities. It shows neither its full importance nor any degree of unity until the end, when the nomad societies, the distinctive product of the steppes, begin to make their contribution to world history. By 1000 BC the ancient civilizations of the first generation had largely run their courses and left their permanent mark on mankind. The nomad societies, on the other hand, had at that time no long history behind them, but were destined during the next two thousand years and more

to intervene catastrophically in the affairs of many civilizations. To trace their origin is thus a historical task of the highest interest, and only in our time has it become possible to do so.

European knowledge of the steppes in ancient times began with the study of the Greek descriptions of the Scythians given in the *Histories* of Herodotus (written in the fifth century BC), and in the medical essay, *Airs, Waters and Places*, of about the same date and attributed to Hippocrates. These could be supplemented from the later historians who deal with the Huns, and from such European writers as Carpini, Rubruquis and Marco Polo, who described the Tartars in the Middle Ages.

From the eighteenth century onward the Greek sources began to be tested by excavation of the great mounds of the Russian Steppe, which revealed burials corresponding closely with those mentioned by Herodotus, and described later in this chapter. At the same time archaeological exploration of the Near East brought to light Assyrian and other records, in which information was found of nomad invasions, confirming and supplementing Herodotus. In the Far East, Chinese records have yielded some evidence concerning the nomads early in the first millennium BC. Meanwhile prehistoric archaeology has been continued in Russian territories by Soviet scholars, who have added greatly to our knowledge and finally provided a general framework for the entire history of the ancient nomads. Nomadism as a developed way of life, however, arose relatively late from a background of more or less settled agricultural communities, and it is to the origins of these that we must first turn.

The Beginnings

In Siberia and Mongolia the Palaeolithic (Old Stone Age) traditions lingered long, and even at a period contemporary with the beginnings of civilization in Western Asia, man was still a hunter without the opportunity for agriculture, using spears and arrows tipped with bone, various bone tools, rounded stone axes, and a crude pottery. In the remoter parts around Lake Baikal and in Manchuria, skeletons of the same period are found with remains that show only the primitive hunting and fishing economy of late palaeolithic type, such as is described in chapter I. Further south stone tools of the so-called 'microlithic' type and arrowheads have been found in the Gobi and Ordos regions. Before the pottery-making phase this culture extended southward through Central Asia and the Aral region to the Indian Ocean. It represents an advance on the Palaeolithic, and had evidently spread from the south-west through the eastern half of the steppes, probably in moister conditions than those that now prevail. The steppes even then appear as a corridor allowing the spread of population and techniques over great distances to the east. In the west these early periods are already beginning to be dominated by stone-using cultures involving animal husbandry and grain cultivation, described below.

Agriculture and Herding

The most plausible theory for the origin of herding is that it arose from agriculture in places where the wild animals grew accustomed to feeding on plants cultivated by men. This would most naturally happen in countries of little rainfall, where the best watered ground near springs or rivers would often be occupied by human cultivators. Though they would not be welcome at first, the animals under stress of hunger would be persistent visitors and become familiar with the sight of man. These would be the best conditions for catching them alive and keeping them for later eating. The value of females for milk would soon be obvious, and eventually also the usefulness of the larger and stronger animals for work.

The earliest known agriculture, at any rate of cereals, began as we have seen in Western Asia, before the seventh millennium BC, precisely in these dry conditions, and on occasion (as at Jericho) round about sources of water. As early as the fifth millennium (and perhaps before) sheep, goats and cattle, and later even the onager or wild ass, appear to have been tamed, to judge from bones on the sites. If stock-breeding arose as part of the first neolithic culture in Western Asia, we have also a readier explanation for the development of specialized herding on its southern fringe in Arabia and North Africa, where the known history of nomadism begins earlier. It is most important for our purpose that though the onager and the ass are native to the Near East, the horse is not, so that horsebreeding cannot have originated there.

Chronological Table of cultures and movements on the Northern Steppes 3000 BC – AD 100

	SOUTH RUSSIA	CAUCASIA and NEAR EAST	KAZAKHSTAN and WESTERN SIBERIA
	Neolithic on steppes with mixed farming Whites on steppes, mongoloid element in forests	Neolithic mixed farming with transhumance N. of Caucasus. Full civilization in Near East with copper and bronze	Neolithic mixed farming scattered in suitable places Mongoloids in forest, whites on steppes
3000 BC	*Tripolye A* *(I)* *Tripolyan culture* introduced from west, in Ukraine *Painted pottery*		
2750			
2500	*Tripolye B I* *(II)*		*Afanasievo culture* on steppe
		Mesopotamian influence in Caucasia; copper imports Early Indo-Europeans on Caucasian steppe? *Large barrows: pit-graves. Pastoralism in North Caucasia. Ochre burials* Nalchik, Maikop and similar Kuban burials	
2250	*Tripolye B II* *(III)*	COPPER AGE IN CAUCASIA BEGINS	
	Pastoral societies spreading on Pontic coast Ochre burials. Pit-graves Usatovo Mariupol COPPER AGE		COPPER AGE
2000	*Tripolye C* *(IV)* *Catacomb graves* on Pontic coast in SE End of Tripolyan culture	Connection of Caucasia with Near East broken. Indic branch of Indo-Europeans crosses Caucasus, while Iranian branch remains north of it Kuban-Terek culture on Caucasian steppe *Catacomb graves. Chariots in Near East*	
1750	Ochre burials become general on Pontic steppe Pastoral peoples dominant Cimmerians?	BRONZE AGE *North Caucasian Dolmens* Cimmerians in North Caucasia and on Caucasian steppe? Riding for war becomes commoner in Near East	*Andronovo culture* on steppe BRONZE AGE
1500		but charioteering still dominant	
1250	Cimmerians dominant on Pontic steppe Links with Hallstatt culture in Central Europe *Mounted nomadism beginning*	*Hittite Empire falls* IRON AGE BEGINS IN NEAR EAST Iranian peoples begin to spread south through Caucasia to north-western Iran *Mounted nomadism beginning on Caucasian steppe?*	*Late Andronovo culture* on steppe Indo-Europeans begin to spread eastward
1000	Cimmerians dominant on Pontic steppe Timber graves on Volga steppe Early Scythian mounted nomads Scythians move west, ? pressure from Sarmatians Scythians begin to oust Cimmerians from Pontic steppe	*Koban culture* in northern Caucasia and astride the range. *Gandsha Karabagh* culture in Transcaucasia and *Talysh culture* in Azerbaijan show affinities with *Luristan culture* of Zagros Mts. Caucasian forerun- ners of Animal Style?	Mounted nomadism spreading eastward Pontic-Tocharian migration? *Late Andronovo culture* disappearing Sarmatian peoples becoming dominant and begin- ning to press westward later toward the Volga
750	Cimmerians migrate towards Armenia Scythian horde occupies Pontic steppe and crosses Caucasus Scythians return over Caucasus Royal burials in Kuban and then on Dniepr *Animal style flourishes on Pontic steppe*	Cimmerians devastate Urartu, threaten Assyria, overrun Phrygia, Lydia and Greek territories on coast. *Transcaucasian Lelvar culture*. Scythians cross Caucasus; ally with Assyria. Medes defeat Assyria and Scythians. Persian empire dominant *Ziwiye Treasure*	Sarmatian peoples
500	Royal Horde of Scythians attacked unsuccessfully by Darius of Persia Scythian trade with Greek cities; contact with Celts and Thracians Scythians ousted from Pontic steppe by Sarmatians	Sarmatians on Caucasian steppe Persian empire falls to Alexander	*Siberian Animal Style*
250	Sarmatians on Pontic steppe and in Hungary encounter Celts and Germans		Sarmatians
0			
100 AD	Sarmatians		Huns moving westward, eventually to reach South Russia in fourth century AD

CENTRAL ASIA, ZUNGARIA, PAMIR, TURKESTAN, ARAL REGION	ALTAI, UPPER YENISEI, TARIM BASIN	FAR EAST	
Neolithic mixed farming except in mountains and deserts	Mesolithic, or neolithic, stone-technique but hunting and fishing economy. Mongoloids in forests, whites on steppes	Mesolithic in north Beginning of neolithic toward China *Serovo culture* in Siberia. Hunting and fishing	3000 BC
Anau I in Turkestan *Painted Pottery* *Kelteminar culture* in Aral region. Neolithic with painted pottery but largely hunting and fishing			
Anau II in Turkestan COPPER AGE		*Kitoi culture* in Siberia, hunting and fishing Neolithic stone-technique	2750
Anau III in Turkestan *Late Kelteminar culture* in Aral region	*Afanasievo culture*, mainly stockbreeding Ochre burials	*Glazkovo culture* in Siberia, hunting and fishing	2500
			2250
BRONZE AGE		Painted pottery in China *Late Glazkovo culture* in Siberia	2000
Tazabagyab culture in Aral region		*Yang Shao culture* on Upper Hwang-Ho *Lung Shan culture* on Lower Hwang-Ho, with black polished pottery	
Andronovo culture in north	BRONZE AGE *Andronovo culture* of mixed farming, increasing settlement	BRONZE AGE *Shang state* founded in Hwang-Ho valley	1750
		Chariots used in warfare Pressure of Shang state on neighbours including those to the north	1500
			1250
Karasuk culture in some places	Mongoloids of North Chinese type begin to appear in burials. *Karasuk culture* of mixed farming with strong stockbreeding element	North-westward migration of shepherd tribes with some agriculture from North Chinese border into Siberia *Chou Dynasty* in China	
Mounted nomadism spreading eastward to Zungaria and Pamir *Late Andronovo culture disappearing* in north Chorasmian region south of Aral settled from Iran	Mounted nomads reach Altai and Minusinsk *Karasuk culture disappearing*	Chinese influence spreading northward Mounted nomads perhaps on western edge of Kansu (Pontic-Tocharian migration?)	1000
Saka peoples Persian Empire in conflict with Saka peoples	Sarmatian poeples? *Maiemir culture* in Altai begins *Tagar culture* in Minusinsk begins	Sarmatian peoples on the NW edge of China? Also Yue-Chi (Tocharians)?	750
Central Asian Animal Style	Pazyryk tombs in Altai begin. *Animal Style of Altai and Minusinsk* Some mongoloids beginning to be mounted nomads in Altai Later Pazyryk tombs contain Chinese fabrics	*Animal Style of Ordos and Southern Gobi* Sarmatian influence Hsiung-Nu become mounted nomads? Mounted nomadism beginning in E. Siberia and Manchuria?	500
Sakas Huns in central Asia	TARIM BASIN Han Dynasty's campaigns Cities of Tarim region submit: inhabitants Iranian? Little Yue-Chi settle	China: *Chou dynasty falls. Han Empire* Constant threat of Mongolian Hsiung-Nu Hsiung-Nu drive Yue-Chi west; after their confederacy broken, move west as Huns Manchurian mounted nomads later enemies of Hsiung-Nu	250
			0
			100 AD

During the fourth and third millennia BC peoples with subsistence based on mixed farming, making pottery and using stone tools, began to spread towards the northern steppes. One route along which these new techniques of living spread lay north-eastward through Iran to Turkestan, where near Merv the settlement of Anau had a long history. Another route ran north-westward through southern Asia Minor, across the Aegean to Greece, and so through the Balkans to the Danube valley and South Russia. It is less easy to trace a direct northward spread through the difficult country of Armenia and the Caucasus. From South Russia, where the Tripolye culture was in existence probably from the beginning of the third millennium, and from Central Asia, neolithic cultures apparently reached North China and neighbouring regions.

The neolithic basis assumed for stockbreeding is thus likely to have existed at suitable places throughout the northern steppes at least from the third millennium onwards, and this could have developed on the fringes of cultivation into specialized herding. It is clear that in suitable conditions this could arise anywhere from the neolithic mixed economy, and also from any similar economy in the early stages of the use of metal, as in the Bronze and Early Iron Ages.

 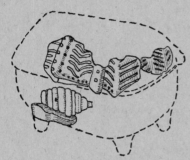

Pottery models of Tripolye houses with gabled roofs, and with designs on the walls similar to the pottery. (fig. 1)

The Tripolye Culture (c. 3000-1700 BC)

This culture is important not only because of its early date, but because of its difference from succeeding cultures, which were nomadic. It takes its name from Tripolye, near Kiev, where it was first excavated, and was the product of communities that carried on mixed farming of the neolithic pattern on the fertile wind-blown soil or loess, stretching from the lower Danube round the eastern end of the Carpathians and across Bessarabia and the Ukraine as far as the Dniepr, and for some distance beyond. The painted pottery, clay models of houses and clay figurines made by the Tripolye people show their affinity with the neolithic peoples of the Balkans. Four main stages can be recognized (referred to here as Phases I-IV), between approximate limits of 3000 and 1700 BC; the earlier date is rather hypothetical but is supported by recent C 14 tests. Nearly all the details known are derived from settlements and not from burials.

Life was based on the cultivation of wheats, barley and millet, and on the breeding of cattle, goats, sheep, and pigs, the last unsuited to a nomadic existence and native to wooded country. The bones of horses occur at all levels, and the tame horses of this culture are probably the earliest in history. They were apparently at first kept for meat, but later are likely to have carried and drawn loads. Wheeled vehicles are not known from these sites, but there are clay models of sledges. The camel was known toward the end of the Tripolye phase, no doubt as an import from the east. In the refuse of food, the percentage of game-bones declines steadily. Fishing is attested by fish-hooks of bone or copper from the earliest sites, and small perforated pieces of clay are probably net-sinkers. Copper was first used for fish-hooks, rings, bangles and beads, and later for axes, adzes, picks and broad daggers with a central rib. There is no sign yet of the plough drawn by animals.

The settlements were generally in defensible positions on spurs of loess above river valleys. The most representative sites are in the region of wooded steppe, not on the barer steppe or near the coast. At Vladimirovka on the Bug the largest village known contained (in Phase III) as many as two hundred houses in five concentric circles. Their sites are represented by platforms of baked clay resulting from the burning and collapse of walls and floors. Post-holes for timber frames define rectangular floors varying between 7 x 4 m. and 27 x 6.5 m. The walls were of wattle and clay or of compacted earth, coloured over, and the roofs probably of thatch. A middle-sized house

(Phase II) contained two separate rooms, each with a clay oven 2 m. square, set against the wall, while the largest known house at Vladimirovka contained five rooms, four with one oven and the fifth with two. The floors are of well smoothed and hard baked clay, and on the underside show the imprint of close-set timbers that supported them. It is not certain whether there was empty space under the timbers, as has sometimes been claimed; they may simply have rested on the earth. These floors were proof against damp, rodents and insects.

Among the fixtures, the clay ovens were constructed on frames of saplings, which left their impression on the inner surface. The frames would no doubt perish with continual heating, but by the same process the clay would become nearly as hard as earthenware. Apart from baking bread and cooking, the ovens no doubt served in winter as stoves to warm the houses. Beside them were wide raised benches of baked clay, which could be used as shelves, and would also have been convenient for sitting and sleeping. Near the centre of the floor in every room was a low clay platform about 0.25 m. high, shaped like a cross when viewed from above, and adorned with engraved lines or with paint. These have been interpreted as altars for offerings. The cross-shape is stout and rounded, and recalls the shapes of altars known from Minoan sites on Crete, such as Mallia (pl. 3).

Though the 'altars' themselves have been found only at Vladimirovka, models of them occur elsewhere as parts of complete clay model huts, also belonging to this period *(fig. 1)*. A very remarkable round model hut from Popudnia stands on short legs, which again suggests that the original building was raised on piles, and has a sort of porch. It contains an altar, an oven, three vessels on a bench, and two small female figurines, one of a woman grinding with a stone quern by the porch, and another, seated by the oven, who may be the protecting goddess of the house. This seeming dolls' house no doubt had a religious or magical purpose, and is now exceedingly helpful to archaeologists (pl. 2).

Ovens, benches, and altars were apparently the only fixtures. The movable objects were, typically, querns for grinding grain; jars for holding liquids, flour and seeds, other pottery, tools as described, needles, spindle-weights and a great number of clay statuettes, nearly all of them female. The statuettes are usually found near the ovens or the altars. Many of them were no doubt used for the rites of an agricultural religion. The commoner type of figurine is nude, and may represent the mother-goddess, as in the Balkans, the Aegean, and Western Asia. These may have been dressed for ritual occasions. Others seem to represent women, and have painted on them belts, which could have held up skirts, a sort of bodice, and a style of hairdressing that suggests a chignon *(fig. 2)*. Traces of plant fibres and wool from excavations confirm the existence of clothing of these materials. The figurines show that the feminine influence was strong. Though the remains include battle-axes, it is not likely that war was common or serious among such communities.

Ordinary domestic pottery of a plain kind was made, probably by the women, from stocks of prepared clay, such as were discovered in some houses. Professionally made pottery was red or orange, with elaborate, often spiral, designs painted on in darker colours, some-

Head of painted pottery figurine from one of the houses at Vladimirovka, showing the style of hairdressing. (fig. 2)

times over a white slip. This was fired in vertical kilns such as one whose remains were found at Erösd in Transylvania, stacked with vases (pl. 2, left).

The last stages of the village however show that settled life was increasingly abandoned. Large settlements disappeared, agriculture declined into second place as a source of livelihood, and the painted pottery gave way to another type. The Tripolye culture must have been broken up by immigrants who had a pastoral culture and a different structure of society.

Further east, in Siberia there is still no evidence for any settled culture as old as the Tripolye, but there, and on the drier steppes, any remains would have been much more easily destroyed by cattle and winds. Yet it is of some significance that the Chinese Yang Shao culture of painted pottery occupied similar sites on loess terraces overlooking rivers, and in the Aral region the neolithic hunters and fishers of Kelteminar used a red painted pottery.

The Rise of Pastoral Societies

Thus far we have followed the slow spread over the northern steppes of settled agricultural communities derived from those of Western Asia. We now come to the beginning of pastoral societies on the northern steppes, which at their furthest development were as different from the settled cultures of the Near East as were the nomads of the southern deserts. In the west this process is also connected with another of special significance, the rise and spread of the peoples speaking Indo-European languages, to whom many of the northern nomads belonged.

The evidence for these earliest pastoralists comes almost wholly from graves, often under mounds or barrows forming groups or cemeteries, the monuments of these ancient peoples, visible even today on the wide steppe-land. The disentangling of the different cultural traditions over the vast area where the various groups had once moved with their flocks and herds is not an easy task, but what can be deduced is set out below.

The Usatovo Culture

As early as Phase III of the Tripolye culture in South Russia, the earliest known form of a different society was growing up on its fringes toward the Black Sea and the Caucasus. At Usatovo near Odessa remains were found of a society, probably with a more marked social stratification, which made greater use of metal and buried its chiefs under conspicuous mounds or barrows in cemeteries. The bodies were interred in a contracted position on one side, or on their backs, in a central shaft encircled by slabs set on edge. Slaves or dependants were killed and buried in accessory graves before the earth was heaped over the whole, and bones of animals and statuettes were buried in separate pits. Flat graves elsewhere, perhaps those of cultivators, consisted of shallow pits under flat slabs. Degenerate pottery and figurines of Tripolye style were found in both kinds of burial, and also a coarse ware bearing cord-impressions which some have thought characteristic of the early Indo-European peoples. Animal bones were very numerous and represented far more horses and far fewer pigs than Tripolye remains. The new type of pottery and selection of animal bones represent a pastoral element. Copper, in the form of daggers, flat axes, quadrangular awls and spiral rings, is much more abundant; some of the spirals are also of silver. The type of copper object distributed along the coast suggests a source overseas.

The Ochre-Grave Cultures

Further south and east remains are found of other cultures that have something in common with that of Usatovo but no Tripolye basis. They are distinguished usually by their barrow-graves, and by the habit of covering their dead with red ochre. Some of the 'ochre-graves', as they are called, are covered with long mounds and contain skeletons reddened with ochre arranged in groups. At Mariupol, on the Sea of Azov, 120 adults and 6 children were buried in a long communal grave; at Volnishki near Dniepropetrovsk 130 skeletons were buried together; and at Nalchik in North Caucasia 130 contracted skeletons were found, both under long mounds. A knobbed stone mace-head at Mariupol and copper rings, probably worn as hair ornaments, and carnelian beads at Nalchik show trading connections with the Near East, where such things could be obtained.

These various forms of burial are almost the only evidence we have of these peoples. Russian archaeologists have classified them as the cultures of shaft-graves, pit-graves and timber-graves, though the pit-graves (or catacomb-graves) are confined to the coast of the Black Sea and the basin of the Don. During this period, from the end of the third millennium and through the second, the richly furnished burials of the chieftains of the Caucasian Copper Age appear, again under large barrows. Finds from domestic sites, of the period of pit-graves under round barrows (burials, as the name implies, in a simple pit in the ground), show that cattle, sheep and goats were bred and millet cultivated. In a barrow at Storozhevaya Mogila near Dniepropetrovsk remains of a wooden cart with two solid wheels, used as a hearse, were found, which shows that wheeled vehicles had begun to be used on the Pontic steppe by the end of the third millennium, as also at Budakalász in Hungary, where a grave contained a clay model of a four-wheeled cart. At Ul in the Caucasus a clay model of a covered waggon may be dated about 1800 BC. Developed nomadism on the northern steppes was scarcely possible without waggons to transport families and their belongings (see p. 322 and *fig. 13*).

Afanasievo

Eastward in Siberia and Inner Asia during the same period developments are illustrated from the best explored region, the basin of the Upper Yenisei above the zone of forests.

Here remains representing communities living from perhaps 3000 to 1700 BC have been named by archaeologists the Afanasievo phase, after the locality of Afanasievaya Gora. We only know these peoples' graves, in the form of oval or rectangular trenches covered with stone slabs. Some burials are communal, some individual. The skeletons, as in the earliest herdsmen's graves on the Dniepr, are tall and long-headed, and in the Altai region, to which this culture also extends, some skulls are of the so-called Cro-Magnon type, long but with short broad faces. Again, as in South Russia, the dead are buried on their backs or on their sides in contracted position, and covered with ochre. In the Altai region the graves are in chambers roofed with stone slabs or tree trunks and covered with small barrows. Apart from tools of bone or antler, and bones of cattle, sheep and horses, these graves contain simple red pots, mostly with conical bases, recalling pottery styles from Transcaucasia, Persia and Transcaspia, and also copper plates, needles and spiral ornaments. Cultural links therefore are with the west and south-west among these earliest stockbreeders of Siberia. They were quite different from the neolithic mongoloids of which archaeological traces have been found to the north-east.

The Andronovo Culture

The next stage, dated provisionally from 1700 BC onward, is named after Andronovo on the Yenisei. It is best represented in the Minusinsk depression, an enclave of grassland in the forest, and in various forms covers the western Altai, the Semirechie, the Aral region, and Kazakhstan. It is known chiefly from burial grounds varying between three and fifty graves. The graves are marked with stone slabs or by small barrows surrounded with circles of stones. The burial chambers are lined with stone or tree trunks, and the dead usually lie in a bent position, but some were cremated. The racial type of the skeletons is again European, now for the first time with an admixture of the round-headed white race from the Pamir. These people made large flat-bottomed vases of a smooth brown pottery ornamented with triangles, diamonds, swastikas and other geometrical designs, or with meanders. Arrowheads are often of bone but sometimes of copper, like the occasional axes, knives, daggers and sickles, and moulds for casting these have been found. Gold is very common, and is used for covering plates of copper or bronze.

Remains of the horse and camel show that stockbreeding was important, but the copper sickles and stone hoes also indicate agriculture. One wealthy grave contained horses, probably to be ridden by the privileged dead. Some settlements have been found, with large houses and an open space by the village believed to be for laying out loaves. There is evidence everywhere of a tendency to form settled communities, except in eastern Kazakhstan. Russian prehistorians regard the phase as the greatest development of mixed economy in Siberia and Central Asia, though much later than the rather similar economy of Tripolye in the west. In Western Siberia, Kazakhstan and the Aral region it lasted for a long time. In the Yenisei basin and in the Altai, on the other hand, by 1100 BC or a little later a new culture appears, named after Karasuk in Minusinsk, which has important links with China.

The South Russian Region (2500-1000 BC)

From these communities of the third and second millennium BC, whose material equipment as known from their graves does not provide us with anything more than the rather humdrum products of peasant activity and skills, we can turn to look once again in the south Russian region, this time to the country north of the Caucasus, between the Black Sea and the Caspian. Here we encounter barrow burials again, but with a rich and varied equipment buried with the dead which make them merit the title of Royal Tombs.

A development in the prestige and wealth of the people of the ochre-graves must have begun towards the end of the third millennium in northern Caucasia, where wealthy chiefs' tombs show clear links with the Near East, in the form of luxury goods imported or copied from foreign originals. These tombs are situated in the basin of the Kuban River, on the northern side of the Caucasus. The burials resemble that already described at Nalchik, but are much richer and contain far fewer bodies. They are in fact the first princely burials or Royal Tombs, of a kind recurring at times for centuries afterwards among the pastoral warriors of the steppes, and show a much sharper distinction of rank between chiefs and subjects, such as arose when pastoral societies in their turn became wealthy.

Silver vessel with figures of panthers wearing collars. From the Royal Tomb, Maikop; compare pl. 6. (fig. 3)

The Maikop Burial

The most famous of these burials, and apparently the earliest (probably about 2300 BC), is that at Maikop on the Byelaya. Under a mound 10.65 m. high, at the level of the ground and within a ring of vertical slabs of limestone, was the main burial in what had been a rectangular wooden chamber 5.33 m. x 3.73 m. Before all the wood had rotted and the earth fallen in from above, the grave had been walled and roofed with beams, and its floor laid with broken stones, and outside a large wooden structure had been built enclosing it. The inner space had been divided into a northern and a southern compartment, and the northern compartment again into a western and an eastern half.

In the middle of the southern compartment lay a man's skeleton with knees drawn up and head to the south, as in most of these burials, and thickly covered with ochre. The body was strewn with gold ornaments, and beside it lay rods of gold and silver tubing with small figures of bulls in gold or silver (pl. 4). There were also beads of gold, turquoise and carnelian with the body, gold studs, rings of gold wire, and pierced disks of silver and gold. Vessels of gold or silver, or of stone adorned with these metals, stood along the eastern and western walls, some crushed by the earth on the collapse of the burial chamber.

From this collection of treasures about the body the burial could be reconstructed as it would have appeared when the tomb was closed and the great mound piled on the timber structures. The chieftain was probably wrapped in coloured robes, such as those later to be mentioned from Novosvobodnaya, and wore on his head a tiara of cloth or felt ornamented in front with two diadems, studded with golden rosettes, that were found near it (fig. 4). The rods, each made of three fitted sections of gold or silver tubing, seem to have been the

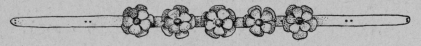

Golden rosettes from Maikop. These were probably mounted on felt or cloth as a diadem. (fig. 4)

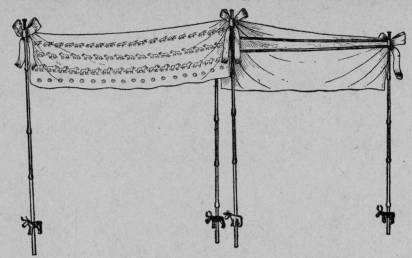

Maikop: reconstruction of the canopy that covered the chieftain's bier. For the gold bulls on the carrying poles see pl. 4. (fig. 5)

frame of a processional canopy held over the waggon or bier by four bearers. As carried in the procession, these four rods had been uprights, held at the bottom by bearers. Their lowest sections ran down through the bull-figures and projected a hand's breadth below, so that the figures would have rested on the bearers' hands, facing forwards. Through slits in the top sections, which were crowned with gold or silver caps, also found, ribbons had been passed to hold on the canopy. Two other rods without bulls or caps had been cross-pieces, perhaps fastened with ribbons, stretching from front to back (fig. 5).

In the tomb, the canopy that once covered this frame had been laid as a pall over the dead. Sixty-eight gold plaques of two sizes, representing lions, and nineteen similar ones representing bulls, all of them pierced with a few holes round the edges, lay among the bones. These had been sewn to the canopy, probably to front and rear flaps only, since more would have been needed for the whole cloth. The gold disks had also been sewn on, while the beads had belonged to necklaces or bracelets.

Among the vessels were two egg-shaped silver vases with necks. On one (pl. 6) is incised a most remarkable design—nothing less than a complicated landscape. In the background is a jagged range of mountains, interrupted by two palm-trees and a bear reared up between them; in the foreground two streams flow down into a round lake. Across this scene walk two processions of animals: in one a bull, a wild steppe horse, and a lion with a bird of prey on its back, while another bull faces the opposite way; in the other a boar, a tiger perhaps, and two wild mouflon sheep. The second vessel shows in procession a bull, a mouflon, panthers apparently with collars, and a duck-like bird (fig. 3).

Among weapons were an axe-adze, a straight-bladed axe and a cross-bladed adze, all of copper, the last two of Mesopotamian type, and evidently the symbols of power and authority of the chieftain in life. Flint arrowheads lay by the body.

Of the other two chambers, the eastern one contained the skeleton of a woman with earrings of gold wire, beads of gold and carnelian, and vessels of copper, and the western a man's skeleton with beads and a large earthenware jar. These are likely to have been servants, put to death to accompany their master.

Other Burials

The burial at Maikop, though most remarkable and exciting, is not unique. Two graves discovered under great mounds at Tsarskaya, now Novosvobodnaya, were similarly those of chieftains or members of princely classes. These differed from that of Maikop in having chambers which were of stone and not wood (like the 'dolmens' of the northern Caucasus mentioned below), but contained similar weapons. One was gabled, like a miniature house, the other was flat-roofed, and both had two compartments, the larger in each case containing the body. Ochre was spread over the bodies and in one case even on a wall of the chamber. Among the weapons were curious socketed fork-heads of copper, rather like pitch-forks, but with their points bent into hooks; one was even adorned with human figures. In the second grave the skeleton was still wrapped in a black fur coat with the hair outside and a silver collar; under this was a cloak of camel's wool with black stripes, and under that again a linen garment

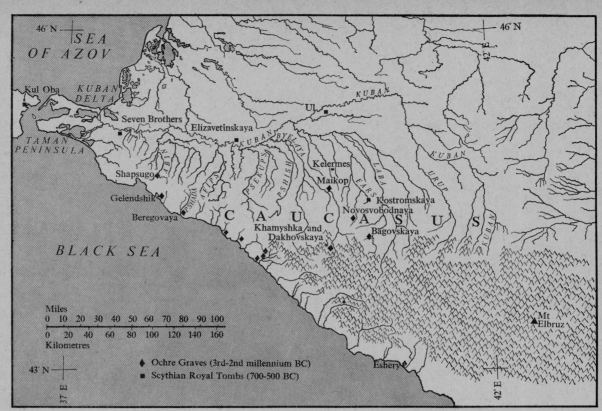

Maikop and associated early ochre-graves in the Kuban Basin. The map also shows Scythian royal burials of some 1500 years later (see p. 325). (fig. 6)

with a purplish-red border. These precious surviving fragments show how much we have lost of the craftsmanship in furs and textiles of these peoples.

These princely burials resemble in many respects others south of the Caucasus at Alaca Hüyük (described in chapter VI). Their contents recall the treasures at Troy II in Asia Minor and the finds at Hissar in Iran. All are related to Mesopotamian royal burials in their conception and in the style of some of their contents, particularly the bronze weapons. The design of landscape and animals on one of the Maikop vases has general affinities with Near Eastern work, and the lions, tigers, and panthers as subjects point in the same direction. It is likely that the vases and plaques are imports, or the work of a craftsman from Western Asia. No burials equalling these in splendour are known on the steppe in the Kuban region or near it until the Scythian period, more than a millennium later, when contact with the Near East was again close. The semi-precious stones used for beads include carnelians from India or Iran, lazurite from Central Asia, and meerschaum from Anatolia.

In this region archaeologists have determined a sequence of cultures from the early second millennium BC onwards, named Nalchik, Kuban, and Kuban-Terek, of which the last extends right across the Caucasian steppe. Later in the Kuban stage (after 1500 BC) the connection with the Near East was broken off, and the peoples of these regions were thrown upon their own resources in metallurgy. They made connections instead with the Danubian region and the Urals for new supplies, apparently not yet knowing those of Transcaucasia.

In the North Caucasus stone-built tombs known as 'dolmens' were being built at this time. They are usually built in the form of a square or oblong stone cist, roofed with a similar slab and pierced through one wall with a hole for offerings. But some are boxes hollowed out of one massive rock. Their connections seem to be Asiatic rather than European or West Mediterranean. The best known are those of Gelendshik, Beregovaya, Dakhovskaya and Storozhevaya, and of the avenue at Novosvobodnaya *(fig. 7, 8)*. They contained copper or bronze weapons, such as spearheads, axes and daggers, but also arrowheads and small blades of flint.

The First Indo-European Migrations (c. 1900-1000 BC)

During the long period of rising pastoral societies the Indo-European peoples, who all show traces of such a phase in their history, must first have come into prominence. Attempts have been made to equate linguistics and archaeology north of the Black Sea and the Caucasus, and to suggest that the corded pottery and the battle axes of stone or metal that spread through eastern Europe at this time, particularly on the fringes of the old Tripolye and Danubian cultures, were made by speakers of Indo-European tongues. It is likely that the Indo-European languages arose on the Pontic and Caucasian steppes, not far from Anatolia, where Hittite and related languages of the Hittite Empire have left written traces beginning early in the second millennium, as we saw in chapter VI.

Though the route by which the Hittites entered Anatolia cannot yet be traced archaeologically, it is a reasonable guess that they

Stone burial chamber with 'porthole': Gelendshik, Caucasus. (fig. 7)

Decorated porthole slab from a dolmen near Storozhevaya, Caucasus. (fig. 8)

arrived about 1900 BC by way of the Caucasus. The same route was probably taken by the ruling element among the people known as the Kassites in the Zagros Mountains, who seem to have had Indo-European names. It was also no doubt followed by a much stronger group, the Aryans, later of India and Iran, evidence of whose language appears early in the second millennium south-east of the Hittites in the country of the Hurrians, originally a Caucasian people. People with Indo-European names ruled the Mitannian kingdom in northern Iraq and Syria in the middle of the second millennium. Others passed on through Iran to found the Sanskrit-speaking Aryan society of India. Corded pottery found in the stone cist-graves of Kayakent near Derbent has been claimed as evidence that the Aryans passed the Caucasus by this route along the Caspian coast. Some Indo-European names of Mitannian kings appear with Caucasian suffixes in Hittite texts. The name of the ancient Sindians of the Kuban delta may be the Sanskrit *sindhava*, 'men of the river'. It is suggested that these Indo-Europeans remained in their old home when the majority passed southward, to arrive eventually on the banks of another river that they likewise called Sindhu and we call the Indus.

Karasuk stele at Tasmin, Minusinsk. (fig. 9)

Another movement of Indo-Europeans passed southward later to settle in Iran, after which their whole group has since been named Iranians. Some Iranians remained north of the Caucasus and became mounted nomads; other Indo-Europeans to take up nomadism were some of the Thracians and also the Tocharians.

The Conditions of Nomadism: (1) Waggons and Chariots

In spite of the important part played in the development of a characteristic economy by the pastoral peoples so far described, the peoples of the steppes did not exert their greatest effect on the outside world until the rise of mounted nomadism, which is the culmination of ancient life on the steppes. But the change follows closely on the full development of an earlier use of the horse in war for drawing the light chariot with spoked wheels.

In Mesopotamia the Sumerians had by 3000 BC or so converted the waggon to military use as a heavy war-car, with solid wheels, drawn by onagers. The horse appears to have been introduced for drawing a new light kind of war-chariot with spoked wheels by the Hurrians of North Syria, already mentioned, or rather by their Indo-European rulers. It is a plausible suggestion that the Indo-Europeans brought the horse to south of the Caucasus early in the second millennium, and that the Hurrians as their allies and subjects developed the light chariot in this suitably timbered region for the faster and more manageable animal. The war-chariot as a revolutionary weapon invented on the edge of Near Eastern civilization became a decisive factor in warfare in the Near East itself, in Europe, and also, as is now apparent, so far away as China.

How it reached China is not certain, but it appears (as we saw in chapter IX) in the armies of the later rulers of the Shang Dynasty at Anyang in the twelfth century BC. Traces of chariots have been found in Shang tombs, and the early form of the Chinese script current at this date contains a sign for chariot.

The Karasuk Culture (c. 1000 BC)

The population of the Minusinsk region now shows a great increase, and physical remains appear of a mongoloid type, but usually with some special traits not found in the peoples of the Siberian forests, but belonging to the northern borders of China. The skeletons are slight and the skulls small, low, and narrow in the face. The animal bones in the graves show an increase of sheepbreeding, but the many large pots suitable for grain storage suggest that agriculture continued. A monumental stone upright or *stele* near Znamenka shows a covered waggon drawn by a single horse. The camel was used extensively but there appears to be no reason for considering these people nomadic, in spite of the evidence for sheepbreeding.

The graves are shallow stone cists, and contain pottery with round or pointed bottoms, not flat bottoms as in Andronovo graves. The vessels are finely made, smooth and thin-walled, suggesting Chinese influence. But the strongest links with China are in metal work, particularly in the types of bronze knife which occur also at Anyang, on the Ordos steppe, and in Mongolia *(fig. 10)*. The knives are sometimes S-shaped with points curved back, but more commonly inward curving, with the handles terminating in rings, in animal heads, or in jingles. Sometimes the animal terminals are not merely heads, but standing figures, single or in rows. Knives and daggers with such

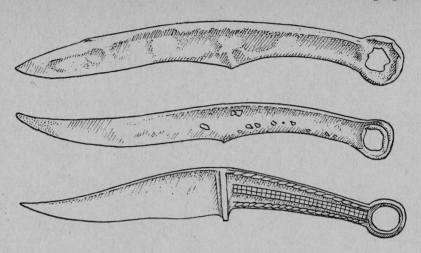

handles suggest a Chinese element in the famous Animal Style which, as we shall see, is characteristic of the mounted nomads in the next phase, and is their notable contribution to the world's decorative art.

Peculiar to this Karasuk culture are the curious stone *stelae* shaped like sabres and carved on their sides with human faces, on which a pattern of radiating lines is again attributed to Chinese influence *(fig. 9)*. Some form of the Karasuk culture is also found in the region of Semirechie and in the Tien Shan. But further west Kazakhstan and Siberia west of the Altai are still occupied by a late form of the Andronovo culture until about 800 BC.

The Second Indo-European Migrations (c. 900 BC)

Both these groups of peoples were next to be disturbed and overrun from the west by a new immigration of peoples of European type. It has been suggested that the beginning of this process may have been a movement of tribes from South Russia to the Tarim Basin in Chinese Turkestan, inferred by certain archaeologists from a wide survey of objects found in China and neighbouring countries which have no ancestry in Eastern Asia, and also do not belong to the Scytho-Sarmatian period that follows from the sixth or fifth century BC. They include axes, picks, daggers, belt clasps, crossed tubes for harness, metal buttons, buckets, and such decorative motifs as wolf's teeth, characteristic of the Late Bronze and Early Iron Age peoples of eastern Europe, including Caucasia. Perhaps their carriers were Indo-Europeans, now riders, including bands of those peoples known to the classical writers as Cimmerians, Thracians, Illyrians and maybe even early Germans. There may also have been among them the ancestors of the Tocharian people of the Tarim Basin, who spoke an Indo-European language and were part of the white-skinned Yue Chi horde mentioned later by Chinese sources. This movement would have taken place after 900 BC, and would be part of the last phase of the great secondary expansion of Indo-European peoples from Eastern and Central Europe which began about 1200 BC.

The Conditions of Nomadism: (2) Riding

Thus for the opening of the next era in the history of the steppes we are brought back once more to South Russia and the Caucasus, where mounted fighters had begun to be decisive in battle and to create societies of mounted nomads. For this step not only the earlier taming of the horse for work, but probably also its use with chariots by the Aryans in the Near East was a necessary preparation. There is evidence that riding of other animals was known earlier in the Near East than on the steppes, but it did not become common for civil or for military purposes until the horse had been introduced in convenient numbers by the Aryans, at first for driving.

Evidence for riding becomes more abundant late in the second millennium. For example a Hurrian relief from Tell Halaf of the fifteenth or fourteenth century BC shows a mounted warrior. A Kassite seal of the thirteenth century from Luristan appears to show a mounted archer in fantastic form. Mycenaean potsherds from Ras Shamra (Ugarit) in Syria of the fourteenth or thirteenth century may show riders in formation. In the eleventh century Nebuchadnezzar I of Babylon mentions riding horses. At the other end of Asia, a Shang grave near the site of Anyang, dated to the eleventh century, contained a single man's skeleton buried with weapons and jade ornaments and the skeleton of a single horse and of a dog. He appears to have been

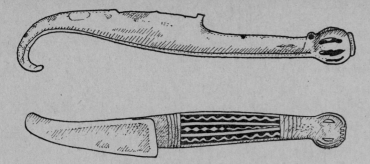

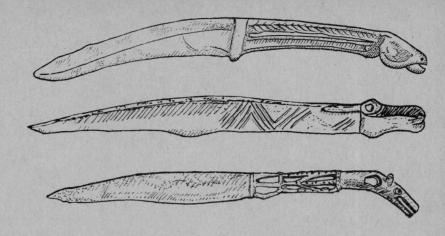

Three groups of bronze knives, c. 1500 BC onwards, suggest contacts be-tween China, Mongolia and the Karasuk culture in the Minusinsk basin. Left, ring-headed, the earliest form; above, jingle-headed; right, more elaborately decorated with animal heads. In each group the first is from Anyang, the second from the Ordos, the third (left and right) from Minusinsk. (fig. 10)

a foreign rider, a hunter and warrior, and perhaps a nomad. Riding in Shang China, if it was introduced from the west, raises the same problems of transmission as chariot-driving. But cavalry are not mentioned in Chinese sources for centuries after this date.

On this evidence it appears that regular riding was coming into fashion in the Near East at any rate after the fourteenth century BC, and that it spread thence through the mountain zone to the steppes. But neither this, nor even cavalry, is mounted nomadism. According to some, riding was first developed beyond this point by the peoples, partly Aryan and partly of older local origin, of Transcaucasia and northern Iran (pl. 10, fig. 11). Mounted warriors went not only south from this region into the Near East as conquerors and mercenaries, but north as plunderers against the pastoralists of the steppes, who did not yet ride as a general habit. The pastoral peoples could make no effective resistance to the attacks of cavalry, and were bound either to yield their flocks and herds as plunder, and so lose their livelihood, or to submit to the rule of their mounted enemies, paying tribute in cattle. If they wished to resist they were obliged to become mounted fighters themselves. In either case there would come into being communities of mounted warriors who controlled many subject tribes and large flocks and herds on the steppes. The more these took to the open steppes, the more purely nomadic they would become. Since the new form of military power depended on great herds of horses with enormous requirements in good fresh pasture, military needs would be added to the motives for conquering more areas of fertile steppe. This development could spread rapidly in all directions where the country was suitable, and soon reach the limits of the western steppes.

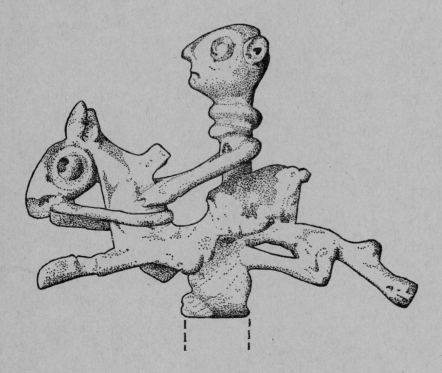

Head of a bronze pin from the Kuban Basin in the Caucasus, showing a rider at full gallop. About 1000 BC. (fig. 11)

Impact of the Nomads on Previous Cultures

In this way the first of a long succession of nomad empires would be formed. The process has been compared to the known spread of mounted fighting among the Indians of the American prairies, once these had learned the art from the Spaniards in the south. The Pontic-Tocharian migration described above might have been the beginning of this advance. These communities of riders spread through the territories of the unwarlike late Andronovo and Karasuk cultures of mixed farmers and herders. Recent evidence favours the theory that these mounted warriors were the first Indo-Europeans to reach Siberia and Inner Asia.

There is nothing in common between the remains of the Andronovo culture and those of the first Aryans in Iran. The 'timber-grave' culture of the Pontic steppe (see above, p. 319) just before the Scythian period is also different from the Andronovo. On the northern edge of Kazakhstan in the centre of the Andronovo culture, Andronovo pottery is succeeded suddenly by another style, a change that should be the result of political and military events. The Andronovo culture persists only in fortified places on the wooded edge of the steppes, where the agricultural tradition continues west of the Altai. It is likely that the people there first fell under the rule of the nomad Sarmatians, related to and contemporary with the Scythians, and finally suffered a military disaster. In Minusinsk the white element in the population (perceptible in skull types) is suddenly reinforced from no nearby source. Near Karaganda at Dyndybay forms of pottery like those of Andronovo exist side by side with forms which are new to the Asiatic steppe and like those of northern Caucasia and South Russia. In the Aral region the Iranian movement comes northward from Iran itself. On the borders of China there were movements of nomads in the Chou period (first millennium BC), and Chinese sources mention their red hair and green eyes.

The Cimmerians (c. 800 BC)

The mounted nomads created a peculiar form of society which outlasted the ancient civilizations of the Near East and of the classical world. It was perfectly adapted to the steppes, especially where they would not support agriculture; where agriculture was possible and the cultivators were tenacious, the nomads levied tribute from them, as in South Russia. It was a tribal society, in which particular tribes of nomads became for a time Royal Hordes and ruled other nomads in feudal fashion. One Royal Horde could easily be overthrown, and then with all its subjects become itself subject to a new Royal Horde. The later history of the steppes consists of a repetition of this change on varying scales, and of collisions between the nomads and civilized peoples. Hunting peoples from the forests were also recruited to nomadism by direct example. All the peoples were in continual movement over their ranges of pasture, but did not migrate unless they were driven.

On the South Russian steppes the first approximation to a mounted nomad power was that of people known in classical sources as the Cimmerians, who ruled north of the Caucasus and on the Pontic steppes, with an extension into Hungary. From the names of the chiefs, preserved in Assyrian accounts of their attacks on Near Eastern peoples, it is now commonly taken that the rulers were Iranians, though their subjects were probably of other groups also, for instance Thracians and Caucasians. The origin of the Cimmerians

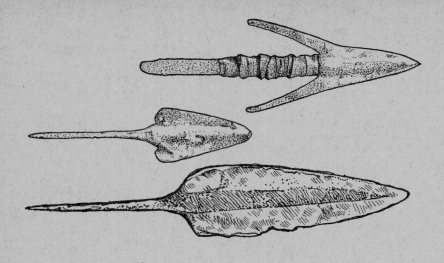

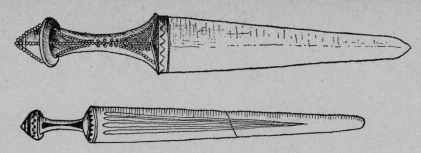

Stylistic links between Koban and Luristanian metalwork: (left) bronze arrowheads from Transcaucasia (first two) and Luristan show affinities in the shape and in the bold tang. (Above) dagger from Gandsha and bronze sword from Davshanli of pre-Scythian types. Compare the Scythian sword opposite. (Right) bronze battle-axes from Koban, for contrasting with the Scythian example in fig. 17. The engraved decoration includes fabulous animals and an archer. About 1000–800 BC. (fig. 12)

is hard to trace. They may have originated in the North Caucasian culture, advancing northwards to conquer the Pontic steppes and part of the Danubian plain where new types of harness equipment of Koban style appear c. 800 BC.

The link between Koban and Luristanian metal-work (pl. 8, 9, *fig. 12*) suggests that the Cimmerians penetrated into Iran, while grave finds on the Dniepr and Don have also been attributed to them. Finally the Don Basin catacomb-graves have been taken as Cimmerian, the succeeding timber-graves being early Scythian, c. 900 BC, or later.

In general history the Cimmerians are chiefly famous for their invasion of Asia Minor in 680-670 BC, which according to Herodotus was the result of their flight from the Scythians. They left the Pontic steppes and crossed the Caucasus, leaving a small remnant behind fortifications in the Taman Peninsula, east of the straits of Kerch, the ancient Cimmerian Bosporus. In spite of Herodotus, the movement of peoples may have begun earlier than the Scythian invasion of their country. But at any rate he must be correct in saying that they crossed the mountains further west than the Scythians, who went by the Caspian coast to Media. An alternative route would lead them into Armenia, and it is there that they appear late in the eighth century on the northern border of the kingdom of Urartu as the Gimirrai or Gamir of Assyrian records. The crown prince Sennacherib reports to his father Sargon (721-705 BC), at war with Urartu, that its king Rusas has been heavily defeated by the Cimmerians in the north (pl. 11).

The Cimmerians, while occupying northern Urartu, appear finally as allies of the Urartians against Assyria and then advance westward. In 695 BC they destroyed the kingdom of Phrygia and afterwards dominated Central Anatolia in the time of Sennacherib (704-681 BC). They overran Lydia, devastated the Greek cities of the coast, such as Ephesus, Magnesia and Smyrna, and finally turned south against Cilicia, then an Assyrian province.

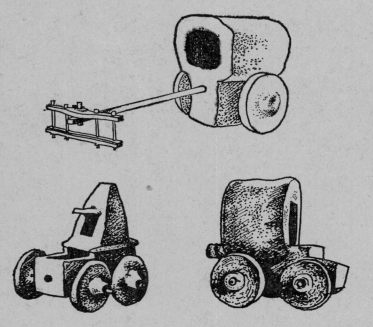

Pottery models of early covered waggons; above, from Tri Brata, Kalmuk Steppe, c. 2000 BC; below, Scythian, from Kerch, c. 600 BC. (fig. 13)

In the Scythian period the Siberian and Central Asian steppes were occupied by Sarmatian peoples akin to the Scythians. All these people were mounted nomads, and their decorative art included some version of the Animal Style described below. All wore the tunic, trousers, boots and cap, and carried the bowcases, bows, arrows, swords and axes represented as theirs in Greek and Persian art. In metallurgy some had adopted iron besides bronze, while others still used bronze only. For transport they had elaborate waggons, in South Russia sometimes with two or even three compartments *(fig. 13)*.

The Scythians

In South Russia the Scythians occupied the former Cimmerian territory, except the Taman Peninsula and part of the Crimea, and for a time they did not cross the Dniestr to Bessarabia and the Danube valley and further, where later remains of theirs are found. Archaeologically the earliest Scythians are a problem, because they did not develop their distinctive art style until the sixth century, as dated by Greek objects found with its oldest specimens, and the style has no ancestry in South Russia. If we identify the catacomb tombs as Cimmerian, we can regard the timber-graves that follow them as early Scythian. These, like the catacomb-graves, extend into Caucasia and even round the eastern end of the range through Daghestan. In Transcaucasia they would represent Scythians of an earlier immigration direct from the Volga steppe, who perhaps drove on the Median and Persian tribes into Iran.

The main Scythian migration under the Royal Horde, the only one known to Herodotus, flowed first into South Russia. Then, drawn perhaps by their kinsmen's stories of rich plunder, the Scythians passed the mountains to invade Western Asia. The main body arrived in the Mannaean country around Lake Urmia, but some at least must have destroyed the Urartian town of Teishebani (modern Karmir Blur in Soviet Armenia), where their distinctive trilobate arrowheads *(fig. 14)* were found sticking in the walls. The remains show that other Scythians were among the defenders. The Scythians remained in Western Asia for a generation or two during the last days of Assyria. The two nations became allies, and remained allied until the last. After the time of Esarhaddon and Ashurbanipal the Scythians plundered some of the provinces of the weakened Assyrian Empire, but were still, if Herodotus is right, so far its allies and guests that Cyaxares the Mede had to break their power before he could destroy Nineveh in 612 BC. After their defeat by the Medes, they returned through the Caucasus to the Pontic steppes, leaving some of their number behind in the Armenian districts of Scythene and Sacasene, and elsewhere. They had given Western Asia its first taste of domination by mounted nomads.

The Animal Style

We now come to one of the most exciting manifestations of the nomad peoples of the steppes—their creation of an individual and vigorous art style which still has power to intrigue and fascinate. It is an art of pattern and ornament, in which naturalistic motifs, especially those based on animals, are subordinated to a strong sense of rhythm and design, and built up into fantastic arrangements of compelling aesthetic quality. It is the antithesis of the naturalistic art of the village and urban communities of the settled agriculturalists: human repre-

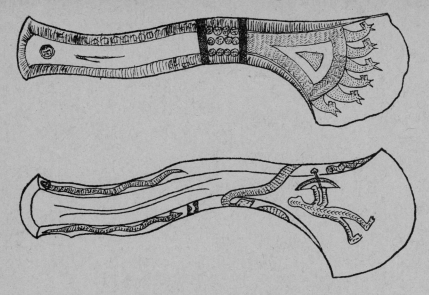

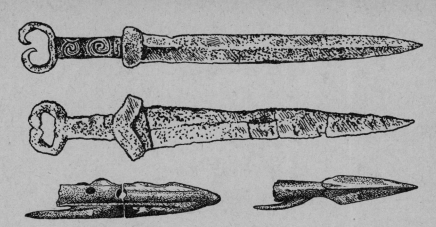

Bronze Scythian swords with eared hilts recalling those of the Early Iron Age in Central Europe (7th–6th century BC). Below, bronze trilobate barbed and socketed arrowheads of Scythian types (same date). Compare these weapons with the earlier types in fig. 12 opposite. (fig. 14)

sentations scarcely exist, portraiture never, and literal transcripts of nature are shunned. Just as the pattern of life of the nomad contrasts at every point with that of the farmer or townsman, so too the pattern of the art produced on the steppes has its individual and arresting qualities. Made by people on the move, it is lavished on portable objects such as decorations on weapons or the equipment for horse and rider; the outcome of a heroic society, it is an art of display and ostentation. Precious metals, especially gold, are used in profusion: it is essentially an aristocratic art, like that of the Celts described in chapter XII.

Our knowledge of Scythian art is almost wholly gained by the excavation of the royal or semi-royal tombs of their nobility and aristocracy, where, as we shall see, the dead were buried with barbaric pomp. These tombs began to be made by the Scythians in the Kuban Basin, and later on the Dniepr, only after their return from Western Asia. There are several strands of tradition which combine to make Scythian art what it is, a unique creation resulting in something new, rich and strange.

One strand came from Anatolia; for instance the antlered stag, a favourite Scythian theme, appears already with head and neck treated somewhat in the Scythian fashion on stone reliefs from Alaca Hüyük in Anatolia of about the fourteenth century BC, and even earlier from the Royal Tombs there as a metal figure to be fastened on a pole-top in the Scythian manner (pl. 5). From the Transcaucasian Bronze Age various sites of the native Gandsha-Karabagh culture, such as Kayakent, have produced bronze belt-plates bearing animal figures that seem to show a development from formal geometric shape and arrangement to livelier and freer forms more akin to the Scythian. A bronze belt found near Kiev combines Transcaucasian animal forms with something like animal combat between a stag and a beast of prey and a heraldic opposition of beasts *(fig. 15)*. Another animal style is

that of the Lelvar culture of the Transcaucasian Iron Age, but this is different, and has human figures of bowmen as the reliefs of Alaca Hüyük have (pl. 7), and even chariots. The Koban culture has fantastic animal figures, used particularly to decorate bronze belt-plates and axe-blades, but it also has representations of bowmen, and it delights in small bronze figures of riders. Further south the bronzes of Luristan have representations of animals and even animal-combats, executed in a style which seems to anticipate the Scythian, but they also have human figures as a prominent feature (pl. 12, 13, 16).

A more definitely Near Eastern contribution is suggested by the figures on gold plate found in the treasure of Ziwiye in Kurdistan, the ancient Mannaean country. There the artist has combined animal figures recognizable as Scythian with features of Assyrian and Mannaean art, so that it has been suggested that the treasure belonged to Bartatua, the Scythian king allied to the Assyrians around 670 BC. This is certainly the nearest approach to the early Scythian style of the Kuban (pl. 14, 15, 17, 19).

Something like the Scythian Animal Style was adopted in various forms by all the mounted nomads as far as the borders of China by the end of the first millennium. The animal figures no doubt had a religious significance for peoples who believed in animal ancestors, or in spirits in animal form having magic powers of helping the soul to reach the next world. They may also have been the badges of an intertribal caste of mounted warriors who carried them wherever they ruled (pl. 30).

The Royal Tombs

The tombs of the Scythian kings and chiefs have long been famous in archaeology. In construction they have much in common with the far older barrows of the Kuban already described, while in contents they show an analogous mixture of northern and Near Eastern objects

Forerunners of the Scythian animal style. Above: bronze belt-plate from Kiev, combining Caucasian and Scythian features; 10th century BC. Below: *bronze belt-plate from Kayakent (10th century BC) contrasted with a fantastic animal figure of the Koban culture. (fig. 15)*

and styles. This continuity in idea cannot be traced on the steppes, and should probably be sought in Western Asia, which now provides a new impulse.

The most notable groups of tombs are in the Kuban basin, often in the same places as the first great barrows (see map, p. 321), in the Taman Peninsula, in the Crimea, and on the Dniepr where they extend to the neighbourhood of Kiev. Other burials occur in the Danubian plain, and outlying single graves even in North Germany; there are more on the Don and Donetz and further east by the Volga to the Urals. From the Kuban westward, as time passes, the contents show increasing Greek influence.

The Account of Herodotus

A celebrated description of the tombs and the funeral rites is given by Herodotus, who is to a great extent confirmed by excavation. This is as follows: 'The tombs of the kings are in the land of the Gerrhi. There, when their king dies, they dig a great square pit. When they have prepared this they take up the corpse, its body smeared over with wax and its belly slit open, cleaned out, and filled with chopped frankincense, parsley and anise, and then sewn up again, and bring it on a waggon to another tribe. These who receive the corpse when it is brought do as the Royal Scythians. They cut a piece out of their ears, cut their hair short, slash their arms, slit their foreheads and noses, and thrust arrows through their left hands. Then they convey the corpse to another tribe among their subjects, and the tribe first reached goes with them. When they have gone round all the tribes with the corpse, they are among the Gerrhi, who live furthest off of all their subjects, and among the tombs.

'When they have laid the corpse upon a mattress in its chamber, they stick spears into the ground on all sides. Then they lay beams across and cover these with wicker, and in the remaining space of the tomb they strangle and bury one concubine, the cupbearer, a cook, a groom, an attendant and a messenger; they also bury the pick of everything else and golden vessels. They use no silver or bronze. When they have done this, they heap up a great mound, vying with one another and full of eagerness to make it as great as they can. Then when a year has passed they do as follows. They take the most suitable of the other attendants—these are true-born Scythians and are called to attend him by the king himself, for they have no bought slaves—and strangle fifty of them and fifty of the finest horses. They take out their entrails, clean them, fill them with chaff and sew them up. Then they put half the rim of a wheel with the hollow side upward on two stakes, and

the other half-rim on two others, fixing many such frames, drive stout stakes lengthwise through the horses to their necks and hoist them onto the rims. The front rims support the horses' shoulders and the rear ones their thighs and bellies, while both pairs of legs hang free. They put reins and bridles on the horses, draw these forward and tie them to pegs. They then hoist every one of the strangled youths onto his horse, after driving a vertical stake through him by the spine to the neck, and part of this stake that projects downward they fasten into a socket in the other stake that runs through the horse. When they have set up riders in this style round the tomb they ride off.'

Herodotus also says that after a funeral the Scythians used to purify themselves by inhaling the fumes of hemp from seeds scattered on red-hot stones inside tents of felt. As they did this they howled in delight at the vapour-bath. This custom he hardly understands.

This account can be compared with the results of excavation. The circles of impaled horses and riders, if they existed, would soon be destroyed by beasts and birds and the weather. But later nomad peoples in Siberia have had the custom of impaling horses for sacrifice until very recent times. The tombs themselves confirm Herodotus in many details. The profusion of finds is such that one or two burials, briefly described, must stand for all.

Scythian Burials in the Kuban

In the Kuban region an earlier stage is represented by such burials as those of Kostromskaya and Kelermes. At Kostromskaya the burial chamber was marked out by four great posts. Beams were laid cross-wise about them to form a square of side 10 ft. 6 ins. and held in place by rows of much smaller and shorter posts. Roof beams were added between the posts sloping upward to form the frame of a pyramidal roof. In the square about 7 ft. below ground were the dead man's belongings: an iron scale hauberk with copper scales on the shoulders and lower edge, four iron spearheads, a thin round shield of iron adorned in the centre with a cast gold plaque of a deer (pl. 23), two leather quivers, some bronze arrowheads, several copper and iron bits, and a large whetstone and pottery, all deliberately broken. The square space had been filled with earth, rolled hard, which contained 13 skeletons but nothing with them. At the very bottom was a small chamber closed with two slabs of stone, but this was empty. The wooden structure had apparently been set alight before the earth was heaped on it. Outside the square were the skeletons of 22 horses buried in pairs, some with bits in their mouths (*fig. 16*).

In one barrow at Kelermes the chief's body was untouched. He

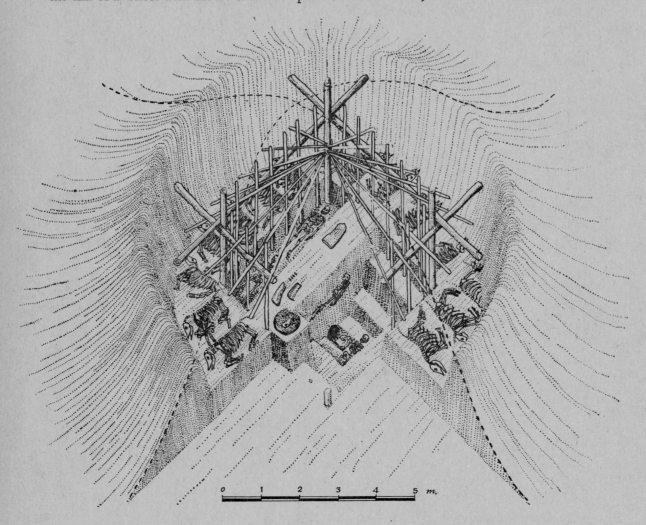

0 1 2 3 4 5 *m.*

The Scythian royal tomb at Kostromskaya (6th century BC). The framework of the timber mortuary house is shown, containing on the ground-level, among other objects, a circular iron shield decorated with the gold stag of pl. 23, chain mail, two leather quivers and iron spear-heads. The dead man was buried in a subterranean chamber, while above were thirteen skeletons of sacrificed victims. Outside the mortuary house were the skeletons of twenty-two sacrificed horses, laid in pairs. The whole was covered with a great earthen mound, and provides dramatic confirmation of Herodotus' description of such burials. (fig. 16)

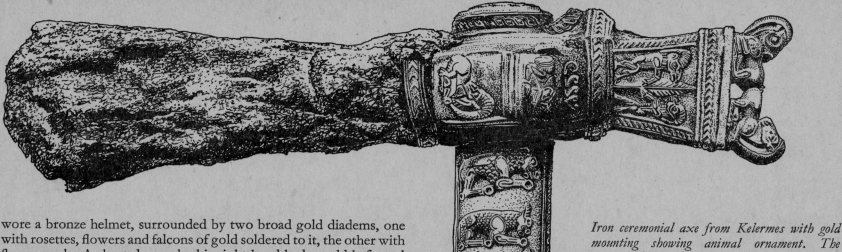

wore a bronze helmet, surrounded by two broad gold diadems, one with rosettes, flowers and falcons of gold soldered to it, the other with flowers only. A short dagger by his right hand had a gold haft, and a gold sheath with a row of monsters and genii, and on its side projection a crouching stag. An iron axe *(fig. 17)* was decorated on haft and head with genii and beasts in gold. To the left was a golden panther surrounded by iron scales; its eyes and nostrils were filled by glass pastes with stones inset, and its ears decorated with glass pastes set in cloisons of gold. The dagger and panther were in the Mesopotamian style of the eighth and seventh centuries BC.

The Chertomlyk Burial

Of the royal tombs on the Dniepr, the great burial of Chertomlyk may be taken as an example. The mound was 60 ft. high and 1100 ft. round, and the main chamber measured 15 ft. 7 ins. at the top, widening downwards to a depth of 35 ft. 6 ins. Four side-chambers opened out from this, one from each corner, and the fourth of these again into a fifth. In the main chamber, which had been very much plundered, were traces of a coffin or bier painted red and bright blue. In the southeast chamber were a cauldron, remains of a skeleton, knives, arrows, traces of a carpet, gold plates and strips which had been sewn to clothes, and iron hooks in the walls and ceilings for hanging clothes. In the north-east chamber were six amphorae, a bronze mirror, a skeleton with a bronze torque, earrings and finger-rings of gold, remains of a whip-handle of ivory and gold, 399 gold strips representing animals, monsters, and in a few cases scenes from Greek myth,

Iron ceremonial axe from Kelermes with gold mounting showing animal ornament. The crouching stags recall pl. 23, 24. Seventh or sixth century BC. (fig. 17)

and many more gold ornaments. In the south-west chamber lay a skeleton with a golden torque bearing 12 figures of lions, remains of a hood and 25 gold plates, in the form of griffins, bracelets, a brass-plated belt, greaves, vessels of gold and bronze, a quiver with arrows, and a whip. Beside this was another skeleton with similar equipment. In the north-west chamber, on remains of a bier painted dark and light blue, lay a woman's skeleton with earrings and gold plates by the head, and covered there and on the upper body with a purple veil bearing 57 gold plates outlining the shape of a hood. By this lay a man's skeleton with bracelets and knives. In the west of the chamber was the famous Chertomlyk vase, made of silver and engraved with plants and birds, and also with a frieze representing Scythians breaking in horses, surmounted with another frieze of griffins *(fig. 18)*. By it was a great silver dish engraved with acanthus leaves and the figure of a woman. The last two are Greek work. In the fifth chamber were cauldrons and a heap of gold, and plunder from the king's body, including the great gold plates from his bowcase and sword-sheath engraved with Greek scenes and griffins (pl. 22). Outside this group were three graves of horses bridled with gold and silver and two of grooms with silver or gold torques and quivers of arrows.

We can now imagine the funeral procession, led by standard-bearers with beast emblems mounted on poles and others waving bronze rattles on poles and shrieking (pl. 27). The king's body would follow on a waggon, probably under a canopy supported by poles with beast emblems, adorned with gold plaques of beasts and monsters, and hung with bells. The concubines, the servants and the grooms with saddled and bridled horses would come next, and finally the great crowd of cropped and gashed mourners wailing and howling. At the tomb the women, servants and grooms would be strangled, the horses killed with a blow from an axe on the head. The royal body in its festal robe would be laid on its bier in the centre of the chamber, at full length with its head to the east, and weapons and vessels full of food placed ready to hand. The walls would be hung with brightly dyed and embroidered felt and the floor covered with carpets to reproduce the sumptuous interior of the royal tent. The grooms and horses nearby in their places of burial would be ready to accompany their master with due pomp on his journey through the afterworld.

The Chertomlyk vase. Round the shoulder is a frieze, showing Scythians breaking in horses. Greek workmanship, 4th century BC. (fig. 18)

The Pazyryk Burials

The ritual has now been further illustrated by finds of normally perishable materials intact in the famous tombs of Pazyryk in the High Altai, where nomads related to the Scythians buried their chiefs under stone-topped barrows. The stone has had the effect of freezing the contents in ice, very little altered for more than twenty-three centuries, particularly where more water was let in through robbers' shafts. The chambers are of the usual square timber-lined kind, and the contents are closely like those of the South Russian tombs, though much less rich in metal *(fig. 19)*. The influence of Western Asia of the Persian period is strongly present, and in the place of added Greek influence there is here Chinese. A few notable examples of the finds must suffice.

The horses buried round the chambers were in many cases not the small Mongolian breed of the steppes, but tall thoroughbred animals such as were famous in Bactria and Media, and their stomachs contained the remains of grain, not of the expected grass, showing they had been carefully stabled and fed. In some cases they wore masks of leather and felt, representing reindeer or griffins, which were evidently of magical importance.

The most remarkable tomb was the second. The floor and walls had been largely covered with black felt secured with pegs and bronze nails. The furniture included low wooden tables that could be taken to pieces, wooden food-vessels, a drum shaped like an hour-glass and ornamented with gold leaf, and a stringed instrument like a lute. A double coffin 4.20 m. long lay empty, covered with birch bark and leather appliqué, and lined with black felt and carpet; it would have taken two bodies end to end. Among articles of clothing were a long woman's coat of squirrel fur, hairs outward, edged with horse-hide, and a matching stomacher edged with sable and other fur; a long wide man's shirt of plant fibres; and two pairs of women's fur boots, one of leopard skin and ornamented on soft soles with a pattern of crystals, so that they may have been worn in cross-legged position to show the soles turned upward.

On top of an original layer of clear ice, and held in a mass of dirty yellow ice from the later inflow, lay the bodies of the chief and his wife, torn from their coffin. The woman was about forty years old, tall and graceful and of European type. Her hair had been shaved off and her head trepanned to remove the brain, which had been replaced with plant material, after which the scalp was sewn up again; her entrails had been removed through a long slit in the belly and similarly replaced with plant material before the skin was sewn up again. A long plait of her hair, soft, black, and wavy, lay near by in a case of its own. The man was about sixty, of mongoloid type and powerfully built. He had been killed in battle by two axe-strokes through his skull, and had been scalped before his own men recovered him and fitted him out with a false scalp sewn on. He too had been embalmed, and in

Tomb 5 at Pazyryk. Outside the rifled tomb are the remains of a four-wheeled waggon, decorated with felt hangings, and the skeletons of the sacrificed horses. See also pl. 32–41. About 500 BC. (fig. 19)

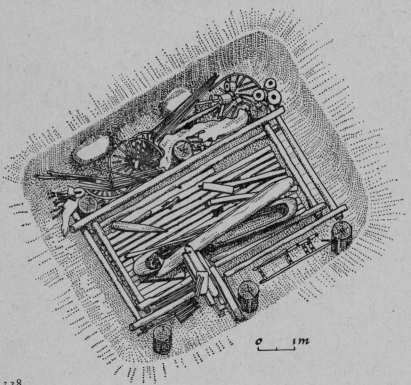

Upper part of the chieftain's body from Tomb 2, Pazyryk, showing tattoo patterns in the nomadic animal style. (fig. 20)

early life had been tattooed with designs in the best Animal Style, the pigment having penetrated the muscle before he grew fat. His chin was adorned with a false beard of horse hair, hanging from a strip and thickly and lumpily dyed with black. The embalming process is exactly as described by Herodotus. A bronze cauldron filled with large stones and seeds of charred hemp also bears out Herodotus' account of the Scythian inhaling of hashish for religious purposes.

Bronze cauldron from Tomb 2, Pazyryk, containing stones and charred hemp-seeds. (fig. 21)

In the fifth burial were some astonishing textiles. A deep red and yellow pile carpet 4 square metres in size and almost certainly Persian, is decorated with plant ornaments in the middle and with two bands of figures, the inner one a procession of stags, and the outer a procession of riders in hoods, tunics and tight trousers on horses with clipped manes and feather head-dresses (pl. 39). Among appliqué felt hangings two are pre-eminent. One shows a curious lion-bodied monster with wings, a human head, and antlers, fighting a fantastic giant bird. On the other (pl. 32) a rider, wearing a short cloak and tight trousers and bareheaded, approaches a figure seated on a throne, shaven headed, wearing a fur cap and a long robe, while a 'tree of life' stands close by. A felt chariot-cover bears representations of tethered swans in undoubtedly Chinese style (pl. 35).

These finds show that the Scythian way of life was reproduced in full detail in at least one other region of the steppe and must have been well known to less fortunate hordes.

Later Nomadic Empires

The Royal Horde of Scythians ruled in barbaric wealth over the nomads and cultivators of the Pontic steppe, and foiled the attempt of Darius of Persia to invade its territory in the fifth century. In the fourth century it was gradually displaced by Sarmatians from beyond the Don (pl. 26). The Sarmatians and then the Altaic Huns, Avars, Turks and Mongols from beyond Zungaria continued the same tradition of mounted nomadism on an increasing scale, ruling great empires not only on the steppes, but often in the countries on their borders. They conquered their empires with cavalry, and, so long as they retained the habits of nomads, regarded their subjects very much as cattle. It is only in recent centuries that the Russian and Chinese states between them have broken the power of the nomads and begun to put an end even to their distinctive mode of life.

XII BARBARIAN EUROPE

From the first farmers to the Celts

T.G.E. POWELL

Barbarian Europe: the main cultural developments from the Neolithic Period to the Roman Conquests

	c. 4000–2500 BC	c. 1800	c. 1500	c. 1200	c. 700	c. 400–100 BC
ATLANTIC EUROPE	The W. Mediterranean *Cardium* Ware culture — The *Western* Neolithic culture	Megalithic tombs and collective burial. Continuity of Neolithic plus primitive bronze and copper using cultures	Early Bronze Age of Ireland — Regional Bronze Age cultures with Mediterranean trade.		Spread westwards of *Urnfield* and *Hallstatt* cultures	
MIDDLE EUROPE	Aegean & Balkan Neol. *Danubian Neol. I* — *First Northern* or *Funnel-Beaker* culture — Regional *Danubian* cultures	Early copper and bronze workers with Anatolian and Pontic connections. Wheeled vehicles. Baden-Pecél culture and others	'Tell'-villages of Middle and Lower Danubian regions with cremation urnfields	Chieftains' barrow burials: principally Wessex and Leubingen cultures — South-eastward intrusion of *Tumulus* culture. Destruction of Mid-Danubian 'tell'-villages. — Expansion from Mid-Danube of cremation rite and new types of bronzes: *Urnfield* Late Bronze Age	Iron-using economy becomes general: *Hallstatt* culture	
EASTERN GRASSLANDS	Painted-Pottery cultures				Scythians	Sarmatians

Vertical labels (far left): Interrelated Eastern Mediterranean and Anatolian *Neolithic* cultures · Cereal cultivation and cattle-breeding with no use of metals

Vertical/diagonal labels: Pastoralists: *Bell Beaker* culture · Prospectors and traders: *Corded-Ware–Battle-Axe* cultures · Oriental bronze horse-harness: Thraco-Cimmerian riders? · Florescence of the Celts: *La Tène* culture

Map labels: Orton, Torrs, New Grange, Tara, Mangerton, Mold, Trawsfynydd, Desborough, Avebury, Stonehenge, Aylesford, Mané-er-Hroek, Fritzdorf, Waldalgesheim, Bassé, Yutz, Koblenz, Rodenbach, Reinheim, Mont Lassois, Kappel-am-Rhein, Vilsingen, Heuneburg, La Tène, Gomadingen, Camp de Château, Hallstatt, Ingolstadt, Strělice, Bratislava, Budakalász, Strettweg, Hajdúsámson, Kökénydomb, Roquepertuse, Marseilles, Antequerra, Eisleben, Leubingen, Dobritz, Unětice, Jungfernhöle, Gundestrup, Trundholm, Brå, Maltbæk, Mycenae

Geographic labels: JUTLAND, BALTIC SEA, ELBE, ODER, VISTULA, RHINE, SEINE, SAÔNE, RHONE, ALPS, PYRENEES, CARPATHIANS, TISZA, KÖRÖS, MAROS, DANUBE, MEDITERRANEAN SEA, BLACK SEA

Scale: Miles 0 100 200 300 400 500 / Kilometres 0 100 200 300 400 500 600 700 800

The anonymous prehistoric peoples

who were our own immediate ancestors in Europe lived, some five thousand years ago, in the region of equable climate and deciduous woodland north of the Pyrenees, the Alps and the Balkans. Cut off by the mountain ranges from the more advanced communities to the south, they were at first but small groups of primitive stone-using cultivators and herdsmen, never far above the subsistence level, and moving on as the soil became exhausted by their 'slash and burn' methods of clearance. The great rivers were the principal routes of penetration and expansion, and their flood plains offered the most suitable lands for cultivation and settlement. Chief among them was the Danube.

Simple forms and impressed decoration characterize the pottery of the Danubian Neolithic, though later wares were painted before firing, in the Anatolian and Mesopotamian tradition. The three groups on the right represent regional variations: the first group is from a grave near Pest, Hungary; the flask and bowl (centre) are from the Jungfernhöhle cave in Franconia; the lowest group comes from two separate finds in Württemberg. The gourd shape of the pot in the middle of this group is typical of the Danubian I period. (1)

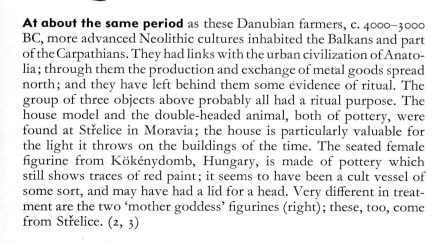

At about the same period as these Danubian farmers, c. 4000–3000 BC, more advanced Neolithic cultures inhabited the Balkans and part of the Carpathians. They had links with the urban civilization of Anatolia; through them the production and exchange of metal goods spread north; and they have left behind them some evidence of ritual. The group of three objects above probably all had a ritual purpose. The house model and the double-headed animal, both of pottery, were found at Střelice in Moravia; the house is particularly valuable for the light it throws on the buildings of the time. The seated female figurine from Kökénydomb, Hungary, is made of pottery which still shows traces of red paint; it seems to have been a cult vessel of some sort, and may have had a lid for a head. Very different in treatment are the two 'mother goddess' figurines (right); these, too, come from Střelice. (2, 3)

The tulip-beaker and kneading-plate above come from Michelsberg, near Untergrombach, in Baden, South Germany. This hill-top site, with rampart and ditch enclosure, gives its name to a late Western Neolithic culture widespread in west central Europe. (4)

Of all the neolithic monuments of Britain none, except Stonehenge, is more famous than Avebury, in Wiltshire. The air photograph below (looking south) shows the great rampart and inner ditch of this, the largest site of its kind, about 1400 yards in diameter. Avebury was probably a ritual site, like Stonehenge; some remaining uprights of the great stone circle can be seen near the inner lip of the ditch in the right foreground. From the southern entrance, alongside the road, an avenue of paired monoliths, the West Kennet Avenue, runs over a somewhat irregular course for nearly a mile and a half to terminate at a smaller circular sanctuary, once of timber as well as stone uprights, on Overton Hill. (5)

The Bell Beaker folk spread widely over west and central Europe early in the 2nd millennium BC. A special characteristic of their equipment is a guard of stone or bone to protect the left forearm against the recoil of a bowstring. The example above (centre) is particularly finely made and decorated. Below it is a vessel of birch wood from a Corded Ware grave near Eisleben, Germany; footed pottery bowls of similar shape have been found in several roughly contemporary cultures. (6)

In fineness of fabric and decoration, the Bell Beaker pottery is among the highest products of late neolithic Europe. Above is an outstanding example of the pottery that gave this widespread culture its name: the decoration was carried out before firing, with a small toothed tool. This pot was found in the long barrow at West Kennet, Wiltshire, not far from Avebury. (7)

The megalithic tradition of building in large stone blocks spread throughout the Mediterranean and Western Europe in the later Neolithic. Decoration in a curvilinear style was also common both in tombs and the great temples which were such a special feature of Malta in the 2nd millennium BC. The picture above shows part of the most impressive of these, Tarxien. (8)

Designs painstakingly chopped out with a pocking technique sometimes decorate these megalithic tombs, as well as slab-lined tombs under round tumuli. The designs may show cult symbols, such as the hut shrine with axes from Brittany (right, above), or, in a conscious effort at decoration, may recall painted frescoes as in the chambered tomb at Gavr' Inis, Morbihan (right, below). (9, 10)

Emphasized by a white filling material in the incisions, this stone slab (above) even more strongly resembles a textile design. It is from a recently discovered tumulus tomb on the Dölauer Heide, near Halle. Such individual tombs as this recall the steppe traditions of princely burial before 2000 BC, described in chapter XI. (11)

The intricate design of spirals below decorates a great stone placed before the entrance of the corbelled New Grange tomb. (12)

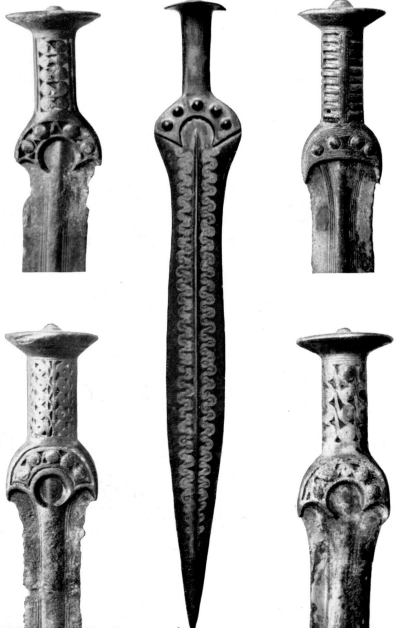

the Saxo-Thuringian chieftains of north central Europe controlled many important trade routes. Their territory lay across the amber route from the Baltic to the Mediterranean, and the route presumably travelled by the traders in tin from the west, as well as those who brought bronze and gold from the metal-working centres of middle Europe. Thus they found themselves able to command a generous supply of the trappings of wealth.

Typical of the luxury enjoyed by the chieftains of Central Europe at this time are the spiral-headed gold cloak-pin (left) from Trassem in the Saar valley, which shows Anatolian influence, and the hoard of bronze weapons and ornaments (above) from Dieskau, Sachsen-Anhalt. The flat axe to the right of the centre is an Irish import, and the long, thin double axes are a ritual form which derives from Aegean origins. (13, 14)

The cut-and-thrust sword with its typical leaf shape, seen in the centre of the plate to the left, was an original contribution to armament by the advanced Bronze Age weapon smiths of eastern Europe. The one shown was found at Hajdúsámson in Hungary. The decoration of the Danish bronze hilts in the same picture also shows the influence of eastern Europe and—in the spirals—ultimately of Mycenae. These features would have spread north to the somewhat later Bronze Age of Scandinavia by way of the amber trade route. (15)

The influence of Mycenae and the Aegean was felt not only in Scandinavia but also in the west. The gold cup from Fritzdorf, near Bonn (below), has a handle of decorated sheet gold, fixed with rivets exactly in the style of the one from Rillaton in Cornwall, which is shown opposite. Its horizontal ribbing is a Mycenaean technique to give added strength. It was probably made by a native craftsman who had learned the trick from more sophisticated imports. (16, 17)

Ornaments of gold were typical possessions of the wealthier British Bronze Age chieftains of the 1st millennium BC. The massive and ornate gold collar in the painting above has been reconstructed from fragments of repoussé gold work found at Mold in North Wales, and now in the British Museum. North Wales at that time, lying between the main centres of Wessex and Ireland, was as well placed as the chieftains of Saxo-Thuringia for amassing wealth and power from control of trade routes. Many other finds of gold work in or near the Vale of Clwyd suggest that this was the main 'port of entry' for the river-washed gold that was being brought into Britain from Ireland. (18)

'Basket' earrings in sheet gold with incised ornament are widely associated with the Bell Beaker culture in Britain (mid-2nd millennium BC). The ones above are based on finds from Orton, Scotland, which were probably of Irish gold. (19)

Moon-shaped collars of sheet gold, called lunulae, with engraved ornament on the edges and the horns, are a typical product of 2nd-millennium Ireland, then a rich source of gold. They were exported to the Low Countries and Britain, and copies have been found in Denmark. (20)

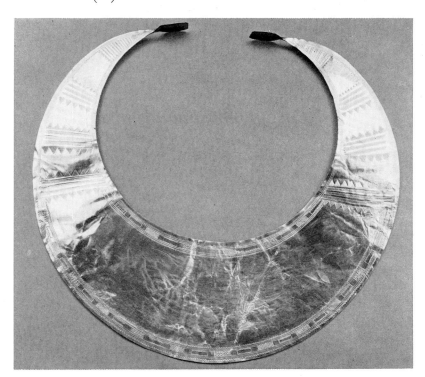

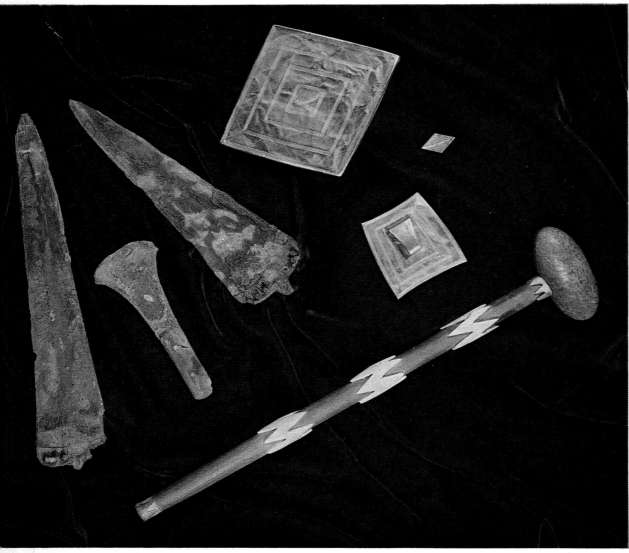

A rich grave of the early Wessex Bronze Age, Bush Barrow in Wiltshire, dominates a group of barrows to the east of Stonehenge. The riveted round-heeled daggers (left) resemble the contemporary weapons from the Saale-Elbe region, which was itself in close touch with the Únětice culture of Bohemia. The gold objects, particularly the hooked buckle catch, also have parallels in Central Europe, and the zigzag bone mountings on the reconstructed handle of the ceremonial mace once more suggest contacts with Hungary and Mycenae. Bush Barrow is a warrior chieftain's grave of the Bronze Age, typical of many. Such chieftains, besides being pastoralists, had strong trading connections with the Continent, and a religious centre and meeting-place at Stonehenge. (21)

A unique monument of Neolithic and Bronze Age Britain, Stonehenge, on the chalk downs of Wiltshire (left) was the culmination of British circular sanctuaries. Excavation has revealed a number of rearrangements and additions, from the first bank-and-ditch enclosure of the late Neolithic, somewhere between 1900 and 1700 BC, to the final, Bronze Age, complex of circle and horseshoe which must have been completed about 1500 BC.

The stones are sarsens, weighing up to 50 tons, from the Marlborough Downs some 18 miles to the north, and dolerite and other stone from South Wales. The transport and erection of these massive monoliths, the symmetry of the plan, and the skilful cutting of tongue-and-groove joints suggest supervision by an experienced architect or master-builder. A clue to this was given by the discovery in 1953 of carvings of bronze axe-blades and a bronze dagger possibly of Aegean type on one of the stones—a 'signature' which may point to one centre of the axe-cult, Mycenae, where the masonry of the shaft-graves offers a near parallel to this form of construction. (22)

How Stonehenge was built is, and must probably remain, a matter of guesswork. About eighty large bluestone blocks, each weighing anything up to 5 tons, are known to have come from the Prescelly Mountains in Pembrokeshire, a distance of 135 miles as the crow flies; though they could have been brought some of the way by water, coastwise and up the Avon, the last stage of their journey must have been a long, grinding haul on sledges. The painting below reconstructs a small part of the immense labour involved. The overseer's weapons, mace, shield and belt buckle are based on the Bush Barrow find (pl. 21, opposite); his necklace of amber, shale and faience on a find at Upton Lovel, Wilts.

To symbolize the possibility hinted at in the caption to pl. 22, a Mycenaean master architect is shown on the extreme right, watching the work. (23)

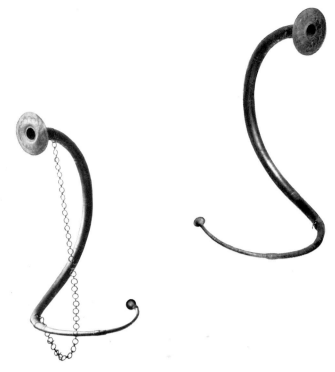

More sophisticated craftmanship in metal came to the northern barbarians of Europe from the south and east, originating pro: bly in what is now Hungary, under East Mediterranean influence. e gold vessels above are Danish, 10th–9th century BC. They c central European forms but the handle is purely Danish. (24)

Bronze trumpets (above), called *lurs*, are characteristic of the 'baroque' Danish Late Bronze Age, and different types of long horns have also been found in graves or ritual deposits in Britain and Ireland. (25)

A position of prayer seems to be indicated by these cast bronze figurines (left) from the end of the Bronze Age in Denmark. Kneeling, with the left arm held across the body, they suggest a ritual attitude that can also be seen in later Celtic art. All three are wearing neck rings, and the female on the left, whose eyes are inlaid with gold leaf, also has a short skirt of a kind that has been found in women's graves of the earlier Bronze Age. (26)

Wheels with spokes were a Bronze Age innovation, first seen in barbarian Europe in the 13th or 12th century BC. From Trundholm, Denmark, comes the bronze model (below), the object of recent vandalism, of a horse drawing a disk, covered with gold leaf, presumed to represent the sun. (27)

Further evidence of wheeled vehicles comes to light in Late Bronze Age graves of the Urnfield culture, so called from the spread of the rites of cremation and urn burial. The cult car above (8th–7th century BC) was found in a cremation grave at Strettweg, Austria. The dominating female figure and some of her attendants may be forerunners of personalities in later Celtic and Teutonic myths. (28)

The oldest witness to the wheel in Europe is the pottery model cart on the right, which thus takes on a importance out of all proportion to its beauty. It was found in a grave at Budakalász, Hungary, and its probable date is about 1900 BC. Solid wheels were also in use about that time on the South Russian steppes. The cremation urn in the shape of a wheeled cauldron (Peckatel, Mecklenburg, before 1000 BC) shows more developed wheels, but still with only four spokes. (29, 30)

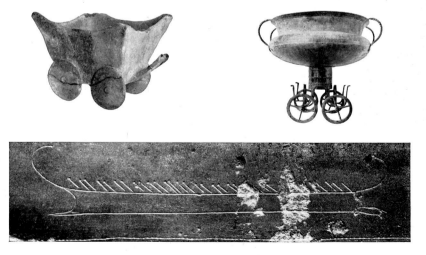

The ancestor of the 'long ship' of the Vikings is first depicted in this engraving (right) on a sword found in a bog at Rørby, Denmark. The blade had a strange curled end to the tip, a form otherwise known only in its pair near by, in a flint copy, and in examples from the Near East. (31)

Miniature gold-leaf boats from Nors, Denmark. Dating from the last part of the Bronze Age or perhaps the Early Iron Age, some of the boats have strakes and possibly shields inscribed on their sides. The idea of the funerary boat seems to have been early established in the North, which must have relied to a large degree on the sea not only as a source of food but as a major means of trade. (32)

The technical skill achieved by native craftsmen of the 'Urnfield' culture is well shown in the hoard of bronze vessels (above right) from a Late Bronze Age grave near Dresden, and the later, Early Iron Age bowl in beaten gold of the 6th century BC. As the Hallstatt chieftains of the Rhône-Rhine-Danube headwaters area grew wealthy from the export of copper and salt, they not only imported objects from abroad but also patronized native-born craftsmen who adapted foreign styles to the taste of their patrons, particularly in beaten metal-work. These vessels above were probably for wine, love of which was a barbarian characteristic right up to Roman times (33, 34)

The 'Hallstatt duck', a favourite motif in decorative work of this period, can be seen on the bronze pail below, from the cemetery that grew up round the Hallstatt salt mines. Combined, as here, with solar symbols, it may perhaps have been connected with some sort of sun worship; its head can occasionally be seen forming a finial for a boat in which the sun is riding. (35)

In the depths of a Salzkammergut hillside, Early Hallstatt copper workings have been preserved by flooding of the mine shafts. The reconstruction opposite, based on information thus obtained, shows the tools used to get and break up the ore (which was first rendered friable by fire), the log troughs to carry it away, and the open-air smelting-ovens. Notched ladders have been found, and even the miners' leather clothing, to say nothing of their excrement, analysis of which shows that, despite the wealth which must have accrued from the export of the refined copper as well as salt to southern Europe, the workers' diet was extremely frugal. (38)

The warrior element in Hallstatt society can be seen in the sword below—now for the first time made of iron instead of the softer bronze. Inlaid with geometric gold ornament on hilt and pommel, it is very different in form from the earlier Bronze Age swords of pl. 15. Armour was not in general use yet, and the helmet, face mask and breastplate on the right, from a Late Hallstatt grave at Krollhügel, Germany, must have been an innovation from the classical world. The face mask, which may have been fixed to a coffin, oddly recalls the gold masks of the Mycenaean shaft-graves. (36, 37)

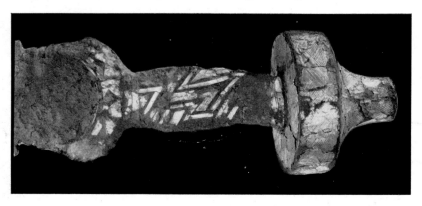

Much new light has been thrown on princely barbarian life in the 6th and early 5th centuries BC by excavations at the Late Hallstatt stronghold (above) overlooking the Danube on the Heuneburg. This was the seat of a wealthy community whose trading relations with the Greeks of Massilia (Marseilles) are indicated not only by imported drinking vessels and wine jars, but by a bastioned defensive wall above the steeper slopes of the plateau. This was built of mud-brick—something wholly exotic to this part of Europe and clearly introduced from the Mediterranean. (39)

◄ **The most impressive** of the Late Hallstatt tombs, marking the west-ward spread of what we can now definitaly call the Celts, was found near the headwaters of the Seine, beneath the hilltop fort of Mont Lassois. Here a princess lay on a funerary cart, its wheels stacked against the walls of the wood-lined pit. The painting on the left re-constructs the scene as she was laid to rest, covered with a rich velvet pall, a golden diadem on her head. Beside her stood a spectacular bronze *krater*, or mixing vessel for wine, about five feet high. This tomb underlines not only the Celtic love of finery and good living, but also their trading contacts with Italy and the Greeks. (40)

The first true art style north of the Alps is the La Tène style of the second half of the Iron Age—the art of the Celts, which grew out of the society of the Heuneburg and Mont Lassois. This gold disk from Auvers (above) dates from the 5th century BC and shows how the classical element, here exemplified by the complex palmette design, mingled with native Hallstatt and nomad motifs to produce the true La Tène style. (41)

The moustachioed Celtic face, seen here on a gold finger ring from Rodenbach, is a favourite La Tène motif. The splendid neck torc and bracelets below come from a late 4th century BC grave at Waldalges-heim. This grave has given its name to the second phase of La Tène art, which, after a mixed early style (as in pl. 46), was based almost entirely on decorative classical motifs. (42, 43)

A final element in European Celtic art is the plastic, almost Disney-like abstraction of human and animal forms. The grotesque owl mask below is part of the handle of a great bronze cauldron found at Brå, in eastern Jutland. (44)

Grazing cattle, a boar chasing a rabbit, and other animals incised on the shoulder of this Iron Age flask from Matzhausen (above) are less in the true La Tène style than in that of Adriatic metal-work. (47)

Sharp angles and dark burnished colour characterize early Iron Age pottery from Northern France (above). Later, the potters of the Marne region—the first in northern Europe to use the wheel—broke away from the more geometric style of their Hallstatt predecessors to produce freer curvilinear designs such as the pot on the left. (45)

Among the finest and earliest products of Celtic craftsmanship are these two bronze wine flagons (below) found at Basse-Yutz on the Moselle. They are a perfect example of the adoption and adaptation of Italic styles, being La Tène copies of a typical Etruscan shape. Classical motifs, such as the palmettes on the neck and at the base of the handle, are mingled with elements from the east such as the panther-like handle, and pure Celtic touches—the human mask which forms its tail, and the duck swimming up the spout. (46)

A hoard of gold coins from the great Celtic 'oppidum' of Manching, near Ingolstadt on the Danube, with a typical Late La Tène jar. Local Celtic chieftains minted their own coinage, based on a Macedonian design. (48)

The peak of European barbarism

is the heroic society of the Celts—an organized and sophisticated society that was moving away from the traditional semi-nomadic pastoralism to a life of wealth and luxury with at any rate some elements of urban civilization. From the beginning of the 4th century BC, when Celts invaded North Italy, the archaeological evidence can be supported and supplemented by descriptions from Greek and Latin writers.

One of the most outstanding of the early La Tène graves so far found is the princess's grave discovered in 1954 at Reinheim near Saarbrücken. Among the many magnificent pieces of jewellery it contained were those shown on the right, which include a neck torc with a twisted hoop, two penannular bracelets and two finger rings. Stylistic comparison with the objects found in the Waldalgesheim grave (pl. 43) suggest that his gravet is the older, probably belonging to the beginning of the 4th century BC. (49)

◄ **The first signs** of La Tène chieftains in Britain are found amongst the chariot burials of the north-east of England. Both there and in Southern Scotland the La Tène style developed into a more flamboyant version of the Waldalgesheim phase. A good example of this is the bronze pony cap (opposite) from Torrs, Kirkcudbrightshire—a fine British piece of about 250 BC. Here the classical palmette can still be seen, much debased but still recognizable. (50)

British craftsmen of the centuries around the birth of Christ had a particular skill in the making of elaborate bronze hand mirrors. In the so-called Mayer Mirror (below), now in Liverpool, we see the basic triple design and the cross or 'basketry' hatching which are the hallmarks of the early style, of the 2nd-1st centuries BC. (51)

More flamboyant and more 'cluttered' in its design, this mirror (below) from Desborough dates from the 1st century AD. It retains the basic three-part design, but this has become almost lost in a welter of elaboration. Compare the complex handle with the simplicity of the earlier design. It is interesting, too, to notice that in the later mirror the pattern is picked out with cross-hatching, whereas in the Mayer mirror the pattern itself stands out against a cross-hatched background. (52)

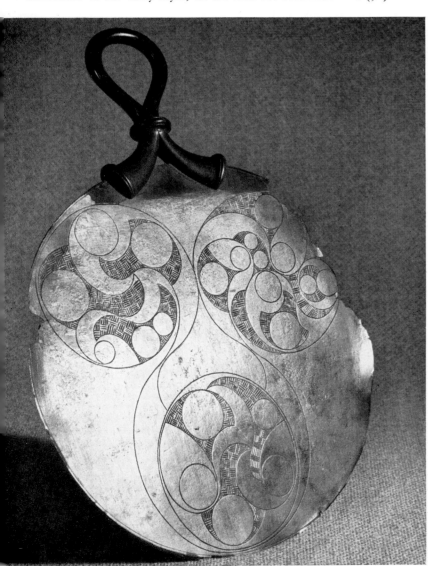

Towards the end of the La Tène period signs begin to appear of degeneration of the geometric and animal styles. The ten-inch-high bronze bucket above (left) was found in a cremation cemetery in Kent, and may originate from the Marne. The palmettes and human head mountings are, in a way, effete, as though invention was dying. The tankard (above, right) dates from the 1st century AD. (53, 54)

Julius Caesar himself wrote (though quite mistakenly) that the religion of the Celts had many parallels with that of the Romans. The stone finial above (centre) in the shape of a two-headed Hermes was found at Roquepertuse, at the mouth of the Rhône, and illustrates the partly classical influence on Celtic religious sculpture. This is only one of many expressions of Celtic veneration of the head. (55)

The most precious treasure of Danish antiquity is a large silver cauldron (above) from Gundestrup, North Jutland. Like so many other Danish finds, it was originally a votive deposit, left on the surface of a bog. Though the people of the period were well aware of the hidden wealth of the bogs, theft of these sacrifices was unthinkable until the beginnings of modern archaeology.

The Gundestrup cauldron, 27 inches across at the rim, is made of silver—in the Celtic world the rarest precious metal of all. On the plates which cover the walls are depicted half-length figures of gods and goddesses, some of whom hold human figures suspended in the air. Around the inside of the cauldron further strange scenes are depicted. Of the three plates visible in this picture, the loose one on the rounded bottom and the left-hand wall-plate show scenes from

a bull-hunt, while on the other a god is seen receiving a human sacrifice, as a procession of horsemen and foot soldiers passes by to the sound of trumpets. This superb piece, probably made some time at the beginning of our era, is of vital importance in any attempt to understand the art and religion of our Celtic ancestors. Despite Italic and Gaulish parallels, the source of this splendid cauldron is probably further to the east. Similar base plates have been found in South Russia (one with a Greek inscription), and we know from classical sources that the silver deposits of the eastern Danube were highly prized. It seems at least likely, therefore, that the cauldron comes from as far east as the borders of Hungary, the meeting-place of the classical, nomadic and Celtic elements that had been the three roots of La Tène art. (56)

From the first farmers to the Celts

T. G. E. POWELL

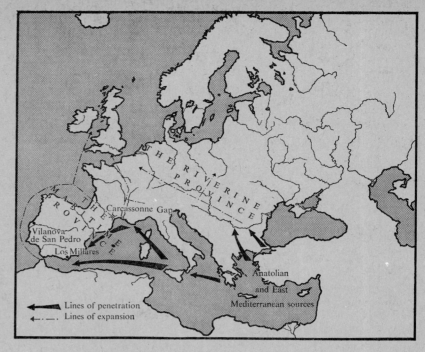

Cultivators of the fourth and third millennia BC, showing lines of penetration and expansion. (fig. 1)

IN THIS CHAPTER we are not concerned with any complete, final achievement of an ancient people whose civilization may now be regarded as contributory in greater or less degree to something yet to come. We have to do only with raw material, with rustic and barbarous populaces who came later to profit by what had been developed elsewhere, but who already possessed in themselves that capacity which ultimately brought forth European civilization as it has been understood for the past thousand years. That is the abiding interest of the early beginnings of Europe, and it is the relevance to history of those anonymous prehistoric peoples who had already conditioned the grand design of historical Europe in such fields as linguistic provinces, social systems, and patterns of rural economy.

The Teutonic peoples who finally overran the Roman Empire in the fifth century AD, and from whose political regroupings medieval Europe took shape, were not the only barbarian people to have descended upon the northern Mediterranean shores from the other side of the Alps. At the end of the fifth century BC, and for nearly two hundred years thereafter, there had been periodic incursions by the Celts. They had threatened even the survival of Rome, and had penetrated through the Balkans to Asia Minor. These were both fully historical events recorded by Greek and Latin writers, but from remoter times still, going back to the thirteenth century BC, there is evidence in archaeology, and in Egyptian memorials, for a period of great upheavals and expansions, an epoch that would seem to have been of prime significance for the future character of Europeans, forging new links between the barbarians in the wilderness north of the great mountain ranges, and their more advanced cousins dwelling in Greece, Italy, and the Iberian Peninsula.

The geographical domain of the European barbarians was essentially that of the temperate climatic zone of the continent; the region of equable temperatures and deciduous woodland lying north of the great mountain ranges already mentioned. The Atlantic, with its moisture-laden winds, formed the boundary to the west, and that to the north was the Baltic and the beginnings of the coniferous forest zone with its severer climate. The eastern boundary is less definable, as here the great Eurasiatic plain runs continuously except where blocked by the Carpathians. The great rivers were the principal means of penetration and intercommunication, and their flood plains offered the most suitable lands for cultivation and settlement. Chief amongst these was the Danube, and then the Elbe and the Rhine. The Rhône and Seine on the western flank, and the Oder and Vistula on the eastern, also played their part, as did many others.

Neolithic farmers

Barbarian, but not savage, life in Europe began with the intrusion from Asia Minor and from eastern Mediterranean lands of the first farming communities. These were at first but small groups of primitive plot-cultivators and cow-keepers. They kept close to the rivers, moving from one spot to another, incapable of gaining a livelihood except by the simplest methods, burning forest patches to make clearings for their sowing, while the cropping of their animals helped further to reduce new growth of high tree cover. This process had begun in Europe during the fourth millennium BC, and some evidence points to a start perhaps a thousand years earlier, but while the riverine province, with the Danube as its axial feature, provides the oldest, fullest, and most significant information, it is important to distinguish, from the beginning, another region of early colonization.

This may be called the maritime province, and it embraced at first the shores of the western Mediterranean basin, with the Rhône valley as an important means of access northward, but, later, it extended to all the coast-lands of the Atlantic approached both from the Straits of Gibraltar and by way of the Carcassonne gap, whence the pioneering of sea routes opened the way to Brittany, Cornwall, and Ireland. In the maritime province the ecological background differed in many respects from that within the continental land-mass; the colonists tended to become isolated around selected landfalls, their environment restricted intercourse, and largely ruled out conflicting cultural influences or interferences, so that the earliest traditions of Mediterranean peasant life survived for long periods in various degrees of dilution *(fig. 1)*.

An ancient Mediterranean practice that was developed spectacularly in the far west by some neolithic groups, but not certainly along the Rhône axis, was the rite of collective burial. Natural caves were originally used in the East and Central Mediterranean, but even before the expansion to the west, artificial rock-cut tombs had come into use. In the newly-colonized regions both rock-cut tombs, and burial chambers constructed of large stone slabs—megalithic chamber tombs—were widely used, and became the most enduring witnesses of their builders. It seems that the peasant farmers of the maritime provice were engrossed in a cult of the dead, and the propitiation of an earth-mother, to an extent that absorbed a greater effort than any other aspect of their lives.

In the Iberian peninsula the introduction of metal working, in copper and the alloy bronze, was brought about by further colonizations, but seemingly on a very small scale, from the eastern Mediterranean. These people brought a rudimentary skill for the exploitation of surface ores, and the casting of primitive axes and knives or daggers. They also built for themselves defended settlements in the manner of their oriental homelands, as at Los Millares in Almeria (almost a little township with its bastioned defensive wall), and at Vilanova de San Pedro near Lisbon. The mother-goddess cult of the Neolithic groups amongst whom they settled was now further enriched through the introduction of newer forms of representation in idol and amulet, and the more advanced constructional techniques of dry-stone walling and corbel roof were applied to tomb building. At Los Millares (c. 2300 BC) the cemetery of the settlement consisted of a cluster of finely built dry-stone and corbel-vault tombs with passage and chamber, and elsewhere the new techniques were used jointly with megalithic construction to achieve ever more impressive monuments.

The principal theatre of European barbarism may now be brought into view, and we have already noted the riverine and forested character of this inland province. Amongst the earliest Neolithic peoples who ventured into Greece and the Balkans were some whose ceramic styles belonged to the impressed ware family, and, somewhat later, there arrived other groups who decorated their pottery by painting, before firing in the kiln, as in the tradition of their Anatolian and Mesopotamian forebears. These two elements of the Neolithic population of the most south-eastern parts of Europe contributed in various combinations amongst themselves and with the assumed pre-pottery Neolithic colonists, to the emergence, probably in the fourth millennium BC, of the major Neolithic cultures of the Danubian zone who formed the first foundations for the whole future cultural and economic aspect of middle Europe.

The early Danubian culture itself is characterized by its simple pottery forms often decorated with spiral patterns executed by incision on the soft paste before firing (pl. 1). The stone equipment was suitable for wood working, and the farming practice was of the primitive slash-and-burn kind involving great waste of soil and devastation of cleared land. Although the nature of their cultivation forbade residence of any long duration in one place, the Danubians are known from excavations to have erected substantial wooden houses. These were long rectangular post-built structures, with a door or doors midway in the longer sides *(fig. 2)*. The early Danubian farmers rarely made figurines or other cult objects. Their dead were buried separately, the corpse being flexed and accompanied with grave offerings. Cremation was very occasionally employed.

This Danubian province eventually split up into several regional groups which can be distinguished one from another by their pottery. These cultures are largely contemporary, in the later half of the third millennium BC, with a group of more evolved Neolithic cultures extending throughout the Balkans and into the Carpathian basin. These had stronger Anatolian connections, and possessed a fuller ritual apparatus in figurines of a mother-goddess and of domestic animals (pl. 2, 3). The pottery was generally painted, but on the finished surface after firing (see p. 61). The influence of this group becomes increasingly important especially in the production and exchange of metal goods, and in maintaining many links south-eastwards with the zone of urban civilization in Anatolia and beyond. By

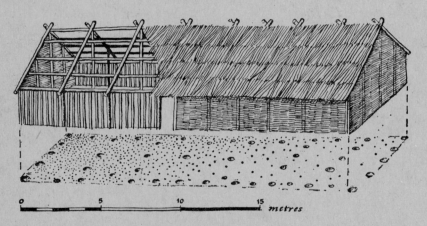

Köln-Lindenthal: ground plan and reconstruction of typical early Danubian Neolithic 'long house' from a lakeside settlement. This type is standard throughout the Danubian loess province from the southern Netherlands to Czechoslovakia. (fig. 2)

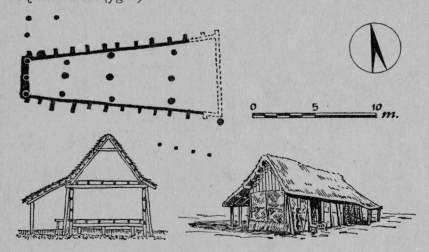

Deiringsen-Ruploh, Westphalia: ground plan, reconstructed perspective and cross-section of a wedge-shaped house of the later Neolithic. This particular plan occurs also in the later neolithic villages of Poland. (fig. 3)

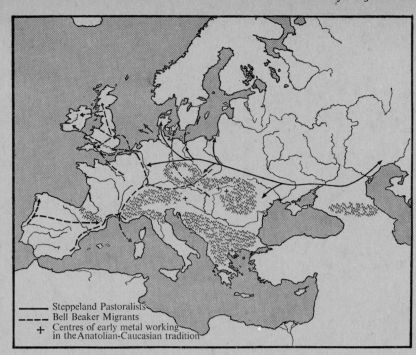

Warriors and traders of the early 2nd millennium BC: principal lines of movement. (fig. 4)

the opening of the second millennium BC the whole of temperate Europe was peopled, if only thinly, by groups of cultivators and flock raisers. The ever increasing forest clearance for a type of cultivation that itself brought about land exhaustion, and the consequent establishment of a different ecology with lighter flora, became a major factor in bringing about certain changes that were to have a permanent effect on barbarian life in temperate Europe. In its effect on rural economy this change led to an alteration in balance between cereal cultivation and cattle raising. Larger herds came into being; there was more pasturage available to them, and this in turn may have led to the manuring of cultivation plots. Barley rather than wheat became the principal crop, but as no field systems survive for study from this remote period it seems unwise to say that there was an actual decline in plot cultivation; perhaps only a change in kind. This move to a predominantly pastoral life was something that developed amongst the late Danubian and certain more northern Neolithic communities evidently without external pressures. The pressures were more likely to have come from amongst themselves in competition for grazing lands, and the opportunities for individual enrichment through cattle stealing. A fragmentation in social structure is indicated by the replacement, in many regions, of the Danubian long house by small single, or two-roomed, cabins suitable for more independent and patriarchal households *(fig. 3)*.

Movements from the Steppe: the domestic horse

The grasslands, especially across the southern fringe of the north European plain, outside the wall of the Carpathians, led directly into the heart of temperate Europe from the east, and from this quarter came people and ideas that were to hold a dominant position for the remaining span of European barbarism. On the Pontic steppelands there had already developed, by the opening of the second millennium BC, a series of interrelated pastoral peoples who extended from the Caucasus north-eastward around the Caspian, and north-westward around the Black Sea. Those nearest the Caucasus were acquainted with copper tools and weapons, but the more peripheral tribes made do without. By a process involving common traditions, and by copying one from another the ceremonial of greater chieftains, a characteristic rite of individual burial under a monumental mound, a *tumulus* or barrow, came to be widespread, and this, together with traits in ceramic styles, shapes of stone battle-axe copied from Caucasian metal prototypes *(fig. 5)*, and the appearance of the horse as a domesticated animal, now all make their appearance in Europe. There is no necessity to invoke a horde of invading horsemen from the steppes. In fact the horse was unlikely to have been ridden at speed at this period. It was still too small, undernourished, and ill-bred for that accomplishment, but its use as a draught animal had already been achieved.

By the nineteenth century BC there had been established a great zone of mainly pastoralist peoples running south-east to north-west from the Caucasus to Jutland. In the first phase, long distances had been covered by small bodies of forceful migrants so that common types of weapons and pottery are widespread. In the ensuing period regional forms came into being, and it is possible to distinguish the more dominant groups through their advantageous geographical locations as well as by their range of material equipment, and their relations with neighbouring, but differing, communities.

It would be wrong to suppose that this eastern element consisted merely of disruptive nomads; recent work has shown that cereal cultivation also played some part in their economy, that, at least at certain times of the year, they dwelt in solidly built wooden cabins, and that fortifications were not unknown. When metal objects came into their possession, the first steps towards a bronze-using economy were taken, and it will be seen how their descendants played a leading rôle as patrons and traders for the copper-smelter and bronze-smith.

There is a case for thinking that these grassland warriors spoke languages, or interrelated dialects, that belonged to the Indo-European language group.

In Saxo-Thuringia, the greatest concentration of grave mounds, and other finds, lies in the area immediately west of the river Saale, and here the intruders found an already large and mixed population, with very varied, and often remarkable, ceramic styles derived in the main from Danubian and Northern traditions. The process of fusion, resulting in greater uniformity of material culture within each natural area, was here, and elsewhere, now about to take place, but with this distinctive mark, that elaborate tumulus burial was to continue as the symbol of the warrior overlord.

Amongst the regional groups that became established in temperate Europe, the Saxo-Thuringian is of special importance. Here some of the graves are of particular interest in throwing light on the house types of the living. Both in wooden and stone remains, a two-roomed

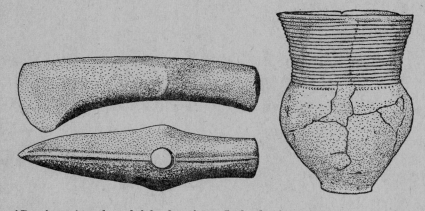

'Battle-axe' and corded beaker from Jutland: the two main types of the single-grave warrior herdsmen of the late Neolithic. The median ridge and drooping blade of the axe are an imitation of the (presumed) copper prototypes of eastern Europe and Anatolia. (fig. 5)

cabin is represented, and the dead man was placed in the inner room as befitting the place of sleep. In two graves, which had walls formed of large stone slabs, the walls were decorated with incised designs suggestive of textile hangings, and showing objects normally suspended by cords from pegs. The most graphic tomb is that found at Göhlitzsch where the man's bow, quiver with arrows, and battle axe are all depicted on the walls as well as the representation of hangings. In a recently discovered tomb on the Dölauer Heide, a larger and more profusely decorated stone-lined grave came to light (pl. 11). Colouring material as well as incisions were here employed. The inner part of the Dölauer Heide grave had been floored with timber planks, and on this the corpse had been laid. The part of the floor nearest the door had no covering over the earth, and so a two-roomed, or room-and-porch type of small house seems indicated. The mode of burial illustrated in these two tombs reflects clearly the steppeland tradition of the richer forms of sepulture where the practice of erecting both wooden and stone houses for the dead, suitably equipped with creature comforts, extended over a long period. It is necessary to instance only the great tumulus burial at Maikop, dating to the end of the third millennium BC, and the Scythian princely tomb at Chertomlyk of the fourth century BC (chapter XI).

Only brief mention can be made of the Bell Beaker culture whose bearers were also widespread in temperate Europe, but with a more central and western distribution than the pastoralists of Pontic origin just described. (fig. 4) The beaker is a finely made pottery vessel of distinctive shape and decoration, and the anonymous people, who have been labelled with the name given to their most characteristic material product, are considered to have originated in the Iberian Peninsula. This is a very complex matter, but there is no doubt that the Bell Beaker people had very close contacts with other peoples and cultures throughout the region between the Rhine and the Elbe to the middle Danube (pl. 6, 7).

The typical Bell Beaker grave is a pit in which the corpse was placed in a crouched position accompanied by a beaker, and perhaps

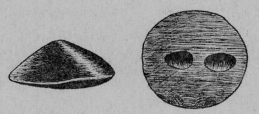

Conical button of jet, showing (right) the 'V'-perforation associated with the Bell Beaker folk of Iberia, Central Europe and Britain. (fig. 6)

a metal knife-dagger, pin, or bracelet. Gold earrings are known in graves from Bohemia to Britain and Portugal. The buttons in bone and shale with V-perforations which are so widespread a feature of Beaker equipment would seem to have been first introduced in the form of amber buttons from the East Baltic, and clothing fastened with buttons is an essentially northern, cold-climate device (fig. 6). Where the Bell Beaker people penetrated into the far west, and into the western Mediterranean, they seem to have had no difficulty in placing their dead, with typical accompaniments, in the collective tombs, rock-cut or megalithic, of the older inhabitants.

The Transition to Bronze Age Cultures

One further component in the first flowering of European Bronze Age barbarism remains to be noticed. In the country within the Carpathian shield, accessible across the Middle Danube from the Balkans, and ultimately from the Aegean, there had come into being a number of interrelated cultures whose general aspect might be said to have been Neolithic with an ever increasing openness to exotic influences from the south-east. The Moravian-Slovakian Painted Ware had been an early example of this, but then followed a period in which several contemporary cultures of mixed local and exotic origins were lodged in all the Middle Danubian lands, and in whose archaeological material appeared the first copper ornaments—small wire spirals and rings for clothes, hair or fingers (pl. 14), and quite substantial shaft-hole axe-adzes which are more likely to have been tools than weapons. The Baden culture (about 2000 BC) is important in this setting, and its pottery is remarkable for skilfully-made high handled cups (fig. 7) and larger vessels which suggest in their shape a metal prototype perhaps to be looked for in Anatolia. These people are now also known to have possessed wheeled carts, as is witnessed by the finding of an admirably detailed pottery model cart at a site in Hungary (pl. 29). The domestic horse was also at home amongst

High-handled 'Baden' cup from Leobersdorf in Austria. The shape suggests an Anatolian metal prototype. (fig. 7)

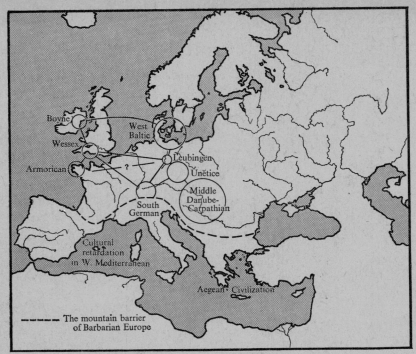

Barbarian Europe in the High Bronze Age (c. 1550–1300 BC). The circles represent the principal culture-groups and the lines their interconnections. (fig. 8)

the Baden people, and complete skeletons have been found in ritual burials along with those of humans and oxen; in one case at least, in Slovakia, a dog received formal burial above a group of humans. These occurrences of the horse, and of wheeled vehicles, would suggest that there had also been some contribution directly from the Causasian-Black Sea region penetrating around the southern edge of the Carpathians to the Middle Danube. Evidence is in fact rapidly increasing for the importance of Caucasian technical ideas spreading westwards at this period.

The gradual exploration of the hill country, lying generally to the north of the middle course of the Danube, led to the discovery of copper ores in many localities. The earliest, and richest, would appear to have been in Transylvania for it was along the lower courses of such rivers as the Körös and Maros, tributaries of the Tisza, and on the banks of that river itself, that settlements sprang up whose inhabitants were clearly engaged in metallurgy as well as

The amber route from Jutland to the Mediterranean. (fig. 9)

some form of stable husbandry. East and south of Bratislava, on the Middle Danube, lies a region of 'tells'; villages of mud-brick houses that were occupied over a long period of time, being rebuilt on the same foundations, and so coming to form small artificial hills. Nowhere further north or west did comparable village sites ever come into existence in prehistoric times, so that the cultural sequences revealed in the stratigraphy of these village mounds, and the correlations that may be established between these and the grave offerings in associated cemeteries, are of the highest value in attempting the interpretation of the developing European Bronze Age.

The Bronze Age

The term *European Bronze Age* can be valued as something more than the retention of an old-fashioned descriptive label, not only because it was an epoch in which bronze became the principal substance for hard-edge tools and weapons but also because the exploitation of, and long-distance trade in, metals, and in rarer luxury commodities such as gold and amber, made possible the propagation of ideas and common objectives that could not have been realized under former circumstances.

The ever-widening operations of metal workers, beginning in the early second millennium BC and now moving into Bohemia and towards the Elbe, and into the Alpine Zone, together with the varied activities of pastoralists and traders already noted, brought about a series of new culture-groups.

Clothing of the Danish Bronze Age, based on finds from tree-trunk coffin burials under Jutland barrows. The woman wears a woollen shift and skirt, and a decorated bronze belt plate. The warrior has a woollen cap and cloak, and a sword in a wooden sheath. (fig. 10)

The Únětice Culture

We may now come to those Bronze Age cultures which exhibit the first examples of a general pattern of European barbarism, and which can reasonably be dated, with some variations according to region, in the early part of the sixteenth century BC. First there is the province of the Únětice (Aunjetitz) culture, so called from the graves found at this place in Bohemia. Originally this culture was confined to metal working people of more south-easterly origins, but in its later stages, and when it had spread along the Elbe and crossed over to the Saale basin, it was adopted by the local (Saxo-Thuringian) warrior pastoralists whose chieftains now found themselves in a position to command a generous supply of bronze weapons, and trappings, and gold ornaments in the form of weighty bracelets, cloak pins, and rings. This is the Leubingen variant of the Únětice culture, and is so called from a rich tumulus burial at that place. Leubingen and some four other outstandingly rich tumulus burials in the Saale region (and others in Western Poland) belong to a relatively late stage in the life of the Únětice culture, but it is first important to appreciate the reasons for this wealth, and there appear to be two principal factors: the availability of salt in the region, and the advantageous geographical position at the crossing of long-distance trade routes. Through this area, too, passed the amber route from Jutland on its way to the Adriatic and thence to Mycenaean Greece, and it was this commerce probably more than any other factor that enlivened and enriched the Saxo-Thuringian scene *(fig. 9)*.

The westward connections of the Leubingen group extended to Britain, and indirectly to Ireland, and from these islands one may deduce that there came to the Saale gold and bronze, or tin, as raw materials, as well as the occasional importation of actual insular manufactures such as Irish bronze axes with their distinctive decoration (pl. 14).

The Northern Bronze Age

The rise of the Bronze Age in Denmark, and the west Baltic area generally, must next be mentioned. The amber supplies that fed the first southern markets had been provided by neolithic communities. As there are no natural sources of metal in the north, it must have been principally by trading amber that the west Baltic people were able to import metal goods, and then, later, the metal in ingot form so that a remarkable home industry, with its own characteristic northern types, came into being. The importation of metal objects began about the beginning of the fifteenth century BC and the home industry about a century later. The numerous tumulus burials of men and women of the Danish Bronze Age during the later fifteenth and fourteenth centuries BC, are remarkable for their wealth of bronze weapons and ornaments, amber beads, and occasional gold (pl. 24–27, 31, *fig. 10*).

The European High Bronze Age

A series of interdependent and chronologically overlapping cultures within particular geographical regions may be envisaged dominating the scene in trans-Alpine Europe for some three centuries after 1600 BC. The overlords in all cases shared some degree of common ancestry in the Neolithic warrior pastoralists, and the tradition of tumulus burial was maintained, but now greatly enriched through the deposition with the dead of costly belongings. *(fig. 8)*

The Middle Danubian region must not be forgotten in this period for events there, somewhat later, were to have a considerable effect on all the adjacent parts of Europe. The settled village communities between the Tisza and the Transylvanian mountains meanwhile continued to flourish, and throughout the Hungarian plain, in Slovakia, and in much of Rumania, a whole series of interrelated cultures can be distinguished. These shared the general characteristics of the bronze industry as it was throughout the Middle Danubian region, but it is particularly in the great variety of ceramic types, with individual geographical distributions, that the complexity of the cultural traditions can be detected. The whole region continued to be tied most closely with lands further south-east. Judging from the contents of the large cemeteries of flat cremation graves, the social system did not include headmen of the category described amongst the tumulus-building peoples further north and west. Personal adornment with gold beads, bracelets, and arm, finger, and hair rings, was by no means strange to the people of the Middle Danubian cultures. Theirs was the gold of the Transylvanian rivers, but amber was either not available or not acceptable, although small beads of faience from Egypt or the Levant found their way here as they did even as far as Britain and Ireland. The real treasure of the Middle Danubian peoples can be estimated less from their dwelling places or graves during their period of prosperity than from the caches which they were obliged to make in times of trouble, at least one of which seems to have occurred in the thirteenth century BC.

Craftsmen

We should turn now to some short discussion of the craftsmanship of the developed Bronze Age, for here was the first evocation of skill to produce not only efficient and useful objects such as tools and weapons, but things of beauty for personal adornment and household embellishment. Work in gold certainly takes pride of place, and whatever was thought of amber and faience in one region or another, gold was universally esteemed and treated in characteristic styles from place to place. In the Leubingen group, heavy solid gold bracelets with chased rib ornament, large gold pins with loop heads, and spiral wire rings of various sizes, were the fashion, but gold was available in such quantity that at least one hoard containing a ritual axe made in this metal has been found. Moving to Britain and Ireland, and in the latter island to a source of river-washed gold comparable in richness (for at least a time) to Transylvania, we find quite different fashions. In the Wessex culture of the southern chalkland area of Britain, which is roughly contemporary with the Leubingen

group, there are no bracelets or pins in gold, but fine sheet plaques for sewing on clothes (pl. 21). Otherwise, at least in the tumulus graves, gold was lavished on objects of magical value, amulets such as small disks of amber with sheet gold edging, and miniature 'halberd charms' consisting of an amber shaft with gold binding, mounting a small triangular bronze blade. Gold sheet covering for conical buttons should also be mentioned, and buttons of this shape, with V-perforations, in shale continue an ancestral Beaker fashion *(fig. 6)*.

In Wessex, even more remarkable, are some few drinking vessels in precious substances. At Rillaton in Cornwall, on the western flank of the Wessex culture area, there was found a grave with a typical bronze dagger, and a gold cup (pl. 17) with horizontally ribbed, or corrugated, surface, and a handle of sheet gold held in position by carefully executed rivets with lozenge-shaped washers between the wall of the vessel and the rivet heads. The strengthening of the walls of thin gold vessels by corrugation was a device worked out in the Aegean, and although the Rillaton cup is not similar in shape to any surviving gold cups from that region, it is very close in technical workmanship to cups from shaft grave IV at Mycenae. The Rillaton cup must be regarded as the product of a native goldsmith working under the influence of more sophisticated imports, but whether in southern Britain, or elsewhere in trans-Alpine Europe, it is hard to say. A recent discovery at Fritzdorf near Bonn has brought to light a large gold cup (pl. 16) with smooth surfaces, but with a handle that in shape and decoration, as well as in its method of attachment, is almost identical with that from Rillaton. The shape of the Fritzdorf cup is however related to a Wessex form known best in finely carved shale cups with handles, and from one of amber. These all have an ovoid body with shoulder and a curving neck above. The finest amber cup in Britain came from a Wessex culture grave near Hove, in Sussex. Its general shape is hemispherical with carefully modelled rim and shoulder grooving, and a well-developed handle which displays close connections with those of the vessels already described. In the Wessex culture we see, even more clearly than in Saxo-Thuringia, the range of costly paraphernalia characteristic of a barbarian heroic society; weapons, personal adornment, and drinking vessels are all present, and will be found to have remained the distinguishing marks of aristocratic patronage of the skilled crafts for the duration of barbarian Europe.

In Ireland no gold objects have been found in graves, but a number of remarkable sheet-gold ornaments of crescentic shape, the *lunulae* so called, have come to light under rocks and in peat bogs. These objects have finely engraved geometric ornament executed along the edges of the crescent and over the terminal horns (pl. 20). In shape it would seem that the *lunulae* are gold versions of the principle of the bead crescentic necklace known elsewhere in amber and jet. The *lunula* was exported to Britain and western France, and there are attenuated copies in gold from Denmark. Also amongst the earlier Irish gold work are small disks with radial decoration, and holes for sewing on cloth. Such things have been found in Bell Beaker graves in southern Britain, and these, together with simple 'basket' earrings of which a few have been found in Ireland, suggest that the natural gold sources of Ireland were discovered by Beaker traders amongst the first of metal-minded prospectors reaching Ireland (pl. 19).

It will be as well to mention here another type of gold ornament originating from Irish goldsmiths which should not be placed as early as the objects just now described, but which seem proper to the setting of the High Bronze Age rather than later times. These are torcs made from rods of solid gold, and known by the name 'Tara torc' from the finding at that place of two very large and weighty specimens.

The technique involved in the making of Tara torcs is particularly interesting. The cylindrical rod of gold was grooved longitudinally and flanges were then hammered up so that the rod now became cruciform in section. The whole thing was then twisted so that the flanges appeared as diagonal fluting, but the terminals were left plain. This technique is generally accepted as having been a device to produce a scintillating effect that was achieved by Aegean goldsmiths by soldering two angular bent strips of sheet gold together and then twisting them. The secret of soldering gold did not reach the north-western isles until much later centuries.

Returning now to mainland Europe, the Fritzdorf cup reminds us that in the Rhine valley one may also look for barbarian patrons of the goldsmith, and in the important hoard of bronze weapons from

Trassem, which should date to the fourteenth century BC, comes the magnificent gold pin with triple spiral head. This piece may not of course be of native manufacture, for spiral-headed pins were made earlier in Anatolia, and this may be an import (pl. 13). Of bronze weapons no survey can be attempted that might cover all the remarkable achievements in casting throughout the various barbarian provinces, and two only will be chosen as outstanding. First there are the elegant battle-axes of the Middle Danubian-Transylvanian group, sometimes decorated with spiral ornament derived from Mycenaean styles, and secondly there are the daggers and swords of the second period of the Danish Bronze Age with wonderfully intricate spiral ornament cast on the hilts, which were sometimes further enriched with inlays of amber and gold. These Danish masterpieces are reflections, of course, of the amber trade with the far south (pl. 15).

Western Tombs

In a far distant quarter, but important for the present sketch, are the great Passage Graves of southern Spain, such as the Cueva del Romeral at Antequerra, and its peers, in construction and size, in Atlantic Europe, such as Ile Longue in the Golfe du Morbihan, and, most particularly, New Grange and its monumental neighbours, which stand above the river Boyne near the east coast of Ireland. There are a number of reasons for believing these very large and skilfully built Passage Graves to date to the middle part of the second millennium BC, and so to be largely contemporary with Mycenaean civilization and the High Bronze Age of middle Europe (pl. 8–12). We do not know whether these particular tombs were raised for individuals, or for families in the old collective sense. The magical art that was cut on the walls of some of the larger tombs in Brittany, and which is found in somewhat different guise in Ireland, is related in the main to the ancient theme of the earth-mother-goddess, but at New Grange and some few other tombs, the decoration includes bold spirals, a motif foreign to the older art, and used with a much greater regard for a sense of monumental decoration, in a manner recalling the Mycenae grave-slabs and the contemporary Maltese temples. All this, together with outstanding achievement in building technique, is best exemplified in the tomb at New Grange, and it may be wondered whether this is not the indigenous westerly counterpart to the tombs of rich chieftains of the Leubingen-Wessex kind.

The End of the Bronze Age

The downfall of heroic societies has usually come about as the result of internal dissensions and of individual rapacity, in so far as these can be observed in historical times, and the same processes may well have been operative in Bronze Age Europe. Our lack of information on the dwellings of the Leubingen and Wessex chieftains, for instance, makes it impossible to tell if any of their houses or strongholds were abandoned or sacked. Whatever the initial circumstances

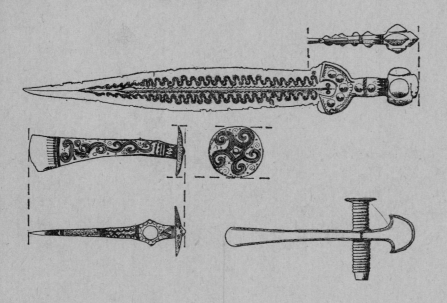

Weapons from the Apa hoard of the Carpathian full Bronze Age, roughly contemporary with Hajdúsámson (pl. 15). The slender-shafted battle axe is an early type, contrasting with the disc-ended example; again the spirals, adopted by the Northern 'baroque' Bronze Age, recall Mycenae. (fig. 11)

Fortified island settlement of the Late ('Urnfield') Bronze Age at Wasserburg-Buchau, Württemberg, with defensive works and a cluster of farmsteads. The largest building (centre) may have been a chieftain's house (fig. 12).

may have been, there is evidence for the destruction and abandonment of the tell-villages, and other defended settlements throughout the Middle Danubian region, and down into the Balkans. To this phase belong a number of rich gold hoards, and collections of weapons, all evidently hidden and never recovered, and a new weapon, the slashing sword, was evolved in response to the new conditions of prolonged unrest. The cut-and-thrust sword, as opposed to thrusting swords and rapiers, was an original contribution to armament by the barbarians of central Europe, and it spread in many variations of form over the whole continent as well as into the lands of the eastern Mediterranean (pl. 15, *fig. 11*).

Urnfield Cultures

We must now consider briefly the trend of events in the Upper Danubian region during and after the thirteenth century BC. The folk of the Tumulus Bronze Age cultures of all this region had been open to the influences of the superior crafts of the Middle Danubian higher barbarism before they moved east to destroy it. There was therefore some approximation in ceramic styles and metal artefacts in favoured areas, but this should not obscure the evidence for actual movements of Middle Danubian farmers westwards along the fertile riverine soils which the pastoralists had largely avoided. These newcomers were not displaced tell-villagers so much as people from western Hungary and Slovakia, related culturally and economically to the tell-village sphere, but themselves living in less permanent settlements—either small strongholds on hill-tops, defended farmsteads of timber-built houses, or perhaps in as yet undiscovered village conglomerations using timber, not mud-brick *(fig. 12)*.

Again, the cremation rite, involving urn burial with increasingly large cemeteries, or urnfields, makes its appearance, hence a widely used term 'Urnfield Cultures' for all cultures of this type throughout the drainage area of the Upper Danube, and extending therefrom to the Rhine, and eventually to the Rhône, Seine, and the Low Countries. Not only have we to do with an important augmentation of the population in this 'North Alpine' zone, as it has been called, but with eventual fusions of communities, Tumulus and Urnfield, in certain areas. Marked economic changes, in improved agricultural practice, and in the exploitation of metal, together with improved casting techniques and tool forms, also took place.

By the time the Urnfield cultures were being established in the Upper Danubian region certain oriental influences had begun to make themselves felt. This was no doubt the outcome of the opening up of the lands of the eastern Mediterranean to the barbarians, and the carrying home of sophisticated metalwork, and of craftsmen able to produce it. In particular may be mentioned cups and larger vessels of bronze sheet metal, and even ritual vessels mounted on miniature wheels having Levantine prototypes (pl. 28, 29, 30). The influence of metal vessels with burnished surfaces and twisted wire handles is seen in ceramic forms amongst early Urnfield pottery. A new fashion in personal adornment is marked by the appearance of the first safety-pin brooches made of bronze wire *(fig. 13)*, and a favourite decorative motif, a stylized duck, the so-called 'Hallstatt duck', now comes into evidence (pl. 35, fig. 18). The origins of the brooch and the duck may both be looked for in Greece during the last phases of Mycenaean prosperity. Somewhat later came ideas of body armour in sheet bronze, cuirasses and greaves, helmets, and shields, and the description of Goliath might do as well for any well-equipped barbarian warrior in the Late Bronze Age north of the Alps as for one campaigning in Israel (pl. 37).

It may have been in the twelfth century BC that the two-wheeled war chariot was introduced to middle Europe; the evidence is indirect, and no actual remains have been recognized so far. The Hittites and Mycenaean Greeks had been well acquainted with this vehicle, but its construction depended on a standard of carpentry and bronze casting that had not been reached north of the Alps much before this time. Bronze mounts for four-spoked wheels, and later, complete bronze wheels originally possessing wooden tyres have been found in Urnfield culture contexts, but these may just as well have belonged to four-wheeled vehicles as to any other type *(fig. 15, 16)*.

By the opening of the first millennium BC, the North Alpine Urnfield culture-province had extended virtually to the estuary of the Rhine, and eventually in the late eighth century it reached beyond the Pyrenees to Catalonia. The populace were no longer displaced migrants but rather colonists seeking more land. Cereal cultivation, or pastoralism, according to environment, were the bases of economy but specialist groups, in particular miners and smiths, had come into existence in response to a greatly enlarged bronze industry. The break-up of the old Mediterranean markets for raw materials had released for home barbarian consumption metal resources that hitherto had been drawn southwards, and the introduction of improved techniques had contributed materially to the provision of a greatly increased range in uses to which bronze could be put (pl. 38).

Even the remote islands, Britain and Ireland, came, within the tenth century, to experience some of these changes and some two hundred years later, insular bronze-smiths were beginning to produce fine sheet-metal vessels that must have marked a great advance in the preparation of food and drink *(fig. 17)*.

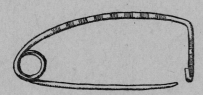

Safety-pin brooch, or fibula, of the so-called 'violin-bow' type, from Strbci, S. Bosnia. One of the new pin types introduced at the end of the Bronze Age, it has close parallels in such pre-classical Greek connections as the Kerameikos cemetery (see chapter V, p. 156). (fig. 13)

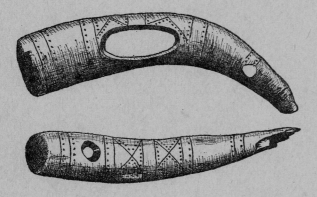

Decorated antler cheek-piece of the High Bronze Age, from a stratified settlement 'tell' at Füzesabony, Hungary. Objects of this class offer some of the earliest evidence for the harnessing, if not for the riding, of horses in Central Europe. (fig. 14)

Carved design from one of several decorated stone slabs forming part of the construction of a chieftain's tomb at Kivik, S. Sweden. Dated about 1200 BC, it is the first evidence for the two-wheeled chariot in the North. (fig. 15)

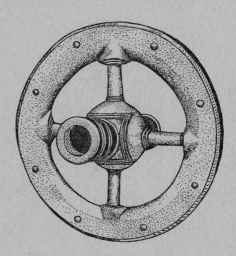

Reconstruction of a bronze-cast wheel from a late Urnfield settlement on the shores of L. Neuchâtel. Slats held a wooden rim or tyre. (fig. 16)

The Hallstatt Culture

By the middle of the seventh century BC, there had arisen in Bohemia and Bavaria martial groups whose warriors were buried accompanied for the first time by iron swords, although bronze ones remained in use for some time as well. The greater chieftains were entombed in a wood-built chamber under a great tumulus, and lying on the body of a cart or waggon, of which the wheels had usually been removed but placed within the tomb. Iron swords and spears, and pottery vessels with joints of pork and beef, had also been placed in the chamber together with the bronze harness for a pair of horses, and sometimes for a third. The antecedents of these iron-using chieftains and warriors is not clear; the bulk of their material culture carries on the Urnfield modes, but iron, cart burial with horse harness, and inhumation, are new features, and can at the moment be explained in various ways as representing nothing more than culture contact between local potentates and the Etruscans, now established in Italy, or with peoples of the Steppe. Alternatively, a case can be made for actual incomers from the east following the horsemen of the previous century, but this view is not supported here. The acquisition of iron, knowledge of which may well have come up through the Balkans, undoubtedly made these people the most powerful north of the Alps, and their overlordship of the Urnfield populace during the ensuing two centuries may well account for the emergence of the Celts as a nation.

The Hallstatt culture has been so called from the place of that name in the Salzkammergut in Upper Austria where, in the nineteenth century, a very rich cemetery was excavated yielding iron swords and daggers, quantities of fine bronze vessels (pl. 35), many of them being imports from Italy, and of course great quantities of pottery. Both cremation and inhumation graves were present, and on stylistic and typological grounds, two main phases could be distinguished. The exceptional community represented by these graves owed its wealth to an export trade in salt which was mined, and extracted from springs, at the head of the valley. The value of salt in the contemporary world may be gauged by the wealth of exotic objects received in return.

It was in the second phase of the Hallstatt culture, beginning in the mid-sixth century BC, that the impact of Greek trade from the colony

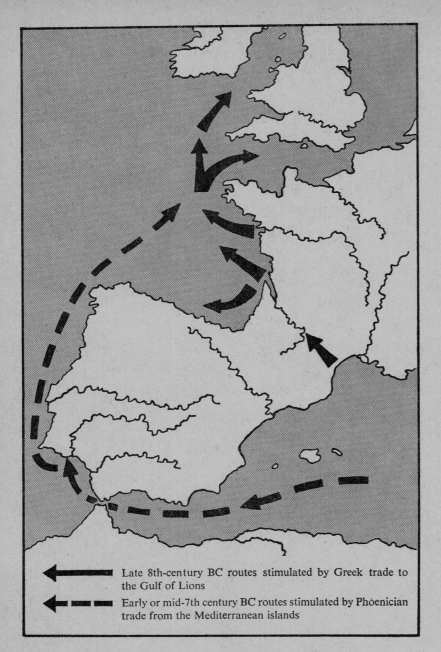

The presumed use of the western seaways. (fig. 17)

The 'Hallstatt duck' and 'solar boat' symbols. Above: detail of an early La Tène bronze torc from northern France; compare the Hallstatt bucket in pl. 35. Below: detail of decoration on a Late Bronze Age (Urnfield) bronze basin from Rossin, Pomerania. (fig. 18)

at Marseilles (*Massilia*) reached up the Rhône and Saône to the Swiss Lakes and the Upper Danube, and here the waggon-burying chieftains are found in their graves with actual Greek imports, such as bronze wine jugs, while in their strongholds Greek pottery wine cups and wine amphorae are found scattered as sherds amongst native wares. Gold ornaments, and cups, make their appearance in the tombs now for the first time, but these are of native manufacture, and bear witness to an accumulation of wealth amongst these chieftains which they had not previously enjoyed.

The beginning of the trade between the late Hallstatt people of the Rhône-Rhine-Danube headwaters area is marked by two important waggon graves in which were found the fragments of bronze Rhodian wine-jugs *(fig. 19)*. These tombs, at Vilsingen in Hohenzollern, and Kappel-am-Rhein in Baden, may be dated between 560 and 520 BC, and contemporary with them is the first phase in the late Hallstatt stronghold at the Heuneburg, Kr. Saulgau, in Württemberg, a fortified eminence overlooking the Danube. The modern excavations at the Heuneburg have thrown a flood of new light on the nature of princely barbarian life in the sixth and early fifth centuries BC, and we are justified in calling the inhabitants of this region Celts, for they are one and the same people recorded by Herodotus and other Greek writers from the fifth century onwards. The most astonishing fact revealed by excavation at the Heuneburg was the second rebuilding of the defences when a great mud-brick wall, with forward-projecting square bastions, crowned the steeper slopes of the hill. This wall was tied in to an immense timber and earth rampart of native type which barred the gentler approach on one side. The mud-brick construction is of course something wholly exotic to this part of Europe and was clearly introduced from the Mediterranean. One must suppose that the local ruler engaged builders who themselves were Greeks, or Greek-trained, and one cannot but wonder whether the desire to erect such a fortification in an area climatically not suitable for mud-brick, had not arisen because the ruler had seen such walls on a visit to the far south (pl. 39).

The Heuneburg may have been a unique stronghold in so far as brick fortifications were concerned, but the wine amphorae, and 'Black Figure', later to be succeeded by 'Red Figure', Greek painted wares, are known from other hill-top sites such as the Camp de Château in the French Jura, and the routes by which all these luxury objects travelled from Massilia are now fairly certainly known to have been land routes following, at higher levels, the banks of the Rhône and Saône. At the turn of the sixth and fifth centuries BC, an important stronghold had been established on Mont Lassois, near Châtillon-sur-Seine, close to the headwaters of that river. Black Figure pottery also found its way to this place, but interest principally centres on the very rich tomb found at Vix not far from the foot of the hill, where a young woman, one may well say a princess, had been buried. Here also a wood-built chamber had been constructed, over which a tumulus had been heaped. The lady rested on the body of a vehicle whose four wheels had been removed and placed against one wall. She was adorned with a gold penannular ornament, either for the neck or head, and probably of eastern Greek workmanship. Her native jewellery was confined to a few insignificant bronze brooches, but she was accompanied by a fabulous collection of bronze vessels, chief amongst which was an immense and elaborate *krater* or mixing vessel of Greek workmanship. There were also present a Greek pottery cup, and an Etruscan bronze beaked flagon of a type that was to be increasingly imported across the Alps in the succeeding half century. The Vix tomb is considered to date to about 500 BC (pl. 40).

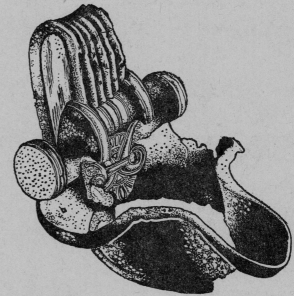

Fragment of an imported bronze Rhodian flagon from the Hallstatt waggon grave at Vilsingen, Hohenzollern, which may have preceded the actual transport of Greek 'Black Figure' drinking cups such as those in pl. 40. (fig. 19)

Reconstruction of a defended farmstead of the Early Iron Age at Little Woodbury, Wiltshire. In the corn-growing country of southern England this kind of one-family dwelling was common, and contrasts with the highly organized 'oppida' of the Continent. (fig. 20)

Lakeside settlement at Milton Crannog, S.W. Scotland (reconstruction). In the north and in Ireland, settlements such as this continued well into the Roman occupation. (fig. 21)

The La Tène Culture

The principal point in enumerating these finds of exotic craftsmanship in a European barbarian setting is to show how the accumulation of influences from the Mediterranean world brought about the creation of the first true art style north of the Alps, known archaeologically as that of La Tène. This undoubtedly found its birth amongst patrons and craftsmen in such centres of power and wealth as represented by the Heuneburg and Mont Lassois. In fact the spark may have been touched off not at either of these places but on the Middle Rhine, for it is from chieftains' tombs, mainly in the vicinity of Koblenz, that the earliest and finest examples of metal work, gold and bronze, in the La Tène style have been found. In these tombs, the four-wheeled waggon gives place to the two-wheeled chariot, and this is perhaps another aspect of Etruscan influence. The earliest La Tène chariot graves on the Middle Rhine, and in Champagne, date from about 450 BC, or shortly thereafter. Some few have produced Red Figure cups, and genuine Etruscan beaked flagons of bronze and other objects, but very soon the Celtic craftsmen had mastered the art sufficiently to make excellent copies of the Etruscan flagons (pl. 46), and to improve upon them in the barbaric taste of their patrons. Grotesque animal handles, and coral inlay are conspicuous, and at the same time a linear and plastic art based on plant motifs (pl. 41), seen in Greek and Etruscan exemplars, is developed with a special flair for asymmetry, and curvilinear abstract designs incorporating allusions to animal and human shapes (pl. 44). Drinking vessels, helmets, and chariot fittings were amongst the principal fields for this new art in bronze, while in gold, neck ornaments, the torc, and bracelets were the chief objects. Some women's graves were as rich as men's, or more so, as is witnessed by that found in recent years at Reinheim near Saarbrücken (pl. 49).

However much it is possible to distinguish Greek, Etruscan, and Scythian, or other oriental, contributions to La Tène art, it is something quite unitary, and all the borrowings have been so changed and adapted to new purposes that no accusation of mere copying can be levelled.

The site of La Tène, from which the culture and the art style take their names, lies at the north-eastern end of the Lake of Neuchâtel. During the nineteenth century the lowering of the lake level revealed timber posts, and a great quantity of iron weapons, but relatively few other objects. It is now considered that this was a votive deposit on a large scale, but in the manner of others since discovered, and such ritual offerings bear out the testimony of Classical writers who ascribe this kind of practice to the Celts. The votive deposit at La Tène was made in the second century BC, and the site does not lie within the boundaries of the earliest province of the culture. The name has been retained, however, as a general label for the whole culture, and the art style.

The peak of European prehistoric barbarism is reached in the Celts, with their tradition of heroic society including kings, craftsmen, and chariotry. From the opening of the fourth century BC, when Celtic tribes invaded northern Italy, these people come ever more closely within the range of written history so that the archaeological evidence can be filled out through the observations of Greek and Latin writers. But the Celts also expanded into as yet more remote parts of Europe and not least into Britain and Ireland. In Britain, between the third and the first century BC, they created a lively and individual school of La Tène art (pl. 48, 50–54), and in Ireland they were able to retain their ancient language, and social system, undisturbed by Rome, so that at the beginning of the Middle Ages the traditional literature of the Irish was still cast in the modes of heroic Celtic life as it had been many centuries earlier on the continent. Of the oral learning and legal systems of the Celts there is not room here to write, but no impression of European barbarism can be complete on the material evidence alone, and we must see the arms and fortifications, the gold ornaments, and the drinking vessels, against a background of rural populaces bound to each other in a customary system of family relationships and social obligations to serve and protect; the whole knit together by ritual and magical sanctions. It is indeed in these last observances, and in the corporations of learned and sacred persons who maintained them in Celtic society, the druids, seers, and bards, that the continuity of European barbarism from perhaps as early as the beginning of the second millennium BC can be followed down even into the post-Roman period (pl. 55, 56).

Beyond the world of the Celts lay other major groups of peoples and languages, not yet crystallized as nations, but, in subsequent time, to play to the end of the Roman Empire the rôle that the Celts had played to Graeco-Etruscan civilization. Through trade and pillage the Teutonic tribes, and later still the Slavs, were to possess themselves of those substances and concepts of an Heroic Age that led to the formation of nations, and to the civilization of Europe as we have known it *(fig. 22)*.

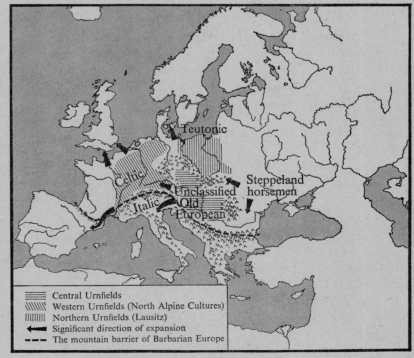

The linguistic and cultural zones of Barbarian Europe in the early 1st millennium BC. (fig. 22)

XIII THE CRIMSON-TIPPED FLOWER

The birth and growth of New World civilization

G. H. S. BUSHNELL

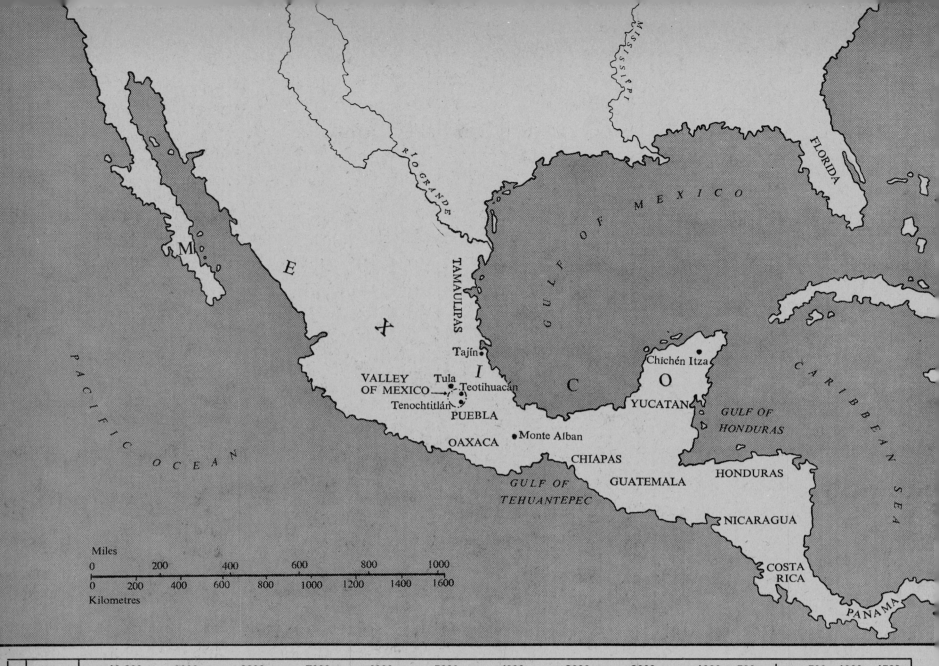

		BC 10,000	9000	8000	7000	6000	5000	4000	3000	2000	1000	500 BC | AD	500	1000	1500
NORTH AMERICA	**East & Plains**	(Clovis points)		(Folsom points)				Beginning of settlements Shell mounds		*? Beginnings of pottery and agriculture in East*	*Ceremonial earthworks and rich burials in NE. (Hopewell, Adena)*			*Temple mounds and towns in Mississippi Basin and SE.*
		Big game hunters	*(Various types of point)*			←———— Archaic stage in East ————→ Hunting continues in the Plains								
	South-West											*Basket makers*	*Pueblo Indians, Hohokam etc.*	
	Great Basin	←———————— Gatherers of wild seeds and hunters of small game ————————→												
MIDDLE AMERICA	**Central Mexico**	Mammoth hunters						Agricultural villages. Pottery	First temple mounds (Cuicuilco etc.)	Teoti- huacán Classic	Toltecs	Chichimeca (Aztecs & others)		
	Other Areas							Beginnings of agriculture in N. E. Mexico		Classic Maya in Guatemala, SE. Mexico etc. Monte Alban in Oaxaca	*Mixtecs in Oaxaca Tajin in Vera Cruz Toltec-Maya in Yucatan*			
SOUTH AMERICA		Hunters in Patagonia		Hunters in Peru, Venezuela and Argentina (Ayampitín)		Early fisher farmers	↑ Chavín ↓ N. coast tradition S. coast tradition	Classic Mochica in N. Coast Nazca in S. Coast. Tiahuanaco in S. Andes	Tiahuanaco expansion	Coastal states: Chimú Inca Empire				

PERU AND BOLIVIA

| | BC 10,000 | 9000 | 8000 | 7000 | 6000 | 5000 | 4000 | 3000 | 2000 | 1000 | 500 BC \| AD | 500 | 1000 | 1500 |

The first Americans

crossed the Bering Straits from their Asiatic homeland more than 10,000 years ago. The next step was the development in the American continent of fishing, hunting and food-gathering societies like those of the Palaeolithic and Mesolithic peoples of Europe and Asia. We are then confronted with a series of economies based on cultivation (notably of maize) but emerging quite independently of the early agricultural communities of the Old World. On this substructure there arose, in Middle and South America, the complex civilization encountered by the invading Spaniards in the early 16th century AD—the twin cultural peaks of Mexico and Peru. Although they had a highly organized social structure, and considerable accomplishments in architecture and craftsmanship, there were also some strange technological gaps. The Maya, for example, though they could count in millions, and construct a calendar of extraordinary accuracy, lived to all intents and purposes in the Stone Age.

About 1500 BC the Valley of Mexico, which corresponds to the Federal District and the northern part of the State of Mexico and is now the most heavily populated part of the country, was a great lake, slowly sinking. Around it was a cluster of villages, typical of the early farmers of America.

The only signs of religion in these early farming communities are the numerous female pottery figurines, which are believed to have been used ceremonially to promote the fertility of the crops. The one on the right comes from Tlatilco in the Valley of Mexico. (1, 2)

Where these early farmers came from we do not yet know. This pottery figurine of a baby (above), which was found at Tlatilco, is in the Olmec style, originating on the Gulf coast of Vera Cruz, so there may be a relationship between the two areas. (3)

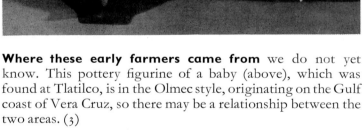

A group of immigrants, probably from the south, settled at Tlatilco in about 1100 BC and influenced the surrounding villages. Rather more sophisticated than their neighbours, they created new types of pottery, including many finely modelled from life. Of the four pieces from this period shown above, the tripod vessel, decorated with red slip, is from Zacatenco, and the others from Tlatilco. The bowl on the left is buff ware with some dull red painting on the area within the incisions; the gourd-shaped bowl, dark brown. The polished black bowl on the right, in the shape of a fish, has traces of red colouring on the belly and fins. (4)

A more complex civilization

began to grow up in the early years of the Christian era, particularly in Middle America (Mexico and parts of adjacent countries of Central America). Out of simple beginnings great religious and ceremonial centres developed among the Maya peoples of this area. From small shrine mounds as at Cuicuilco in the Valley of Mexico grew temple-topped pyramids of great size and fantastic decoration, with a powerful priesthood serving a religion of increasing elaboration. To regulate religious feasts and the agricultural year, the Maya priests devised a calendar more accurate than that of any other ancient civilization.

The Maya religion seems to have developed out of a form of nature worship, designed to promote the fertility of the crops, with a few gods such as those of the rain, the wind, maize with Itzamna, the Old God, head of them all. In the Classic period (roughly, AD 300–900) many more were added; the Classic Maya pantheon included gods of the sun, the moon, death, and even days, months, and the numbers attached to them.

Blood was an acceptable offering to the gods of the Maya, though human sacrifice was comparatively rare. On this carved stone lintel from Menché in Chiapas, the most easterly state of Mexico (probable date, AD 781), a man is seen kneeling before a priest and making an offering of his own blood. This, which must have been a severe test of religious devotion, was done by passing aloe thorns through the tongue on a cord. Blood drops were then caught on a piece of bark paper (in the basket in front of the kneeling man), and offered up to the god as a symbolic human sacrifice. Notice the artificially deformed shape of the skulls—a regular feature of Maya art. (5)

Jade ear ornament (right) of the Classic Maya period from British Honduras, which was on the eastern fringe of the Maya country. Until recently no source of jade was known in Middle America, but it has now been found in the mountains of eastern Guatemala. (6)

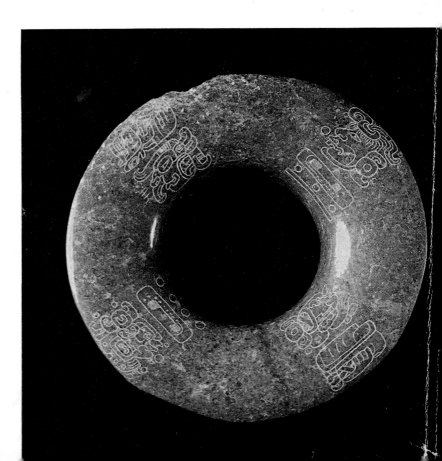

One of the first Maya centres to attract the attention of the archaeologist (as long ago as 1785) was Palenque in the north of the state of Chiapas. Of recent years much work has been done in winning back the buildings from the encroaching jungle and restoring them, and today they are an attraction much visited by tourists. In the 7th century AD Palenque was an important Classic Maya ceremonial centre, as is proved by the abundance of its inscriptions and the unsurpassed refinement of its art and architecture. The Temple of the Sun (below, right), which stood along one side of a ceremonial square, is a very well preserved building of the Classic Maya period, on which much repair work is now being done. The interior consists of two naves running parallel to the front face and spanned by corbelled vaults; the rear nave contains a dedicatory relief with a date corresponding to AD 692. The ornamental roof crest is typical of Maya architecture. The cross-section drawing (below, left) shows the construction of the corbelled vaults, each course of stone projecting out over the one below until a single stone could bridge the gap. With all their intellectual achievements, the Maya never hit upon the true arch. (7, 8)

The astonishing accuracy of the Maya calendar system was due to observation of the heavenly bodies over a long period of time, and to co-operation and consultation between the priests of the various religious centres. These pictures of Altar 'Q' at Copán, Honduras (taken by the English explorer A. P. Maudslay in 1885), show sixteen representatives of Maya centres gathered together at Copán for an astronomical conference. Each representative is seated on a glyph which may denote the name of his town. Carved on the altar top is a date corresponding to AD 776. Copán seems to have been a very important religious centre of the Maya, with large numbers of hieroglyphic stelae ranging in date from AD 616 to 782, all revealing the strange preoccupation of the Maya priesthood with numbers and the measurement of time. The last inscription of Copán dates from AD 800, and shortly afterwards the hierarchy disappeared. Probably, in their overwhelming obsession with time and eternity, they eventually lost the support of an increasingly sceptical peasantry. (9, 10)

A complex mass of pyramids, temples, terraces and courts—such was the magnificent group of buildings at Copán now called the 'Acropolis' (see reconstruction below). Occupying a great platform 12 acres in extent, on the bank of the River Copán, it has been rescued from the jungle and partly restored. It is a tremendous and impressive sight even now; in its heyday it must have been an awe-inspiring symbol of hierarchical power. On the left of the picture is the Great Plaza, containing elaborately carved stelae which probably represented priest-rulers of Copán. Nearer to the Acropolis itself, between two smaller temples, is the court for the ceremonial ball-game. (11)

More than a thousand years before the West had any knowledge of rubber, or rubber balls, the Maya had a game, probably of a ceremonial nature, played with a heavy ball of solid rubber. Its origins are lost in the mists of the past, and we cannot be certain about the rules or the object of the game. The painting above shows the court; on top of the sloping block of masonry on either side are set three macaw heads carved in stone. The object of the game seems to have been to keep the ball in flight using only hips, thighs and elbows; leather padding was sometimes used to protect the hips, which caught the brunt of the bruising. (12)

Along the centre of the ball-court are three carved stone markers. Their purpose we do not know, but from the designs on them (above and below) we can see what the players looked like. The padded leather hip-guards and knee-pads can be clearly seen, and also the ceremonial feather head-dresses. (13, 14)

In the depths of the forests of Chiapas, near the Guatemalan border, a group of Late Classic Maya temples was discovered in 1946, and given the Maya name Bonampak, 'Painted Walls'. In one of these temples, the walls of two rooms were entirely covered with a magnificent series of frescoes, painted with a freedom and realism far removed from the stiff conventions of the carved stelae. Maya murals of the Classic period are rare, and these of Bonampak are an invaluable source of information about these people. The murals form a sequence, and the drawing below, from Room 1, shows their arrangement round the walls and the corbelled vault. The sequence describes

a raid for sacrificial victims, the preparations for the raid and the subsequent ceremonial. The photograph below (a detail from the west wall of Room 1) shows preparation for a dance by impersonators of the gods. In the painting above, a copy reconstructed by the Guatemalan artist Antonio Tejeda, a group of captives seem to be pleading for their lives while a dead man sprawls on the steps. The contrast between the abject, naked prisoner and the ruthless victors in their finery shows a high degree of realism and artistic imagination.

A carved stela at Bonampak bears the Maya date 9.17.15.00, which corresponds to AD 785. (15–17)

In the Great Plaza at Copán (see pl. 11) stand nine elaborately carved stone stelae about 12 feet high, each portraying a stiff, richly dressed figure who may have been a priest-ruler of Copán. Stelae of this kind were erected at Maya centres to mark important dates, usually the end of a *katun*—roughly a 20-year period—or half *katun*. Stela C (above, left) bears a glyph signifying the date AD 782, and stands in the north-west corner of the Plaza. (18)

The largest centre of the Maya civilization, and possibly the earliest, was Tikal, in northern Guatemala. Here, too, stelae and their attendant altars were erected to commemorate milestones in the eternal procession of the years. The one above (right) bears a dedicatory date which probably corresponds to 22nd January, AD 771. The flat treatment of the carving is in strong contrast to pl. 18, which is a near approach to sculpture in the round. (19)

Two richly clad figures are shown on the painted clay beaker (left) from Nebaj, Guatemala, one standing and one half-kneeling, presenting offerings to a dignitary (who is on the other side of the vase). The subdued colours, red and black on a pale yellow background, heighten the illusion of reality created by the fluent drawing. (20)

The Classic Period

came to an end in the 9th century AD. In the south, the priests departed, their temples and stelae were abandoned to the jungle, only visited now and then by peasant farmers to sacrifice to their gods or bury their dead. But farther north, in the peninsula of Yucatán, some of the sanctuaries still carried on and some, about AD 975, were reoccupied by a new people, the Itzá. Who these were we do not know for certain, but it seems likely, from similarities of religion and art, that they were a branch of the warlike Toltecs, who founded the city of Tula about 950. The Toltecs in their turn were overthrown after 200 years by the Chichimec tribes, chief among whom were the Aztecs, rulers of Mexico when the Spaniards came.

War and violence and a military élite were introduced by the Toltecs to the Valley of Mexico. The façade of one of their temples at Tula (above) shows a frieze of ocelots and coyotes, and birds eating human hearts—emblematic of the chief orders of Toltec knights. (21)

Wooden war drum of the Aztecs (above). The carvings depict a struggle between an eagle and a tiger, with a sun symbol between; this may represent the sun between the powers of light and darkness. (23)

The temple of the warriors at Chichén Itzá (above) contains many sculptures of Quetzalcóatl, the feathered serpent god of the people of Teotihuacán, the Toltecs, and the Aztecs. (22)

The Toltecs had distinctive and easily recognizable pottery styles. Mazápan ware, for instance, as in this bowl (above), is decorated with groups of wavy parallel lines in orange on a buff ground. (24)

Human blood was the food of the gods, and Huitzilopochtli, god of the sun and patron of the ruthless, warlike Aztecs, fed on it insatiably. The painting below shows the centre of Tenochtitlán (where Mexico City now stands) with the Great Teocalli, crowned by its twin temples of Huitzilopochtli and Tlaloc. Down the blood-spattered steps of the pyramid sprawl the bodies of slaves and prisoners, after the priests have cut the still beating hearts out of them in sacrifice to the god. It is said that when the last enlargement of this massive pile was dedicated, 20,000 prisoners were sacrificed. At the foot of the steps, warriors are dancing before the chief the mimic dance of the sun, ending in the killing of a bound warrior, the sun impersonator, in their midst. For the sun, in the Aztec mythology, was a young warrior, born of the earth-goddess Coatlicué, whose daily journey began in battle and ended in death—to be revived again with blood. (25)

Sacrificial knife of flint (left); the mosaic-covered handle represents a knight of the Aztec military order of the Eagles. The actual sacrifice is shown (right) in a brutally realistic scene from the Temple of the Jaguars at Chichén Itzá. (26, 27)

Much Aztec pottery too was pervaded with the sinister influence of their religion. Below (right) is the figure of one of the Aztec gods enthroned upon the steps of the *teocalli*, or pyramid. The whistle embellished with a vulture head is of the type played by a victim ascending the steps to the stone of sacrifice. It seems strange that they could approach so grisly an end with music, but the Aztecs believed that those who died in battle, or were sacrificed to the gods, went straight to the highest heaven. (30, 31)

Xipe, the Flayed One, is the god portrayed in this black basalt mask (above). His priests danced in the flayed skin of a sacrificed slave, which—though this seems hard to believe—symbolized the fresh green covering of the earth in spring. The whole skin, even to the face, was used in this repulsive ritual; this is indicated by the tautly stretched 'O' of the dead lips. The worship of Xipe seems to have originated among the Mixtecs of Oaxaca, but the Aztecs absorbed many alien influences in both their religion and their art. (28)

This fine carving (right), of the type known as *hacha*, is a characteristic product of Tajín, on the Gulf coast of Mexico, but *hachas* have been found all the way across the isthmus to the Pacific. It seems likely that the inset decorative ribbons, and the eye, were originally inlaid with some other material. What these curious wedge-shaped carvings were used for is not known. (29)

Ceremonial spear-thrower or *atlatl*, ornamented with gilt relief showing an Aztec eagle knight. In action, the butt of the spear lies in a groove on the reverse side, and the thrower is held with a finger through each of the stone loops. (32)

Pottery imports included graceful Mixtec tripod bowls from Oaxaca (above) and highly polished polychrome ware from Cholula in Puebla (south of Tenochtitlán), like the cup and bowl below. (33, 34)

The Lady Three Flint, named after the year and day of her birth, is shown in this detail from a Mixtec manuscript, giving birth to a child (right-hand edge). She then dives head foremost into a hole in a mountain, leading to a purifying bath, in which she is seen (bottom left) with attendants around. Above this she and her husband the Lord Five Flower receive the homage of two priests. (35)

When Cortes came to Mexico in 1519 he was met by emissaries of the Aztec emperor Montezuma, bearing gifts. One of them was the ceremonial feather shield below, which was presented by Cortes to his own emperor, Charles V, and is now in Vienna. The central figure in the design is a coyote, picked out in gold thread, symbolizing one of the orders of military knights. (38)

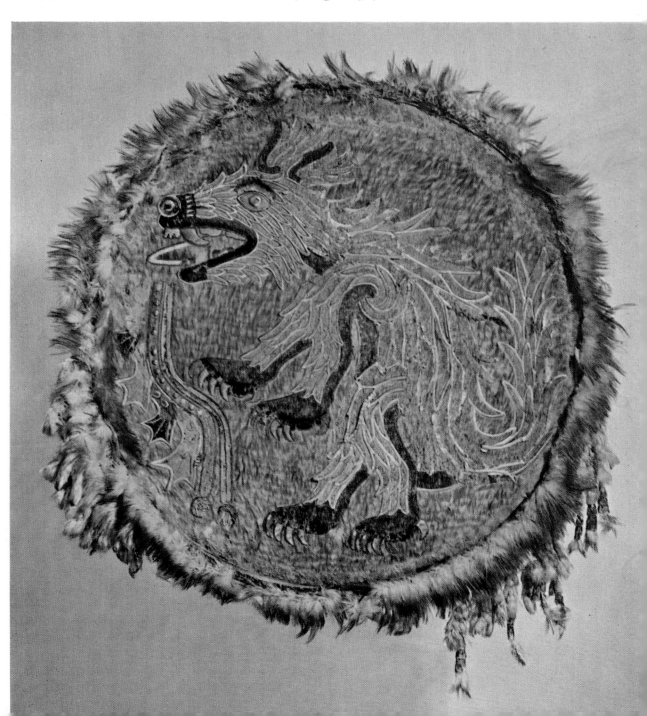

Even local Aztec wares could be light and pleasant. The tripod bowl above, decorated with a black design on an orange ground, was probably made between 1403 and 1507; the jug below (black on dark red), probably later than this. (36, 37)

The only true empire

in ancient America was the empire of the Incas in Peru, but it only came to its full power in the last hundred years before the Spaniards came. Its origins, about which we are only now beginning to learn a little here and there, go back more than three millennia BC, and are governed by the physical shape of the country. Peru is dominated by the great mountain chain of the Andes, sloping steeply down to the Pacific on the west, and to the vast rain forests of the Amazon on the east. Short, fast-flowing rivers empty into the Pacific across a dry, narrow, coastal plain. Here, from about the 3rd millennium BC, groups of settlers began to appear, mostly at the mouths of rivers such as the Moche and Chicama in the north, Nazca and Ica in the south. Here they lived on sea-lions, fish, wild plants and cultivated beans and squash. They grew cotton (but had no looms) and by about 1200 BC they were making pottery. Some 200 years later a group of immigrants, probably from Mexico, brought maize, the loom, and the worship of a puma or jaguar god, with its religious centre at Chavín. Both north and south reached their highest development about the same time as the Classic Maya (about AD 250–750), though they had no hieroglyphics, and probably no elaborate calendar. With greater political integration they were able to organize the irrigation of the dry coastal plain; cities began to develop, and, later, militarism and war.

A fine but unusual example of the Mochica pottery style (right). Jaguar worship is often shown by semi-human figures with feline faces, or even fanged human ones, but the animal itself is rarely shown. (39)

Between the two heights of Mexico and Peru lived many lesser peoples whose history is not so well known as that of the Aztecs or the Inca. Some of them were ruled by chiefs of considerable power and state, whose graves were rich treasure houses. The regions now covered by Costa Rica, Panama, Colombia and Ecuador are famous for their work in gold, especially that of the Quimbaya of Colombia. Of the three Quimbaya objects on the left, the gourd-shaped vase in the centre is of gold, while the other two are made in a gold-copper alloy. The Peruvians and their neighbours could work metal over a thousand years before the Mexicans, who for all practical purposes were still living in the Stone Age at the Spanish conquest. (40)

Richly embroidered textiles are a feature of the southern pre-Classic period cultures of the Nazca and Ica valleys and around Paracas. On the right, draped on a lay figure, is a large and lavishly worked suit of textiles from an early cemetery on the Paracas peninsula. (41)

Painting rather than modelling was used by the potters of south Peru for decoration of their wares. In the group below are a pre-Classical Paracas bowl (left), a two-spouted polychrome jar (Classic Nazca), and a late Ica bowl (centre) with a design in black, white and red reminiscent of textiles. The Nazca people shared the cat-god cults with the peoples of the north, but had also a rich and strange mythology of their own, of which the monster on the jar below may be an illustration. (42)

Peruvian pottery of the Classic period (about AD 250–750) made frequent use of human or animal forms—or strange mixtures of both. Below, on a piece of contemporary gauze textile: left, Mochica stirrup-spouted jar showing a richly dressed corpse; top right, Recuay (N. Highlands) jar with remains of negative painting in black; bottom, Nazca polychrome jar. Of the three jars on the right, the lowest (coast Chavín) represents a bird with feline tusks and some human features; the macaw is Classic Mochica. Chimú, the powerful northern confederacy that grew out of the Mochica (c. 1300) produced the black jar, decadent in its rather lifeless modelling. (43, 44)

near Lake Titicaca a great religious centre grew up at Tiahuanaco, towards the end of the first millennium BC, with skilfully worked masonry and pillar-like statues. Tiahuanaco pottery influenced art styles of the coast towards the end of the Classic period, for the rich and fertile coast lands were a continual attraction to the hardier but less wealthy highlanders. These incursions from the highlands to the plain triggered off a period of political change, with the people gathering together more and more into large towns. Eventually three new states emerged in the north, centre and south of the coastal plain, the Chimú in the north being the most powerful.

Massive stone gateway at Tiahuanaco. The central carved figure, which some say represents a creator god of Peruvian mythology, has round staring eyes from which tears fall. The weeping eyes are a constantly recurring theme wherever Tiahuanaco influence is felt. (45)

Strongly individual painted pottery was made by the Tiahuanacans, one marked feature of which is the parti-coloured black-and-white eyes. The group above includes (left) an early bowl with a puma head and tail on the rim; (centre) a Classic period beaker; (right) post-Classic, decadent beaker in dull black and red on orange slip. (46)

Tiahuanaco influence on coastal wares was strong too, and is easily recognized. The three pieces above, on a piece of Coast Tiahuanaco tapestry, are all from the Central coast. Left and centre, polychrome vessels; right, in black, white and red. The characteristic eyes can be seen on one of the vessels and also on the tapestry. (47)

The Inca dynasty

and its subjects had been settled in and around Cuzco since about AD 1200, but with the accession to the throne of Pachacuti in 1438 they began the career of conquest which led finally to an Inca Empire extending from Quito in the north, right down to central Chile. Throughout their career of conquest and unification they imported not only material loot but also craftsmen, particularly from the Chimú. The Empire, still actively developing when the Spaniards landed in 1532, was a rigidly pyramidal structure, with an absolute Emperor at the head, supported by an hereditary aristocracy and a warrior caste. All this was accomplished by a people who, in contrast to the Aztecs of Mexico, had no means of writing and could only record figures on knotted strings.

Massive polygonal blocks, perfectly joined, are a typical feature of Inca fortifications. The great fortress of Saccsaihuaman (left), overlooking the Inca capital at Cuzco, though it must have been nearly impregnable with a precipice on one side and three rows of ramparts on the other, was probably built more for show than from fear of attack. Some of the stones are more than twenty feet in height. (48)

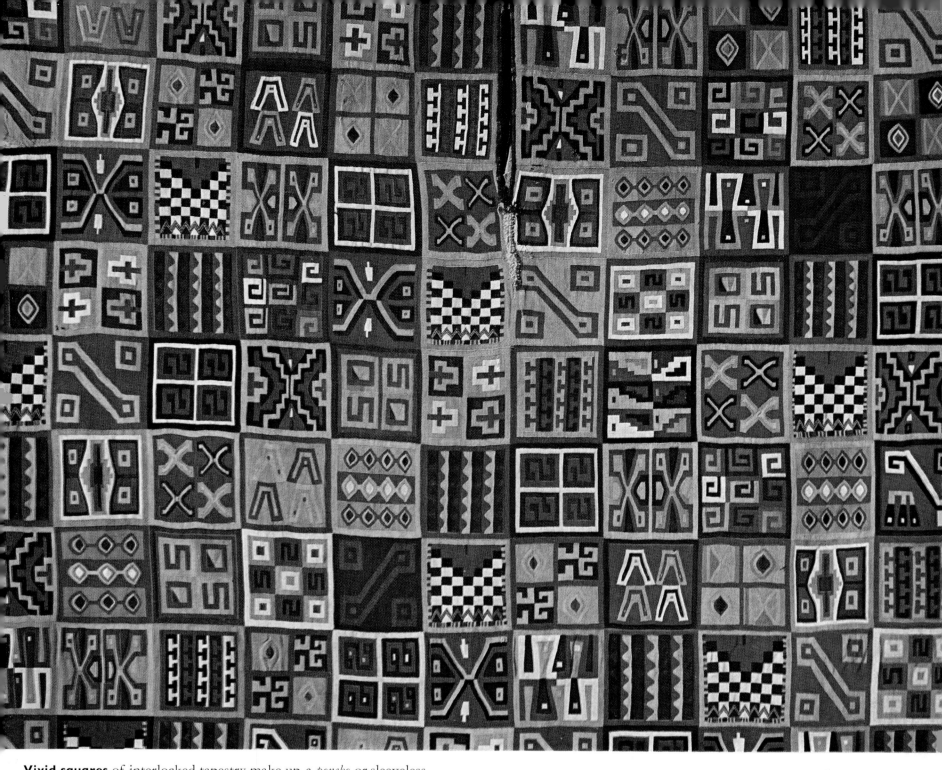

Vivid squares of interlocked tapestry make up a *poncho* or sleeveless shirt of the Inca period from Ica, south coast. (49)

Inca craftsmanship is represented by a polychrome pottery vessel (below, left), a stone dish (top) and an inlaid wooden beaker. (50)

Alpaca in banded agate, from Cuzco (length 5 ½ ins.). Pottery figurines of similar form are still used in fertility ceremonies, being buried in fields and stockyards to increase the herds. (51)

Chimú gold formed a large part of the loot of the Incas in the early part of their career of conquest. On the left is an ornate gold breast ornament from Huarmey in the southern part of the Chimú kingdom. (52)

Captured by the Incas in the middle of the fifteenth century, Chan-Chan, the Chimú capital (below), covered an area of about eleven square miles. The great mud-brick walled compounds, like miniature cities, are believed to have housed separate clans, under their own chiefs. Each compound was divided from the rest by irrigated areas and reservoirs. Large towns such as this were sited where the irrigation canals of two or more valleys could be fed in, for on the arid coastal plain of Peru it was only irrigation that made such centres of population possible. It made them vulnerable too: the Incas from the highlands had only to gain command of their water supply to enforce surrender. (53)

The birth and growth
of New World civilization

G. H. S. BUSHNELL

The spear-thrower is a device for increasing the range of the spear by providing, as it were, an extension to the throwing arm. Invented in palaeolithic times, it was brought to America by the early hunters, and is still in use in Mexico and some other parts of the world. The drawing shows it being used by an Australian aboriginal. (fig. 1)

WHEN COLUMBUS ARRIVED in American waters in 1492, American culture was like a range of mountains, rising from lowlands in Alaska and Tierra del Fuego, through the foothills of the United States and Chile, to the great twin peaks of Mexico and Peru, with lesser heights over the intervening Central and South American areas. In the peak areas, man had reached a high state of culture, and the Inca and the more advanced Mexicans possessed most of the features of a civilized community. At the other extreme were the Eskimo in the north and the tribes of Tierra del Fuego in the south, but though their resources were meagre and their cultures simple, they were highly adapted to their harsh surroundings and must have lived in them for a long time.

The high cultures had many features which the Spaniards could understand. There were hierarchical states, whose rulers lived in considerable splendour, fine buildings, specialist craftsmen, and a religion which played a dominant part in the lives of the people, though its practices were far from being such as they could approve of. On the other hand, the civilizations they encountered lacked iron, the wheel, the plough and the alphabet, and the invaders must have wondered to find a civilized people without those things which they took for granted in their own life, and who had moreover neither horses, cattle, sheep nor pigs, and who ate strange plants. This state of affairs had taken a long time to develop, and it is the purpose of this chapter to outline its growth.

The Setting: Early Man before 5000 BC

The story of man in the New World had begun even before the retreating ice sheets of glacial North America had paused and pushed forward a little between about 9000 and 8000 BC. By this time man was well established in the Continent: how much earlier he came we do not know. There are persistent claims that human beings were present in America between 20,000 and 30,000 years ago; there are fires which man may, or may not, have lit—animals he may, or may not, have killed—and crudely flaked stone objects, which those most qualified to judge think that he did not make. By weight of numbers, these finds have been built up into an impression of probability, but the idol has feet of clay, and a single stratified sequence would do more to support it than any number of doubtful finds.

Before passing on to surer ground a word is necessary about the changes in climate which have taken place in the last 20,000 years. We begin in a time of increasing cold which reached its peak from about 16,000 to 15,000 BC, after which there was a milder interval, followed by another cold peak about 12,000 BC. Then there was another mild interval, followed by the cold period already mentioned, from 9000 to 8000 BC. Each of these cold peaks was less intense than its predecessor, and the Ice Age was coming to an end. Next came a cool, wet period called the Anathermal ('not warm'), gradually warming up until about 5000 BC, and this was followed, until 2000 BC, by a period hotter than the present day, called the Altithermal ('high temperature'), which was associated with desert conditions in western North America, while the East was probably warm and wet, like the contemporary Atlantic Period in Western Europe (see chapter XII). After 2000 BC conditions approached those of the present time.

Man must have come to America first by the Bering Straits, and his access depended on climate. Before boats were invented he had to cross on dry land, and this could only be done in cold periods when so much water was locked up in the ice sheets that the Straits were dry. There were times in the Ice Age, not yet well defined, when Alaska

was also free enough from ice to allow him to find his way south. When between 8000 and 5000 BC the climate became warmer and the oceans filled up, any new migrations would necessarily have been by boat. It is not known when boats were first used to cross the Bering Straits, but they were known by the 7th millennium BC in Northern Europe (see chapter I), so they could have been used here at an early date.

Both before and after the cold period of 9000 to 8000 BC, hunters were roaming parts of the United States in pursuit of large mammals, much in the manner of the ancient hunters of Europe and Asia described in chapter I. They have left their traces on temporary camp sites and places where they killed their prey. The weapons they used were spears tipped with beautifully flaked stone points, which were hurled by means of the spear-thrower, a device still used by the Eskimos, the Australian aborigines and other primitive peoples *(fig. 1)*. The earliest finds, dating from before the cold period, but how much before we do not know, are associated with a type of point called 'Clovis' *(fig. 2)*, and these have been found with the remains of mammoth and horse. During the cold period, man was hunting mammoth in the Valley of Mexico, where the ice was confined to high mountains, and elsewhere there was increased rainfall.

Many finds dating from between 8000 and 5000 BC, when the climate was improving, show that the hunters were ranging over a wide area of the United States from the Great Plains eastward, killing more bison than mammoth. The many varieties of stone point which they used have this in common, that they were large enough to be the heads of spears for killing large animals. One type in particular, the 'Folsom' point, is a household word in American archaeology *(fig. 2)*.

While the hunters lived in the Plains and the East, there were people with rather a different way of life west of the Rocky Mountains, in the Great Basin, Washington, Oregon and California. Gathering wild seeds and plants was more important to them than hunting, and some of the larger animals, such as the bison and the mammoth, were rare or absent. Ground sloth, horse and camel, all of which later became extinct, were hunted in some places, but in others only forms which still survive, like mountain sheep, antelopes, and duck. Fishing

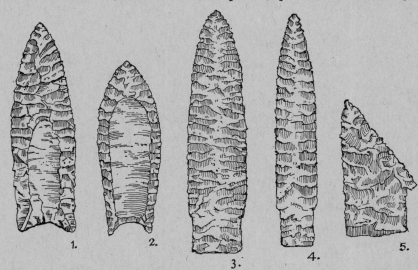

Types of N. American stone artifacts. 1, Clovis; 2, Folsom; 3, Scottsbluff; 4, Eden; 5, Cody Knife. (fig. 2)

was possible only in a few places, but the salmon run was exploited at The Dalles, Oregon, where the Columbia River enters the gorge through the Cascade Range. Some of the most important finds come from dry caves, where materials normally perishable are preserved, and these include rope sandals and specialized types of twined basketry, which are still being made in the West *(fig. 3)*. Although these people probably reached America later than the hunters, they are believed to have been there by 9000 BC, and by 7000 BC some of them were living in much the same way as their successors continued to do until about 1850.

Little is known of the early Americans in the vast area south of Mexico, although they were hunting the ground sloth and the native horse in southern Patagonia by between 7000 and 6000 BC. No traces of their presence have been found in Central America, through which they must surely have passed, for the famous footprints found deep in volcanic ash in Nicaragua (and formerly claimed for this early date) are those of men and animals fleeing from an eruption of a much later time. It may be that they followed the coast and that their remains have been washed away by the rising sea of post-glacial times, or they may have penetrated the highlands, in which case traces of them may yet be found in the caves which abound in Costa Rica and Honduras. Surface finds of points and other stone implements belonging to hunters are scattered widely in South America, and there is a strong presumption that some of these belong to the earliest peoples to reach the Continent, two of the best instances being in Venezuela and on the coast of Peru. Apart from the finds in Southern Patagonia mentioned above, the only material of this sort so far found in a datable context is at Ayampitín in Argentina, of about 5000 BC.

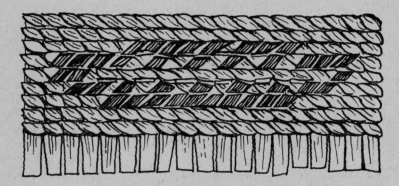

Twined basketry ornamented with a patch of 'false embroidery', shown in black, as still practised by several Indian tribes in western North America. False embroidery appears only on the outside of a basket. (fig. 3)

The Rise of the Farmers

About 5000 BC, but possibly earlier, begins the story of the development of permanent settlements in favoured spots, although it was not until the beginning of agriculture, which came later, that they became widespread. Even when they did, it must not be imagined that hunting and gathering ceased; the buffalo hunters of the Great Plains, the acorn gatherers of California, the Fuegians and the Eskimos remind us that these ways of making a living have lasted into our own times.

In those parts of the eastern United States where the climate of the Altithermal Period was warm and wet, are found sites which show that people were able to live for considerable lengths of time in one place, or at any rate to return to it at frequent intervals over a long period. The remains found on these sites are far from uniform, except in the things they lack, such as pottery, earthworks, substantial buildings, and evidence of agriculture, but they are at a generally similar cultural level, called by archaeologists the Archaic Stage.

Along rivers in Kentucky and Tennessee are mounds built up over a long period from the discarded shells of freshwater mussels, the regular source of food which enabled the people to remain there. Among their possessions were ground stone axes for wood working, stone pestles for grinding wild seeds and berries, and spear-throwers of bone and antler with which they hunted the deer whose bones are found in the shell heaps. In the forests of the North-East, and in and around New York and New England, were bands of people who were probably less settled, although their rubbish heaps show that a few spots were, if not semi-permanent settlements, at least favourite camping places. They had stone slabs, mortars, mullers and pestles for grinding acorns and other plant food, bone hooks and

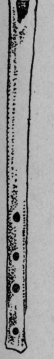

Bone end-blown flute. (fig. 4)

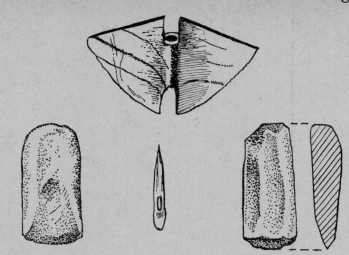

Archaic artifacts from the Eastern U.S.A. Top: banner-stone. Below (l. to r.) : stone gouge; bone needle; bevelled stone adze for woodworking. (fig. 5)

gorges for fishing, stone-tipped spears for hunting, and stone adzes for wood working, to which were added later stone gouges, weights called 'banner-stones' for attachment to spear throwers, bone needles, soapstone vessels and other things *(fig. 5)*.

In both areas the dead were buried, with grave goods of various kinds, in the refuse dumps, and in some cases in the North-East they were accompanied by powdered red ochre, a dog or a second human skull. Turtle-shell rattles, bone flutes and whistles *(fig. 4)*, and necklaces of shell beads and animal teeth, give an indication of interests outside the daily quest for food, and there is evidence of contacts with peoples far away, in the shape of tools and weapons beaten out of native copper from Lake Superior *(fig. 6)*, and shells from Florida. (This does not imply a knowledge of true metal working, which was quite unknown in America until much later. The copper was treated as a malleable stone.) It is unlikely that the various groups of people who lived on these and other sites were descendants of the early hunters of the Great Plains and the East, and it may be that they came from Asia in later migrations, although traces of their passage through the intervening territory still elude us. When agriculture began in this region is uncertain, and the Archaic Stage is assumed to have ended about 2500 BC with the coming of pottery and other features previously lacking.

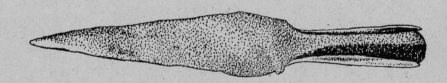

Spear-head beaten out of native copper. Archaic Stage. (fig. 6)

It is always difficult to detect the beginnings of agriculture among archaeological remains, and in a wet climate it may be impossible. Agriculture does not necessarily coincide with the introduction of pottery and other 'neolithic' features as in Britain or in other parts of the Old World, in fact it is known that ground stone tools were used in North America long before, and that in at least two areas pottery was introduced long after. To learn something of the beginnings of cultivation, we must turn to the evidence obtained by excavation in some dry caves in the Sierra de Tamaulipas in north-east Mexico. People who lived here around 2500 BC ate mainly wild plants, grubs and grasshoppers, which made up over 80% of their food. Judging by the discarded bones, about 10% of their diet was composed of the meat of large animals, and there was a residue of 4% of cultivated maize of a primitive variety, and squash. Remains of everything they used have been preserved, grinding stones, crude stone knives and scraping tools, wooden spears with stone points, wooden awls, string, checker mats and coiled baskets. They were food gatherers who did a little gardening.

A very different picture is given by their successors who occupied the caves, after a break, round about 500 BC. They were true farmers, and a much improved maize, beans and squash made up over 60% of their food, besides which they had fine pottery and cotton cloth woven on the loom. A similar state of affairs is seen far away on the arid coast of Peru. The people who settled there about 2500 BC lived chiefly on the harvest of the sea—sea-lions, fish and shell fish—but they also gathered wild plants and cultivated a very few, chiefly cotton, squash and beans, but no maize.

Around 1500 BC there was a great lake in the Valley of Mexico, whose level was slowly falling. On its margins were swamps, and the surrounding hills were clothed with forests of pine and evergreen oak. It was good country to live in, and the people who began to settle there at this time will be taken as our example of the early American farmers. They settled first on the dry ground just beyond the swamps, and eventually formed a group of villages at El Arbillo, Tlatilco, Zacatenco, Copilco, Cuicuilco and other places, some of which were occupied until about 100 BC. We do not yet know where these people came from before they colonized the valley. They cut the scrub with stone axes and probably burnt it, so clearing fields in which they grew maize, beans and squash, tilling the soil with digging-sticks and hoes. In the woods, they hunted deer, peccaries and other animals, with obsidian-tipped spears and perhaps bow and arrow. The lake, the rivers and the swamps provided them with fish, frogs, tortoises and wild fowl, which they caught with net and trap. They collected roots and tubers, prickly pears and other wild fruits, rushes to make mats and reeds and grass for thatching their houses, which were simple rectangles of mud-plastered cane. They ground their maize on rectangular or oval grindstones; they cut up their hides and meat with obsidian knives, and they had bone awls and needles *(fig. 7)*.

They were skilled potters, making their vessels by hand-modelling or coiling, because like all American peoples they did not know the wheel. Their commonest vessels were jars, bowls and tripod bowls, decorated in the earlier stages chiefly by incision with little painting (pl. 4), but paint became more frequent later; finally a polychrome of red designs outlined with white on a buff ground was sometimes used. Judging from figurines, the women wore no clothes in the earliest part of the period, though some are shown wearing short skirts later on, and at all times some of them had ornaments such as ear-plugs, nose-rings, necklaces, anklets and turbans, and some painted their bodies with designs in various colours. The men are shown wearing only a brief loin cloth. Such clothing as they had was woven from local vegetable fibres such as yucca, and in the later stages from cotton brought from lower altitudes. They knew nothing of any metals.

At first the only indications of religion are the numerous female

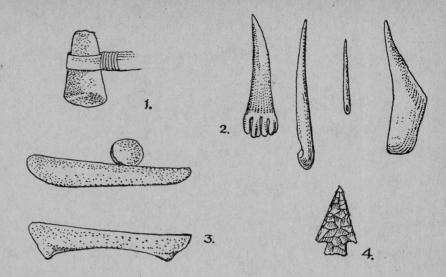

Artifacts of the first farmers in the Valley of Mexico. 1, Polished stone axe-head and method of hafting; 2, Three bone awls and a needle; 3, Two querns, one with its stone muller; 4, Obsidian projectile point. (fig. 7)

figurines of pottery (pl. 1, 2), believed to have been used in cere-monies to promote the fertility of the crops, but by about 600 BC shrines raised on platforms or mounds had begun to be built; these were the forerunners of the prominent pyramids of later times. The best example is at Cuicuilco; it is a terraced circular structure of clay reinforced with large stones, which in its final state, after an enlarge-ment, had four stages, and was approached by ramps, perhaps stair-ways, from East and West. There was a clay altar painted red on the top, presumably sheltered by a thatched roof *(fig. 8)*. Figurines in the shape of an aged man representing the god of fire appear at the same time.

About 1100 BC a group of immigrants, who seem to have come from the south, possibly from the lowlands, settled at Tlatilco and influenced the other villages. Although they must have lived in a very similar way to their neighbours, they were in some ways more sophisticated. They brought new types of pottery, including finely-modelled life forms like fish, armadillo and duck in polished black ware, which are real works of art (pl. 4). They made pottery masks representing fantastic beings, or jaguars and other animals, which were probably worn by magicians or priests. They had new types of figurines; women with children, two-headed women, dancing girls,

Reconstruction of the circular pyramid and shrine at Cuicuilco, Valley of Mexico, as it probably appeared shortly before the eruption of Xitle that buried it. (fig. 8)

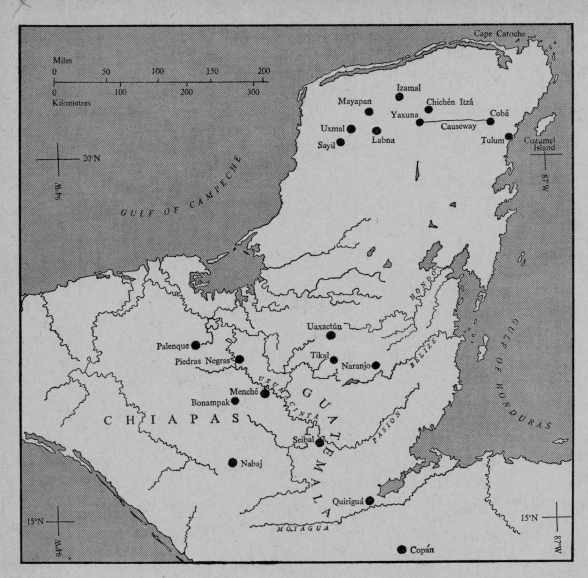

Maya sites in southern Mexico and Guatemala. (fig. 9)

magicians or priests, and even a man dressed to play a ballgame of which we shall hear more later. They made fine figurines of jade. There are many signs of jaguar worship, and some evidence of human sacrifice to supply attendants for the dead.

In brief, the seeds of the higher American civilizations (of what is called the Classic Period) were already growing, when, rather over 2000 years ago, an eruption of the volcano Xitle buried the village of Copilco and the temple-mound of Cuicuilco and caused the abandonment of other sites.

Priestly Rulers: the Maya

In the early centuries of the Christian era, the farming peoples of America were growing up into a more complex sort of civilization. This growth was most marked in two main regions, Middle America comprising Mexico and the adjacent parts of the Central American countries, and Peru.

In Middle America it was a time when ceremonial centres developed to an amazing degree out of simple beginnings like the mound of Cuicuilco. This architectural development was accompanied by the perfection of the arts, and the elaboration of a calendrical system based on astronomical observations and mathematics, and recorded in hieroglyphic writing. All this was dedicated to the service of a religion of increasing elaboration. This epoch, which lasted until about AD 900, is called the Classic Period.

There were important centres in many places, prominent among which were Teotihuacán in the Valley of Mexico, on the opposite side of the lake to the villages described above, and Monte Alban in Oaxaca, but it is the many sanctuaries of the Maya people which will claim most of our attention. These are found in the forested lowlands of Guatemala and the adjacent countries, the uplands of Chiapas, and British Honduras, and the dry limestone plain of the peninsula of Yucatán. The Maya of the present day, who live in the same area, speak one or other of a closely related group of languages, and their ancestors doubtless did much the same; but although this sets them apart from other Mexican and Central American peoples, nevertheless Maya and non-Maya centres were not isolated from one another, because goods were traded far and wide between them.

Pottery from Teotihuacán is found in Maya centres and at Monte Alban, and one of the best Maya jades in the British Museum was found at Teotihuacán.

It must never be forgotten that all the great achievements of ancient American civilization, like those of the Old World, were raised on an agricultural foundation, but that the most important plant here in Middle America was maize, which was unknown in Eurasia at the time. The Maya regarded the maize as the greatest gift of the creator gods, in fact it was itself a god, and to this day they address it as 'Your Grace'. In spite of the poverty of the soil in many places, and the continual struggle against drought in some parts and tropical vegetation in others, it gives so rich a yield that there is much spare time for the maize cultivator, and the remains show that in Classic times this was largely used in the erection and frequent reconstruction of great buildings and the maintenance of the cult. The great centres have sometimes been likened to cities, but they were more like cathedral closes, and the priests and attendants who lived there must have been supported by a vastly greater number of peasants who lived round about on their *milpas*, the clearings in which they grew their maize. Lacking draught animals and the plough, they depended entirely on human labour, and after a few years the growth of weeds, and perhaps exhaustion of the soil, meant that a new *milpa* had to be laboriously cleared by cutting the timber with stone axes and burning the brushwood when dry.

The Classic Period was a time of peace. The great centres were not in defensible positions and there is no sign of any attempt to fortify them. It is true that a section of the splendid Maya wall paintings at Bonampak in Chiapas (pl. 15–17) depicts a fight, but from the context this appears to have been a raid on some less cultured neighbours, perhaps to obtain prisoners for sacrifice in a great ceremony. Each centre had its ruler, a high priest or perhaps a group of priests, who maintained friendly relations with the independent rulers of other centres, forming a ruling caste among themselves. In esoteric knowledge and intellectual capacity they were doubtless far above the peasants who supported them.

The centres were all composed of elements of the same kind—courts, platforms, pyramids, and so on—but they differ greatly in execution. The towering steep pyramids of Tikal give a very different impression from the lower ones at Palenque (pl. 8), and the flat low-relief monoliths (stelae) of Tikal are far from the rounded sculptural forms of Copán (pl. 18, 19). Maya architecture as a whole was concerned with the grouping of great masses about open spaces, and little interest was taken in interiors. The temples which crowned the great pyramids were small and dark inside, roofed with wooden beams, or corbelled vaults in which each successive horizontal course of stone oversails that below it, until finally the remaining gap can be bridged by a single stone. A roof of either kind was generally crowned with a towering mass of masonry with a great carved roof-comb at the top, designed purely for external effect (pl. 7; 8). Stone masonry, corbelled vaults, and hieroglyphic inscriptions carved in stone began rather suddenly among the Maya around AD 300, but it is probable that they had predecessors of more perishable materials, such as stucco-coated rubble and wood.

The carved hieroglyphic inscriptions which are so notable a feature of Maya ceremonial centres were concerned almost entirely with the passage of time under the patronage of the appropriate gods, but the same type of writing was painted on strips of bark-cloth sized with lime, and the three surviving books of such strips or pages (codices, as they are called) contain also astronomical matter and divinatory almanacs. Two factors allowed a beginning to be made with their decipherment, namely the survival of several Maya dialects as spoken languages, and the records left by Diego de Landa, third Bishop of Yucatán, in the middle of the 16th century. Landa gave us a description of the calendar, and the glyphs, or pictographic symbols, of the days and 20-day 'months'. He also tried to reduce Maya glyphs to an alphabet, which they are not. His method was to pronounce the letters of the alphabet, in Spanish, and ask his informant, an educated Maya, to write down glyphs denoting those sounds. The result was not at all what he intended and has led to confusions and controversies which are not yet ended, but indirectly it has resulted in the decipherment of certain glyphs (for example he said 'be'—pronounced 'bay'—for 'b' and his informant drew a foot, the Maya glyph for journey or road). On these foundations, archaeologists, linguists, astronomers and others have by laborious study and brilliant deduction built up little by little our present body of knowledge. Much has been read, but the subject is intensely difficult and many glyphs still evade us. Most appear to represent words, a few perhaps syllables of compound words. They even vary in nature—some make use of the combination of sound and sight which we call 'rebus' writing, some are pictorial, and some ideographic.

A centre of the first rank is Copán, which lies in the extreme south-east of the Maya area in the republic of Honduras. It is in a remote valley where tropical plants flourish in clearings in the forest but the hills round about are clothed with pines. In the 5th century AD, some time after the Classic Period had begun elsewhere, some members of the Maya hierarchy arrived in the valley, where they found people who had maintained a simpler way of life, similar to that of the earliest villages in the Valley of Mexico. By some means, perhaps a religious conversion, they induced them to provide labour for building the first sanctuaries on the site. Time passed, the cultivation of the valley was intensified, and the great ceremonial centre was gradually formed, as well as a multitude of smaller ones scattered over the valley. Eventually there stood a magnificent group of buildings, now called the Acropolis, which centred in a great platform still covering 12 acres, from which rose a complex mass of pyramids, temples, terraces and courts, towering above the river which later cut much of it away. Even in its ruin, partly rescued from the forest and repaired, it is a breath-taking sight, though it is but a shadow of what, in its glory, it must have been (pl. 11).

To the north of the Acropolis lies a great space enclosed by terraces, forming a series of courts. The northernmost of these, the Great Plaza, is 250 feet square, and is bounded on three sides by tiers of stone steps, which perhaps served as seats, with a pyramid in the midst of the fourth. In and about it stand nine stelae, elaborately carved stone monoliths about 12 feet high, each having a stiff, richly-dressed, dignified figure on the front, and hieroglyphic inscriptions on the sides and sometimes on the back (pl. 18). The figures may represent rulers of Copán, who were priests or impersonators of gods; each carries a finely carved bar with a serpent head at either end across his chest, and one, who wears a skirt instead of a breech-clout, may be a woman. Each stela has a carved block, perhaps an altar, standing in

front of it. Stelae, which are also characteristic of other parts of Copán and the other Maya sites, were put up to mark important dates, generally but not always the endings of *katuns*, roughly 20-year periods, or half-*katuns*. Those in the Great Plaza range from AD 616 to 782, but the two earliest, dated 616 and 676, must have been put up before the enclosing terraces were built, because the first was re-erected on top of the western terrace and a niche was formed in the eastern terrace to avoid disturbing the second.

The religion to which all this was dedicated doubtless had its origin in some form of nature worship, designed to promote the fertility of the crops, with a few gods such as those of the rain, the wind and the maize, to which was early added a god of fire, called Itzamna, the Old God, the head of them all *(fig. 10)*. In Classic times there were in addition thirteen gods of the upper world, nine gods of the under-world, four personages known as *bacabs* who stood at the cardinal points and supported the sky, a god of death, gods of the sun, the moon and Venus, and many others. Days, months and the numbers attached to them all had their patron gods, or were themselves deified. Some gods were benevolent, some the reverse, and some gods had more than one aspect; thus Chac, the rain god *(fig. 10)*, is sometimes

Chac, the rain god, and Itzamna, god of fire. Chac has the facial characteristics, particularly the nose, of a tapir. From the Dresden Codex. (fig. 10)

thought of as four Chacs, each associated with a cardinal point and coloured accordingly. The colours were red for east, yellow for south, black for west and white for north, and were constantly associated with these directions, the *bacabs* for example being so coloured.

Judging by what was recorded as happening in later times, the ceremonies included prayer, the burning of incense, dancing, and sacrificial offering, preceded by fasting and continence as a preparation, and ending with feasting. It is certain that men made offerings of their own blood, drawn from tongue, ears and other parts using aloe thorns, sometimes attached to a string (pl. 5), but human sacrifice was comparatively rare. Doubtless precious things like jade were among the offerings. Great ceremonies were accompanied by orchestras with trumpets, drums and rattles.

There was also a ceremonial ball-game, and the court where it was played lies just north of the Acropolis. It was apparently built in the 8th century AD, and was the third to be constructed on the site. It is an elongated rectangular space with the floor spread out slightly at the ends like a Roman I, contained on either side by a block of masonry with a sloping top in which are set three stone macaw heads on either side (pl. 12). Behind each of these blocks rises a temple-crowned platform. Set in the floor along the axis are three weathered stone markers; those from the previous court were found buried underneath in good condition, and they are disks bearing elaborately-carved armoured figures representing players (pl. 13, 14). The game, which involved not more than three players a side and sometimes one only, was played by propelling a heavy solid rubber ball to and fro, but how the Maya scored at this time is not known, although later courts had vertical sides bearing a stone ring, and any player who put the ball through it won outright. The game was played throughout Middle America, but its origin is lost in antiquity and its meaning and the way it was played may well have varied. It survived until the Spanish Conquest and Spanish chroniclers say that the ball could be hit with hips, thighs and elbows, but not with the feet. A constant feature of the dress of

The three main numeral glyph types. Top: 'full figure' Maya hieroglyph from Stela D, Copán, showing the god 9 carrying the baktun glyph. Below (l. to r.): 'conventional' glyph for a baktun (400 tuns of 360 days), and 'face' glyph for numeral 9. (fig. 11)

players is a gauntlet on the right hand, a pad on the right knee, and a shoe on the right foot, but these appear to have been to protect these members from the floor rather than the ball. Apart from these there is great variety; some are shown naked except for a loin cloth and the chroniclers say that they suffered severe bruises and sometimes fatal injuries; others like those on the Copán markers, were well padded and richly adorned. The elaborate nature of the courts and the temples attached to them show that the game had an important function, probably to promote the fertility of the soil. In post-Classic times, when new influences came to the Maya from Central Mexico, it was associated with human sacrifice, and a member of a losing team might have his head cut off by one of the winners. There is no reason to believe that matters were carried to this extreme by the Classic Maya at Copán!

The Maya surpassed all other American peoples in their knowledge of mathematics and astronomy, and in the complexity of their calendar. This could only have been achieved by discipline, self-effacing co-operation between many people over many generations, and a great love of order, and all that we know of the Maya tells us that this is just what their character would lead to. Copán was probably the leading astronomical centre, and its priests knew the length of the solar year to a degree of accuracy slightly greater than the modern or Gregorian calendar we now use. A carved altar there shows representatives from other centres apparently conferring together to decide on the correction necessary to harmonize the conventional 365-day Maya year with the solar year (pl. 9, 10).

Their 365-day year consisted of 18 months of 20 numbered days, plus an unlucky 5-day period. They also observed a 260-day ceremonial cycle of 20 named days combined with the numbers 1 to 13. These two cycles ran on in harmony, and a day named in the two cycles did not repeat itself until 52 years later. They also counted each day from an arbitrary beginning far back in time, which we believe to be 3113 BC, and they expressed this in days (*kins*), periods of 20 days (*uinals*), 360 days (*tuns*), 7200 days (*katuns*) and 144,000 days (*baktuns*). Their normal mathematical system was vigesimal (i.e. based on a unit of 20), but when dealing with time they substituted a factor of 18 for the normal 20 in forming a *tun*, because

it made that unit 360 days, the nearest multiple of 20 to a year. When carving a date they added glyphs to give information about the position of the moon, besides some others of unknown meaning.

As has been said, days, months, numbers, *katuns*, and other periods were under the patronage of gods, a point which is emphasized by a rare type of inscription found on one of the stelae in the Great Plaza at Copán, in which the numbers are shown as gods in the guise of Maya bearers at a pause in their journey through time, when they have laid down their burdens the *baktuns*, *katuns*, etc., and in some cases the forehead bands with which they carried them can be seen. As an example, the top right-hand glyph in this inscription shows the number 9 carrying the *baktun* glyph (*fig. 11*).

Full-figure glyphs of this kind for numbers are rare and those for numbers 1 to 19 are more commonly shown by a head alone (*fig. 11,12*). Numbers of any size can be written by columns of bars and dots in a vigesimal system, using dots for units up to four and bars for five and its multiples up to 15; numbers up to 19 are placed at the bottom, multiples of 20 up to 380 (20 x 19) above them, followed by multiples of 400, and so on. There are even symbols corresponding to our zero, although the Maya thought of it rather differently (*fig. 12*).

Any day, then, was under the patronage of many gods, some well-disposed and some malevolent, and some more powerful than others, and the success of an undertaking would depend on the patrons of the day it began on. It was therefore important to the Maya that the various calendar cycles should be correctly related, and properly synchronized, so that they should know who the patrons of a given day really were. It was also vital to consult a priest who understood the attributes of the gods before starting any important undertaking, and to perform the required ceremonies to propitiate them.

In AD 800 the last hieroglyphic inscription was carved at Copán. No further building was done and shortly afterwards the hierarchy

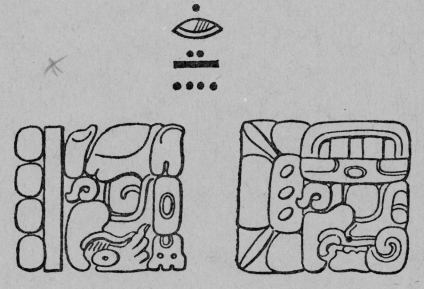

The Maya bar-and-dot system of numbering (top). One dot, 8,000: zero on the 400 line; seven 20's; four units: total, 8,144. Below, glyphs for 9 baktuns (1,296,000 days or 3,600 'short' years) and 'zero' tuns. (Head glyphs for baktun and tun.) (fig. 12)

disappeared. During the century which followed, the same happened at Quiriguá, Piedras Negras, Tikal, Uaxactún and the other southern centres. We do not know why this happened, but the most probable reason is that their religion had grown away from the people, the cult of time was being developed for its own sake, and much of what went on in the sanctuaries did nothing to promote the fertility of the fields. The peasants continued to cultivate the valley, but the Acropolis was abandoned to the forest, and they only visited it from time to time to burn incense to the Chacs or the maize god, or to bury their dead.

The Coming of the Warriors

The southern Maya sanctuaries had been abandoned, but some of those in Yucatán continued and some were reoccupied. Notable among these was Chichén Itzá, an abandoned site which started a new lease of life about AD 975, with the coming of the Itzá. They brought the worship of new gods, involving wars to get sacrificial victims, erotic rites, and a new architectural style which included great colonnades with some columns in the form of a feathered rattlesnake, the symbol of the Mexican god Quetzalcóatl (pl. 22, *fig. 13*). Wall paintings there show two different peoples in conflict, and a carved frieze in the ball court shows their teams lined up facing one another across a disk bearing a death's head, the foremost player of one team holding the head of his opposite number which he has cut off with a stone knife. From the victim's neck sprout serpents surrounding a great plant, doubtless fertilized by his blood. These two peoples were the old Maya of Classic times and the Itzá. Traditions which survived until the 16th century show the feelings of the Maya towards the Itzá, who lacked, they said, sound judgment, orderliness and wisdom, besides introducing lewdness which led to sickness and disaster.

The new architecture at Chichén Itzá and the sculpture which adorned it are so close to those found at Tula, the home of the Toltecs, some 50 miles north of Mexico City, that the Itzá must either have been Toltecs or Maya under Toltec influence. Besides the prominence of feathered serpent columns at both sites, both have paintings of human sacrifice by tearing out the heart, and both have carved friezes showing birds of prey devouring human hearts, with ocelots, and coyotes, typifying the military orders of 'eagles' and 'tigers' which became so prominent in Aztec times (pl. 21). There is an ancient tradition that a being named Quetzalcóatl, believed to be Topiltzin Quetzalcóatl, the first ruler of Tula who was also named after the god, was expelled from his country late in the 10th century, just about the time that Chichén Itzá was reoccupied, and a Maya tradition speaks of the arrival there from the west of a great lord named Kukulcán, meaning feathered serpent in that tongue. Traditions about events long past are unreliable guides by themselves, but these two receive sufficient archaeological support to suggest strongly that they reflect two stages in one migration.

We come back, then, to Central Mexico. The great Classic centre of Teotihuacán was destroyed and partly burnt about AD 950, and it is at least possible that this must be laid at the door of the Toltecs, who were immigrants to the Valley. They are believed to have come from the north-west and to have been the first of a number of related tribes to arrive. They are said to have been barbarians when they came, but if this is so they rapidly acquired much of the civilization of the settled peoples of the Valley, so much so that the later Aztecs looked back on their time as a Golden Age. On the other hand, they introduced war and violence. Their tribal god was called Tezcatlipoca, meaning Smoking Mirror in the Nahua tongue, the god of the night sky, but they adopted the worship of Quetzalcóatl, which they must have learnt from Teotihuacán, where it had long been practised. It is believed that disagreements between the votaries of these gods may have led to the expulsion of Topiltzin, but however this may be, the temple of Quetzalcóatl is one of the most prominent ruins at Tula.

However much the Toltecs may have owed to their predecessors in the Mexican uplands, they had well-marked cultural features of their own. They had a characteristic style of sculpture and easily recognized types of pottery, particularly that known to archaeologists as Mazápan Ware, decorated with groups of wavy parallel lines in orange on a buff ground (pl. 24). They were in a sense a cosmopolitan people with widespread contacts, and they received influences and actual imports from several directions. One of their gods, Xipe, the Flayed One, whose priests danced in the flayed skin of a sacrificed slave, typifying the fresh green covering of the earth in spring, seems to have originated in Oaxaca, although he may have been known in Teotihuacán (pl. 28). Imported wares figure among their pottery, notably a lustrous greyish-black to brown ware, called from its appearance 'Plumbate', which came from the Pacific Coast, and they are credited with the introduction of metal ornaments from as far away as Panama and Colombia. Among the contemporaries of the Toltecs were a people who erected notable buildings at an old ceremonial centre at Tajín in the hot lowlands of Vera Cruz, and certain small stone objects of superb quality from that area are probably their work (pl. 29).

The Toltec domination lasted little more than two centuries. Tula was founded about AD 950, about half a century after their arrival, and was overthrown and burnt about 1150 by a new wave of Nahua-speaking invaders, the Chichimeca, who were closely related to them. They took the sword and they perished by it. Their downfall ushered in a period of chaos, the history of which is complex and not altogether clear. Its decipherment does not depend entirely upon archaeology, since the period is covered by a series of records, some written before the Spanish Conquest in the native picture writing, and others

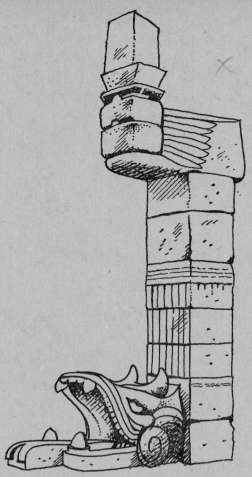

Feathered serpent column from the Temple of the Warriors, Chichén Itzá (see pl. 22). (fig. 13)

embodying native oral traditions, written in Nahua or Spanish in European characters shortly after the Conquest. These manuscripts or codices were painted on bark paper with a surface dressing of lime, and took the form of 'rebus' writing of a sort: thus the Aztec capital, Tenochtitlán, was represented by a cactus *(nochtli)* sprouting from a stone *(tena)*. This recalls their legend that the site was indicated to them by a white eagle representing the god Huitzilopochtli, who perched on a cactus growing from a stone on an island in the Lake of Texcoco. The records are often obscure or contradictory, so the reconstruction of the story is far from easy.

The Aztecs

The Chichimeca were nomads when they arrived. Their language suggests that they came, like their relatives the Toltecs, from the north, but they soon adopted the settled agricultural pattern of life of the previous inhabitants, and it is very likely that some cultural features, notably certain styles and the art of picture writing, came from the Mixtecs of Oaxaca (pl. 35). Among many Chichimec tribes the most prominent were the Culhuas, the Texocans and the Tenochcas, generally called the Aztecs. Their disputes and wars resulted in the disappearance of the Culhuas and the emergence of the Aztecs as the chief tribe among them, a position which they held when the Spaniards arrived in 1519. Their city of Tenochtitlán seems to have been founded about 1300.

The Aztecs were organized in groups, each composed of about 20 families, and a representative of each group was a member of a supreme council. This council elected four military chiefs, from among whom two supreme chiefs were chosen. The first, called Tlatoani, controlled foreign affairs and war, and the other, Cihuacóatl, the internal goverment of the tribe, but both had important religious functions also, and were both chief and priest. Their power was limited, since the Council could depose them if they failed in their duties. The Tlatoani when the Spaniards came was Montezuma, and the pomp and splendour with which he was surrounded led them to believe that he was an absolute monarch. His office was not in theory hereditary, but it had become customary to choose both chiefs from one family. Society was highly specialized. There were the three warrior orders of Eagles, Tigers and Arrows, who held a position of special honour; priests of many grades; a privileged class of merchants who travelled abroad with something approaching diplomatic privileges; and craftsmen of many types. There was an increasing emphasis on militarism, and this was bound up with religion, in which the old pantheon, the gods of agriculture and rain, with Quetzalcóatl, Xipe and the rest *(fig. 14, 15)*, had acquired new aspects, and had been joined by the special gods of the Chichimeca. The patron of the Aztecs was Huitzilopochtli, the sun god, a young warrior who was born anew every morning of Coatlicué, the ghastly old earth-goddess with the skirt of serpents. His elder sister and brothers, the moon and the stars, were provoked to furious jealousy, and each morning he had to overcome them before starting his journey through the sky, borne on a litter as far as the zenith by warriors killed in battle or sacrificed, and thence to the end of the day by women who had died in childbirth. At sunset he died and was gathered again to the earth. The divine struggle was repeated daily, and the sun had to be strong to repulse the multitude of stars with his fiery serpents, the rays or arrows of light, or the world would come to an end as it had four times before, and indeed was doomed to do again on a day called '4 Earthquake.'

In the meantime man had to feed the sun with the food of the gods, the *chalchíuatl* or precious fluid, human blood. The Aztecs were the people of the sun, so it was their special duty and privilege to get prisoners, and to offer him their blood and their hearts. His thirst came to be shared by other gods, hence the notorious ghastly succession of human sacrifices, most of which were performed by cutting out the heart of the victim stretched on a stone before the temple of the god, at the top of its *teocalli* or pyramid. It is said that 20,000 prisoners were slaughtered at the dedication of the last enlargement of the Great Teocalli in Tenochtitlán. The higher the degree of the victim, the more valuable he was for the purpose, and ceremonial conflicts called Wars of Flowers were arranged between the cream of the warriors of different Chichimec tribes to obtain prisoners for sacrifice and to re-enact the Sun's daily war. The warriors did not fear death, because to be killed in battle, or to be sacrificed, was to go direct to the highest heaven (pl. 25–27, 30, 31).

Religion was still bound up with the calendar, and the Aztecs, together with other Central American peoples, shared the 365-day year and the 260-day cycle or *tonalpohualli*, which have been mentioned in connexion with the Maya. These formed a 52-year cycle, but the Aztecs did not know the higher elaborations of the Maya calendar. The ending of the cycle, which was always on a day called 1 *Malinalli* (Grass) in the *tonalpohualli*, was a critical time, since it was feared that it might mark the end of the world, and great precautions were taken. Fires were let out, pottery was broken, pregnant women were shut up in granaries lest they turned into wild animals, and children were kept awake lest they turned into rats. A solemn procession of priests marched up the Hill of the Star near Culhuacán, and waited for a certain star called Yohualtecuhtli, perhaps Aldebaran, to pass the zenith and show that the world would continue. A victim was then sacrificed and fire kindled with a drill on a wooden hearth placed in the gash whence his heart had been removed, to be carried to hearths throughout the land. These cycles have archaeological importance, since they were marked by the reconstruction of temple pyramids, like that of Tenayuca, which was enlarged five times, after the cycles which ended in 1299, 1351, 1403, 1455 and 1507. It has also been suggested that certain dumps of broken pottery date from the same cycle endings, thus providing a chronology of Aztec pottery styles (pl. 36, 37).

There was no Aztec Empire as is sometimes supposed. On their very doorstep were the other Chichimec tribes, with some of whom they had short-lived alliances but as often they fought with them. They exercised an uneasy domination over many tribes from coast to coast, but this amounted to little more than the exaction of tribute, and the tribes remained tribes, ready to break away if opportunity offered. There was no Imperial organization such as the Inca had. Groups of Nahua-speaking peoples were found by the Spaniards scattered throughout Central America right down to the borders of Panama, and these are sometimes considered to be outposts of an Aztec Empire, but they are better thought of in terms of the shortage of land in face of increasing population in the Valley of Mexico. This meant that warriors were willing to establish colonies in the lands of defeated tribes, incidentally helping to keep them docile.

Much of Aztec art reflects the brutality of their religion, and this is seen particularly in their stone carving. Grim-featured gods, Xipe-masks (pl. 28) skulls and serpents all emphasize its grisly character. The

Quetzalcóatl in the guise of Ehecatl, the wind god, and wearing the characteristic mask. From the Codex Magliabechi. (fig. 14)

Tlaloc, the Aztec rain god. From the Codex Magliabechi. (fig. 15)

same applies to mosaic work like the sacrificial knife handle (pl. 26) and the human skull in the British Museum, encrusted with turquoise, black lignite (a variety of coal), red and white shell, and brassy pyrites. Symbolism of the same sort is found on some of the pottery, which includes fine, high-polished polychrome wares brought by trade or tribute from Cholula in Puebla or the Mixtec country in Oaxaca, (pl. 33, 34), as well as local wares, with delicate designs in black on orange or red. Some of the shapes of all these are very light and graceful (pl. 36, 37).

It would be natural to believe that the state of the Aztec tribe bore within it the seeds of disaster, that the continual wars and human sacrifices were too great a burden to bear, and that the common people would sooner or later rise against the chiefs and priests. If this was so, the point had not been reached when the Spaniards put an end to it all. Although specializations had arisen and there were distinctions of rank, it seems that membership of the tribe, the People of the Sun, transcended the differences. All were part of the system, and they took it very much for granted. Every able-bodied man was trained to fight, and he could gain honour and advancement by distinguishing himself in battle and by taking prisoners, and in so doing he participated in the sacrifices.

The Growth of Empire: the Incas

In the long period between the first glimmerings of civilization and the Spanish Conquest, many lesser peoples lived in the great area between the cultural heights of Mexico and Peru. Of the earlier stages we are only now beginning to learn a little here and there, but nearly all these tribes had reached the settled farming stage long before the Conquest, and some, like the Chibcha of Colombia, had banded together in confederacies. Some were ruled by absolute chiefs, who lived in considerable state and were buried in graves which are veritable treasure houses, together with wives and retainers who were sacrificed to go with them. The objects they made were kaleidoscopic in variety of style, and metals, pottery, turquoise, jade and shell were all beautifully worked in many places. The regions now occupied by Costa Rica, Panama, Colombia and Ecuador are all famous for their gold jewellery, and that of the Quimbaya of Colombia (pl. 40) was outstanding in its excellence. Although this metalwork was very abundant, it appears that the earliest people to use metal in the Americas lived in Peru. The welding and soldering as well as the hammering of gold and silver were already employed well back in the first millennium BC, and the use of copper began little later. The introduction of casting has, like other techniques, not been closely dated, but the use of both open moulds and the *cire perdue* process for gold, silver, copper and their alloys was probably known early in the first millennium AD, and bronze came later, perhaps as late as AD 1000. The remarkable fact is that the Peruvians knew and practised some metalworking techniques over 1000 years, some perhaps nearly 2000 years, before the Mexicans, who were for practical purposes living in the Stone Age until almost the end of their independent history.

The Inca Empire was the only true empire in ancient America, but it did not arise until the last century of a long story, which began about 2500 BC, and it cannot be appreciated without some idea of what went before, and of its natural surroundings which are among the most remarkable in the world. The countries which lie along the Andes are lands of contrasts, which are nowhere more marked than in Peru. The great mountain chain with its snow-capped peaks, bleak plateaux and passes, sheltered valleys and deep gorges, forms the backbone of the country, and this is the region from which the Incas came. It falls steeply on either flank, eastwards to the dense forests of the Amazon basin, where no great civilizations ever arose, and westwards to the narrow, arid coastal plain, crossed by valleys which cradled many of the ancient cultures. The valleys are separated from one another by miles of rocks or sand, where it seldom rains in the north and never in the south, and the water they carry down from the mountains could only support small settlements near the mouths of the rivers until the cultivable area was extended by irrigation over large parts of the flat valley floors.

After the early hunters whose presence we have inferred, the first people of whom we have certain knowledge settled at the mouths of the Chicama and other rivers about 2500 BC. Among the rubbish they left behind we find remains which show that they lived on sea-lions, fish, shell fish, wild plants, and cultivated squashes and beans. They also grew cotton, and made nets and small cloths from it by hand, without a loom, and they cooked by roasting on hot stones. About 1200 BC the first pottery was introduced, and two centuries or so later came some new people, perhaps a small group, bringing the knowledge of maize, elaborately modelled pottery, the loom and the worship of a cat god, the puma or the jaguar. They had much in common with Mexico, especially with Tlatilco, and seem to have come from that region. They took control of the old inhabitants, established new settlements away from the sea shore, and built temples to their feline god, the most notable of which is a great stone platform honeycombed with passages at Chavín in the north highlands.

A little later a different artistic tradition grew up in and around the Nazca and Ica Valleys on the south coast. It was distinguished by the use of colour rather than modelling for pottery decoration, applied

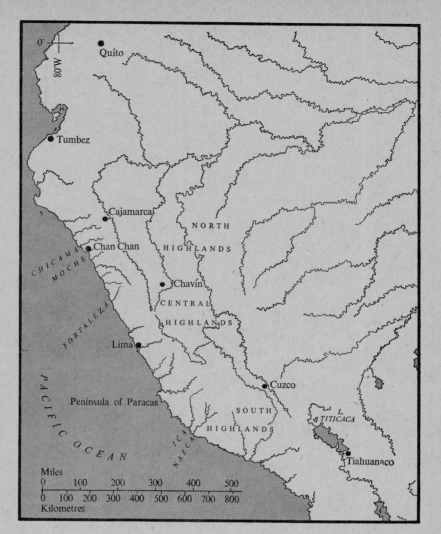

Peru: main sites up to the Inca Empire. (fig. 16)

at first as a resin after firing, and by an abundance of richly coloured and embroidered textiles (pl. 41, 42), lavished on the important dead, some of whom had artificially-deformed skulls and some had been trephined several times during life. Decorations on pottery and textile show that they shared the feline cult with the north, but the cat is accompanied by many fantastic monsters, which bear witness to a rich mythology. The origin of these people is still a mystery.

Both traditions developed, and some time during the first seven or eight centuries AD both reached their highest development. The growth of irrigation resulted in the north in the rise of integrated states in the larger valleys, for irrigation is not possible without control, and one of these, which we call Mochica, spread by conquest from Moche and Chicama over a group of adjacent valleys. Typical of the artistic development is the perfection of pottery modelling with a restrained use of colour in the north, and the use of numerous colours, now applied before firing, in the south. Other areas, such as the central coast, and the north highlands (pl. 43) had their own conventions. This age corresponds in general level, and roughly in time, with the Classic Period of Middle America as already defined, but differs from it in many ways. There is no hieroglyphic writing, and no certain evidence of an elaborate calendar, but metals (gold, silver, copper and their alloys) had long been worked, and militarism was already much in evidence.

Another notable tradition grew up in the south highlands. It is best known by the great religious centre at Tiahuanaco on the bleak uplands near Lake Titicaca, where there is much skilfully worked masonry, the remains of a stone-faced pyramid, stairways and enclosures, also large, pillar-like statues and a carved monolithic gateway (pl. 45). Its painted pottery shows features which are later found far afield, particularly representations of animals and birds with eyes divided vertically into black and white halves (pl. 46, left). Influences from this region reached the central and south parts of the coast by way of the central highlands towards the end of the Classic Period, and showed themselves in various art styles of Tiahuanaco origin which included these features (pl. 47). Subsequently there was a stronger wave of influence from the same quarter, which affected practically the whole coast, obliterating the coastal art styles and the Mochica state. It carried southern building plans, and the custom of burying the dead in crouched mummy bundles, right up to the Mochica area, and is best explained by a religious movement backed by military force, probably about AD 1000.

This is one of the events which serve to knit together the many local developments in Peruvian archaeology, and it may be a parallel to the much later spread of the Inca. Each time, highlanders invaded the coast, and no cases of the contrary are known. There are great differences of altitude between the two regions, and adaptation from one to the other is a great strain, but the easier climatic conditions on the coast resulted in richer cultures, a likely attraction to the highlanders.

Shortly after they were established in the coast, the Tiahuanacoid art styles began to decay. Distinctive designs like the 'party-eyed' animals on pottery and textile lost their character and disappeared, and the polychrome pottery bearing these designs gave place in time to a black, white and red style with geometrical decorations. Eventually three new states emerged in the north, central, and south parts of the coast. It was a time of political change, which witnessed the culmination of a process which began in the previous stage, namely the gathering of the people in large towns on a scale never attempted before. It is best seen in the northern state, the Chimú, called by the inhabitants Chimor, which was by far the largest and most powerful of the three, and it can be exemplified by its great mud-brick capital Chan-Chan, near Trujillo (pl. 53). This covers eleven square miles and contains ten great walled compounds, each like a city in miniature, separated from its fellows by irrigated areas, reservoirs and cemeteries. Each compound contains a palace-like structure and a pyramid, and is believed to have housed a clan or similar division under its chief, who thus had it under control. The largest of these towns were placed where the irrigation canals of two or more valleys could be fed in, giving rise to systems unprecedented in scale.

Artistically it was a time of decadence. Each of the three states had its characteristic pottery style, but only that of the Chimú resembles that which existed before the highland invasion. It shares with its Mochica predecessor the use of elaborate modelling, and forms like the stirrup spout which go right through north coast prehistory, but it is carried out in black ware and the modelling is dull and lifeless (pl. 44). Pottery, textiles and metalwork were all produced in large quantities, and decorated pots in particular were in general use instead of being made, as in the past, chiefly for the dead.

The rise of the Chimú kingdom is believed to have begun early in the 14th century in Moche, Chicama and the neighbouring valleys, and by the middle of the 15th century the king Minchançaman had conquered the coast from Tumbez in the north to the Fortaleza Valley in the south, and perhaps beyond it nearly to Lima.

In the highlands, the Inca dynasty and its subjects had been settled in and around Cuzco since about AD 1200. Like other small highland tribes they had engaged in raids and minor wars on their neighbours, but it was not until they had barely excaped a crushing defeat by the Chanca, another highland group, that they embarked on sustained conquests. These began with the accession to the throne in 1438 of Pachacuti, who had led their resistance to the Chanca. In the next 20 years, he subdued the highlands from near Lake Titicaca in the south-east to Lake Junín in the north-west, and then his son, Topa Inca, was given command of the army and conquered the country up to Quito in the Ecuadorian Andes. Having overrun their highland allies in Cajamarca, he was in strong position to attack the Chimú, since he commanded their water supplies, and their great towns, whose food supply was very vulnerable, were not adapted to threats from that quarter. Minchançaman resisted bitterly but in vain, his capital was looted, he was carried off to live in Cuzco, and one of his sons was installed in his place under Inca control. Subsequent conquests carried the Inca over the rest of the Peruvian coast, into north-west Argentina and down to central Chile, and after Topa Inca's death in 1493 Huayna Capac conquered northern Ecuador, but none of these campaigns had an effect comparable with that of the conquest of the Chimú.

The Inca carried off much Chimú gold and other loot to Cuzco (pl. 52), also craftsmen from whom they learnt various textile and metalworking techniques, and mass production methods especially of pottery. More important is the likelihood that much of the organization of the Empire was based on that of the Chimú, since it was not until after the conquest of the north coast that Topa Inca built it up in the form about which so much has been written. It was an impressive achievement, with its pyramidal structure, its road system, and the integration of many peoples and customs, all accomplished by a people who had no means of writing and could only record figures on knotted strings. Witness to its greatness is borne not only by the Spanish chroniclers but also by its material remains, the great ruins of the Cuzco district and elsewhere (pl. 48), and the wide distribution of bronze tools and the Inca pottery style (pl. 50). If this had been built up from nothing in less than a century, it would have been scarcely credible, but the story needs qualification. The Inca system rose on the foundation of earlier Peruvian civilizations, and most of its elements were not new. Stratified and specialist societies had long existed on the coast, and the Chimú are believed to have ruled through an hereditary aristocracy. On the material side they had, for example, a ready-made road system which the Inca took over. It is, moreover, unlikely that the organization was as standardized as is generally believed; a good instance is the retention by local coast chiefs of their ancestral lands when the standard Inca system was to divide all land between Emperor, religion and people. Nevertheless, when all allowances have been made, the Inca did a remarkable thing in uniting such an enormous and diversified area, organizing its communications and supplies and building up rank upon rank of officials each responsible to the Emperor through his representative in the rank above.

The Empire was a despotism, with an absolute, divine ruler supported by an hereditary aristocracy, but the well-being of its subjects was in the interests of both. The measures taken to ensure this have given rise to the idea that it was a sort of socialistic welfare state, but states of that sort do not move unruly tribes forcibly from their homes to live among docile peoples and send loyal *mitimaes* to take their place, neither do they have one law for the nobles and another for commoners as the Inca did. The lands of the peasant group or *ayllu* were held in common and redistributed among its members each year; this feature, at the agricultural base of the Inca pyramid, was doubtless very ancient, but it was the only egalitarian or theoretically communistic characteristic of the system. There is in fact little profit in comparing the Inca Empire to modern political structures.

The success of the Inca armies cannot be ascribed to superior arms because they fought with the same weapons as their enemies, but a large factor must have been the sustained aggressiveness, which contrasts with the general highland custom of short-lived raids. This was backed by their organizing ability, which enabled them to raise and maintain armed levies, to supply them from their storehouses, and to move them rapidly along their roads to where they wished. Many of their conquests were accomplished by threats and diplomacy, and their fiercest battles were with comparatively small highland tribes like the Cañari of Ecuador.

The persistence of the offensive spirit is doubtless to be ascribed to various motives. The first conquests after the Chanca defeat may well have been undertaken to secure the Inca position, but the consequent increase of power and wealth seem to have bred the taste for more. The aristocracy was polygamous and increased rapidly, and its young men were nurtured in the arts of war. A campaign gave an outlet for their energies, and subsequently provided some with responsible posts in conquered territory. There seem to have been some signs of unrest among the ruling classes, possibly owing to unsatisfied ambition and idleness, a potential source of weakness. The Empire was still in a state of active development when the Spaniards landed in 1532, and what its subsequent history would have been is a matter for speculation. Two main factors undermined its strength. One was the lack of a fixed rule of succession among the Emperor's sons, which resulted in the civil war between Huascar and Atahuallpa when Huayna Capac died before deciding who should succeed him. The other was inherent in the structure itself; all owed allegiance to the Emperor at the head of the pyramid, but there was insufficient cohesion at each level of society. While the Emperor was venerated as a divine monarch this was no weakness, but when a handful of invaders, who cared for none of these things, struck at Atahuallpa, the head and heart of the Empire, they brought it to the dust.

XIV Epilogue:
The heritage of Man

STUART PIGGOTT

WE HAVE COME now to the end of our survey: in it as in a jig-saw puzzle we have attempted to piece together the past, at times bridging the gaps in our material evidence by reasonable surmise, at times being able only to define the limits of our ignorance. Indeed 'the historian can only point like a showman to the things of the past, with their manifold and mysterious message'—or so G. M. Trevelyan, a philospher amongst historians, has concluded. Although in considering our achievements we may wonder what, if any, are the messages conveyed by things, and try our best to read the sermons which lie in stones, the rôle of the historian is certainly that of a guide pointing out for us the main routes taken by history ancient and modern, no less than it is the task of the prehistorian to indicate the significant perspectives of those societies which lie beyond its bounds.

This book then has acted as a pointer, a showman demonstrating the tangible evidence for those many and varied peoples present at the dawn of what we have termed 'civilization'. It is because our evidence has for the most part been archaeological that our view has largely been a technological one. We have, then, looked at early societies in terms of a technological 'model' seeking to define a pattern of development where the raw materials of nature, mineral wealth, plant life and the lesser animals have been exploited and adapted until they have become the servants of man.

But above all, in works of art, ancient man, like his modern descendants, achieved one of the most remarkable of his artificial achievements, the capacity of making an 'image of feeling', 'an image of an experience in which the representation of feeling plays an essential part', whether in the visual form of painting, sculpture, and architecture, or in the composition of prose and poetry, or—and perhaps the most expressive of all—in the creation of music.

But we may well ask ourselves, as a recent writer has done, 'What is most important in history? Is it ideas or faith, technology or great men, property systems or geography?' We have seen that for much of the time and places covered in this book, we have to take what we can get, whether we think it the most important aspect of history or not. In prehistoric, non-literate, societies, or those whose documentary material is scanty and uninformative, ideas and faith do not leave their record in any but the most oblique form (and one peculiarly subject to false inferences); great men lived before Agamemnon, but they are mostly anonymous and undiscoverable in an unlettered past. We may know a little about property systems, and infer more, in early cultures, and without being geographical determinists, we can see how great a part in shaping the earlier of human societies the natural setting played. We are left with technology and art, because it is these human activities that leave tangible remains for us to study where all else is lost. Half a century ago Godley, an Oxford scholar, ironically laughing at his fellow-scholars who were then just appreciating the value of archaeological evidence for the ancient world, wrote:

> For 'tis not verse, and 'tis not prose,
> But earthenware alone
> It is that ultimately shows
> What men have thought and done!

The reader of this book may have felt that this jibe was justified, and that he has been made an unfair cock-shy, to be pelted with potsherds, a latter-day St Stephen without even the crown of martyrdom.

However, we are not free to make a choice of what we might think the most important content of ancient history and prehistory, for as we have seen, what we can know is dictated by the type of evidence. Many are the gaps which remain unfilled and many are those which will always so remain; there are no conceivable means whereby we can recover the language and thoughts of a palaeolithic cave artist, or be apprised of the strategy of the warrior commanding a Middle Bronze Age war-band in Central Europe. The conversations when the first walls of Jericho were building are lost for ever; the war cries of the first hunters in America have long ceased to echo.

Nevertheless, within its limitations archaeology has recovered no negligible portion of the ancient past of mankind. And perhaps the most impressive contribution which the most ancient civilizations and their forerunners have made to the modern world is that of their art. Before the discovery and recognition of this, the western artistic tradition up until the last century was based on a single canon, that of the Greek and Roman world as seen within the aesthetic and moral model which had come to be employed after the Renaissance rediscovery of classical antiquity. The revolution in aesthetic values which has come in our own time has in its essentials been the incidental result of the work of archaeologists and anthropologists in recovering and putting before the artist not only the work of the accepted classical masters, but that of antiquity from the Ice Age to the Scythians, side by side with the comparable achievements of still surviving communities outside the accepted 'civilized' world.

This has enormously enhanced our artistic sensibility, and extended our capability of appreciation and enjoyment far beyond the bounds of less than a century before. There are qualities in ancient non-classical art which may stir us deeply, more profoundly than those within the academic tradition of naturalistic representation and the emphasis on the human body as a persistent symbol. The metal work of the peoples of the steppe, or that of the early Celts; the pottery-painters of the ancient Near East or of Middle America; the stone carvings of the megalith builders of Western Europe—these have still power to move us in what may be a rather disturbing way. They get under our civilized skin, and remind us that our ancestry includes not only Plato and the New Testament, but the sweaty blood-stained rituals of Stone Age hunters' magic, and the irrational terrors of the world of shaman and seer, the talking animals and the personal malevolence of mountain and forest.

So when we contemplate our forefathers, let us remember what a mixed heritage is that of nominally civilized man. Whatever may be our technological achievements, our mastery over natural substances, we must remember that most of our actions, in private and public, are more swayed by the appetites and emotions, the prejudices and apprehensions, of the non-rational past of humanity than by the clear light of conscious reason. The founders of civilization have contributed more to us than merely providing the prerequisites for the technical and material achievements of humanity which we select as the desirable contributions to civilized life. We must, if we look into the past for a clue to our present make-up, do this dispassionately and with a recognition that any human civilization so far known has been a combination of often conflicting qualities. Some of these, in the value-judgments we make within the framework of our own civilization, we rank as good and desirable; others as evil and despicable. But the less reputable contributions to our own culture from antiquity are as important as those which contemporary society holds in esteem, and to form any kind of balanced view, we must study peoples whose cultures we may think primitive or barbarian, as well as those who contributed the intellectual and emotional concepts and feelings which mark man's mastery over himself, as well as over his material environment. There is much of the primitive and barbarian in every civilized society today, as there has been throughout history, and it may well be an unjustified optimism to think this state can be materially altered.

If then we are to try to extract any meaning from history (in its widest sense) let us recognize that it affords us an opportunity for observing the enormous variety of methods which have been evolved by human communities in the past for dealing with the problems of people living in societies, and in relationship not only to other individuals and societies, but to their natural environment. We are ourselves the heirs of that type of society which put technological innovations at a premium, and we have seen how such societies arose from their tentative beginnings in Asia and Europe with the appearance of relatively modern climatic conditions after the final retreat of the ice sheet. In the early civilizations of the Ancient East and of the Aegean we see the beginnings, the foundations, of what was to be further developed into the more familiar civilizations of Greece and Rome, and following that in Europe, medieval Christendom under the Eastern and Western Churches. Side by side by these communities, we have marked the survival of simpler societies, preserving their traditions of relationship to their environment almost unchanged for long periods of time.

In the early civilizations we observe, as we do in those of today, that mixture of components which we have seen are likely to be inevitable, since they are the product of the physiology and psychology of man as an animal. The endemic warfare among contesting groups, the outcome of irrational and emotive promptings, is as insistent in societies we call civilized as in those we stigmatize as barbarian, and it would be a grave error to omit this trait when enumerating others which are conventionally thought of as those characteristic of civilization. The unequalled display of rational powers and intellectual enquiry in classical Greece must be seen in its proper perspective against the irrational pattern of ordinary feeling of the time; the moral authority of the early church can only be understood in terms of the combat between rivals for the magic control of the natural forces and of the universe in which each believed the others to have a real potency. And when we come to look at the present day, how often may we recognize ourselves in the Central European Bronze Age rather than in Augustan Rome, amongst the predatory strand-loopers of early post-Glacial Europe and not with the sages of Periclean Athens.

If this does not lead to uncritical optimism, it should not send us to the other extreme, to say with W. H. Auden:

The earth is an oyster with nothing inside it,
Not to be born is the best for man:
The end of toil is a bailiff's order—
Throw down the mattock and dance when you can.

History helps towards forming a balanced judgment, for at least we can compare our own society with others no longer surviving, and so increase our perspective. But if this perspective is to avoid distortion, we must look at all types of society, for all are human, all relevant. We must look not only on the full light of civilization, but to its dawn.

Select Bibliography

In a subject as necessarily technical as archaeology, and in a book as all-embracing as *The Dawn of Civilization*, it would be impossible to give anything like a complete bibliography. The selection below has been made primarily with an eye to availability, and wherever possible general works in the most common European languages have been given preference. However, in certain areas of the world —China, Russia and South East Asia for example—such summaries are rare or non-existent, and thus specialist references have been noted to fill the gaps.

Introduction: the Man-Made World

ATKINSON, R.J.C. *Archaeology, History and Science* (1960)
Archaeology: Methods and Principles (1961)
BIBBY, G. *The Testimony of the Spade* (1957)
CERAM, C.W. *Picture History of Archaeology* (1958)
CLARK, J.G.D. *The Study of Prehistory* (1954)
Outline of World Prehistory (1961)
COTTRELL, L. (ed.) *Concise Dictionary of Archaeology* (1960)
DANIEL, G.E. *The Three Ages* (1943)
EBERT, M. (ed.) *Reallexikon der Vorgeschichte* I–XV (1924–32)
PIGGOTT, S. *Approach to Archaeology* (1959). For bibliography
SHAPIRO, H.L. (ed.) *Man, Culture, and Society* (revised ed. 1960)
SINGER, C. et al. (ed.) *History of Technology* I (1954)
ZEUNER, F.E. *Dating the Past* (3rd ed. 1958)

I The First Half-Million Years

(Abbreviations: MIA – Materialy i Issledovaniya po Arkheologiyi SSSR; TAPS – Transactions of the American Philosophical Society)

BALOUT, L. *Préhistoire de l'Afrique du Nord* (1955)
BLACK, DAVIDSON et al. 'Fossil man in China' in *Mem. Geol. Survey of China* Ser. A, vol. II (1933)
BORISKOVSKII, P.I. 'Palaeolithic of the Ukraine' in MIA 40 (1953). In Russian
BREUIL, H. *Four Hundred Centuries of Cave Art* (1952)
CLARK, J.D. *The Prehistory of Southern Africa* (1959)
CLARK, J.G.D. *The Mesolithic Settlement of Northern Europe* (1936)
Excavations at Star Carr (1954)
COLE, S. *The Prehistory of East Africa* (1954)
GARROD, D.A.E., & BATE, D.M.A. *The Stone Age of Mount Carmel* (1937)
GARROD, D.A.E. 'The Upper Palaeolithic in the light of recent discovery' in *Proc. Prehist. Soc.* IV (1938), 1–26
GOLOMSHTOK, E.A. 'The Old Stone Age in European Russia' in TAPS n. s. XXIX, Pt. 2 (1938)
GRAZIOSI, P. *Palaeolithic Art* (1960)
LAMING, A. *Lascaux: Paintings and Engravings* (1959)
LEAKEY, L.S.B. *Adam's Ancestors* (4th ed. 1953)
LE GROS CLARK, W.E. *History of the Primates* (6th ed. 1960)
MC BURNEY, C.B.M. *The Stone Age of Northern Africa* (1960)
MOVIUS, H.L. 'The Lower Palaeolithic cultures of Southern and Eastern Asia' in TAPS n. s. XXXVIII, Pt. 4 (1948)
OAKLEY, K.P. *Man the Tool-Maker* (4th ed. 1958)
OBERMAIER, H. *Fossil Man in Spain* (1925)
OKLADNIKOV, A.P. 'Palaeolithic and Neolithic in the USSR' in MIA 59 (1957). In Russian

II Roots in the Soil

(Abbreviations: A & S – Antiquity and Survival; *An. Stud.* – Anatolian Studies; *Ant.* – Antiquity; *Arch. Anz.* – Archäologischer Anzeiger; IEJ – Israel Exploration Journal; JNES – Journal of Near Eastern Studies; PEQ – Palestine Exploration Quarterly)

General
COLE, S. *The Neolithic Revolution* (1960)
BRAIDWOOD, R.J. 'Near Eastern Prehistory' in *Science* 127 (June 1958), 1419–30. Source for the majority of C 14 dates
Prehistoric Men (3rd ed. 1957)
'The achievement and early consequences of food production' in *Cold Spring Harbor Symposia on Quantitative Biology* XXII (1957)
BRAIDWOOD, R.J. & L. 'The earliest village communities of SW Asia' in *Journ. World Hist.* I (1953)
KENYON, K.M. 'Jericho and its setting in Near Eastern History' in *Ant.* XXIX (Dec. 1956), 184ff.
BRAIDWOOD, R.J. 'Jericho and its setting in Near Eastern history' in *Ant.* XXX (June 1957), 73ff.
KENYON, K.M. 'Reply to Prof. Braidwood' in *Ant.* XXX, 82ff.
WHEELER, MORTIMER 'The First Towns?' in *Ant.* XXIX (Sept. 1956), 132ff.
ZEUNER, F.E. 'The Radiocarbon age of Jericho' in *Ant.* XXIX (Dec. 1956), 195f.
'The goats of early Jericho' in PEQ (1955), 70ff.
'Dog and cat in the Neolithic of Jericho' in PEQ (1958), 52f.
MELLAART, J. 'Anatolia and the Balkans' in *Ant.* XXXIV (Dec. 1960), 270ff.
Archaeological sites
ALLBRIGHT, W.F. *Archaeology of Palestine* (1956), 59ff. (Natufian)
BRAIDWOOD *Prehistoric Men*, 113f. (Natufian)
PERROT, J. in IEJ 7 (1957), 125–7 (Eynan)
'Le Mésolithique de Palestine et les récentes découvertes à Eynan' in *A & S* II (1957), 91–110
STEKELIS, M. in IEJ 7 (1957), 125, and IEJ 8 (1958). 131 (Oren)
BRAIDWOOD, R.J. in *Sumer* 7 (1951), 102 (Karim Shahir)
Prehistoric Men, 116f. (Karim Shahir)
In *Sumer* 10 (1954), 123f. (Gird Chai)
SOLECKI, R.S. in *Sumer* 13 (1957), 168ff. (Zawi Chemi, Shanidar)
KENYON, K.M. in PEQ (1956), 70f., and (1957), 101–7 (Jericho Pre-Pottery Neolithic A)
In PEQ (1954), 48 (1955), 110–1, and (1956), 70 (Jericho Pre-Pottery Neolithic B)
BRAIDWOOD, R.J. in *Sumer* 10 (1954), 128–9 (M'Lefaat)
Prehistoric Men, 127 (M'Lefaat)
Alumoth: IEJ 7 (1957), 263–4
Hamadia: PEQ (1958), 46
BRAIDWOOD, R.J. in *Sumer* 7 (1951) 103–6 (Jarmo)
Prehistoric Men, 128f. (Jarmo)
INGHOLT, H. in *Sumer* 13 (1957), 215 (Tell Shemshara)
MILOJČIĆ, V. 'Ergebnisse der Deutschen Ausgrabungen in Thessalien' in *Jahrb. des Römisch-Germanischen Zentralmuseums Mainz* VI (1959)
DIKAIOS, P. *Khirokitia* (1953)
GARSTANG, J. *Prehistoric Mersin* (1953)
BRAIDWOOD, R.J. & L. 'Earliest Village Communities of SW Asia' in *Journ. World Hist.* (1953), 291 (Amuq A)
MELLAART, J. in *An. Stud.* VIII (1958), 150f. (Çukurkent culture)
ibid., 127ff. (Hacilar)
In *Illus. London News* 238, No. 6341 (1961), 229–31 (Hacilar)
MILOJČIĆ, V. in *Arch. Anz.* (1956), 166 (Pre-Pottery Greece)
In *Germania* 34 (1956), 208ff. (Pre-Pottery Greece)
THEOCHARES, D. in *Praktika* 32 (1957), 151ff. (Pre-Pottery Greece). (In Greek)
MILOJČIĆ, V. in *Arch. Anz.* (1955), 172ff., and (1956), 162ff. (Pre- and Proto-Sesklo, Rainbow)
CASKEY, J.L. in *Hesperia* XXVI (1957), 160, and XXVII (1958), 138–9, 143 (Pre- and Proto-Sesklo, Rainbow)
VAN DER BERGHE, L. in *Ex Oriente Lux* 12 (1951–2), 400ff., and 13 (1953–4), 212ff. (Tepe Jarri B and Tell Mushki)
GHIRSMAN, R. *Fouilles de Siyalk* I (1938)
MELLAART, J. in *Annual of Dept. of Ant. of the Hashemite Kingdom of Jordan* III (1956), 24f. (Ghrubba)
KENYON, K.M. in PEQ (1956), 76, and *Ant.* 122 (1957), 76 (Jericho Pottery Neolithic A & B)
DUNAND, M. in *Bull. du Musée de Beyrouth* IX (1949–50), 55ff., 68ff., and XII (1955), 10, 15, and XIII (1956), 74f. (Byblos A, Neol.)
LLOYD, S., & SAFAR, F. in JNES IV (1948), 259ff. (Hassuna)
HERZFELD, E. *Die Ausgrabungen von Samarra* V: 'Die Vorgeschichtlichen Töpfereien' (1930)
BRAIDWOOD, R.J., et al. in JNES III (1944), 47 (Samarra)
MESNIL DU BUISSON, Comte. *Baghuz* (1948)
LLOYD, S., & SAFAR, F. in *Sumer* IV (1948), 115f. (Eridu)
LE BRETON, A. in *Iraq* XIX (1957), 84ff. (Susiana)

III The Birth of Written History

CHILDE, V.G. *New Light on the Most Ancient East* (1952)
FRANKFORT, H. *Art and Architecture of the Ancient Orient* (revised ed. 1958)
SPEISER, E.A. *Excavations at Tepe Gawra* I (1935)
TOBLER, A.J. *Excavations at Tepe Gawra* II (1950)
PERKINS, A.L. *The Comparative Archaeology of Early Mesopotamia* (1949)
LABAT, R. *Manuel d'Epigraphie Akkadienne* (1948)
DRIVER, G.R. *Semitic Writing* (1944)
HEINRICH, E. (ed.) *Vorläufiger Berichten über Uruk-Warka* I–XIV (1929–58)
Kleinfunde aus den Archäischen Tempelschichten in Uruk (1936)
FALKENSTEIN, A. *Uruk Archäische Texte* (1936)
PARROT, A. *Sumer* (1960)
SCHMIDT, E.F. *Excavations at Tepe Hissar, Damghan* (1937)
ARNE, T.J. *Excavations at Shah Tepe, Iran* (1945)
DELOUGAZ, P., & LLOYD, S. *Pre-Sargonid Temples in the Diyala Region* (Oriental Institute, Chicago, 1942)
DELOUGAZ, P. *Pottery from the Diyala Region* (Oriental Institute, Chicago, 1952)
JACOBSEN, T. *The Sumerian King List* (Oriental Institute, Chicago, 1939)
WOOLLEY, C.L., et al. *Excavations at Ur: a Record of Twelve Years' Work* (1954)
WOOLLEY, C.L. (ed.) *Ur Excavations:* II, *The Royal Cemetery* (1934); V, *The Ziggurat and its Surroundings* (1939); IV, *The Early Periods* (1956)
WISEMAN, D.J. *Cylinder Seals of Western Asia* (n. d.)
PARROT, A. *Archéologie Mesopotamienne* (2 vols. 1946, 1953)
CONTENAU, G. *Manuel d'Archéologie Mesopotamienne* I–IV (1927–47)
ANDRAE, W. *Das Wiedererstandene Assur* (1938)
LE BRETON, A. 'The Early Periods at Susa' in *Iraq* XIX (1957)
MALLOWAN, M.E.L. *Twenty-Five Years of Mesopotamian Discovery* (2nd ed. 1959)
POPE, A.U. *A Survey of Persian Art* (4 vols. 1938)
GHIRSHMAN, R. *Iran* (1954)
KRAMER, S.N. *Sumerian Mythology* (1944)
History Begins at Sumer (1958)
The following three periodicals contain much of the source-material for this chapter:
Iraq. Journal of the British School of Archaeology, Iraq I–(1934–). See particularly Vol. XXIV (1960), 'Ur in Retrospect', ed. Mallowan & Wiseman
Sumer. Published by the Iraq Antiquities Dept., 1945–
Mémoires de la Mission Archéologique de Perse I– (1900–)

IV The Rise of the God-Kings

ALDRED, C. *The Egyptians* (1961)
Old Kingdom Art in Ancient Egypt (1949)

BADAWY, A. *A History of Egyptian Architecture* I (1954)

VON BISSING, F.W. et al. *Das Re-Heiligtum des Königs Ne-woserrē* I–III (1905–28)

BORCHARDT, L. *Das Grabdenkmal des Königs Sahu-Rē* (2 vols. 1910–13)

BRUNTON, G. *Mostagedda and the Tasian Culture* (1937)

BRUNTON, G., & CATON-THOMPSON, G. *The Badarian Civilisation* (1928)

CATON-THOMPSON, G., & GARDNER, E.W. *The Desert Fayum* (2 vols. 1934)

DUELL, P. *The Mastaba of Mereruka* (2 vols. 1938)

EMERY, W.B. *The Tomb of Hemaka* (1938)
Great Tombs of the First Dynasty (2 vols. 1949, 1954)

FIRTH, C.M., & QUIBELL, J.E. *The Step Pyramid* (2 vols. 1935–36)

FRANKFORT, H. *Kingship and the Gods* (1948)
The Birth of Civilisation in the Near East (1951)

HAYES, W.C. *The Scepter of Egypt*, Vol. I (1953)

HOLSCHER, U. *Das Grabdenkmal des Königs Chephren* (1912)

MONTET, P. *Les scènes de la vie privée dans les tombeaux égyptiens de l'ancien empire* (1925)

NEWBERRY, P.E. 'Egypt as a field of anthropological research' in *Report of 91st Meeting, British Association* (1923), 175 ff.

PETRIE, W.M.F., & QUIBELL, J.E. *Nagada and Ballas* (1896)

PETRIE, W.M.F. *The Royal Tombs of the First Dynasty*, Pts. I & II (1900–1)
Prehistoric Egypt (1920)

QUIBELL, J.E. *Hierakonpolis*, Pts. I & II (1900–2)
The Tomb of Heay (1913)

SANDFORD, K.S., & ARKELL, W.J. *Paleolithic Man and the Nile Valley* (4 vols. 1929–39)

SMITH, W.S. *History of Egyptian Sculpture and Painting in the Old Kingdom* (1949)

STEINDORFF, G. *Das Grab des Ti* (1913)

VANDIER, J. *Manuel d'archéologie égyptienne* (Vols. I–II 1952, 1955)

WAINWRIGHT, G.A. *The Sky-Religion in Egypt* (1938)

V The First Merchant Venturers

General

SCHAEFFER, C.F.A. *Stratigraphie comparée de l'Asie Occidental* (1949)

FRANKFORT, H. *Art and Architecture of the Ancient Orient* (revised ed. 1958)

CONTENAU, G. *La civilisation phénicienne* (2nd ed. 1949)

BOSSERT, H. *Altsyrien* (1953)

GOETZE, A. *Hethiter, Churriter und Assyrer* (1936)

Byblos

MONTET, P. *Byblos et l'Egypte* (1922)

DUNAND, M. *Fouilles de Byblos* (2 vols. 1937, 1939)

Palestine

ALBRIGHT, W.F. *The Archaeology of Palestine* (2nd ed. 1960)

LAMON, R., & SHIPTON, G.M. *Megiddo*, Pt. I (1939)

KENYON, K.M. *Archaeology in the Holy Land* (1959)

N. Syria

O'CALLAGHAN, R.T. *Aram Naharaim* (1948)

WOOLLEY, C.L. *Alalakh: 1937–1949* (1955)

SMITH, S. *Alalakh and Chronology* (1940)

DUPONT-SOMMER, A. 'Sur les débuts de l'histoire araméenne' *Vetus Testamentum* Suppl. I (1953)

OPPENHEIM, M. *Tell Halaf* (1948)

Ugarit

SCHAEFFER, C.F.A. *Ugaritica* (3 vols. 1939–56)
The Cuneiform Texts of Ras Shamra – Ugarit (1939)
Enkomi-Alasia (1952)

SCHAEFFER, C.F.A., & NONGAYROL, I. *Le palais royal d'Ugarit, textes accadiens et hourrites etc.* (1955)

DUSSAUD, R. *Les découvertes de Ras Shamra (Ugarit) et l'Ancien Testament* (2nd. ed 1941)

Ivories

DECAMPS DE MERTZENFELD, C. *Inventaire commenté des ivoires phéniciennes* (1954)

BARNETT, R.D. *Catalogue of the Nimrûd Ivories* (1957)

MALLOWAN, M.E.L. in *Iraq* XV– (for Nimrûd)

SCHAEFFER, C.F.A. in *Syria* XXXI

Syro-Hittites

LANDSBERGER, B. *Sam'al* (1948)

Ugaritic Literature

GORDON, C.H. *Ugaritic Literature* (1949)

GRAY, J. 'The Legacy of Canaan' *Vetus Test.* Suppl. V (1957)

DRIVER, G.R. *Canaanite Myths and Legends* (1956)

GASTER, T.H. *Thespis* (1950)

The Western Phoenicians

CINTAS, P. *Céramique punique* (1950)
Contribution a l'expansion carthaginoise au Maroc (1954)

ALBRIGHT, W.F. in *Bulletin of the American Schools of Oriental Research* 83 (1941)

FEVRIER, J.G. in *Revue d'Assyriologie* XLIV (1950)

PICARD, G. *Le Monde de Carthage* (1957)

PICARD, G. & C. *Everyday Life in Carthage* (1961)

GARCIA Y BELLIDO, A. *Fenicios y Cartagineses en Occidente* (1942)

Orientalizing Art

DUNBABIN, T.J. *The Greeks and their Eastern Neighbours* (1957)

PARETI, L. *La Tomba Regolini-Galassi* (1947)

MÜHLESTEIN, H. *Die Kunst der Etrusker* (1929)

BLOCH, R. *Etruscan Art* (1959)

Alphabetic Writing

DIRINGER, D. *The Alphabet* (1941)
Writing (1961)

DRIVER, G.R. *Semitic Writing* (1947)

VI Melting Pot of Peoples

SCHLIEMANN, H. *Ilios* (1880)
Troja (1884)

BLEGEN, C.W., et al. *Troy* (4 vols. 1950-58)

HUTCHINSON, R.W. 'Uruk and Yortan' in *Iraq* II (1935), 211

GARSTANG, J. *Prehistoric Mersin* (1952)

BITTEL, K. et al. Boghazköy excavation reports in *Abhandlungen der preussischen Akademie der Wissenschaften* (1935-)

YOUNG, R. Gordion excavation reports published in *Bull. University Museums*, Philadelphia, and *Am. Journ. Archaeology* (1951-)

KOŞAY, H. I. *Les fouilles d'Alaca Hüyük* (1951)

DELAPORTE, L. *Malatya, Arslantepe. La Porte des Lions* (1940)

HOGARTH, D. G., & WOOLLEY, C. L. *Carchemish* (3 vols. 1914-52)

AKURGAL, E. *Spälhethitische Bildkunst* (1949)
Phrygische Kunst (1955)

BOSSERT, H. *Altanatolien* (1942)

GARSTANG J. *The Hittite Empire* (1929)

GURNEY, O.R. *The Hittites* (revised ed. 1961)

LLOYD, S. *Early Anatolia* (1956)
Art of the Ancient Near East (1961)

VIEYRA, M. *Hittite Art* (1955)

NAUMANN, R. *Architektur Kleinasiens* (1956)

RIEMSCHNEIDER, M. *Die Welt der Hethiter* (1954)

ÖZGUÇ, N. & T. *Kültepe Kazisi Raporu* (1953-60)

LLOYD, S. & MELLAART, J. Beycesultan and Hacilar excavation reports in *Anatolian Studies* IV- (1954-)

MELLAART, J. 'The Royal Treasure of Dorak' in *Illus. London News* 235, No. 6278 (1959), 754 ff.

VII The Home of the Heroes

TSOUNTAS, Ch., & MANATT, J. *The Mycenaean Age* (1903)

HALL, H.R. *Aegean Archaeology* (1915)
The Civilization of Greece in the Bronze Age (1928)

BURN, A.R. *Minoans, Philistines and Greeks* (1930)

GLOTZ, G. *La civilisation égéenne* (new ed. 1952)

MATZ, F. 'Die Ägäis' in *Handbuch der Archäologie* IV/2 (1950)

SCHACHERMEYR, F. *Die Ältesten Kulturen Griechenlands* (1955)

BOSSERT, H. Th. *The Art of Ancient Crete* (1937)

ZERVOS, Ch. *L'art de la Crète* (1956)
L'art des Cyclades (1957)

MYRES, J.L. *Who Were the Greeks?* (1930)

LORIMER, H.L. *Homer and the Monuments* (1950)

FORSDYKE, J. *Greece Before Homer* (1956)

WEBSTER, T.B.L. *From Mycenae to Homer* (1958)

VENTRIS, M., & CHADWICK, J. *Documents in Mycenaean Greek* (1956)

CHADWICK, J. *The Decipherment of Linear B* (1958)

NILSSON, M.P. *The Minoan-Mycenaean Religion and its Survival in Greek Religion* (2nd ed. 1950)

EVANS, A.E. *The Palace of Minos at Knossos* (4 vols. 1921-35)

BAIKIE, J. *The Sea-Kings of Crete* (1910)

PENDLEBURY, J.D.S. *The Archaeology of Crete* (1939)
Handbook to the Palace of Minos (2nd ed. 1954)

SCHLIEMANN, H. *Mycenae* (1878)
Tiryns (1886)

MYLONAS, G.E. *Ancient Mycenae: the Capital City of Agamemnon* (1957)

WACE, A.J.B. *Mycenae: an Archaeological History and Guide* (1949)
'Chamber Tombs at Mycenae' in *Archaeologia* 82 (1932)

PERSSON, A.W. *The Royal Tombs at Dendra near Midea* (1931)
New Tombs at Dendra near Midea (1942)

MARINATOS, S. & HIRMER, M. *Crete and Mycenae* (1960)

HOOD, M.S.F. 'Tholos Tombs of the Aegean' in *Antiquity* XXXIV (Sept. 1960)

VIII Ancient India

MARSHALL, J. *Mohenjo-daro and the Indus Civilization* (3 vols. 1931)

MACKAY, E.J.H. *Further Excavations at Mohenjo-daro* (2 vols. 1938)
Chanhu-daro Excavations 1935-36 (1943)

VATS, M.S. *Excavations at Harappā* (2 vols. 1940)

PIGGOTT, S. *Prehistoric India* (1950)

WHEELER, MORTIMER *The Indus Civilization* (2nd ed. 1960)
Early India and Pakistan (1959)

SUBBARAO, B. *The Personality of India* (2nd ed. 1958)

GORDON, D.H. *The Prehistoric Background of Indian Culture* (1958)

Publications of the Dept. of Archaeology, New Delhi: *Ancient India* (1946-); and *Indian Archaeology* (1953-)

IX A Cycle of Cathay

History

CREEL, H.G. *The Birth of China: a Survey of the Formative Period of Chinese Civilization* (1936)

EBERHARD, W. *A History of China* (1950)

HERRMANN, A. *Atlas of China* (1935)

MASPERO, H. *La Chine antique* (1927)

Archaeology

ANDERSSON, J.G. *Children of the Yellow Earth* (1934)

CHENG TÊ-K'UN. *Archaeology in China* I: *Prehistoric China* (1959)
II: *Shang China* (1960)

LI CHI. *The Beginnings of Chinese Civilization* (1957)

WATSON, W. *Archaeology in China* (1960)
China (1961). For full bibliography

Weapons

LOEHR, M. *Chinese Bronze Age Weapons* (1956)

Arts

BACHHOFER, L. *A Short History of Chinese Art* (1944)

WILLETTS, W. *Chinese Art* (2 vols., 1958)

Mythology and Ritual

GRANET, M. *Danses et légendes de la Chine ancienne* (1926)

KARLGREN, B. 'Legends and Cults in Ancient China' in *Bull. Mus. Far Eastern Antiquities, Stockholm* XVIII (1946)

WATERBURY, F. *Early Chinese Symbols and Literature: Vestiges and Speculations* (1942)

Collections and Exhibitions

JENYNS, S. *Chinese Archaic Jades in the British Museum* (1951)

LODGE, J.E., WENLEY, A.G., & POPE, J.A. *Chinese Bronzes Acquired during the Administration of John Ellerton Lodge.* Freer Gallery of Art, Washington (1946)

YETTS, W.P. *The Cull Chinese Bronzes* (1939)

X The Sea-Locked Lands

(Abbreviations: BEFEO - Bulletin de l'Ecole française d'Extrême Orient; RAA - Revue des Arts asiatiques; BMFEAS - Bulletin of the Museum of Far Eastern Antiquities, Stockholm)

COEDÈS, G. *Les états hindouisés d'Indochine et d'Insulinde* (1948). Best general introduction

COLANI, M. *Mégalithes du Haut-Laos* (1935)
'Recherches sur le préhistorique indochinois' in BEFEO XXX (1930)

Select Bibliography

GOETZ, H. *India: Five Thousand Years of Indian Art* (1960)

GOLOUBEW, V. 'L'age du bronze au Tokin et dans le Nord-Annam' in BEFEO XXIX (1929)

'Le tambour métallique de Hoang-ha' in BEFEO XL (1940)

HEEKEREN, H. R. VAN. *The Stone Age of Indonesia* (1957)

The Bronze-Iron Age of Indonesia (1958)

HEGER, F. *Alte Metalltrommeln aus Südost-Asien* (1902)

HEINE-GOLDERN, R. VON. 'Prehistoric research in the Netherlands Indies' in *Science and Scientists in the Netherlands Indies* (1945), 129-67

'L'art prébouddhique de la Chine et de l'Asie du Sud-Est et son influence en Océanie' in *RAA* XI (1937)

'Vorgeschichtliche Grundlagen der kolonialindischen Kunst' in *Wiener Beiträge zur Kunst- und Kulturgeschichte Asiens* VIII (1935)

HOOP, A. Th. à Th. VAN DER. 'De Praehistorie' in *Geschiedenis van Nederlandsch Indië* I (1938)

Megalithic Remains in South Sumatra (1932)

JANSE, O. 'La station et la nécropole "indonésiennes" de Dong-son (Thank-hoa), Annam du Nord' in *RAA* X (1936)

KARLGREN, B. 'The date of the early Dong-son culture' in *BMFEAS* XIV (1942)

KAUDERN, W. *Megalithic Finds in Central Celebes* (1938)

LEVY, P. *Recherches préhistoriques dans la région de Mlu Prei* (1943)

MALLERET, L. *L'archéologie du delte du Mékong* (1959)

PARMENTIER, H. 'Anciens tambours de bronze' in *BEFEO* XVIII (1910)

Proceedings of the Third Congress of Prehistorians of the Far East, Singapore (1940)

QUARITCH-WALES, H. G. *The Making of Greater India* (1951)

Prehistory and Religion in South-East Asia (1957)

STUTTERHEIM, W. F. 'Het zoogenaamde Iingga-heiligdom op Java' in *Verslag 3de Congres Oostersch Genootschap, Leiden* (1923)

TWEEDIE, M. W. F. 'The Stone Age in Malaya' in *Journal of Malayan Branch, Royal Asiatic Society* XXVI ('Monographs on Malay Subjects') (1953)

WAGNER, F. A. *Indonesia: the Art of an Island Group* (1959)

WEN HU. *Selected Bronze Drums found in China and Southeast Asia* (1955). In Chinese

XI The Royal Hordes

(Abbreviations: AA – Artibus Asiae; BMFEAS – Bulletin of the Museum of Far Eastern Antiquities, Stockholm; ESA – Eurasia Septentrionalis Antiqua)

General

GIMBUTAS, M. *The Prehistory of Eastern Europe* I (American School of Prehistoric Research Bulletin 20, 1956)

HANČAR, F. *Das Pferd in prähistorischer und früher historischer Zeit* (1955)

KISELEV, S. V. *Ancient History of Southern Siberia* (1951). In Russian

MINNS, E. H. *Scythians and Greeks* (1913)

MONGAIT, A. *Archaeology in the USSR* (1959)

ROSTOVTZEV, M. *Iranians and Greeks in South Russia* (1922)

TALBOT RICE, T. *The Scythians* (3rd revised ed. 1961)

VERNADSKY, G. *Ancient Russia* (1946)

HANČAR, F. 'Die Skythen als Forschungsproblem' in *Reinecke-Festschrift* (Mainz, 1950), 67-83

JETTMAR, K. 'Les plus anciennes civilisations d'éleveurs des steppes d'Asie centrale' in *Cahiers d'Histoire Mondiale* I No. 4 (1954), 760-83

PHILLIPS, E.D. 'New light on the ancient history of the Eurasian Steppe' in *American Journ. Archaeology* LXI (1957), 269-80

South Russia

PASSEK, T. S. *The Periodization of Tripolyan Settlement* (MIA 10, 1949). In Russian

'Die ersten Ackerbauern' in *Lebende Vergangenheit* (1954), 49-70. In a collection of essays by various writers

ROSTOVTZEV, M. *Skythien und der Bosporus* I (1931)

Caucasia

HANČAR, F. *Urgeschichte Kaukasiens von den Anfängen bis in die Zeit seiner frühen Metallurgie* (1937)

TALLGREN, A. M. 'Sur les monuments mégalithiques du Caucase occidental' in *ESA* IX (1934), 1-45

Anatolia

GOETZE, A. *Kleinasien* (2nd ed. 1957)

LLOYD, S. *Early Anatolia* (1956)

Iran

GHIRSHMAN, R. *Iran from the Earliest Times to the Islamic Conquest* (1954)

Central Asia

JETTMAR, K. 'Archäologische Spuren von Indo-Germanen in Zentralasien' in *Paideuma* V, Heft I (1952), 236-54

Siberia

JETTMAR, K. 'The Karasuk culture and its south eastern affinities' in *BMFEAS* 22 (1950), 83-126

'The Altai before the Turks' in *BMFEAS* 23 (1951), 135-223

GHIRSHMAN, R. 'Summary of S. V. Kiselev *Histoire ancienne de la Sibérie* (Moscow, 1949)' in *AA* XIV/2 (1951), 168-89

GRIAZNOV, M., & BOULGAKOV, A. *L'art ancien de l'Altaï* (1958)

RUDENKO, S. I. *The Culture of the People of the High Altai in the Scythian Period* (1953). In Russian

'Die Schätze der pazyrykschen Kurganen' in *Lebende Vergangenheit* (1954), 129-56

China

KARLGREN, B. 'Some weapons and tools of the Yin Dynasty' in *BMFEAS* XVII (1945), 101 ff.

LOEHR, M. 'Zur Ur- und Vorgeschichte Chinas' in *Saeculum* III, Heft I (1952), 15-55

Special Problems

HARMATTA, J. 'Le problème cimmérien' in *Archaeologiai Értesítő* VII (1946), 79-132

HEINE-GELDERN, R. VON. 'Das Tocharerproblem und die pontische Wanderung' in *Saeculum* II (1951), 225-55

JETTMAR, K. 'Zur Wanderungsgeschichte der Iranier' in *Die Wiener Schule der Völkerkunde, Festschrift zum 25jährigen Bestand* (1954), 327-48

KRETSCHMER, P. 'Inder im Kuban' in *Anzeiger der Akademie der Wissenschaften in Wien* LXXX (1943), 34-42

LEHMANN-HAUPT, C. Article 'Kimmerier' in Pauly-Wissowa *Realencyclopaedi der klassischen Altertumswissenschaft* XI/1 (1921)

PHILLIPS, E. D. 'The legend of Aristeas. Fact and fancy in early Greek notions of East Russia, Siberia and Inner Asia' in *AA* XVIII/2 (1955), 161-77

'A further note on Aristeas' in *AA* XX/2,3 (1957), 159-62

SULIMIRSKI, T. 'Scythian antiquities in Western Asia' in *AA* XVII/3-4 (1954), 282-318

'The Cimmerian problem' in *Univ. London Inst. of Archaeology Bulletin No. 2, 1959* (1960), 45-64

Nomad Art, the Animal Style etc.

BOROVKA, G. *Scythian Art* (1928)

GHIRSHMAN, R. 'Notes Iraniennes IV: le trésor de Sakkez, les origines de l'art mède, et les bronzes de Luristan' in *AA* XIII (1950), 181-206

GODARD, A. *Les Bronzes de Luristan* (1931)

Le Trésor de Ziwiyè (1950)

HANČAR, F. 'Zum Problem des kaukasischen Tierstils' in *Wiener Beiträge zur Kunst- und Kulturgeschichte Asiens* IX (1934)

'Kaukasus-Luristan' in *ESA* IX (1934), 46-112

MINNS, E. H. 'The Art of the Northern Nomads' in *Proc. British Academy* XXVII (1942), 47-100

ROSTOVTZEV, M. *The Animal Style in South Russia and China* (1929)

TALLGREN, A. M. 'Zum Ursprungsgebiet des sogenannten skythischen Tierstils' in *Acta Archaeologica* IV (1933)

CARTER, D. *The Symbol of the Beast* (1957)

XII Barbarian Europe

CHILDE, V. G. *Prehistoric Migrations in Europe* (1950)

The Dawn of European Civilization (6th ed. 1957)

The Prehistory of European Society (1958)

HAWKES, C. F. C. *The Prehistoric Foundations of Europe* (1940)

KIMMIG, W., & HELL, H. *Vorzeit an Rhein und Donau* (1958)

BRAILSFORD, J. W. *Later Prehistoric Antiquities of the British Isles* (1953)

EVANS, J. D. 'Two phases of prehistoric settlement in the Western Mediterranean' in *Univ. London Inst. of Archaeology 13th Annual Report and Bulletin* (1955-56)

PIGGOTT, S. 'Le néolithique occidental et le chalcolithique en France: esquisse préliminaire' in *L'Anthropologie* 57 (1953), 401-43, and 58 (1954), 1-28

The Neolithic Cultures of the British Isles (1954)

DANIEL, G. E. *The Megalith Builders of Western Europe* (1958). For general survey and bibliography

BERNABÒ BREA, L. *Sicily Before the Greeks* (1957)

DE LAET, S. J. *The Low Countries* (1958), 65. For recently excavated Danubian house plans

FORMAN, W. & B., & POULÍK, J. *Prehistoric Art* (n. d.). For excellent illustrations of central European ceramics

GIMBUTAS, M. *The Prehistory of Eastern Europe* I (American School of Prehistoric Research Bulletin 20, 1956), 124-37. For convenient summary and bibliography

HENCKEN, H. *Indo-European Languages and Archaeology* (American Anthropological Association Memoir 84, 1955)

HACHMANN, R. *Die frühe Bronzezeit im westlichen Ostseegebiet und ihre mittel- und südosteuropäischen Beziehungen* (1957)

MOZSOLICS, A. 'Die Ausgrabungen in Tószeg im Jahre 1948' in *Acta Archaeologica Hungarica* II (1952), 35-69

BROHOLM, H. C. *Danske Oldsager* III: *Aeldre Bronzealder* (1952)

KLINDT-JENSEN, O. *Denmark Before the Vikings* (1957)

STONE, J. F. S. *Wessex Before the Celts* (1958). For Wessex culture illustrations

MOZSOLICS, A. 'Archäologische Beiträge zur Geschichte der Grossen Wanderung' in *Acta Archaeologica Hungarica* VIII (1957), 119-56

SMITH, M. A. 'A study in Urnfield interpretations in Middle Europe' in *Zephyrus* VIII (1957), 195-240

HAWKES, C. F. C., & SMITH, M. A. 'On some buckets and cauldrons of the Bronze and Early Iron Ages' in *The Antiquaries' Journal* XXXVII (1957), 131-98

POWELL, T. G. E. *The Celts* (2nd revised ed. 1960). For bibliography

DEHN, W. 'Die Heuneburg an der Oberen Donau und ihre Wehranlagen' in KRAMER, W. (ed.) *Neue Ausgrabungen in Deutschland* (1958), 127-45

KLINDT-JENSEN, O. *Bronzekedelen fra Brå* (1953). In Danish and English

XIII The Crimson-Tipped Flower

WORMINGTON, H. M. *Ancient Man in North America* (4th ed. 1957)

MARTIN, P. S., QUIMBY, G. I., & COLLIER, D. *Indians Before Columbus* (1947). This very useful book now badly needs bringing up to date

MORLEY, S. G. *The Ancient Maya* (3rd ed. 1956)

THOMPSON, J. E. S. *The Rise and Fall of Maya Civilization* (1954)

FEUCHTWANGER, F., & GROTHKIMBALL, I. *The Art of Ancient Mexico* (1954). For the illustrations

LINNÉ, S. *Treasures of Mexican Art* (1956)

VAILLANT, G. C. *The Aztecs of Mexico* (6th ed. 1960)

BUSHNELL, G. H. S. *Peru* (3rd imp. 1960)

MASON, J. A. *The Ancient Civilizations of Peru* (1957)

COE, M. *Mexico* (1961)

STEWARD, J. H. (ed.) *Handbook of South American Indians*, Vol. 2. (Smithsonian Institution, Bureau of American Ethnology, Bulletin 143, 1946)

LOTHROP, S. K. et al. *Pre-Columbian Art* (2nd revised ed. 1959)

List and Sources of Illustrations

In the following list the first set of numerals indicates the page and the second plate and figure numbers. Wherever possible both the find spot and the present location of objects is stated. Owners of copyright are indicated in *italic*. Where no other source of illustration or present location is given these should be understood to be identical with the copyright holder.

The following abbreviations are used for staff illustrators and photographers: CH *Charles Hasler*, DH *Diana Holmes*, ES *Edwin Smith*, ET *Eileen Tweedy*, GC *Gaynor Chapman*, HJP *Hubert J. Pepper*, IMK *Ian Mackenzie Kerr*, JP *Josephine Powell*, JRF *John R. Freeman*, MEW *Martin E. Weaver*, MMH *Marjory Maitland Howard*, MS *Margaret Scott*, PPP *P. P. Pratt*, PRW *Phillip R. Ward*, SS *Shalom Schotten*. The time charts and diagrams have been prepared by the Assistant Editor and SS from drafts supplied by the authors. The title page drawings are by IMK.

Page

114 36. Giza, reburial of Hetep-heres I: gold covered wooden furniture. Cairo Museum. Photo courtesy *Museum of Fine Arts, Boston*
37. Meidum, tomb chapel of Rehotep and Nofret; pair statues. Cairo Museum. Photo *Max Hirmer*
38. Giza, rock-cut chapel of Meresankh III: painted relief of Prince Ka-wab. Photo *Bernard. V. Bothmer*

115 39. Giza, rock-cut chapel of Meresankh III: painted relief; Hetepheres II and Meresankh III in a punt pulling papyrus heads (detail immediately right of 38). Photo *Bernard V. Bothmer*
40. Giza, *serdab* of Methethy: painted wooden statue of Methethy. *William Rockbill Nelson Gallery of Art, Kansas City*

116 41. Saqqara: painted limestone statue of unknown scribe, Dynasty V. Cairo Museum. Photo *Max Hirmer*
42. Giza: limestone diad of Memysabu and wife, Dynasty V–VI. *Metropolitan Museum of Art, New York*
43. Saqqara: limestone triad of Iruka-Ptah, wife and son, Dynasty V. *Brooklyn Museum*

117 44. Saqqara, Mortuary Temple o Weser-kaf: painted limestone fragment from a fowling scene. Cairo Museum. Photo courtesy *Director, Service des Antiquités, Cairo*
Abusir, Funerary Temple of Sahure: 45. Relief fragment showing detail of king's kilt. *Anatomy Museum, University of Aberdeen.* 46. Relief fragment showing king shooting with bow and arrow. *Staatliche Museen, Berlin*

118 47. Hierakonpolis, sanctuary: copper sheathed statue group of Pepy I and ?Mer-en-re detail of head of Pepy. Cairo Museum. Photo *Max Hirmer*
48. ?Saqqara: votive statuette of Pepy I. Brooklyn Museum. Photo *Charles Uht*
49. Abusir: pyramid complex of Nefer-ir-ka-re, Ni-weser-re, and Sahu-re from N. Reconstruction painting MEW after Borchardt

119 50. Abu Gurob: Sun Temple of Ni-weser-re from S. Reconstruction painting MEW after Borchardt
51. ?Saqqara, statuette of Ankhnes-mery-re nursing Pepy II. *Brooklyn Museum*

120– 52. Saqqara, *mastaba* of Mereruka:
1 chamber A 13, E wall; painted limestone relief of work in the fields. Painting Vcevold Strekalovsky courtesy *Oriental Institute, University of Chicago*

120 56. Saqqara, Mortuary Temple of Nefer-her-en-Ptah: painted limestone relief of bird trapping. Photo *Bernard V. Bothmer*
53. Saqqara, tomb of Nebet: limestone relief of attendants of Queen Nebet. Photo *Bernard V. Bothmer*

121 54. Saqqara, *mastaba* of Mereruka: chamber A 13, N wall; reliefs of (above) girls at play, (below) boys at play (in the tomb the first section joins on immediately *below* the second). Drawings Stanley R. Shepherd courtesy *Oriental Institute, University of Chicago*
55. Saqqara, tomb of Ptah-hotep: relief of personifications of pyramid towns and estates bringing gifts. Photo courtesy *Director, Service des Antiquités, Cairo*
57. Saqqara, Mortuary Temple of Nefer-her-en-Ptah: limestone relief of grape harvest. Photo *Bernard V. Bothmer*

122 58. Abydos, tomb of Idi: copper offering table and miniature ritual vessels. British Museum. Photo JRF
59. Unprovenanced: terracotta statuette of porter with trussed gazelle. *Royal Scottish Museum, Edinburgh.* Photo Tom Scott

122 60. Unprovenanced: painted limestone statuette of servant woman grinding corn. *Pelizaeus Museum, Hildesheim*
61. ?Giza, *mastaba* of Ne-inpu-kau: painted limestone statuette of potter at the wheel. *Oriental Institute, University of Chicago*

123 1. Hôsh, Upper Egypt: Predynastic rock-carving. HJP after Winkel

124 2. Naqada, tomb 1419: Amratian ivory comb. Flinders Petrie Collection, University College, University of London. HJP
3. Wady-el-Faiyum: Faiyum 'A' grass basket in storage pit. HJP after Caton-Thompson

125 4. El-Badari, cemetery 5100: Badavian ivory female figurine. British Museum. HJP
5. Gerzean pottery: decorative motifs. HJP after Flinders Petrie and Stevenson Smith

126 Hieroglyphs and transliteration: 6. *hem*, a mason's drill. 7. *deshret*, the Red Crown of Lower Egypt. 8. *hedjet*, the White Crown of Upper Egypt. DH

127 9. Hieroglyph and transliteration: *Ptah*, the god. DH
10. Saqqara, mortuary chapel of Hesy-re: wooden corn measure and striker from a wall painting. HJP after Quibell

128 11. ? Abydos: inscribed star sighting instrument made from a date palm frond. Staatliche Museen, Berlin. HJP after Borchardt
12. Abydos: ivory sandal label of Wedymu. British Museum. HJP

129 13. Saqqara, tomb of ?Merneith: reconstruction of upper works. MEW after Lauer
14. Saqqara, Step Pyramid: chapels and Jubilee court. Reconstruction Cyril Aldred after Lauer
15. Saqqara, Step Pyramid: stone imitation stake fence (detail). HJP after Drioton and Lauer

130 16. Abusir, Valley Temple of Ni-weser-re. Reconstruction MEW after Borchardt
17. Abusir, Pyramid Temple of Sahu-re: cut-away reconstruction of court. PPP after Borchardt

V The First Merchant Venturers

134 Map: Phoenicians in the Mediterranean. CH

135 Byblos, temple deposit: 1. ivory-handled knife and gold foil scabbard; 2. golden ceremonial axe; 3. gold votive jar in form of bull's scrotum. National Museum, Beirut. Photos *EPCO*

136 4. Byblos, royal tomb: collar of beaten gold. Louvre. Photo *Maurice Chuzeville*
5. Byblos: ruins of XIIth Dynasty obelisk temple. Photo Richard Dormer courtesy *Harper's Bazaar*

137 6. Egypt, unprovenanced: bronze statuette of a vassal Mitannian king. Cairo Museum. Photo courtesy *Director, Service des Antiquités, Cairo*
7. Tell Atchana: white magnesite statue of King Idrimi of Alalakh. British Museum. Photo ES

138 8. Phoenician traders in Egypt.
–9 Reconstruction painting GC

139 9. Thebes, tomb of Sobek-hotep: fragment of wall painting. *Trustees of the British Museum*
10. Egypt: Levantine vessels; (left and centre) Sidmant: black flask and red 'spindle bottle'; (right) Kurneh, Thebes: oil horn from tomb. Royal Scottish Museum, Edinburgh. Photo *Tom Scott*

140 11. Hazor, Israel: the Canaanite temple; *stele* from 'Holy of Holies'. Photo Richard Lannoy
12. Hazor, Israel: the Canaanite temple; the god Ba'al and two *stelae* (to the left of 11 above) Photo Y. Yadin courtesy *Anglo-Israeli Exploration Society*
13. Hazor, Israel: the Canaanite temple; basalt bowl and pottery urn. Photo courtesy *Anglo-Israeli Exploration Society*

141 14. North Syria, unprovenanced: bronze figure of the god Teshub. Burrell Collection, *Glasgow City Museum and Art Gallery*
15. Egypt, unprovenanced 12th. cent. tomb: wooden cup in form of woman's head. Burrell Collection, *Glasgow City Museum and Art Gallery*
16. Beirut: limestone lid of a sarcophagus. *Archaeological Museum, Istanbul*

142 17. Enkomi, Cyprus: ivory gamebox with pieces, and two mirror-handles. British Museum. Photo ET
18. Ras Shamra (Ugarit): gold bowl. Louvre. Photo *Maurice Chuzeville*

143 19. Nimrûd: inlaid ivory plaque, showing a lioness attacking a negro boy. British Museum. Photo ET
20. Curium, Cyprus: gold sceptre inlaid with blue and white pastes. *Cyprus Museum, Nicosia*
21. Nimrûd: ivory plaque of a lion in a lily-grove. British Museum. Photo ET

144 22. Nimrûd: ivory panel showing two divine attendants. *Trustees of the British Museum*
23. Nimrûd: ivory panel showing the god Tammuz. Iraq Museum, Baghdad. Photo courtesy *British School of Archaeology, Iraq*
24. Carchemish: grey steatite spoon. British Museum. Photo JRF

145 25. Nimrûd: ivory plaque showing a goddess. Iraq Museum, Baghdad. Photo courtesy *British School of Archaeology, Iraq*
26. Citium, Cyprus: painted jug. Ashmolean Museum, Oxford. Photo ET

146 27. ? Idalions, Cyprus: terracotta statuette of a woman. Louvre. Photo *Maurice Chuzeville*
29. Cyprus: three jugs. *Metropolitan Museum of Art, New York*
30. Cyprus: scent-bottle of Phoenician glass. *Metropolitan Museum of Art, New York*

147 28. Cypro-Phoenician princess at toilet. Reconstruction painting GC

148 31. Aliseda, Spain: gold belt end. *Museo Arqueologico Nacional, Madrid*
32. Praeneste (Palestrina), Italy: 'Bernadini' tomb; part of a shoulder-clasp. Museo Preistorico L. Pigorini. Photo courtesy *Soprintendenza alle Antichità*

149 33. Praeneste (Palestrina), Italy: silver drinking bowl from the Bernardini tomb. Museo Preistorico L. Pigorini. Photo courtesy *Soprintendenza alle Antichità*
34. Carmona, Spain: bone comb. *Hispanic Society of America*
35. Carmona, Spain: ivory panel from a box. *Hispanic Society of America*

150 36. Tharros, Sardinia: grotesque Punic mask. *Trustees of the British Museum*
37. Carthage: Carthaginian gold stater (obverse and reverse). Heberden Coin Room, Ashmolean Museum, Oxford. Photo ET
38. Carthage: Precinct of Tanit. Photo courtesy *Musée Alaoui, Le Bardo, Tunisia*

151 1. Byblos: embossed design from dagger sheath in 1 above. HJP

152 2. Byblos: design from ivory dagger handle in 1 above. HJP

153 3. Tell Atchana: Mitannian cylinder seal showing a king and goddess. HJP after Woolley

156 4. Curium, Cyprus: bronze cauldron stand. British Museum. IMK
5. Tell Halaf: façade of the Temple Palace. PPP after the reconstruction in the Staatliche Museen, Berlin

157 6. Ezzib (*extreme left*) and Carthage: Phoenician glass beads; former, Royal Scottish Museum, Edinburgh; latter, Musée Alaoui, Le Bardo, Tunisia. HJP after Culican and Picard

158 7. Carthage, Precinct of Tanit: cinerary urn and pottery. Musée Alaoui, Le Bardo, Tunisia. HJP

159 8. ?Etruria: frieze of engraved silver Phoenician cup. Museum of Fine Arts, Boston. HJP

160 9. Table: development of the letters A, B, N. SS

VI Melting Pot of Peoples

162 Map: Late Bronze Age cultures in Anatolia. SS

163 1. Alaca Hüyük, tomb L: gold, silver and bronze figurines. Ankara Museum. Photo JP

164 2. Alaca Hüyük, Royal Cemetery: copper finial. Ankara Museum. Photo JP
3. Alaca Hüyük: two open-work gold diadems (left from tomb L, right from tomb K), a gold necklace and mace (both from tomb K). Ankara Museum. Photo JP
4. Alaca Hüyük, tombs K and L: gold flagon, chalice and pin, brooch (tomb L), bracelet, ornament, and copper sun-disc. Ankara Museum. Photo JP

164 5. Alaca Hüyük: the Royal Ceme-
–5 tery. Reconstruction painting GC

165 6. Alaca Hüyük, tomb L: royal tomb. Drawing MEW after Akok

166 7. Horoztepe: tomb group; bronze figurine of woman suckling a child. Ankara Museum. Photo *Selâhattan Öztartan*
8. Horoztepe: tomb group; bronze rattle. Ankara Museum. Photo *Selâhattan Öztartan*
9. Horoztepe: tomp group; bronze pole-mounting. Ankara Museum. Photo *Selâhattan Öztartan*
10. Mahmutlar: tomb group; bronze axes. Ankara Museum. Photo *Hamet Koşay*
11. Mahmutlar: tomb group; base of gold jug. Ankara Museum. Photo *Hamet Koşay*

167 12, 14. Troy (Hissarlik): Level II G 'Priam's Treasure'; gold earrings. Archaeological Museum, Instanbul. Photo JP
13. Troy: Level II G, 'Priam's Treasure'. Mrs Schliemann wearing some of the jewellery. Steel engraving March 31st 1877 *The Queen and Lady's Newspaper*
15. Troy: Level II G, 'Priam's Treasure'; gold bracelet. Archaeological Museum, Istanbul. Photo JP
16. Troy (Hissarlik). Photo *Seton Lloyd*

168 17. Dorak, Tomb II: drawing MEW after Mellaart
18. Dorak, Tomb I: drawing MEW after Mellaart
19. (top centre right) Dorak, Tomb II: sceptres. Drawing *J. Mellaart*
20. (top right) Dorak, Tomb I: sword-hilt. Drawing *J. Mellaart*
21. (bottom right centre) Dorak, Tomb II: ceremonial axe-heads. Drawing *J. Mellaart*
22. (bottom right) Dorak, Tomb I: swords. Drawing *J. Mellaart*
23–26. (left) Dorak: bronze and silver figurines, possibly from Tomb II. Drawing *J. Mellaart*

VII The Home of the Heroes

Index

Page-numbers in **bold** type refer to the main entry;
those in *italic* indicate illustrations